The 60s Music Co

by Dave Kinzer

The 60s Music Compendium
The 60s Music Compendium

Copyright 2017 Dave Kinzer

All rights reserved. This book or any portion thereof may not be reproduced or used in any manner whatsoever without the express written permission of the author except for the use of brief quotations in a book review.

Any method of distribution or reproduction via the internet without the permission of the author is illegal and punishable by law. If you wish to have an electronic version of this book, please purchase an ebook from an authorized ebook reader.

ISBN-13: 978-1974405183
ISBN-10: 1974405184

First Edition

To contact the author, email him at davekinzerbooks@gmail.com and visit his website: www.davekinzer.com.

Dave Kinzer

Also by the author:

Pranked!

The 80s Music Compendium

"*The 80s Music Compendium* is not only an entertaining book for 80s music lovers, but it is informative for music geeks everywhere. ~Nina Blackwood, Original MTV VJ and SiriusXM Radio Host

The 60s Music Compendium
INTRODUCTION

Has American popular music ever had a decade quite like the 1960s? The musical journey you can take from 1960 to 1969 is wild. You can start by taking a listen to the most popular song of 1960: "The Theme from 'A Summer Place'", by Percy Faith. It was number one on the Hot 100 chart for nine weeks. Only one other song in the 60s would stay at the top of the charts that long: the Beatles' "Hey Jude" in 1968. A quick listen (well, not too quick- the "na-na-na" outro of "Hey Jude" is more than a minute longer than "A Summer Place"!) to both of them will reveal that those two songs are nothing alike. It's obvious that *something* changed between 1960-1968.

How did we get to "Hey Jude" from "A Summer Place"? Well, it took awhile, but we got there with a few 1950s remakes, answer songs, and car songs; with over 550 instrumental songs, 163 novelty song, and over 600 one-hit wonders; with dozens of hits from Bobby (Bland, Darin, Goldsboro, Rydell, Vee, and Vinton), guitar legends like Duane Eddy and Jimi Hendrix, British invaders like the Who and the Rolling Stones, country legends like Johnny Cash and Marty Robbins, teen idols like Annette and Paul Anka, family groups like the Beach Boys and the Cowsills, duos (Simon & Garfunkel), trios (Peter, Paul & Mary), quartets (the Four Tops), quintets (the Temptations), and entire choirs (Harry Simeone Chorale).

And let's not forget 1964. That was the year the Supremes started their number one hit streak, the Beach Boys hit their stride, and the Beatles took over the world. You could have a mini-music Hall of Fame with the artists who debuted that year: the Rolling Stones, Herman's Hermits, the Temptations, Petula Clark, the Kinks, and the Four Tops.

It's obvious 1964 would stand up pretty well against any other year for music. And- take it from someone who has listened to all 6,886 Hot 100 hits from the 60s- it would be tough for any other decade to beat the 1960s, musically speaking.

So take a look at the lists, charts, and trivia in the following pages. I hope you rediscover some old classics, and find some great "new" songs that you'd never heard before.

Be sure to check out my other books. They are also available as ebooks. If you have any questions or comments, or would like to illustrate an artist for a future compendium, please email me at davekinzerbooks@gmail.com. Also, be sure to visit my website: www.davekinzer.com.

Thanks for reading!

Dave Kinzer

One more thing...

For the purposes of this book, a song is only considered to have been a "hit" if it appeared on Billboard's Hot 100 chart between 1960-1969. If a song didn't appear on the Hot 100, then it won't be included in any list, no matter how great that song is. What if a song debuted in December of 1959, but was also popular in 1960? Then I look at what year the song hit its peak position. So a song that peaked on the charts in December of 1959 but hung around on the charts into January of 1960 will not appear in this book. A song like "El Paso" by Marty Robbins, however, will be listed in this book even though it debuted in November of 1959 because it reached its peak position (#1) in January of 1960.

TABLE OF CONTENTS	PAGE
GENRES	1
Country Songs	1
Novelty Songs	7
Live Songs	11
Car Songs	14
Patriotic Songs	15
Medleys	15
Comedy Songs	16
Religious Songs	17
Songs That Tell Stories	17
Blues	20
Jazz	23
Christmas Songs	26
INSTRUMENTAL SONGS	27
Instrumental Songs (No Voices)	28
Instrumental Songs (With Voices)	38
Instrumental Songs with Featured Instruments	42
Break-In Songs	42
Songs from TV Shows	43
Songs from Movies/Musicals	44
REMAKES	54
1950s Remakes	54
1960s Remakes	64
Songs That Hit the Hot 100 Chart Twice	75
INSTRUMENTS	77
Accordion	77
Banjo	78
Barred Instruments	80
Clarinet	90
Clavioline (Musitron)	91
Flute	91
The Longest Guitar Solos of the 1960s	97
Guitar (Slide)	100
Harmonica	102
Harp	107
Harpsichord	110
Horns	113
Kazoo	143
Mandolin	143
Oboe	144
Orchestra	145
Organ	169

Piano	193
Saxophone	237
Sitar	268
Tubular/Church Bells	269
Ukulele	271
Vibraslap	271
Violin	272
Miscellaneous Instruments	303
TOP ARTISTS OF THE 1960s	**305**
The Beach Boys	307
The Beatles	308
Chuck Berry	314
James Brown	315
Ray Charles	316
Sam Cooke	317
The Four Seasons	318
Connie Francis	319
Aretha Franklin	321
Brenda Lee	322
Elvis Presley	323
The Rolling Stones	325
The Supremes	326
MUSIC THEORY	**328**
Songs with Call & Response	328
Songs that Modulate	331
Songs with Ostinatos	334
Songs with a Countermelody	340
Songs with an Unusual Time Signature	342
VOICE	**342**
Songs with Falsetto	342
Songs with Chipmunk Voices	346
Songs with Whistling	347
Songs with 100% Speaking	349
Songs with Yodeling	350
SINGERS	**350**
Songs with an Adult Choir	350
Songs with a Children's Choir	353
Male/Female Duets	353
Male/Male Duets	357
Female/Female Duets	360
MISCELLANEOUS	**360**
Songs with Sound Effects	360
Answer Songs	362
Songs About Dances	364

Songs with Deaths	367
Songs with False Endings	369
Songs with Mistakes	370
Songs Recorded by More Than One Artist That Debuted in the Hot 100 in the Same Year	371
Songs That Borrow from Other Creative Works	377
Songs That Borrow from Classical Works	381
Songs with Foreign Languages	383
SONGS OF EXTREME DURATION	**386**
The Longest Songs of the 1960s	386
The Shortest Songs of the 1960s	388
BEST/WORST LISTS	**391**
Songs That Deserved to Make the Top 40	391
The Best Instrumental Songs of the 1960s	395
The Best 241 Songs of the 1960s	397
The Worst Songs of the 1960s	403
Singers Who Also Acted in Movies/TV	405
One-Hit Wonders	408
Artists Who Used a Stage Name	423
1960s Artists Who are Related to Other Hot 100 Artists	428
Groups with Strange Names	434
Artists with Posthumous Hits	434
Artists from Foreign Countries	435
Artists Whose Hits Each Charted Lower Than Their Previous Hits	438
Artists with the Most Hits Only in the 1960s	439
Other Trivia/Facts	440
Sources	442

GENRES

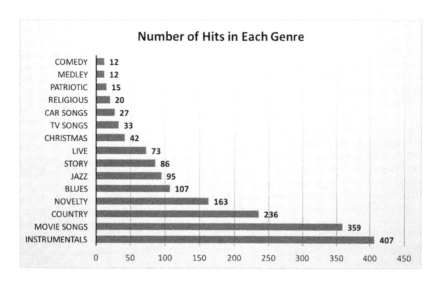

COUNTRY SONGS

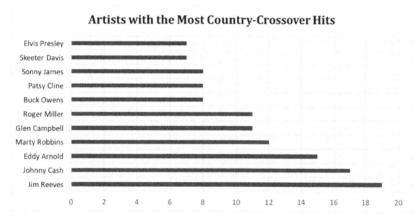

SONG	ARTIST	COUNTRY CHART	HOT 100
1960			
El Paso	Marty Robbins	#1 in 1959	#1
Are You Lonesome Tonight?	Elvis Presley	#22	#1
Everybody's Somebody's Fool	Connie Francis	#24	#1
Stuck on You	Elvis Presley	#27	#1
He'll Have to Go	Jim Reeves	#1	#2
Sink the Bismark	Johnny Horton	#6	#3
North to Alaska	Johnny Horton	#1	#4
The Old Lamplighter	The Browns	#20	#5
Please Help Me, I'm Falling	Hank Locklin	#1	#8
Big Iron	Marty Robbins	#5	#26
Just One Time	Don Gibson	#2	#29
Am I Losing You	Jim Reeves	#8	#31
I'm Getting' Better	Jim Reeves	#3	#37

COUNTRY SONGS (cont'd)

(I Can't Help You) I'm Falling Too	Skeeter Davis	#2	#39
Mary Don't You Weep	Stonewall Jackson	#12	#41
I Missed Me	Jim Reeves	#3	#44
No Love Have I	Webb Pierce	#4	#54
Send Me the Pillow You Dream On	The Browns	#23	#56
Alabam	Cowboy Copas	#1	#63
Jenny Lou	Sonny James	#22	#67
Is It Wrong (For Loving You)	Webb Pierce	#11	#69
Far, Far Away	Don Gibson	#11	#72
Five Brothers	Marty Robbins	#26	#74
Second Honeymoon	Johnny Cash	#15	#79
I Know One	Jim Reeves	#6	#82
Why I'm Walkin'	Stonewall Jackson	#6	#83
Riverboat	Faron Young	#4	#83
Straight A's in Love	Johnny Cash	#16	#84
Rockin', Rollin' Ocean	Hank Snow	#22	#87
(Doin' The) Lovers Leap	Webb Pierce	#17	#93
Sweet Dreams	Don Gibson	#6 in 1961	#93
Fallen Angel	Webb Pierce	#4	#99
She's Just A Whole Lot Like You	Hank Thompson	#14	#99
1961			
Don't Worry	Marty Robbins	#1	#3
Walk on By	Leroy Van Dyke	#1	#5
Crazy	Patsy Cline	#2	#9
You're the Reason	Bobby Edwards	#4	#11
I Fall to Pieces	Patsy Cline	#1	#12
Wings of a Dove	Ferlin Husky	#1 in 1960	#12
Hello Walls	Faron Young	#1	#12
Sea of Heartbreak	Don Gibson	#2	#21
My Last Date (With You)	Skeeter Davis	#4	#26
In the Middle of a Heartache	Wanda Jackson	#6 in 1962	#27
Right or Wrong	Wanda Jackson	#9	#29
What'd I Say	Jerry Lee Lewis	#27	#30
Three Hearts in a Tangle	Roy Drusky	#2	#35
Jimmy Martinez	Marty Robbins	#24	#51
It's Your World	Marty Robbins	#3	#51
Sleepy-Eyed John	Johnny Horton	#9	#54
Mom and Dad's Waltz	Patti Page	#21	#58
Lonesome Number One	Don Gibson	#2	#59
The Blizzard	Jim Reeves	#4	#62
The Comancheros	Claude King	#7	#71
What Would You Do?	Jim Reeves	#15	#73
Tender Years	George Jones	#1	#76

COUNTRY SONGS (cont'd)

Big River, Big Man	Claude King	#7	#82
Tennessee Flat Top Box	Johnny Cash	#11	#84
I'll Just Have a Cup of Coffee (Then I'll Go)	Claude Gray	#4	#84
You're the Reason	Joe South	#16	#87
Losing Your Love	Jim Reeves	#2 in 1962	#89
Backtrack	Faron Young	#8	#89
(How Can I Write on Paper) What I Feel in My Heart	Jim Reeves	#7 in 1962	#92
What About Me	Don Gibson	#22	#100
1962			
It Keeps Right on A-hurtin'	Johnny Tillotson	#4	#3
Wolverton Mountain	Claude King	#1	#6
She's Got You	Patsy Cline	#1	#14
Devil Woman	Marty Robbins	#1	#16
Don't Go Near the Indians	Rex Allen	#4	#17
Send Me the Pillow You Dream On	Johnny Tillotson	#11	#17
Ruby Ann	Marty Robbins	#1 in 1963	#18
Shame on Me	Bobby Bare	#18	#23
If a Woman Answers (Hang Up the Phone)	Leroy Van Dyke	#3	#35
I'm the Girl from Wolverton Mountain	Jo Ann Campbell	#24	#38
Go on Home	Patti Page	#13	#42
That's My Pa	Ben Colder (Sheb Wooley)	#1	#51
When I Get Thru with You (You'll Love Me Too)	Patsy Cline	#10	#53
The Burning of Atlanta	Claude King	#10	#53
If I Cried Every Time You Hurt Me	Wanda Jackson	#28	#58
Don't Go Near the Eskimos	Ben Colder (Sheb Wooley)	#18	#62
I've Been Everywhere	Hank Snow	#1	#68
Love Can't Wait	Marty Robbins	#12	#69
So Wrong	Patsy Cline	#14	#85
Mama Sang a Song	Bill Anderson	#1	#89
Imagine That	Patsy Cline	#21	#90
Adios Amigo	Jim Reeves	#2	#90
The Waltz You Saved for Me	Ferlin Husky	#13	#94
I'm Gonna Change Everything	Jim Reeves	#2	#95
Honky-Tonk Man	Johnny Horton	#11	#96
Does He Mean That Much to You?	Eddy Arnold	#5 in 1963	#98
1963			
The End of the World	Skeeter Davis	#2	#2
From a Jack to a King	Ned Miller	#2	#6
I Can't Stay Mad at You	Skeeter Davis	#14	#7
Still	Bill Anderson	#1	#8
500 Miles Away from Home	Bobby Bare	#5 in 1964	#10
Abilene	George Hamilton IV	#1	#15
Detroit City	Bobby Bare	#6	#16

COUNTRY SONGS (cont'd)

Ring of Fire	Johnny Cash	#1	#17
Six Days on the Road	Dave Dudley	#2	#32
I'm Saving My Love	Skeeter Davis	#9	#41
The Matador	Johnny Cash	#2	#44
Sweet Dreams (Of You)	Patsy Cline	#5	#44
Tips of My Fingers	Roy Clark	#10	#45
8 X 10	Bill Anderson	#2	#53
Beggin to You	Marty Robbins	#1 in 1964	#74
Leavin' on Your Mind	Patsy Cline	#8	#83
Don't Let Me Cross Over	Carl Butler & Pearl	#1 in 1962	#88
Guilty	Jim Reeves	#3	#91
Cigarettes and Coffee Blues	Marty Robbins	#14	#93
The Minute You're Gone	Sonny James	#9	#95
Cowboy Boots	Dave Dudley	#3	#95
Make the World Go Away	Ray Price	#3	#100
1964			
Ringo	Lorne Greene	#21	#1
Miller's Cave	Bobby Bare	#4	#33
Understand Your Man	Johnny Cash	#1	#35
He Says the Same Things to Me	Skeeter Davis	#17	#47
Gonna Get Along Without You Now	Skeeter Davis	#8	#48
It Ain't Me, Babe	Johnny Cash	#4 in 1965	#58
Four Strong Winds	Bobby Bare	#3 in 1965	#60
Long Gone Lonesome Blues	Hank Williams, Jr.	#5	#67
I Guess I'm Crazy	Jim Reeves	#1	#82
Saginaw, Michigan	Lefty Frizzell	#1	#85
Endless Sleep	Hank Williams, Jr.	#46	#90
You're the Only World I Know	Sonny James	#1 in 1965	#91
I Don't Care (Just as Long as You Love Me)	Buck Owens	#1	#92
I Won't Forget You	Jim Reeves	#3 in 1965	#93
Have I Stayed Away Too Long	Bobby Bare	#47	#94
My Heart Skips a Beat	Buck Owens	#1	#94
1965			
King of the Road	Roger Miller	#1	#4
Make the World Go Away	Eddy Arnold	#1	#6
Engine Engine 9	Roger Miller	#2	#7
England Swings	Roger Miller	#3	#8
May the Bird of Paradise Fly Up Your Nose	"Little" Jimmy Dickens	#1	#15
I've Got a Tiger By the Tail	Buck Owens	#1	#25
The Entertainer	Tony Clarke	#15	#31
One Dyin' and a Buryin'	Roger Miller	#10	#34
10 Little Bottles	Johnny Bond	#2	#43
Do What You Do Do Well	Ned Miller	#7	#52

COUNTRY SONGS (cont'd)

What's He Doing in My World	Eddy Arnold	#1	#60
Is It Really Over?	Jim Reeves	#1	#79
Orange Blossom Special	Johnny Cash	#3	#80
Before You Go	Buck Owens	#1	#83
This Is It	Jim Reeves	#1	#88
Girl on the Billboard	Del Reeves	#1	#96
The Race Is On	George Jones	#3	#96
Yakety Axe	Chet Atkins	#4	#98
I've Got Five Dollars and It's Saturday Night	George Jones & Gene Pitney	#16	#99
1966			
Flowers on the Wall	The Statler Brothers	#2	#4
Almost Persuaded	David Houston	#1	#24
Husbands and Wives	Roger Miller	#5	#26
I Want to Go with You	Eddy Arnold	#1	#36
You Can't Roller Skate in a Buffalo Herd	Roger Miller	#35	#40
The Last Word in Lonesome Is Me	Eddy Arnold	#2	#40
The Tip of My Fingers	Eddy Arnold	#3	#43
Distant Drums	Jim Reeves	#1	#45
The One on the Right Is on the Left	Johnny Cash	#2	#46
Somebody Like Me	Eddy Arnold	#1	#53
Waitin' in Your Welfare Line	Buck Owens	#1	#57
Almost Persuaded No. 2	Ben Colder (Sheb Wooley)	#6	#58
My Uncle Used to Love Me but She Died	Roger Miller	#39	#58
Blue Side of Lonesome	Jim Reeves	#1	#59
Snow Flake	Jim Reeves	#2	#66
Think of Me	Buck Owens	#1	#74
Giddyup Go	Red Sovine	#1	#82
Heartbreak Hotel	Roger Miller	#55	#84
Don't Touch Me	Jeannie Seely	#2	#85
Everybody Loves a Nut	Johnny Cash	#17	#96
I'm Living in Two Worlds	Bonnie Guitar	#9	#99
1967			
By the Time I Get to Phoenix	Glen Campbell	#2	#26
Walkin' in the Sunshine	Roger Miller	#7	#37
Misty Blue	Eddy Arnold	#3	#57
Danny Boy	Ray Price	#9	#60
Gentle on My Mind	Glen Campbell	#30	#62
There Goes My Everything	Jack Greene	#1	#65
Turn the World Around	Eddy Arnold	#1	#66
You Mean the World to Me	David Houston	#1	#75
Lonely Again	Eddy Arnold	#1	#87
Here Comes Heaven	Eddy Arnold	#2	#91
Sam's Place	Buck Owens	#1	#92

COUNTRY SONGS (cont'd)

Little Old Wine Drinker Me	Robert Mitchum	#9	#96
I'll Never Find Another You	Sonny James	#1	#97
1968			
Harper Valley P.T.A.	Jeannie C. Riley	#1	#1
Skip a Rope	Henson Cargill	#1	#25
U.S. Male	Elvis Presley	#55	#28
Dreams of the Everyday Housewife	Glen Campbell	#3	#32
Folsom Prison Blues	Johnny Cash	#1	#32
The Straight Life	Bobby Goldsboro	#37	#36
I Wanna Live	Glen Campbell	#1	#36
Little Green Apples	Roger Miller	#6	#39
Hey Little One	Glen Campbell	#13	#54
The Girl Most Likely	Jeannie C. Riley	#6	#55
D-I-V-O-R-C-E	Tammy Wynette	#1	#63
I Walk Alone	Marty Robbins	#1	#65
Harper Valley P.T.A. (Later That Same Day)	Ben Colder (Sheb Wooley)	#24	#67
Your Time Hasn't Come Yet, Baby	Elvis Presley	#50	#72
Here Comes the Rain, Baby	Eddy Arnold	#4	#74
It's Over	Eddy Arnold	#4	#74
Vance	Roger Miller	#15	#80
Born to Be with You	Sonny James	#1	#81
Then You Can Tell Me Goodbye	Eddy Arnold	#1	#84
Rosanna's Going Wild	Johnny Cash	#2	#91
What's Made Milwaukee Famous (Has Made a Loser Out of Me)	Jerry Lee Lewis	#2	#94
Another Place Another Time	Jerry Lee Lewis	#4	#97
Have a Little Faith	David Houston	#1	#98
They Don't Make Love Like They Used To	Eddy Arnold	#10	#99
1969			
A Boy Named Sue	Johnny Cash	#1	#2
Wichita Lineman	Glen Campbell	#1	#3
In the Ghetto	Elvis Presley	#60	#3
Galveston	Glen Campbell	#1	#4
Ruby, Don't Take Your Love to Town	Kenny Rogers & The First Edition	#39	#6
Yesterday, When I was Young	Roy Clark	#9	#19
Stand By Your Man	Tammy Wynette	#1	#19
Try a Little Kindness	Glen Campbell	#2	#23
Reuben James	Kenny Rogers & The First Edition	#46	#26
Where's the Playground Susie	Glen Campbell	#28	#26
True Grit	Glen Campbell	#9	#35
Memories	Elvis Presley	#56	#35
Clean Up Your Own Backyard	Elvis Presley	#74	#35
Let It Be Me	Glen Campbell & Bobbie Gentry	#14	#36

COUNTRY SONGS (cont'd)

Don't It Make You Want to Go Home	Joe South & The Believers	#27	#41
Daddy Sang Bass	Johnny Cash	#1	#42
Blistered	Johnny Cash	#4	#50
Get Rhythm	Johnny Cash	#23	#60
Since I Me You, Baby	Sonny James	#1	#65
(I'm So) Afraid of Losing You Again	Charley Pride	#1	#74
Singing My Song	Tammy Wynette	#1	#75
See Ruby Fall	Johnny Cash	#4	#75
There Never Was a Time	Jeannie C. Riley	#5	#77
Mr. Walker, It's All Over	Billie Jo Spears	#4	#80
The Ways to Love a Man	Tammy Wynette	#1	#81
Kay	John Wesley Ryles I	#9	#83
The Wedding Cake	Connie Francis	#33	#91
All I Have to Offer You (Is Me)	Charley Pride	#1	#91
Only the Lonely	Sonny James	#1	#92
The Carroll County Accident	Porter Wagoner	#2	#92
Running Bear	Sonny James	#1	#94
Big in Vegas	Buck Owens	#5	#100

NOVELTY SONGS

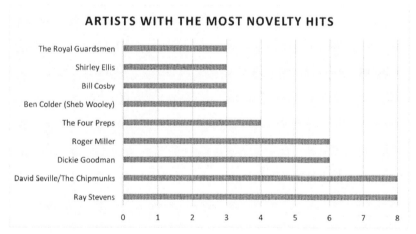

SONG	ARTIST	HOT 100
1960		
Mr. Custer	Larry Verne	#1
Alley-Oop	Hollywood Argyles	#1
Itsy Bitsy Teenie Weenie Yellow Polka Dot Bikini	Brian Hyland	#1
Let's Think About Living	Bob Luman	#7
Yogi	The Ivy Three	#8
Happy-Go-Lucky-Me	Paul Evans	#10
Alley-Oop	Dante & The Evergreens	#15
Rudolph the Red Nosed Reindeer	The Chipmunks	#21

NOVELTY SONGS (cont'd)

Delaware	Perry Como	#22
Got a Girl	The Four Preps	#24
There's Something on Your Mind (Part 2)	Bobby Marchan	#31
Hot Rod Lincoln	Charlie Ryan	#33
Alvin's Orchestra	The Chipmunks	#33
Bad Man's Blunder	The Kingston Trio	#37
The Chipmunk Song	The Chipmunks	#45
The Puppet Song	Frankie Avalon	#56
Alley-Oop	The Dyna-Sores	#59
Psycho	Bobby Hendricks	#73
Kookie Little Paradise	The Tree Swingers	#73
Time Machine	Dante & The Evergreens	#73
Mister Livingston	Larry Verne	#75
Mumblin' Mosie	The Johnny Otis Show	#80
Werewolf	The Frantics	#83
Shoppin' for Clothes	The Coasters	#83
Side Car Cycle	Charlie Ryan	#84
Alvin for President	The Chipmunks	#95
The Yen Yet Song	Gary Cane	#99
The Old Payola Roll Blues (Side 1)	Stan Freberg/Jesse White	#99
1961		
The Boll Weevil Song	Brook Benton	#2
Does Your Chewing Gum Lose Its Flavor (On the Bedpost Over Night)	Lonnie Donegan	#5
Baby Sittin' Boogie	Buzz Clifford	#6
Who Put the Bomp (In the Bomp, Bomp, Bomp)	Barry Mann	#7
More Money for You and Me	The Four Preps	#17
Little Egypt (Ying-Yang)	The Coasters	#23
"Nag"	The Halos	#25
Frogg	The Brothers Four	#32
Jeremiah Peabody's Poly Unsaturated Quick Dissolving Fast Acting Pleasant Tasting Green and Purple Pills	Ray Stevens	#35
Rudolph the Red Nosed Reindeer	The Chipmunks	#47
A Dollar Down	The Limeliters	#60
The Touchables	Dickie Goodman	#60
Alvin's Harmonica	The Chipmunks	#73
Donald Where's Your Troosers	Andy Stewart	#77
Top Forty, News, Weather and Sports	Mark Dinning	#81
Dedicated (To the Songs I Love)	The 3 Friends	#89
Dear Mr. D.J. Play It Again	Tina Robin	#95
Santa and the Touchables	Dickie Goodman	#99
Everybody's Cryin'	Jimmie Beaumont	#100
1962		
Monster Mash	Bobby "Boris" Pickett	#1

NOVELTY SONGS (cont'd)

Ahab the Arab	Ray Stevens	#5
Small Sad Sam	Phil McLean	#21
My Boomerang Won't Come Back	Charlie Drake	#21
Monsters' Holiday	Bobby "Boris" Pickett	#30
The Alvin Twist	The Chipmunks	#40
Ben Crazy	Dickie Goodman	#44
Santa Claus Is Watching You	Ray Stevens	#45
I'm Going Back to School	Dee Clark	#52
Happy Jose (Ching-Ching)	Jack Ross	#57
Dr. Ben Basey	Mickey Shorr	#60
The Big Draft	The Four Preps	#61
Don't Go Near the Eskimos	Ben Colder (Sheb Wooley)	#62
Road Hog	John D. Loudermilk	#65
My Daddy Is President	Little Jo Ann	#67
Twistin' All Night Long	Danny & The Juniors w/Freddy Cannon	#68
Lose Her	Bobby Rydell	#69
That Greasy Kid Stuff	Janie Grant	#74
Callin' Doctor Casey	John D. Loudermilk	#83
Pop Goes the Weasel	Anthony Newley	#85
Alvin's Harmonica	The Chipmunks	#87
Keep Your Hands in Your Pockets	The Playmates	#88
Further More	Ray Stevens	#91
Sam's Song	Dean Martin & Sammy Davis Jr.	#94
The John Birch Society	Chad Mitchell Trio	#99
1963		
Tie Me Kangaroo Down, Sport	Rolf Harris	#3
Pepino the Italian Mouse	Lou Monte	#5
On Top of Spaghetti	Tom Glazer	#14
Mr. Bass Man	Johnny Cymbal	#16
Martian Hop	The Ran-Dells	#16
Long Tall Texan	Murry Kellum	#51
Who Stole the Keeshka?	The Matys Bros.	#55
Speed Ball	Ray Stevens	#59
Little Eeefin Annie	Joe Perkins	#76
Jenny Brown	The Smothers Brothers	#84
Detroit City No. 2	Ben Colder (Shep Wooley)	#90
Nick Teen and Al K. Hall	Rolf Harris	#95
The Lone Teen Ranger	Jerry Landis	#97
1964		
Dang Me	Roger Miller	#7
Chug-A-Lug	Roger Miller	#9
Haunted House	Gene Simmons	#11
Beans in My Ears	The Serendipity Singers	#30

NOVELTY SONGS (cont'd)

Rip Van Winkle	The Devotions	#36
We Love You Beatles	The Carefrees	#39
The Marvelous Toy	Chad Mitchell Trio	#43
T'ain't Nothin' to Me	The Coasters	#64
The Dodo	Jumpin' Gene Simmons	#83
My Boyfriend Got a Beatle Haircut	Donna Lynn	#83
A Letter to the Beatles	The Four Preps	#85
The Boy with the Beatle Hair	The Swans	#85
One Piece Topless Bathing Suit	The Rip Chords	#96
1965		
The Name Game	Shirley Ellis	#3
The Jolly Green Giant	The Kingsmen	#4
The Clapping Song (Clap Pat Clap Slap)	Shirley Ellis	#8
May the Bird of Paradise Fly Up Your Nose	"Little" Jimmy Dickens	#15
Leader of the Laundromat	The Detergents	#19
Do-Wacka-Do	Roger Miller	#31
Kansas City Star	Roger Miller	#31
10 Little Bottles	Johnny Bond	#43
Ode to the Little Brown Shack Out Back	Billy Edd Wheeler	#50
N-E-R-V-O-U-S	Ian Whitcomb	#60
The Puzzle Song (A Puzzle in Song)	Shirley Ellis	#78
Inky Dinky Spider (The Spider Song)	The Kids Next Door	#84
Lip Sync (To the Tongue Twisters)	Len Barry	#84
The Crusher	The Novas	#88
Double-O-Seven	The Detergents	#89
I Want My Baby Back	Jimmy Cross	#92
Girl on the Billboard	Del Reeves	#96
1966		
Snoopy vs. the Red Baron	The Royal Guardsmen	#2
Yellow Submarine	The Beatles	#2
They're Coming to Take Me Away, Ha-Haaa!	Napoleon XIV	#3
You Can't Roller Skate in a Buffalo Herd	Roger Miller	#40
The One on the Right Is on the Left	Johnny Cash	#46
The Eggplant That Ate Chicago	Dr. West's Medicine Show and Junk Band	#52
I'm a Nut	Leroy Pullins	#57
Almost Persuaded No. 2	Ben Colder (Sheb Wooley)	#58
My Uncle Used to Love Me but She Died	Roger Miller	#58
Juanita Banana	The Peels	#59
I Love Onions	Susan Christie	#63
Batman	Jan & Dean	#66
There's Something on Your Mind	Baby Ray	#69
Batman & His Grandmother	Dickie Goodman	#70
Downtown	Mrs. Miller	#82

NOVELTY SONGS (cont'd)

Freddie Feelgood (And His Funky Little Five Piece Band)	Ray Stevens	#91
Superman	Dino, Desi & Billy	#94
A Lover's Concerto	Mrs. Miller	#95
Everybody Loves a Nut	Johnny Cash	#96
1967		
Little Ole Man (Uptight-Everything's Alright)	Bill Cosby	#4
Skinny Legs and All	Joe Tex	#10
Ding Dong! The Witch Is Dead	The Fifth Estate	#11
Stand By Me	Spyder Turner	#12
The Return of the Red Baron	The Royal Guardsmen	#15
Knight in Rusty Armour	Peter & Gordon	#15
Hooray for the Salvation Army Band	Bill Cosby	#71
Mairzy Doats	The Innocence	#75
They're Here	Boots Walker	#77
Ten Commandments	Prince Buster	#81
1968		
Tip-Toe Thru' the Tulips with Me	Tiny Tim	#17
Here Comes the Judge	Pigmeat Markham	#19
Loving You Has Made Me Bananas	Guy Marks	#51
Here Come the Judge	The Magistrates	#54
Thank U Very Much	The Scaffold	#69
Snoopy for President	The Royal Guardsmen	#85
Funky North Philly	Bill Cosby	#91
1969		
Gitarzan	Ray Stevens	#8
Along Came Jones	Ray Stevens	#27
Moonflight	Vik Venus	#38
On Campus	Dickie Goodman	#45
Mah-Na-Mah-Na	Piero Umiliani	#55
Bubble Gum Music	Rock & Roll Dubble Bubble	#74
My Wife, My Dog, My Cat	The Maskman & The Agents	#91
One Eye Open	The Maskman & The Agents	#95
Theme from Electric Surfboard	Brother Jack McDuff	#95
Luna Trip	Dickie Goodman	#95
It's A Funky Thing-Right On (Part 1)	Herbie Mann	#95
Big Bruce	Steve Greenberg	#97

LIVE SONGS

SONG	ARTIST	HOT 100
1960		
How High the Moon (Part 1)	Ella Fitzgerald	#76

LIVE SONGS (cont'd)

1961
Does Your Chewing Gum Lose Its Flavor (On the Bedpost Over Night)	Lonnie Donegan	#5
More Money for You and Me	The Four Preps	#17

1962
Cinderella	Jack Ross	#16
Lizzie Borden	Chad Mitchell Trio	#44
The Big Draft	The Four Preps	#61
The John Birch Society	Chad Mitchell Trio	#99

1963
Fingertips - Pt. 2	Little Stevie Wonder	#1
Hello Muddah, Hello Fadduh! (A Letter from Camp)	Allan Sherman	#2
If I Had a Hammer	Trini Lopez	#3
The Jive Samba	Cannonball Adderley	#66
Bill Bailey, Won't You Please Come Home	Ella Fitzgerald	#75
Hootenanny Saturday Night	The Brothers Four	#89
We Shall Overcome	Joan Baez	#90

1964
Memphis	Johnny Rivers	#2
Maybelline	Johnny Rivers	#12
Money	The Kingsmen	#16
Kansas City	Trini Lopez	#23
Oh Baby Don't You Weep (Part 1)	James Brown	#23
My Girl Sloopy	The Vibrations	#26
20-75	Willie Mitchell	#31
Hello Muddah, Hello Fadduh! (A Letter from Camp) (New 1964 version)	Allan Sherman	#59
Something You Got	Ramsey Lewis Trio	#63
T'ain't Nothin' to Me	The Coasters	#64
Little Boxes	Pete Seeger	#70
Baby What You Want Me to Do	Etta James	#82
High Heel Sneakers	Jerry Lee Lewis	#91
Oh, Rock My Soul (Part I)	Peter, Paul & Mary	#93
Jailer, Bring Me Water	Trini Lopez	#94
Please, Please, Please	James Brown	#95
It's a Sin to Tell a Lie	Tony Bennett	#99

1965
Seventh Son	Johnny Rivers	#7
Hang on Sloopy	Ramsey Lewis Trio	#11
Midnight Special	Johnny Rivers	#20
Crazy Downtown	Allan Sherman	#40
10 Little Bottles	Johnny Bond	#43
Makin' Whoopee	Ray Charles	#46
Ode to the Little Brown Shack Out Back	Billy Edd Wheeler	#50
(Here They Come) From All Over the World	Jan & Dean	#56

LIVE SONGS (cont'd)

High Heel Sneakers	Stevie Wonder	#59
Land of a Thousand Dances (Part 1)	Thee Midniters	#67
I Gotta Woman (Part One)	Ray Charles	#79
The Drinking Man's Diet	Allan Sherman	#98
1966		
(I Washed My Hands In) Muddy Water	Johnny Rivers	#19
A Hard Day's Night	Ramsey Lewis Trio	#29
The Ballad of Irving	Frank Gallop	#34
Hi Heel Sneakers - Pt. 1	Ramsey Lewis Trio	#70
I'll Go Crazy	James Brown	#73
La Bamba - Part 1	Trini Lopez	#86
Lost Someone	James Brown	#94
Off to Dublin in the Green	Abbey Tavern Singers	#94
1967		
Skinny Legs and All	Joe Tex	#10
Mercy, Mercy, Mercy	"Cannonball" Adderley	#11
Shake	Otis Redding	#47
Soothe Me	Sam & Dave	#56
Because of You	Chris Montez	#71
Why? (Am I Treated So Bad)	"Cannonball" Adderley	#73
Dancing in the Street	Ramsey Lewis	#84
Sweet Soul Medley - Part 1	The Magnificent Men	#90
1968		
Goin' Out of My Head/Can't Take My Eyes Off You	The Lettermen	#7
Folsom Prison Blues	Johnny Cash	#32
The Star-Spangled Banner	Jose Feliciano	#50
I Have a Dream	Rev. Martin Luther King	#88
1969		
A Boy Named Sue	Johnny Cash	#2
Papa's Got a Brand New Bag	Otis Redding	#21
Day Is Done	Peter, Paul & Mary	#21
Crossroads	Cream	#28
With Pen in Hand	Vikki Carr	#35
The Pledge of Allegiance	Red Skelton	#44
Get Rhythm	Johnny Cash	#60
Since I Met You, Baby	Sonny James	#65
Just a Little Love	B.B. King	#76
Hold Me	The Baskerville Hounds	#88

CAR SONGS

This section was a little difficult to compile, as it is somewhat subjective determining what exactly makes a song a car song. Should a song be considered a car song just because there is a car in the title or in the lyrics? I don't think so. Take "Cab Driver" by The Mills Brothers. Yes, there's a car in the song, but it doesn't play a particularly important role in the song. Although there is a car in the song, it is not the focus of the lyrics. To be included in this list, a car must be the focus of the lyrics or the story. "Stick Shift" is included because sound effects related to cars are heard throughout the song.

SONG	ARTIST	HOT 100
1960		
Tell Laura I Love Her	Ray Peterson	#7
Hot Rod Lincoln	Johnny Bond	#26
Hot Rod Lincoln	Charlie Ryan	#33
Side Car Cycle	Charlie Ryan	#84
1961		
Stick Shift	The Duals	#25
1962		
Route 66 Theme	Nelson Riddle	#30
Road Hog	John D. Loudermilk	#65
409	Beach Boys	#76
1963		
Little Deuce Coupe	The Beach Boys	#15
Shut Down	The Beach Boys	#23
The Scavenger	Dick Dale	#98
1964		
The Little Old Lady (From Pasadena)	Jan & Dean	#3
G.T.O.	Ronny & The Daytonas	#4
Hey Little Cobra	The Rip Chords	#4
Fun, Fun, Fun	The Beach Boys	#5
Dead Man's Curve	Jan & Dean	#8
Drag City	Jan & Dean	#10
No Particular Place to Go	Chuck Berry	#10
Maybelline	Johnny Rivers	#12
Three Window Coupe	The Rip Chords	#28
Custom Machine	Bruce & Terry	#85
1965		
Bucket "T"	Ronny & The Daytonas	#54
Dear Dad	Chuck Berry	#95
1966		
Mustang Sally	Wilson Pickett	#23
Tijuana Taxi	Herb Alpert	#38
1967		
My Old Car	Lee Dorsey	#97

CAR SONGS (cont'd)

1969		
Chitty Chitty Bang Bang	Paul Mauriat	#76

PATRIOTIC SONGS

SONG	ARTIST	HOT 100
1960		
There's a Star Spangled Banner Waving #2 (The Ballad of Francis Powers)	Red River Dave	#64
Ballad of the Alamo	Bud & Travis	#64
Johnny Freedom	Johnny Horton	#69
1961		
God, Country and My Baby	Johnny Burnette	#18
1962		
P.T. 109	Jimmy Dean	#8
The Burning of Atlanta	Claude King	#53
This Land Is Your Land	Ketty Lester	#97
1966		
The Ballad of the Green Berets	Ssgt Barry Sadler	#1
1967		
An Open Letter to My Teenage Son	Victor Lundberg	#10
Gallant Men	Senator Everett McKinley Dirksen	#29
A Letter to Dad	Every Father's Teenage Son	#93
1968		
Battle Hymn of the Republic	Andy Williams	#33
The Star-Spangled Banner	Jose Feliciano	#50
America Is My Home - Pt. 1	James Brown	#52
1969		
This Is My Country	The Impressions	#25

MEDLEYS

A medley is a song that consists of parts of at least two other songs.

SONG	ARTIST	HOT 100
1961		
More Money for You and Me	The Four Preps	#17
1962		
The Big Draft	The Four Preps	#61
1966		
Devil with a Blue Dress On & Good Golly Miss Molly	Mitch Ryder & The Detroit Wheels	#4
Jenny Take a Ride!	Mitch Ryder & The Detroit Wheels	#10

MEDLEYS (cont'd)

1967		
Lovey Dovey/You're So Fine	Bunny Sigler	#86
Sweet Soul Medley - Part 1	The Magnificent Men	#90
1968		
Goin' Out of My Head/Can't Take My Eyes Off You	The Lettermen	#7
My Girl/Hey Girl	Bobby Vee	#35
(You've Got) Personality and Chantilly Lace	Mitch Ryder	#87
1969		
Aquarius/Let the Sunshine In	The 5th Dimension	#1
Good Old Rock 'N Roll	Cat Mother & The All Night News Boys	#21
I Can Sing a Rainbow/Love Is Blue	The Dells	#22

COMEDY SONGS

SONG	ARTIST	HOT 100
1960		
The Big Time Spender (Parts I & II)	Cornbread & Biscuits	#75
1961		
The Astronaut (Parts 1 & 2)	Jose Jimenez	#19
1962		
Cinderella	Jack Ross	#16
Lizzie Borden	Chad Mitchell Trio	#44
1963		
Hello Mudduh, Hello Fadduh! (A Letter from Camp)	Allan Sherman	#2
1964		
Hello Muddah, Hello Fadduh! (A Letter from Camp) (New 1964 version)	Allan Sherman	#59
1965		
Crazy Downtown	Allan Sherman	#40
The Drinking Man's Diet	Allan Sherman	#98
1966		
The Ballad of Irving	Frank Gallop	#34
1967		
Wild Thing	Senator Bobby	#20
Mellow Yellow	Senator Bobby & Senator McKinley	#99
1969		
Kick Out the Jams	MC5	#82

RELIGIOUS SONGS

SONG	ARTIST	HOT 100
1960		
Run Samson Run	Neil Sedaka	#28
Just a Closer Walk with Thee	Jimmie Rodgers	#44
Adam and Eve	Paul Anka	#90
A Closer Walk	Pete Fountain	#93
1961		
Saved	LaVern Baker	#37
1962		
Shadrack	Brook Benton	#19
Mama Sang a Song	Stan Kenton	#32
Mama Sang a Song	Walter Brennan	#38
Walk on the Wild Side	Brook Benton	#43
The Lost Penny	Brook Benton	#77
Mama Sang a Song	Bill Anderson	#89
1964		
Oh, Rock My Soul (Part I)	Peter, Paul & Mary	#93
1965		
Amen	The Impressions	#7
1966		
Wade in the Water	Ramsey Lewis	#19
1968		
Amen	Otis Redding	#36
A Working Man's Prayer	Arthur Prysock	#74
1969		
Oh Happy Day	Edwin Hawkins Singers	#4
Jesus Is a Soul Man	Lawrence Reynolds	#28
Kum Ba Yah	Tommy Leonetti	#54
Dammit Isn't God's Last Name	Frankie Laine	#86

SONGS THAT TELL STORIES

SONG	ARTIST	HOT 100
1960		
El Paso	Marty Robbins	#1
Mr. Custer	Larry Verne	#1
Running Bear	Johnny Preston	#1
Sink the Bismark	Johnny Horton	#3
North to Alaska	Johnny Horton	#4
Tell Laura I Love Her	Ray Peterson	#7

SONGS THAT TELL STORIES (cont'd)

Down By the Station	The Four Preps	#13
Big Iron	Marty Robbins	#26
Hot Rod Lincoln	Johnny Bond	#26
Run Samson Run	Neil Sedaka	#28
Hot Rod Lincoln	Charlie Ryan	#33
Ballad of the Alamo	Marty Robbins	#34
Run Red Run	The Coasters	#36
Bad Man's Blunder	The Kingston Trio	#37
Mary Don't You Weep	Stonewall Jackson	#41
I Shot Mr. Lee	The Bobbettes	#52
The Puppet Song	Frankie Avalon	#56
Everglades	The Kingston Trio	#60
There's a Star Spangled Banner Waving #2 (The Ballad of Francis Powers)	Red River Dave	#64
Ballad of the Alamo	Bud & Travis	#64
The Wreck of the "John B"	Jimmie Rodgers	#64
Delia Gone	Pat Boone	#66
(The Clickity Clack Song) Four Little Heels	Brian Hyland	#73
The Old Oaken Bucket	Tommy Sands	#73
Five Brothers	Marty Robbins	#74
Mister Livingston	Larry Verne	#75
Side Car Cycle	Charlie Ryan	#84
1961		
Big Bad John	Jimmy Dean	#1
Ebony Eyes	The Everly Brothers	#8
Frankie and Johnny	Brook Benton	#20
What a Surprise	Johnny Maestro	#33
Jimmy Martinez	Marty Robbins	#51
The Touchables	Dickie Goodman	#60
The Blizzard	Jim Reeves	#62
A Scottish Soldier (Green Hills of Tyrol)	Andy Stewart	#69
A Little Dog Cried	Jimmie Rodgers	#71
The Comancheros	Claude King	#71
A Cross Stands Alone	Jimmy Witter	#89
Johnny Willow	Fred Darian	#96
The Battle of Gettysburg	Fred Darian	#100
1962		
(The Man Who Shot) Liberty Valance	Gene Pitney	#4
Old Rivers	Walter Brennan	#5
P.T. 109	Jimmy Dean	#8
I've Got Bonnie	Bobby Rydell	#18
Shadrack	Brook Benton	#19
Small Sad Sam	Phil McLean	#21
Cajun Queen	Jimmy Dean	#22

SONGS THAT TELL STORIES (cont'd)

Steel Men	Jimmy Dean	#41
That's My Pa	Sheb Wooley	#51
The Burning of Atlanta	Claude King	#53
The Ballad of Thunder Road	Robert Mitchum	#65
1963		
It's My Party	Lesley Gore	#1
Puff the Magic Dragon	Peter, Paul & Mary	#2
Harry the Hairy Ape	Ray Stevens	#17
Stewball	Peter, Paul & Mary	#35
Speed Ball	Ray Stevens	#59
Give Us Your Blessing	Ray Peterson	#70
The Folk Singer	Tommy Roe	#84
1964		
Ringo	Lorne Greene	#1
Last Kiss	J. Frank Wilson & The Cavaliers	#2
Dead Man's Curve	Jan & Dean	#8
Miller's Cave	Bobby Bare	#33
Rip Van Winkle	The Devotions	#36
The Marvelous Toy	Chad Mitchell Trio	#43
1965		
Laurie (Strange Things Happen)	Dickey Lee	#14
Give Us Your Blessing	The Shangri-Las	#29
I Want My Baby Back	Jimmy Cross	#92
Girl on the Billboard	Del Reeves	#96
1966		
Snoopy vs. the Red Baron	The Royal Guardsmen	#2
The Ballad of Irving	Frank Gallop	#34
Billy and Sue	B.J. Thomas	#34
1967		
The Return of the Red Baron	The Royal Guardsmen	#15
Stag-O-Lee	Wilson Pickett	#22
Hooray for the Salvation Army Band	Bill Cosby	#71
1968		
Harper Valley P.T.A.	Jeannie C. Riley	#1
The Unicorn	The Irish Rovers	#7
The Ballad of Bonnie and Clyde	Georgie Fame	#7
Delilah	Tom Jones	#15
Vance	Roger Miller	#80
The Biplane, Ever More	The Irish Rovers	#91
1969		
A Boy Named Sue	Johnny Cash	#2
Pinball Wizard	The Who	#19

SONGS THAT TELL STORIES (cont'd)

Along Came Jones	Ray Stevens	#27
The Carroll County Accident	Porter Wagoner	#92
Running Bear	Sonny James	#94
Big Bruce	Steve Greenberg	#97

BLUES

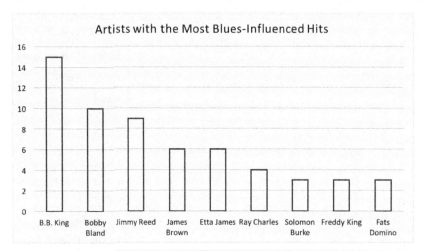

SONG	ARTIST	HOT 100
1960		
Mule Skinner Blues	Fendermen	#5
All I Could Do Was Cry	Etta James	#33
Baby What You Want Me to Do	Jimmy Reed	#37
Heartbreak (It's Hurtin' Me)	Jon Thomas	#48
If I Can't Have You	Etta James & Harvey Fuqua	#52
Honey Hush	Joe Turner	#53
Someday (You'll Want Me to Want You)	Della Reese	#56
The Bells	James Brown	#68
Cry Cry Cry	Bobby Bland	#71
Hush-Hush	Jimmy Reed	#75
Spoonful	Etta James & Harvey Fuqua	#78
I Idolize You	Ike & Tina Turner	#82
You've Got the Power	James Brown w/Bea Ford	#86
Found Love	Jimmy Reed	#88
Nobody Knows You When You're Down and Out	Nina Simone	#93
Smokie- Part 2	Bill Doggett	#95
Don't Let the Sun Catch You Cryin'	Ray Charles	#95
If You Need Me	Fats Domino	#98
1961		
All in My Mind	Maxine Brown	#19
Funny	Maxine Brown	#25

BLUES (cont'd)

Hide Away	Freddy King	#29
Ain't That Just Like a Woman	Fats Domino	#33
Rainin' in My Heart	Slim Harpo	#34
Bewildered	James Brown	#40
Smile	Timi Yuri	#42
I Pity the Fool	Bobby Bland	#46
Fool That I Am	Etta James	#50
Bright Lights Big City	Jimmy Reed	#58
I've Got News for You	Ray Charles	#66
I Hear You Knocking	Fats Domino	#67
Close Together	Jimmy Reed	#68
Son-In-Law	Louise Brown	#76
Wabash Blues	The Viscounts	#77
Big Boss Man	Jimmy Reed	#78
You Don't Know What It Means	Jackie Wilson	#79
Milk Cow Blues	Ricky Nelson	#79
Driving Wheel	Junior Parker	#85
Lonesome Whistle Blues	Freddy King	#88
I Can't Take It	Mary Ann Fisher	#92
She Really Loves You	Timi Yuri	#93
You've Got to Love Her with a Feeling	Freddy King	#93
1962		
Lie to Me	Brooke Benton	#13
Stop the Wedding	Etta James	#34
Stormy Monday Blues	Bobby Bland	#43
Lost Someone	James Brown	#48
Boom Boom	John Lee Hooker	#60
Who Will the Next Fool Be	Bobby Bland	#76
Good Lover	Jimmy Reed	#77
Aw Shucks, Hush Your Mouth	Jimmy Reed	#93
Shake a Hand	Ruth Brown	#97
1963		
Cry Baby	Garnet Mimms & The Enchanters	#4
Part Time Love	Little Johnny Taylor	#19
Cry to Me	Betty Harris	#23
I Got What I Wanted	Brook Benton	#28
Shame, Shame, Shame	Jimmy Reed	#52
I'm a Woman	Peggy Lee	#54
Got You on My Mind	Cookie & His Cupcakes	#94
1964		
Goodbye Baby (Baby Goodbye)	Solomon Burke	#33
Rock Me Baby	B.B. King	#34
Slip-In Mules (No High Heel Sneakers)	Sugar Pie DeSanto	#48

BLUES (cont'd)

The Price	Solomon Burke	#57
If Somebody Told You	Anna King	#67
Baby What You Want Me to Do	Etta James	#82
Beautician Blues	B.B. King	#82
Never Trust a Woman	B.B. King	#90
The Feeling Is Gone	Bobby Bland	#91
Night Time Is the Right Time	Rufus & Carla	#94
How Blue Can You Get	B.B. King	#97
Help the Poor	B.B. King	#98
The Things That I Used to Do	James Brown	#99
Trouble I've Had	Clarence Ashe	#99
Strange Things Happening	Little Junior Parker	#99
1965		
One Monkey Don't Stop No Show	Joe Tex	#65
Blind Man	Bobby Bland	#78
I'm a Fool to Care	Ray Charles	#84
Blind Man	Little Milton	#86
You're Gonna Make Me Cry	O.V. Wright	#86
Have Mercy Baby	James Brown	#92
Think	Jimmy McCracklin	#95
Blue Shadows	B.B. King	#97
Black Night	Bobby Bland	#99
1966		
Let's Go Get Stoned	Ray Charles	#31
Don't Answer the Door - Part 1	B.B. King	#72
Black Nights	Lowell Fulsom	#91
I'm Your Hoochie Cooche Man (Part 1)	Jimmy Smith	#94
Your Good Thing (Is About to End)	Mable John	#95
I Feel a Sin Coming On	Solomon Burke	#97
1967		
Dirty Man	Laura Lee	#68
Cry to Me	Freddie Scott	#70
Eight Men, Four Women	O.V. Wright	#80
Feel so Bad	Little Milton	#91
The Jungle	B.B. King	#94
Somebody's Sleeping in My Bed	Johnnie Taylor	#96
1968		
Paying the Cost to Be the Boss	B.B. King	#39
I'm Gonna Do What They Do to Me	B.B. King	#74
You Put It on Me	B.B. King	#82
The Woman I Love	B.B. King	#94
Driftin' Blues	Bobby Bland	#96

BLUES (cont'd)

1969		
Your Good Thing (Is About to End)	Lou Rawls	#18
Rockin' in the Same Old Boat	Bobby Bland	#58
Chains of Love	Bobby Bland	#60
Why I Sing the Blues	B.B. King	#61
I've Been Loving You Too Long	Ike & Tina Turner	#68
Nothing Can Take the Place of You	Brook Benton	#74
Get Off My Back Women	B.B. King	#74
Just a Little Love	B.B. King	#76
I Can't Be All Bad	Johnny Adams	#89

JAZZ

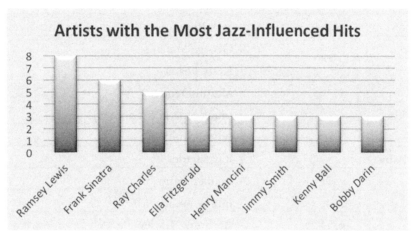

SONG	ARTIST	HOT 100
1960		
Georgia On My Mind	Ray Charles	#1
Beyond the Sea	Bobby Darin	#6
Pennies from Heaven	The Skyliners	#24
Ol' Mac Donald	Frank Sinatra	#25
Mack the Knife	Ella Fitzgerald	#27
Don't Go to Strangers	Etta James	#36
Don't Fence Me In	Tommy Edwards	#45
My Love	Nat "King" Cole/Stan Kenton	#47
Wake Me When It's Over	Andy Williams	#50
Hardhearted Hannah	Ray Charles	#55
Nice 'N' Easy	Frank Sinatra	#60
Delia Gone	Pat Boone	#66
Theme from "The Dark at the Top of the Stairs"	Ernie Freeman	#70
Time After Time	Frankie Ford	#75
How High the Moon (Part 1)	Ella Fitzgerald	#76
Cry Me A River	Janice Harper	#91
A Closer Walk	Pete Fountain	#93

JAZZ (cont'd)

1961

Take Five	Dave Brubeck Quartet	#25
Lost Love	H.B. Barnum	#35
Exodus	Eddie Harris	#36
Water Boy	Don Shirley Trio	#40
I'll Be Seeing You	Frank Sinatra	#58
Granada	Frank Sinatra	#64
I Don't Want Nobody (To Have My Love but You)	Ella Johnson with Buddy Johnson	#78
Our Love Is Here to Stay	Dinah Washington	#89
Canadian Sunset	Etta James	#91
Won'cha Come Home, Bill Bailey	Della Reese	#98

1962

Midnight in Moscow	Kenny Ball	#2
Cinderella	Jack Ross	#16
Teach Me Tonight	George Maharis	#25
But Not for Me	Ketty Lester	#41
A Taste of Honey	Martin Denny	#50
Me and My Shadow	Frank Sinatra & Sammy Davis Jr.	#64
Midnight Special, Part 1	Jimmy Smith	#69
But on the Other Hand Baby	Ray Charles	#72
Ev'rybody's Twistin'	Frank Sinatra	#75
Ol' Man River	Jimmy Smith	#82
Pop Goes the Weasel	Anthony Newley	#85
You're Nobody 'Til Somebody Loves You	Dinah Washington	#87
The Green Leaves of Summer	Kenny Ball	#87
A Taste of Honey	Victor Feldman Quartet	#88
March of the Siamese Children	Kenny Ball	#88
I Found a New Baby	Bobby Darin	#90
Baby It's Cold Outside	Ray Charles & Betty Carter	#91
The Basie Twist	Count Basie	#94
Sam's Song	Dean Martin & Sammy Davis Jr.	#94

1963

Watermelon Man	Mongo Santamaria	#10
Misty	Lloyd Price	#21
Cast Your Fate to the Wind	Vince Guaraldi Trio	#22
I Got a Woman	Freddie Scott	#48
Bossa Nova U.S.A.	Dave Brubeck Quartet	#69
Bill Bailey, Won't You Please Come Home	Ella Fitzgerald	#75
I Can't Stop Loving You	Count Basie	#77
Now!	Lena Horne	#92
Banzai Pipeline	Henry Mancini	#93
Don't Fence Me In	George Maharis	#93
True Blue Lou	Tony Bennett	#99

JAZZ (cont'd)

1964

The Pink Panther Theme	Henry Mancini	#31
Charade	Sammy Kaye	#36
I Still Get Jealous	Louis Armstrong	#45
Something You Got	Ramsey Lewis Trio	#63
The Cat	Jimmy Smith	#67
Billie Baby	Lloyd Price	#84
Be Anything (But Be Mine)	Gloria Lynne	#88
A Shot in the Dark	Henry Mancini	#97
It's a Sin to Tell a Lie	Tony Bennett	#99

1965

The "In" Crowd	Ramsey Lewis Trio	#5
Goldfinger	Shirley Bassey	#8
Cast Your Fate to the Wind	Sounds Orchestral	#10
Red Roses for a Blue Lady	Bert Kaempfert	#11
You're Nobody till Somebody Loves You	Dean Martin	#25
Makin' Whoopee	Ray Charles	#46
A Time to Love - A Time to Cry (Petite Fleur)	Lou Johnson	#59
Watermelon Man	Gloria Lynne	#62
Soul Sauce (Guacha Guaro)	Cal Tjader	#88
Love Me Now	Brook Benton	#100

1966

Wade in the Water	Ramsey Lewis	#19
A Hard Day's Night	Ramsey Lewis Trio	#29
Up Tight	Ramsey Lewis	#49
Mame	Bobby Darin	#53
Bye Bye Blues	Bert Kaempfert	#54
Hi Heel Sneakers - Pt. 1	Ramsey Lewis Trio	#70
Smokey Joe's La La	Googie Rene Combo	#77
Mame	Louis Armstrong	#81
A Man and a Woman	Tamiko Jones w/Herbie Mann	#88
Uptight (Everything's Alright)	The Jazz Crusaders	#95
Secret Love	Richard "Groove" Holmes	#99

1967

Why? (Am I Treated So Bad)	"Cannonball" Adderley	#73
Day Tripper	Ramsey Lewis	#74
Night and Day	Sergio Mendes & Brasil '66	#82
Dancing in the Street	Ramsey Lewis	#84
Ode to Billy Joe	Ray Bryant	#89
Peas 'N' Rice	Freddie McCoy	#92

1968

Listen Here	Eddie Harris	#45

JAZZ (cont'd)		
1969		
Camel Back	A.B. Skhy	#100

CHRISTMAS SONGS

Quite a few Christmas songs hit the Hot 100 from 1960-1962. Then, Christmas songs were relegated to their own chart, and most did not appear on the Hot 100 for the rest of the decade. Evidently, the songs from 1964 and 1969 listed below were not officially classified as Christmas songs.

SONG	ARTIST	HOT 100
1960		
Rockin' Around the Christmas Tree	Brenda Lee	#14
Rudolph the Red Nosed Reindeer	The Chipmunks	#21
The Little Drummer Boy	Harry Simeone	#24
White Christmas	Bing Crosby	#27
Jingle Bell Rock	Bobby Helms	#36
Adeste Fideles (Oh, Come, All Ye Faithful)	Bing Crosby	#45
The Chipmunk Song	The Chipmunks	#45
Twistin' Bells	Santo & Johnny	#49
Christmas Auld Lang Syne	Bobby Darin	#51
Silent Night	Bing Crosby	#54
Rudolph the Red Nosed Reindeer	The Melodeers	#71
The Christmas Song (Merry Christmas to You)	Nat "King" Cole	#80
Child of God	Bobby Darin	#95
White Christmas	The Drifters	#96
Blue Christmas	The Browns	#97
1961		
White Christmas	Bing Crosby	#12
Jingle Bell Rock	Bobby Rydell & Chubby Checker	#21
The Little Drummer Boy	Harry Simeone	#22
Baby's First Christmas	Connie Francis	#26
The Chipmunk Song	The Chipmunks	#39
Jingle Bell Rock	Bobby Helms	#41
Little Altar Boy	Vic Dana	#45
Rudolph the Red Nosed Reindeer	The Chipmunks	#47
Rockin' Around the Christmas Tree	Brenda Lee	#50
Please Come Home for Christmas	Charles Brown	#76
The Little Drummer Boy	Jack Halloran Singers	#96
Santa and the Touchables	Dickie Goodman	#99
1962		
Santa Claus Is Coming to Town	The Four Seasons	#23
The Little Drummer Boy	Harry Simeone	#28
Monsters' Holiday	Bobby "Boris" Pickett	#30
White Christmas	Bing Crosby	#38

CHRISTMAS (cont'd)

The Chipmunk Song	The Chipmunks	#40
Santa Claus Is Watching You	Ray Stevens	#45
Jingle Bell Rock	Bobby Helms	#56
Rockin' Around the Christmas Tree	Brenda Lee	#59
The Christmas Song (Merry Christmas to You)	Nat "King" Cole	#65
Rudolph the Red Nosed Reindeer	The Chipmunks	#77
White Christmas	The Drifters	#88
Jingle Bell Rock	Bobby Rydell & Chubby Checker	#92
Silent Night, Holy Night	Mahalia Jackson	#99
1964		
The Marvelous Toy	Chad Mitchell Trio	#43
1969		
Greensleeves	Mason Williams	#90

INSTRUMENTAL

Instrumental songs were very popular in the 1960s. Approximately one out of every twenty hits was an instrumental song.

Instrumental songs are those that have instruments only- no singing. However, some songs have been (incorrectly) classified as instrumental if they don't have much singing, or if they don't have singing with words. In other words, some songs are considered instrumental if they have "oohing" and "ahhhs" instead of lyrics. Even though this isn't accurate, since a true instrumental song will have no voices at all, I've created two instrumental lists. The first list below contains the instrumental songs that had no voices at all. The second list has those songs with voices.

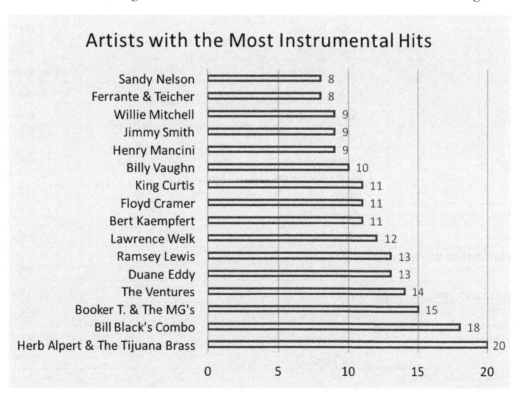

INSTRUMENTAL SONGS (NO VOICES)

SONG	ARTIST	HOT 100
1960		
Theme from "A Summer Place"	Percy Faith	#1
Walk - Don't Run	The Ventures	#2
Because They're Young	Duane Eddy	#4
White Silver Sands	Bill Black's Combo	#9
Don't Be Cruel	Bill Black's Combo	#11
Tracy's Theme	Spencer Ross	#13
Beatnik Fly	Johnny & The Hurricanes	#15
Perfidia	The Ventures	#15
Blue Tango	Bill Black's Combo	#16
Smokie - Part 2	Bill Black's Combo	#17
Josephine	Bill Black's Combo	#18
Look for a Star	Billy Vaughn	#19
Mr. Lucky	Henry Mancini	#21
Bulldog	The Fireballs	#24
Bonnie Came Back	Duane Eddy	#26
Peter Gunn	Duane Eddy	#27
Summer Set	Monte Kelly	#30
Ruby Duby Du	Tobin Matthews	#30
Theme for Young Lovers	Percy Faith	#35
Gonzo	James Booker	#43
Shazam!	Duane Eddy	#45
Caravan	Santo & Johnny	#48
Down Yonder	Johnny & The Hurricanes	#48
Twistin' Bells	Santo & Johnny	#49
The Sundowners	Billy Vaughn	#51
Harlem Nocturne	The Viscounts	#52
National City	Joiner, Arkansas Junior High School Band	#53
Chattanooga Choo Choo	Ernie Fields	#54
Rocking Goose	Johnny & The Hurricanes	#60
Theme from "The Dark at the Top of the Stairs"	Ernie Freeman	#70
Skokiaan (South African Song)	Bill Haley & His Comets	#70
Rambling	The Ramblers	#73
Brontosaurus Stomp	The Piltdown Men	#75
Night Theme	The Mark II	#75
La Montana (If She Should Come to You)	Frank De Vol	#77
Bongo Bongo Bongo	Preston Epps	#78
Kommotion	Duane Eddy	#78
Night Train	The Viscounts	#82

INSTRUMENTAL SONGS (NO VOICES) (cont'd)

Werewolf	The Frantics	#83
Beautiful Obsession	Sir Chauncey	#89
Stranger from Durango	Richie Allen	#90
You Are My Sunshine	Johnny & The Hurricanes	#91
Midnight Lace- Part One	Ray Conniff	#92
Theme from "The Sundowners"	Mantovani	#93
A Closer Walk	Pete Fountain	#93
Smokie- Part 2	Bill Doggett	#95
Revival	Johnny & The Hurricanes	#97
Vaquero (Cowboy)	The Fireballs	#99
Beachcomber	Bobby Darin	#100
1961		
Apache	Jorgen Ingmann	#2
Wheels	The String-A-Longs	#3
Yellow Bird	Arthur Lyman Group	#4
Mexico	Bob Moore	#7
Let There Be Drums	Sandy Nelson	#7
"Pepe"	Duane Eddy	#18
Bonanza	Al Caiola	#19
Hearts of Stone	Bill Black's Combo	#20
Bumble Boogie	B. Bumble and The Stingers	#21
Ole Buttermilk Sky	Bill Black's Combo	#25
Stick Shift	Duals	#25
Take Five	Dave Brubeck Quartet	#25
Quite a Party	The Fireballs	#27
Hide Away	Freddy King	#29
Ram-Bunk-Shush	The Ventures	#29
Main Theme from Exodus (Ari's Theme)	Mantovani	#31
Lost Love	H.B. Barnum	#35
Brass Buttons	The String-A-Longs	#35
The Magnificent Seven	Al Caiola	#35
Exodus	Eddie Harris	#36
Never on Sunday	Don Costa	#37
Like, Long Hair	Paul Revere & The Raiders	#38
Water Boy	Don Shirley Trio	#40
African Waltz	Cannonball Adderley	#41
Movin'	Bill Black's Combo	#41
Should I	The String-A-Longs	#42
Up A Lazy River	Si Zentner	#43
Underwater	The Frogmen	#44
San-Ho-Zay	Freddy King	#47
The Charleston	Ernie Fields	#47

INSTRUMENTAL SONGS (NO VOICES) (cont'd)

Blue Moon	The Ventures	#54
Anna	Jorgen Ingmann	#54
Cherry Pink and Apple Blossom White	Jerry Murad's Harmonicats	#56
Honky Tonk (Part 2)	Bill Doggett	#57
That's the Way with Love	Piero Soffici	#59
Orange Blossom Special	Billy Vaughn	#63
Back Beat No. 1	The Rondels	#66
Lullaby of the Leaves	The Ventures	#69
Come September	Billy Vaughn	#73
Cerveza	Bert Kaempfert	#73
Wabash Blues	The Viscounts	#77
Night Train	Richard Hayman	#80
La Dolce Vita	Ray Ellis	#81
Flamingo Express	The Royaltones	#82
Theme from "Silver City"	The Ventures	#83
Ja-Da	Johnny & The Hurricanes	#86
Boogie Woogie	B. Bumble and The Stingers	#89
Hop Scotch	Santo and Johnny	#90
Honky Train	Bill Black's Combo	#92
Image - Part 1	Hank Levine	#98
1962		
The Stripper	David Rose	#1
Stranger on the Shore	Mr. Acker Bilk	#1
Telstar	The Tornadoes	#1
Midnight in Moscow	Kenny Ball	#2
Green Onions	Booker T. & The MG's	#3
Alley Cat	Bent Fabric	#7
Percolator (Twist)	Billy Joe & The Checkmates	#10
Rinky Dink	Baby Cortez	#10
Desafinado	Stan Getz/Charlie Byrd	#15
Soul Twist	King Curtis & Noble Knights	#17
Tuff	Ace Cannon	#17
I've Got a Woman (Part 1)	Jimmy McGriff	#20
Walk on the Wild Side (Part 1)	Jimmy Smith	#21
Nut Rocker	B. Bumble & The Stingers	#23
Twist-Her	Bill Black's Combo	#26
Theme from Ben Casey	Valjean	#28
Drums are My Beat	Sandy Nelson	#29
The Jam (Part 1)	Bobby Gregg	#29
Route 66 Theme	Nelson Riddle	#30
Surfer's Stomp	The Mar-Kets	#31
The Ballad of Paladin	Duane Eddy	#33
Blues (Stay Away from Me)	Floyd Cramer	#36

INSTRUMENTAL SONGS (NO VOICES) (cont'd)

Afrikaan Beat	Bert Kaempfert	#42
Swingin' Gently	Earl Grant	#44
Flying Circle	Frank Slay	#45
Maria	Roger Williams	#48
Balboa Blue	The Mar-Kets	#48
Baby Elephant Walk	Lawrence Welk	#48
A Taste of Honey	Martin Denny	#50
Sweet Sixteen Bars	Earl Grant	#55
Above the Stars	Mr. Acker Bilk	#59
Let's Go Trippin'	Dick Dale	#60
Beach Party	King Curtis & Noble Knights	#60
Hot Pepper	Floyd Cramer	#63
…And Then There Were Drums	Sandy Nelson	#65
Patricia- Twist	Perez Prado	#65
Happy Weekend	Dave "Baby" Cortez	#67
Drummin' Up a Storm	Sandy Nelson	#67
Midnight Special, Part 1	Jimmy Smith	#69
Jivin' Around	Al Casey Combo	#71
Unsquare Dance	Dave Brubeck Quartet	#74
The Birth of the Beat	Sandy Nelson	#75
Midnight	Johnny Gibson	#76
Deep in the Heart of Texas	Duane Eddy	#78
So What	Bill Black's Combo	#78
Ol' Man River	Jimmy Smith	#82
Drum Stomp	Sandy Nelson	#86
Baby Elephant Walk	The Miniature Men	#87
The Green Leaves of Summer	Kenny Ball	#87
A Taste of Honey	Victor Feldman Quartet	#88
March of the Siamese Children	Kenny Ball	#88
A Taste of Honey	Victor Feldman Quartet	#88
Amor	Roger Williams	#88
Shimmy, Shimmy Walk, Part 1	The Megatons	#88
Potato Peeler	Bobby Gregg	#89
Let's Go	Floyd Cramer	#90
Sugar Blues	Ace Cannon	#92
White Silver Sands	Bill Black's Combo	#92
Cookin'	Al Casey Combo	#92
Limelight	Mr. Acker Bilk	#92
The Twist	Ernie Freeman	#93
The Basie Twist	Count Basie	#94
Pop-Eye Stroll	Mar-Keys	#94
Play the Thing	Marlowe Morris Quintet	#95
Theme from "Hatari!"	Henry Mancini	#95

INSTRUMENTAL SONGS (NO VOICES) (cont'd)

Let Me Entertain You	Ray Anthony	#96
Guitar Boogie Shuffle Twist	The Virtues	#96
Fiesta	Dave "Baby" Cortez	#96
Zero-Zero	Lawrence Welk	#98
Lisa	Ferrante & Teicher	#98
Tequila Twist	The Champs	#99
Til There Was You	Valjean	#100
Drown in My Own Tears	Don Shirley	#100
Sweet Georgia Brown	Carroll Bros.	#100
1963		
Wipe Out	The Surfaris	#2
Washington Square	The Village Stompers	#2
Pipeline	Chantay's	#4
Memphis	Lonnie Mack	#5
Maria Elena	Los Indios Tabajaras	#6
Wild Weekend	The Rebels	#8
More	Kai Winding	#8
Fly Me to the Moon - Bossa Nova	Joe Harnell	#14
Cast Your Fate to the Wind	Vince Guaraldi Trio	#22
Wiggle Wobble	Les Cooper	#22
Wham!	Lonnie Mack	#24
Bust Out	The Busters	#25
Yakety Sax	Boots Randolph	#35
The Lonely Surfer	Jack Nitzsche	#39
Love for Sale	Arthur Lyman Group	#43
Monkey-Shine	Bill Black's Combo	#47
Point Panic	The Surfaris	#49
Sting Ray	The Routers	#50
All About My Girl	Jimmy McGriff	#50
Do It - Rat Now	Bill Black's Combo	#51
Dawn	David Rockingham Trio	#62
Ridin' the Wind	The Tornados	#63
Chicken Feed	Bent Fabric	#63
Back at the Chicken Shack, Part 1	Jimmy Smith	#63
Gravy Waltz	Steve Allen	#64
Jack the Ripper	Link Wray	#64
Sax Fifth Avenue	Johnny Beecher	#65
The Jive Samba	Cannonball Adderley	#66
Meditation (Meditacao)	Charlie Byrd	#66
Hobo Flats - Part 1	Jimmy Smith	#69
Bossa Nova U.S.A.	Dave Brubeck Quartet	#69
Only You (And You Alone)	Mr. Acker Bilk	#77
I Can't Stop Loving You	Count Basie	#77

INSTRUMENTAL SONGS (NO VOICES) (cont'd)

Chinese Checkers	Booker T. & The MG's	#78
Jellybread	Booker T. & The MG's	#82
Boss	The Rumblers	#87
Rockin' Crickets	Rockin' Rebels	#87
Hot Cakes! 1st Serving	Dave "Baby" Cortez	#91
Rumble	Jack Nitzsche	#91
The 2,000 Pound Bee (Part 2)	The Ventures	#91
Banzai Pipeline	Henry Mancini	#93
Saltwater Taffy	Lonnie Mack	#93
Summertime	Chris Columbo Quintet	#93
Baja	The Astronauts	#94
M.G. Blues	Jimmy McGriff	#95
Theme from "Any Number Can Win"	Jimmy Smith	#96
Diane	Joe Harnell	#97
The Last Minute (Pt. 1)	Jimmy McGriff	#99
Every Beat of My Heart	James Brown	#99
Breakwater	Lawrence Welk	#100
1964		
Out of Limits	The Marketts	#3
Java	Al Hirt	#4
Walk-Don't Run '64	The Ventures	#8
Shangri-La	Robert Maxwell	#15
Penetration	Pyramids	#18
20-75	Willie Mitchell	#31
The Pink Panther Theme	Henry Mancini	#31
Slaughter on Tenth Avenue	The Ventures	#35
Charade	Sammy Kaye	#36
Charade	Henry Mancini	#36
Tall Cool One	The Wailers	#38
Teen Beat '65	Sandy Nelson	#44
Soul Serenade	King Curtis	#51
Ringo's Theme (This Boy)	George Martin	#53
I Want to Hold Your Hand	Boston Pops Orchestra	#55
I'll Remember (In the Still of the Night)	Santo & Johnny	#58
The James Bond Theme	Billy Strange	#58
Something You Got	Ramsey Lewis Trio	#63
Peg O' My Heart	Robert Maxwell	#64
Comin' On	Bill Black's Combo	#67
The Cat	Jimmy Smith	#67
Pink Dominos	The Crescents	#69
Who's Afraid of Virginia Woolf? (Part I)	Jimmy Smith	#72
Little Queenie	Bill Black's Combo	#73

INSTRUMENTAL SONGS (NO VOICES) (cont'd)

Song	Artist	Chart
Kiko	Jimmy McGriff	#79
From Russia with Love	The Village Stompers	#81
Always in My Heart	Los Indios Tabajaras	#82
Searchin'	Ace Cannon	#84
The Mexican Shuffle	Herb Alpert & The Tijuana Brass	#85
Vanishing Point	The Marketts	#90
So Far Away	Hank Jacobs	#91
Tequila	Bill Black's Combo	#91
The Dartell Stomp	The Mustangs	#92
All My Loving	The Hollyridge Strings	#93
Soul Dressing	Booker T. & The MG's	#95
Fiddler on the Roof	The Village Stompers	#97
Mo-Onions	Booker T. & The MG's	#97
A Shot in the Dark	Henry Mancini	#97
1965		
The "In" Crowd	Ramsey Lewis Trio	#5
A Taste of Honey	Herb Alpert & The Tijuana Brass	#7
Cast Your Fate to the Wind	Sounds Orchestral	#10
A Walk in the Black Forest	Horst Jankowski	#12
Hungry for Love	San Remo Golden Strings	#27
Hawaii Tattoo	The Waikikis	#33
Cleo's Back	Jr. Walker/The All Stars	#43
Goldfinger	Billy Strange	#55
Boot-Leg	Booker T. & The MG's	#58
Moon Over Naples	Bert Kaempfert	#59
Buckaroo	Buck Owens	#60
Try Me	James Brown	#63
Apache '65	The Arrows/Davie Allan	#64
Peanuts (La Cacahuata)	The Sunglows	#64
Diamon Head	The Ventures	#70
Goldfinger	John Barry	#72
Apples and Bananas	Lawrence Welk	#75
Stand By Me	Earl Grant	#75
Canadian Sunset	Sounds Orchestral	#76
The Sidewinder, Part 1	Lee Morgan	#81
Percolatin'	Willie Mitchell	#85
I'm Satisfied	San Remo Golden Strings	#89
Hawaii Honeymoon	The Waikikis	#91
Mexican Pearls	Billy Vaughn	#94
Goldfinger	Jack LaForge	#96
Buster Browne	Willie Mitchell	#96
El Pussy Cat	Mongo Santamaria	#97
Yakety Axe	Chet Atkins	#98

INSTRUMENTAL SONGS (NO VOICES) (cont'd)

1966

Zorba the Greek	Herb Alpert & The Tijuana Brass	#11
Wade in the Water	Ramsey Lewis	#19
What Now My Love	Herb Alpert & The Tijuana Brass	#24
Summer Samba (So Nice)	Walter Wanderley	#26
Spanish Flea	Herb Alpert & The Tijuana Brass	#27
A Hard Day's Night	Ramsey Lewis Trio	#29
The Phoenix Love Theme (Senza Fine)	The Brass Ring	#32
Tijuana Taxi	Herb Alpert & The Tijuana Brass	#38
Misty	"Groove" Holmes	#44
Up Tight	Ramsey Lewis	#49
Cleo's Mood	Jr. Walker/The All Stars	#50
The Fife Piper	The Dynatones	#53
Bye Bye Blues	Bert Kaempfert	#54
Lara's Theme from "Dr. Zhivago"	Roger Williams	#65
Hi Heel Sneakers - Pt. 1	Ramsey Lewis Trio	#70
The Loop	Johnny Lytle	#80
My Sweet Potato	Booker T. & The MG's	#85
Hot Shot	The Buena Vistas	#87
Philly Dog	The Mar-Keys	#89
Bad Eye	Willie Mitchell	#92
Philly Dog	Herbie Mann	#93
Uptight (Everything's Alright)	The Jazz Crusaders	#95
What Now My Love	"Groove" Holmes	#96
Secret Love	Richard "Groove" Holmes	#99
Theme from The Wild Angels	Davie Allan/The Arrows	#99
I Can't Give You Anything but Love	Bert Kaempfert	#100

1967

Mercy, Mercy, Mercy	"Cannonball" Adderley	#11
Music to Watch Girls By	Bob Crewe Generation	#15
I Was Kaiser Bill's Batman	Whistling Jack Smith	#20
Groovin'	Booker T. & The MG's	#21
Casino Royale	Herb Alpert & The Tijuana Brass	#27
Ode to Billy Joe	The Kingpins	#28
The Happening	Herb Alpert & The Tijuana Brass	#32
A Banda (Ah Bahn-da)	Herb Alpert & The Tijuana Brass	#35
Hip Hug-Her	Booker T. & The MG's	#37
Blues' Theme	Davie Allan/The Arrows	#37
Wade in the Water	Herb Alpert & The Tijuana Brass	#37
Windy	Wes Montgomery	#44
Soul Man	Ramsey Lewis	#49
You've Got to Pay the Price	Al Kent	#49

INSTRUMENTAL SONGS (NO VOICES) (cont'd)

Slim Jenkin's Place	Booker T. & The MG's	#70
Why? (Am I Treated So Bad)	"Cannonball" Adderley	#73
Spreadin' Honey	Watts 103rd St. Rhythm Band	#73
Day Tripper	Ramsey Lewis	#74
Knucklehead	Bar-Kays	#76
Dancing in the Street	Ramsey Lewis	#84
For What It's Worth	King Curtis & Kingpins	#87
Birds of Britain	Bob Crewe Generation	#89
Ode to Billy Joe	Ray Bryant	#89
To Sir, with Love	Herbie Mann	#93
Alligator Bogaloo	Lou Donaldson	#93
Slippin' & Slidin'	Willie Mitchell	#96
Along Comes Mary	Baja Marimba Band	#96
Devil's Angels	Davie Allan/The Arrows	#97
Georgy Girl	Baja Marimba Band	#98
1968		
Grazing in the Grass	Hugh Masekela	#1
Love Is Blue	Paul Mauriat	#1
Classical Gas	Mason Williams	#2
The Horse	Cliff Nobles & Co.	#2
Soul-Limbo	Booker T. & The MG's	#17
Soul Serenade	Willie Mitchell	#23
Mission-Impossible	Lalo Schifrin	#41
My Favorite Things	Herb Alpert & The Tijuana Brass	#45
Prayer Meetin'	Willie Mitchell	#45
Listen Here	Eddie Harris	#45
Carmen	Herb Alpert & The Tijuana Brass	#51
The Impossible Dream	Roger Williams	#55
Foggy Mountain Breakdown (Theme from Bonnie & Clyde)	Flatt & Scruggs	#55
Love in Every Room	Paul Mauriat	#60
Burning Spear	The Soulful Strings	#64
Alfie	Eivets Rednow (Stevie Wonder)	#66
Up-Up and Away	Hugh Masekela	#71
Puffin' on down the Track	Hugh Masekela	#71
Cabaret	Herb Alpert & The Tijuana Brass	#72
I Was Made to Love Her	Stevie Wonder	#76
United (Part 1)	The Music Makers	#78
Unchain My Heart	Herbie Mann	#81
Turn On Your Love Light	Bill Black's Combo	#82
The Mule	The James Boys	#82
I Heard It Thru the Grapevine	King Curtis & Kingpins	#83
(Sittin' On) The Dock of the Bay	King Curtis & Kingpins	#84

INSTRUMENTAL SONGS (NO VOICES) (cont'd)

It's Crazy	Eddie Harris	#88
Georgia on My Mind	Wes Montgomery	#91
Up-Hard	Willie Mitchell	#91
Harper Valley P.T.A.	King Curtis & Kingpins	#93
Baroque-A-Nova	Mason Williams	#96
The Worm	Jimmy McGriff	#97
1969		
Soulful Strut	Young-Holt Unlimited	#3
Hawaii Five-O	The Ventures	#4
Time Is Tight	Booker T. & The MG's	#6
Hang 'Em High	Booker T. & The MG's	#9
Keem-O-Sabe	The Electric Indian	#16
Cissy Strut	The Meters	#23
Groovy Grubworm	Harlow Wilcox	#30
Sophisticated Cissy	The Meters	#34
Mrs. Robinson	Booker T. & The MG's	#37
The Minotaur	Dick Hyman	#38
Lowdown Popcorn	James Brown	#41
Memphis Underground	Herbie Mann	#44
Apricot Brandy	Rhinoceros	#46
Riot	Hugh Masekela	#55
Who's Making Love	Young-Holt Unlimited	#57
Ease Back	The Meters	#61
30-60-90	Willie Mitchell	#69
Truck Stop	Jerry Smith	#71
Julia	Ramsey Lewis	#76
Chitty Chitty Bang Bang	Paul Mauriat	#76
Theme from "A Summer Place"	The Ventures	#83
Slum Baby	Booker T. & The MG's	#88
Greensleeves	Mason Williams	#90
Switch It On	Cliff Nobles & Co.	#93
If I Only Had Time	Nick DeCaro	#95
Theme from Electric Surfboard	Brother Jack McDuff	#95
Feeling Alright	Mongo Santamaria	#96
Galveston	Roger Williams	#99
Camel Back	A.B. Skhy	#100

INSTRUMENTAL SONGS (WITH VOICES)

SONG	ARTIST	HOT 100
1960		
Last Date	Floyd Cramer	#2
Theme from "The Apartment"	Ferrante & Teicher	#10
Never on Sunday	Don Costa	#19
Last Date	Lawrence Welk	#21
Theme from "The Unforgiven" (The Need for Love)	Don Costa	#27
The Madison Time - Part 1	Ray Bryant Combo	#30
Too Much Tequila	The Champs	#30
On the Beach	Frank Chacksfield	#47
Temptation	Roger Williams	#56
Amapola	Jacky Noguez	#63
(Let's Do) The Hully Gully Twist	Bill Doggett	#66
Theme from "The Sundowners"	Felix Slatkin	#70
Teensville	Chet Atkins	#73
One Mint Julep	Chet Atkins	#82
Midnight Lace	Ray Ellis	#84
Watcha' Gonna Do	Nat "King" Cole	#92
Teenage Hayride	Tender Slim	#93
Theme from "Adventures in Paradise"	Jerry Byrd	#97
Midnight Lace	David Carroll	#98
1961		
Calcutta	Lawrence Welk	#1
Wonderland by Night	Bert Kaempfert	#1
Exodus	Ferrante & Teicher	#2
Last Night	Mar-Keys	#3
On the Rebound	Floyd Cramer	#4
San Antonio Rose	Floyd Cramer	#8
Tonight	Ferrante & Teicher	#8
One Mint Julep	Ray Charles	#8
Wonderland by Night	Louis Prima	#15
Wheels	Billy Vaughn	#28

INSTRUMENTAL SONGS (WITH VOICES) (cont'd)

(Ghost) Riders in the Sky	Ramrods	#30
Tenderly	Bert Kaempfert	#31
The Graduation Song… Pomp and Circumstance	Adriam Kimberly	#34
Love Theme from "One Eyed Jacks"	Ferrante & Teicher	#37
Theme from Dixie	Duane Eddy	#39
Now and Forever	Bert Kaempfert	#48
My Blue Heaven	Duane Eddy	#50
Theme from "My Three Sons"	Lawrence Welk	#55
Theme from "Tunes of Glory"	The Cambridge Strings	#60
Morning After	Mar-Keys	#60
Berlin Melody	Billy Vaughn	#61
Your Last Goodbye	Floyd Cramer	#63
Yellow Bird	Lawrence Welk	#71
The Guns of Navarone	Joe Reisman	#74
Searchin'	Jack Eubanks	#83
Blue Tomorrow	Billy Vaughn	#84
Ring of Fire	Duane Eddy	#84
Drivin' Home	Duane Eddy	#87
Riders in the Sky	Lawrence Welk	#87
Tunes of Glory	Mitch Miller	#88
Late Date	The Parkays	#89
Theme from "The Great Imposter"	Henry Mancini	#90
Hang On	Floyd Cramer	#95
Green Grass of Texas	The Texans	#100

1962

The Lonely Bull	Herb Alpert & The Tijuana Brass	#6
Swingin' Safari	Billy Vaughn	#13
Let's Go (Pony)	The Routers	#19
Chattanooga Choo Choo	Floyd Cramer	#36
Limbo Rock	The Champs	#40
Runaway	Lawrence Welk	#56
Happy Jose (Ching-Ching)	Jack Ross	#57
The White Rose of Athens	David Carroll	#61
Lolita Ya-Ya	The Ventures	#61
That Happy Feeling	Bert Kaempfert	#67
Chapel by the Sea	Billy Vaughn	#69
Worried Mind	Ray Anthony	#74
All Night Long	Sandy Nelson	#75
Lovesick Blues	Floyd Cramer	#87
Smile	Ferrante & Teicher	#94
Hully Gully Guitar	Jerry Reed	#99

1963

| Our Winter Love | Bill Pursell | #9 |

INSTRUMENTAL SONGS (WITH VOICES) (cont'd)

Watermelon Man	Mongo Santamaria	#10
Hot Pastrami with Mashed Potatoes - Part 1	Joey Dee & The Starliters	#36
Java	Floyd Cramer	#49
Cottonfields	Ace Cannon	#67
Organ Shout	Dave "Baby" Cortez	#76
Red Pepper I	Roosevelt Fountain	#78
Antony and Cleopatra Theme	Ferrante & Teicher	#83
Theme from "Lawrence of Arabia"	Ferrante & Teicher	#84
Scarlett O'Hara	Lawrence Welk	#89
Yeh-Yeh!	Mongo Santamaria	#92
Preacherman	Charlie Russo	#92
Marching Thru Madrid	Herb Alpert & The Tijuana Brass	#96
1964		
Cotton Candy	Al Hirt	#15
Sugar Lips	Al Hirt	#30
Comin' in the Back Door	Baja Marimba Band	#41
Do Anything You Wanna (Part I)	Harold Betters	#74
Scratchy	Travis Wammack	#80
Stockholm	Lawrence Welk	#91
The Son of Rebel Rouser	Duane Eddy	#97
1965		
Hang on Sloopy	Ramsey Lewis Trio	#11
Red Roses for a Blue Lady	Bert Kaempfert	#11
Twine Time	Alvin Cash & The Crawlers	#14
Three O'Clock in the Morning	Bert Kaempfert	#33
Hole in the Wall	The Packers	#43
3rd Man Theme	Herb Alpert & The Tijuana Brass	#47
Fancy Pants	Al Hirt	#47
Al's Place	Al Hirt	#57
Honky Tonk '65	Lonnie Mack	#78
Soul Sauce (Guacha Guaro)	Cal Tjader	#88
Simpel Gimpel	Horst Jankowski	#91
The Organ Grinder's Swing	Jimmy Smith w/ Kenny Burrell & Grady Tate	#92
The Silence (Il Silenzio)	Al Hirt	#96
1966		
No Matter What Shape (Your Stomach's In)	The T-Bones	#3
Baby Scratch My Back	Slim Harpo	#16
Batman Theme	The Marketts	#17
The Work Song	Herb Alpert & The Tijuana Brass	#18
Flamingo	Herb Alpert & The Tijuana Brass	#28
Batman Theme	Neal Hefti	#35
Ghost Riders in the Sky	Baja Marimba Band	#52
Secret Agent Man	The Ventures	#54

INSTRUMENTAL SONGS (WITH VOICES) (cont'd)

Sippin' 'N Chippin'	The T-Bones	#62
Michelle	Bud Shank	#65
Smokey Joe's La La	Googie Rene Combo	#77
Spanish Harlem	King Curtis	#89
Count Down	Dave "Baby" Cortez	#91
Rib Tip's (Part 1)	Andre Williams	#94
1967		
Soul Finger	Bar-Kays	#17
Hey, Leroy, Your Mama's Callin' You	Jimmy Castor	#31
Memphis Soul Stew	King Curtis	#33
The Dis-Advantages of You	The Brass Ring	#36
Wack Wack	The Young Holt Trio	#40
Spooky	Mike Sharpe	#57
Jump Back	King Curtis	#63
One, Two, Three	Ramsey Lewis	#67
Precious Memories	The Romeos	#67
Funky Donkey	Pretty Purdie	#87
Give Everybody Some	The Bar-Kays	#91
Peas 'N' Rice	Freddie McCoy	#92
Temptation	Boots Randolph	#93
Lapland	The Baltimore & Ohio Marching Band	#94
1968		
The Good, the Bad and the Ugly	Hugo Montenegro	#2
Ame Caline (Soul Coaxing)	Raymond Lefevre	#37
Cold Feet	Albert King	#67
Horse Fever	Cliff Nobles & Co.	#68
Hang 'Em High	Hugo Montenegro	#82
Valley of the Dolls	King Curtis	#83
Here Come Da Judge	The Buena Vistas	#88
Since You've Been Gone	Ramsey Lewis	#98
1969		
Love Theme from Romeo & Juliet	Henry Mancini	#1
Quentin's Theme	The Charles Randolph Grean Sounde	#13
The Popcorn	James Brown	#30
Cloud Nine	Mongo Santamaria	#32
Mah-Na-Mah-Na	Piero Umiliani	#55
Jingo	Santana	#56
Kool and the Gang	Kool & The Gang	#59
Getting the Corners	The T.S.U. Toronadoes	#75
Zazueira (Za-zoo-wher-a)	Herb Alpert & The Tijuana Brass	#78
Moonlight Sonata	Henry Mancini	#87
Land of 1000 Dances	The Electric Indian	#95

INSTRUMENTAL SONGS WITH FEATURED INSTRUMENTS

Many instrumental songs feature orchestras, horns, organs, guitars, or saxophones. Here are a few instrumentals that featured some rarely used instruments (for pop songs, at least). The 3 songs that feature whistling are listed below as well.

YEAR	SONG	ARTIST	HOT 100	FEATURED INSTRUMENT
1960	Amapola	Jacky Noguez	#63	Accordion
1961	Calcutta	Lawrence Welk	#1	Accordion
1963	Washington Square	The Village Stompers	#2	Banjo
1964	From Russia with Love	The Village Stompers	#81	Banjo
1968	Foggy Mountain Breakdown (Theme from Bonnie & Clyde)	Flatt & Scruggs	#55	Banjo
1960	A Closer Walk	Pete Fountain	#93	Clarinet
1962	Stranger on the Shore	Mr. Acker Bilk	#1	Clarinet
1962	Baby Elephant Walk	Lawrence Welk	#48	Clarinet
1962	Above the Stars	Mr. Acker Bilk	#59	Clarinet
1963	Only You (And You Alone)	Mr. Acker Bilk	#77	Clarinet
1969	Camel Back	A.B. Skhy	#100	Clavinet
1962	Telstar	The Tornadoes	#1	Clavioline
1963	Chinese Checkers	Booker T. & The MG's	#78	Electric Piano
1962	Zero-Zero	Lawrence Welk	#98	Kazoo
1960	Never on Sunday	Don Costa	#19	Mandolin
1962	Zero-Zero	Lawrence Welk	#98	Whistling
1962	Sweet Georgia Brown	Carroll Bros.	#100	Whistling
1961	Tunes of Glory	Mitch Miller	#88	Whistling

BREAK-IN SONGS

Break-in songs are a strange part of popular music history. A break-in song is one that consists of parts of a bunch of different songs, but they are different from medleys. Typically, a medley will only have parts of 2-4 different songs, and each part will be an entire verse or chorus. Break-in songs will commonly consist of parts of ten or more songs. Each part will usually only be a few seconds long. These parts are then joined together by spoken dialogue that is usually telling some silly story.

The break-in song was never extremely popular, though Dickie Goodman made a career out of them. From 1956-1977 he had 17 hits- all break-in songs.

YEAR	SONG	ARTIST	HOT 100
1961	The Touchables in Brooklyn	Dickie Goodman	#42
1961	The Touchables	Dickie Goodman	#60
1961	Santa and the Touchables	Dickie Goodman	#99
1962	Ben Crazy	Dickie Goodman	#44
1962	Dr. Ben Basey	Mickey Shorr	#60
1966	Batman & His Grandmother	Dickie Goodman	#70
1969	Moonflight	Vik Venus	#38
1969	On Campus	Dickie Goodman	#45

| 1969 | Luna Trip | Dickie Goodman | #95 |

SONGS FROM TV SHOWS

This list includes songs that were official theme songs for TV shows, but also songs that were featured during a show or a commercial.

SONG	ARTIST	HOT 100	TV SHOW
1960			
Tracy's Theme	Spencer Ross	#13	"Philadelphia Story"
Mr. Lucky	Henry Mancini	#21	"Mr. Lucky"
Peter Gunn	Duane Eddy	#27	"Peter Gunn"
Theme from "Adventures in Paradise"	Jerry Byrd	#97	"Adventures in Paradise"
1961			
Bonanza	Al Caiola	#19	"Bonanza"
Theme from "My Three Sons"	Lawrence Welk	#55	
1962			
Stranger on the Shore	Mr. Acker Bilk	#1	"Stranger on the Shore"
A Swingin' Safari	Billy Vaughn and His Orchestra	#13	"Match Game"
Theme from Ben Casey	Valjean	#28	"Ben Casey"
Route 66 Theme	Nelson Riddle and His Orchestra	#30	"Route 66"
The Ballad of Paladin	Duane Eddy	#33	"Have Gun-Will Travel"
Bonanza!	Johnny Cash	#94	"Bonanza!"
1963			
The Ballad of Jed Clampett	Lester Flatt/Earl Scruggs	#44	"Beverly Hillbillies"
Hootenanny Saturday Night	The Brothers Four	#89	"Hootenanny"
1964			
A Holly Jolly Christmas	Burl Ives	#13	"Rudolph the Red-Nosed Reindeer"
Shangri La	Robert Maxwell	#15	"Mad Men"
Young and in Love	Chris Crosby	#53	"Dr. Kildare"
Rome Will Never Leave You	Richard Chamberlain	#99	"Dr. Kildare"
1965			
Action	Freddy Cannon	#13	"Where the Action Is"
Whipped Cream	Herb Alpert & The Tijuana Brass	#68	"The Dating Game"
1966			
Secret Agent Man	Johnny Rivers	#3	"Secret Agent"
Five O'Clock World	The Vogues	#4	"The Drew Carey Show"
Batman Theme	The Marketts	#17	
Spanish Flea	Herb Alpert & The Tijuana Brass	#27	"The Dating Game"
Batman Theme	Neal Hefti	#35	
Secret Agent Man	The Ventures	#54	"Secret Agent"

SONGS FROM TV SHOWS (cont'd)

1967			
The First Christmas	Danny Thomas	#24	"Cricket on the Hearth"
Music to Watch Girls By	Andy Williams	#34	Diet Pepsi commercial
1968			
Mission-Impossible	Lalo Schifrin	#41	"Mission Impossible"
1969			
Hawaii Five-O	The Ventures	#4	"Hawaii Five-O"
Quentin's Theme	The Charles Randolph Grean Sounde	#13	"Dark Shadows"
Seattle	Perry Como	#38	"Here Comes the Brides"
Mah-Na-Mah-Na	Piero Umiliani	#55	"Benny Hill Show"

SONGS FROM MOVIES/MUSICALS

This list includes songs used in movies, movie musicals, and broadway musicals. The movies aren't limited to 1960s movies. For example, the Token's "The Lion Sleeps Tonight" is included for its use in the 1994 movie "The Lion King", while "The Way You Look Tonight", by the Lettermen is included for its use in the 1936 movie "Swing Time".

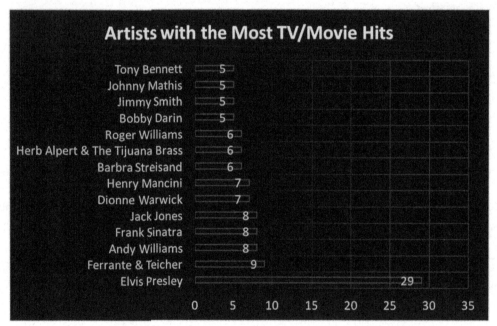

SONG	ARTIST	HOT 100	MOVIE/MUSICAL
1960			
Theme from "A Summer Place"	Percy Faith	#1	
North to Alaska	Johnny Horton	#4	"North to Alaska"
Because They're Young	Duane Eddy	#4	"Because They're Young"
Swingin' School	Bobby Rydell	#5	"Because They're Young"
Lonely Blue Boy	Conway Twitty	#6	"Danny"
Kiddio	Brook Benton	#7	"Mr. Rock and Roll"
Theme from "The Apartment"	Ferrante & Teicher	#10	
Look for a Star	Garry Miles	#16	"Circus of Horrors"

SONGS FROM MOVIES/MUSICALS (cont'd)

Over the Rainbow	The Demensions	#16	"Wizard of Oz"
Look for a Star	Billy Vaughn and His Orchestra	#19	"Circus of Horrors"
Never on Sunday	Don Costa and His Orchestra and Chorus	#19	"Never on Sunday"
Artificial Flowers	Bobby Darin	#20	"Tenderloin"
Hello Young Lovers	Paul Anka	#23	"The King and I"
Look for a Star - Part 1	Garry Mills	#26	"Circus of Horrors"
Theme from "The Unforgiven" (The Need for Love)	Don Costa and His Orchestra and Chorus	#27	"The Unforgiven"
Look for a Star - Part 1	Garry Mills	#26	"Circus of Horrors"
Ruby	Ray Charles	#28	"Ruby Gentry"
Look for a Star	Deane Hawley	#29	"Circus of Horrors"
When You Wish Upon a Star	Dion and The Belmonts	#30	"Pinocchio"
Ruby Duby Du	Tobin Matthews	#30	"Key Witness"
Ballad of the Alamo	Marty Robbins	#34	"The Alamo"
Waltzing Matilda	Jimmie Rodgers	#41	"On the Beach"
Ruby Duby Du from "Key Witness"	Charles Wolcott	#41	
Shazam!	Duane Eddy	#45	"Because They're Young"
Wake Me When It's Over	Andy Williams	#50	"Wake Me When It's Over"
Anyway the Wind Blows	Doris Day	#50	"Please Don't Eat The Daisies"
The Sundowners	Billy Vaughn	#51	"The Sundowners"
One Boy	Joanie Sommers	#54	"Bye Bye Birdie"
Ruby	Adam Wade	#58	"Ruby Gentry"
Ballad of the Alamo	Bud and Travis	#64	"The Alamo"
How to Handle a Woman	Johnny Mathis	#64	"Camelot"
The Green Leaves of Summer	The Brothers Four	#65	"The Alamo"
Theme from "The Sundowners"	Felix Slatkin	#70	
Do You Mind?	Andy Williams	#70	"Let's Get Married"
Theme from "The Dark at the Top of the Stairs"	Ernie Freeman	#70	
Too Young to Go Steady	Connie Stevens	#71	"Strip for Action"
Gloria's Theme	Adam Wade	#74	"Butterfield 8"
Climb Every Mountain	Tony Bennett	#74	"The Sound of Music"
My Hero	Harold Melvin and The Blue Notes	#78	"The Chocolate Soldier"
Maria	Johnny Mathis	#78	"West Side Story"
I'll Be Seeing You	The Five Satins	#79	"Right This Way"
Make Someone Happy	Perry Como	#80	"Do Re Mi"
Come Rain or Come Shine	Ray Charles	#83	"St. Louis Woman"
The Sound of Music	Patti Page	#90	"The Sound of Music"
Adam and Eve	Paul Anka	#90	"The Private Lives of Adam & Eve"
Do You Mind?	Anthony Newley	#91	"Let's Get Married"
Midnight Lace- Part One	Ray Conniff	#92	"Midnight Lace"
Theme from The Sundowners	Mantovani	#93	
Midnight Lace	David Carroll and His Orchestra	#98	"Midnight Lace"

SONGS FROM MOVIES/MUSICALS (cont'd)

1961

Song	Artist	Chart	Movie/Musical
The Lion Sleeps Tonight	The Tokens	#1	"The Lion King"
Exodus	Ferrante & Teicher	#2	"Exodus"
Where the Boys Are	Connie Francis	#4	"Where the Boys Are"
Tonight	Ferrante & Teicher	#8	"West Side Story"
Let's Get Together	Hayley Mills	#8	"Parent Trap"
Moon River	Jerry Butler	#11	"Breakfast at Tiffany's"
Never on Sunday	The Chordettes	#13	"Never on Sunday"
The Way You Look Tonight	The Lettermen	#13	"Swing Time"
Flaming Star	Elvis Presley	#14	"Flaming Star"
Pepe	Duane Eddy	#18	"Pepe"
Don't Blame Me	The Everly Brothers	#20	"Clowns in Clover"
That Old Black Magic	Bobby Rydell	#21	"Star-Spangled Rhythm"
Wild in the Country	Elvis Presley	#26	"Wild in the Country"
Main Theme from Exodus (Ari's Theme)	Mantovani	#31	
Lonely Man	Elvis Presley	#32	"Wild in the Country"
The Magnificent Seven	Al Caiola	#35	"The Magnificent Seven"
Exodus	Eddie Harris	#36	"Exodus"
Love Theme from "One Eyed Jacks"	Ferrante & Teicher	#37	
Smile	Timi Yuro	#42	"Modern Times"
Tonight	Eddie Fisher	#44	"West Side Story"
The Second Time Around	Frank Sinatra	#50	"High Time"
I'll Be Seeing You	Frank Sinatra	#58	"Right This Way"
Theme from "Tunes of Glory"	The Cambridge Strings	#60	
The Exodus Song (This Land Is Mine)	Pat Boone	#64	Theme song from the movie "Exodus"
Come September	Billy Vaughn and His Orchestra	#73	"Come September"
The Guns of Navarone	Joe Reisman	#74	"The Guns of Navarone"
Summertime	The Marcels	#78	"Porgy and Bess" (opera)
La Dolce Vita	Ray Ellis	#81	"La Dolce Vita"
Kissin Game	Dion	#82	"Teenage Millionaire"
Ring of Fire	Duane Eddy	#84	"Ring of Fire"
Theme from "Goodbye Again"	Ferrante & Teicher	#85	
If I Knew	Nat "King" Cole	#86	"The Unsinkable Molly Brown"
Tunes of Glory	Mitch Miller	#88	"Tunes of Glory"
This World We Love In (Il Cielo In Una Stanza)	Mina	#90	"Girl with a Suitcase"
Theme from "The Great Imposter"	Henry Mancini	#90	
Girls Girls Girls (Part II)	The Coasters	#96	"Girls! Girls! Girls!"
Can't Help Lovin' That Girl of Mine	The Excels	#100	"Show Boat"

1962

Song	Artist	Chart	Movie/Musical
Return to Sender	Elvis Presley	#2	"Girls! Girls! Girls!"
Can't Help Falling in Love	Elvis Presley	#2	"Blue Hawaii"
Al Di La'	Emilio Pericoli	#6	"Rome Adventure"

SONGS FROM MOVIES/MUSICALS (cont'd)

Title	Artist	Chart	Movie/Musical
Shout - Part 1	Joey Dee & The Starliters	#6	"Hey, Let's Twist"
Theme from "Dr. Kildare" (Three Stars Will Shine Tonight)	Richard Chamberlain	#10	
Town Without Pity	Gene Pitney	#13	"Town Without Pity"
Follow That Dream	Elvis Presley	#15	"Follow That Dream"
What Kind of Fool am I	Sammy Davis Jr.	#17	"Stop the World- I Want to Get Off"
What Kind of Love Is This	Joey Dee & The Starliters	#18	"Two Tickets to Paris"
Hey, Let's Twist	Joey Dee & The Starliters	#20	"Hey, Let's Twist"
Walk on the Wild Side Part 1	Jimmy Smith	#21	"Walk on the Wild Side"
Rock-A-Hula Baby ("Twist" Special)	Elvis Presley	#23	"Blue Hawaii"
Seven Day Weekend	Gary (U.S.) Bonds	#27	"It's Trad-Dad"
King of the Whole Wide World	Elvis Presley	#30	"Kid Galahad"
Multiplication	Bobby Darin	#30	"Come September"
If a Man Answers	Bobby Darin	#32	"If a Man Answers"
Pocketful of Miracles	Frank Sinatra	#34	"Pocketful of Miracles"
Chattanooga Choo Choo	Floyd Cramer	#36	"Sun Valley Serenade"
But Not for Me	Ketty Lester	#41	"Girl Crazy"
Walk on the Wild Side	Brook Benton	#43	"Walk on the Wild Side"
Lizzie Borden	Chad Mitchell Trio	#44	"New Faces of 1952"
Baby Elephant Walk	Lawrence Welk and His Orchestra	#48	"Hatari!"
Maria	Roger Williams	#48	"West Side Story"
The Boys' Night Out	Patti Page	#49	"Boys' Night Out"
A Taste of Honey	Denny Martin and His Orchestra	#50	"A Taste of Honey"
Above the Stars	Mr. Acker Bilk	#59	"The Wonderful World of the Brothers Grimm"
Lolita Ya-Ya	The Ventures	#61	"Lolita"
The White Rose of Athens	David Carroll and His Orchestra	#61	"Dreamland of Desire"
(Theme from) A Summer Place	Dick Roman	#64	
Roly Poly	Joey Dee & The Starliters	#74	"Hey, Let's Twist"
Ol' Man River	Jimmy Smith	#82	"Show Boat"
What Kind of Fool am I	Anthony Newley	#85	"Stop the World- I Want to Get Off"
Marianna	Johnny Mathis	#86	"The Counterfeit Traitor"
Baby Elephant Walk	The Miniature Men	#87	"Hatari!"
A Taste of Honey	Victor Feldman Quartet	#88	"A Taste of Honey"
March of the Siamese Children	Kenny Ball	#88	"The King and I"
Summertime	Ricky Nelson	#89	"Porgy and Bess"
What Kind of Fool am I	Robert Goulet	#89	"Stop the World- I Want to Get Off"
Baby It's Cold Outside	Ray Charles	#91	"Neptune's Daughter"
Smile	Ferrante & Teicher	#94	"Modern Times"
Theme from "Hatari!"	Henry Mancini and His Orchestra	#95	"Hatari!"
Let Me Entertain You	Ray Anthony	#96	"Gypsy"
Lisa	Ferrante & Teicher	#98	"Lisa"
Lover Come Back	Doris Day	#98	"Lover Come Back"

SONGS FROM MOVIES/MUSICALS (cont'd)

Where Do You Come From	Elvis Presley	#99	"Girls! "Girls! Girls!"
Theme from Taras Bulba (The Wishing Star)	Jerry Butler	#100	
Till There was You	Valjean	#100	"The Music Man"

1963

In Dreams	Roy Orbison	#7	"Blue Velvet"
More	Kai Winding & Orchestra	#8	"Mondo Cane"
Zip-A-Dee Doo-Dah	Bob B. Soxx and The Blue Jeans	#8	"Song of the South"
Bossa Nova Baby	Elvis Presley	#8	"Fun in Acapulco"
One Broken Heart for Sale	Elvis Presley	#11	"It Happened at the World's Fair"
Days of Wine and Roses	Andy Williams	#26	"Days of Wine and Roses"
Days of Wine and Roses	Henry Mancini and His Orchestra	#33	"Days of Wine and Roses"
More	Vic Dana	#42	Italian documentary ""Mondo Cane"
September Song	Jimmy Durante	#51	"Knickerbocker Holiday"
They Remind Me Too Much of You	Elvis Presley	#53	"It Happened at the World's Fair"
As Long as She Needs Me	Sammy Davis Jr.	#59	"Oliver!"
Hi-Lili, Hi-Lo	Richard Chamberlain	#64	"Lili"
I Could Have Danced All Night	Ben E. King	#72	"My Fair Lady"
Call Me Irresponsible	Jack Jones	#75	"Papa's Delicate Condition"
Call Me Irresponsible	Frank Sinatra	#78	"Papa's Delicate Condition"
Antony and Cleopatra Theme	Ferrante & Teicher	#83	"Cleopatra"
Theme from "Lawrence of Arabia"	Ferrante & Teicher	#84	
Toys in the Attic	Joe Sherman	#85	"Toys in the Attic"
Al Di La	Connie Francis	#90	"Rome Adventure"
Toys in the Attic	Jack Jones	#92	"Toys in the Attic"
It's a Mad, Mad, Mad, Mad World	The Shirelles	#92	"It's a Mad, Mad, Mad, Mad World"
Theme from "Any Number Can Win"	Jimmy Smith	#96	
31 Flavors	The Shirelles	#97	"It's a Mad, Mad, Mad, Mad World"
True Love	Richard Chamberlain	#98	"High Society"

1964

Hello, Dolly!	Louis Armstrong	#1	"Hello, Dolly!"
People	Barbra Streisand	#5	"Funny Girl"
Hooray for Santa Claus	Al Hirt	#6	"Santa Claus Conquers the Martians"
Kissin' Cousins	Elvis Presley	#12	"Kissin' Cousins"
Today	The New Christy Minstrels	#17	"Advance to the Rear"
Ebb Tide	Lenny Welch	#25	"Sweet Bird of Youth"
On the Street Where You Live	Andy Williams	#28	"My Fair Lady"
Al-Di-La	Ray Charles Singers	#29	"Rome Adventure"
The Pink Panther Theme	Henry Mancini	#31	"The Pink Panther"

SONGS FROM MOVIES/MUSICALS (cont'd)

Who Can I Turn To (When Nobody Needs Me)	Tony Bennett		"The Roar of the Greasepaint"
You'll Never Walk Alone	Patti LaBelle	#34	"Carousel"
Charade	Sammy Kaye and His Orchestra	#36	"Charade"
Funny Girl	Barbra Streisand	#44	"Funny Girl"
Looking for Love	Connie Francis	#45	"Looking for Love"
I Wanna Be with You	Nancy Wilson	#57	"Golden Boy"
The James Bond Theme	Billy Strange	#58	from the "James Bond" movies
Where Love has Gone	Jack Jones	#62	"Where Love has Gone"
Love with the Proper Stranger	Jack Jones	#62	"Love with the Proper Stranger"
Almost There	Andy Williams	#67	"I'd Rather Be Rich"
The Cat	Jimmy Smith	#67	"Joy House"
A House Is Not a Home	Dionne Warwick	#71	"A House is Not a Home"
Who's Afraid of Virginia Woolf? (Part 1)	Jimmy Smith	#72	"Who's Afraid of Virginia Woolf?"
A House Is Not a Home	Brook Benton	#75	"A House is Not a Home"
Stay with Me	Frank Sinatra	#81	"The Cardinal"
From Russia with Love	The Village Stompers	#81	"From Russia with Love"
Always in My Heart	Los Indios Tabajaras	#82	"Always in My Heart"
A Taste of Honey	Tony Bennett	#94	"A Taste of Honey"
Fiddler on the Roof	The Village Stompers	#97	"Fiddler on the Roof"
A Shot in the Dark	Henry Mancini	#97	"Pink Panther"
Charade	Andy Williams	#100	"Charade"
People	Nat "King" Cole	#100	"Funny Girl"
1965			
What's New Pussycat?	Tom Jones	#3	"What's New Pussycat?"
Catch Us If You Can	Dave Clark Five	#4	"Having a Wild Weekend"
Ferry Cross the Mersey	Gerry and The Pacemakers	#6	"Ferry Cross the Mersey"
Taste of Honey	Herb Alpert & The Tijuana Brass	#7	"A Taste of Honey"
Amen	The Impressions	#7	"Lilies of the Field"
Hush, Hush, Sweet Charlotte	Patti Page	#8	"Hush, Hush, Sweet Charlotte"
Goldfinger	Shirley Bassey	#8	"Goldfinger"
Baby the Rain Must Fall	Glenn Yarbrough	#12	"Baby the Rain Must Fall"
Sunshine, Lollipops and Rainbows	Lesley Gore	#13	"Ski Party"
Some Enchanted Evening	Jay & The Americans	#13	"South Pacific"
Theme from "A Summer Place"	The Lettermen	#16	
Do the Clam	Elvis Presley	#21	"Girl Happy"
It's Gonna Be Alright	Gerry and The Pacemakers	#23	"Ferry Cross the Mersey"
If I Loved You	Chad & Jeremy	#23	"Carousel"
Dear Heart	Andy Williams	#24	"Dear Heart"
Dear Heart	Jack Jones	#30	"Dear Heart"

SONGS FROM MOVIES/MUSICALS (cont'd)

Song	Artist	Chart	Movie/Musical
If I Ruled the World	Tony Bennett	#34	"Pickwick"
Smile	Jerry Butler	#42	"Modern Times"
You'll Never Walk Alone	Gerry and The Pacemakers	#48	"Carousel"
Angel	Johnny Tillotson	#51	"Those Calloways"
He Touched Me	Barbra Streisand	#53	"Drat! The Cat!"
Sinner Man	Trini Lopez	#54	"Marriage on the Rocks"
It Feels so Right	Elvis Presley	#55	"Tickle Me"
Goldfinger	Billy Strange	#55	"Goldfinger"
(Here They Come) From All Over the World	Jan & Dean	#56	From concert film "T.A.M.I. Show"
Theme from "Harlow" (Lonely Girl)	Bobby Vinton	#61	
Who Can I Turn To	Dionne Warwick	#62	"The Roar of the Greasepaint"
Married Man	Richard Burton	#64	"Baker Street"
Here I Am	Dionne Warwick	#65	"What's New Pussycat?"
Super-cali-fragil-istic-expi-ali-docious	Julie Andrews-Dick Van Dyke	#66	"Mary Poppins"
Try to Remember	Ed Ames	#73	"The Fantasticks"
Dear Heart	Henry Mancini and His Orchestra	#77	"Dear Heart"
Why Did I Choose You	Barbra Streisand	#77	"The Yearling"
Funny Little Butterflies	Patty Duke	#77	"Billie"
Forget Domani	Frank Sinatra	#78	"The Yellow Rolls Royce"
Forget Domani	Connie Francis	#79	"The Yellow Rolls Royce"
Hello, Dolly!	Bobby Darin	#79	"Hello, Dolly!"
Chim, Chim, Cheree	New Christy Minstrels	#81	"Mary Poppins"
Justine	The Righteous Brothers	#85	"A Swingin' Summer"
I Have Dreamed	Chad & Jeremy	#91	"The King and I"
Try to Remember	The Brothers Four	#91	"The Fantasticks"
Pass Me By	Peggy Lee	#93	"Father Goose"
Love Theme from "The Sandpiper" (The Shadow of Your Smile)	Tony Bennett	#95	
Goldfinger	Jack LaForge	#96	"Goldfinger"
Try to Remember	Roger Williams	#97	"The Fantasticks"
On a Clear Day You Can See Forever	Johnny Mathis	#98	"On a Clear Day You Can See Forever"
1966			
When a Man Loves a Woman	Percy Sledge	#1	"Platoon"
Strangers in the Night	Frank Sinatra	#1	"A Man Could Get Killed"
Yellow Submarine	The Beatles	#2	"Yellow Submarine"
Born Free	Roger Williams	#7	"Born Free"
Somewhere, My Love	Ray Conniff	#9	"Dr. Zhivago"
I've Got You Under My Skin	The Four Seasons	#9	"Born to Dance"
Zorba the Greek	Herb Alpert & The Tijuana Brass	#11	"Zorba the Greek"
The More I See You	Chris Montez	#16	"Billy Rose's Diamond Horseshoe"
Mame	Herb Alpert & The Tijuana Brass	#19	"Mame"
Love Letters	Elvis Presley	#19	"Love Letters"

SONGS FROM MOVIES/MUSICALS (cont'd)

Frankie and Johnny	Elvis Presley	#25	"Frankie and Johnny"
Thunderball	Tom Jones	#25	"Thunderball"
Somewhere	Len Barry	#26	"West Side Story"
Alfie	Cher	#32	"Alfie"
The Phoenix Love Theme (Senza Fine)	The Brass Ring	#32	"Flight of the Phoenix"
There Will Never Be Another You	Chris Montez	#33	"Iceland"
The Impossible Dream (The Quest)	Jack Jones	#35	"Man of La Mancha"
Time After Time	Chris Montez	#36	"It Happened in Brooklyn"
Spinout	Elvis Presley	#40	"Spinout"
I Want to Be with You	Dee Dee Warwick	#41	"Golden Boy"
All That I Am	Elvis Presley	#41	"Spinout"
Please Don't Stop Loving Me	Elvis Presley	#45	"Frankie and Johnny"
In the Arms of Love	Andy Williams	#49	"What Did You Do in the War, Daddy?"
My Little Red Book	Love	#52	"What's New Pussycat"
Mame	Bobby Darin	#53	"Mame"
A Day in the Life of a Fool	Jack Jones	#62	French movie "Black Orpheus"
Lara's Theme from "Dr. Zhivago"	Roger Williams	#65	
I Only Have Eyes for You	The Lettermen	#72	"Dames"
Promise Her Anything	Tom Jones	#74	"Promise Her Anything"
On the Good Ship Lollipop	The Four Seasons	#87	"Bright Eyes"
A Man and a Woman	Tamiko Jones	#88	French movie "A Man and a Woman"
Where am I Going?	Barbra Streisand	#94	"Sweet Charity"
Theme from "The Wild Angels"	Davie Allan/The Arrows	#99	
1967			
To Sir with Love	Lulu	#1	"To Sir with Love"
The Happening	The Supremes	#1	"The Happening"
Georgy Girl	The Seekers	#2	"Georgy Girl"
I Got Rhythm	The Happenings	#3	"Girl Crazy"
This Is My Song	Petula Clark	#3	"A Countess From Hong Kong"
My Cup Runneth Over	Ed Ames	#8	"I Do, I Do"
Ding Dong! The Witch Is Dead	The Fifth Estate	#11	"Wizard of Oz"
Alfie	Dionne Warwick	#15	"Alfie"
Darling Be Home Soon	The Lovin' Spoonful	#15	"You're a Big Boy Now"
The Look of Love	Dusty Springfield	#22	"Casino Royale"
Glad to Be Unhappy	The Mamas & The Papas	#26	"On Your Toes"
Casino Royale	Herb Alpert & The Tijuana Brass	#27	"Casino Royale"
In the Heat of the Night	Ray Charles	#33	"In the Heat of the Night"
All	James Darren	#35	"Run for Your Wife"
Anything Goes	Harpers Bizarre	#43	"Anything Goes"
You Only Live Twice	Nancy Sinatra	#44	"You Only Live Twice"
Chattanooga Choo Choo	Harpers Bizarre	#45	"Sun Valley Serenade"

SONGS FROM MOVIES/MUSICALS (cont'd)

Title	Artist	Chart	Movie/Musical
This Town	Frank Sinatra	#53	"The Cool Ones"
Glory of Love	Otis Redding	#60	"Guess Who's Coming to Dinner"
Wish Me a Rainbow	Gunter Kallmann Chorus	#63	"This Property Is Condemned"
Long Legged Girl (With the Short Dress On)	Elvis Presley	#63	"Double Trouble"
Tony Rome	Nancy Sinatra	#83	"Tony Rome"
Sunrise, Sunset	Roger Williams	#84	"Fiddler on the Roof"
Walk Tall	2 of Clubs	#92	"Doctor, You've Got to Be Kidding"
Stout-Hearted Men	Barbra Streisand	#92	"The New Moon"
The Shadow of Your Smile	Boots Randolph	#93	"The Sandpiper"
To Sir, with Love	Herbie Mann	#93	"To Sir, with Love"
The Jokers	Peter and Gordon	#97	"The Jokers"
Devil's Angels	Davie Allan/The Arrows	#97	"Devil's Angels"
Georgy Girl	Baja Marimba Band	#98	"Georgy Girl"
Live for Life	Jack Jones	#99	"Live for Life"

1968

Title	Artist	Chart	Movie/Musical
Harper Valley P.T.A.	Jeannie C. Riley	#1	"Harper Valley P.T.A."
Mrs. Robinson	Simon & Garfunkel	#1	"The Graduate"
The Good, the Bad and the Ugly	Hugo Montenegro	#2	"The Good, the Bad, and the Ugly"
(Theme from) Valley of the Dolls	Dionne Warwick	#2	
The Look of Love	Sergio Mendes & Brasil '66	#4	"Casino Royale"
Scarborough Fair	Simon & Garfunkel	#11	"The Graduate"
Tip-Toe Thru' the Tulips with Me	Tiny Tim	#17	"Gold Diggers of Broadway"
Promises, Promises	Dionne Warwick	#19	"Promises, Promises"
Shape of Things to Come	Max Frost and The Troopers	#22	"Wild in the Streets"
Born Free	The Hesitations	#38	"Born Free"
People	The Tymes	#39	"Funny Girl"
The Impossible Dream	The Hesitations	#42	"Man of La Mancha"
Guitar Man	Elvis Presley	#43	"Clambake"
My Favorite Things	Herb Alpert & The Tijuana Brass	#45	"Sound of Music"
Bring a Little Lovin'	Los Bravos	#51	"Bravos II"
The Impossible Dream	Roger Williams	#55	"Man of la Mancha"
Foggy Mountain Breakdown	Flatt & Scruggs	#55	"Bonnie & Clyde"
Porpois Song	The Monkees	#62	"Head"
Anyone for Tennis	Cream	#64	"The Savage Seven"
Alfie	Eivets Rednow (Stevie Wonder)	#66	"Alfie"
Stay Away	Elvis Presley	#67	"Stay Away"
Down Here on the Ground	Lou Rawls	#69	"Cool Hand Luke"
A Little Less Conversation	Elvis Presley	#69	"Live a Little, Love a Little"
Let Yourself Go	Elvis Presley	#71	"Speedway"
Cabaret	Herb Alpert & The Tijuana Brass	#72	"Cabaret"
Your Time Hasn't Come Yet, Baby	Elvis Presley	#72	"Speedway"

SONGS FROM MOVIES/MUSICALS (cont'd)

Song	Artist	Chart	Movie/Musical
You Put It on Me	B.B. King	#82	"For Love of Ivy"
Hang 'Em High	Hugo Montenegro	#82	"Hang 'Em High"
Where Do I Go	Carla Thomas	#86	"Hair"
Montage from How Sweet It Is (I Know That You Know)	The Love Generation	#86	"How Sweet It Is"
Climb Every Mountain	The Hesitations	#90	"The Sound of Music"
You'll Never Walk Alone	Elvis Presley	#90	"Carousel"
Almost in Love	Elvis Presley	#95	"Live a Little, Love a Little"
The B.B. Jones	B.B. King	#98	"For Love of Ivy"
1969			
Aquarius/Let the Sunshine In (The Flesh Failures)	The 5th Dimension	#1	"Hair"
Love Theme from "Romeo and Juliet"	Henry Mancini and His Orchestra	#1	"Romeo & Juliet"
Hair	The Cowsills	#2	"Hair"
Jean	Oliver	#2	"The Prime of Miss Jean Brodie"
Good Morning Starshine	Oliver	#3	"Hair"
Easy to Be Hard	Three Dog Night	#4	"Hair"
Everybody's Talkin'	Nilsson	#6	"Midnight Cowboy"
Time Is Tight	Booker T. & The MG's	#6	"Up Tight"
Hang 'Em High	Booker T. & The MG's	#9	"Hang 'Em High"
I've Gotta Be Me	Sammy Davis Jr.	#11	"Golden Rainbow"
The Windmills of Your Mind	Dusty Springfield	#31	"The Thomas Crown Affair"
Clean Up Your Own Back Yard	Elvis Presley	#35	"The Trouble with Girls (And How to Get Into It)"
True Grit	Glen Campbell	#35	"True Grit"
Something in the Air	Thunderclap Newman	#37	"The Magic Christian"
The April Fools	Dionne Warwick	#37	"The April Fools"
Mrs. Robinson	Booker T. & The MG's	#37	"The Graduate"
You'll Never Walk Alone	Brooklyn Bridge	#51	"Carousel"
Mah-Na-Mah-Na	Piero Umiliani	#55	"Sweden Heaven and Hell"
Ballad of Easy Rider	The Byrds	#65	"Easy Rider"
Chitty Chitty Bang Bang	Paul Mauriat	#76	"Chitty Chitty Bang Bang"
Goodbye Columbus	The Association	#80	"Goodbye Columbus"
Theme from "A Summer Place"	The Ventures	#83	
Farewell Love Scene	Romeo & Juliet Soundtrack	#86	"Romeo & Juliet"
Good Morning Starshine	Strawberry Alarm Clock	#87	"Hair"
Wake Up	The Chambers Brothers	#92	"The April Fools"
Ain't Got No; I Got Life	Nina Simone	#94	"Hair"
Love Theme from "Romeo and Juliet" (A Time for Us)	Johnny Mathis	#96	

REMAKES

For this category, I am listing only remakes of songs that previously landed on any of the main Billboard charts. Billboard started these charts ("Best Sellers in Stores", "Most Played by Disc Jockeys", and "Most Played in Juke Boxes") in 1955. The Hot 100 chart began in 1958. As a result, any cover of a song that appeared on a chart pre-1955 will not be listed. For example, Frank Sinatra's 1962 hit "Me and My Shadow" was a big hit for Jack Smith, but it won't be listed below, as that song is from 1927.

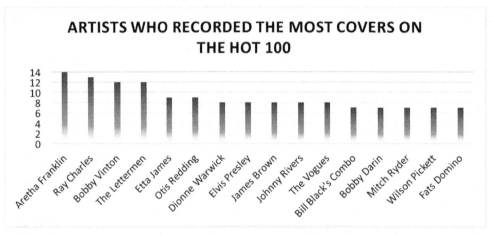

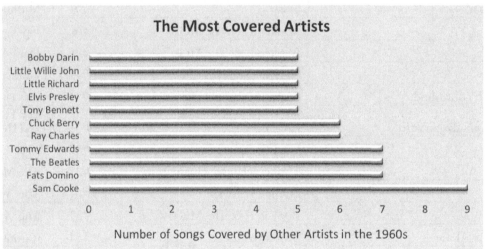

1950s REMAKES

SONG	ARTIST	60s CHART	50s ARTIST	YEAR	50s CHART
1960					
At My Front Door	Dee Clark	#56	The El Dorados	1955	#17
Earth Angel	Johnny Tillotson	#57	The Penguins	1955	#8
Pledging My Love	Johnny Tillotson	#63	Johnny Ace	1955	#17
Cry Me a River	Janice Harper	#91	Julie London	1955	#9
Beyond the Sea	Bobby Darin	#6	Roger Williams	1956	#37
Don't Be Cruel	Bill Black's Combo	#11	Elvis Presley	1956	#1
Mack the Knife	Ella Fitzgerald	#27	Dick Hyman Trio	1956	#8

1950s REMAKES (cont'd)

Don't Go to Strangers	Etta James	#36	Vaughn Monroe	1956	#38
You Don't Know Me	Lenny Welch	#45	Jerry Vale	1956	#14
I Walk the Line	Jaye P. Morgan	#66	Johnny Cash	1956	#17
Too Young to Go Steady	Connie Stevens	#71	Nat "King" Cole	1956	#21
Be-Bop-A-Lula	The Everly Brothers	#74	Gene Vincent	1956	#7
Since I Met You Baby	Bobby Vee	#81	Ivory Joe Hunter	1956	#12
Let It Be Me	The Everly Brothers	#7	Jill Corey w/Jimmy Carroll	1957	#57
White Silver Sands	Bill Black's Combo	#9	Don Rondo	1957	#7
			Dave Gardner	1957	#22
Lucille	The Everly Brothers	#21	Little Richard	1957	#21
Rudolph the Red-Nosed Reindeer	The Chipmunks	#21	Gene Autry	1957	#70
Think	James Brown	#33	The "5" Royales	1957	#66
Red Sails in the Sunset	The Platters	#36	Tab Hunter	1957	#57
Whole Lot of Shakin' Going On	Chubby Checker	#42	Jerry Lee Lewis	1957	#3
My Shoes Keep Walking Back to You	Guy Mitchell	#45	Ray Price	1957	#63
Whole Lot of Shakin' Going On	Conway Twitty	#55	Ray Price	1957	#63
Little Bitty Pretty One	Frankie Lymon	#58	Thurston Harris	1957	#6
Is It Wrong (For Loving You)	Webb Pierce	#69	Warner Mack	1957	#61
Rudolph the Red-Nosed Reindeer	The Melodeers	#71	Gene Autry	1957	#70
Volare (Nel Blu Dipinto Di Blu)	Bobby Rydell	#4	Domenico Modugno	1958	#1
			Dean Martin	1958	#12
Old MacDonald	Frank Sinatra	#25	The Chargers	1958	#95
What am I Living For	Conway Twitty	#26	Chuck Willis	1958	#9
City Lights	Debbie Reynolds	#55	Ray Price	1958	#71
Someday You'll Want Me to Want You	Della Reese	#56	Jodie Sands	1958	#95
Send Me the Pillow You Dream On	The Browns	#56	Hank Locklin	1958	#77
I Can't Help It (If I'm Still in Love with You)	Adam Wade	#64	Margaret Whiting	1958	#74
Someday You'll Want Me to Want You	Brook Benton	#93	Jodie Sands	1958	#95
Are You Lonesome Tonight	Elvis Presley	#1	Jaye P. Morgan	1959	#65
Peter Gunn	Duane Eddy	#27	Ray Anthony	1959	#8
Love Walked In	Dinah Washington	#30	The Flamingos	1959	#88
There's Something on Your Mind	Bobby Marchan	#31	Big Jay McNeely	1959	#44
Ebb Tide	The Platters	#56	Bobby Freeman	1959	#93
I'll Be Seeing You	The Five Satins	#79	Tommy Sands	1959	#51
Wheel of Fortune	LaVern Baker	#83	The Knightsbridge Strings	1959	#88
1961					
Hearts of Stone	Bill Black's Combo	#20	The Charms	1955	#15
That Old Black Magic	Bobby Rydell	#21	Sammy Davis, Jr.	1955	#13
Cherry Pink and Apple Blossom White	Jerry Murad's Harmonicats	#56	Perez Prado	1955	#1
Ling, Ting, Tong	Buddy Knox	#65	The Charms	1955	#26
I Hear You Knocking	Fats Domino	#67	Gale Storm	1955	#2

1950s REMAKES (cont'd)

Seventeen	Frankie Ford	#72	Boyd Bennett	1955	#5
Ko Ko Mo (I Love You So)	The Flamingos	#92	The Crew-Cuts	1955	#6
Blue Moon	The Marcels	#1	Elvis Presley	1956	#55
Heartaches	The Marcels	#7	Somethin' Smith & The Redheads	1956	#71
Corinna, Corinna	Ray Peterson	#9	Joe Turner	1956	#41
Lazy River	Bobby Darin	#14	Roberta Sherwood	1956	#57
Heart and Soul	The Cleftones	#18	Johnny Maddox	1956	#57
Heart and Soul	Jan & Dean	#25	Johnny Maddox	1956	#57
Rock-A-Bye Your Baby with a Dixie Melody	Aretha Franklin	#37	Jerry Lewis	1956	#10
Lazy River	Si Zentner (Up A)	#43	Roberta Sherwood	1956	#57
My Blue Heaven	Duane Eddy	#50	Fats Domino	1956	#19
Blue Moon	Herb Lance	#50	Elvis Presley	1956	#55
Roll Over Beethoven	The Velaires	#51	Chuck Berry	1956	#29
Blue Moon	The Ventures	#54	Elvis Presley	1956	#55
I Don't Want Nobody (To Have My Love but You)	Ella Johnson w/Buddy Johnson	#78	Woody Herman	1956	#75
Canadian Sunset	Etta Jones	#91	Hugo Winterhalter and His Orchestra	1956	#2
Girl in My Dreams	The Capris	#92	The Cliques	1956	#45
Let the Four Winds Blow	Fats Domino	#15	Roy Brown	1957	#29
Jingle Bell Rock	Bobby Rydell & Chubby Checker	#21	Bobby Helms	1957	#6
Ram-Bunk-Shush	The Ventures	#29	Bill Doggett	1957	#67
Trust in Me	Etta James	#30	Chris Connor	1957	#95
Don't Get Around Much Anymore	The Belmonts	#57	Tab Hunter	1957	#74
Peanuts	Rick & The Keens	#60	Little Joe & The Thrillers	1957	#22
Trees	The Platters	#62	Al Hibbler	1957	#92
Teardrops in My Heart	Joe Barry	#63	Teresa Brewer	1957	#64
Summertime	The Marcels	#78	Sam Cooke	1957	#81
Searchin'	Jack Eubanks	#83	The Coasters	1957	#3
What Will I Tell My Heart	The Harptones	#96	Fats Domino	1957	#64
Please Love Me Forever	Cathy Jean & The Roommates	#12	Tommy Edwards	1958	#61
One Summer Night	The Diamonds	#22	The Danleers	1958	#7
Count Every Star	Donnie & The Dreamers	#35	The Rivieras	1958	#73
Bewildered	James Brown	#40	Mickey & Sylvia	1958	#57
It's Too Soon to Know	Etta James	#54	Pat Boone	1958	#4
Dream	Etta James	#55	Betty Johnson	1958	#19
(I Love You) For Sentimental Reasons	The Cleftones	#61	Sam Cooke	1958	#17
Cerveza	Bert Kaempfert	#73	Boots Brown	1958	#23
For Your Love	The Wanderers	#93	Ed Townsend	1958	#13
Little Drummer Boy	Jack Holloran Singers	#96	Harry Simeone	1958	#13
Yellow Bird	The Arthur Lyman Group	#4	The Mills Brothers	1959	#70

1950s REMAKES (cont'd)

Tragedy	The Fleetwoods	#10	Thomas Wayne	1959	#5
Frankie and Johnny	Brook Benton	#20	Johnny Cash	1959	#57
Lovey Dovey	Buddy Knox	#25	Clyde McPhatter	1959	#49
What'd I Say	Jerry Lee Lewis	#30	Ray Charles	1959	#6
Smile	Timi Yuro	#42	Tonyu Bennett	1959	#73
I'll Be Seeing You	Frank Sinatra	#58	Tommy Sands	1959	#51
Danny Boy	Andy Williams	#64	Sil Austin	1959	#59
Yellow Bird	Lawrence Welk	#71	The Mills Brothers	1959	#70
Leave My Kitten Alone	Johnny Preston	#73	Little Willie John	1959	#60
Dedicated to the One I Love	"5" Royales	#81	The Shirelles	1959	#83
Lover's Question	Ernestine Anderson	#98	Clyde McPhatter	1959	#6
1962					
White Christmas	The Drifters	#88	Bing Crosby	1954	#13
You Win Again	Fats Domino	#22	The Paulette Sisters	1955	#92
Teach Me Tonight	George Maharis	#25	The DeCastro Sisters	1955	#2
You Don't Know Me	Ray Charles	#2	Jerry Vale	1956	#14
Love Me Tender	Richard Chamberlain	#21	Elvis Presley	1956	#1
Till	The Angels	#14	Percy Faith and His Orchestra	1957	#63
Little Bitty Pretty One	Clyde McPhatter	#25	Thurston Harris	1957	#6
What's the Reason	Bobby Edwards	#71	Fats Domino	1957	#50
Summertime	Ricky Nelson	#89	Sam Cooke	1957	#81
Four Walls	Kay Starr	#92	Jim Reeves	1957	#11
White Silver Sands (Twistin')	Bill Black's Combo	#92	Dave Gardner	1957	#22
Stardust	Frank Sinatra	#98	Nat "King" Cole	1957	#79
Silent Night	Mahalia Jackson	#99	Bing Crosby	1957	#54
I Can't Stop Loving You	Ray Charles	#1	Don Gibson	1958	#81
Send Me the Pillow You Dream On	Johnny Tillotson	#17	Hank Locklin	1958	#77
I Can't Help It (If I'm Still in Love with You)	Johnny Tillotson	#24	Margaret Whiting	1958	#74
Your Cheatin' Heart	Ray Charles	#29	George Hamilton IV	1958	#72
Susie Darlin'	Tommy Roe	#35	Robin Luke	1958	#5
Count Every Star	Linda Scott	#41	The Rivieras	1958	#73
Baby Face	Bobby Darin	#42	Little Richard	1958	#41
La Paloma	Chubby Checker (Twist)	#72	Billy Vaughn	1958	#20
Twilight Time	Andy Williams	#86	The Platters	1958	#1
Dream	Dinah Washington	#92	Betty Johnson	1958	#19
Sweet Little Sixteen	Jerry Lee Lewis	#95	Chuck Berry	1958	#2
Shake a Hand	Ruth Brown	#97	Mike Pedicin Quintet	1958	#71
You're a Sweetheart	Dinah Washington	#98	Little Willie John	1958	#66
Shout	Joey Dee	#6	The Isley Brothers	1959	#47
My Own True Love	The Duprees	#13	Jimmy Clanton	1959	#33
What'd I Say	Bobby Darin	#24	Ray Charles	1959	#6

1950s REMAKES (cont'd)

My Melancholy Baby	The Marcels	#58	Tommy Edwards	1959	#26
Goodnight Irene	Jerry Reed	#79	Billy Williams	1959	#75
La Bamba	The Tokens	#85	Ritchie Valens	1959	#22
Smile	Ferrante & Teicher	#94	Tony Bennett	1959	#73
Funny	Gene McDaniels	#99	Jesse Belvin	1959	#81
Till There was You	Valjean	#100	Anita Bryant	1959	#30
1963					
Ain't That a Shame	The Four Seasons	#22	Fats Domino	1955	#10
Unchained Melody	Vito & The Salutations	#66	Les Baxter	1955	#1
			Al Hibbler	1955	#3
Only You (And You Alone)	Mr. Acker Bilk	#77	The Platters	1955	#5
You Don't Have to Be a Baby to Cry	The Caravelles	#3	"Tennessee" Ernie Ford	1956	#78
Que Sera, Sera (Whatever Will Be, Will Be)	High Keyes	#47	Doris Day	1956	#2
Armen's Theme	Bobby Vee (Yesterday and You)	#55	Joe Reisman	1956	#46
Hi-Lili, Hi-Lo	Richard Chamberlain	#64	Dick Hyman Trio	1956	#78
I'm in Love Again	Ricky Nelson	#67	Fats Domino	1956	#3
I Could Have Danced All Night	Ben E. King	#72	Dinah Shore	1956	#93
Graduation Day	Bobby Pickett	#88	The Rover Boys	1956	#16
			The Four Freshmen	1956	#17
Don't Be Cruel	Barbara Lynn	#93	Elvis Presley	1956	#1
True Love	Richard Chamberlain	#98	Jane Powell	1956	#15
Deep Purple	Nino Tempo & April Stevens	#1	Billy Ward	1957	#20
Wonderful! Wonderful!	The Tymes	#7	Johnny Mathis	1957	#14
Send Me Some Lovin'	Sam Cooke	#13	Little Richard	1957	#54
Over the Mountain (Across the Sea)	Bobby Vinton	#21	Johnnie & Joe	1957	#8
Without Love (There Is Nothing)	Ray Charles	#29	Clyde McPhatter	1957	#19
Goodnight My Love	The Fleetwoods	#32	The McGuire Sisters	1957	#32
C.C. Rider	LaVern Baker	#34	Chuck Willis	1957	#12
Red Sails in the Sunset	Fats Domino	#35	Tab Hunter	1957	#57
Come Go with Me	Dion	#48	The Dell-Vikings	1957	#4
Bony Moronie	The Appalachians	#62	Larry Williams	1957	#14
Lucky Lips	Cliff Richard	#62	Ruth Brown	1957	#25
Summertime	Chris Columbo Quintet	#93	Sam Cooke	1957	#81
Drip Drop	Dion	#6	The Drifters	1958	#58
Talk to Me, Talk to Me	Sunny & The Sunglows	#11	Little Willie John	1958	#20
All I Have to Do Is Dream	Richard Chamberlain	#14	Everly Brothers	1958	#1
Everybody Loves a Lover	The Shirelles	#19	Doris Day	1958	#6
Shake a Hand	Jackie Wilson & Linda Hopkins	#42	Mike Pedicin Quintet	1958	#71
I Can't Stop Loving You	Count Basie	#63	Don Gibson	1958	#81
Rumble	Jack Nitzsche	#91	Link Wray	1958	#16
Ten Commandments of Love	James MacArthur	#94	Harvey & The Moonglows	1958	#22

1950s REMAKES (cont'd)

Frankie and Johnny	Sam Cooke	#14	Johnny Cash	1959	#57
Misty	Lloyd Price	#21	Johnny Mathis	1959	#12
Here I Stand	The Rip Chords	#51	Wade Flemons w/The Newcomers	1959	#80
I'm Movin' On	Matt Lucas	#56	Ray Charles	1959	#40
Gotta Travel On	Timi Yuro	#64	Billy Grammer	1959	#4
Rockin' Crickets	Rockin' Rebels	#87	The Hot-Toddys	1959	#57
1964					
Maybellene	Johnny Rivers	#12	Chuck Berry	1955	#5
Sincerely	The Four Seasons	#75	The McGuire Sisters	1955	#1
It's a Sin to Tell a Lie	Tony Bennett	#99	Somethin' Smith & The Redheads	1955	#7
On the Street Where You Live	Andy Williams	#28	Vic Damone	1956	#4
Look Homeward Angel	The Monarchs	#47	Four Esquires	1956	#55
Gonna Get Along Without Ya Now	Skeeter Davis	#48	Patience & Prudence	1956	#11
Tear Fell	Ray Charles	#50	Teresa Brewer	1956	#5
Gonna Get Along Without Ya Now	Tracey Dey	#51	Patience & Prudence	1956	#11
In the Still of the Nite	Santo & Johnny	#58	The Five Satins	1956	#24
Roll Over Beethoven	The Beatles	#68	Chuck Berry	1956	#29
Out of Sight, Out of Mind	Sunny & The Sunliners	#71	The Five Keys	1956	#23
Slippin' and Slidin'	Jim & Monica	#96	Little Richard	1956	#33
Let It Be Me	Betty Everett & Jerry Butler	#5	Jill Corey w/Jimmy Carroll	1957	#57
Shangri-La	Robert Maxwell	#15	The Four Coins	1957	#11
Shangri-La	Vic Dana	#27	The Four Coins	1957	#11
Alone (Why Must I Be Alone)	The Four Seasons	#28	Shepherd Sisters	1957	#18
Stardust	Nino Tempo & April Stevens	#32	Nat "King" Cole	1957	#79
Searchin'	Ace Cannon	#84	The Coasters	1957	#3
Pretend You Don't See Her	Bobby Vee	#97	Jerry Vale	1957	#45
It's All in the Game	Cliff Richard	#25	Tommy Edwards	1958	#1
For Your Precious Love	Garnet Mimms	#26	Jerry Butler & The Impressions	1958	#11
Do You Want to Dance	Del Shannon	#43	Bobby Freeman	1958	#5
Good Golly, Miss Molly	Swinging Blue Jeans	#43	Little Richard	1958	#10
Love Is All We Need	Vic Dana	#53	Tommy Edwards	1958	#15
Tea for Two	Nino Temp & April Stevens	#56	Tommy Dorsey (Cha Cha)	1958	#7
Carol	Tommy Roe	#61	Chuck Berry	1958	#18
The Book of Love	The Raindrops	#62	The Monotones	1958	#5
Johnny B. Goode	Dion	#71	Chuck Berry	1958	#8
We Belong Together	Jimmy Velvet	#75	Robert & Johnny	1958	#32
Endless Sleep	Hank Williams Jr.	#90	Jody Reynolds	1958	#5
Tequila	Bill Black's Combo	#91	The Champs	1958	#1
Rockin' Robin	The Rivieras	#96	Bobby Day	1958	#2
There, I've Said It Again	Bobby Vinton	#1	Sam Cooke	1959	#81

1950s REMAKES (cont'd)

What'd I Say	Elvis Presley	#21	Ray Charles	1959	#6
Ebb Tide	Lenny Welch	#25	Bobby Freeman	1959	#93
Tennessee Waltz	Sam Cooke	#35	Jerry Fuller	1959	#63
I Still Get Jealous	Louis Armstrong	#45	Joni James	1959	#63
Since I Don't Have You	Chuck Jackson	#47	The Skyliners	1959	#12
Who Cares	Fats Domino	#63	Don Gibson	1959	#43
Try Me	Jimmy Hughes	#65	James Brown	1959	#48
Little Queenie	Bill Black's Combo	#73	Chuck Berry	1959	#80
Frankie and Johnny	Greenwood County Singers	#75	Johnny Cash	1959	#57
Dream Lover	Paris Sisters	#91	Bobby Darin	1959	#2
Shout	Lulu	#94	The Isley Brothers	1959	#47
Night Time Is the Right Time	Rufus Thomas & Carla Thomas	#94	Ray Charles	1959	#95

1965

Unchained Melody	The Righteous Brothers	#4	Les Baxter	1955	#1
			Al Hibbler	1955	#3
No Arms Can Ever Hold You	The Bachelors	#27	Georgie Shaw	1955	#23
			Pat Boone	1955	#26
			The Gaylords	1955	#67
It's Almost Tomorrow	Jimmy Velvet	#93	Snooky Lanson	1955	#20
Fever	The McCoys	#7	Little Willie John	1956	#24
Two Different Worlds	Lenny Welch	#61	Don Rondo	1956	#11
Canadian Sunset	Sounds Orchestral	#76	Hugo Winterhalter/Eddie Heywood	1956	#2
Honky Tonk	Lonnie Mack	#78	Bill Doggett	1956	#2
Let the Good Times Roll	Roy Orbison	#81	Shirley & Lee	1956	#20
I Want You to Be My Girl (Boy)	The Exciters	#98	Frankie Lymon	1956	#13
Silhouettes	Herman's Hermits	#5	The Rays	1957	#3
Long Lonely Nights	Bobby Vinton	#17	Lee Andrews	1957	#45
			Clyde McPhatter	1957	#49
Diana	Bobby Rydell	#98	Paul Anka	1957	#1
Over and Over	Dave Clark Five	#1	Bobby Day	1958	#41
			Thurston Harris	1958	#96
Do You Want to Dance	The Beach Boys	#12	Bobby Freeman	1958	#5
Send Me the Pillow You Dream On	Dean Martin	#22	Hank Locklin	1958	#77
To Know Him (You) Is to Love Him (You)	Peter & Gordon	#24	The Teddy Bears	1958	#1
Jealous Heart	Connie Francis	#47	Tab Hunter	1958	#62
Secretly	The Lettermen	#64	Jimmie Rodgers	1958	#3
Are You Sincere	Trini Lopez	#85	Andy Williams	1958	#3
Maybe	The Shangri-Las	#91	The Chantels	1958	#15
For Your Love	Sam & Bill	#95	Ed Townsend	1958	#13
Love Potion Number Nine	The Searchers	#3	The Clovers	1959	#23
Heartaches By the Number	Johnny Tillotson	#35	Guy Mitchell	1959	#1

1950s REMAKES (cont'd)

(All of a Sudden) My Heart Sings	Mel Carter	#38	Paul Anka	1959	#15
Smile	Betty Everett & Jerry Butler	#42	Tony Bennett	1959	#73
(I'll Be with You In) Apple Blossom Time	Wayne Newton	#52	Tab Hunter	1959	#31
Cry	Ray Charles	#58	Knightsbridge Strings	1959	#53
Petite Fleur	Lou Johnson (Time to Love)	#59	Chris Barber	1959	#5
Misty	The Vibrations	#63	Johnny Mathis	1959	#12
Danny Boy	Patti LaBelle & Her Blue Belles	#76	Sil Austin	1959	#59
My Man	Barbra Streisand	#79	Peggy Lee	1959	#81
Danny Boy	Jackie Wilson	#94	Sil Austin	1959	#59
You Can't Be True Dear	Patti Page	#94	Mary Kaye Trio	1959	#75
1966					
He	The Righteous Brothers	#18	Al Hibbler	1955	#5
Band of Gold	Mel Carter	#32	Kit Carson	1955	#11
Tell Me Why	Elvis Presley	#33	The Crew Cuts	1956	#45
			Gale Storm	1956	#52
Memories are Made of This	The Drifters	#48	Dean Martin	1956	#1
Young Love	Lesley Gore	#50	Sonny James	1956	#1
Heartbreak Hotel	Roger Miller	#84	Elvis Presley	1956	#1
I'll Be Home	The Platters	#97	Pat Boone	1956	#4
Summertime	Billy Stewart	#10	Sam Cooke	1957	#81
C.C. Rider	The Animals	#10	Chuck Willis	1957	#12
C.C. Rider	Bobby Powell	#76	Chuck Willis	1957	#12
Goodnight My Love	Ben E. King	#91	The McGuire Sisters	1957	#32
Good Golly, Miss Molly	Mitch Ryder & The Detroit Wheels (medley)	#4	Little Richard	1958	#10
Come On Let's Go	The McCoys	#22	Ritchie Valens	1958	#42
Flamingo	Herb Alpert	#28	Gaylords (L'Amore)	1958	#98
Love Is All We Need	Mel Carter	#50	Tommy Edwards	1958	#15
For Your Precious Love	Jerry Butler	#99	Jerry Butler & The Impressions	1958	#11
See You in September	The Happenings	#3	The Tempos	1959	#23
Ebb Tide	The Righteous Brothers	#5	Bobby Freeman	1959	#93
Cry	Ronnie Dove	#18	Knightsbridge Strings	1959	#53
Misty	"Groove" Holmes	#44	Johnny Mathis	1959	#12
Please Mr. Sun	The Vogues	#48	Tommy Edwards	1959	#11
There's Something on Your Mind	Baby Ray	#69	Big Jay McNeely	1959	#44
I Only Have Eyes for You	The Lettermen	#72	The Flamingos	1959	#11
La Bamba	Trini Lopez	#86	Ritchie Valens	1959	#22
Big Hurt	Del Shannon	#94	Miss Toni Fisher	1959	#3
1967					
Sixteen Tons	Tom Jones	#68	"Tennessee" Ernie Ford	1955	#1
I Want You to Be My Baby	Ellie Greenwich	#83	Georgia Gibbs	1955	#14

The 60s Music Compendium

1950s REMAKES (cont'd)

			Lillian Briggs	1955	#18
Let the Good Times Roll	Bunny Sigler (medley)	#22	Shirley & Lee	1956	#20
Love Me Tender	Percy Sledge	#40	Elvis Presley	1956	#1
Why Do Fools Fall in Love	The Happenings	#41	Frankie Lymon & The Teenagers	1956	#6
You Don't Know Me	Elvis Presley	#44	Jerry Vale	1956	#14
Gonna Get Along Without Ya Now	Trini Lopez	#93	Patience & Prudence	1956	#11
Slippin' and Slidin'	Willie Mitchell	#96	Little Richard	1956	#33
Love Is Strange	Peaches & Herb	#13	Mickey & Sylvia	1957	#11
Love Me Forever	Roger Williams	#60	The Four Esquires	1957	#25
Let It Be Me	Sweet Impressions	#94	Jill Corey w/Jimmy Carroll	1957	#57
Please Love Me Forever	Bobby Vinton	#6	Tommy Edwards	1958	#61
For Your Love	Peaches & Herb	#20	Ed Townsend	1958	#13
For Your Precious Love	Oscar Toney, Jr.	#23	Jerry Butler & The Impressions	1958	#11
What am I Living For	Percy Sledge	#91	Chuck Willis	1958	#9
I Can't Help It (If I'm Still in Love with You)	B.J. Thomas	#94	Margaret Whiting	1958	#74
Dedicated to the One I Love	The Mamas & The Papas	#2	The Shirelles	1959	#83
Stagger Lee	Wilson Pickett	#22	Lloyd Price	1959	#1
Kansas City	James Brown	#55	Wilbert Harrison	1959	#1
Danny Boy	Ray Price	#60	Sil Austin	1959	#59
You're So Fine	Bunny Sigler (medley)	#86	The Falcons	1959	#17
Lovey Dovey	Bunny Sigler (medley)	#86	Clyde McPhatter	1959	#49
There Must Be a Way	Jimmy Roselli	#93	Joni James	1959	#33
Shout	Lulu & The Luvers	#96	The Isley Brothers	1959	#47
1968					
Unchained Melody	The Sweet Inspirations	#73	Les Baxter	1955	#1
			Al Hibbler	1955	#3
Born to Be with You	Sonny James	#81	The Chordettes	1956	#5
My Special Angel	The Vogues	#7	Bobby Helms	1957	#7
Suzie-Q	Creedence Clearwater Revival	#11	Dale Hawkins	1957	#27
Till	The Vogues	#27	Percy Faith and His Orchestra	1957	#63
You Send Me	Aretha Franklin	#56	Sam Cooke	1957	#1
Without Love (There Is Nothing)	Oscar Toney, Jr.	#90	Clyde McPhatter	1957	#19
Summertime Blues	Blue Cheer	#14	Eddie Cochran	1958	#8
For Your Precious Love	Jackie Wilson & Count Basie	#49	Jerry Butler & The Impressions	1958	#11
Ten Commandments of Love	Peaches & Herb	#55	Harvey & The Moonglows	1958	#22
Bluebirds Over the Mountain	The Beach Boys	#61	Ersel Hickey	1958	#74
Do You Want to Dance	The Mamas & The Papas	#76	Bobby Freeman	1958	#5
Chantilly Lace	Mitch Ryder (medley)	#87	The Big Bopper	1958	#6
Just as Much as Ever	Bobby Vinton	#24	Bob Beckham	1959	#32
Battle Hymn of the Republic	Andy Williams	#33	The Mormon Tabernacle Choir	1959	#13

1950s REMAKES (cont'd)

Song	Artist	Peak	Original Artist	Year	Orig Peak
Put Your Head on My Shoulder	The Lettermen	#44	Paul Anka	1959	#2
Lovey Dovey	Otis Redding & Carla Thomas	#60	Clyde McPhatter	1959	#49
Personality	Mitch Ryder (medley)	#87	Lloyd Price	1959	#2
Battle of New Orleans	Harpers Bizarre	#95	Johnny Horton	1959	#1
1969					
Earth Angel	The Vogues	#42	The Penguins	1955	#8
Moments to Remember	The Vogues	#47	The Four Lads	1955	#2
Sincerely	Paul Anka	#80	The McGuire Sisters	1955	#1
Only You (And You Alone)	Bobby Hatfield	#95	The Platters	1955	#5
No, Not Much!	The Vogues	#34	The Four Lads	1956	#2
Out of Sight, Out of Mind	Little Anthony & The Imperials	#52	The Five Keys	1956	#23
Chains of Love	Bobby Bland	#60	Pat Boone	1956	#10
In the Still of the Nite	Paul Anka	#64	The Five Satins	1956	#24
Sine I Met You Baby	Sonny James	#65	Ivory Joe Hunter	1956	#12
When You Dance	Jay & The Americans	#70	The Turbans	1956	#33
No, Not Much!	Smoke Ring	#85	The Four Lads	1956	#2
Goodnight My Love	Paul Anka	#27	The McGuire Sisters	1957	#32
Let It Be Me	Glen Campbell & Bobbie Gentry	#36	Jill Corey w/Jimmy Carroll	1957	#57
And That Reminds Me	The Four Seasons	#45	Kay Starr	1957	#9
Shangri-La	The Lettermen	#64	The Four Coins	1957	#11
Greensleeves	Mason Williams	#90	Beverley Sisters	1957	#41
To Know Him (You) Is to Love Him (You)	Bobby Vinton	#34	The Teddy Bears	1958	#1
Looking Back	Joe Simon	#70	Nat "King" Cole	1958	#5
Ten Commandments of Love	Little Anthony & The Imperials	#82	Harvey & The Moonglows	1958	#22
Great Balls of Fire	Tiny Tim	#85	Jerry Lee Lewis	1958	#2
I Can't Help It (If I'm Still in Love with You)	Al Martino	#97	Margaret Whiting	1958	#74
Along Came Jones	Ray Stevens	#27	Coasters	1959	#9
Lover's Question	Otis Redding	#48	Clyde McPhatter	1959	#6
Tragedy	Brian Hyland	#56	Thomas Wayne	1959	#5
Hushabye	Jay & The Americans	#62	The Mystics	1959	#20
Shout	The Chambers Brothers	#83	The Isley Brothers	1959	#47
Guess Who	Ruby Winters	#99	Jesse Belvin	1959	#31

1960s REMAKES

Here's a great trivia question: What was the first song written by John Lennon and Paul McCartney to chart in the U.S.? If you said "I Want to Hold Your Hand", you'd be wrong! Good guess, but still wrong. That was the first Beatles' hit in the U.S., which was, of course, written by Lennon and McCartney. However, the first song written by Lennon/McCartney to hit the Hot 100 chart was actually "From Me to You" released by Del Shannon in 1963. So even though he didn't write it, his version was the first to appear on the Hot 100 chart, which is why I have the Beatles' version listed as the cover, and Shannon's version listed as the original.

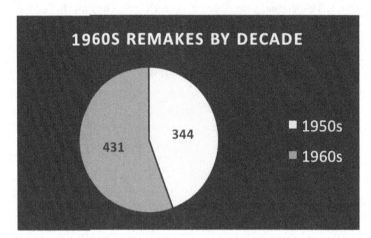

SONG	ARTIST	HOT 100	ORIGINAL 60s ARTIST	YEAR	HOT 100
1961					
One Mint Julep	Ray Charles	#8	Chet Atkins	1960	#82
Never on Sunday	The Chordettes	#13	Don Costa	1960	#19
Temptation	The Everly Brothers	#27	Roger Williams	1960	#56
Twistin' U.S.A.	Chubby Checker	#68	Danny & The Juniors	1960	#27
Night Train	Richard Hayman	#80	The Viscounts	1960	#82
Never on Sunday	Lale Anderson (Ein Schiff)	#88	Don Costa	1960	#19
Won't You Come Home Bill Bailey	Della Reese	#98	Bobby Darin	1960	#19
1962					
You Are My Sunshine	Ray Charles	#7	Johnny & The Hurricanes	1960	#91
Irresistible You	Bobby Darin	#15	Bobby Peterson	1960	#96
I was Such a Fool (To Fall in Love with You)	Connie Francis	#24	The Flamingos	1960	#71
Jambalaya (On the Bayou)	Fats Domino	#30	Bobby Comstock	1960	#90
Night Train	James Brown	#35	The Viscounts	1960	#82
Chattanooga Choo Choo	Ernie Fields	#36	Ernie Fields	1960	#54
Maria	Roger Williams	#48	Johnny Mathis	1960	#78
Theme from "A Summer Place"	Dick Roman	#64	Percy Faith	1960	#1
Mashed Potatoes	Steve Alaimo	#81	Nat Kendrick (Do The)	1960	#84
Green Leaves of Summer	Kenny Ball	#87	Brothers Four	1960	#65
Fools Rush In	Etta James	#87	Brook Benton	1960	#24
I Really Don't Want to Know	Solomon Burke	#93	Tommy Edwards	1960	#18
The Twist	Ernie Freeman	#93	Chubby Checker	1960	#1

1960s REMAKES (cont'd)

When I Fall in Love	The Lettermen	#7	Etta Jones	1961	#65
Runaway	Lawrence Welk	#56	Del Shannon	1961	#1
Glory of Love	Don Gardner & Dee Dee Ford	#75	The Roommates	1961	#49
Amor	Roger Williams	#88	Ben E. King	1961	#18
Don't Cry, Baby	Aretha Franklin	#92	Etta James	1961	#61
Three Hearts in a Tangle	James Brown	#93	Roy Drusky	1961	#35
Bonanza	Johnny Cash	#94	Al Caiola	1961	#19
1963					
Blue Velvet	Bobby Vinton	#1	The Statues	1960	#84
Fools Rush In	Ricky Nelson	#12	Brook Benton	1960	#24
String Along	Ricky Nelson	#25	Fabian	1960	#39
Sweet Dreams	Patsy Cline	#44	Don Gibson	1960	#93
I Really Don't Want to Know	Esther Phillips	#61	Tommy Edwards	1960	#18
Won't You Come Home Bill Bailey	Ella Fitzgerald	#75	Bobby Darin	1960	#19
Eternally	The Chantels	#77	Sarah Vaughan	1960	#41
Don't Fence Me In	George Maharis	#93	Tommy Edwards	1960	#45
You Can't Sit Down	The Dovells	#3	Philip Upchurch Combo	1961	#29
No One	Ray Charles	#21	Connie Francis	1961	#34
Signed, Sealed and Delivered	James Brown	#77	Rusty Draper	1961	#91
Trouble in Mind	Aretha Franklin	#86	Nina Simone	1961	#92
Every Beat of My Heart	James Brown	#99	The Pips	1961	#6
			Gladys Knight & The Pips	1961	#45
Michael	Steve Alaimo	#100	The Highwaymen	1961	#1
Cry to Me	Betty Harris	#23	Solomon Burke	1962	#44
I Got a Woman	Freddie Scott	#48	Jimmy McGriff	1962	#20
I Got a Woman	Ricky Nelson	#49	Jimmy McGriff	1962	#20
Funny How Time Slips Away	Johnny Tillotson	#50	Jimmy Elledge	1962	#22
Cotton Fields	Ace Cannon	#67	The Highwaymen	1962	#13
Al Di La'	Connie Francis	#90	Emilio Pericoli	1962	#6
Detroit City	Ben Colder (Sheb Wooley)	#90	Bobby Bare	1963	#16
1964					
Mountain of Love	Johnny Rivers	#9	Harold Dorman	1960	#21
Money (That's What I Want)	The Kingsmen	#16	Barrett Strong	1960	#23
Stay	The Four Seasons	#16	Maurice Williams	1960	#1
Handy Man	Del Shannon	#22	Jimmy Jones	1960	#2
Forever	Pete Drake	#25	The Little Dippers	1960	#9
He'll Have to Go (Stay)	Solomon Burke	#51	Jeanne Black	1960	#4
(I Do The) Shimmy Shimmy	The Orlons	#66	Bobby Freeman	1960	#37
To Each His Own	The Tymes	#78	The Platters	1960	#21
Baby What You Want Me to Do	Etta James	#82	Jimmy Reed	1960	#37
Hey Little One	J. Frank Wilson	#85	Dorsey Burnette	1960	#48
Gee	The Pixies Three	#87	Jan & Dean	1960	#81

1960s REMAKES (cont'd)

Have You Ever Been Lonely (Have You Ever Been Blue)	The Caravelles	#94	Teresa Brewer	1960	#84
Where or When	The Lettermen	#98	Dion & The Belmonts	1960	#3
Let's Have a Party	The Rivieras	#99	Wanda Jackson	1960	#37
California Sun	The Rivieras	#5	Joe Jones	1961	#89
My Heart Belongs to Only You	Bobby Vinton	#9	Jackie Wilson	1961	#65
Right or Wrong	Ronnie Dove	#14	Wanda Jackson	1961	#29
Very Thought of You	Ricky Nelson	#26	Little Willie John	1961	#61
Michael	Trini Lopez	#42	The Highwaymen	1961	#1
Milord	Bobby Darin	#45	Edith Piaf	1961	#88
Big Boss Man	Gene Chandler	#92	Jimmy Reed	1961	#78
Mr. Lonely	Bobby Vinton	#1	Buddy Greco	1962	#64
Twist and Shout	The Beatles	#2	The Isley Brothers	1962	#17
Do You Love Me	Dave Clark Five	#11	The Contours	1962	#3
Funny How Time Slips Away	Joe Hinton	#13	Jimmy Elledge	1962	#22
Al Di La'	Ray Charles Singers	#29	Emilio Pericoli	1962	#6
Snap Your Fingers	Barbara Lewis	#71	Joe Henderson	1962	#8
Taste of Honey	Tony Bennett	#94	Martin Denny	1962	#50
Memphis	Johnny Rivers	#2	Lonnie Mack	1963	#5
Love Me with All Your Heart	Ray Charles Singers	#3	Steve Allen (Cuando Calienta)	1963	#85
Java	Al Hirt	#4	Floyd Cramer	1963	#49
Diane	The Bachelors	#10	Joe Harnell	1963	#97
Needles and Pins	The Searchers	#13	Jackie DeShannon	1963	#84
Reach Out for Me	Dionne Warwick	#20	Lou Johnson	1963	#74
From Me to You	The Beatles	#41	Del Shannon	1963	#77
Little Latin Lupe Lu	The Kingsmen	#46	The Righteous Brothers	1963	#49
Just One Look	The Hollies	#98	Doris Troy	1963	#10
I'm Confessin' (That I Love You)	Nino Tempo & April Stevens	#99	Frank Ifield	1963	#58
1965					
Wonderful World	Herman's Hermits	#4	Sam Cooke	1960	#12
I'll Be There	Gerry & The Pacemakers	#14	Bobby Darin	1960	#79
Theme from "A Summer Place"	The Lettermen	#16	Percy Faith	1960	#1
Midnight Special	Johnny Rivers	#20	Paul Evans	1960	#16
Bumble Bee	The Searchers	#21	LaVern Baker	1960	#46
Just a Little Bit	Roy Head	#39	Rosco Gordon	1960	#64
New Orleans	Eddie Hodges	#44	U.S. Bonds	1960	#6
Road Runner	The Gants	#46	Bo Diddley	1960	#75
Have Mercy Baby	James Brown	#92	The Bobbettes	1960	#66
I Like It Like That	Dave Clark Five	#7	Chris Kenner	1961	#2
I Understand (Just How You Feel)	Freddie & The Dreamers	#36	The G-Clefs	1961	#9
Apache	Davie Allan	#64	Sonny James	1961	#87
You Can Have Her (Him)	The Righteous Brothers	#65	Roy Hamilton	1961	#12
You Can Have Her (Him)	Dionne Warwick	#75	Roy Hamilton	1961	#12

1960s REMAKES (cont'd)

Stand By Me	Earl Grant	#75	Ben E. King	1961	#4
Cupid	Johnny Rivers	#76	Sam Cooke	1961	#17
Orange Blossom Special	Johnny Cash	#80	Billy Vaughn	1961	#63
I'm a Fool to Care	Ray Charles	#84	Oscar Black	1961	#94
			Joe Barry	1961	#24
You Can Have Her (Him)	Timi Yuro	#96	Roy Hamilton	1961	#12
Little Bit of Soap	Garnet Mimms	#95	The Jarmels	1961	#12
No One	Brenda Lee	#98	Connie Francis	1961	#34
Taste of Honey	Herb Alpert	#7	Martin Denny	1962	#50
I Will	Dean Martin	#10	Vic Dana	1962	#47
Thou Shalt Not Steal	Dick & DeeDee	#13	John D. Loudermilk	1962	#73
Make It Easy on Yourself	Walker Bros.	#16	Jerry Butler	1962	#20
Lemon Tree	Trini Lopez	#20	Peter, Paul & Mary	1962	#35
You're Nobody Till Somebody Loves You	Dean Martin	#25	Dinah Washington	1962	#87
Where Have All the Flowers Gone	Johnny Rivers	#26	The Kingston Trio	1962	#21
Bring It on Home to Me	The Animals	#32	Sam Cooke	1962	#13
Boom Boom	The Animals	#43	John Lee Hooker	1962	#60
Lipstick Traces (On a Cigarette)	The O'Jays	#48	Benny Spellman	1962	#80
Silver Threads and Golden Needles	Jody Miller	#54	The Springfields	1962	#20
I Got a Woman	Ray Charles	#79	Jimmy McGriff	1962	#20
Cast Your Fate to the Wind	Sounds Orchestral	#10	Vince Guaraldi Trio	1963	#22
Don't Think Twice, It's All Right	The Wonder Who?	#12	Peter, Paul & Mary	1963	#9
Yeh, Yeh	Georgie Fame	#21	Mongo Santamaria	1963	#92
Give Us Your Blessings	The Shangri-Las	#29	Ray Peterson	1963	#70
Land of 1000 Dances	Cannibal & The Headhunters	#30	Chris Kenner	1963	#77
When a Boy Falls in Love	Sam Cooke	#52	Mel Carter	1963	#44
Watermelon Man	Gloria Lynne	#62	Mongo Santamaria	1963	#10
Land of 1000 Dances	Thee Midniters	#67	Chris Kenner	1963	#77
Fly Me to the Moon	LaVern Baker	#84	Joe Harnell (Bossa Nova)	1963	#14
Fly Me to the Moon	Tony Bennett	#84	Joe Harnell (Bossa Nova)	1963	#14
Cast Your Fate to the Wind	Steve Alaimo	#89	Vince Guaraldi Trio	1963	#22
Yakety Sax (Axe)	Chet Atkins	#98	Boots Randolph	1963	#35
Hang on Sloopy	The McCoys	#1	The Vibrations (My Girl Sloopy)	1964	#26
It Ain't Me, Babe	The Turtles	#8	Johnny Cash	1964	#58
Hang on Sloopy	The Ramsey Lewis Trio	#11	The Vibrations (My Girl Sloopy)	1964	#26
Sha-La-La	Manfred Mann	#12	The Shirelles	1964	#69
You'll Never Walk Alone	Gerry & The Pacemakers	#48	Patti LaBelle & Her Blue Belles	1964	#34
Hang on Sloopy	Little Caesar & The Consuls (My Girl Sloopy)	#50	The Vibrations (My Girl Sloopy)	1964	#26
(There's) Always Something There to Remind Me	Sandie Shaw	#52	Lou Johnson	1964	#49
And I Love Her (Him)	Esther Phillips	#54	The Beatles	1964	#12

1960s REMAKES (cont'd)

Something You Got	Chuck Jackson & Maxine Brown	#55	Alvin Robinson	1964	#52
Hi-Heel Sneakers	Stevie Wonder	#59	Tommy Tucker	1964	#11
Who Can I Turn To	Dionne Warwick	#62	Tony Bennett	1964	#33
Hello, Dolly!	Bobby Darin	#79	Louis Armstrong	1964	#1
From a Window	Chad & Jeremy	#97	Billy J. Kramer	1964	#23
Crying in the Chapel	Elvis Presley	#3	Adam Wade	1965	#88
1966					
Sloop John B	The Beach Boys	#3	Jimmie Rodgers	1960	#64
Sweet Dreams	Tommy McLain	#15	Don Gibson	1960	#93
I Really Don't Want to Know	Ronnie Dove	#22	Tommy Edwards	1960	#18
Time After Time	Chris Montez	#36	Frankie Ford	1960	#75
Money (That's What I Want)	Jr. Walker	#52	Barrett Strong	1960	#23
Georgia on My Mind	The Righteous Brothers	#62	Ray Charles	1960	#1
He Don't Love You (Like I Love You)	The Righteous Brothers	#91	Jerry Butler	1960	#7
Barbara-Ann	The Beach Boys	#2	The Regents	1961	#13
Crying	Jay & The Americans	#25	Roy Orbison	1961	#2
Hurt	Little Anthony & The Imperials	#51	Timi Yuro	1961	#4
(Ghost) Riders in the Sky	Baja Marimba Band	#52	The Ramrods	1961	#30
Little Bit of Soap	The Exciters	#58	The Jarmels	1961	#12
Take Good Care of Her	Mel Carter	#78	Adam Wade	1961	#7
Spanish Harlem	King Curtis	#89	Ben E. King	1961	#10
Look in My Eyes	3 Degrees	#97	The Chantels	1961	#14
I'm So Lonesome I Could Cry	B.J. Thomas	#8	Johnny Tillotson	1962	#89
Love Letters	Elvis Presley	#19	Ketty Lester	1962	#5
Hide & Go Seek	Sheep	#58	Bunker Hill	1962	#33
If You Gotta Make a Fool of Somebody	Maxine Brown	#63	James Ray	1962	#22
She (He) Cried	The Shangri-Las	#65	Jay & The Americans	1962	#5
You're Nobody Till Somebody Loves You	The Wonder Who?	#96	Dinah Washington	1962	#87
Land of 1000 Dances	Wilson Pickett	#6	Chris Kenner	1963	#77
Blowin' in the Wind	Stevie Wonder	#9	Peter, Paul & Mary	1963	#2
Go Away Little Girl	The Happenings	#12	Steve Lawrence	1963	#1
Little Latin Lupe Lu	Mitch Ryder & The Detroit Wheels	#17	The Righteous Brothers	1963	#49
Louie Louie	The Sandpipers	#30	The Kingsmen	1963	#2
Love Me with All Your Heart	The Bachelors	#38	Steve Allen (Cuando Calienta)	1963	#85
Tip of My Fingers	Eddy Arnold	#43	Roy Clark	1963	#45
Cast Your Fate to the Wind	Shelby Flint	#61	Vince Guaraldi Trio	1963	#22
Every Day I Have to Cry Some	The Gentrys	#77	Steve Alaimo	1963	#46
Killer Joe	The Kingsmen	#77	Rocky Fellers	1963	#16
Still	The Sunrays	#93	Bill Anderson	1963	#8
Tell Him (Her)	Dean Parrish	#97	The Exciters	1963	#4

1960s REMAKES (cont'd)

Fly Me to the Moon	Sam & Bill	#98	Joe Harnell (Bossa Nova)	1963	#14
Meditation (Meditacao)	Claudine Longet	#98	Charlie Byrd	1963	#66
A Hard Day's Night	Ramsey Lewis Trio	#29	The Beatles	1964	#1
She (He) Understands Me	Bobby Vinton	#40	Johnny Tillotson	1964	#31
I Wanna Be with You	Dee Dee Warwick	#41	Nancy Wilson	1964	#57
Sugar and Spice	The Cryan Shames	#49	The Searchers	1964	#44
Whenever He (She) Holds You	Patty Duke	#64	Bobby Goldsboro	1964	#39
Hi-Heel Sneakers	Ramsey Lewis Trio	#70	Tommy Tucker	1964	#11
Harlem Shuffle	The Traits	#94	Bob & Earl	1964	#44
Good Lovin'	The Young Rascals	#1	The Olympics	1965	#81
Pied Piper	Crispian St. Peters	#4	Changin' Times	1965	#87
As Tears Go By	The Rolling Stones	#6	Marianne Faithfull	1965	#22
Gloria	Shadows of Knight	#10	Them	1965	#93
How Sweet It Is (To Be Loved By You)	Jr. Walker	#18	Marvin Gaye	1965	#6
Trains and Boats and Planes	Dionne Warwick	#22	Billy J. Kramer	1965	#47
Summer Wind	Frank Sinatra	#25	Wayne Newton	1965	#78
Somewhere	Len Barry	#26	P.J. Proby	1965	#91
(I Can't Get No) Satisfaction	Otis Redding	#31	The Rolling Stones	1965	#1
Lover's Concerto	Sarah Vaughan	#63	The Toys	1965	#2
Downtown	Mrs. Miller	#82	Petula Clark	1965	#1
Respect	The Rationals	#92	Otis Redding	1965	#35
Lover's Concerto	Mrs. Miller	#95	The Toys	1965	#2
1967					
You Got What It Takes	Dave Clark Five	#7	Marv Johnson	1960	#10
Feel so Fine	Bunny Sigler (medley)	#22	Johnny Preston	1960	#14
My Girl Josephine	Jerry Jaye	#29	Fats Domino	1960	#14
Lawdy Miss Clawdy	The Buckinghams	#41	Gary Stites	1960	#47
Chattanooga Choo Choo	Harpers Bizarre	#45	Ernie Fields	1960	#54
You Are My Sunshine	Mitch Ryder	#88	Johnny & The Hurricanes	1960	#91
Temptation	Boots Randolph	#93	Roger Williams	1960	#56
Stand By Me	Spyder Turner	#12	Ben E. King	1961	#4
You Must Have Been a Beautiful Baby	Dave Clark Five	#35	Bobby Darin	1961	#5
Portrait of My Love	The Tokens	#36	Steve Lawrence	1961	#9
Big Boss Man	Elvis Presley	#38	Jimmy Reed	1961	#78
Soothe Me	Sam & Dave	#56	The Sims Twins	1961	#42
Glory of Love	Otis Redding	#60	The Roommates	1961	#49
Just Out of Reach (Of My Two Open Arms)	Percy Sledge	#66	Solomon Burke	1961	#24
Daddy's Home	Chuck Jackson & Maxine Brown	#91	Shep & The Limelites	1961	#2
I Feel So Bad	Little Milton	#91	Elvis Presley	1961	#5
Release Me	Engelbert Humperdinck	#4	Esther Phillips	1962	#8
Try a Little Tenderness	Otis Redding	#25	Aretha Franklin	1962	#100

1960s REMAKES (cont'd)

Song	Artist	Chart	Original Artist	Year	Chart
I Found a Love	Wilson Pickett	#32	The Falcons	1962	#75
Turn on Your Love Light	Oscar Toney, Jr.	#65	Bobby Bland	1962	#28
Little Bit Now	Dave Clark Five	#67	The Majors	1962	#63
Cry to Me	Freddie Scott	#70	Solomon Burke	1962	#44
Shame on Me	Chuck Jackson	#76	Bobby Bare	1962	#23
Only Love Can Break a Heart	Margaret Whiting	#96	Gene Pitney	1962	#2
Shake a Tail Feather	James & Bobby Purify	#25	The Five Du-Tones	1963	#51
Detroit City	Tom Jones	#27	Bobby Bare	1963	#16
I (Who Have Nothing)	Terry Knight	#46	Ben E. King	1963	#29
Lonely Drifter	Pieces of Eight	#59	The O'Jays	1963	#93
Our Winter Love	The Lettermen	#72	Bill Pursell	1963	#9
Mockingbird	Aretha Franklin	#94	Inez Foxx w/Charlie Foxx	1963	#7
Baby I Need Your Loving	Johnny Rivers	#3	Four Tops	1964	#11
When You're Young and in Love	The Marvelettes	#23	Ruby & The Romantics	1964	#48
Everybody Needs Somebody to Love	Wilson Pickett	#29	Solomon Burke	1964	#58
In the Misty Moonlight	Dean Martin	#46	Jerry Wallace	1964	#19
Jump Back	King Curtis	#63	Rufus Thomas	1964	#49
Dancing in the Street	The Mamas & Papas	#73	Martha & The Vandellas	1964	#2
Dancing in the Street	Ramsey Lewis	#84	Martha & The Vandellas	1964	#2
Tell Him	Patti Drew	#85	The Drew-Vels	1964	#90
Respect	Aretha Franklin	#1	Otis Redding	1965	#35
Tracks of My Tears	Johnny Rivers	#10	The Miracles	1965	#16
Too Many Fish in the Sea	Mitch Ryder & The Detroit Wheels (medley)	#24	The Marvelettes	1965	#25
Yesterday	Ray Charles	#25	The Beatles	1965	#1
Chapel in the Moonlight	Dean Martin	#25	The Bachelors	1965	#32
You Were on My Mind	Crispian St. Peters	#36	We Five	1965	#3
Shake	Otis Redding (live)	#47	Sam Cooke	1965	#7
Get Together	The Youngbloods	#62	We Five	1965	#31
Ooh Baby Baby	The Five Stairsteps	#63	The Miracles	1965	#16
1-2-3	Ramsey Lewis	#67	Len Barry	1965	#2
Shadow of Your Smile	Boots Randolph	#93	Tony Bennett	1965	#95
I'll Never Find Another You	Sonny James	#97	The Seekers	1965	#4
Alfie	Dionne Warwick	#15	Cher	1966	#32
Wild Thing	Senator Bobby	#20	The Troggs	1966	#1
Knock on Wood	Otis Redding & Carla Thomas	#30	Eddie Floyd	1966	#28
What Now My Love	Mitch Ryder	#30	Sonny & Cher	1966	#14
Wade in the Water	Herb Alpert	#37	Ramsey Lewis	1966	#19
You Keep Me Hangin' On	Vanilla Fudge	#67	The Supremes	1966	#1
Day Tripper	Ramsey Lewis	#74	The Beatles	1966	#5
Hold On! I'm a Comin'	Chuck Jackson & Maxine Brown	#91	Sam & Dave	1966	#21
Hey Joe	Cher	#94	Leaves	1966	#31
96 Tears	Big Maybelle	#96	? & The Mysterians	1966	#1

1960s REMAKES (cont'd)

Along Comes Mary	Baja Marimba Band	#96	Association	1966	#7
Mellow Yellow	Senator Bobby & Senator McKinley	#99	Donovan	1966	#2
1968					
Am I That Easy to Forget	Engelbert Humperdinck	#18	Debbie Reynolds	1960	#25
Hey Little One	Glen Campbell	#54	Dorsey Burnette	1960	#48
Mountain of Love	Ronnie Dove	#67	Harold Dorman	1960	#21
Million to One	The Five Stairsteps	#68	Jimmy Charles	1960	#5
To Each His Own	Frankie Laine	#82	The Platters	1960	#21
Chain Gang	Jackie Wilson & Count Basie	#84	Sam Cooke	1960	#2
Climb Every Mountain	The Hesitations	#90	Tony Bennett	1960	#74
Georgia on My Mind	Wes Montgomery	#91	Ray Charles	1960	#1
Turn Around, Look at Me	The Vogues	#7	Glen Campbell	1961	#62
I Love How You Love Me	Bobby Vinton	#9	Paris Sisters	1961	#5
Halfway to Paradise	Bobby Vinton	#23	Tony Orlando	1961	#39
Will You Love Me Tomorrow	The Four Seasons	#24	The Shirelles	1961	#1
Take Good Care of My Baby	Bobby Vinton	#33	Bobby Vee	1961	#1
Music, Music, Music	The Happenings	#96	The Sensations	1961	#54
Bring It on Home to Me	Eddie Floyd	#17	Sam Cooke	1962	#13
Sealed with a Kiss	Gary Lewis & The Playboys	#19	Brian Hyland	1962	#3
Breaking Up Is Hard to Do	The Happenings	#67	Neil Sedaka	1962	#1
Turn on Your Love Light	Human Beinz	#80	Bobby Bland	1962	#28
Unchain My Heart	Herbie Mann	#81	Ray Charles	1962	#9
Turn on Your Love Light	Bill Black's Combo	#82	Bobby Bland	1962	#28
Release Me	Johnny Adams	#82	Esther Phillips	1962	#8
Hey, Girl	Bobby Vee (medley)	#35	Freddie Scott	1963	#10
Fly Me to the Moon	Bobby Womack	#52	Joe Harnell (Bossa Nova)	1963	#14
Soulville	Aretha Franklin	#83	Dinah Washington	1963	#92
Up on the Roof	The Cryan' Shames	#85	The Drifters	1963	#5
Goin' Out of My Head	The Lettermen (medley)	#7	Little Anthony & The Impreials	1964	#6
Soul Serenade	Willie Mitchell	#23	King Curtis	1964	#51
Come See About Me	Jr. Walker	#24	The Supremes	1964	#1
			Nella Dodds	1964	#74
Hi-Heel Sneakers	Jose Feliciano	#25	Tommy Tucker	1964	#11
Security	Etta James	#35	Otis Redding	1964	#97
(There's) Always Something There to Remind Me	Dionne Warwick	#65	Lou Johnson	1964	#49
Nitty Gritty	Ricardo Ray	#90	Shirley Ellis	1964	#8
You'll Never Walk Alone	Elvis Presley	#90	Patti LaBelle & Her Blue Belles	1964	#34
(You Can't Let the Boy Overpower) The Man in You	Chuck Jackson	#94	The Miracles	1964	#59
Sally was a Good Old Girl	Trini Lopez	#99	Fats Domino	1964	#99
See Saw	Aretha Franklin	#14	Don Covay	1965	#44

1960s REMAKES (cont'd)

My Girl	Bobby Vee (medley)	#35	The Temptations	1965	#1
Amen	Otis Redding	#36	The Impressions	1965	#7
In the Midnight Hour	The Mirettes	#45	Wilson Pickett	1965	#21
I Got You Babe	Etta James	#69	Sonny & Cher	1965	#1
She's About a Mover	Otis Clay	#97	Sire Douglas Quintet	1965	#13
You Keep Me Hangin' On	Vanill Fudge	#6	The Supremes	1966	#1
Walk Away Renee	Four Tops	#14	The Left Banke	1966	#5
If I Were a Carpenter	Four Tops	#20	Bobby Darin	1966	#8
I'm Gonna Make You Love Me	Madeline Bell	#26	Dee Dee Warwick	1966	#88
Eleanor Rigby	Ray Charles	#35	The Beatles	1966	#11
Born Free	The Hesitations	#38	Roger Williams	1966	#7
Impossible Dream	The Hesitations	#42	Jack Jones	1966	#35
United	Peaches & Herb	#46	The Intruders (We'll Be)	1966	#78
Impossible Dream	Roger Williams	#55	Jack Jones	1966	#35
I Put a Spell on You	Creedence Clearwater Revival	#58	Alan Price Set	1966	#80
Alfie	Stevie Wonder	#66	Cher	1966	#32
It's Over	Eddy Arnold	#74	Jimmie Rodgers	1966	#37
United	Music Makers	#78	The Intruders (We'll Be)	1966	#78
Reach Out I'll Be There	Merrilee Rush	#79	Four Tops	1966	#1
Any Way That You Want Me	American Breed	#88	Liverpool Five	1966	#98
You Don't Have to Say You Love Me	The Four Sonics	#89	Dusty Springfield	1966	#4
I Heard It Through the Grapevine	Marvin Gaye	#1	Gladys Knight & The Pips	1967	#2
For Once in My Life	Stevie Wonder	#2	Tony Bennett	1967	#91
Spooky	Classics IV	#3	Mike Sharpe	1967	#57
Light My Fire	Jose Feliciano	#3	The Doors	1967	#1
Hush	Deep Purple	#4	Billy Joe Royal	1967	#52
Look of Love	Sergio Mendes	#4	Dusty Springfield	1967	#22
Can't Take My Eyes Off You	The Lettermen (medley)	#7	Frankie Valli	1967	#2
I Say a Little Prayer	Aretha Franklin	#10	Dionne Warwick	1967	#4
Piece of My Heart	Big Brother & The Holding Company	#12	Erma Franklin	1967	#62
Take Me for a Little While	Vanilla Fudge	#38	Patti LaBelle & The Bluebelles	1967	#89
Kentucky Woman	Deep Purple	#38	Neil Diamond	1967	#22
Gentle on My Mind	Patti Page	#66	Glen Campbell	1967	#62
For Once in My Life	Jackie Wilson	#70	Tony Bennett	1967	#91
Up-Up and Away	Hugh Masekela	#71	The 5th Dimension	1967	#7
To Love Somebody	The Sweet Inspirations	#74	The Bee Gees	1967	#17
I Was Made to Love Her	King Curtis	#76	Stevie Wonder	1967	#2
I Heard It Through the Grapevine	King Curtis	#83	Gladys Knight & The Pips	1967	#2
Then You Can Tell Me Goodbye	Eddy Arnold	#84	The Casinos	1967	#6
Some Kind of Wonderful	Fantastic Johnny C	#87	The Soul Brothers Six	1967	#91
Never My Love	The Sandpebbles	#98	The Association	1967	#2

1960s REMAKES (cont'd)

Song	Artist	Peak	Original Artist	Year	Orig. Peak
Keep the Ball Rollin'	Al Hirt	#100	Jay & The Techniques	1967	#14
Whiter Shade of Pale	The Hesitations	#100	Procol Harum	1967	#5
New Orleans	Neil Diamond	#51	U.S. Bonds	1968	#51
Lady Madonna	Fats Domino	#100	The Beatles	1968	#4
1969					
This Magic Moment	Jay & The Americans	#6	The Drifters	1960	#16
Forever	Mercy	#79	Billy Walker	1960	#83
Theme from "A Summer Place"	The Lettermen	#83	Percy Faith	1960	#1
Million to One	Brian Hyland	#90	Jimmy Charles	1960	#5
Only the Lonely	Sonny James	#92	Roy Orbison	1960	#2
Greenfields	The Vogues	#92	The Brothers Four	1960	#2
I Need You Now	Ronnie Dove	#93	100 Strings & Joni James	1960	#98
Running Bear	Sonny James	#94	Johnny Preston	1960	#1
I Don't Want to Cry	Ruby Winters	#97	Chuck Jackson	1961	#36
Baby It's You	Smith	#5	The Shirelles	1962	#8
I'll Try Something New	Supremes & Temptations	#25	The Miracles	1962	#39
Try a Little Tenderness	Three Dog Night	#29	Aretha Franklin	1962	#100
Hey! Baby	Jose Feliciano	#71	Bruce Channel	1962	#1
Silver Threads and Golden Needles	The Cowsills	#74	The Springfields	1962	#20
Let Me Be the One	Peaches & Herb	#74	The Paris Sisters	1962	#87
Any Day Now	Percy Sledge	#86	Chuck Jackson	1962	#23
Let's Dance	Ola & The Janglers	#92	Chris Montez	1962	#4
Rhythm of the Rain	Gary Lewis & The Playboys	#63	The Cascades	1963	#3
In My Room	Sagittarius	#86	The Beach Boys	1963	#23
Land of 1000 Dances	Electric Indian	#95	Chris Kenner	1963	#77
That's How Heartaches are Made	The Marvelettes	#97	Baby Washington	1963	#40
Baby, I Love You	Andy Kim	#9	The Ronettes	1964	#24
Share Your Love with Me	Aretha Franklin	#13	Bobby Bland	1964	#42
Nitty Gritty	Gladys Knight & The Pips	#19	Shirley Ellis	1964	#8
What Kind of Fool Do You Think I Am	Bill Deal	#23	The Tams	1964	#9
Walk on By	Isaac Hayes	#30	Dionne Warwick	1964	#6
You'll Never Walk Alone	Brooklyn Bridge	#51	Patti LaBelle & Her Blue Belles	1964	#34
Hold Me	Baskerville Hounds	#88	P.J. Proby	1964	#70
Hurt So Bad	The Lettermen	#12	Little Anthony & The Imperials	1965	#10
You've Lost That Lovin' Feelin'	Dionne Warwick	#16	The Righteous Brothers	1965	#1
Papa's Got a Brand New Bag	Otis Redding	#21	James Brown	1965	#8
Shotgun	Vanilla Fudge	#68	Jr. Walker	1965	#4
Turn! Turn! Turn!	Judy Collins	#69	The Byrds	1965	#1
Tracks of My Tears	Aretha Franklin	#71	The Miracles	1965	#16
I'm Gonna Make You Love Me	Supremes & Temptations	#2	Dee Dee Warwick	1966	#88
Eleanor Rigby	Aretha Franklin	#17	The Beatles	1966	#11
Your Good Thing (Is About to End)	Lou Rawls	#18	Mable John	1966	#95

1960s REMAKES (cont'd)

Song	Artist	Peak	Original Artist	Year	Peak
I Can Hear Music	The Beach Boys	#24	The Ronettes	1966	#100
Don't Touch Me	Bettye Swann	#38	Jeannie Seely	1966	#85
California Dreamin'	Bobby Womack	#43	The Mamas & The Papas	1966	#4
Any Way That You Want Me	Evie Sands	#53	Liverpool Five	1966	#98
River Deep-Mountain High	Deep Purple	#53	Ike & Tina Turner	1966	#88
Don't Forget About Me	Dusty Springfield	#64	Barbara Lewis	1966	#91
This Old Heart of Mine	Tammi Terrell	#67	The Isley Brothers	1966	#12
Poor Side of Town	Al Wilson	#75	Johnny Rivers	1966	#1
Almost Persuaded	Etta James	#79	David Houston	1966	#24
My World Is Empty Without You	Jose Feliciano	#87	The Supremes	1966	#5
Let's Call It a Day Girl	Bobby Vee	#92	Razor's Edge	1966	#77
Oh How Happy	Blinky & Edwin Starr	#92	Shades of Blue	1966	#12
You Keep Me Hangin' On	Wilson Pickett	#92	The Supremes	1966	#1
You've Made Me So Very Happy	Blood, Sweat & Tears	#2	Brenda Holloway	1967	#39
The Letter	The Arbors	#20	The Box Tops	1967	#1
River Is Wide	The Grassroots	#31	Forum	1967	#45
(I Wanna) Testify	Johnnie Taylor	#36	Parliaments	1967	#20
By the Time I Get to Phoenix	Isaac Hayes	#37	Glen Campbell	1967	#26
You've Got to Pay the Price	Gloria Taylor	#49	Al Kent	1967	#49
Purple Haze	Dion	#65	Jimi Hendrix	1967	#65
Gentle on My Mind	Aretha Franklin	#76	Glen Campbell	1967	#62
By the Time I Get to Phoenix	The Mad Lads	#84	Glen Campbell	1967	#26
Who Do You Love	Quicksilver Messenger Service	#91	The Woolies	1967	#95
Me About You	Lovin' Spoonful	#91	Mojo Men	1967	#83
My Special Prayer	Percy Sledge	#93	Joe Simon	1967	#87
Here We Go Again	Nancy Sinatra	#98	Ray Charles	1967	#15
Grazing in the Grass	Friends of Distinction	#3	Hugh Masekela	1968	#1
This Guy's (Girl's) in Love with You	Dionne Warwick	#7	Herb Alpert	1968	#1
Hang 'Em High	Booker T. & The MG's	#9	Hugo Montenegro	1968	#82
The Weight	Aretha Franklin	#19	Jackie DeShannon	1968	#55
Workin' On a Groovy Thing	The 5th Dimension	#20	Patti Drew	1968	#62
Hey Jude	Wilson Pickett	#23	The Beatles	1968	#1
Abraham, Martin and John	The Miracles	#33	Dion	1968	#4
Abraham, Martin and John	Moms Mabley	#35	Dion	1968	#4
With Pen in Hand	Vikki Carr	#35	Billy Vera	1968	#43
Sunday Mornin'	Oliver	#35	Spanky & Our Gang	1968	#30
Mrs. Robinson	Booker T. & The MG's	#37	Simon & Garfunkel	1968	#1
(Sittin' On) The Dock of the Bay	The Dells	#42	Otis Redding	1968	#1
Honey	O.C. Smith	#44	Bobby Goldsboro	1968	#1
The Weight	The Supremes & Temptations	#46	Jackie DeShannon	1968	#55
Who's Making Love	Young-Holt Unlimited	#57	Johnnie Taylor	1968	#5
I Can't Make It Alone	Lou Rawls	#63	Bill Medley	1968	#95

1960s REMAKES (cont'd)					
Born to Be Wild	Wilson Pickett	#64	Steppenwolf	1968	#2
Where Do I Go	The Happenings (medley)	#66	Carla Thomas	1968	#86
(Sittin' On) The Dock of the Bay	Sergio Mendes	#66	Otis Redding	1968	#1
Both Sides Now	Dion	#91	Judy Collins	1968	#8
MacArthur Park	Waylon Jennings & The Kimberlys	#93	Richard Harris	1968	#2
Good Morning Starshine	Strawberry Alarm Clock	#87	Oliver	1969	#3
Feeling Alright	Mongo Santamaria	#96	Joe Cocker	1969	#69
Galveston	Roger Williams	#99	Glen Campbell	1969	#4

SONGS THAT HIT THE HOT 100 CHART TWICE

SONG	ARTIST	HOT 100	YEAR SONG PREVIOUSLY CHARTED	PREVIOUS CHART POSITION
1960				
Little Drummer Boy	Harry Simeone	#24	1958	#13
White Christmas	Bing Crosby	#26	1954	#13
Jingle Bell Rock	Bobby Helms	#36	1957	#6
The Chipmunk Song	The Chipmunks	#45	1958	#1
Let the Good Times Roll	Shirley & Lee	#48	1956	#20
Silent Night	Bing Crosby	#54	1957	#54
In the Still of the Nite	The Five Satins	#81	1956	#24
Over the Mountain; Across the Sea	Johnnie & Joe	#89	1957	#8
Thousand Miles Away	The Heartbeats	#96	1957	#53
1961				
Dedicated to the One I Love	The Shirelles	#3	1959	#83
White Christmas	Bing Crosby	#12	1954	#13
Little Drummer Boy	Harry Simeone	#22	1958	#13
Never on Sunday	Don Costa	#37	1960	#19
The Chipmunk Song	The Chipmunks	#39	1958	#1
Jingle Bell Rock	Bobby Helms	#41	1957	#6
Rudolph the Red-Nosed Reindeer	The Chipmunks	#47	1960	#21
Rockin' Around the Christmas Tree	Brenda Lee	#50	1960	#14
Honky Tonk	Bill Doggett (Part 2)	#57	1956 (Parts 1 & 2)	#2
Leave My Kitten Alone	Little Willie John	#60	1959	#60
Alvin's Harmonica	The Chipmunks	#73	1959	#3
Tonite, Tonite	The Mello-Kings	#95	1957	#77
All I Have to Do Is Dream	The Everly Brothers	#96	1958	#1
In the Still of the Nite	The Five Satins	#99	1956	#24
1962				
The Twist	Chubby Checker	#1	1960	#1

SONGS THAT HIT THE HOT 100 CHART TWICE (cont'd)

Little Drummer Boy	Harry Simeone	#28	1958	#13
Dreamy Eyes	Johnny Tillotson	#35	1959	#63
White Christmas	Bing Crosby	#38	1954	#13
Summertime, Summertime	The Jamies	#38	1958	#26
The Chipmunk Song	The Chipmunks	#40	1958	#1
Jingle Bell Rock	Bobby Helms	#56	1957	#6
Rockin' Around the Christmas Tree	Brenda Lee	#59	1960	#14
Patricia	Perez Prado (Twist)	#65	1958	#1
The Christmas Song	Nat "King" Cole	#65	1960	#80
Ballad of Thunder Road	Robert Mitchum	#65	1958	#62
Rudolph the Red-Nosed Reindeer	The Chipmunks	#77	1960	#21
Alvin's Harmonica	The Chipmunks	#87	1959	#3
Maria	Johnny Mathis	#88	1960	#78
White Silver Sands (Twistin')	Bill Black's Combo	#92	1960	#9
Jingle Bell Rock	Bobby Rydell & Chubby Checker	#92	1961	#21
Shout	The Isley Brothers	#94	1959	#47
Tequila	The Champs (Tequila Twist)	#99	1958	#1
1964				
Walk Don't Run	The Ventures	#8	1960	#2
Tall Cool One	The Wailers	#38	1959	#36
Teen Beat	Sandy Nelson	#44	1959	#4
Hello Mudduh, Hello Fadduh! (A Letter from Camp)	Allan Sherman	#59	1963	#2
Wonder of You	Ray Peterson	#70	1959	#25
It Will Stand	The Showmen	#80	1962	#61
I Can't Get You Out of My Heart	Al Martino	#99	1959	#44
1965				
Try Me	James Brown	#63	1959	#48
4-By the Beatles	The Beatles	#68	1964	#92
So What	Bill Black's Combo	#89	1962	#78
Autumn Leaves	Roger Williams	#92	1955	#1
1966				
Wipe Out	The Surfaris	#16	1963	#2
Harlem Nocturne	The Viscounts	#39	1960	#52
Rainbow	Gene Chandler	#69	1963	#47
Gloria	Them	#71	1965	#93
Feel It	Sam Cooke	#95	1961	#56
Louie Louie	The Kingsmen	#97	1963	#2
1967				
Just One Look	The Hollies	#44	1964	#98
Release Me	Esther Phillips	#93	1962	#8
1968				
You Keep Me Hangin' On	Vanill Fudge	#6	1967	#67

SONGS THAT HIT THE HOT 100 CHART TWICE (cont'd)

Gentle on My Mind	Glen Campbell	#39	1967	#62
Light My Fire	The Doors	#87	1967	#1
Come Rain or Come Shine	Ray Charles	#98	1960	#83
1969				
Get Together	The Youngbloods	#5	1967	#62
I'll Never Fall in Love Again	Tom Jones	#6	1967	#49
But It's Alright	J.J. Jackson	#45	1966	#22
In-A-Gadda-Da-Vida	Iron Butterfly	#68	1968	#30
I Do Love You	Billy Stewart	#94	1965	#26

INSTRUMENTS

The following section lists songs that feature a particular instrument. It may not list every single song that used, for example, a piano, but it will have the songs that featured the piano. In other words, if the sound of the piano isn't obvious and easy to hear, then I left it off the list. For the sake of space, I did this for every instrument.

In addition, the piano, organ, harmonica, and guitar sections list songs that featured solos by those instruments.

If a song has an instrument like the flute, violin, or harp that is part of an orchestra, then the song will be listed under the "orchestra" section. If a song has one of those instruments <u>without</u> an orchestra as well, then it will be listed in that particular instrument's section.

ACCORDION

SONG	ARTIST	HOT 100
1960		
Baciare Baciare (Kissing Kissing)	Dorothy Collins	#43
Amapola	Jacky Noguez	#63
1961		
Calcutta	Lawrence Welk	#1
Flaming Star	Elvis Presley	#14
Lonely Man	Elvis Presley	#32
Transistor Sister	Freddy Cannon	#35
Donald Where's Your Troosers	Andy Stewart	#77
Sugar Bee	Cleveland Crochet	#80
(A Ship Will Come) Ein Schiff Wird Kommen	Lale Anderson	#88
1962		
Zero-Zero	Lawrence Welk	#98
1963		
Pepino the Italian Mouse	Lou Monte	#5
Who Stole the Keeshka?	The Matys Bros.	#55
Pepin's Friend Pasqual (The Italian Pussy-Cat)	Lou Monte	#78
From the Bottom of My Heart (Dammi, Dammi, Dammi)	Dean Martin	#91

ACCORDION (cont'd)

1964		
Milord	Bobby Darin	#45
Rome Will Never Leave You	Richard Chamberlain	#99
I Can't Get You Out of My Heart	Al Martino	#99
Charade	Andy Williams	#100
1965		
What's New Pussycat?	Tom Jones	#3
My Cherie	Al Martino	#88
1966		
Wouldn't It Be Nice	The Beach Boys	#8
God Only Knows	The Beach Boys	#39
I'll Be Gone	Pozo Seco Singers	#92
Dommage, Dommage (Too Bad, Too Bad)	Jerry Vale	#93
Dommage, Dommage (Too Bad, Too Bad)	Paul Vance	#97
1967		
How Can I Be Sure	The Young Rascals	#4

1968		
The Unicorn	The Irish Rovers	#7
A Man Without Love	Engelbert Humperdinck	#19
Les Bicyclettes de Belsize	Engelbert Humperdinck	#31
(Puppet Song) Whiskey on a Sunday	The Irish Rovers	#75
1969		
Where Do You Go To (My Lovely)	Peter Sarstedt	#70

BANJO

SONG	ARTIST	HOT 100
1960		
Happy-Go-Lucky-Me	Paul Evans	#10
Run Samson Run	Neil Sedaka	#28
Mary Don't You Weep	Stonewall Jackson	#41
Lonely Wind	The Drifters	#54
Banjo Boy	Jan & Kjeld	#58
Alabam	Cowboy Copas	#63
Johnny Freedom	Johnny Horton	#69
Banjo Boy	Dorothy Collins	#79
Riverboat	Faron Young	#83
Banjo Boy	Art Mooney	#100
1961		
Sleepy-Eyed John	Johnny Horton	#54
A Dollar Down	The Limeliters	#60

BANJO (cont'd)

Big River, Big Man	Claude King	#82
1962		
Midnight in Moscow	Kenny Ball	#2
P.T. 109	Jimmy Dean	#8
B'wa Nina (Pretty Girl)	The Tokens	#55
Blue Water Line	The Brothers Four	#68
The Green Leaves of Summer	Kenny Ball	#87
This Land Is Your Land	New Christy Minstrels	#93
The John Birch Society	Chad Mitchell Trio	#99
1963		
Washington Square	The Village Stompers	#2
Reverend Mr. Black	The Kingston Trio	#8
On Top of Spaghetti	Tom Glazer	#14
I'll Take You Home	The Drifters	#25
Saturday Night	New Christy Minstrels	#29
Desert Pete	The Kingston Trio	#33
Hootenanny	The Glencoves	#38
The Ballad of Jed Clampett	Lester Flatt/Earl Scruggs	#44
Hootenanny Saturday Night	The Brothers Four	#89
1964		
Hello, Dolly!	Louis Armstrong	#1
So Long Dearie	Louis Armstrong	#56
Winkin', Blinkin' and Nod	The Simon Sisters	#73
From Russia with Love	The Village Stompers	#81
Fiddler on the Roof	The Village Stompers	#97
1965		
Inky Dinky Spider (The Spider Song)	The Kids Next Door	#84
1966		
Flowers on the Wall	The Statler Brothers	#4
Lady Godiva	Peter & Gordon	#6
Stop Stop Stop	The Hollies	#7
Happy Summer Days	Ronnie Dove	#27
History Repeats Itself	Buddy Starcher	#39
1967		
Morningtown Ride	The Seekers	#44
1968		
Those Were the Days	Mary Hopkins	#2
Money	The Lovin' Spoonful	#48
Snoopy for President	The Royal Guardsmen	#85
Do the Best You Can	The Hollies	#93
Battle of New Orleans	Harpers Bizarre	#95

BANJO (cont'd)

1969		
I Guess the Lord Must Be in New York City	Nilsson	#34
Good Clean Fun	The Monkees	#82
July You're a Woman	Pat Boone	#100

BARRED INSTRUMENTS

Barred instruments are xylophones, metallophones, marimbas, glockenspiels and other similar instruments.

SONG	ARTIST	HOT 100
1960		
He'll Have to Go	Jim Reeves	#2
Puppy Love	Paul Anka	#2
My Home Town	Paul Anka	#8
Stairway to Heaven	Neil Sedaka	#9
Theme from "The Apartment"	Ferrante & Teicher	#10
Summer's Gone	Paul Anka	#11
Look for a Star	Billy Vaughn	#19
Never on Sunday	Don Costa	#19
Like Strangers	The Everly Brothers	#22
Delaware	Perry Como	#22
Another Sleepless Night	Jimmy Clanton	#22
Togetherness	Frankie Avalon	#26
Am I Losing You	Jim Reeves	#31
I'm Getting' Better	Jim Reeves	#37
In the Still of the Night	Dion & The Belmonts	#38
Waltzing Matilda	Jimmie Rodgers	#41
I Missed Me	Jim Reeves	#44
Bumble Bee	LaVern Baker	#46
On the Beach	Frank Chacksfield	#47
Christmas Auld Lang Syne	Bobby Darin	#51
Silent Night	Bing Crosby	#54
Always It's You	The Everly Brothers	#56
Someday (You'll Want Me to Want You)	Della Reese	#56
Don't Deceive Me	Ruth Brown	#62
I Can't Help It	Adam Wade	#64
The Old Oaken Bucket	Tommy Sands	#73
Night Theme	The Mark II	#75
Promise Me a Rose (A Slight Detail)	Anita Bryant	#78
Banjo Boy	Dorothy Collins	#79
I Know One	Jim Reeves	#83
Adam And Eve	Paul Anka	#90

BARRED INSTRUMENTS (cont'd)

The Last One to Know	The Fleetwoods	#96

1961

Daddy's Home	Shep & The Limelites	#2
Crying	Roy Orbison	#2
Run to Him	Bobby Vee	#2
Yellow Bird	Arthur Lyman Group	#4
Calendar Girl	Neil Sedaka	#4
This Time	Troy Shondell	#6
Tonight	Ferrante & Teicher	#8
When We Get Married	The Dreamlovers	#10
Spanish Harlem	Ben E. King	#10
Little Devil	Neil Sedaka	#11
Moon River	Henry Mancini	#11
Hello Walls	Faron Young	#12
Look in My Eyes	The Chantels	#14
Let Me Belong to You	Brian Hyland	#20
Jingle Bell Rock	Bobby Rydell & Chubby Checker	#21
Angel on My Shoulder	Shelby Flint	#22
There She Goes	Jerry Wallace	#26
Right or Wrong	Wanda Jackson	#29
The Graduation Song… Pomp and Circumstance	Adriam Kimberly	#34
Kissin' on the Phone	Paul Anka	#35
Love Theme from "One Eyed Jacks"	Ferrante & Teicher	#37
Ready for Your Love	Shep & The Limelites	#42
Starlight, Starbright	Linda Scott	#44
A Perfect Love	Frankie Avalon	#47
The Wayward Wind	Gogi Grant	#50
First Taste of Love	Ben E. King	#53
Three Steps from the Altar	Shep & The Limelites	#58
Tonight I Won't Be There	Adam Wade	#61
Granada	Frank Sinatra	#64
My Claire de Lune	Steve Lawrence	#68
Summer Souvenirs	Karl Hammel Jr.	#68
The Charanga	Merv Griffin	#69
A Little Dog Cried	Jimmie Rodgers	#71
Yellow Bird	Lawrence Welk	#71
Let True Love Begin	Nat "King" Cole	#73
The Guns of Navarone	Joe Reisman	#74
Who Else but You	Frankie Avalon	#82
Kissin Game	Dion	#82
Dream Boy	Annette	#87
(A Ship Will Come) Ein Schiff Wird Kommen	Lale Anderson	#88

BARRED INSTRUMENTS (cont'd)

Losing Your Love	Jim Reeves	#89
Canadian Sunset	Etta James	#91
Girl in My Dreams	The Capris	#92
It's All Right	Sam Cooke	#93
Image - Part 1	Hank Levine	#98
I Love You Yes I Do	Bull Moose Jackson	#98
1962		
Only Love Can Break a Heart	Gene Pitney	#2
Can't Help Falling in Love	Elvis Presley	#2
Happy Birthday, Sweet Sixteen	Neil Sedaka	#5
Next Door to an Angel	Neil Sedaka	#5
Gina	Johnny Mathis	#6
You Beat Me to the Punch	Mary Wells	#9
Percolator (Twist)	Billy Joe & The Checkmates	#10
Love Me Warm and Tender	Paul Anka	#12
Shadrack	Brook Benton	#19
Make It Easy on Yourself	Jerry Butler	#20
Monsters' Holiday	Bobby "Boris" Pickett	#30
Pocketful of Miracles	Frank Sinatra	#34
Don't You Believe It	Andy Williams	#39
Cry to Me	Solomon Burke	#44
King of Clowns	Neil Sedaka	#45
I Will	Vic Dana	#47
Baby Elephant Walk	Lawrence Welk	#48
You Threw a Lucky Punch	Gene Chandler	#49
A Taste of Honey	Martin Denny	#50
Just Tell Her Jim Said Hello	Elvis Presley	#55
I Keep Forgettin'	Chuck Jackson	#55
Keep Your Love Locked (Deep in Your Heart)	Paul Petersen	#58
If I Didn't Have a Dime (To Play the Jukebox)	Gene Pitney	#58
Our Anniversary	Shep & The Limelites	#59
Oh My Angel	Bertha Tillman	#61
If I Should Lose You	Dreamlovers	#62
The Alley Cat Song	David Thorne	#76
Tears from an Angel	Troy Shondell	#77
March of the Siamese Children	Kenny Ball	#88
For All We Know	Dinah Washington	#88
Still Waters Run Deep	Brook Benton	#89
What Kind of Fool am I?	Robert Goulet	#89
Adios Amigo	Jim Reeves	#90
Island in the Sky	Troy Shondell	#92
The Waltz You Saved for Me	Ferlin Husky	#94
What Did Daddy Do	Shep & The Limelites	#94

BARRED INSTRUMENTS (cont'd)

The Wonderful World of the Young	Andy Williams	#99
Night Time	Pete Antell	#100

1963

Our Day Will Come	Ruby & The Romantics	#1
Sukiyaki	Kyu Sakamoto	#1
Blue Velvet	Bobby Vinton	#1
Hello Mudduh, Hello Fadduh! (A Letter from Camp)	Allan Sherman	#2
Rhythm of the Rain	The Cascades	#3
Tell Him	The Exciters	#4
Up on the Roof	The Drifters	#5
Those Lazy-Hazy-Crazy Days of Summer	Nat "King" Cole	#6
Wonderful! Wonderful!	The Tymes	#7
Take These Chains from My Heart	Ray Charles	#8
That Sunday, That Summer	Nat "King" Cole	#12
Pretty Paper	Roy Orbison	#15
My Summer Love	Ruby & The Romantics	#16
Alice in Wonderland	Neil Sedaka	#17
My Coloring Book	Kitty Kallen	#18
The Good Life	Tony Bennett	#18
My Coloring Book	Sandy Stewart	#20
Wait Til' My Bobby Gets Home	Darlene Love	#26
Love (Makes the World Go 'Round)	Paul Anka	#26
First Quarrel	Paul & Paula	#27
Bad Girl	Neil Sedaka	#33
(Today I Met) The Boy I'm Gonna Marry	Darlene Love	#39
Puddin N' Tain (Ask Me Again, I'll Tell You the Same)	The Alley Cats	#43
Love for Sale	Arthur Lyman Group	#43
Lovesick Blues	Frank Ifield	#44
Coney Island Baby	The Excellents	#51
A Fine Fine Boy	Darlene Love	#53
How Can I Forget	Jimmy Holiday	#57
Teenage Heaven	Johnny Cymbal	#58
I'm Confessin' (That I Love You)	Frank Ifield	#58
As Long as She Needs Me	Sammy Davis Jr.	#59
First Day Back at School	Paul & Paula	#60
The Last Leaf	The Cascades	#60
Sax Fifth Avenue	Johnny Beecher	#65
Enamorado	Keith Colley	#66
(I Cried At) Laura's Wedding	Barbara Lynn	#68
Molly	Bobby Goldsboro	#70
Ask Me	Maxine Brown	#75
Get Him	The Exciters	#76
Something Old, Something New	Paul & Paula	#77

BARRED INSTRUMENTS (cont'd)

Call Me Irresponsible	Frank Sinatra	#78
Sooner or Later	Johnny Mathis	#84
Love Me All the Way	Kim Weston	#88
Did You Have a Happy Birthday?	Paul Anka	#89
I'll Search My Heart	Johnny Mathis	#90
Guilty	Jim Reeves	#91
Banzai Pipeline	Henry Mancini	#93
Saturday Sunshine	Burt Bacharach	#93
Never Love a Robin	Bobby Vee	#99
Please Don't Kiss Me Again	The Charmettes	#100
1964		
Rag Doll	The Four Seasons	#1
Where Did Our Love Go	The Supremes	#1
Chapel of Love	The Dixie Cups	#1
There! I've Said It Again	Bobby Vinton	#1
Dawn (Go Away)	The Four Seasons	#3
Forget Him	Bobby Rydell	#4
The Girl from Ipanema	Getz/Gilberto	#5
The Shoop Shoop Song (It's in His Kiss)	Betty Everett	#6
Walk on By	Dionne Warwick	#6
My Heart Belongs to Only You	Bobby Vinton	#9
Good Times	Sam Cooke	#11
I'm So Proud	The Impressions	#14
Clinging Vine	Bobby Vinton	#17
Once Upon a Time	Marvin Gaye & Mary Wells	#19
Walking in the Rain	The Ronettes	#23
You'll Never Get to Heaven if You Break My Heart	Dionne Warwick	#34
The New Girl in School	Jan & Dean	#37
Stay Awhile	Dusty Springfield	#38
Comin' in the Back Door	Baja Marimba Band	#41
Angelito	Rene & Rene	#43
When You're Young and in Love	Ruby & The Romantics	#48
My True Carrie, Love	Nat "King" Cole	#49
Good Night Baby	The Butterflys	#51
The Little Boy	Tony Bennett	#52
Anyone Who Knows What Love Is (Will Understand)	Irma Thomas	#52
Bye Bye Barbara	Johnny Mathis	#53
I Wanna Be with You	Nancy Wilson	#57
Hello Muddah, Hello Fadduh! (A Letter from Camp) (New 1964 version)	Allan Sherman	#59
Thank You Baby	The Shirelles	#63
True Love Goes On and On	Burl Ives	#66
It's All Over	Walter Jackson	#67

BARRED INSTRUMENTS (cont'd)

Song	Artist	Chart
Almost There	Andy Williams	#67
A House Is Not a Home	Dionne Warwick	#71
A House Is Not a Home	Brook Benton	#75
The Anaheim, Azusa & Cucamonga Sewing Circle, Book Review and Timing Association	Jan & Dean	#77
The Cheer Leader	Paul Petersen	#78
For Your Sweet Love	The Cascades	#86
Maybe Tonight	The Shirelles	#88
Society Girl	The Rag Dolls	#91
Here She Comes	The Tymes	#92
Have You Ever Been Lonely (Have You Ever Been Blue)	The Caravelles	#94
Willyam, Willyam	Dee Dee Sharp	#97
The Magic of Our Summer Love	The Tymes	#99
The Clock	Baby Washington	#100

1965

Song	Artist	Chart
I Hear a Symphony	The Supremes	#1
Stop! In the Name of Love	The Supremes	#1
Downtown	Petula Clark	#1
You've Lost That Lovin' Feelin'	The Righteous Brothers	#1
I Got You Babe	Sonny & Cher	#1
It's the Same Old Song	Four Tops	#5
What the World Needs Now Is Love	Jackie DeShannon	#7
A Taste of Honey	Herb Alpert & The Tijuana Brass	#7
Hold Me, Thrill Me, Kiss Me	Mel Carter	#8
Hurt So Bad	Little Anthony/Imperials	#10
Nothing but Heartaches	The Supremes	#11
Don't Think Twice	The Wonder Who (The Four Seasons)	#12
Run, Baby Run (Baby, Goodbye)	The Newbeats	#12
A Walk in the Black Forest	Horst Jankowski	#12
Bye, Bye, Baby (Baby, Goodbye)	The Four Seasons	#12
People Get Ready	The Impressions	#14
Theme from "A Summer Place"	The Lettermen	#16
Take Me Back	Little Anthony/Imperials	#16
Nothing Can Stop Me	Gene Chandler	#18
Just You	Sonny & Cher	#20
Say Something Funny	Patty Duke	#22
Have You Looked into Your Heart	Jerry Vale	#24
Dear Heart	Andy Williams	#24
Kiss Away	Ronnie Dove	#25
Where Do You Go	Cher	#25
You Really Know How to Hurt a Guy	Jan & Dean	#27
Dear Heart	Jack Jones	#30

BARRED INSTRUMENTS (cont'd)

A Change Is Gonna Come	Sam Cooke	#31
New York's a Lonely Town	The Trade Winds	#32
(All of a Sudden) My Heart Sings	Mel Carter	#38
It's Gonna Take a Miracle	The Royalettes	#41
Angel	Johnny Tillotson	#51
Dusty	The Rag Dolls	#55
It's Too Late, Baby Too Late	Arthur Prysock	#56
Summer Sounds	Robert Goulet	#58
What's He Doing in My World	Eddy Arnold	#60
Married Man	Richard Burton	#64
Bring a Little Sunshine (To My Heart)	Vic Dana	#66
You Can Have Her	The Righteous Brothers	#67
Remember When	Wayne Newton	#69
Hey-Da-Da-Dow	The Dolphins	#69
I Want to Meet Him	The Royalettes	#72
The Girl from Peyton Place	Dickey Lee	#73
Roses and Rainbows	Danny Hutton	#73
Real Live Girl	Steve Alaimo	#77
Why Did I Choose You	Barbra Streisand	#77
Gotta Have Your Love	The Sapphires	#77
Chim, Chim, Cheree	New Christy Minstrels	#81
Are You Sincere	Trini Lopez	#85
Soul Sauce (Guacha Guaro)	Cal Tjader	#88
Tommy	Reparata & The Delrons	#92
What Are We Going to Do?	David Jones	#93
Sad Tomorrows	Trini Lopez	#94
Mexican Pearls	Billy Vaughn	#94
The Shadow of Your Smile	Tony Bennett	#95
Me Without You	Mary Wells	#95
You're Next	Jimmy Witherspoon	#98
The Drinking Man's Diet	Allan Sherman	#98
Right Now and Not Later	Shangri-Las	#99
Love Me Now	Brook Benton	#100
1966		
Cherish	The Association	#1
Beauty Is Only Skin Deep	The Temptations	#3
Sloop John B.	The Beach Boys	#3
No Matter What Shape (Your Stomach's In)	The T-Bones	#3
I'm Your Puppet	James & Bobby Purify	#6
I'm So Lonesome I Could Cry	B.J. Thomas	#8
Love Is like an Itching in My Heart	The Supremes	#9
Whispers (Getting' Louder)	Jackie Wilson	#11
Love Makes the World Go Round	Deon Jackson	#11

BARRED INSTRUMENTS (cont'd)

Title	Artist	#
This Old Heart of Mine (Is Weak for You)	Isley Brothers	#12
Oh How Happy	Shades of Blue	#12
The Duck	Jackie Lee	#14
Rhapsody in the Rain	Lou Christie	#16
The Work Song	Herb Alpert & The Tijuana Brass	#18
When Liking Turns to Loving	Ronnie Dove	#18
Cry	Ronnie Dove	#18
Mame	Herb Alpert & The Tijuana Brass	#19
The Joker Went Wild	Brian Hyland	#20
Popsicle	Jan & Dean	#21
But It's Alright	J.J. Jackson	#22
Call Me	Chris Montez	#22
What Now My Love	Herb Alpert & The Tijuana Brass	#24
All Strung Out	Nino Tempo & April Stevens	#26
Flamingo	Herb Alpert & The Tijuana Brass	#28
Where Were You When I Needed You	The Grass Roots	#28
I Love You Drops	Vic Dana	#30
Band of Gold	Mel Carter	#32
The Phoenix Love Theme (Senza Fine)	The Brass Ring	#32
Time After Time	Chris Montez	#36
Tijuana Taxi	Herb Alpert & The Tijuana Brass	#38
Younger Girl	The Critters	#42
Take This Heart of Mine	Marvin Gaye	#44
In Our Time	Nancy Sinatra	#46
On This Side of Goodbye	The Righteous Brothers	#47
There's No Living Without Your Loving	Peter & Gordon	#50
Hurt	Little Anthony/Imperials	#51
Ghost Riders in the Sky	Baja Marimba Band	#52
Better Use Your Head	Little Anthony/Imperials	#54
Lullaby of Love	The Poppies	#56
Wiederseh'n	Al Martino	#57
Can You Please Crawl out Your Window?	Bob Dylan	#58
Tears	Bobby Vinton	#59
Nobody's Baby Again	Dean Martin	#60
Cast Your Fate to the Wind	Shelby Flint	#61
Sippin' 'N Chippin'	The T-Bones	#62
Baby, Do the Philly Dog	The Olympics	#63
Lara's Theme from "Dr. Zhivago"	Roger Williams	#65
Dianne, Dianne	Ronny & The Daytonas	#69
Lonely Summer	The Shades of Blue	#72
Promise Her Anything	Tom Jones	#74
Melody for an Unknown Girl	The Unknowns	#74
We Know We're in Love	Lesley Gore	#76

BARRED INSTRUMENTS (cont'd)

Let's Call It a Day Girl	The Razor's Edge	#77
(We'll Be) United	The Intruders	#78
Happiness	Shades of Blue	#78
Something I Want to Tell You	Johnny & The Expressions	#79
The Loop	Johnny Lytle	#80
Petticoat White (Summer Sky Blue)	Bobby Vinton	#81
Free Again	Barbra Streisand	#83
Stop, Look and Listen	The Chiffons	#85
Living for You	Sonny & Cher	#87
Hot Shot	The Buena Vistas	#87
Spanish Harlem	King Curtis	#89
Goodnight My Love	Ben E. King	#91
It's That Time of the Year	Len Barry	#91
It's Not the Same	Anthony & The Imperials	#92
Big Time	Lou Christie	#95
Alfie	Cilla Black	#95
Because I Love You	Billy Stewart	#96
Sam, You Made the Pants Too Long	Barbra Streisand	#98
I Struck It Rich	Len Barry	#98
That's the Tune	The Vogues	#99
Open Up Your Door	Richard & The Young Lions	#99
Such a Sweet Thing	Mary Wells	#99
1967		
The Rain, the Park & Other Things	The Cowsills	#2
San Francisco (Be Sure to Wear Flowers in Your Hair)	Scott McKenzie	#4
Boogaloo Down Broadway	Fantastic Johnny C	#7
98.6	Keith	#7
My Cup Runneth Over	Ed Ames	#8
In and Out of Love	The Supremes	#9
Tell It to the Rain	The Four Seasons	#10
(The Lights Went Out In) Massachusetts	The Bee Gees	#11
Music to Watch Girls By	Bob Crewe Generation	#15
Ain't No Mountain High Enough	Marvin Gaye & Tammi Terrell	#19
Let's Fall in Love	Peaches & Herb	#21
Hypnotized	Linda Jones	#21
Make Me Yours	Bettye Swann	#21
The Last Waltz	Engelbert Humperdinck	#25
Sunday for Tea	Peter & Gordon	#31
The Happening	Herb Alpert & The Tijuana Brass	#32
There's Got to Be a Word!	The Innocence	#34
A Banda (Ah Bahn-da)	Herb Alpert & The Tijuana Brass	#35
Blue Autumn	Bobby Goldsboro	#35

BARRED INSTRUMENTS (cont'd)

Song	Artist	Position
Girls in Love	Gary Lewis/Playboys	#39
Everybody Needs Love	Gladys Knight & The Pips	#39
Don't Let the Rain Fall down on Me	The Critters	#39
Daddys Little Girl	Al Martino	#42
I Fooled You This Time	Gene Chandler	#45
You Wanted Someone to Play With (I Wanted Someone to Love)	Frankie Laine	#48
Funny Familiar Forgotten Feelings	Tom Jones	#49
Tiny Bubbles	Don Ho	#57
When You're Gone	Brenda & The Tabulations	#58
Oooh, Baby Baby	The Five Stairsteps	#63
Wish Me a Rainbow	The Gunter Kallmann Chorus	#63
I Feel Good (I Feel Bad)	Lewis & Clarke Expedition	#65
It's a Happening World	The Tokens	#69
Because of You	Chris Montez	#71
Mairzy Doats	The Innocence	#75
Tony Rome	Nancy Sinatra	#83
Full Measure	The Lovin' Spoonful	#87
Dancin' Out of My Heart	Ronnie Dove	#87
You're All I Need	Bobby Bland	#88
Goin' Back	The Byrds	#89
Hey Love	Stevie Wonder	#90
Sing Along with Me	Tommy Roe	#91
Peas 'N' Rice	Freddie McCoy	#92
To Be a Lover	Gene Chandler	#94
Shake Hands and Walk Away Cryin'	Lou Christie	#95
Along Comes Mary	Baja Marimba Band	#96
Georgy Girl	Baja Marimba Band	#98
When the Good Sun Shines	Elmo & Almo	#98
When the Snow Is on the Roses	Ed Ames	#98
1968		
Scarborough Fair/Canticle	Simon & Garfunkel	#11
Words	The Bee Gees	#15
Soul-Limbo	Booker T. & The MG's	#17
D.W. Washburn	The Monkees	#19
We Can Fly	The Cowsills	#21
How'd We Ever Get This Way	Andy Kim	#21
Dreams of the Everyday Housewife	Glen Campbell	#32
Help Yourself	Tom Jones	#35
Friends	The Beach Boys	#47
Carmen	Herb Alpert & The Tijuana Brass	#51
Loving You Has Made Me Bananas	Guy Marks	#51
Storybook Children	Billy Vera & Judy Clay	#54
I Can't Believe I'm Losing You	Frank Sinatra	#60

BARRED INSTRUMENTS (cont'd)

Bluebirds Over the Mountain	The Beach Boys	#61
Isn't It Lonely Together	O.C. Smith	#63
Burning Spear	The Soulful Strings	#64
My Way of Life	Frank Sinatra	#64
I'll Be Sweeter Tomorrow (Than I Was Today)	The O'Jays	#66
Barefoot in Baltimore	Strawberry Alarm Clock	#67
Down Here on the Ground	Lou Rawls	#69
Mrs. Bluebird	Eternity's Children	#69
Cabaret	Herb Alpert & The Tijuana Brass	#72
It's Over	Eddy Arnold	#74
Apologize	Ed Ames	#79
Up On the Roof	The Cryan' Shames	#85
Montage from How Sweet It Is (I Know That You Know)	The Love Generation	#86
Billy You're My Friend	Gene Pitney	#92
Almost in Love	Elvis Presley	#95
No One Knows	Every Mother's Son	#96
1969		
Na Na Hey Hey Kiss Him Goodbye	Steam	#1
Wedding Bell Blues	The 5th Dimension	#1
Sweet Caroline (Good Times Never Seemed So Good)	Neil Diamond	#4
I'm Livin' in Shame	The Supremes	#10
Baby, I'm for Real	The Originals	#14
With Pen in Hand	Vikki Carr	#35
So Good Together	Andy Kim	#36
Echo Park	Keith Barbour	#40
Shangri-La	The Lettermen	#64
Don't Forget to Remember	Bee Gees	#73

CLARINET

SONG	ARTIST	HOT 100
1960		
A Closer Walk	Pete Fountain	#93
1961		
Theme from "My Three Sons"	Lawrence Welk	#55
1962		
Stranger on the Shore	Mr. Acker Bilk	#1
Walk on the Wild Side (Part 1)	Jimmy Smith	#21
Stranger on the Shore	Andy Williams	#38
Baby Elephant Walk	Lawrence Welk	#48
Above the Stars	Mr. Acker Bilk	#59

CLARINET (cont'd)

Yes Indeed	Pete Fountain	#69
1963		
Mecca	Gene Pitney	#12
Only You (And You Alone)	Mr. Acker Bilk	#77
1964		
Hey Girl Don't Bother Me	The Tams	#41
Garden in the Rain	Vic Dana	#97
1965		
A Time to Love - A Time to Cry (Petite Fleur)	Lou Johnson	#59
1966		
Sloop John B.	The Beach Boys	#3
1967		
The 59th Street Bridge Song (Feelin' Groovy)	Harpers Bizarre	#13
1968		
Hey Jude	The Beatles	#1
Those Were the Days	Mary Hopkins	#2

CLAVIOLINE (MUSITRON)

YEAR	SONG	ARTIST	HOT 100
1961	Runaway	Del Shannon	#1
1961	Hats off to Larry	Del Shannon	#5
1962	Telstar	The Tornadoes	#1
1962	She's Everything (I Wanted You to Be)	Ral Donner	#19
1964	Handy Man	Del Shannon	#22
1964	I'll Touch a Star	Terry Stafford	#25
1964	Do You Want to Dance	Del Shannon	#43
1967	Baby You're a Rich Man	The Beatles	#34

FLUTE

SONG	ARTIST	HOT 100
1960		
Harbor Lights	The Platters	#8
I Love the Way You Love	Marv Johnson	#9
You Got What It Takes	Marv Johnson	#10
How About That	Dee Clark	#33
Don't Go to Strangers	Etta James	#36
Waltzing Matilda	Jimmie Rodgers	#41
Gonzo	James Booker	#43
Kookie Little Paradise	Jo Ann Campbell	#61

FLUTE (cont'd)

All the Love I've Got	Marv Johnson	#63
There's a Star Spangled Banner Waving #2 (The Ballad of Francis Powers)	Red River Dave	#64
Ain't Gonna Be That Way	Adam Wade	#74
Let the Good Times Roll	Ray Charles	#78
The Brigade of Broken Hearts	Paul Evans	#81
Don't Let the Sun Catch You Cryin'	Ray Charles	#95
Theme from "Adventures In Paradise"	Jerry Byrd	#97
1961		
Tragedy	The Fleetwoods	#10
A Tear	Gene McDaniels	#31
It's Too Soon to Know	Etta James	#54
When I Fall in Love	Etta Jones	#65
Summer Souvenirs	Karl Hammel Jr.	#68
The Charanga	Merv Griffin	#69
The Next Kiss (Is the Last Goodbye)	Conway Twitty	#72
Muskrat	The Everly Brothers	#82
1962		
P.T. 109	Jimmy Dean	#8
Conscience	James Darren	#11
Close to Cathy	Mike Clifford	#12
Swingin' Safari	Billy Vaughn	#13
What Kind of Fool am I	Sammy Davis Jr.	#17
Dear Ivan	Jimmy Dean	#24
Where are You	Dinah Washington	#36
Stubborn Kind of Fellow	Marvin Gaye	#46
The Burning of Atlanta	Claude King	#53
That Happy Feeling	Bert Kaempfert	#67
That Happy Feeling	Bert Kaempfert	#67
I'll Take You Home	The Corsairs	#68
Bermuda	Linda Scott	#70
Desafinado (Slightly Out of Tune)	Pat Thomas	#78
Pop Goes the Weasel	Anthony Newley	#85
Jane, Jane, Jane	The Kingston Trio	#93
Stardust	Frank Sinatra	#98
The Moon Was Yellow	Frank Sinatra	#99
Sweet Thursday	Johnny Mathis	#99
1963		
Be True to Your School	The Beach Boys	#6
Fly Me to the Moon - Bossa Nova	Joe Harnell	#14
El Watusi	Ray Barretto	#17
The Good Life	Tony Bennett	#18
Hey There Lonely Boy	Ruby & The Romantics	#27

FLUTE (cont'd)

Hitch Hike	Marvin Gaye	#30
Young Wings Can Fly (Higher Than You Know)	Ruby & The Romantics	#47
September Song	Jimmy Durante	#51
Don't Wait Too Long	Tony Bennett	#54
As Long as She Needs Me	Sammy Davis Jr.	#59
This Is My Prayer	Theola Kilgore	#60
My Block	The Four Pennies	#67
This Is All I Ask	Tony Bennett	#70
I'll Search My Heart	Johnny Mathis	#90
I Cried	Tammy Montgomery (Tammie Terrell)	#99
1964		
There! I've Said It Again	Bobby Vinton	#1
We'll Sing in the Sunshine	Gale Garnett	#4
People	Barbra Streisand	#5
See the Funny Little Clown	Bobby Goldsboro	#9
What Kind of Fool (Do You Think I Am)	The Tams	#9
The Pink Panther Theme	Henry Mancini	#31
Whenever He Holds You	Bobby Goldsboro	#39
Comin' in the Back Door	Baja Marimba Band	#41
Look Homeward Angel	The Monarchs	#47
Where Love Has Gone	Jack Jones	#62
You Lied to Your Daddy	The Tams	#70
Winkin', Blinkin' and Nod	The Simon Sisters	#73
It's All Right (You're Just in Love)	The Tams	#79
A Little Toy Balloon	Danny Williams	#84
Can't Get Over (The Bossa Nova)	Eydie Gorme	#87
Be Anything (But Be Mine)	Gloria Lynne	#88
I've Got the Skill	Jackie Ross	#89
I Can't Wait Until I See My Baby	Justine Washington	#93
Pretend You Don't See Her	Bobby Vee	#97
1965		
Ferry Cross the Mersey	Gerry & The Pacemakers	#6
Say Something Funny	Patty Duke	#22
You Really Know How to Hurt a Guy	Jan & Dean	#27
Come Tomorrow	Manfred Mann	#50
And I Love Him	Esther Phillips	#54
A Time to Love - A Time to Cry (Petite Fleur)	Lou Johnson	#59
Good Lovin'	The Olympics	#81
Pied Piper	The Changin' Times	#87
Quiet Nights of Quiet Stars	Andy Williams	#92
Pass Me By	Peggy Lee	#93
The Shadow of Your Smile	Tony Bennett	#95

FLUTE (cont'd)

1966

Good Vibrations	The Beach Boys	#1
Poor Side of Town	Johnny Rivers	#1
Sloop John B.	The Beach Boys	#3
California Dreamin'	Mamas & Papas	#4
The Pied Piper	Crispian St. Peters	#4
Walk Away Renee	The Left Banke	#5
The Men in My Little Girl's Life	Mike Douglas	#6
Along Comes Mary	The Association	#7
(Come 'Round Here) I'm the One You Need	The Miracles	#17
Walkin' My Cat Named Dog	Norma Tanega	#22
Alfie	Cher	#32
Caroline, No	The Beach Boys	#32
Long Live Our Love	The Shangri-Las	#33
A Symphony for Susan	The Arbors	#51
The Fife Piper	The Dynatones	#53
Come Back	The Five Stairsteps	#61
Free Again	Barbra Streisand	#83
A Man and a Woman	Tamiko Jones w/Herbie Mann	#88
Philly Dog	Herbie Mann	#93
Let's Go Steady Again	Sam Cooke	#97
Meditation (Meditacao)	Claudine Longet	#98

1967

The Happening	The Supremes	#1
Penny Lane	The Beatles	#1
Baby I Need Your Lovin'	Johnny Rivers	#3
It Must Be Him	Vikki Carr	#3
Creeque Alley	Mamas & Papas	#5
Ding Dong! The Witch Is Dead	The Fifth Estate	#11
Words	The Monkees	#11
There Is a Mountain	Donovan	#11
The 59th Street Bridge Song (Feelin' Groovy)	Harpers Bizarre	#13
To Love Somebody	The Bee Gees	#17
It's Now Winters Day	Tommy Roe	#23
She's Still a Mystery	The Lovin' Spoonful	#27
You've Made Me so Very Happy	Brenda Holloway	#39
Bowling Green	The Everly Brothers	#40
Why Do Fools Fall in Love	The Happenings	#41
In the Misty Moonlight	Dean Martin	#46
No Fair at All	The Association	#51
Spooky	Mike Sharpe	#57
Turn the World Around	Eddy Arnold	#66
My Special Prayer	Joe Simon	#87

FLUTE (cont'd)

Title	Artist	Chart
Danger! She's a Stranger	The Five Stairsteps	#89
Sing Along with Me	Tommy Roe	#91
Up-Up and Away	Johnny Mann Singers	#91
To Sir, with Love	Herbie Mann	#93
Holiday for Clowns	Brian Hyland	#94
How Can You Mistreat the One You Love	Jean & The Darlings	#96
Along Comes Mary	Baja Marimba Band	#96
There Goes the Lover	Gene Chandler	#98
Georgy Girl	Baja Marimba Band	#98
1968		
Light My Fire	Jose Feliciano	#3
Fool on the Hill	Sergio Mendes & Brasil '66	#6
Turn Around, Look at Me	The Vogues	#7
Ain't Nothing Like the Real Thing	Marvin Gaye & Tammi Terrell	#8
Everything That Touches You	The Association	#10
Mighty Quinn (Quinn the Eskimo)	Manfred Mann	#10
Like to Get to Know You	Spanky & Our Gang	#17
Hi-Heel Sneakers	Jose Feliciano	#25
Special Occasion	Smokey Robinson & The Miracles	#26
To Give (The Reason I Live)	Frankie Valli	#29
Lalena	Donovan	#33
The Straight Life	Bobby Goldsboro	#36
Mission-Impossible	Lalo Schifrin	#41
Dancing Bear	Mamas & Papas	#51
Safe in My Garden	Mamas & Papas	#53
Me, The Peaceful Heart	Lulu	#53
In Need of a Friend	The Cowsills	#54
Look, Here Comes the Sun	The Sunshine Company	#56
Lost	Jerry Butler	#62
Destination: Anywhere	The Marvelettes	#63
Burning Spear	The Soulful Strings	#64
Breaking up Is Hard to Do	The Happenings	#67
Impossible Mission (Mission Impossible)	Soul Survivors	#68
I Say Love	The Royal Guardsmen	#72
Mornin' Glory	Bobbie Gentry & Glen Campbell	#74
Unchain My Heart	Herbie Mann	#81
Snoopy for President	The Royal Guardsmen	#85
Tell Someone You Love Them	Dino, Desi & Billy	#92
The Shadow of Your Love	The 5 Stairsteps & Cubie	#94
People World	Jim & Jean	#94
Springfield Plane	Kenny O'Dell	#94
Battle of New Orleans	Harpers Bizarre	#95
Baroque-A-Nova	Mason Williams	#96

FLUTE (cont'd)

Do Your Own Thing	Brook Benton	#99
1969		
Aquarius/Let the Sunshine In	The 5th Dimension	#1
Grazing in the Grass	Friends of Distinction	#3
Hawaii Five-O	The Ventures	#4
My Cherie Amour	Stevie Wonder	#4
Sweet Cherry Wine	Tommy James & The Shondells	#7
This Girl's in Love with You	Dionne Warwick	#7
This Girl Is a Woman Now	Gary Puckett & The Union Gap	#9
My Whole World Ended (The Moment You Left Me)	David Ruffin	#9
Going Up the Country	Canned Heat	#11
Going in Circles	Friends of Distinction	#15
Soul Deep	The Box Tops	#18
Undun	The Guess Who	#22
Sweet Cream Ladies, Forward March	The Box Tops	#28
Abergavenny	Shannon (Marty Wilde)	#47
What Is a Man	Four Tops	#53
(We've Got) Honey Love	Martha & The Vandellas	#56
Ice Cream Song	The Dynamics	#59
Glad She's a Woman	Bobby Goldsboro	#61
Happy Heart	Petula Clark	#62
Pretty World	Sergio Mendes & Brasil '66	#62
Purple Haze	Dion	#63
Hey! Baby	Jose Feliciano	#71
Poor Side of Town	Al Wilson	#75
Gentle on My Mind	Aretha Franklin	#76
Can't Find the Time	Orpheus	#80
Kay	John Wesley Ryles I	#83
The Thought of Loving You	The Crystal Mansion	#84
My World Is Empty Without You	Jose Feliciano	#87
Green Fields	The Vogues	#92
Theme from Electric Surfboard	Brother Jack McDuff	#95
Turn Around and Love You	Rita Coolidge	#96
Sausalito	Al Martino	#99

THE LONGEST GUITAR SOLOS OF THE 1960s

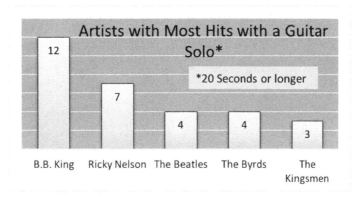

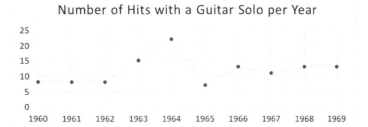

YEAR	SONG	ARTIST	HOT 100	LENGTH OF SOLO(S)
1969	Who Do You Love	Quicksilver Messenger Service	#91	81 seconds
1968	All Along the Watchtower	Jimi Hendrix	#20	66 seconds
1969	Crossroads	Cream	#28	63, 44 seconds
1968	Summertime Blues	Blue Cheer	#14	61 seconds
1966	Don't Answer the Door - Part 1	B.B. King	#72	54 seconds
1968	Hurdy Gurdy Man	Donovan	#5	52 seconds
1968	I Put a Spell on You	Creedence Clearwater Revival	#58	50, 31 seconds
1968	The Woman I Love	B.B. King	#94	46 seconds
1967	Purple Haze	Jimi Hendrix	#65	43 seconds
1961	You've Got to Love Her with a Feeling	Freddy King	#93	42 seconds
1964	No Particular Place to Go	Chuck Berry	#10	41, 22 seconds
1962	The Waltz You Saved for Me	Ferlin Husky	#94	41 seconds
1968	White Houses	Eric Burdon/Animals	#67	39 seconds
1969	Just a Little Love	B.B. King	#76	38, 36 seconds
1967	Get Together	The Youngbloods	#62	38 seconds
1968	Suzie Q. (Part One)	Creedence Clearwater Revival	#11	37, 29, 27 seconds
1962	Soldier Boy	The Shirelles	#1	37 seconds
1966	Black Nights	Lowell Fulsom	#91	37 seconds
1967	Feel so Bad	Little Milton	#91	37 seconds
1967	The Jungle	B.B. King	#94	37 seconds

THE LONGEST GUITAR SOLOS OF THE 1960s (cont'd)

1969	Silver Threads and Golden Needles	The Cowsills	#74	37 seconds
1966	Eight Miles High	The Byrds	#14	36, 24 seconds
1965	Turn! Turn! Turn! (To Everything There Is a Season)	The Byrds	#1	36 seconds
1960	Don't Go to Strangers	Etta James	#36	34 seconds
1968	You Put It on Me	B.B. King	#82	34 seconds
1969	I'm Tired	Savoy Brown	#74	34 seconds
1960	Sandy	Larry Hall	#15	33 seconds
1964	Hi-Heel Sneakers	Tommy Tucker	#11	33 seconds
1964	Slow Down	The Beatles	#25	33 seconds
1965	Blue Shadows	B.B. King	#97	33 seconds
1964	Slip-In Mules (No High Heel Sneakers)	Sugar Pie DeSanto	#48	32 seconds
1969	Someday Soon	Judy Collins	#55	32 seconds
1969	Badge	Cream	#60	32 seconds
1964	Little Marie	Chuck Berry	#54	31 seconds
1965	Apple of My Eye	Roy Head & The Traits	#32	31 seconds
1966	Just Like Me	Paul Revere & The Raiders	#11	31 seconds
1966	Come On Up	The Rascals	#43	31 seconds
1969	Kick Out the Jams	MC5	#82	31 seconds
1969	Hold Me	The Baskerville Hounds	#88	31 seconds
1968	Crown of Creation	Jefferson Airplane	#64	30, 28 seconds
1960	I Forgot More About Her Than You'll Ever Know	Sonny James	#80	30 seconds
1963	Meditation (Meditacao)	Pat Boone	#91	30 seconds
1966	Neighbor, Neighbor	Jimmy Hughes	#65	30 seconds
1967	Have You Seen Her Face	The Byrds	#74	30 seconds
1969	Time Was	Canned Heat	#67	30 seconds
1963	Fools Rush In	Ricky Nelson	#12	29 seconds
1963	I Got a Woman	Ricky Nelson	#49	29 seconds
1964	My Bonnie (My Bonnie Lies Over the Ocean)	The Beatles	#26	29 seconds
1964	Rock Me Baby	B.B. King	#34	29 seconds
1962	If a Man Answers	Bobby Darin	#32	28 seconds
1962	Dear Hearts and Gentle People	The Springfields	#95	28 seconds
1963	Baby, What's Wrong	Lonnie Mack	#93	28 seconds
1964	It's All Over Now	The Rolling Stones	#26	28 seconds
1964	Hold Me	P.J. Proby	#70	28 seconds
1968	Kentucky Woman	Deep Purple	#38	28 seconds
1969	Mr. Limousine Driver	Grand Funk Railroad	#97	28 seconds
1963	Louie Louie	The Kingsmen	#2	27 seconds
1963	I'm In Love Again	Ricky Nelson	#67	27 seconds
1964	Time Is on My Side	The Rolling Stones	#6	27 seconds
1967	Somebody to Love	Jefferson Airplane	#5	27 seconds
1967	San Franciscan Nights	Eric Burdon/Animals	#9	27 seconds
1967	You are My Sunshine	Mitch Ryder	#88	27 seconds
1969	You, I	The Rugbys	#24	27 seconds

THE LONGEST GUITAR SOLOS OF THE 1960s (cont'd)

Year	Title	Artist	Chart	Duration
1963	If You Can't Rock Me	Ricky Nelson	#100	26 seconds
1964	Little Latin Lupe Lu	The Kingsmen	#46	26 seconds
1965	Do the Clam	Elvis Presley	#21	26 seconds
1968	Coo Coo	Big Brother & The Holding Company	#84	26 seconds
1968	San Francisco Girls (Return of the Native)	Fever Tree	#91	26 seconds
1968	Paying the Cost to Be the Boss	B.B. King	#39	25, 23 seconds
1962	Ruby Ann	Marty Robbins	#18	25 seconds
1962	Aw Shucks, Hush Your Mouth	Jimmy Reed	#93	25 seconds
1964	Have I the Right?	The Honeycombs	#5	25 seconds
1964	Gonna Send You Back to Georgia (A City Slick)	Timmy Shaw	#41	25 seconds
1967	Tramp	Lowell Fulsom	#52	25 seconds
1968	I'm Gonna Do What They Do to Me	B.B. King	#74	25 seconds
1963	The Dog	Rufus Thomas	#87	24 seconds
1964	Gonna Send You Back to Walker (Gonna Send You Back to Georgia)	The Animals	#57	24 seconds
1967	Don't Do It	Micky Dolenz	#75	24 seconds
1969	Why I Sing the Blues	B.B. King	#61	24 seconds
1960	Secret of Love	Elton Anderson	#88	23 seconds
1962	Peppermint Twist - Part 1	Joey Dee & The Starliters	#1	23 seconds
1963	String Along	Ricky Nelson	#25	23 seconds
1963	Don't Wait Too Long	Tony Bennett	#54	23 seconds
1964	Why (Doncha Be My Girl)	The Chartbusters	#92	23 seconds
1964	I Don't Care (Just as Long as You Love Me)	Buck Owens	#92	23 seconds
1964	My Heart Skips a Beat	Buck Owens	#94	23 seconds
1965	I'm a Fool	Dino, Desi & Billy	#17	23 seconds
1965	I Can't Stop	The Honeycombs	#48	23 seconds
1966	Secret Agent Man	Johnny Rivers	#3	23 seconds
1967	My Back Pages	The Byrds	#30	23 seconds
1968	Just Dropped In (To See What Condition My Condition Was In)	The First Edition/Kenny Rogers	#5	23 seconds
1968	Journey to the Center of the Mind	The Amboy Dukes	#16	23 seconds
1969	Time Machine	The Grand Funk Railroad	#48	23 seconds
1969	Get Off My Back Women	B.B. King	#74	23 seconds
1960	Mule Skinner Blues	Fendermen	#5	22 seconds
1961	Son-In-Law	Louise Brown	#76	22 seconds
1963	Old Enough to Love	Ricky Nelson	#94	22 seconds
1964	I Saw Her Standing There	The Beatles	#14	22 seconds
1966	Hanky Panky	Tommy James & The Shondells	#1	22 seconds
1966	Happenings Ten Years Time Ago	The Yardbirds	#30	22 seconds
1966	My Babe	Roy Head & The Traits	#99	22 seconds
1961	Tennessee Flat-Top Box	Johnny Cash	#84	21, 21, 25 seconds
1960	Be Bop A-Lula	The Everly Brothers	#74	21, 19 seconds
1961	Ling-Ting-Tong	Buddy Knox	#65	21 seconds

THE LONGEST GUITAR SOLOS OF THE 1960s (cont'd)

1961	Milk Cow Blues	Ricky Nelson	#79	21 seconds
1963	Your Baby's Gone Surfin'	Duane Eddy	#93	21 seconds
1964	Kansas City	Trini Lopez	#23	21 seconds
1964	Johnny B. Goode	Dion	#71	21 seconds
1964	Beautician Blues	B.B. King	#82	21 seconds
1966	Shapes of Things	The Yardbirds	#11	21 seconds
1966	Please Don't Fight It	Dino, Desi & Billy	#60	21 seconds
1966	What Goes On	The Beatles	#81	21 seconds
1968	Pictures of Matchstick Men	The Status Quo	#12	21 seconds
1960	Just One Time	Don Gibson	#29	20 seconds
1960	Train of Love	Annette	#36	20 seconds
1960	Whole Lot of Shakin' Going On	Conway Twitty	#55	20 seconds
1961	Stick with Me Baby	The Everly Brothers	#41	20 seconds
1961	Well-A, Well-A	Shirley & Lee	#77	20 seconds
1961	Sugar Bee	Cleveland Crochet	#80	20 seconds
1961	Signed, Sealed and Deliverd	Rusty Draper	#91	20 seconds
1962	Honky-Tonk Man	Johnny Horton	#96	20 seconds
1963	Walk Right In	The Rooftop Singers	#1	20 seconds
1963	Mecca	Gene Pitney	#12	20 seconds
1963	Surfer Joe	The Surfaris	#62	20 seconds
1964	Money	The Kingsmen	#16	20 seconds
1964	Run, Run, Run	The Gestures	#44	20 seconds
1965	Bring It on Home to Me	The Animals	#32	20 seconds
1966	Bad Little Woman	The Shadows of Knight	#91	20 seconds

GUITAR (SLIDE)

SONG	ARTIST	HOT 100
1960		
Paper Roses	Anita Bryant	#5
Pineapple Princess	Annette	#11
Anymore	Teresa Brewer	#31
Little Coco Palm	Jerry Wallace	#36
(I Can't Help You) I'm Falling Too	Skeeter Davis	#39
My Shoes Keep Walking Back to You	Guy Mitchell	#45
I Forgot More About Her Than You'll Ever Know	Sonny James	#80
Why I'm Walkin'	Stonewall Jackson	#83
Honky-Tonk Girl	Johnny Cash	#92
Theme from "Adventures In Paradise"	Jerry Byrd	#97
Fallen Angel	Webb Pierce	#99
She's Just A Whole Lot Like You	Hank Thompson	#99

GUITAR (SLIDE) (cont'd)

1961		
I Fall to Pieces	Patsy Cline	#12
I Dreamed of a Hill-Billy Heaven	Tex Ritter	#20
In the Middle of a Heartache	Wanda Jackson	#27
No One	Connie Francis	#34
Three Hearts in a Tangle	Roy Drusky	#35
What Would You Do?	Jim Reeves	#73
Tender Years	George Jones	#76
I'll Never Be Free	Kay Starr	#94
Cowboy Jimmy Joe (Die Sterne Der Prarie)	Lolita	#94
1962		
Alley Cat	Bent Fabric	#7
Mama Sang a Song	Bill Anderson	#89
The Waltz You Saved for Me	Ferlin Husky	#94
1963		
Still	Bill Anderson	#8
Don't Let Me Cross Over	Carl Butler & Pearl	#88
1964		
Pearly Shells (Popo O Ewa)	Burl Ives	#60
1965		
Hawaii Tattoo	The Waikikis	#33
10 Little Bottles	Johnny Bond	#43
Before You Go	Buck Owens	#83
Hawaii Honeymoon	The Waikikis	#91
1966		
My Heart's Symphony	Gary Lewis/Playboys	#13
Almost Persuaded	David Houston	#24
Almost Persuaded No. 2	Ben Colder (Sheb Wooley)	#58
Think of Me	Buck Owens	#74
Giddyup Go	Red Sovine	#82
Don't Touch Me	Jeannie Seely	#85
I'm Living in Two Worlds	Bonnie Guitar	#99
1967		
Nashville Cats	Lovin' Spoonful	#8
Jackson	Nancy Sinatra & Lee Hazlewood	#14
There Goes My Everything	Jack Greene	#65
My Elusive Dreams	David Houston & Tammy Wynette	#89
1968		
I Met Her in Church	The Box Tops	#37
D-I-V-O-R-C-E	Tammy Wynette	#63
Harper Valley P.T.A. (Later That Same Day)	Ben Colder (Sheb Wooley)	#67
You Ain't Going Nowhere	The Byrds	#74
What's Made Milwaukee Famous (Has Made a Loser Out of Me)	Jerry Lee Lewis	#94

GUITAR (SLIDE) (cont'd)

Have a Little Faith	David Houston	#98
1969		
The Boxer	Simon & Garfunkel	#7
Lay Lady Lay	Bob Dylan	#7
Stand By Your Man	Tammy Wynette	#19
Tonight I'll Be Staying Here with You	Bob Dylan	#50
Someday Soon	Judy Collins	#55
Maybe the Rain Will Fall	The Cascades	#61
Listen to the Band	The Monkees	#63
(I'm So) Afraid of Losing You Again	Charley Pride	#74
Singing My Song	Tammy Wynette	#75
There Never Was a Time	Jeannie C. Riley	#77
The Ways to Love a Man	Tammy Wynette	#81
Kay	John Wesley Ryles I	#83
Love Is Just a Four-Letter Word	Joan Baez	#86
All I Have to Offer You (Is Me)	Charley Pride	#91
Only the Lonely	Sonny James	#92
The Carroll County Accident	Porter Wagoner	#92
Home to You	Earth Opera	#97
Here We Go Again	Nancy Sinatra	#98

HARMONICA

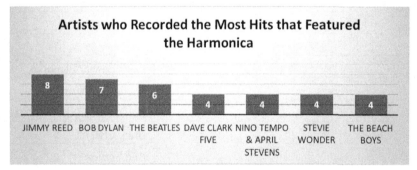

SONG	ARTIST	HOT 100	LENGTH OF SOLO
1960			
One of Us (Will Weep Tonight)	Patti Page	#31	
Baby What You Want Me to Do	Jimmy Reed	#37	27, 10 sec.
Fannie Mae	Buster Brown	#38	
Hush-Hush	Jimmy Reed	#75	28 sec.
Is You Is or Is You Ain't My Baby	Buster Brown	#81	
Midnight Lace	Ray Ellis	#84	
Found Love	Jimmy Reed	#88	25 sec.
Midnight Lace- Part One	Ray Conniff	#92	

HARMONICA (cont'd)

1961

Heartaches	The Marcels	#7	
Moon River	Jerry Butler	#11	
Moon River	Henry Mancini	#11	30, 27 sec.
I Just Don't Understand	Ann-Margret	#17	22 sec.
Candy Man	Roy Orbison	#25	24 sec.
Rainin' in My Heart	Slim Harpo	#34	24 sec.
It's All Because	Linda Scott	#50	
Sleepy-Eyed John	Johnny Horton	#54	
I Never Knew	Clyde McPhatter	#56	
Cherry Pink and Apple Blossom White	Jerry Murad's Harmonicats	#56	
Bright Lights Big City	Jimmy Reed	#58	28 sec.
Close Together	Jimmy Reed	#68	
For Me and My Gal	Freddy Cannon	#71	37, 22 sec.
Alvin's Harmonica	The Chipmunks	#73	
Big Boss Man	Jimmy Reed	#78	33 sec.
Night Train	Richard Hayman	#80	
Searchin'	Jack Eubanks	#83	
And the Heavens Cried	Ronnie Savoy	#84	

1962

Hey! Baby	Bruce Channel	#1	15 sec.
Sealed with a Kiss	Brian Hyland	#3	21 sec.
I Remember You	Frank Ifield	#5	
When the Boy in Your Arms (Is the Boy in Your Heart)	Connie Francis	#10	
Lie to Me	Brooke Benton	#13	
Love Me Tender	Richard Chamberlain	#21	
Small Sad Sam	Phil McLean	#21	
Cajun Queen	Jimmy Dean	#22	
If You Gotta Make a Fool of Somebody	James Ray	#22	
Warmed Over Kisses (Left Over Love)	Brian Hyland	#25	
Little Black Book	Jimmy Dean	#29	24 sec.
Johnny Will	Pat Boone	#35	
Steel Men	Jimmy Dean	#41	
Itty Bitty Pieces	James Ray	#41	
Number One Man	Bruce Channel	#52	
Chapel by the Sea	Billy Vaughn	#69	
Somebody Have Mercy	Sam Cooke	#70	
Stranger on the Shore	The Drifters	#73	18 sec.
How Can I Meet Her?	The Everly Brothers	#75	10 sec.
Good Lover	Jimmy Reed	#77	26 sec.
Shimmy, Shimmy Walk, Part 1	The Megatons	#88	
I'm So Lonesome I Could Cry	Johnny Tillotson	#89	
Summertime	Ricky Nelson	#89	

HARMONICA (cont'd)

Lover Come Back to Me	The Cleftones	#95	
Come on Baby	Bruce Channel	#98	27 sec.
Sugar Babe	Buster Brown	#99	35, 35 sec.

1963

Deep Purple	Nino Tempo & April Stevens	#1	
Fingertips - Pt. 2	Little Stevie Wonder	#1	20 sec.
You're the Reason I'm Living	Bobby Darin	#3	
What Will My Mary Say	Johnny Mathis	#9	
My Coloring Book	Kitty Kallen	#18	
I Got What I Wanted	Brook Benton	#28	
Blue Bayou	Roy Orbison	#29	
Workout Stevie, Workout	Little Stevie Wonder	#33	24, 17 sec.
Shame, Shame, Shame	Jimmy Reed	#52	17 sec.
I'm Confessin' (That I Love You)	Frank Ifield	#58	
I'm Afraid to Go Home	Brian Hyland	#63	
I Will Love You	Richard Chamberlain	#65	
Hobo Flats - Part 1	Jimmy Smith	#69	
From Me to You	Del Shannon	#77	
Toys in the Attic	Joe Sherman	#85	26 sec.

1964

Love Me Do	The Beatles	#1	18, 12 sec.
My Boy Lollipop	Millie Small	#2	14 sec.
Please Please Me	The Beatles	#3	
We'll Sing in the Sunshine	Gale Garnett	#4	
Mountain of Love	Johnny Rivers	#9	20 sec.
When I Grow Up (To Be a Man)	The Beach Boys	#9	
Whispering	Nino Tempo & April Stevens	#11	
Maybelline	Johnny Rivers	#12	
As Usual	Brenda Lee	#12	
Hey Harmonica Man	Stevie Wonder	#29	19, 19, 15 sec.
Stardust	Nino Tempo & April Stevens	#32	
Thank You Girl	The Beatles	#35	
I Rise, I Fall	Johnny Tillotson	#36	
From Me to You	The Beatles	#41	
Not Fade Away	The Rolling Stones	#48	
The World I Used to Know	Jimmie Rodgers	#51	
I Should Have Known Better	The Beatles	#53	
I Knew It All the Time	Dave Clark Five	#53	25, 25 sec.
It Ain't Me, Babe	Johnny Cash	#58	12 sec.
Four Strong Winds	Bobby Bare	#60	15 sec.
Johnny B. Goode	Dion	#71	
There's a Place	The Beatles	#74	

HARMONICA (cont'd)

It'll Never Be over for Me	Baby Washington	#98	
I'm Confessin' (That I Love You)	Nino Tempo & April Stevens	#99	
Strange Things Happening	Little Junior Parker	#99	

1965

Over and Over	Dave Clark Five	#1	11 sec.
Eve of Destruction	Barry McGuire	#1	
Like a Rolling Stone	Bob Dylan	#2	
Catch Us if You Can	Dave Clark Five	#4	25 sec.
Hush, Hush, Sweet Charlotte	Patti Page	#8	
Baby Don't Go	Sonny & Cher	#8	
Laugh, Laugh	The Beau Brummels	#15	
I'm a Man	The Yardbirds	#17	25 sec.
I've Been Loving You Too Long (To Stop Now)	Otis Redding	#21	14 sec.
Paper Tiger	Sue Thompson	#23	
Dream on Little Dreamer	Perry Como	#25	
Voodoo Woman	Bobby Goldsboro	#27	
It's Alright	Adam Faith w/The Roulettes	#31	10 sec.
Mystic Eyes	Them	#33	33, 12 sec.
The Dawn of Correction	The Spokesmen	#36	10 sec.
Peaches "N" Cream	The Ikettes	#36	12 sec.
What Color (Is a Man)	Bobby Vinton	#38	
You Tell Me Why	The Beau Brummels	#38	
Subterranean Homesick Blues	Bob Dylan	#39	
Ain't It True	Andy Williams	#40	
Roses Are Red My Love	The "You Know Who" Group!	#43	10 sec.
Sinner Man	Trini Lopez	#54	
Lovin' Place	Gale Garnett	#54	
High Heel Sneakers	Stevie Wonder	#59	15 sec.
Child of Our Times	Barry McGuire	#72	
Orange Blossom Special	Johnny Cash	#80	42 sec.
Let the Good Times Roll	Roy Orbison	#81	
I Still Love You	The Vejtables	#84	
Justine	The Righteous Brothers	#85	15 sec.
The Sins of a Family	P.F. Sloan	#87	
Pied Piper	The Changin' Times	#87	
Good Time Music	The Beau Brummels	#97	29 sec.
Talk About Love	Adam Faith	#97	13 sec.
Stay Away from My Baby	Ted Taylor	#99	

1966

Good Vibrations	The Beach Boys	#1	
Daydream	The Lovin' Spoonful	#2	
Rainy Day Women #12 & 35	Bob Dylan	#3	
Psychotic Reaction	Count Five	#5	

HARMONICA (cont'd)

Title	Artist	Chart	Duration
Dirty Water	The Standells	#11	12 sec.
Baby Scratch My Back	Slim Harpo	#16	
I Want You	Bob Dylan	#20	
Walkin' My Cat Named Dog	Norma Tanega	#22	
Just Like a Woman	Bob Dylan	#33	
Day for Decision	Johnny Sea	#35	
Satisfied with You	Dave Clark Five	#50	15 sec.
The Eggplant That Ate Chicago	Dr. West's Medicine Show and Junk Band	#52	
You're Gonna Miss Me	Thirteenth Floor Elevators	#55	
I'm a Nut	Leroy Pullins	#57	10 sec.
Can You Please Crawl out Your Window?	Bob Dylan	#58	
I Love Onions	Susan Christie	#63	
Set You Free This Time	The Byrds	#79	
Moulty	The Barbarians	#90	
Respect	The Rationals	#92	13 sec.
I'm Your Hoochie Cooche Man (Part 1)	Jimmy Smith	#94	
One Too Many Mornings	Beau Brummels	#95	
1967			
Groovin'	The Young Rascals	#1	
I Was Made to Love Her	Stevie Wonder	#2	34 sec.
Skinny Legs and All	Joe Tex	#10	
Heroes and Villains	The Beach Boys	#12	16 sec.
Jackson	Nancy Sinatra & Lee Hazlewood	#14	
You Got to Me	Neil Diamond	#18	10 sec.
Too Much of Nothing	Peter, Paul & Mary	#35	
Little Ole Wine Drinker, Me	Dean Martin	#38	
Big Boss Man	Elvis Presley	#38	11 sec.
Laudy Miss Claudy	The Buckinghams	#41	26 sec.
This Town	Frank Sinatra	#53	
Plastic Man	Sonny & Cher	#74	
Knucklehead	Bar-Kays	#76	
Leopard-Skin Pill-Box Hat	Bob Dylan	#81	
Little Old Wine Drinker Me	Robert Mitchum	#96	
The Jokers	Peter & Gordon	#97	
1968			
The Good, the Bad and the Ugly	Hugo Montenegro	#2	
For Once in My Life	Stevie Wonder	#2	
On the Road Again	Canned Heat	#16	19 sec.
Friends	The Beach Boys	#47	
Alfie	Eivets Rednow (Stevie Wonder)	#66	
Let Yourself Go	Elvis Presley	#71	
Turn on Your Love Light	The Human Beinz	#80	

HARMONICA (cont'd)

Song	Artist	Hot 100	
Funky North Philly	Bill Cosby	#91	
Do the Best You Can	The Hollies	#93	
Living in the U.S.A.	Steve Miller Band	#94	20 sec.
What's Made Milwaukee Famous (Has Made a Loser Out of Me)	Jerry Lee Lewis	#94	
1969			
And When I Die	Blood, Sweat & Tears	#2	
The Boxer	Simon & Garfunkel	#7	
Polk Salad Annie	Tony Joe White	#9	
Cinnamon	Derek (Johnny Cymbal)	#11	
See	The Rascals	#27	
Roosevelt and Ira Lee (Night of the Mossacin)	Tony Joe White	#44	14 sec.
Time Machine	The Grand Funk Railroad	#48	27 sec.
Back Door Man	Derek (Johnny Cymbal)	#59	
Crumbs Off the Table	The Glass House	#59	
I Want to Take You Higher	Sly & The Family Stone	#60	18 sec.
Don't Waste My Time	John Mayall	#81	
Never Comes the Day	The Moody Blues	#91	
Alice's Rock & Roll Restaurant*	Arlo Guthrie	#97	*Bass harmonica

HARP

SONG	ARTIST	HOT 100
1960		
Alone at Last	Jackie Wilson	#8
Over the Rainbow	The Demensions	#16
To Each His Own	The Platters	#21
Starbright	Johnny Mathis	#25
Ruby	Ray Charles	#28
Red Sails in the Sunset	The Platters	#36
Eternally	Sarah Vaughan	#41
My Love for You	Johnny Mathis	#47
Ebb Tide	The Platters	#56
One of the Lucky Ones	Anita Bryant	#62
Sleepy Lagoon	The Platters	#65
Gloria's Theme	Adam Wade	#74
The Christmas Song (Merry Christmas to You)	Nat "King" Cole	#80
1961		
I Dreamed of a Hill-Billy Heaven	Tex Ritter	#20
Halfway to Paradise	Tony Orlando	#39
The Tear of the Year	Jackie Wilson	#44
Human	Tommy Hunt	#48
Trees	The Platters	#62

HARP (cont'd)

The Lonely Crowd	Teddy Vann	#76
Theme from "Goodbye Again"	Ferrante & Teicher	#85
If I Knew	Nat "King" Cole	#86
Wasn't the Summer Short?	Johnny Mathis	#89

1962

Stranger on the Shore	Mr. Acker Bilk	#1
Al Di La'	Emilio Pericoli	#6
What Kind of Fool am I	Sammy Davis Jr.	#17
I'll Try Something New	The Miracles	#39
I Could Have Loved You so Well	Ray Peterson	#57
Above the Stars	Mr. Acker Bilk	#59
Lollipops and Roses	Jack Jones	#66
The Lost Penny	Brook Benton	#77
Marianna	Johnny Mathis	#86
Oh! What It Seemed to Be	The Castells	#91
Limelight	Mr. Acker Bilk	#92
The Moon Was Yellow	Frank Sinatra	#99

1963

The Grass Is Greener	Brenda Lee	#17
Alice in Wonderland	Neil Sedaka	#17
In My Room	The Beach Boys	#23
Young Wings Can Fly (Higher Than You Know)	Ruby & The Romantics	#47
September Song	Jimmy Durante	#51
Don't Wait Too Long	Tony Bennett	#54
This Is All I Ask	Tony Bennett	#70
Call Me Irresponsible	Jack Jones	#75
Call Me Irresponsible	Frank Sinatra	#78
Faded Love	Jackie DeShannon	#97

1964

People	Barbra Streisand	#5
Dead Man's Curve	Jan & Dean	#8
Shangri-La	Robert Maxwell	#15
It's All in the Game	Cliff Richard	#25
Shangri-La	Vic Dana	#27
On the Street Where You Live	Andy Williams	#28
You'll Never Walk Alone	Patti LaBelle & The Blue Belles	#34
Love Is All We Need	Vic Dana	#53
Bye Bye Barbara	Johnny Mathis	#53
Ringo's Theme (This Boy)	George Martin	#53
Love with the Proper Stranger	Jack Jones	#62
Where Love Has Gone	Jack Jones	#62
I Should Care	Gloria Lynne	#64
Peg O' My Heart	Robert Maxwell	#64

HARP (cont'd)

Garden in the Rain	Vic Dana	#97
The Magic of Our Summer Love	The Tymes	#99

1965

Walk Away	Matt Monro	#23
Dear Heart	Jack Jones	#30
This Little Bird	Marianne Faithfull	#32
It's Gonna Take a Miracle	The Royalettes	#41
Nobody Knows What's Goin' On (In My Mind but Me)	The Chiffons	#49
Good Times	Jerry Butler	#64
Here I Am	Dionne Warwick	#65
I Want to Meet Him	The Royalettes	#72
Try to Remember	Ed Ames	#73
The World Through a Tear	Neil Sedaka	#76
Somewhere	P.J. Proby	#91

1966

Look Through My Window	Mamas & Papas	#24
The Dangling Conversation	Simon & Garfunkel	#25
It Was a Very Good Year	Frank Sinatra	#28
I Love You Drops	Vic Dana	#30
Mind Excursion	The Trade Winds	#51
(We'll Be) United	The Intruders	#78
Painter	Lou Christie	#81
Free Again	Barbra Streisand	#83
The Answer to My Prayer	Neil Sedaka	#89
Dommage, Dommage (Too Bad, Too Bad)	Jerry Vale	#93

1967

The Rain, the Park & Other Things	The Cowsills	#2
Mirage	Tommy James & The Shondells	#10
Lazy Day	Spanky & Our Gang	#14
Holiday	The Bee Gees	#16
To Love Somebody	The Bee Gees	#17
More Love	Smokey Robinson & The Miracles	#23
Why Do Fools Fall in Love	The Happenings	#41
Daddys Little Girl	Al Martino	#42
It's a Happening World	The Tokens	#69

1968

(Theme from) Valley of the Dolls	Dionne Warwick	#2
Abraham, Martin and John	Dion	#4
Fool on the Hill	Sergio Mendes & Brasil '66	#6
Over You	Gary Puckett & The Union Gap	#7
Scarborough Fair	Sergio Mendes & Brasil '66	#16
A Man Without Love	Engelbert Humperdinck	#19
I Get the Sweetest Feeling	Jackie Wilson	#34

HARP (cont'd)

Sherry Don't Go	The Lettermen	#52
Love Is Blue	Al Martino	#57
I Can't Believe I'm Losing You	Frank Sinatra	#60
For Once in My Life	Jackie Wilson	#70
Love Is Blue (L'Amour Est Bleu)	Claudine Longet	#71
I Am Your Man	Bobby Taylor	#85
The Father of Girls	Perry Como	#92
Lonely Is the Name	Sammy Davis, Jr.	#93
The Choice	The O'Jays	#94
1969		
Jean	Oliver	#2
Love Me Tonight	Tom Jones	#13
My Way	Frank Sinatra	#27
Goodnight My Love	Paul Anka	#27
True Grit	Glen Campbell	#35
Woman Helping Man	The Vogues	#47
Welcome Me Love	The Brooklyn Bridge	#48
Rain in My Heart	Frank Sinatra	#62
Julia	Ramsey Lewis	#76
Sincerely	Paul Anka	#80
Can't Find the Time	Orpheus	#80
First Hymn from Grand Terrace	Mark Lindsay	#81
In My Room	Sagittarius	#86
From Both Sides Now	Dion	#91

HARPSICHORD

SONG	ARTIST	HOT 100
1961		
Calcutta	Lawrence Welk	#1
That's It- I Quit- I'm Movin' On	Sam Cooke	#31
Language of Love	John D. Loudermilk	#32
Theme from "My Three Sons"	Lawrence Welk	#55
1962		
All Alone Am I	Brenda Lee	#3
Summertime, Summertime	The Jamies	#38
Hot Pepper	Floyd Cramer	#63
Callin' Doctor Casey	John D. Loudermilk	#83
1963		
Blue Bayou	Roy Orbison	#29
Your Used to Be	Brenda Lee	#32

HARPSICHORD (cont'd)

He's So Heavenly	Brenda Lee	#73
Graduation Day	Bobby Pickett	#88
Scarlett O'Hara	Lawrence Welk	#89
Breakwater	Lawrence Welk	#100
1964		
When I Grow Up (To Be a Man)	The Beach Boys	#9
Blue Winter	Connie Francis	#24
Long Gone Lonesome Blues	Hank Williams, Jr.	#67
The Anaheim, Azusa & Cucamonga Sewing Circle, Book Review and Timing Association	Jan & Dean	#77
Dream Lover	The Paris Sisters	#91
Stockholm	Lawrence Welk	#91
It's a Cotton Candy World	Jerry Wallace	#99
1965		
What's New Pussycat?	Tom Jones	#3
Everybody Loves a Clown	Gary Lewis/Playboys	#4
For Your Love	The Yardbirds	#6
Laurie (Strange Things Happen)	Dickey Lee	#14
Summer Nights	Marianne Faithfull	#24
Come and Stay with Me	Marianne Faithfull	#26
It's Gonna Be Fine	Glenn Yarbrough	#54
Silver Threads and Golden Needles	Jody Miller	#54
Al's Place	Al Hirt	#57
Whenever a Teenager Cries	Reparata & The Delrons	#60
Apples and Bananas	Lawrence Welk	#75
Play with Fire	The Rolling Stones	#96
1966		
Walk Away Renee	The Left Banke	#5
Sugar Town	Nancy Sinatra	#5
Green Grass	Gary Lewis/Playboys	#8
My Heart's Symphony	Gary Lewis/Playboys	#13
Little Man	Sonny & Cher	#21
Who Am I	Petula Clark	#21
Lady Jane	The Rolling Stones	#24
Where Were You When I Needed You	The Grass Roots	#28
I Hear Trumpets Blow	The Tokens	#30
Caroline, No	The Beach Boys	#32
Help Me Girl	The Outsiders	#37
God Only Knows	The Beach Boys	#39
Dum-De-Da	Bobby Vinton	#40
Please Don't Ever Leave Me	The Cyrkle	#59
You Are She	Chad & Jeremy	#87

HARPSICHORD (cont'd)

1967

Title	Artist	Chart
Windy	The Association	#1
Dedicated to the One I Love	Mamas & Papas	#2
Ding Dong! The Witch Is Dead	The Fifth Estate	#11
Heroes and Villains	The Beach Boys	#12
Dandelion	The Rolling Stones	#14
7 Rooms of Gloom	Four Tops	#14
Epistle to Dippy	Donovan	#19
Lady Bird	Nancy Sinatra & Lee Hazlewood	#20
Casino Royale	Herb Alpert & The Tijuana Brass	#27
She's Still a Mystery	The Lovin' Spoonful	#27
Sunday for Tea	Peter & Gordon	#31
The Girl I Knew Somewhere	The Monkees	#39
Wake Up, Wake Up	The Grass Roots	#68
Constant Rain (Chove Chuva)	Sergio Mendes & Brasil '66	#71
Got to Have You Back	Isley Brothers	#93
Fortune Teller	The Hardtimes	#97
Happy and Me	Don & The Goodtimes	#98
Take Me in Your Arms and Love Me	Gladys Knight & The Pips	#98

1968

Title	Artist	Chart
Love Is Blue	Paul Mauriat	#1
Fool on the Hill	Sergio Mendes & Brasil '66	#6
Reach Out of the Darkness	Friend & Lover	#10
Scarborough Fair/Canticle	Simon & Garfunkel	#11
Different Drum	Stone Poneys feat. Linda Ronstadt	#13
Who Will Answer?	Ed Ames	#19
Will You Love Me Tomorrow	The Four Seasons	#24
Love Me Two Times	The Doors	#25
Peace Brother Peace	Bill Medley	#48
In Need of a Friend	The Cowsills	#54
Love Is Blue	Al Martino	#57
You've Got to Be Loved	The Montanas	#58
Sleepy Joe	Herman's Hermits	#61
My Way of Life	Frank Sinatra	#64
Love Is Blue (L'Amour Est Bleu)	Claudine Longet	#71
Do You Wanna Dance	Mamas & Papas	#76
In Another Land	Bill Wyman	#87
1941	Tom Northcott	#88
Love Is Blue (L'Amour Est Bleu)	Manny Kellem	#96

1969

Title	Artist	Chart
Love Theme from Romeo & Juliet	Henry Mancini	#1
Quentin's Theme	The Charles Randolph Grean Sounde	#13

HARPSICHORD (cont'd)		
Ball of Fire	Tommy James & The Shondells	#19
Muddy River	Johnny Rivers	#41
(We've Got) Honey Love	Martha & The Vandellas	#56

HORNS

SONG	ARTIST	HOT 100
1960		
You Talk Too Much	Joe Jones	#3
Way Down Yonder in New Orleans	Freddie Cannon	#3
Go, Jimmy, Go	Jimmy Clanton	#5
Question	Lloyd Price	#19
(You've Got To) Move Two Mountains	Marv Johnson	#20
Clementine	Bobby Darin	#21
Runaround	The Fleetwoods	#23
Hello Young Lovers	Paul Anka	#23
Look for a Star - Part 1	Garry Mills	#26
A Fool in Love	Ike & Tina Turner	#27
Run Samson Run	Neil Sedaka	#28
Jump Over	Freddy Cannon	#28
Ruby Duby Du	Tobin Matthews	#30
The Madison Time - Part 1	Ray Bryant Combo	#30
Chattanooga Shoe Shine Boy	Freddy Cannon	#34
Just Come Home	Hugo & Luigi	#35
Little Coco Palm	Jerry Wallace	#36
Heartbreak (It's Hurtin' Me)	Little Willie John	#38
Swingin' on a Rainbow	Frankie Avalon	#39
Sticks and Stones	Ray Charles	#40
I Love You in the Same Old Way	Paul Anka	#40
Waltzing Matilda	Jimmie Rodgers	#41
For Love	Lloyd Price	#43
Walking the Floor Over You	Pat Boone	#44
Dear John	Pat Boone	#44
Don't Fence Me In	Tommy Edwards	#45
My Love	Nat "King" Cole/Stan Kenton	#47
Anyway the Wind Blows	Doris Day	#50
National City	Joiner, Arkansas Junior High School Band	#53
Honey Hush	Joe Turner	#53
Hardhearted Hannah	Ray Charles	#55
The Puppet Song	Frankie Avalon	#56

HORNS (cont'd)

At My Front Door	Dee Clark	#56
Someday (You'll Want Me to Want You)	Della Reese	#56
Humdinger	Freddy Cannon	#59
The Urge	Freddy Cannon	#60
I Don't Know What It Is	The Bluenotes	#61
Delia Gone	Pat Boone	#66
The Bells	James Brown	#68
Comin' Down with Love	Mel Gadson	#69
Cry Cry Cry	Bobby Bland	#71
Psycho	Bobby Hendricks	#73
Time After Time	Frankie Ford	#75
Spoonful	Etta James & Harvey Fuqua	#78
Let the Good Times Roll	Ray Charles	#78
Let the Good Times Roll	Ray Charles	#78
Just Call Me (And I'll Understand)	Lloyd Price	#79
Make Someone Happy	Perry Como	#80
Mumblin' Mosie	The Johnny Otis Show	#80
The Brigade of Broken Hearts	Paul Evans	#81
Gee	Jan and Dean	#81
Forever	Billy Walker	#83
Tuxedo Junction	Frankie Avalon	#83
My Little Marine	Jamie Horton	#84
Before I Grow Too Old	Fats Domino	#84
The Girl with the Story in Her Eyes	Safaris	#85
You've Got the Power	James Brown w/Bea Ford	#86
I've Been Loved Before	Shirley & Lee	#88
House of Bamboo	Earl Grant	#88
Cry Me A River	Janice Harper	#91
You Are My Sunshine	Johnny & The Hurricanes	#91
Mediterranean Moon	The Rays	#95
Smokie- Part 2	Bill Doggett	#95
The Whiffenpoof Song	Bob Crewe	#96
Livin' Dangerously	The McGuire Sisters	#97
The Last Dance	The McGuire Sisters	#99
1961		
Mother-In-Law	Ernie K-Doe	#1
Hit the Road Jack	Ray Charles	#1
Wonderland by Night	Bert Kaempfert	#1
Last Night	Mar-Keys	#3
But I Do	Clarence Henry	#4
Mama Said	The Shirelles	#4
School Is Out	Gary (U.S.) Bonds	#5
One Mint Julep	Ray Charles	#8

HORNS (cont'd)

One Track Mind	Bobby Lewis	#9
Tragedy	The Fleetwoods	#10
You Always Hurt the One You Love	Clarence Henry	#12
(He's My) Dreamboat	Connie Francis	#14
Lazy River	Bobby Darin	#14
Wonderland by Night	Louis Prima	#15
More Money for You and Me	The Four Preps	#17
Cupid	Sam Cooke	#17
All In My Mind	Maxine Brown	#19
Tenderly	Bert Kaempfert	#31
Anybody but Me	Brenda Lee	#31
The Graduation Song… Pomp and Circumstance	Adriam Kimberly	#34
Transistor Sister	Freddy Cannon	#35
The Bilbao Song	Andy Williams	#37
Saved	LaVern Baker	#37
Nature Boy	Bobby Darin	#40
African Waltz	Cannonball Adderley	#41
Havin' Fun	Dion	#42
Hollywood	Connie Francis	#42
Up A Lazy River	Si Zentner	#43
I Pity the Fool	Bobby Bland	#46
Under the Moon of Love	Curtis Lee	#46
Watch Your Step	Bobby Parker	#51
Te-Ta-Te-Ta-Te	Ernie K-Doe	#53
Muskrat Ramble	Freddy Cannon	#54
I Never Knew	Clyde McPhatter	#56
Lonely Street	Clarence Henry	#57
Them That Got	Ray Charles	#58
Berlin Melody	Billy Vaughn	#61
Teardrops in My Heart	Joe Barry	#63
On Bended Knees	Clarence Henry	#64
I've Got News for You	Ray Charles	#66
Welcome Home	Sammy Kaye	#68
I Cried My Last Tear	Ernie K-Doe	#69
Little Miss Stuck-Up	The Playmates	#70
For Me and My Gal	Freddy Cannon	#71
The Comancheros	Claude King	#71
Don't Cry No More	Bobby Bland	#71
Seventeen	Frankie Ford	#72
Cerveza	Bert Kaempfert	#73
Milord	Teresa Brewer	#74
I Don't Want Nobody (To Have My Love but You)	Ella Johnson with Buddy Johnson	#78
Here Comes the Night	Ben E. King	#81

HORNS (cont'd)

You're the Boss	LaVern Baker/Jimmy Ricks	#81
Rockin' Bicycle	Fats Domino	#83
I'm Gonna Move to the Outskirts of Town	Ray Charles	#84
Driving Wheel	Junior Parker	#85
La Pachanga	Audrey Arno	#87
California Sun	Joe Jones	#89
Wishin' on a Rainbow	Phill Wilson	#91
You've Got to Love Her with a Feeling	Freddy King	#93
I'm a Fool to Care	Oscar Black	#94
Free Me	Johnny Preston	#97
Won'cha Come Home, Bill Bailey	Della Reese	#98
I Love You Yes I Do	Bull Moose Jackson	#98
1962		
Midnight in Moscow	Kenny Ball	#2
I Know (You Don't Love Me No More)	Barbara George	#3
Norman	Sue Thompson	#3
Her Royal Majesty	James Darren	#6
The Lonely Bull	Herb Alpert & The Tijuana Brass	#6
Venus in Blue Jeans	Jimmy Clanton	#7
You Are My Sunshine	Ray Charles	#7
Snap Your Fingers	Joe Henderson	#8
That's Old Fashioned (That's the Way Love Should Be)	The Everly Brothers	#9
Unchain My Heart	Ray Charles	#9
Twist, Twist Senora	Gary (U.S.) Bonds	#9
Love Came to Me	Dion	#10
Town Without Pity	Gene Pitney	#13
I'll Never Dance Again	Bobby Rydell	#14
Revenge	Brook Benton	#15
Irresistible You	Bobby Darin	#15
Cinderella	Jack Ross	#16
Twist and Shout	The Isley Brothers	#17
James (Hold the Ladder Steady)	Sue Thompson	#17
I Left My Heart in San Francisco	Tony Bennett	#19
Hide 'Nor Hair	Ray Charles	#20
Point of No Return	Gene McDaniels	#21
Johnny Jingo	Hayley Mills	#21
Walk on the Wild Side (Part 1)	Jimmy Smith	#21
If You Gotta Make a Fool of Somebody	James Ray	#22
Twistin' Matilda (And the Channel)	Jimmy Soul	#22
Shame on Me	Bobby Bare	#23
What'd I Say (Part 1)	Bobby Darin	#24
Teach Me Tonight	George Maharis	#25
The Push and Kick	Mark Valentino	#27

HORNS (cont'd)

Title	Artist	Page
Turn on Your Love Light	Bobby Bland	#28
That Stranger Used to Be My Girl	Trade Martin	#28
Multiplication	Bobby Darin	#30
If a Man Answers	Bobby Darin	#32
Itty Bitty Pieces	James Ray	#41
At the Club	Ray Charles	#44
Hit Record	Brook Benton	#45
Flying Circle	Frank Slay	#45
You Talk About Love	Barbara George	#46
I Don't Love You No More (I Don't Care About You)	Jimmy Norman	#47
Balboa Blue	The Mar-Kets	#48
Baby Elephant Walk	Lawrence Welk	#48
Tra La La La La	Ike & Tina Turner	#50
I Keep Forgettin'	Chuck Jackson	#55
Happy Jose (Ching-Ching)	Jack Ross	#57
Keep Your Love Locked (Deep in Your Heart)	Paul Petersen	#58
Careless Love	Ray Charles	#60
The Big Draft	The Four Preps	#61
Meet Me at the Twistin' Place	Johnnie Morisette	#63
Me and My Shadow	Frank Sinatra & Sammy Davis Jr.	#64
Just Got to Know	Jimmy McCracklin	#64
Patricia- Twist	Perez Prado	#65
If You Were a Rock and Roll Record	Freddy Cannon	#67
Why Did You Leave Me?	Vince Edwards	#68
Somebody Have Mercy	Sam Cooke	#70
Down in the Valley	Solomon Burke	#71
La Paloma Twist	Chubby Checker	#72
But on the Other Hand Baby	Ray Charles	#72
Big Love	Joe Henderson	#74
Worried Mind	Ray Anthony	#74
Ev'rybody's Twistin'	Frank Sinatra	#75
All Night Long	Sandy Nelson	#75
Who Will the Next Fool Be	Bobby Bland	#76
Sweet and Lovely	April Stevens & Nino Tempo	#77
Nothing New (Same Old Thing)	Fats Domino	#77
A Little Too Much	Clarence Henry	#77
Goodnight, Irene	Jerry Reed	#79
Did You Ever See a Dream Walking	Fats Domino	#79
Lipstick Traces (On a Cigarette)	Benny Spellman	#80
Mashed Potatoes U.S.A.	James Brown	#82
Ol' Man River	Jimmy Smith	#82
I'm Hanging Up My Heart for You	Solomon Burke	#85
Pop Goes the Weasel	Anthony Newley	#85

HORNS (cont'd)

Ain't That Loving You	Bobby Bland	#86
You're Nobody 'Til Somebody Loves You	Dinah Washington	#87
The Green Leaves of Summer	Kenny Ball	#87
March of the Siamese Children	Kenny Ball	#88
Keep Your Hands in Your Pockets	The Playmates	#88
There Is No Greater Love	The Wanderers	#88
Shimmy, Shimmy Walk, Part 1	The Megatons	#88
You Should'a Treated Me Right	Ike & Tina Turner	#89
Let's Go	Floyd Cramer	#90
Baby It's Cold Outside	Ray Charles & Betty Carter	#91
Further More	Ray Stevens	#91
Don't Cry, Baby	Aretha Franklin	#92
Dream	Dinah Washington	#92
I Found Love	Jackie Wilson & Linda Hopkins	#93
Three Hearts in a Tangle	James Brown	#93
The Searching Is Over	Joe Henderson	#94
The Basie Twist	Count Basie	#94
Rough Lover	Aretha Franklin	#94
Sam's Song	Dean Martin & Sammy Davis Jr.	#94
A Sunday Kind of Love	Jan & Dean	#95
You Don't Miss Your Water	William Bell	#95
Dear Hearts and Gentle People	The Springfields	#95
Theme from "Hatari!"	Henry Mancini	#95
Cold, Cold Heart	Dinah Washington	#96
Hail to the Conquering Hero	James Darren	#97
Popeye Joe	Ernie K-Doe	#99
Mama (He Treats Your Daughter Mean)	Ruth Brown	#99
1963		
It's My Party	Lesley Gore	#1
Fingertips - Pt. 2	Little Stevie Wonder	#1
Washington Square	The Village Stompers	#2
Sally, Go 'Round the Roses	The Jaynetts	#2
It's All Right	The Impressions	#4
Busted	Ray Charles	#4
Judy's Turn to Cry	Lesley Gore	#5
Baby Workout	Jackie Wilson	#5
It's Up to You	Ricky Nelson	#6
Two Lovers	Mary Wells	#7
More	Kai Winding	#8
Mickey's Monkey	The Miracles	#8
The Monkey Time	Major Lance	#8
(Down At) Papa Joe's	The Dixiebelles	#9
Our Winter Love	Bill Pursell	#9

HORNS (cont'd)

Title	Artist	#
Pride and Joy	Marvin Gaye	#10
Watermelon Man	Mongo Santamaria	#10
Little Town Flirt	Del Shannon	#12
Birdland	Chubby Checker	#12
Hey Little Girl	Major Lance	#13
Frankie and Johnny	Sam Cooke	#14
Laughing Boy	Mary Wells	#15
Killer Joe	The Rocky Fellers	#16
Wildwood Days	Bobby Rydell	#17
Harry the Hairy Ape	Ray Stevens	#17
Ring of Fire	Johnny Cash	#17
Have You Heard	The Duprees	#18
Don't Set Me Free	Ray Charles	#20
Misty	Lloyd Price	#21
Little Band of Gold	James Gilreath	#21
No One	Ray Charles	#21
You Lost the Sweetest Boy	Mary Wells	#22
Call On Me	Bobby Bland	#22
Call On Me	Bobby Bland	#22
Wham!	Lonnie Mack	#24
Only in America	Jay & The Americans	#25
First Quarrel	Paul & Paula	#27
Linda	Jan & Dean	#28
Without Love (There Is Nothing)	Ray Charles	#29
Come and Get These Memories	Martha & The Vandellas	#29
Hitch Hike	Marvin Gaye	#30
Witchcraft	Elvis Presley	#32
Shake! Shake! Shake!	Jackie Wilson	#33
Your Old Stand By	Mary Wells	#40
Shake a Hand	Jackie Wilson & Linda Hopkins	#42
Treat My Baby Good	Bobby Darin	#43
Lovesick Blues	Frank Ifield	#44
The Matador	Johnny Cash	#44
Locking Up My Heart	The Marvelettes	#44
Every Day I Have to Cry	Steve Alaimo	#46
Monkey-Shine	Bill Black's Combo	#47
Que Sera, Sera (Whatever Will Be, Will Be)	The High Keyes	#47
Java	Floyd Cramer	#49
Little Latin Lupe Lu	The Righteous Brothers	#49
You're Good for Me	Solomon Burke	#49
Don't Make My Baby Blue	Frankie Laine	#51
Do It - Rat Now	Bill Black's Combo	#51
Pin a Medal on Joey	James Darren	#54

HORNS (cont'd)

I'm a Woman	Peggy Lee	#54
Like the Big Guys Do	The Rocky Fellers	#55
Sometimes You Gotta Cry a Little	Bobby Bland	#56
Baby Get It (And Don't Quit It)	Jackie Wilson	#61
Two Sides (To Every Story)	Etta James	#63
Gravy Waltz	Steve Allen	#64
Can't Nobody Love You	Solomon Burke	#66
The Jive Samba	Cannonball Adderley	#66
Hobo Flats - Part 1	Jimmy Smith	#69
Sweet Impossible You	Brenda Lee	#70
This Is All I Ask	Tony Bennett	#70
Man's Temptation	Gene Chandler	#71
Cindy's Gonna Cry	Johnny Crawford	#72
I'm the One Who Loves You	The Impressions	#73
Breath Taking Guy	The Supremes	#75
My Babe	The Righteous Brothers	#75
I Can't Stop Loving You	Count Basie	#77
Pepin's Friend Pasqual (The Italian Pussy-Cat)	Lou Monte	#78
Chinese Checkers	Booker T. & The MG's	#78
Pay Back	Etta James	#78
Hey Lover	Debbie Dovale	#81
Any Other Way	Chuck Jackson	#81
Little Tin Soldier	The Toy Dolls	#84
The Dog	Rufus Thomas	#87
Guilty	Jim Reeves	#91
Rumble	Jack Nitzsche	#91
Look at Me	Dobie Gray	#91
Yeh-Yeh!	Mongo Santamaria	#92
The Brightest Smile in Town	Ray Charles	#92
I'm Not a Fool Anymore	T.K. Hulin	#92
Soulville	Dinah Washington	#92
Preacherman	Charlie Russo	#92
Banzai Pipeline	Henry Mancini	#93
Surfer Street	The Allisons	#93
Don't Fence Me In	George Maharis	#93
Lonely Drifter	The O'Jays	#93
Saturday Sunshine	Burt Bacharach	#93
Don't Be Cruel	Barbara Lynn	#93
Don't Mention My Name	The Shepherd Sisters	#94
Someone Somewhere	Junior Parker	#95
Marching Thru Madrid	Herb Alpert & The Tijuana Brass	#96
At the Shore	Johnny Caswell	#97
Baby, We've Got Love	Johnnie Taylor	#98

HORNS (cont'd)

River's Invitation	Percy Mayfield	#99
Every Beat of My Heart	James Brown	#99
True Blue Lou	Tony Bennett	#99
Oo-La-La-Limbo	Danny & The Juniors	#99
Two Wrongs Don't Make a Right	Mary Wells	#100
1964		
Hello, Dolly!	Louis Armstrong	#1
My Guy	Mary Wells	#1
Chapel of Love	The Dixie Cups	#1
My Boy Lollipop	Millie Small	#2
Dancing in the Street	Martha & The Vandellas	#2
The Little Old Lady (From Pasadena)	Jan & Dean	#3
Come a Little Bit Closer	Jay & The Americans	#3
Out of Limits	The Marketts	#3
Suspicion	Terry Stafford	#3
Java	Al Hirt	#4
C'mon and Swim	Bobby Freeman	#5
Um, Um, Um, Um, Um, Um	Major Lance	#5
The Shoop Shoop Song (It's in His Kiss)	Betty Everett	#6
Navy Blue	Diane Renay	#6
Quicksand	Martha & The Vandellas	#8
The Nitty Gritty	Shirley Ellis	#8
Good News	Sam Cooke	#11
The Way You Do the Things You Do	The Temptations	#11
People Say	The Dixie Cups	#12
Talking About My Baby	The Impressions	#12
Funny (How Time Slips Away)	Joe Hinton	#13
I'm So Proud	The Impressions	#14
Southtown, U.S.A.	The Dixiebelles	#15
You Must Believe Me	The Impressions	#15
Try It Baby	Marvin Gaye	#15
You're a Wonderful One	Marvin Gaye	#15
Cotton Candy	Al Hirt	#15
Abigail Beecher	Freddy Cannon	#16
What's the Matter with You Baby	Marvin Gaye & Mary Wells	#17
The Matador	Major Lance	#20
Ain't Nothing You Can Do	Bobby Bland	#20
When the Lovelight Starts Shining Through His Eyes	The Supremes	#23
Walking in the Rain	The Ronettes	#23
Out of Sight	James Brown	#24
Sidewalk Surfin'	Jan & Dean	#25
My Girl Sloopy	The Vibrations	#26
Girl (Why You Wanna Make Me Blue)	The Temptations	#26

HORNS (cont'd)

Remember Me	Rita Pavone	#26
I Like It Like That	The Miracles	#27
Baby Don't Do It	Marvin Gaye	#27
Kiss Me Sailor	Diane Renay	#29
Sugar Lips	Al Hirt	#30
Cousin of Mine	Sam Cooke	#31
20-75	Willie Mitchell	#31
I'll Be in Trouble	The Temptations	#33
That's What Love Is Made Of	The Miracles	#35
Tra La La La Suzy	Dean & Jean	#35
Understand Your Man	Johnny Cash	#35
Tennesse Waltz	Sam Cooke	#35
I Don't Wanna Be a Loser	Lesley Gore	#37
Giving Up	Gladys Knight & The Pips	#38
You Should Have Seen the Way He Looked at Me	The Dixie Cups	#39
Baby, Don't You Cry (The New Swingova Rhythm)	Ray Charles	#39
Sweet William	Millie Small	#40
Can You Do It	The Contours	#41
Comin' in the Back Door	Baja Marimba Band	#41
Wow Wow Wee (He's the Boy for Me)	The Angels	#41
Live Wire	Martha & The Vandellas	#42
Don't Ever Leave Me	Connie Francis	#42
He's in Town	The Tokens	#43
Angelito	Rene & Rene	#43
Harlem Shuffle	Bob & Earl	#44
I Still Get Jealous	Louis Armstrong	#45
Ain't It the Truth	Mary Wells	#45
Milord	Bobby Darin	#45
I Can't Stand It	Soul Sisters	#46
Can Your Monkey Do the Dog	Rufus Thomas	#48
Ain't Doing Too Bad (Part 1)	Bobby Bland	#49
She Want T' Swim	Chubby Checker	#50
My Baby Don't Dig Me	Ray Charles	#51
Good Night Baby	The Butterflys	#51
You're No Good	Betty Everett	#51
Baby Baby Baby	Anna King-Bobby Byrd	#52
Smack Dab in the Middle	Ray Charles	#52
Something You Got	Alvin Robinson	#52
Young and in Love	Chris Crosby	#53
Hurt by Love	Inez Foxx	#54
S-W-I-M	Bobby Freeman	#56
So Long Dearie	Louis Armstrong	#56

HORNS (cont'd)

One Way Love	The Drifters	#56
Everybody Needs Somebody to Love	Solomon Burke	#58
It Ain't Me, Babe	Johnny Cash	#58
The James Bond Theme	Billy Strange	#58
Hello Muddah, Hello Fadduh! (A Letter from Camp) (New 1964 version)	Allan Sherman	#59
What Good Am I Without You	Marvin Gaye & Kim Weston	#61
La La La La La	The Blendells	#62
Who Cares	Fats Domino	#63
Thank You Baby	The Shirelles	#63
Yesterday's Hero	Gene Pitney	#64
Shimmy Shimmy	The Orlons	#66
I Can't Hear You	Betty Everett	#66
If Somebody Told You	Anna King	#67
I've Got No Time to Lose	Carla Thomas	#67
The Cat	Jimmy Smith	#67
Girls	Major Lance	#68
It Ain't No Use	Major Lance	#68
Tell Me Baby	Garnet Mimms	#69
Oh! Baby (We Got a Good Thing Goin')	Barbara Lynn	#69
Chained and Bound	Otis Redding	#70
Snap Your Fingers	Barbara Lewis	#71
Who's Afraid of Virginia Woolf? (Part I)	Jimmy Smith	#72
It's All Over	Ben E. King	#72
(That's) What the Nitty Gritty Is	Shirley Ellis	#72
Look Away	Garnet Mimms	#73
Come See About Me	Nella Dodds	#74
(It's No) Sin	The Duprees	#74
Do Anything You Wanna (Part I)	Harold Betters	#74
Yesterday's Gone	The Overlanders	#75
Leaving Here	Eddie Holland	#76
The Anaheim, Azusa & Cucamonga Sewing Circle, Book Review and Timing Association	Jan & Dean	#77
Mexican Drummer Man	Herb Alpert & The Tijuana Brass	#77
Since I Found a New Love	Little Johnny Taylor	#78
Do-Wah-Diddy	The Exciters	#78
From Russia with Love	The Village Stompers	#81
Beautician Blues	B.B. King	#82
My Dreams	Brenda Lee	#85
The Mexican Shuffle	Herb Alpert & The Tijuana Brass	#85
Up Above My Head (I Hear Music in the Air)	Al Hirt	#85
Lazy Lady	Fats Domino	#86
Somebody Stole My Dog	Rufus Thomas	#86
Sometimes I Wish I Were a Boy	Lesley Gore	#86

HORNS (cont'd)

Stop Takin' Me for Granted	Mary Wells	#88
I've Got the Skill	Jackie Ross	#89
Going Back to Louisiana	Bruce Channel	#89
Lovers Always Forgive	Gladys Knight & The Pips	#89
Never Trust a Woman	B.B. King	#90
Vanishing Point	The Marketts	#90
Ask Me	Inez Foxx	#91
I Wanna Thank You	The Enchanters	#91
The Feeling Is Gone	Bobby Bland	#91
Here She Comes	The Tymes	#92
Soul Hootenanny Pt. I	Gene Chandler	#92
Somebody New	Chuck Jackson	#93
I Can't Wait Until I See My Baby	Justine Washington	#93
That's Where It's At	Sam Cooke	#93
Big Boss Line	Jackie Wilson	#94
Night Time Is the Right Time	Rufus & Carla	#94
Jailer, Bring Me Water	Trini Lopez	#94
A Taste of Honey	Tony Bennett	#94
Caldonia	James Brown	#95
Please, Please, Please	James Brown	#95
Security	Otis Redding	#97
Fiddler on the Roof	The Village Stompers	#97
A Shot in the Dark	Henry Mancini	#97
Good Time Tonight	The Soul Sisters	#98
Jamaica Ska	The Ska Kings	#98
All Grown Up	The Crystals	#98
Help the Poor	B.B. King	#98
The Things That I Used to Do	James Brown	#99
Strange Things Happening	Little Junior Parker	#99
Just a Moment Ago	Soul Sisters	#100
1965		
Stop! In the Name of Love	The Supremes	#1
1 2 3	Len Barry	#2
Treat Her Right	Roy Head	#2
A Lover's Concerto	The Toys	#2
Let's Hang On	The Four Seasons	#3
California Girls	The Beach Boys	#3
What's New Pussycat?	Tom Jones	#3
The Name Game	Shirley Ellis	#3
I Got You (I Feel Good)	James Brown	#3
Rescue Me	Fontella Bass	#4
Hold What You've Got	Joe Tex	#5
Amen	The Impressions	#7

HORNS (cont'd)

Title	Artist	Position
You've Got Your Troubles	The Fortunes	#7
Shake	Sam Cooke	#7
A Taste of Honey	Herb Alpert & The Tijuana Brass	#7
The Clapping Song (Clap Pat Clap Slap)	Shirley Ellis	#8
The Boy from New York City	The Ad Libs	#8
Nowhere to Run	Martha & The Vandellas	#8
Papa's Got a Brand New Bag (Part 1)	James Brown	#8
It's Not Unusual	Tom Jones	#10
Nothing but Heartaches	The Supremes	#11
Action	Freddy Cannon	#13
Laurie (Strange Things Happen)	Dickey Lee	#14
Marie	The Bachelors	#15
Do the Freddie	Freddie & The Dreamers	#18
Give Him a Great Big Kiss	The Shangri-Las	#18
Agent Double-O-Soul	Edwin Starr	#21
In the Midnight Hour	Wilson Pickett	#21
I've Been Loving You Too Long (To Stop Now)	Otis Redding	#21
Got to Get You off My Mind	Solomon Burke	#22
Oo Wee Baby, I Love You	Fred Hughes	#23
I Want To (Do Everything for You)	Joe Tex	#23
We're Gonna Make It	Little Milton	#25
Too Many Fish in the Sea	The Marvelettes	#25
Tonight's the Night	Solomon Burke	#28
Woman's Got Soul	The Impressions	#29
I Found a Girl	Jan & Dean	#30
The Entertainer	Tony Clarke	#31
Kansas City Star	Roger Miller	#31
Sugar Dumpling	Sam Cooke	#32
Three O'Clock in the Morning	Bert Kaempfert	#33
Wild One	Martha & The Vandellas	#34
I'll Always Love You	The Spinners	#35
Respect	Otis Redding	#35
You've Been in Love Too Long	Martha & The Vandellas	#36
I'm a Happy Man	The Jive Five	#36
Peaches "N" Cream	The Ikettes	#36
I Do	The Marvelows	#37
Just a Little Bit	Roy Head	#39
Crazy Downtown	Allan Sherman	#40
It's Got the Whold World Shakin'	Sam Cooke	#41
Mr. Pitiful	Otis Redding	#41
Who's Cheating Who?	Little Milton	#43
Seesaw	Don Covay/Goodtimers	#44
New Orleans	Eddie Hodges	#44

HORNS (cont'd)

Title	Artist	Page
Thanks a Lot	Brenda Lee	#45
You Better Get It	Joe Tex	#46
Can You Jerk Like Me	The Contours	#47
Boo-Ga-Loo	Tom & Jerrio	#47
3rd Man Theme	Herb Alpert & The Tijuana Brass	#47
Fancy Pants	Al Hirt	#47
Meeting Over Yonder	The Impressions	#48
Come On Do the Jerk	The Miracles	#50
You Got What It Takes	Joe Tex	#51
Voice Your Choice	The Radiants	#51
Little Bell	The Dixie Cups	#51
The 81	Candy & The Kisses	#51
Don't Fight It	Wilson Pickett	#53
Goldfinger	Billy Strange	#55
Something You Got	Chuck Jackson & Maxine Brown	#55
(Here They Come) From All Over the World	Jan & Dean	#56
Al's Place	Al Hirt	#57
Boot-Leg	Booker T. & The MG's	#58
I Can't Work No Longer	Billy Butler & The Chanters	#60
If You've Got a Heart	Bobby Goldsboro	#60
Danger Heartbreak Dead Ahead	The Marvelettes	#61
Watermelon Man	Gloria Lynne	#62
These Hands (Small but Mighty)	Bobby Bland	#63
He Was Really Sayin' Something	The Velvelettes	#64
I Need You	The Impressions	#64
Love Is a 5-Letter Word	James Phelps	#66
Land of a Thousand Dances (Part 1)	Thee Midniters	#67
Whipped Cream	Herb Alpert & The Tijuana Brass	#68
See You at the "Go-Go"	Dobie Gray	#69
Temptation 'Bout to Get Me	The Knight Bros.	#70
He's a Lover	Mary Wells	#74
The Letter	Sonny & Cher	#75
You Can Have Him	Dionne Warwick	#75
Gotta Have Your Love	The Sapphires	#77
You Better Go	Derek Martin	#78
Blind Man	Bobby Bland	#78
The Puzzle Song (A Puzzle in Song)	Shirley Ellis	#78
Hello, Dolly!	Bobby Darin	#79
The Sidewinder, Part 1	Lee Morgan	#81
Good Lovin'	The Olympics	#81
Bring Your Love to Me	The Righteous Brothers	#83
The Record (Baby I Love You)	Ben E. King	#84
Lip Sync (To the Tongue Twisters)	Len Barry	#84

HORNS (cont'd)

Percolatin'	Willie Mitchell	#85
Keep on Trying	Bobby Vee	#85
Just One More Day	Otis Redding	#85
Blind Man	Little Milton	#86
Someone Is Watching	Solomon Burke	#89
Chains of Love	The Drifters	#90
Follow Me	The Drifters	#91
Ain't No Big Thing	Radiants	#91
Can't Let You Out of My Sight	Chuck Jackson & Maxine Brown	#91
Ain't It a Shame	Major Lance	#91
Good Times	Gene Chandler	#92
Stop! Look What You're Doing	Carla Thomas	#92
Tommy	Reparata & The Delrons	#92
For You	The Spellbinders	#93
Ain't No Telling	Bobby Bland	#93
Pass Me By	Peggy Lee	#93
Too Hot to Hold	Major Lance	#93
Don't Have to Shop Around	The Mad Lads	#93
I've Cried My Last Tear	The O'Jays	#94
Only Love (Can Save Me Now)	Solomon Burke	#94
Don't Let Your Left Hand Know	Joe Tex	#95
A Little Bit of Soap	Garnet Mimms	#95
Me Without You	Mary Wells	#95
Back Street	Edwin Starr	#95
We're Doing Fine	Dee Dee Warwick	#96
Do I Make Myself Clear	Etta James & Sugar Pie DeSanto	#96
Buster Browne	Willie Mitchell	#96
Can't You Just See Me	Aretha Franklin	#96
Finders Keepers, Losers Weepers	Nella Dodds	#96
I Believe I'll Love On	Jackie Wilson	#96
The Silence (Il Silenzio)	Al Hirt	#96
Teasin' You	Willie Tee	#97
How Nice It Is	Billy Stewart	#97
Long Live Love	Sandie Shaw	#97
El Pussy Cat	Mongo Santamaria	#97
I Want You to Be My Boy	The Exciters	#98
Cross My Heart	Bobby Vee	#99
Black Night	Bobby Bland	#99
Love Me Now	Brook Benton	#100
1966		
These Boots Are Made for Walkin'	Nancy Sinatra	#1
You Keep Me Hangin' On	The Supremes	#1
When a Man Loves a Woman	Percy Sledge	#1

HORNS (cont'd)

Winchester Cathedral	New Vaudeville Band	#1
The Ballad of the Green Berets	SSgt. Barry Sadler	#1
Sunny	Bobby Hebb	#2
Mellow Yellow	Donovan	#2
Beauty Is Only Skin Deep	The Temptations	#3
Uptight (Everything's Alright)	Stevie Wonder	#3
See You in September	The Happenings	#3
Rainy Day Women #12 & 35	Bob Dylan	#3
Black Is Black	Los Bravos	#4
That's Life	Frank Sinatra	#4
Time Won't Let Me	The Outsiders	#5
Sugar Town	Nancy Sinatra	#5
Land of 1000 Dances	Wilson Pickett	#6
Lady Godiva	Peter & Gordon	#6
I'm Your Puppet	James & Bobby Purify	#6
How Does That Grab You, Darlin'?	Nancy Sinatra	#7
Barefootin'	Robert Parker	#7
Wouldn't It Be Nice	The Beach Boys	#8
(I Know) I'm Losing You	The Temptations	#8
Working in the Coal Mine	Lee Dorsey	#8
Blowin' in the Wind	Stevie Wonder	#9
Working My Way Back to You	The Four Seasons	#9
Love Is like an Itching in My Heart	The Supremes	#9
Have You Seen Your Mother, Baby, Standing in the Shadow?	The Rolling Stones	#9
Summertime	Billy Stewart	#10
Petula Clark	A Sign of the Times	#11
Zorba the Greek	Herb Alpert & The Tijuana Brass	#11
Going to a Go-Go	The Miracles	#11
Love Makes the World Go Round	Deon Jackson	#11
The Cheater	Bob Kuban	#12
A Hazy Shade of Winter	Simon & Garfunkel	#13
Opus 17 (Don't You Worry 'Bout Me)	The Four Seasons	#13
Ain't Too Proud to Beg	The Temptations	#13
634-5789 (Soulsville, U.S.A.)	Wilson Pickett	#13
Love Is a Hurtin' Thing	Lou Rawls	#13
B-A-B-Y	Carla Thomas	#14
The Duck	Jackie Lee	#14
(You Don't Have To) Paint Me a Picture	Gary Lewis/Playboys	#15
Respectable	The Outsiders	#15
I Got the Feelin' (Oh No No)	Neil Diamond	#16
Warm and Tender Love	Percy Sledge	#17
Attack	The Toys	#18
The Work Song	Herb Alpert & The Tijuana Brass	#18

HORNS (cont'd)

Mame	Herb Alpert & The Tijuana Brass	#19
Wade in the Water	Ramsey Lewis	#19
Nothing's Too Good for My Baby	Stevie Wonder	#20
Hold On! I'm a Comin'	Sam & Dave	#21
But It's Alright	J.J. Jackson	#22
It's Too Late	Bobby Goldsboro	#23
Holy Cow	Lee Dorsey	#23
Mustang Sally	Wilson Pickett	#23
What Now My Love	Herb Alpert & The Tijuana Brass	#24
Frankie and Johnny	Elvis Presley	#25
Somewhere	Len Barry	#26
Open the Door to Your Heart	Darrell Banks	#27
Like a Baby	Len Barry	#27
Flamingo	Herb Alpert & The Tijuana Brass	#28
The "A" Team	SSgt. Barry Sandler	#28
Knock on Wood	Eddie Floyd	#28
Fa-Fa-Fa-Fa-Fa (Sad Song)	Otis Redding	#29
Help Me Girl	Eric Burdon/Animals	#29
A Sweet Woman Like You	Joe Tex	#29
Secret Love	Billy Stewart	#29
I'll Take Good Care of You	Garnet Mimms	#30
It Tears Me Up	Percy Sledge	#30
Satisfaction	Otis Redding	#31
It's Only Love	Tommy James & The Shondells	#31
I Chose to Sing the Blues	Ray Charles/The Raeletts	#32
Second Hand Rose	Barbra Streisand	#32
The Phoenix Love Theme (Senza Fine)	The Brass Ring	#32
Long Live Our Love	The Shangri-Las	#33
Under Your Spell Again	Johnny Rivers	#35
Batman Theme	Neal Hefti	#35
Recovery	Fontella Bass	#37
Help Me Girl	The Outsiders	#37
(When She Needs Good Lovin') She Comes to Me	The Chicago Loop	#37
Tijuana Taxi	Herb Alpert & The Tijuana Brass	#38
(You're Gonna) Hurt Yourself	Frankie Valli	#39
S.Y.S.L.J.F.M. (The Letter Song)	Joe Tex	#39
Ain't Gonna Lie	Keith	#39
I'm Comin' Home, Cindy	Trini Lopez	#39
The Dedication Song	Freddy Cannon	#41
Andrea	The Sunrays	#41
Michael	The C.O.D.'s	#41
Get Out of My Life, Woman	Lee Dorsey	#44
Distant Drums	Jim Reeves	#45

HORNS (cont'd)

Up and Down	The McCoys	#46
Whole Lot of Shakin' in My Heart (Since I Met You)	The Miracles	#46
Memories are Made of This	The Drifters	#48
Stop Her on Sight (S.O.S.)	Edwin Starr	#48
Up Tight	Ramsey Lewis	#49
Don't Be a Drop-Out	James Brown	#50
Got My Mojo Working (Part 1)	Jimmy Smith	#51
Ghost Riders in the Sky	Baja Marimba Band	#52
Ninety-Nine and a Half (Won't Do)	Wilson Pickett	#53
Money Won't Change You (Part 1)	James Brown	#53
Bye Bye Blues	Bert Kaempfert	#54
Solitary Man	Neil Diamond	#55
The Love You Save (May Be Your Own)	Joe Tex	#56
I Know You Better Than That	Bobby Goldsboro	#56
Juanita Banana	The Peels	#59
Little Boy (In Grown Up Clothes)	The Four Seasons	#60
Cast Your Fate to the Wind	Shelby Flint	#61
Break Out	Mitch Ryder & The Detroit Wheels	#62
I'm Too Far Gone (To Turn Around)	Bobby Bland	#62
Cloudy Summer Afternoon (Raindrops)	Barry McGuire	#62
That's Enough	Rosco Robinson	#62
Let Me Be Good to You	Carla Thomas	#62
My Ship Is Comin' In	The Walker Bros.	#63
You've Got My Mind Messed Up	James Carr	#63
Baby, Do the Philly Dog	The Olympics	#63
Ain't Nobody Home	Howard Tate	#63
I've Got to Do a Little Bit Better	Joe Tex	#64
Said I Wasn't Gonna Tell Nobody	Sam & Dave	#64
Poverty	Bobby Bland	#65
Neighbor, Neighbor	Jimmy Hughes	#65
Love Is Me, Love Is You	Connie Francis	#66
Batman	Jan & Dean	#66
I Believe I'm Gonna Make It	Joe Tex	#67
The Teaser	Bob Kuban	#70
It Hurts Me	Bobby Goldsboro	#70
Get Away	Georgie Fame	#70
Winchester Cathedral	Dana Rollin	#71
I'll Go Crazy	James Brown	#73
Promise Her Anything	Tom Jones	#74
I Want Someone	The Mad Lads	#74
I Got to Handle It	The Capitols	#74
Bring Back the Time	B.J. Thomas	#75
Good Time Charlie	Bobby Bland	#75

HORNS (cont'd)

Title	Artist	Page
Hey You! Little Boo-Ga-Loo	Chubby Checker	#76
We Know We're in Love	Lesley Gore	#76
C.C. Rider	Bobby Powell	#76
Killer Joe	The Kingsmen	#77
Love Takes a Long Time Growing	Deon Jackson	#77
Let's Call It a Day Girl	The Razor's Edge	#77
I Surrender	Fontella Bass	#78
Tired of Being Lonely	Sharpees	#79
Painter	Lou Christie	#81
Mame	Louis Armstrong	#81
This Golden Ring	The Fortunes	#82
Headline News	Edwin Starr	#84
Uptight (Everything's Alright)	Nancy Wilson	#84
Just a Little Misunderstanding	The Contours	#85
Pouring Water on a Drowning Man	James Carr	#85
La Bamba - Part 1	Trini Lopez	#86
On the Good Ship Lollipop	The Wonder Who (The Four Seasons)	#87
Get Back	Roy Head	#88
Heart's Desire	Billy Joe Royal	#88
He Wore the Green Beret	Nancy Ames	#89
The Pain Gets a Little Deeper	Darrow Fletcher	#89
Philly Dog	The Mar-Keys	#89
You Don't Know Like I Know	Sam & Dave	#90
He Will Break Your Heart	The Righteous Brothers	#91
Going Nowhere	Los Bravos	#91
Dear Mrs. Applebee	Flip Cartridge	#91
Don't Forget About Me	Barbara Lewis	#91
Black Nights	Lowell Fulsom	#91
Too Slow	The Impressions	#91
It's That Time of the Year	Len Barry	#91
Bad Eye	Willie Mitchell	#92
Follow Your Heart	The Manhattans	#92
Questions and Answers	The In Crowd	#92
Think Twice	Jackie Wilson & LaVern Baker	#93
Philly Dog	Herbie Mann	#93
Drive My Car	Bob Kuban	#93
Rib Tip's (Part 1)	Andre Williams	#94
Yesterday Man	Chris Andrews	#94
I'm Your Hoochie Cooche Man (Part 1)	Jimmy Smith	#94
Harlem Shuffle	The Traits	#94
Stand in for Love	The O'Jays	#95
You're Nobody Till Somebody Loves You	The Wonder Who? (The Four Seasons)	#96
Tell Her	Dean Parrish	#97

HORNS (cont'd)

Peak of Love	Bobby McClure	#97
I Feel a Sin Coming On	Solomon Burke	#97
I Spy (For the FBI)	Jame Thomas	#98
I Struck It Rich	Len Barry	#98
Love Attack	James Carr	#99
Mine Exclusively	The Olympics	#99
Day Tripper	The Vontastics	#100
I Can Hear Music	The Ronettes	#100
Greetings (This Is Uncle Sam)	The Monitors	#100
We Got the Winning Hand	Little Milton	#100
I Can't Give You Anything but Love	Bert Kaempfert	#100
Safe and Sound	Fontella Bass	#100

1967

The Happening	The Supremes	#1
Penny Lane	The Beatles	#1
Kind of a Drag	The Buckinghams	#1
Sweet Soul Music	Arthur Conley	#2
Can't Take My Eyes Off You	Frankie Valli	#2
Soul Man	Sam & Dave	#2
She'd Rather Be with Me	The Turtles	#3
I Got Rhythm	The Happenings	#3
Little Ole Man (Uptight-Everything's Alright)	Bill Cosby	#4
Baby I Love You	Aretha Franklin	#4
I Second That Emotion	Smokey Robinson & The Miracles	#4
Creeque Alley	Mamas & Papas	#5
Mercy, Mercy, Mercy	The Buckinghams	#5
Words of Love	Mamas & Papas	#5
Then You Can Tell Me Goodbye	The Casinos	#6
The Beat Goes On	Sonny & Cher	#6
Apples, Peaches, Pumpkin Pie	Jay & The Techniques	#6
You Got What It Takes	Dave Clark Five	#7
Cold Sweat (Part 1)	James Brown	#7
98.6	Keith	#7
You Better Sit Down Kids	Cher	#9
I Never Loved a Man (The Way I Love You)	Aretha Franklin	#9
A Girl Like You	The Young Rascals	#10
Jimmy Mack	Martha & The Vandellas	#10
Skinny Legs and All	Joe Tex	#10
Ding Dong! The Witch Is Dead	The Fifth Estate	#11
Mercy, Mercy, Mercy	"Cannonball" Adderley	#11
Get on Up	The Esquires	#11
Hey Baby (They're Playing Our Song)	The Buckinghams	#12
Stand By Me	Spyder Turner	#12

HORNS (cont'd)

My Mammy	The Happenings	#13
Thank the Lord for the Night Time	Neil Diamond	#13
Keep the Ball Rollin'	Jay & The Techniques	#14
Knight in Rusty Armour	Peter & Gordon	#15
Soul Finger	Bar-Kays	#17
(I Wanna) Testify	The Parliaments	#20
Hypnotized	Linda Jones	#21
Make Me Yours	Bettye Swann	#21
Let the Good Times Roll & Feel So Good	Bunny Sigler	#22
And Get Away	The Esquires	#22
Ups and Downs	Paul Revere & The Raiders	#22
Kentucky Woman	Neil Diamond	#22
Niki Hoeky	P.J. Proby	#23
Too Many Fish in the Sea & Three Little Fishes	Mitch Ryder & The Detroit Wheels	#24
Step out of Your Mind	The American Breed	#24
Shake a Tail Feather	James & Bobby Purify	#25
Tramp	Otis & Carla	#26
Everybody Needs Somebody to Love	Wilson Pickett	#29
So You Want to Be a Rock 'N' Roll Star	The Byrds	#29
Bring It Up	James Brown	#29
Dead End Street	Lou Rawls	#29
Knock on Wood	Otis & Carla	#30
What a Woman in Love Won't Do	Sandy Posey	#31
Shake, Rattle & Roll	Arthur Conley	#31
The Happening	Herb Alpert & The Tijuana Brass	#32
I Found a Love - Part 1	Wilson Pickett	#32
Memphis Soul Stew	King Curtis	#33
Show Me	Joe Tex	#35
You Must Have Been a Beautiful Baby	Dave Clark Five	#35
The Dis-Advantages of You	The Brass Ring	#36
Portrait of My Love	The Tokens	#36
Wade in the Water	Herb Alpert & The Tijuana Brass	#37
Ride, Ride, Ride	Brenda Lee	#37
Are You Lonely for Me	Freddy Scott	#39
Love Me Tender	Percy Sledge	#40
Get It Together (Part 1)	James Brown	#40
I'll Try Anything	Dusty Springfield	#40
Laudy Miss Claudy	The Buckinghams	#41
Peace of Mind	Paul Revere & The Raiders	#42
Papa Was Too	Joe Tex	#44
Chattanooga Choo Choo	Harpers Bizarre	#45
I Fooled You This Time	Gene Chandler	#45
I'm in Love	Wilson Pickett	#45

HORNS (cont'd)

Song	Artist	#
Show Business	Lou Rawls	#45
Let Yourself Go	James Brown	#46
Shake	Otis Redding	#47
Together	The Intruders	#48
Soul Man	Ramsey Lewis	#49
My Babe	Ronnie Dove	#50
Hush	Billy Joe Royal	#52
More Than the Eye Can See	Al Martino	#54
Woman Like That, Yeah	Joe Tex	#54
Okolona River Bottom Band	Bobby Gentry	#54
Shout Bamalama	Mickey Murray	#54
Soul Dance Number Three	Wilson Pickett	#55
Kansas City	James Brown	#55
You Can Bring Me All Your Heartaches	Lou Rawls	#55
(Open Up the Door) Let the Good Times In	Dean Martin	#55
I Am the Walrus	The Beatles	#56
Why (Am I Treated So Bad)	The Sweet Inspirations	#57
Mercy, Mercy, Mercy	Marlena Shaw	#58
Lonely Drifter	Pieces of Eight	#59
Glory of Love	Otis Redding	#60
What've I Done (To Make You Mad)	Linda Jones	#61
Go-Go Girl	Lee Dorsey	#62
Long Legged Girl (With the Short Dress On)	Elvis Presley	#63
Jump Back	King Curtis	#63
The Whole World Is a Stage	The Fantastic Four	#63
Funky Broadway Part 1	Dyke & The Blazers	#65
Girl Don't Care	Gene Chandler	#66
One, Two, Three	Ramsey Lewis	#67
Soul Time	Shirley Ellis	#67
Look at Granny Run, Run	Howard Tate	#67
A Little Bit Now	Dave Clark Five	#67
Fall in Love with Me	Bettye Swann	#67
Dirty Man	Laura Lee	#68
It's a Happening World	The Tokens	#69
Just Look What You've Done	Brenda Holloway	#69
Baby I'm Lonely	The Intruders	#70
You Can't Stand Alone	Wilson Pickett	#70
Cry to Me	Freddie Scott	#70
Am I Grooving You	Freddie Scott	#71
Hooray for the Salvation Army Band	Bill Cosby	#71
Stranded in the Middle of No Place	The Righteous Brothers	#72
Peek-A-Boo	New Vaudeville Band	#72
Deadend Street	The Kinks	#73

HORNS (cont'd)

Whole Lotta Woman	Arthur Conley	#73
Why? (Am I Treated So Bad)	"Cannonball" Adderley	#73
Plastic Man	Sonny & Cher	#74
Day Tripper	Ramsey Lewis	#74
I Stand Accused (Of Loving You)	The Glories	#74
Every Day I Have the Blues	Billy Stewart	#74
One Hurt Deserves Another	The Raeletts	#76
Daylight Savin' Time	Keith	#79
Do the Thing	Lou Courtney	#80
All Your Goodies are Gone (The Loser's Seat)	The Parliaments	#80
Mr. Pleasant	The Kinks	#80
Forget It	The Sandpebbles	#81
Lady Friend	The Byrds	#82
Brink of Disaster	Lesley Gore	#82
I Want You to Be My Baby	Ellie Greenwich	#83
Tip Toe	Robert Parker	#83
Me About You	The Mojo Men	#83
I Dig Girls	J.J. Jackson	#83
Tony Rome	Nancy Sinatra	#83
Wanted: Lover, No Experience Necessary	Laura Lee	#84
Lovey Dovey/You're So Fine	Bunny Sigler	#86
Funky Donkey	Pretty Purdie	#87
Baby, Help Me	Percy Sledge	#87
You're All I Need	Bobby Bland	#88
Lonesome Road	The Wonder Who?	#89
Sweet Soul Medley - Part 1	The Magnificent Men	#90
Daddy's Home	Chuck Jackson & Maxine Brown	#91
What am I Living For	Percy Sledge	#91
Get the Message	Brian Hyland	#91
Give Everybody Some	The Bar-Kays	#91
Hold On I'm Coming	Chuck Jackson & Maxine Brown	#91
Girls Are out to Get You	The Fascinations	#92
On a Saturday Night	Eddie Floyd	#92
She Took You for a Ride	Aaron Neville	#92
Tears, Tears, Tears	Ben E. King	#93
Alligator Bogaloo	Lou Donaldson	#93
The Jungle	B.B. King	#94
Different Strokes	Syl Johnson	#95
Everybody Loves a Winner	William Bell	#95
She Shot a Hole in My Soul	Clifford Curry	#95
Make Love to Me	Johnny Thunder & Ruby Winters	#96
How Can You Mistreat the One You Love	Jean & The Darlings	#96
You Always Hurt Me	The Impressions	#96

HORNS (cont'd)

Mercy, Mercy, Mercy	Larry Williams & Johnny Watson	#96
Ten Little Indians	The Yardbirds	#96
Along Comes Mary	Baja Marimba Band	#96
Somebody's Sleeping in My Bed	Johnnie Taylor	#96
Love Is a Doggone Good Thing	Eddie Floyd	#97
I'm a Fool for You	James Carr	#97
Come on Sock It to Me	Syl Johnson	#97
Don't Rock the Boat	Eddie Floyd	#98
Thread the Needle	Clarence Carter	#98
Georgy Girl	Baja Marimba Band	#98
Desiree'	The Left Banke	#98
I Got What You Need	Kim Weston	#99
Two in the Afternoon	Dino, Desi & Billy	#99
Last Minute Miracle	The Shirelles	#99
He Ain't Give You None	Freddie Scott	#100
Think	Vicki Anderson & James Brown	#100
Good Day Sunshine	Claudine Longet	#100
Requiem for the Masses	The Association	#100
1968		
Grazing in the Grass	Hugh Masekela	#1
Tighten Up	Archie Bell & The Drells	#1
People Got to Be Free	The Rascals	#1
Fire	Arthur Brown	#2
Little Green Apples	O.C. Smith	#2
The Horse	Cliff Nobles & Co.	#2
Valleri	The Monkees	#3
A Beautiful Morning	The Rascals	#3
Midnight Confessions	The Grass Roots	#5
Bend Me, Shape Me	The American Breed	#5
Who's Making Love	Johnnie Taylor	#5
Who's Making Love	Johnnie Taylor	#5
Girl Watcher	The O'Kaysions	#5
I Got the Feelin'	James Brown	#6
Think	Aretha Franklin	#7
The Ballad of Bonnie and Clyde	Georgie Fame	#7
Angel of the Morning	Merrilee Rush & The Turnabouts	#7
Dance to the Music	Sly & The Family Stone	#8
I Wonder What She's Doing Tonite	Tommy Boyce & Bobby Hart	#8
I Can't Stop Dancing	Archie Bell & The Drells	#9
Say It Loud - I'm Black and I'm Proud (Part 1)	James Brown	#10
Everything That Touches You	The Association	#10
Take Time to Know Her	Percy Sledge	#11
If You Can Want	Smokey Robinson & The Miracles	#11

HORNS (cont'd)

Baby, Now That I Found You	The Foundations	#11
Sweet Blindness	The 5th Dimension	#13
We're a Winner	The Impressions	#14
Funky Street	Arthur Conley	#14
She's Lookin' Good	Wilson Pickett	#15
Love Makes a Woman	Barbara Acklin	#15
Ain't No Way	Aretha Franklin	#16
Darlin'	The Beach Boys	#19
Never Give You Up	Jerry Butler	#20
(The Lament of the Cherokee) Indian Reservation	Don Fardon	#20
Love Power	The Sandpebbles	#22
I Will Always Think About You	The New Colony Six	#22
Fool for You	The Impressions	#22
Tell Mama	Etta James	#23
I'm a Midnight Mover	Wilson Pickett	#24
Court of Love	The Unifics	#25
Special Occasion	Smokey Robinson & The Miracles	#26
Choo Choo Train	The Box Tops	#26
The Snake	Al Wilson	#27
Alice Long (You're Still My Favorite Girlfriend)	Tommy Boyce & Bobby Hart	#27
Yester Love	Smokey Robinson & The Miracles	#31
Lover's Holiday	Peggy Scott & Jo Jo Benson	#31
Two Little Kids	Peaches & Herb	#31
Chained	Marvin Gaye	#32
Hitch It to the Horse	Fantastic Johnny C	#34
You Met Your Match	Stevie Wonder	#35
Security	Etta James	#35
1432 Franklin Pike Circle Hero	Bobby Russell	#36
Paying the Cost to Be the Boss	B.B. King	#39
Strawberry Shortcake	Jay & The Techniques	#39
Time for Livin'	The Association	#39
Green Light	The American Breed	#39
The Son of Hickory Holler's Tramp	O.C. Smith	#40
Mission-Impossible	Lalo Schifrin	#41
I Found a True Love	Wilson Pickett	#42
Cover Me	Percy Sledge	#42
A Man and a Half	Wilson Pickett	#42
Give a Damn	Spanky & Our Gang	#43
Here I Am Baby	The Marvelettes	#44
Do the Choo Choo	Archie Bell & The Drells	#44
In the Midnight Hour	The Mirettes	#45
Understanding	Ray Charles	#46
You Don't Know What You Mean to Me	Sam & Dave	#48

HORNS (cont'd)

If You Don't Want My Love	Robert John	#49
For Your Precious Love	Jackie Wilson & Count Basie	#50
Carmen	Herb Alpert & The Tijuana Brass	#51
Hard to Handle	Otis Redding	#51
Bring a Little Lovin'	Los Bravos	#51
Keep the One You Got	Joe Tex	#52
America Is My Home - Pt. 1	James Brown	#52
Can't You See Me Cry	The New Colony Six	#52
L. David Sloane	Michele Lee	#52
Goodbye Baby (I Don't Want to See You Cry)	Tommy Boyce & Bobby Hart	#53
Can't You Find Another Way (Of Doing It)	Sam & Dave	#54
Peace of Mind	Nancy Wilson	#55
Got What You Need	Fantastic Johnny C	#56
You Send Me	Aretha Franklin	#56
Good Combination	Sonny & Cher	#56
Hey Hey Bunny	John Fred	#57
Sound Asleep	The Turtles	#57
Back on My Feet Again	The Foundations	#59
I'll Never Do You Wrong	Joe Tex	#59
We're Rolling On (Part 1)	The Impressions	#59
Lovey Dovey	Otis & Carla	#60
I Promise to Wait My Love	Martha & The Vandellas	#62
Looking for a Fox	Clarence Carter	#62
Sudden Stop	Percy Sledge	#63
A Man Needs a Woman	James Carr	#63
That's a Lie	Ray Charles	#64
Good Time Girl	Nancy Sinatra	#65
(There's) Always Something There to Remind Me	Dionne Warwick	#65
Keep On Dancing	Alvin Cash	#66
Two-Bit Manchild	Neil Diamond	#66
Breaking up Is Hard to Do	The Happenings	#67
Funky Walk Part I (East)	Dyke & The Blazers	#67
Cinderella Rockefella	Esther & Abi Ofarim	#68
I Got You Babe	Etta James	#69
A Little Less Conversation	Elvis Presley	#69
Up-Up and Away	Hugh Masekela	#71
Puffin' on down the Track	Hugh Masekela	#71
Cabaret	Herb Alpert & The Tijuana Brass	#72
I'm Gonna Do What They Do to Me	B.B. King	#74
Competition Ain't Nothin'	Little Carl Carlton	#75
I Was Made to Love Her	Stevie Wonder	#76
Love Machine	The O'Kaysions	#76
Stop	Howard Tate	#76

HORNS (cont'd)

Hitchcock Railway	Jose Feliciano	#77
Reach Out	Merrilee Rush	#79
Don't Make the Good Girls Go Bad	Della Humphrey	#79
Give Me One More Chance	Wilmer & The Dukes	#80
There Was a Time	Gene Chandler	#82
The Mule	The James Boys	#82
Sweet Young Thing Like You	Ray Charles	#83
I Heard It Thru the Grapevine	King Curtis & Kingpins	#83
Do What You Gotta Do	Nina Simone	#83
Ready, Willing and Able	The American Breed	#84
Chain Gang	Jackie Wilson & Count Basie	#84
Snoopy for President	The Royal Guardsmen	#85
Soul Drippin'	The Mauds	#85
Young Boy	Brenda Greene	#86
Ain't Nothin' but a House Party	The Show Stoppers	#87
(She's) Some Kind of Wonderful	Fantastic Johnny C	#87
A Little Rain Must Fall	The Epic Splendor	#87
(You've Got) Personality and Chantilly Lace	Mitch Ryder	#87
Here Come Da Judge	The Buena Vistas	#88
1941	Tom Northcott	#88
It's Crazy	Eddie Harris	#88
Anyway That You Want Me	The American Breed	#88
Nitty Gritty	Ricardo Ray	#90
Don't Pat Me on the Back and Call Me Brother	KaSandra	#91
Stay Close to Me	Five Stairsteps & Cubie	#91
Soul Meeting	The Soul Clan	#91
Up-Hard	Willie Mitchell	#91
Funky North Philly	Bill Cosby	#91
Love Explosion	Troy Keyes	#92
Tell Someone You Love Them	Dino, Desi & Billy	#92
Listen, They're Playing My Song	Ray Charles	#92
Hard to Handle	Patti Drew	#93
M'Lady	Sly & The Family Stone	#93
Give My Love a Try	Linda Jones	#93
Love in Them There Hills	The Vibrations	#93
Harper Valley P.T.A.	King Curtis & Kingpins	#93
Life	Sly & The Family Stone	#93
(You Can't Let the Boy Overpower) The Man in You	Chuck Jackson	#94
Help Yourself (To All of My Lovin')	James & Bobby Purify	#94
The Choice	The O'Jays	#94
Springfield Plane	Kenny O'Dell	#94
Send My Baby Back	Freddie Hughes	#94
The Woman I Love	B.B. King	#94

HORNS (cont'd)

Bring Back Those Rockabye Baby Days	Tiny Tim	#95
Battle of New Orleans	Harpers Bizarre	#95
Music Music Music	The Happenings	#96
The Worm	Jimmy McGriff	#97
She's About a Mover	Otis Clay	#97
Blessed Are the Lonely	Robert Knight	#97
I Worry About You	Joe Simon	#98
Jesse Brady	The McCoys	#98
Have a Little Faith	David Houston	#98
Lady Madonna	Fats Domino	#100
Keep the Ball Rollin'	Al Hirt	#100
1969		
Everyday People	Sly & The Family Stone	#1
And When I Die	Blood, Sweat & Tears	#2
It's Your Thing	The Isley Brothers	#2
Take a Letter Maria	R.B. Greaves	#2
You've Made Me So Very Happy	Blood, Sweat & Tears	#2
Spinning Wheel	Blood, Sweat & Tears	#2
Crystal Blue Persuasion	Tommy James & The Shondells	#2
Soulful Strut	Young-Holt Unlimited	#3
Worst That Could Happen	Brooklyn Bridge	#3
Little Woman	Bobby Sherman	#3
Hawaii Five-O	The Ventures	#4
Baby It's You	Smith	#5
Twenty-Five Miles	Edwin Starr	#6
This Magic Moment	Jay & The Americans	#6
Color Him Father	The Winstons	#7
Sweet Cherry Wine	Tommy James & The Shondells	#7
Gitarzan	Ray Stevens	#8
Tracy	The Cuff Links	#9
Polk Salad Annie	Tony Joe White	#9
I'm Gonna Make You Mine	Lou Christie	#10
Backfield in Motion	Mel & Tim	#10
Mother Popcorn (You Got to Have a Mother for Me) Part 1	James Brown	#11
More Today Than Yesterday	Spiral Starecase	#12
If I Can Dream	Elvis Presley	#12
The Chokin' Kind	Joe Simon	#13
Too Weak to Fight	Clarence Carter	#13
Lo Mucho Que Te Quiero (The More I Love You)	Rene & Rene	#14
Cherry Hill Park	Billy Joe Royal	#15
I'd Wait a Million Years	The Grass Roots	#15
Friendship Train	Gladys Knight & The Pips	#17
Your Good Thing (Is About to End)	Lou Rawls	#18

HORNS (cont'd)

Song	Artist	#
Soul Deep	The Box Tops	#18
The Nitty Gritty	Gladys Knight & The Pips	#19
But You Know I Love You	The First Edition/Kenny Rogers	#19
Don't Let the Joneses Get You Down	The Temptations	#20
Take Care of Your Homework	Johnnie Taylor	#20
Papa's Got a Brand New Bag	Otis Redding	#21
Let a Man Come in and Do the Popcorn (Part One)	James Brown	#21
There's Gonna Be a Showdown	Archie Bell & The Drells	#21
What Kind of Fool Do You Think I Am	Bill Deal/The Rhondels	#23
I Turned You On	The Isley Brothers	#23
A Ray of Hope	The Rascals	#24
Heaven Knows	The Grass Roots	#24
I'll Try Something New	Supremes & Temptations	#25
This Is My Country	The Impressions	#25
Sweet Cream Ladies, Forward March	The Box Tops	#28
Cloud Nine	Mongo Santamaria	#32
Is It Something You've Got	Tyrone Davis	#34
Clean Up Your Own Back Yard	Elvis Presley	#35
I Don't Know Why	Stevie Wonder	#39
Lowdown Popcorn	James Brown	#41
Muddy River	Johnny Rivers	#41
Don't Let Love Hang You Up	Jerry Butler	#44
I'll Hold Out My Hand	The Clique	#45
The Weight	Supremes & Temptations	#46
I'd Rather Be An Old Man's Sweetheart (Than a Young Man's Fool)	Candi Station	#46
Buying a Book	Joe Tex	#47
A Lover's Question	Otis Redding	#48
I Could Never Be President	Johnnie Taylor	#48
Welcome Me Love	The Brooklyn Bridge	#48
When He Touches Me (Nothing Else Matters)	Peaches & Herb	#49
What You Gave Me	Marvin Gaye & Tammi Terrell	#49
Lovin' Things	The Grassroots	#49
You Got to Pay the Price	Gloria Taylor	#49
We Gotta All Get Together	Paul Revere & The Raiders	#50
You'll Never Walk Alone	The Brooklyn Bridge	#51
In the Bad, Bad Old Days (Before You Loved Me)	The Foundations	#51
You Don't Have to Walk in the Rain	The Turtles	#51
Can't Take My Eyes Off You	Nancy Wilson	#52
No One for Me to Turn To	The Spiral Staircase	#52
Muddy Mississippi Line	Bobby Goldsboro	#53
Riot	Hugh Masekela	#55
Get It from the Bottom	The Steelers	#56
Tell All the People	The Doors	#57

HORNS (cont'd)

Rockin' in the Same Old Boat	Bobby Bland	#58
Move in a Little Closer, Baby	Mama Cass	#58
Turn On a Dream	The Box Tops	#58
Hey Joe	Wilson Pickett	#59
Crumbs Off the Table	The Glass House	#59
I Want to Take You Higher	Sly & The Family Stone	#60
While You're out Looking for Sugar?	The Honey Cone	#62
I Can't Make It Alone	Lou Rawls	#63
Listen to the Band	The Monkees	#63
Till You Get Enough	Watts 103rd Street Rhythm Band	#67
Just Ain't No Love	Barbara Acklin	#67
Girls It Ain't Easy	The Honey Cone	#68
Questions 67 and 68	Chicago	#71
Tracks of My Tears	Aretha Franklin	#71
Love Man	Otis Redding	#72
Baby, Don't Be Looking in My Mind	Joe Simon	#72
We'll Cry Together	Maxine Brown	#73
Grits Ain't Groceries (All Around the World)	Little Milton	#73
Bubble Gum Music	Rock & Roll Dubble Bubble	#74
Life and Death in G & A	Abaco Dream	#74
Getting the Corners	The T.S.U. Toronadoes	#75
I'm Gonna Hold On Long as I Can	The Marvelettes	#76
Gentle on My Mind	Aretha Franklin	#76
He Called Me Baby	Ella Washington	#77
If It Wasn't for Bad Luck	Ray Charles & Jimmy Lewis	#77
Zazueira (Za-zoo-wher-a)	Herb Alpert & The Tijuana Brass	#78
San Francisco Is a Lonely Town	Joe Simon	#79
Am I the Same Girl	Barbara Acklin	#79
Black Berries - Pt 1	The Isley Brothers	#79
I'm Still a Struggling Man	Edwin Starr	#80
Someday Man	The Monkees	#81
I Want to Love You Baby	Peggy Scott & Jo Jo Benson	#81
Back in the U.S.S.R.	Chubby Checker	#82
It's My Thing (You Can't Tell Me Who to Sock It To)	Marva Whitney	#82
Was It Good to You	The Isley Brothers	#83
By the Time I Get to Phoenix	The Mad Lads	#84
Swingin' Tight	Bill Deal/The Rhondels	#85
Anything You Choose	Spanky & Our Gang	#86
Any Day Now	Percy Sledge	#86
It's Hard to Get Along	Joe Simon	#87
Give It Away	Chi-Lites	#88
That's Your Baby	Joe Tex	#88
Sing a Simple Song	Sly & The Family Stone	#89

HORNS (cont'd)

Born Again	Sam & Dave	#92
You Keep Me Hanging On	Wilson Pickett	#92
Wake Up	The Chambers Brothers	#92
Switch It On	Cliff Nobles & Co.	#93
Too Many Cooks (Spoil the Soup)	100 Proof (Aged in Soul)	#94
Let Me Love You	Ray Charles	#94
I Love My Baby	Archie Bell & The Drells	#94
That's the Way	Joe Tex	#94
Ain't Got No; I Got Life	Nina Simone	#94
All God's Children Got Soul	Dorothy Morrison	#95
Idaho	The Four Seasons	#95
Too Experienced	Eddie Lovette	#95
Theme from Electric Surfboard	Brother Jack McDuff	#95
It's Been a Long Time	Betty Everett	#96
And She's Mine	Spanky & Our Gang	#97
Just a Little Bit	Little Milton	#97
God Knows I Love You	Nancy Sinatra	#97
Big Bruce	Steve Greenberg	#97
St. Louis	The Easybeats	#100
Camel Back	A.B. Skhy	#100
July You're a Woman	Pat Boone	#100
Memphis Train	Buddy Miles	#100

KAZOO

YEAR	SONG	ARTIST	HOT 100
1962	You Belong to Me	The Duprees	#7
1962	Little Diane	Dion	#8
1962	Zero-Zero	Lawrence Welk	#98
1966	The Eggplant That Ate Chicago	Dr. West's Medicine Show and Junk Band	#52
1966	I Love Onions	Susan Christie	#63
1967	Wild Thing	Senator Bobby	#20

MANDOLIN

SONG	ARTIST	HOT 100
1960		
Never on Sunday	Don Costa	#19
1961		
Dance On Little Girl	Paul Anka	#10

MANDOLIN (cont'd)

Don't Read the Letter	Patti Page	#65
1962		
The Lonely Bull	Herb Alpert & The Tijuana Brass	#6
1965		
Forget Domani	Frank Sinatra	#78
1966		
Wouldn't It Be Nice	The Beach Boys	#8
1967		
Sit Down, I Think I Love You	The Mojo Men	#36
1968		
Up On the Roof	The Cryan' Shames	#85
1969		
Runnin' Blue	The Doors	#64
The Wedding Cake	Connie Francis	#91

OBOE

SONG	ARTIST	HOT 100
1960		
On the Beach	Frank Chacksfield	#47
1962		
Ahab the Arab	Ray Stevens	#5
1964		
Don't Let the Sun Catch You Crying	Gerry & The Pacemakers	#4
I Don't Want to See You Again	Peter & Gordon	#16
The Anaheim, Azusa & Cucamonga Sewing Circle, Book Review and Timing Association	Jan & Dean	#77
A Taste of Honey	Tony Bennett	#94
1965		
I Got You Babe	Sonny & Cher	#1
As Tears Go By	Marianne Faithfull	#22
1966		
Sweet Talkin' Guy	The Chiffons	#10
It Was a Very Good Year	Frank Sinatra	#28
Please Don't Ever Leave Me	The Cyrkle	#59
Out of This World	The Chiffons	#67
A Corner in the Sun	Walter Jackson	#83
Free Again	Barbra Streisand	#83
It's an Uphill Climb to the Bottom	Walter Jackson	#88
Don't Forget About Me	Barbara Lewis	#91
1967		
Penny Lane	The Beatles	#1

OBOE (cont'd)

The 59th Street Bridge Song (Feelin' Groovy)	Harpers Bizarre	#13
Dandelion	The Rolling Stones	#14
Pretty Ballerina	The Left Banke	#15
Tell Me to My Face	Keith	#37
Turn the World Around	Eddy Arnold	#66
Two in the Afternoon	Dino, Desi & Billy	#99
1968		
Love Is Blue	Paul Mauriat	#1
Abraham, Martin and John	Dion	#4
Over You	Gary Puckett & The Union Gap	#7
Jennifer Juniper	Donovan	#26
Does Your Mama Know About Me	Bobby Taylor	#29
Eleanor Rigby	Ray Charles	#35
With Pen in Hand	Billy Vera	#43
Look, Here Comes the Sun	The Sunshine Company	#56
You've Got to Be Loved	The Montanas	#58
1969		
Galveston	Glen Campbell	#4
My Whole World Ended (The Moment You Left Me)	David Ruffin	#9
Where's the Playground Susie	Glen Campbell	#26
True Grit	Glen Campbell	#35
Let It Be Me	Glen Campbell & Bobbie Gentry	#36
By the Time I Get to Phoenix	Isaac Hayes	#37
Change of Heart	Dennis Yost/Classics IV	#49
Glad She's a Woman	Bobby Goldsboro	#61
Didn't You Know (You'd Have to Cry Sometime)	Gladys Knight & The Pips	#63
Greensleeves	Mason Williams	#90
From Both Sides Now	Dion	#91

ORCHESTRA

Songs in this list will feature at least two of the four families of instruments in orchestras. Most commonly, you will hear strings paired with brass or woodwinds. For songs with violins only, check out the "violin" list.

SONG	ARTIST	HOT 100
1960		
Theme from "A Summer Place"	Percy Faith	#1
Night	Jackie Wilson	#4
Beyond the Sea	Bobby Darin	#6
The Village of St. Bernadette	Andy Williams	#7
Alone at Last	Jackie Wilson	#8
My Home Town	Paul Anka	#8

ORCHESTRA (cont'd)

Title	Artist	Page
Harbor Lights	The Platters	#8
In My Little Corner of the World	Anita Bryant	#10
Theme from "The Apartment"	Ferrante & Teicher	#10
Tracy's Theme	Spencer Ross	#13
Lady Luck	Lloyd Price	#14
Not One Minute More	Della Reese	#16
Look for a Star	Billy Vaughn	#19
Never on Sunday	Don Costa	#19
Artificial Flowers	Bobby Darin	#20
To Each His Own	The Platters	#21
Mr. Lucky	Henry Mancini	#21
Pennies from Heaven	The Skyliners	#24
Ol' Mac Donald	Frank Sinatra	#25
Starbright	Johnny Mathis	#25
Theme from "The Unforgiven" (The Need for Love)	Don Costa	#27
White Christmas	Bing Crosby	#27
Ruby	Ray Charles	#28
Summer Set	Monte Kelly	#30
Dutchman's Gold	Walter Brennan w/Billy Vaughn	#30
Where Are You	Frankie Avalon	#32
Alvin's Orchestra	The Chipmunks	#33
Talk That Talk	Jackie Wilson	#34
Theme for Young Lovers	Percy Faith	#35
Red Sails in the Sunset	The Platters	#36
Adeste Fideles (Oh, Come, All Ye Faithful)	Bing Crosby	#45
On the Beach	Frank Chacksfield	#47
My Love for You	Johnny Mathis	#47
Wake Me When It's Over	Andy Williams	#50
Christmas Auld Lang Syne	Bobby Darin	#51
The Sundowners	Billy Vaughn	#51
One Boy	Joanie Sommers	#54
Temptation	Roger Williams	#56
Ebb Tide	The Platters	#56
Little Bitty Pretty One	Frankie Lymon	#58
Nice 'N' Easy	Frank Sinatra	#60
Kookie Little Paradise	Jo Ann Campbell	#61
How to Handle a Woman	Johnny Mathis	#64
Sleepy Lagoon	The Platters	#65
Two Thousand, Two Hundred, Twenty-Three Miles	Patti Page	#67
And Now	Della Reese	#69
Theme from "The Sundowners"	Felix Slatkin	#70
Gloria's Theme	Adam Wade	#74
Maria	Jonny Mathis	#78

ORCHESTRA (cont'd)

I Know What God Is	Perry Como	#81
River, Stay 'Way from My Door	Frank Sinatra	#82
Never Let Me Go	Lloyd Price	#82
Serenata	Sarah Vaughan	#82
Come Rain or Come Shine	Ray Charles	#83
Wheel of Fortune	LaVern Baker	#83
Happy Shades of Love	Freddie Cannon	#83
Senza Mamma (With No One)	Connie Francis	#87
(You Better) Know What You're Doin'	Lloyd Price	#90
Adam And Eve	Paul Anka	#90
The Sound of Music	Patti Page	#90
Cry Me A River	Janice Harper	#91
Theme from The Sundowners	Mantovani	#93
What Do You Want?	Bobby Vee	#93
Midnight Lace	David Carroll	#98
1961		
Running Scared	Roy Orbison	#1
Exodus	Ferrante & Teicher	#2
Tower of Strength	Gene McDaniels	#5
Portrait of My Love	Steve Lawrence	#9
Don't Bet Money Honey	Linda Scott	#9
As If I Didn't Know	Adam Wade	#10
I Don't Know Why	Linda Scott	#12
Wonderland By Night	Anita Bryant	#18
My Kind of Girl	Matt Monro	#18
Bonanza	Al Caiola	#19
I'll Never Smile Again	The Platters	#25
Main Theme from Exodus (Ari's Theme)	Mantovani	#31
That's It- I Quit- I'm Movin' On	Sam Cooke	#31
The Magnificent Seven	Al Caiola	#35
Love Theme from "One Eyed Jacks"	Ferrante & Teicher	#37
Rock-a-Bye Your Baby with a Dixie Melody	Aretha Franklin	#37
Tonight	Eddie Fisher	#44
A Perfect Love	Frankie Avalon	#47
The Charleston	Ernie Fields	#47
Now and Forever	Bert Kaempfert	#48
The Second Time Around	Frank Sinatra	#50
It's All Because	Linda Scott	#50
The Wayward Wind	Gogi Grant	#50
I'll Be Seeing You	Frank Sinatra	#58
That's the Way with Love	Piero Soffici	#59
Trees	The Platters	#62
How May Tears	Bobby Vee	#63

ORCHESTRA (cont'd)

Granada	Frank Sinatra	#64
The Exodus Song (This Land Is Mine)	Pat Boone	#64
Somewhere Along the Way	Steve Lawrence	#67
Alvin's Harmonica	The Chipmunks	#73
Come September	Billy Vaughn	#73
The Guns of Navarone	Joe Reisman	#74
La Dolce Vita	Ray Ellis	#81
Theme from "Silver City"	The Ventures	#83
Point of No Return	Adam Wade	#85
Theme from "Goodbye Again"	Ferrante & Teicher	#85
If I Knew	Nat "King" Cole	#86
Here in My Heart	Al Martino	#86
Wasn't the Summer Short?	Johnny Mathis	#89
Mr. Pride	Chuck Jackson	#91
Why Not Now	Matt Monro	#92
Linda	Adam Wade	#94
Oh Mein Papa	Dick Lee	#94
In Time	Steve Lawrence	#94
Impossible	Gloria Lynne	#95
Image - Part 1	Hank Levine	#98
1962		
The Stripper	David Rose	#1
Stranger on the Shore	Mr. Acker Bilk	#1
Only Love Can Break a Heart	Gene Pitney	#2
Next Door to an Angel	Neil Sedaka	#5
Cindy's Birthday	Johnny Crawford	#8
Release Me	"Little Esther" Phillips	#8
Chip Chip	Gene McDaniels	#10
Theme from "Dr. Kildare" (Three Stars Will Shine Tonight)	Richard Chamberlain	#10
Close to Cathy	Mike Clifford	#12
Love Me Warm and Tender	Paul Anka	#12
Swingin' Safari	Billy Vaughn	#13
Til	The Angels	#14
What Kind of Fool am I	Sammy Davis Jr.	#17
What Kind of Love Is This	Joey Dee & The Starliters	#18
Route 66 Theme	Nelson Riddle	#30
Spanish Lace	Gene McDaniels	#31
I'll See You in My Dreams	Pat Boone	#32
The Ballad of Paladin	Duane Eddy	#33
Pocketful of Miracles	Frank Sinatra	#34
Stranger on the Shore	Andy Williams	#38
Count Every Star	Linda Scott	#41
Two of a Kind	Sue Thompson	#42

ORCHESTRA (cont'd)

Afrikaan Beat	Bert Kaempfert	#42
Walk on the Wild Side	Brook Benton	#43
Maria	Roger Williams	#48
Where Have You Been (All My Life)	Arthur Alexander	#58
Above the Stars	Mr. Acker Bilk	#59
The White Rose of Athens	David Carroll	#61
I Lost My Baby	Joey Dee	#61
(Theme from) A Summer Place	Dick Roman	#64
Mr. Lonely	Buddy Greco	#64
Let Me Call You Sweetheart	Timi Yuro	#66
Lollipops and Roses	Jack Jones	#66
My Daddy Is President	Little Jo Ann	#67
That Happy Feeling	Bert Kaempfert	#67
Chapel by the Sea	Billy Vaughn	#69
Tears and Laughter	Dinah Washington	#71
Don't Worry 'Bout Me	Vincent Edwards	#72
What King of Fool am I	Anthony Newley	#85
Pop Goes the Weasel	Anthony Newley	#85
Marianna	Johnny Mathis	#86
Love Is the Sweetest Thing	Saverio Saridis	#86
Fools Rush In	Etta James	#87
I Surrender, Dear	Aretha Franklin	#87
For All We Know	Dinah Washington	#88
Amor	Roger Williams	#88
What Kind of Fool am I?	Robert Goulet	#89
This Land Is Your Land	Ketty Lester	#97
Stardust	Frank Sinatra	#98
Lisa	Ferrante & Teicher	#98
You're a Sweetheart	Dinah Washington	#98
Portrait of a Fool	Conway Twitty	#98
Sweet Thursday	Johnny Mathis	#99
Til There Was You	Valjean	#100
Theme from Taras Bulba (The Wishing Star)	Jerry Butler	#100
1963		
Sukiyaki	Kyu Sakamoto	#1
Hello Mudduh, Hello Fadduh! (A Letter from Camp)	Allan Sherman	#2
Up on the Roof	The Drifters	#5
She's a Fool	Lesley Gore	#5
Losing You	Brenda Lee	#6
My Dad	Paul Petersen	#6
On Broadway	The Drifters	#9
Danke Schoen	Wayne Newton	#13
Send Me Some Lovin'	Sam Cooke	#13

ORCHESTRA (cont'd)

Song	Artist	Ref
Fly Me to the Moon - Bossa Nova	Joe Harnell	#14
I Wanna Be Around	Tony Bennett	#14
Wonderful Summer	Robin Ward	#14
Painted, Tainted Rose	Al Martino	#15
The Grass Is Greener	Brenda Lee	#17
Twenty Four Hours from Tulsa	Gene Pitney	#17
Follow the Boys	Connie Francis	#17
My Coloring Book	Kitty Kallen	#18
The Good Life	Tony Bennett	#18
Prisoner of Love	James Brown	#18
Cry to Me	Betty Harris	#23
My Whole World Is Falling Down	Brenda Lee	#24
I'll Take You Home	The Drifters	#25
Days of Wine and Roses	Andy Williams	#26
I (Who Have Nothing)	Ben E. King	#29
Every Step of the Way	Johnny Mathis	#30
Two Tickets to Paradise	Brook Benton	#32
Days of Wine and Roses	Henry Mancini	#33
Be True to Yourself	Bobby Vee	#34
Red Sails in the Sunset	Fats Domino	#35
The Lonely Surfer	Jack Nitzsche	#39
The Love of a Boy	Timi Yuro	#44
I Got a Woman	Freddie Scott	#48
September Song	Jimmy Durante	#51
Don't Wait Too Long	Tony Bennett	#54
Yesterday and You (Armen's Theme)	Bobby Vee	#55
Night Life	Rusty Draper	#57
China Nights (Shina No Yoru)	Kyu Sakamoto	#58
As Long as She Needs Me	Sammy Davis Jr.	#59
I Really Don't Want to Know	"Little Esther" Phillips	#61
Hi-Lili, Hi-Lo	Richard Chamberlain	#64
Be Mad Little Girl	Bobby Darin	#64
Amy	Paul Petersen	#65
I Will Love You	Richard Chamberlain	#65
Rat Race	The Drifters	#71
I Could Have Danced All Night	Ben E. King	#72
You Never Miss Your Water (Till the Well Runs Dry)	"Little Esther" Phillips & "Big Al" Downing"	#73
Call Me Irresponsible	Jack Jones	#75
Come Dance with Me	Jay & The Americans	#76
Only You (And You Alone)	Mr. Acker Bilk	#77
Willie Can	Sue Thompson	#78
Call Me Irresponsible	Frank Sinatra	#78
Funny Man	Ray Stevens	#81

ORCHESTRA (cont'd)

Antony and Cleopatra Theme	Ferrante & Teicher	#83
Sooner or Later	Johnny Mathis	#84
Sad, Sad Girl and Boy	The Impressions	#84
Theme from "Lawrence of Arabia"	Ferrante & Teicher	#84
This Empty Place	Dionne Warwick	#84
I Will Live My Life for You	Tony Bennett	#85
Trouble in Mind	Aretha Franklin	#86
Scarlett O'Hara	Lawrence Welk	#89
Gone with the Wind	The Duprees	#89
I'll Search My Heart	Johnny Mathis	#90
Al Di La	Connie Francis	#90
From the Bottom of My Heart (Dammi, Dammi, Dammi)	Dean Martin	#91
It's a Mad, Mad, Mad, Mad World	The Shirelles	#92
Now!	Lena Horne	#92
Diane	Joe Harnell	#97
True Love	Richard Chambelain	#98
1964		
Mr. Lonely	Bobby Vinton	#1
Don't Let the Sun Catch You Crying	Gerry & The Pacemakers	#4
People	Barbra Streisand	#5
Walk on By	Dionne Warwick	#6
Wishin' and Hopin'	Dusty Springfield	#6
Goin' Out of My Head	Little Anthony/Imperials	#6
A Summer Song	Chad & Jeremy	#7
I Love You More and More Every Day	Al Martino	#9
Selfish One	Jackie Ross	#11
I Only Want to Be with You	Dusty Springfield	#12
Tell Me Why	Bobby Vinton	#13
Wives and Lovers	Jack Jones	#14
Saturday Night at the Movies	The Drifters	#18
Just Be True	Gene Chandler	#19
Rhythm	Major Lance	#24
Blue Winter	Connie Francis	#24
Be Anything (But Be Mine)	Connie Francis	#25
For Your Precious Love	Garnet Mimms & The Enchanters	#26
You're My World	Cilla Black	#26
I Wish You Love	Gloria Lynne	#28
On the Street Where You Live	Andy Williams	#28
Need to Belong	Jerry Butler	#31
The Pink Panther Theme	Henry Mancini	#31
Who Can I Turn To (When Nobody Needs Me)	Tony Bennett	#33
Always Together	Al Martino	#33
Charade	Henry Mancini	#36

ORCHESTRA (cont'd)

Bless Our Love	Gene Chandler	#39
Funny Girl	Barbra Streisand	#44
In the Summer of His Years	Connie Francis	#46
Look Homeward Angel	The Monarchs	#47
Since I Don't Have You	Chuck Jackson	#47
(There's) Always Something There to Remind Me	Lou Johnson	#49
That Girl Belongs to Yesterday	Gene Pitney	#49
He'll Have to Go	Solomon Burke	#51
The Little Boy	Tony Bennett	#52
Ringo's Theme (This Boy)	George Martin	#53
I Want to Hold Your Hand	Boston Pops Orchestra	#55
Giving Up On Love	Jerry Butler	#56
Sole Sole Sole	Siw Malmkvist-Umberto Marcato	#58
Love with the Proper Stranger	Jack Jones	#62
Where Love Has Gone	Jack Jones	#62
I Should Care	Gloria Lynne	#64
It's All Over	Walter Jackson	#67
One Girl	Garnet Mimms	#67
Almost There	Andy Williams	#67
A House Is Not a Home	Dionne Warwick	#71
Please	Frank Ifield	#71
Everybody Knows	Steve Lawrence	#72
Don't Take Your Love from Me	Gloria Lynne	#76
The Cheer Leader	Paul Petersen	#78
A World Without Love	Bobby Rydell	#80
Stay with Me	Frank Sinatra	#81
L-O-V-E	Nat "King" Cole	#81
Where Does Love Go	Freddie Scott	#82
Stranger in Your Arms	Bobby Vee	#83
(I'm Watching) Every Little Move You Make	Little Peggy March	#84
Billie Baby	Lloyd Price	#84
A Little Toy Balloon	Danny Williams	#84
Taste of Tears	Johnny Mathis	#87
Be Anything (But Be Mine)	Gloria Lynne	#88
Soon I'll Wed My Love	John Gary	#89
All My Loving	The Hollyridge Strings	#93
When Joanna Loved Me	Tony Bennett	#94
Pretend You Don't See Her	Bobby Vee	#97
Big Party	Barbara & The Browns	#97
Charade	Andy Williams	#100
People	Nat "King" Cole	#100
1965		
My Girl	The Temptations	#1

ORCHESTRA (cont'd)

Song	Artist	Chart
I Hear a Symphony	The Supremes	#1
Downtown	Petula Clark	#1
I Know a Place	Petula Clark	#3
Unchained Melody	The Righteous Brothers	#4
Ferry Cross the Mersey	Gerry & The Pacemakers	#6
What the World Needs Now Is Love	Jackie DeShannon	#7
Goldfinger	Shirley Bassey	#8
I Go to Pieces	Peter & Gordon	#9
Hurt So Bad	Little Anthony/Imperials	#10
I Will	Dean Martin	#10
Red Roses for a Blue Lady	Vic Dana	#10
Let's Lock the Door (And Throw Away the Key)	Jay & The Americans	#11
Red Roses for a Blue Lady	Bert Kaempfert	#11
Baby the Rain Must Fall	Glenn Yarbrough	#12
My Baby	The Temptations	#13
Last Chance to Turn Around	Gene Pitney	#13
Some Enchanted Evening	Jay & The Americans	#13
People Get Ready	The Impressions	#14
I'll Be There	Gerry & The Pacemakers	#14
My Girl Has Gone	The Miracles	#14
True Love Ways	Peter & Gordon	#14
Willow Weep for Me	Chad & Jeremy	#15
Theme from "A Summer Place"	The Lettermen	#16
Make It Easy on Yourself	The Walker Bros.	#16
Tracks of My Tears	The Miracles	#16
My Love, Forgive Me (Amore, Scusami)	Robert Goulet	#16
Since I Lost My Baby	The Temptations	#17
Nothing Can Stop Me	Gene Chandler	#18
It's Growing	The Temptations	#18
Sunday and Me	Jay & The Americans	#18
Houston	Dean Martin	#20
Goodnight	Roy Orbison	#21
Say Something Funny	Patty Duke	#22
You'd Better Come Home	Petula Clark	#22
Send Me the Pillow You Dream On	Dean Martin	#22
As Tears Go By	Marianne Faithfull	#22
Walk Away	Matt Monro	#23
Red Roses for a Blue Lady	Wayne Newton	#23
Have You Looked into Your Heart	Jerry Vale	#24
Dear Heart	Andy Williams	#24
To Know You Is to Love You	Peter & Gordon	#24
Home of the Brave	Jody Miller	#25
You're Nobody till Somebody Loves You	Dean Martin	#25

ORCHESTRA (cont'd)

Here It Comes Again	The Fortunes	#27
You Really Know How to Hurt a Guy	Jan & Dean	#27
Hungry for Love	San Remo Golden Strings	#27
Looking Through the Eyes of Love	Gene Pitney	#28
Dear Heart	Jack Jones	#30
A Change Is Gonna Come	Sam Cooke	#31
I Must Be Seeing Things	Gene Pitney	#31
(Remember Me) I'm the One Who Loves You	Dean Martin	#32
My Town, My Guy and Me	Lesley Gore	#32
I Miss You So	Little Anthony/Imperials	#34
If I Ruled the World	Tony Bennett	#34
Heartaches by the Number	Johnny Tillotson	#35
I Don't Wanna Lose You Baby	Chad & Jeremy	#35
Princess in Rags	Gene Pitney	#37
Come See	Major Lance	#40
Gene Chandler	What Now	#40
It's Gonna Take a Miracle	The Royalettes	#41
Smile	Betty Everett & Jerry Butler	#42
Sandie Shaw	Girl Don't Come	#42
At the Club	The Drifters	#43
Anytime at All	Frank Sinatra	#46
If I Didn't Love You	Chuck Jackson	#46
I'll Take You Where the Music's Playing	The Drifters	#51
What Do You Want with Me	Chad & Jeremy	#51
Moonlight and Roses (Bring Mem'ries of You)	Vic Dana	#51
I Live for the Sun	The Sunrays	#51
When a Boy Falls in Love	Sam Cooke	#52
(There's) Always Something There to Remind Me	Sandie Shaw	#52
I'll Be with You in Apple Blossom Time	Wayne Newton	#52
Now That You've Gone	Connie Stevens	#53
He Touched Me	Barbra Streisand	#53
Never, Never Leave Me	Mary Wells	#54
Hello Pretty Girl	Ronnie Dove	#54
And I Love Him	Esther Phillips	#54
One Step at a Time	Maxine Brown	#55
Tell Her (You Love Her Each Day)	Frank Sinatra	#57
Don't Come Running Back to Me	Nancy Wilson	#58
Summer Sounds	Robert Goulet	#58
No Pity (In the Naked City)	Jackie Wilson	#59
Moon Over Naples	Bert Kaempfert	#59
Two Different Worlds	Lenny Welch	#61
Who Can I Turn To	Dionne Warwick	#62
Misty	The Vibrations	#63

ORCHESTRA (cont'd)

Married Man	Richard Burton	#64
Looking with My Eyes	Dionne Warwick	#64
Getting Mighty Crowded	Betty Everett	#65
Here I Am	Dionne Warwick	#65
Super-cali-fragil-istic-expi-ali-docious	Julie Andrews-Dick Van Dyke	#66
Bring a Little Sunshine (To My Heart)	Vic Dana	#66
A Lifetime of Loneliness	Jackie DeShannon	#66
Remember When	Wayne Newton	#69
Our World	Johnny Tillotson	#70
All of My Life	Lesley Gore	#71
Goldfinger	John Barry	#72
I Want to Meet Him	The Royalettes	#72
Darling Take Me Back	Lenny Welch	#72
Just Yesterday	Jack Jones	#73
Try to Remember	Ed Ames	#73
If You Wait for Love	Bobby Goldsboro	#75
Just One Kiss from You	The Impressions	#76
Why Did I Choose You	Barbra Streisand	#77
Dear Heart	Henry Mancini	#77
Summer Wind	Wayne Newton	#78
My Man	Barbra Streisand	#79
Forget Domani	Connie Francis	#79
Don't Pity Me	Peter & Gordon	#83
I'm a Fool to Care	Ray Charles	#84
If You Don't (Love Me, Tell Me So)	Barbara Mason	#85
Are You Sincere	Trini Lopez	#85
The Crying Game	Brenda Lee	#87
Crying in the Chapel	Adam Wade	#88
I'm Satisfied	San Remo Golden Strings	#89
Somewhere	P.J. Proby	#91
Losing You	Dusty Springfield	#91
No Faith, No Love	Mitty Collier	#91
You Can't Hurt Me No More	Gene Chandler	#92
Quiet Nights of Quiet Stars	Andy Williams	#92
Sad Tomorrows	Trini Lopez	#94
Mexican Pearls	Billy Vaughn	#94
Danny Boy	Jackie Wilson	#94
The Shadow of Your Smile	Tony Bennett	#95
Suddenly I'm All Alone	Walter Jackson	#96
Run to My Lovin' Arms	Lenny Welch	#96
Goldfinger	Jack LaForge	#96
Tears Keep On Falling	Jerry Vale	#96

ORCHESTRA (cont'd)

You Can't Take It Away	Fred Hughes	#96
Try to Remember	Roger Williams	#97
The Drinking Man's Diet	Allan Sherman	#98
I Need You So	Chuck Jackson & Maxine Brown	#98
On a Clear Day You Can See Forever	Johnny Mathis	#98

1966

Strangers in the Night	Frank Sinatra	#1
My Love	Petula Clark	#1
You Don't Have to Say You Love Me	Dusty Springfield	#4
Five O'Clock World	The Vogues	#4
My World Is Empty Without You	The Supremes	#5
The Men in My Little Girl's Life	Mike Douglas	#6
What Becomes of the Brokenhearted	Jimmy Ruffin	#7
It's a Man's Man's Man's World	James Brown	#8
I've Got You Under My Skin	The Four Seasons	#9
I Couldn't Live Without Your Love	Petula Clark	#9
A Place in the Sun	Stevie Wonder	#9
Coming on Strong	Brenda Lee	#11
Whispers (Getting' Louder)	Jackie Wilson	#11
This Old Heart of Mine (Is Weak for You)	Isley Brothers	#12
The Sun Ain't Gonna Shine (Anymore)	The Walker Bros.	#13
Woman	Peter & Gordon	#14
Spanish Eyes	Al Martino	#15
Shake Me, Wake Me (When It's Over)	Four Tops	#18
Cry	Ronnie Dove	#18
All I See Is You	Dusty Springfield	#20
Who Am I	Petula Clark	#21
My Baby Loves Me	Martha & The Vandellas	#22
Crying	Jay & The Americans	#25
Summer Wind	Frank Sinatra	#25
Backstage	Gene Pitney	#25
Thunderball	Tom Jones	#25
It Was a Very Good Year	Frank Sinatra	#28
Make Me Belong to You	Barbara Lewis	#28
Girl on a Swing	Gerry & The Pacemakers	#28
Get Ready	The Temptations	#29
Distant Shores	Chad & Jeremy	#30
Go Ahead and Cry	The Righteous Brothers	#30
Band of Gold	Mel Carter	#32
You've Been Cheatin'	The Impressions	#33
Come Running Back	Dean Martin	#35
Day for Decision	Johnny Sea	#35
The Impossible Dream (The Quest)	Jack Jones	#35

ORCHESTRA (cont'd)

Tar and Cement	Verdelle Smith	#38
Love Me with All of Your Heart	The Bachelors	#38
Are You There (With Another Girl)	Dionne Warwick	#39
God Only Knows	The Beach Boys	#39
I Want to Be with You	Dee Dee Warwick	#41
Games That Lovers Play	Eddie Fisher	#45
On This Side of Goodbye	The Righteous Brothers	#47
Can I Trust You?	The Bachelors	#49
You You You	Mel Carter	#49
World of Fantasy	The Five Stairsteps	#49
Have I Stayed Too Long	Sonny & Cher	#49
In the Arms of Love	Andy Williams	#49
Young Love	Lesley Gore	#50
There's No Living Without Your Loving	Peter & Gordon	#50
Love Is All We Need	Mel Carter	#50
Hurt	Little Anthony/Imperials	#51
Dear Lover	Mary Wells	#51
A Symphony for Susan	The Arbors	#51
Somebody Like Me	Eddy Arnold	#53
Mame	Bobby Darin	#53
Wiederseh'n	Al Martino	#57
Not Responsible	Tom Jones	#58
The Wheel of Hurt	Al Martino	#59
Come Back	The Five Stairsteps	#61
Baby What I Mean	The Drifters	#62
Whenever She Holds You	Patty Duke	#64
Stay with Me	Lorraine Ellison	#64
He Cried	The Shangri-Las	#65
Can't Satisfy	The Impressions	#65
Out of This World	The Chiffons	#67
All or Nothing	Patti LaBelle & The Bluebells	#68
I Can Make It with You	Jackie DeShannon	#68
The Proud One	Frankie Vallie	#68
Love (Makes Me Do Foolish Things)	Martha & The Vandellas	#70
What Am I Going to Do Without Your Love	Martha & The Vandellas	#71
Baby What Do You Want Me to Do	Barbara Lewis	#74
Livin' Above Your Head	Jay & The Americans	#76
Just Yesterday	Al Martino	#77
Ain't Gonna Cry No More	Brenda Lee	#77
Take Good Care of Her	Mel Carter	#78
Come On and See Me	Tammi Terrell	#80
Tomorrow Never Comes	B.J. Thomas	#80
A Corner in the Sun	Walter Jackson	#83

ORCHESTRA (cont'd)

Song	Artist	Chart
Free Again	Barbra Streisand	#83
Don't Look Back	The Temptations	#83
Come and Get Me	Jackie DeShannon	#83
May My Heart Be Cast into Stone	The Toys	#85
Living for You	Sonny & Cher	#87
(I'm Just a) Fool for You	Gene Chandler	#88
I'm Gonna Make You Love Me	Dee Dee Warwick	#88
River Deep-Mountain High	Ike & Tina Turner	#88
It's an Uphill Climb to the Bottom	Walter Jackson	#88
Georgia Rose	Tony Bennett	#89
Spanish Harlem	King Curtis	#89
Since I Lost the One I Love	The Impressions	#90
So Much Love	Steve Alaimo	#92
Put Yourself in My Place	The Elgins	#92
It's Not the Same	Anthony & The Imperials	#92
Where Am I Going?	Barbra Streisand	#94
To Make a Big Man Cry	Roy Head	#95
Alfie	Cilla Black	#95
Let's Go Steady Again	Sam Cooke	#97
I'll Be Home	The Platters	#97
Sam, You Made the Pants Too Long	Barbra Streisand	#98
Meditation (Meditacao)	Claudine Longet	#98
Such a Sweet Thing	Mary Wells	#99
1967		
All You Need Is Love	The Beatles	#1
The Letter	The Box Tops	#1
Somethin' Stupid	Nancy & Frank Sinatra	#1
Daydream Believer	The Monkees	#1
This Is My Song	Petula Clark	#3
It Must Be Him	Vikki Carr	#3
I Say a Little Prayer	Dionne Warwick	#4
How Can I Be Sure	The Young Rascals	#4
There's a Kind of Hush	Herman's Hermits	#4
Release Me (And Let Me Love Again)	Engelbert Humperdinck	#4
Don't You Care	The Buckinghams	#6
(Your Love Keeps Lifting Me) Higher and Higher	Jackie Wilson	#6
Strawberry Fields Forever	The Beatles	#8
(You Make Me Feel Like) A Natural Woman	Aretha Franklin	#8
An Open Letter to My Teenage Son	Victor Lundberg	#10
Honey Chile	Martha & The Vandellas	#11
You Know What I Mean	The Turtles	#12
Love Is Strange	Peaches & Herb	#13
Everlasting Love	Robert Knight	#13

ORCHESTRA (cont'd)

It Takes Two	Marvin Gaye and Kim Weston	#14
Darling Be Home Soon	The Lovin' Spoonful	#15
Music to Watch Girls By	Bob Crewe Generation	#15
Love Eyes	Nancy Sinatra	#15
Holiday	The Bee Gees	#16
Color My World	Petula Clark	#16
California Nights	Lesley Gore	#16
To Love Somebody	The Bee Gees	#17
I've Passed This Way Before	Jimmy Ruffin	#17
I Make a Fool of Myself	Frankie Valli	#18
Lady Bird	Nancy Sinatra & Lee Hazlewood	#20
There Goes My Everything	Engelbert Humperdinck	#20
For Your Love	Peaches & Herb	#20
Let's Fall in Love	Peaches & Herb	#21
More Love	Smokey Robinson & The Miracles	#23
Like an Old Time Movie	Scott McKenzie	#24
Neon Rainbow	The Box Tops	#24
In the Chapel in the Moonlight	Dean Martin	#25
I Like the Way	Tommy James	#25
Yesterday	Ray Charles	#25
Love Bug Leave My Heart Alone	Martha & The Vandellas	#25
The Cat in the Window (The Bird in the Sky)	Petula Clark	#26
Casino Royale	Herb Alpert & The Tijuana Brass	#27
She's Still a Mystery	The Lovin' Spoonful	#27
Gallant Men	Senator Everett McKinley Dirksen	#29
What Now My Love	Mitch Ryder	#30
The World We Knew (Over and Over)	Frank Sinatra	#30
The Other Man's Grass Is Always Greener	Petula Clark	#31
Child of Clay	Jimmie Rodgers	#31
Since You Showed Me How to Be Happy	Jackie Wilson	#32
The Sweetest Thing This Side of Heaven	Chris Bartley	#32
Travlin' Man	Stevie Wonder	#32
Music to Watch Girls By	Andy Williams	#34
All	James Darren	#35
A Banda (Ah Bahn-da)	Herb Alpert & The Tijuana Brass	#35
Making Memories	Frankie Laine	#35
Don't Blame the Children	Sammy Davis, Jr.	#37
Mr. Dream Merchant	Jerry Butler	#38
You've Made Me so Very Happy	Brenda Holloway	#39
Girls in Love	Gary Lewis/Playboys	#39
Lady	Jack Jones	#39
Daddys Little Girl	Al Martino	#42
Melancholy Music Man	The Righteous Brothers	#43

ORCHESTRA (cont'd)

Title	Artist	Page
Anything Goes	Harpers Bizarre	#43
Rock 'N' Roll Woman	Buffalo Springfield	#44
The River Is Wide	The Forum	#45
In the Misty Moonlight	Dean Martin	#46
You Wanted Someone to Play With (I Wanted Someone to Love)	Frankie Laine	#48
Another Night	Dionne Warwick	#49
King Midas in Reverse	The Hollies	#51
A Beautiful Story	Sonny & Cher	#53
This Town	Frank Sinatra	#53
I Want to Love You for What You Are	Ronnie Dove	#54
You Gave Me Something (And Everything's Alright)	The Fantastic Four	#55
I'm Gonna Miss You	The Artistics	#55
Washed Ashore (On a Lonely Island in the Sea)	The Platters	#56
I Am the Walrus	The Beatles	#56
Suzanne	Noel Harrison	#56
Misty Blue	Eddy Arnold	#57
Graduation Day	The Arbors	#59
Love Me Forever	Roger Williams	#60
I Dig You Baby	Jerry Butler	#60
Time, Time	Ed Ames	#61
O-O, I Love You	The Dells	#61
Just One Smile	Gene Pitney	#64
Keep a Light in the Window Till I Come Home	Solomon Burke	#64
Summer and Sandy	Lesley Gore	#65
Ooh Baby	Deon Jackson	#65
Turn the World Around	Eddy Arnold	#66
To Share Your Love	Fantastic Four	#68
Stranded in the Middle of No Place	The Righteous Brothers	#72
I'll Make Him Love Me	Barbara Lewis	#72
Now I Know	Jack Jones	#73
Give Me Time	Dusty Springfield	#76
Laura (Tell Me What He's Got That I Ain't Got)	Brook Benton	#78
Can't Help but Love You	The Standells	#78
I Love You More Than Words Can Say	Otis Redding	#78
The Beginning of Loneliness	Dionne Warwick	#79
I'm Indestructible	Jack Jones	#81
I've Lost You	Jackie Wilson	#82
You, No One but You	Frankie Laine	#83
Love Me	Bobby Hebb	#84
I Don't Want to Lose You	Jackie Wilson	#84
Dancin' Out of My Heart	Ronnie Dove	#87
For What It's Worth	King Curtis & Kingpins	#87
You are My Sunshine	Mitch Ryder	#88

ORCHESTRA (cont'd)

Birds of Britain	Bob Crewe Generation	#89
Heart Be Still	Lorraine Ellison	#89
Speak Her Name	Walter Jackson	#89
Danger! She's a Stranger	The Five Stairsteps	#89
Where Is the Party	Helena Ferguson	#90
Just Be Sincere	Jackie Wilson	#91
For Once in My Life	Tony Bennett	#91
Here Comes Heaven	Eddy Arnold	#91
Up-Up and Away	Johnny Mann Singers	#91
When Love Slips Away	Dee Dee Warwick	#92
Stout-Hearted Men	Barbra Streisand	#92
To Sir, with Love	Herbie Mann	#93
I Could Be So Happy	The Magnificent Men	#93
There Must Be a Way	Jimmy Roselli	#93
I Can't Make It Anymore	Spyder Turner	#95
People Like You	Eddie Fisher	#97
When the Snow Is on the Roses	Ed Ames	#98
1968		
Hey Jude	The Beatles	#1
Judy in Disguise (With Glasses)	John Fred	#1
This Guy's in Love with You	Herb Alpert	#1
Love Is Blue	Paul Mauriat	#1
I Heart It Through the Grapevine	Marvin Gaye	#1
MacArthur Park	Richard Harris	#2
Lady Willpower	Gary Puckett & The Union Gap	#2
Classical Gas	Mason Williams	#2
Cry Like a Baby	The Box Tops	#2
Those Were the Days	Mary Hopkins	#2
Young Girl	Gary Puckett & The Union Gap	#2
(Theme from) Valley of the Dolls	Dionne Warwick	#2
Light My Fire	Jose Feliciano	#3
Stoned Soul Picnic	The 5th Dimension	#3
The Look of Love	Sergio Mendes & Brasil '66	#4
Abraham, Martin and John	Dion	#4
Woman, Woman	Gary Puckett & The Union Gap	#4
Fool on the Hill	Sergio Mendes & Brasil '66	#6
Cowboys to Girls	The Intruders	#6
My Special Angel	The Vogues	#7
Over You	Gary Puckett & The Union Gap	#7
Goin' Out of My Head/Can't Take My Eyes Off You	The Lettermen	#7
Turn Around, Look at Me	The Vogues	#7
Ain't Nothing Like the Real Thing	Marvin Gaye & Tammi Terrell	#8
Do You Know the Way to San Jose	Dionne Warwick	#10

ORCHESTRA (cont'd)

Song	Artist	#
Stay in My Corner	The Dells	#10
Susan	The Buckinghams	#11
Summer Rain	Johnny Rivers	#14
Walk Away Renee	Four Tops	#14
Sky Pilot (Part One)	Eric Burdon/Animals	#14
Words	The Bee Gees	#15
Kiss Me Goodbye	Petula Clark	#15
Delilah	Tom Jones	#15
She's a Heartbreaker	Gene Pitney	#16
Like to Get to Know You	Spanky & Our Gang	#17
Always Together	The Dells	#18
Sweet Inspiration	The Sweet Inspirations	#18
A Man Without Love	Engelbert Humperdinck	#19
Promises, Promises	Dionne Warwick	#19
Who Will Answer?	Ed Ames	#19
The Autumn of My Life	Bobby Goldsboro	#19
We Can Fly	The Cowsills	#21
Keep On Lovin' Me Honey	Marvin Gaye & Tammi Terrell	#24
Hi-Heel Sneakers	Jose Feliciano	#25
(Love Is Like A) Baseball Game	The Intruders	#26
I'm Gonna Make You Love Me	Madeline Bell	#26
Some Velvet Morning	Nancy Sinatra & Lee Hazlewood	#26
Till	The Vogues	#27
Mr. Businessman	Ray Stevens	#28
To Give (The Reason I Live)	Frankie Valli	#29
Does Your Mama Know About Me	Bobby Taylor	#29
Shame, Shame	Magic Lanterns	#29
Face It Girl, It's Over	Nancy Wilson	#29
Sunday Mornin'	Spanky & Our Gang	#30
Some Things You Never Get Used To	The Supremes	#30
Les Bicyclettes de Belsize	Engelbert Humperdinck	#31
Dreams of the Everyday Housewife	Glen Campbell	#32
Best of Both Worlds	Lulu	#32
Lalena	Donovan	#33
Who Is Gonna Love Me?	Dionne Warwick	#33
The Lesson	Vikki Carr	#34
I Get the Sweetest Feeling	Jackie Wilson	#34
Help Yourself	Tom Jones	#35
My Girl/Hey Girl	Bobby Vee	#35
The Straight Life	Bobby Goldsboro	#36
I Met Her in Church	The Box Tops	#37
Don't Give Up	Petula Clark	#37
It Should Have Been Me	Gladys Knight & The Pips	#40

ORCHESTRA (cont'd)

I've Never Found a Girl (To Love Me Like You Do)	Eddie Floyd	#40
I Wish It Would Rain	Gladys Knight & The Pips	#41
The Impossible Dream	The Hesitations	#42
I'm Sorry	The Delfonics	#42
Brown Eyed Woman	Bill Medley	#43
With Pen in Hand	Billy Vera	#43
Not Enough Indians	Dean Martin	#43
Wear It on Our Face	The Dells	#44
Put Your Head on My Shoulder	The Lettermen	#44
My Favorite Things	Herb Alpert & The Tijuana Brass	#45
United	Peaches & Herb	#46
Peace Brother Peace	Bill Medley	#48
No Sad Songs	Joe Simon	#49
Look to Your Soul	Johnny Rivers	#49
Jelly Jungle (Of Orange Marmalada)	Lemon Pipers	#51
I Can Remember	James & Bobby Purify	#51
Loving You Has Made Me Bananas	Guy Marks	#51
To Wait for Love	Herb Alpert	#51
It's Nice to Be with You	The Monkees	#51
Unwind	Ray Stevens	#52
Fly Me to the Moon	Bobby Womack	#52
Somebody Cares	Tommy James & The Shondells	#53
In Need of a Friend	The Cowsills	#54
Storybook Children	Billy Vera & Judy Clay	#54
The Ten Commandments of Love	Peaches & Herb	#55
I Guess I'll Have to Cry, Cry, Cry	James Brown	#55
The Impossible Dream	Roger Williams	#55
I Love You Madly	Fantastic Four	#56
Look, Here Comes the Sun	The Sunshine Company	#56
I Ain't Got to Love Nobody Else	The Masqueraders	#57
Back in Love Again	The Buckinghams	#57
Love Is Blue	Al Martino	#57
Brooklyn Roads	Neil Diamond	#58
You've Got to Be Loved	The Montanas	#58
American Boys	Petula Clark	#59
Don't Change Your Love	Five Stairsteps & Cubie	#59
I Can't Believe I'm Losing You	Frank Sinatra	#60
Dreams of the Everyday Housewife	Wayne Newton	#60
You've Still Got a Place in My Heart	Dean Martin	#60
Right Relations	Johnny Rivers	#61
Be Young, Be Foolish, Be Happy	The Tams	#61
I Loved and I Lost	The Impressions	#61
Isn't It Lonely Together	O.C. Smith	#63

ORCHESTRA (cont'd)

My Way of Life	Frank Sinatra	#64
Baby Make Your Own Sweet Music	Jay & The Techniques	#64
The Yard Went on Forever	Richard Harris	#64
(There's) Always Something There to Remind Me	Dionne Warwick	#65
Alfie	Eivets Rednow (Stevie Wonder)	#66
I'll Be Sweeter Tomorrow (Than I Was Today)	The O'Jays	#66
Mountains of Love	Ronnie Dove	#67
A Million to One	Five Stairsteps & Cubie	#68
Hold On	Radiants	#68
Pick Up the Pieces	Carla Thomas	#68
Down Here on the Ground	Lou Rawls	#69
For Once in My Life	Jackie Wilson	#70
Don't Cry My Love	The Impressions	#71
Let Me Be Lonely	Dionne Warwick	#71
Love Is Blue (L'Amour Est Bleu)	Claudine Longet	#71
Everybody Got to Believe in Somebody	Sam & Dave	#73
Do Unto Me	James & Bobby Purify	#73
My Shy Violet	The Mills Brothers	#73
Here Comes the Rain, Baby	Eddy Arnold	#74
Mornin' Glory	Bobbie Gentry & Glen Campbell	#74
It's Over	Eddy Arnold	#74
Let's Make a Promise	Peaches & Herb	#75
Message from Maria	Joe Simon	#75
That Kind of Woman	Merrilee Rush	#76
Apologize	Ed Ames	#79
On the Way Home	Buffalo Springfield	#82
Hang 'Em High	Hugo Montenegro	#82
At the Top of the Stairs	The Formations	#83
Do What You Gotta Do	Bobby Vee	#83
Then You Can Tell Me Goodbye	Eddy Arnold	#84
Montage from How Sweet It Is (I Know That You Know)	The Love Generation	#86
Baby You're so Right for Me	Brenda & The Tabulations	#86
Where Do I Go	Carla Thomas	#86
Lili Marlene	Al Martino	#87
Something's Missing	5 Stairsteps & Cubie	#88
Look Over Your Shoulder	The O'Jays	#89
Climb Every Mountain	The Hesitations	#90
Rosanna's Going Wild	Johnny Cash	#91
Your Heart Is Free Just Like the Wind	Vikki Carr	#91
Hey Boy Take a Chance on Love	Ruby Andrews	#92
If You Ever Leave Me	Jack Jones	#92
Billy You're My Friend	Gene Pitney	#92
Forget Me Not	Martha & The Vandellas	#93

ORCHESTRA (cont'd)

Lonely Is the Name	Sammy Davis, Jr.	#93
The Shadow of Your Love	The 5 Stairsteps & Cubie	#94
I've Got Love for My Baby	Young Hearts	#94
Almost in Love	Elvis Presley	#95
Love Is Blue (L'Amour Est Bleu)	Manny Kellem	#96
Don't Sign the Paper Baby (I Want You Back)	Jimmy Delphs	#96
7:30 Guided Tour	The Five Americans	#96
Isn't It Lonely Together	Robert Knight	#97
Dear Delilah	Grapefruit	#98
Young Birds Fly	The Cryan' Shames	#99
Do Your Own Thing	Brook Benton	#99
They Don't Make Love Like They Used To	Eddy Arnold	#99
Louisiana Man	Bobbie Gentry	#100
1969		
Suspicious Minds	Elvis Presley	#1
Love Theme from Romeo & Juliet	Henry Mancini	#1
Wedding Bell Blues	The 5th Dimension	#1
In the Year 2525	Zager & Evans	#1
Aquarius/Let the Sunshine In	The 5th Dimension	#1
Traces	Classics IV/Dennis Yost	#2
Hot Fun in the Summertime	Sly & The Family Stone	#2
In the Ghetto	Elvis Presley	#3
Grazing in the Grass	Friends of Distinction	#3
Touch Me	The Doors	#3
Wichita Lineman	Glen Campbell	#3
Galveston	Glen Campbell	#4
Put a Little Love in Your Heart	Jackie DeShannon	#4
My Cherie Amour	Stevie Wonder	#4
Sweet Caroline (Good Times Never Seemed So Good)	Neil Diamond	#4
Hooked on a Feeling	B.J. Thomas	#5
These Eyes	The Guess Who?	#6
Color Him Father	The Winstons	#7
This Girl's in Love with You	Dionne Warwick	#7
Baby, Baby Don't Cry	Smokey Robinson & The Miracles	#8
This Girl Is a Woman Now	Gary Puckett & The Union Gap	#9
My Whole World Ended (The Moment You Left Me)	David Ruffin	#9
Is That All There Is	Peggy Lee	#11
I've Gotta Be Me	Sammy Davis Jr.	#11
Hurt so Bad	The Lettermen	#12
Goodbye	Mary Hopkins	#13
Love Me Tonight	Tom Jones	#13
Black Pearl	Sonny Charles & The Checkmates, Ltd.	#13
My Pledge of Love	The Joe Jeffrey Group	#14

ORCHESTRA (cont'd)

Title	Artist	
Baby, I'm for Real	The Originals	#14
Don't Give in to Him	Gary Puckett & The Union Gap	#15
Going in Circles	Friends of Distinction	#15
You've Lost That Lovin' Feeling	Dionne Warwick	#16
Keem-O-Sabe	The Electric Indian	#16
Morning Girl	The Neon Philharmonic	#17
What's the Use of Breaking Up	Jerry Butler	#20
Workin' On a Groovy Thing	The 5th Dimension	#20
Day Is Done	Peter, Paul & Mary	#21
Choice of Colors	The Impressions	#21
I Can Sing a Rainbow/Love Is Blue	The Dells	#22
Happy Heart	Andy Williams	#22
Try a Little Kindness	Glen Campbell	#23
You Gave Me a Mountain	Frankie Laine	#24
There'll Come a Time	Betty Everett	#26
Where's the Playground Susie	Glen Campbell	#26
My Way	Frank Sinatra	#27
Goodnight My Love	Paul Anka	#27
Walk on By	Isaac Hayes	#30
It's Getting Better	Mama Cass	#30
The River Is Wide	The Grassroots	#31
Will You Be Staying After Sunday	The Pepperment Rainbow	#32
Abraham, Martin and John	Smokey Robinson & The Miracles	#33
No, Not Much	The Vogues	#34
Daddy's Little Man	O.C. Smith	#34
Nothing but a Heartache	The Flirtations	#34
Ready or Not Here I Come (Can't Hide from Love)	The Delfonics	#35
True Grit	Glen Campbell	#35
Sunday Mornin'	Oliver	#35
Abraham, Martin and John	Moms Mabley	#35
Memories	Elvis Presley	#35
Let It Be Me	Glen Campbell & Bobbie Gentry	#36
Make Your Own Kind of Music	Mama Cass Elliot	#36
The Beginning of My End	The Unifics	#36
Testify (I Wonna)	Johnnie Taylor	#36
By the Time I Get to Phoenix	Isaac Hayes	#37
World (Part 1)	James Brown	#37
The April Fools	Dionne Warwick	#37
I'm a Better Man	Engelbert Humperdinck	#38
Seattle	Perry Como	#38
Does Anybody Know I'm Here	The Dells	#38
Love Will Find a Way	Jackie DeShannon	#40
You Got Yours and I'll Get Mine	The Delfonics	#40

ORCHESTRA (cont'd)

Don't It Make You Want to Go Home	Joe South & The Believers	#41
Earth Angel (Will You Be Mine)	The Vogues	#42
The Way It Used to Be	Engelbert Humperdinck	#42
Odds and Ends	Dionne Warwick	#43
The Pledge of Allegiance	Red Skelton	#44
Honey (I Miss You)	O.C. Smith	#44
Wishful Sinful	The Doors	#44
Moments to Remember	The Vogues	#47
Woman Helping Man	The Vogues	#47
Friend, Lover, Woman, Wife	O.C. Smith	#47
Abergavenny	Shannon (Marty Wilde)	#47
Change of Heart	Dennis Yost/Classics IV	#49
Playgirl	Thee Prophets	#49
I Could Never Lie to You	The New Colony Six	#50
Out of Sight, Out of Mind	Little Anthony/Imperials	#52
Any Way That You Want Me	Evie Sands	#53
What Is a Man	Four Tops	#53
Love of the Common People	The Winstons	#54
Tomorrow Tomorrow	The Bee Gees	#54
Don't Wake Me Up in the Morning, Michael	Pepperment Rainbow	#54
(We've Got) Honey Love	Martha & The Vandellas	#56
Tragedy	Brian Hyland	#56
Foolish Fool	Dee Dee Warwick	#57
I've Lost Everything I've Ever Loved	David Ruffin	#58
Chains of Love	Bobby Bland	#60
Glad She's a Woman	Bobby Goldsboro	#61
Happy Heart	Petula Clark	#62
Rain in My Heart	Frank Sinatra	#62
Let Yourself Go	The Friends of Distinction	#63
Didn't We	Richard Harris	#63
Purple Haze	Dion	#63
Without Her	Herb Alpert	#63
Shangri-La	The Lettermen	#64
Runnin' Blue	The Doors	#64
In the Still of the Night	Paul Anka	#64
I Want You to Know	The New Colony Six	#65
(Sittin' On) The Dock of the Bay	Sergio Mendes & Brasil '66	#66
The Greatest Love	Dorsey Burnette	#67
One Night Affair	The O'Jays	#68
The Colour of My Love	Jefferson	#68
Proud Mary	The Checkmates, Ltd. feat. Sonny Charles	#69
The Young Folks	The Supremes	#69
I Still Believe in Tomorrow	John & Anne Ryder	#70

ORCHESTRA (cont'd)

Title	Artist	#
Looking Back	Joe Simon	#70
Hey! Baby	Jose Feliciano	#71
Somebody Loves You	The Delfonics	#72
I Take a Lot of Pride in What I Am	Dean Martin	#75
Love's Been Good to Me	Frank Sinatra	#75
Poor Side of Town	Al Wilson	#75
Chitty Chitty Bang Bang	Paul Mauriat	#76
I Can't Say No to You	Betty Everett	#78
Eternity	Vikki Carr	#79
Goin' Out of My Head	Frank Sinatra	#79
Sincerely	Paul Anka	#80
Can't Find the Time	Orpheus	#80
First Hymn from Grand Terrace	Mark Lindsay	#81
She's Got Love	Thomas & Richard Frost	#83
You Don't Need Me for Anything Anymore	Brenda Lee	#84
She's a Lady	John Sebastian	#84
Seven Years	The Impressions	#84
The Thought of Loving You	The Crystal Mansion	#84
Happy	Paul Anka	#86
Dammit Isn't God's Last Name	Frankie Laine	#86
Never Gonna Let Him Know	Debbie Taylor	#86
Eloise	Barry Ryan	#86
My World Is Empty Without You	Jose Feliciano	#87
My Balloon's Going Up	Archie Bell & The Drells	#87
Moonlight Sonata	Henry Mancini	#87
We Must Be in Love	Five Stairsteps & Cubie	#88
Look at Mine	Petula Clark	#89
One Woman	Johnny Rivers	#89
Greensleeves	Mason Williams	#90
Sunday	The Moments	#90
Gotta Get to Know You	Bobby Bland	#91
You've Got the Power	The Esquires	#91
Breakfast in Bed	Dusty Springfield	#91
Me About You	The Lovin' Spoonful	#91
From Both Sides Now	Dion	#91
Brown Arms in Houston	Orpheus	#91
Son of a Travelin' Man	Ed Ames	#92
Hallways of My Mind	The Dells	#92
Let's Call It a Day Girl	Bobby Vee	#92
California Girl (And the Tennessee Square)	Tompall & The Glaser Brothers	#92
No One Better Than You	Petula Clark	#93
How I Miss You Baby	Bobby Womack	#93
I'll Never Fall in Love Again	Burt Bacharach	#93

ORCHESTRA (cont'd)

I Need You Now	Ronnie Dove	#93
MacArthur Park	Waylon Jennings & The Kimberlys	#93
Funny Feeling	The Delfonics	#94
Let Me Be the Man My Daddy Was	Chi-Lites	#94
Land of 1000 Dances	The Electric Indian	#95
Only You (And You Alone)	Bobby Hatfield	#95
Turn Around and Love You	Rita Coolidge	#96
Love Theme from "Romeo and Juliet" (A Time for Us)	Johnny Mathis	#96
I Don't Want to Cry	Ruby Winters	#97
It's a Groovy World	The Unifics	#97
Galveston	Roger Williams	#99
My Little Chickadee	The Foundations	#99
Sausalito	Al Martino	#99
Saturday Night at the World	Mason Williams	#99

ORGAN

ARTISTS WHO RECORDED THE MOST HITS THAT FEATURED THE ORGAN

- 13 — Booker T. & The MG's
- 13 — Jr. Walker/The All Stars
- 11 — Jackie Wilson
- 11 — James Brown
- 11 — The Beach Boys
- 11 — Wilson Pickett
- 10 — Dave Clark Five
- 10 — Jimmy Smith
- 10 — Tommy James & The Shondells
- 9 — Bill Black's Combo
- 9 — Solomon Burke
- 9 — The Animals
- 9 — Willie Mitchell

SONG	ARTIST	HOT 100	LENGTH OF SOLO
1960			
Everybody's Somebody's Fool	Connie Francis	#1	
Tell Laura I Love Her	Ray Peterson	#7	
White Silver Sands	Bill Black's Combo	#9	
Don't Be Cruel	Bill Black's Combo	#11	
Sleep	Little Willie John	#13	18 sec.
Doggin' Around	Jackie Wilson	#15	
Beatnik Fly	Johnny & The Hurricanes	#15	
Blue Tango	Bill Black's Combo	#16	
Look for a Star	Garry Miles	#16	
Josephine	Bill Black's Combo	#18	

ORGAN (cont'd)

Song	Artist	Rank
Look for a Star	Billy Vaughn	#19
Mr. Lucky	Henry Mancini	#21
T.L.C. Tender Love and Care	Jimmie Rodgers	#24
Look for a Star - Part 1	Garry Mills	#26
Look for a Star	Deane Hawley	#29
Heartbreak (It's Hurtin' Me)	Little Willie John	#38
Gonzo	James Booker	#43
Just a Closer Walk with Thee	Jimmie Rodgers	#44
Down Yonder	Johnny & The Hurricanes	#48
Heartbreak (It's Hurtin' Me)	Jon Thomas	#48
National City	Joiner, Arkansas Junior High School Band	#53
Rocking Goose	Johnny & The Hurricanes	#60
There's a Star Spangled Banner Waving #2 (The Ballad of Francis Powers)	Red River Dave	#64
(Let's Do) The Hully Gully Twist	Bill Doggett	#66
Think Me a Kiss	Clyde McPhatter	#66
Theme from "The Dark at the Top of the Stairs"	Ernie Freeman	#70
Rambling	The Ramblers	#73
The Old Oaken Bucket	Tommy Sands	#73
House of Bamboo	Earl Grant	#88
I'll Take Care of You	Bobby Bland	#89
You Are My Sunshine	Johnny & The Hurricanes	#91
Midnight Lace- Part One	Ray Conniff	#92
White Christmas	The Drifters	#96
Revival	Johnny & The Hurricanes	#97
1961		
Wooden Heart	Joe Dowell	#1
Wonderland by Night	Bert Kaempfert	#1
Last Night	Mar-Keys	#3
Dum Dum	Brenda Lee	#4
Every Beat of My Heart	Pips	#6
San Antonio Rose	Floyd Cramer	#8
One Mint Julep	Ray Charles	#8
Wonderland by Night	Louis Prima	#15
Wonderland By Night	Anita Bryant	#18
I'm Comin on Back to You	Jackie Wilson	#19
Hearts of Stone	Bill Black's Combo	#20
I Dreamed of a Hill-Billy Heaven	Tex Ritter	#20
Please Tell Me Why	Jackie Wilson	#20
Just for Old Time's Sake	The McGuire Sisters	#20
Just Out of Reach (Of My Two Open Arms)	Solomon Burke	#24
Ole Buttermilk Sky	Bill Black's Combo	#25
Foot Stomping - Part 1	The Flares	#25

ORGAN (cont'd)

You Can't Sit Down (Part 2)	Philip Upchurch Combo	#29	
Anybody but Me	Brenda Lee	#31	
Years from Now	Jackie Wilson	#37	
Bewildered	James Brown	#40	
Every Beat of My Heart	Gladys Knight & The Pips	#45	
Now and Forever	Bert Kaempfert	#48	
Don't Get Around Much Anymore	The Belmonts	#57	14 sec.
Yes, I'm Lonesome Tonight	Dodie Stevens	#60	
Morning After	Mar-Keys	#60	
I Won't Be There	Adam Wade	#61	
The Girl's a Devil	The Dukays	#64	15 sec.
I've Got News for You	Ray Charles	#66	37 sec.
Welcome Home	Sammy Kaye	#68	
A Little Dog Cried	Jimmie Rodgers	#71	
Wabash Blues	The Viscounts	#77	
I'm Gonna Move to the Outskirts of Town	Ray Charles	#84	42 sec.
Ja-Da	Johnny & The Hurricanes	#86	
I Can't Do It By Myself	Anita Bryant	#87	
Riders in the Sky	Lawrence Welk	#87	
Late Date	The Parkays	#89	
Our Love Is Here to Stay	Dinah Washington	#89	
A Cross Stands Alone	Jimmy Witter	#89	
Theme from "The Great Imposter"	Henry Mancini	#90	
Honky Train	Bill Black's Combo	#92	
1962			
Soldier Boy	The Shirelles	#1	
Peppermint Twist - Part 1	Joey Dee & The Starliters	#1	
Limbo Rock	Chubby Checker	#2	
Green Onions	Booker T. & The MG's	#3	
Palisades Park	Freddy Cannon	#3	
Let's Dance	Chris Montez	#4	19 sec.
Al Di La'	Emilio Pericoli	#6	
Shout- Part 1	Joey Dee & The Starliters	#6	
Baby It's You	The Shirelles	#8	18 sec.
The Cha-Cha-Cha	Bobby Rydell	#10	
Rinky Dink	Baby Cortez	#10	
Soul Twist	King Curtis & Noble Knights	#17	
Tuff	Ace Cannon	#17	
Torture	Kris Jensen	#20	
I've Got a Woman (Part 1)	Jimmy McGriff	#20	
Any Day Now (My Wild Beautiful Bird)	Chuck Jackson	#23	
To a Sleeping Beauty	Jimmy Dean	#26	
Most People Get Married	Patti Page	#27	

ORGAN (cont'd)

Title	Artist	Chart	Time
The Jam (Part 1)	Bobby Gregg	#29	
Blues (Stay Away from Me)	Floyd Cramer	#36	
Comin' Home Baby	Mel Torme	#36	20 sec.
But Not for Me	Ketty Lester	#41	
Swingin' Gently	Earl Grant	#44	
Every Night (Without You)	Paul Anka	#46	
Lost Someone	James Brown	#48	
Baby Elephant Walk	Lawrence Welk	#48	
Moments	Jennell Hawkins	#50	
Sweet Sixteen Bars	Earl Grant	#55	
Beach Party	King Curtis & Noble Knights	#60	
The Swiss Maid	Del Shannon	#64	
If You Were a Rock and Roll Record	Freddy Cannon	#67	
Happy Weekend	Dave "Baby" Cortez	#67	
I'll Take You Home	The Corsairs	#68	
Lose Her	Bobby Rydell	#69	
Midnight Special, Part 1	Jimmy Smith	#69	
I Just Can't Help It	Jackie Wilson	#70	
Jivin' Around	Al Casey Combo	#71	
Down in the Valley	Solomon Burke	#71	
Roly Poly	Joey Dee & The Starliters	#74	15 sec.
Glory of Love	Don Gardner/Dee Dee Ford	#75	
Ol' Man River	Jimmy Smith	#82	
I'm Hanging Up My Heart for You	Solomon Burke	#85	
Baby Elephant Walk	The Miniature Men	#87	
Lovesick Blues	Floyd Cramer	#87	
Shimmy, Shimmy Walk, Part 1	The Megatons	#88	
Getting Ready for the Heartbreak	Chuck Jackson	#88	18 sec.
Let's Go	Floyd Cramer	#90	
Walk on with the Duke	The Duke of Earl (Gene Chandler)	#91	
The Twist	Ernie Freeman	#93	
I Really Don't Want to Know	Solomon Burke	#93	
Shout- Part 1	The Isley Brothers	#94	
Play the Thing	Marlowe Morris Quintet	#95	
You Don't Miss Your Water	William Bell	#95	
Little Young Lover	The Impressions	#96	
Fiesta	Dave "Baby" Cortez	#96	
The (Bossa Nova) Bird	The Dells	#97	
My Time for Cryin'	Maxine Brown	#98	
Silent Night, Holy Night	Mahalia Jackson	#99	
Don't Stop the Wedding	Ann Cole	#99	
Drown in My Own Tears	Don Shirley	#100	

ORGAN (cont'd)

1963

Title	Artist	Chart	Time
Our Day Will Come	Ruby & The Romantics	#1	
My Boyfriend's Back	The Angels	#1	
Sugar Shack	Jimmy Gilmer/Fireballs	#1	
You Can't Sit Down	The Dovells	#3	
Surfin' U.S.A.	The Beach Boys	#3	11 sec.
Rhythm of the Rain	The Cascades	#3	15 sec.
Hello Stranger	Barbara Lewis	#3	
Loop de Loop	Johnny Thunder	#4	
Foolish Little Girl	The Shirelles	#4	
Judy's Turn to Cry	Lesley Gore	#5	
Young Lovers	Paul & Paula	#6	
Two Faces Have I	Lou Christie	#6	
Blame It on the Bossa Nova	Eydie Gorme	#7	
More	Kai Winding	#8	
Bossa Nova Baby	Elvis Presley	#8	
Little Red Rooster	Sam Cooke	#11	
Hot Pastrami	The Dartells	#11	
I Saw Linda Yesterday	Dickey Lee	#14	
My Summer Love	Ruby & The Romantics	#16	
Wildwood Days	Bobby Rydell	#17	
Prisoner of Love	James Brown	#18	
Cross Fire!	The Orlons	#19	
You Lost the Sweetest Boy	Mary Wells	#22	
If My Pillow Could Talk	Connie Francis	#23	15 sec.
Please Don't Talk to the Lifeguard	Diane Ray	#31	
Goodnight My Love	The Fleetwoods	#32	
Shake! Shake! Shake!	Jackie Wilson	#33	
Workout Stevie, Workout	Little Stevie Wonder	#33	
Bad Girl	Neil Sedaka	#33	
Wild!	Dee Dee Sharp	#33	
Hot Pastrami with Mashed Potatoes - Part 1	Joey Dee & The Starliters	#36	
Drownin' My Sorrows	Connie Francis	#36	11 sec.
Down the Aisle (Wedding Song)	Patti LaBelle & The Blue Belles	#37	
That's How Heartaches Are Made	Baby Washington	#40	
Shake a Hand	Jackie Wilson & Linda Hopkins	#42	
Rock Me in the Cradle of Love	Dee Dee Sharp	#43	23 sec.
Some Kinda Fun	Chris Montez	#43	
Betty in Bermudas	The Dovells	#50	17 sec.
All About My Girl	Jimmy McGriff	#50	
Everybody Monkey	Freddy Cannon	#52	
These Foolish Things	James Brown	#55	
Groovy Baby	Billy Abbott	#55	

ORGAN (cont'd)

Song	Artist	Chart	Time
Surf Party	Chubby Checker	#55	13 sec.
Baby Get It (And Don't Quit It)	Jackie Wilson	#61	
Dawn	David Rockingham Trio	#62	
Ridin' the Wind	The Tornados	#63	
Back at the Chicken Shack, Part 1	Jimmy Smith	#63	
Sax Fifth Avenue	Johnny Beecher	#65	
Can't Nobody Love You	Solomon Burke	#66	
Enamorado	Keith Colley	#66	
(I Cried At) Laura's Wedding	Barbara Lynn	#68	
Hobo Flats - Part 1	Jimmy Smith	#69	
I Am a Witness	Tommy Hunt	#71	
Man's Temptation	Gene Chandler	#71	
He's So Heavenly	Brenda Lee	#73	
Tell Me the Truth	Nancy Wilson	#73	
Organ Shout	Dave "Baby" Cortez	#76	
Red Pepper I	Roosevelt Fountain	#78	
Forever	The Marvelettes	#78	
Jellybread	Booker T. & The MG's	#82	
Dance, Dance, Dance	Joey Dee	#89	
Hot Cakes! 1st Serving	Dave "Baby" Cortez	#91	
Saltwater Taffy	Lonnie Mack	#93	
Summertime	Chris Columbo Quintet	#93	
Dear Abby	The Hearts	#94	
Spring	Birdlegs & Pauline	#94	
M.G. Blues	Jimmy McGriff	#95	
Theme from "Any Number Can Win"	Jimmy Smith	#96	
Hello Jim	Paul Anka	#97	
Black Cloud	Chubby Checker	#98	
The Last Minute (Pt. 1)	Jimmy McGriff	#99	
Dance, Everybody, Dance	The Dartells	#99	
Every Beat of My Heart	James Brown	#99	
Two Wrongs Don't Make a Right	Mary Wells	#100	
Baby, You're Driving Me Crazy	Joey Dee	#100	
1964			
A World Without Love	Peter & Gordon	#1	20 sec.
My Guy	Mary Wells	#1	
Do Wah Diddy Diddy	Manfred Mann	#1	
The House of the Rising Sun	The Animals	#1	12 sec.
Dancing in the Street	Martha & The Vandellas	#3	
Because	Dave Clark Five	#3	13 sec.
Love Me with All of Your Heart	Ray Charles Singers	#3	
Out of Limits	The Marketts	#3	
Popsicles and Icicles	The Murmaids	#4	

ORGAN (cont'd)

Can't You See That She's Mine	Dave Clark Five	#4	
Bits and Pieces	Dave Clark Five	#5	
California Sun	The Rivieras	#5	
Fun, Fun, Fun	The Beach Boys	#5	12 sec.
C'mon and Swim	Bobby Freeman	#6	
(Just Like) Romeo & Juliet	The Reflections	#6	
Navy Blue	Diane Renay	#6	13 sec.
Time Is on My Side	The Rolling Stones	#6	
It Hurts to Be in Love	Gene Pitney	#7	12 sec.
Walk-Don't Run '64	The Ventures	#8	
Save It for Me	The Four Seasons	#10	11 sec.
Haunted House	Gene Simmons	#11	
Do You Love Me	Dave Clark Five	#11	
Hi-Heel Sneakers	Tommy Tucker	#11	
Ask Me	Elvis Presley	#12	
Try It Baby	Marvin Gaye	#15	
Shangri-La	Robert Maxwell	#15	
Money	The Kingsmen	#16	
Wish Someone Would Care	Irma Thomas	#17	
I'm Crying	The Animals	#19	
What'd I Say	Elvis Presley	#21	
When the Lovelight Starts Shining Through His Eyes	The Supremes	#23	
The Very Thought of You	Ricky Nelson	#26	
My Girl Sloopy	The Vibrations	#26	
Shangri-La	Vic Dana	#27	
Alone	The Four Seasons	#28	
What's Easy for Two Is so Hard for One	Mary Wells	#29	
Al-Di-La	Ray Charles Singers	#29	
Sugar Lips	Al Hirt	#30	
20-75	Willie Mitchell	#31	
You'll Never Walk Alone	Patti LaBelle & The Blue Belles	#34	
That's What Love Is Made Of	The Miracles	#35	
Tra La La La Suzy	Dean & Jean	#35	
Slaughter on Tenth Avenue	The Ventures	#35	
Charade	Sammy Kaye	#36	
Puppy Love	Barbara Lewis	#38	
I Had a Talk with My Man	Mitty Collier	#41	
Death of an Angel	The Kingsmen	#42	27 sec.
Wendy	The Beach Boys	#44	11 sec.
Little Latin Lupe Lu	The Kingsmen	#44	
Party Girl	The Monarchs	#47	
Slip-In Mules (No High Heel Sneakers)	Sugar Pie DeSanto	#48	
Gonna Get Along Without You Now	Skeeter Davis	#48	

ORGAN (cont'd)

Jump Back	Rufus Thomas	#49	
She Want T' Swim	Chubby Checker	#50	
Baby Baby Baby	Anna King-Bobby Byrd	#52	
Anyone Who Knows What Love Is (Will Understand)	Irma Thomas	#52	
Love Is All We Need	Vic Dana	#53	
The French Song	Lucille Starr	#54	
Bon-Doo-Wah	The Orlons	#55	
S-W-I-M	Bobby Freeman	#56	
Gonna Send You Back to Walker (Gonna Send You Back to Georgia)	The Animals	#57	
Invisible Tears	Ray Conniff	#57	
Our Everlasting Love	Ruby & The Romantics	#64	
Peg O' My Heart	Robert Maxwell	#64	
Little Honda	The Beach Boys	#65	
Loving You More Every Day	Etta James	#65	
Try Me	Jimmy Hughes	#65	
Comin' On	Bill Black's Combo	#67	
If Somebody Told You	Anna King	#67	
The Cat	Jimmy Smith	#67	
Come to Me	Otis Redding	#69	
Who's Afraid of Virginia Woolf? (Part I)	Jimmy Smith	#72	
It's All Over	Ben E. King	#72	
Beach Girl	Pat Boone	#72	
California Bound	Ronny & The Daytonas	#72	
Do Anything You Wanna (Part I)	Harold Betters	#74	
Yesterday's Gone	The Overlanders	#75	
Kiko	Jimmy McGriff	#79	
I See You	Cathy & Joe	#82	
Till the End of Time	Ray Charles Singers	#83	
The Dodo	Jumpin' Gene Simmons	#83	
My Boyfriend Got a Beatle Haircut	Donna Lynn	#83	
Searchin'	Ace Cannon	#84	
(I'm Watching) Every Little Move You Make	Little Peggy March	#84	
My Dreams	Brenda Lee	#85	
(The Story of) Woman, Love and a Man (Part 1)	Tony Clarke	#88	
Here's a Heart	The Diplomats	#89	16 sec.
Never Trust a Woman	B.B. King	#90	
Vanishing Point	The Marketts	#90	
Tell Him	The Drew-Vels	#90	
High Heel Sneakers	Jerry Lee Lewis	#91	
I Wanna Thank You	The Enchanters	#91	
So Far Away	Hank Jacobs	#91	
I Wanna Be Loved	Dean & Jean	#91	

ORGAN (cont'd)

I Didn't Know What Time It Was	The Crampton Sisters	#92	
The Dartell Stomp	The Mustangs	#92	
Run, Run, Run	The Supremes	#93	
Little Donna	The Rivieras	#93	
Soul Dressing	Booker T. & The MG's	#95	
Like Columbus Did	The Reflections	#96	
Long Tall Shorty	Tommy Tucker	#96	
Rockin' Robin	The Rivieras	#96	
Lover's Prayer	Wallace Brothers	#97	
Garden in the Rain	Vic Dana	#97	
Mo-Onions	Booker T. & The MG's	#97	
Across the Street	Lenny O'Henry	#98	
It'll Never Be over for Me	Baby Washington	#98	
The Magic of Our Summer Love	The Tymes	#99	
Let's Have a Party	The Rivieras	#99	16 sec.
The Clock	Baby Washington	#100	11 sec.
You Were Wrong	Z.Z. Hill	#100	
1965			
This Diamond Ring	Gary Lewis/Playboys	#1	
Like a Rolling Stone	Bob Dylan	#2	
California Girls	The Beach Boys	#3	
Keep On Dancing	The Gentrys	#4	
Catch Us if You Can	Dave Clark Five	#4	
Shotgun	Jr. Walker/The All Stars	#4	
Hold What You've Got	Joe Tex	#5	
Positively 4th Street	Bob Dylan	#7	
Keep Searchin' (We'll Follow the Sun)	Del Shannon	#9	11 sec.
I'm Yours	Elvis Presley	#11	22 sec.
Red Roses for a Blue Lady	Bert Kaempfert	#11	
Sha La La	Manfred Mann	#12	
Liar, Liar	The Castaways	#12	
We Gotta Get Out of This Place	The Animals	#13	
She's About a Mover	Sir Douglas Quintet	#13	
Come Home	Dave Clark Five	#14	
Twine Time	Alvin Cash & The Crawlers	#14	
I Knew You When	Billy Joe Royal	#14	
Don't Let Me Be Misunderstood	The Animals	#15	
Sitting in the Park	Billy Stewart	#24	
Here Comes the Night	Them	#24	
Ju Ju Hand	Sam The Sham & The Pharaohs	#26	
I Do Love You	Billy Stewart	#26	
Shake and Fingerpop	Jr. Walker/The All Stars	#29	
The Entertainer	Tony Clarke	#31	

ORGAN (cont'd)

Song	Artist	Page	Notes
Sugar Dumpling	Sam Cooke	#32	
Bring It on Home to Me	The Animals	#32	
One More Time	Ray Charles Singers	#32	
Mystic Eyes	Them	#33	
Ring Dang Doo	Sam The Sham & The Pharaohs	#33	
Three O'Clock in the Morning	Bert Kaempfert	#33	
Do the Boomerang	Jr. Walker/The All Stars	#36	
Boom Boom	The Animals	#43	16 sec.
Cleo's Back	Jr. Walker/The All Stars	#43	
Hole in the Wall	The Packers	#43	
Thanks a Lot	Brenda Lee	#45	
Seven Letters	Ben E. King	#45	
Steppin' Out	Paul Revere & The Raiders	#46	
3rd Man Theme	Herb Alpert & The Tijuana Brass	#47	
Annie Fanny	The Kingsmen	#47	
Lipstick Traces (On a Cigarette)	The O'Jays	#48	
Come Tomorrow	Manfred Mann	#50	
Please Let Me Wonder	The Beach Boys	#52	
Bucket "T"	Ronny & The Daytonas	#54	18, 17 sec.
Lovin' Place	Gale Garnett	#54	
A Woman Can Change a Man	Joe Tex	#56	
Wishing It Was You	Connie Francis	#57	
She's Coming Home	The Zombies	#58	
Boot-Leg	Booker T. & The MG's	#58	
High Heel Sneakers	Stevie Wonder	#59	
The Barracuda	Alvin Cash & The Crawlers	#59	
Dance with Me	The Mojo Men	#61	
It's Wonderful to Be in Love	The Ovations	#61	
Try Me	James Brown	#63	
He's My Guy	Irma Thomas	#63	
The Climb	The Kingsmen	#65	
It's a Man Down There	G.L. Crockett	#67	
Georgie Porgie	Jewel Akens	#68	
Lovely, Lovely (Loverly, Loverly)	Chubby Checker	#70	
The Loser	The Skyliners	#72	
Did You Ever	The Hullaballoos	#74	13 sec.
Apples and Bananas	Lawrence Welk	#75	
Stand By Me	Earl Grant	#75	
The World Through a Tear	Neil Sedaka	#76	
Honky Tonk '65	Lonnie Mack	#78	
Tossing & Turning	The Ivy League	#83	
Percolatin'	Willie Mitchell	#85	
Just One More Day	Otis Redding	#85	

ORGAN (cont'd)

Come Back Baby	Roddie Joy	#86	19 sec.
You're Gonna Make Me Cry	O.V. Wright	#86	
Hawaii Honeymoon	The Waikikis	#91	
The Organ Grinder's Swing	Jimmy Smith w/ Kenny Burrell & Grady Tate	#92	
Gloria	Them	#93	
I Want You Back Again	The Zombies	#95	18 sec.
Break Up	Del Shannon	#95	16 sec.
Buster Browne	Willie Mitchell	#96	
How Nice It Is	Billy Stewart	#97	
In the Meantime	Georgia Fame	#97	
Diana	Bobby Rydell	#98	
Right Now and Not Later	Shangri-Las	#99	
This Sporting Life	Ian Whitcomb	#100	
1966			
Good Lovin'	The Young Rascals	#1	21 sec.
Good Vibrations	The Beach Boys	#1	
96 Tears	? & The Mysterians	#1	
You Keep Me Hangin' On	The Supremes	#1	
When a Man Loves a Woman	Percy Sledge	#1	
Paint It, Black	The Rolling Stones	#1	
Summer in the City	The Lovin' Spoonful	#1	
We Can Work It Out	The Beatles	#1	
Winchester Cathedral	New Vaudeville Band	#1	
The Ballad of the Green Berets	SSgt. Barry Sadler	#1	
I'm a Believer	The Monkees	#1	
Bang Bang (My Baby Shot Me Down)	Cher	#2	
Red Rubber Ball	The Cyrkle	#2	
Did You Ever Have to Make Up Your Mind?	The Lovin' Spoonful	#2	
Snoopy Vs. the Red Baron	The Royal Guardsmen	#2	
Sloop John B.	The Beach Boys	#3	
No Matter What Shape (Your Stomach's In)	The T-Bones	#3	
I Am a Rock	Simon & Garfunkel	#3	
She's Just My Style	Gary Lewis/Playboys	#3	
That's Life	Frank Sinatra	#4	
The Pied Piper	Crispian St. Peters	#4	
Devil with a Blue Dress On & Good Golly Miss Molly	Mitch Ryder & The Detroit Wheels	#4	
Time Won't Let Me	The Outsiders	#5	
Hungry	Paul Revere & The Raiders	#6	
I'm Your Puppet	James & Bobby Purify	#6	
Don't Mess with Bill	The Marvelettes	#7	
Wouldn't It Be Nice	The Beach Boys	#8	
Sweet Pea	Tommy Roe	#8	

ORGAN (cont'd)

Title	Artist	#	
Sure Gonna Miss Her	Gary Lewis/Playboys	#9	
Jenny Take a Ride!	Mitch Ryder & The Detroit Wheels	#10	
See See Rider	Eric Burdon/Animals	#10	
Just Like Me	Paul Revere & The Raiders	#11	
Don't Bring Me Down	The Animals	#12	
Born a Woman	Sandy Posey	#12	
A Hazy Shade of Winter	Simon & Garfunkel	#13	
Sweet Dreams	Tommy McLain	#15	
Respectable	The Outsiders	#15	
Warm and Tender Love	Percy Sledge	#17	
Double Shot (Of My Baby's Love)	Swingin' Medallions	#17	14 sec.
Batman Theme	The Marketts	#17	
Little Latin Lupe Lu	Mitch Ryder & The Detroit Wheels	#17	
At the Scene	Dave Clark Five	#18	
How Sweet It Is (To Be Loved By You)	Jr. Walker/The All Stars	#18	
The Work Song	Herb Alpert & The Tijuana Brass	#18	
(I Washed My Hands in) Muddy Water	Johnny Rivers	#19	
Love Letters	Elvis Presley	#19	
The Little Girl I Once Knew	The Beach Boys	#20	
You Better Run	The Young Rascals	#20	
(I'm A) Road Runner	Jr. Walker/The All Stars	#20	
The Hair on My Chinny Chin Chin	Sam the Sham & The Pharaohs	#22	
I Need Somebody	? & The Mysterians	#22	
Mustang Sally	Wilson Pickett	#23	
Summer Wind	Frank Sinatra	#25	
Summer Samba (So Nice)	Walter Wanderley	#26	
I See the Light	The Five Americans	#26	
Searching for My Love	Bobby Moore & The Rhythm Aces	#27	
The "A" Team	SSgt. Barry Sandler	#28	
Help Me Girl	Eric Burdon/Animals	#29	
Pretty Flamingo	Manfredd Mann	#29	
It's Only Love	Tommy James & The Shondells	#31	
Let's Go Get Stoned	Ray Charles	#31	
The Rains Came	Sir Douglas Quintet	#31	
The Phoenix Love Theme (Senza Fine)	The Brass Ring	#32	
Just Like a Woman	Bob Dylan	#33	
Inside-Looking Out	The Animals	#34	
Billy and Sue	B.J. Thomas	#34	
Batman Theme	Neal Hefti	#35	
Help Me Girl	The Outsiders	#37	
Ain't That a Groove (Part 1)	James Brown	#42	
Come On Up	The Rascals	#43	
Sometimes Good Guys Don't Wear White	The Standells	#43	

ORGAN (cont'd)

5 D (Fifth Dimension)	The Byrds	#44	
Outside the Gates of Heaven	Lou Christie	#45	
She Blew a Good Thing	The Poets	#45	
Peter Rabbit	Dee Jay & The Runaways	#45	18 sec.
You're the One	The Marvelettes	#48	
The Philly Freeze	Alvin Cash & The Registers	#49	
Cleo's Mood	Jr. Walker/The All Stars	#50	
Spread It on Thick	The Gentrys	#50	
Got My Mojo Working (Part 1)	Jimmy Smith	#51	99 sec.
A Young Girl	Noel Harrison	#51	
Money (That's What I Want) Part 1	Jr. Walker/The All Stars	#52	
I Ain't Gonna Eat Out My Heart Anymore	The Young Rascals	#52	
Evol-Not Love	The Five Americans	#52	
Younger Girl	The Hondells	#52	
(You Make Me Feel) So Good	The McCoys	#53	
Money Won't Change You (Part 1)	James Brown	#53	
Lullaby of Love	The Poppies	#56	
Changes	Crispian St. Peters	#57	
This Can't Be True	Eddie Holman	#57	
Sippin' 'N Chippin'	The T-Bones	#62	
Break Out	Mitch Ryder & The Detroit Wheels	#62	
Said I Wasn't Gonna Tell Nobody	Sam & Dave	#64	
Teenager's Prayer	Joe Simon	#66	
I Believe I'm Gonna Make It	Joe Tex	#67	
Lonely Soldier	Mike Williams	#69	
The Teaser	Bob Kuban	#70	
Get Away	Georgie Fame	#70	
She Drives Me out of My Mind	Swingin' Medallions	#71	
Don't Answer the Door - Part 1	B.B. King	#72	
I Want Someone	The Mad Lads	#74	
Everyday I Have to Cry	The Gentrys	#77	
I Put a Spell on You	Alan Price Set	#80	24 sec.
I Confess	New Colony Six	#80	
The Loop	Johnny Lytle	#80	
Stop, Look and Listen	The Chiffons	#85	18 sec.
Pouring Water on a Drowning Man	James Carr	#85	
I'm Gonna Make You Love Me	Dee Dee Warwick	#88	
Moulty	The Barbarians	#90	
(He's) Raining in My Sunshine	Jay & The Americans	#90	
You're Just About to Lose Your Clown	Ray Charles	#91	
Bad Little Woman	The Shadows of Knight	#91	
Going Nowhere	Los Bravos	#91	
Count Down	Dave "Baby" Cortez	#91	

ORGAN (cont'd)

Bad Eye	Willie Mitchell	#92	
My Answer	Jimmy McCracklin	#92	
It's-A-Happening	The Magic Mushrooms	#93	
Drive My Car	Bob Kuban	#93	
The Boogaloo Party	The Flamingos	#93	
Yesterday Man	Chris Andrews	#94	
No Man Is an Island	The Van Dykes	#94	
The Big Hurt	Del Shannon	#94	
Superman	Dino, Desi & Billy	#94	
Stand in for Love	The O'Jays	#95	
Baby Come On Home	Solomon Burke	#96	
What Now My Love	"Groove" Holmes	#96	
Function at the Junction	Shorty Long	#97	
Peak of Love	Bobby McClure	#97	
Any Way That You Want Me	Liverpool Five	#98	
Baby I Love You	Jimmy Holiday	#98	
Secret Love	Richard "Groove" Holmes	#99	
Open Up Your Door	Richard & The Young Lions	#99	
Love Attack	James Carr	#99	
It Was a Very Good Year	Della Reese	#99	
Billy Stewart	Mountain of Love	#100	
Takin' All I Can Get	Mitch Ryder & The Detroit Wheels	#100	
Greetings (This Is Uncle Sam)	The Monitors	#100	
We Got the Winning Hand	Little Milton	#100	
1967			
Incense and Peppermints	Strawberry Alarm Clark	#1	
Kind of a Drag	The Buckinghams	#1	12 sec.
Respect	Aretha Franklin	#1	
Light My Fire	The Doors	#1	
The Letter	The Box Tops	#1	
A Little Bit Me, A Little Bit You	The Monkees	#2	11 sec.
Sweet Soul Music	Arthur Conley	#2	
Never My Love	The Association	#2	
Little Bit O' Soul	The Music Explosion	#2	
Expressway (To Your Heart)	Soul Survivors	#4	
I Think We're Alone Now	Tommy James & The Shondells	#4	
Western Union	The Five Americans	#5	
(We Ain't Got) Nothin' Yet	Blues Magoos	#5	
A Whiter Shade of Pale	Procol Harum	#5	28, 26, 23 sec.
Don't You Care	The Buckinghams	#6	
Then You Can Tell Me Goodbye	The Casinos	#6	14 sec.
The Beat Goes On	Sonny & Cher	#6	
Come on Down to My Boat	Every Mothers' Son	#6	

ORGAN (cont'd)

Song	Artist	Chart	Notes
Apples, Peaches, Pumpkin Pie	Jay & The Techniques	#6	
Please Love Me Forever	Bobby Vinton	#6	
You Got What It Takes	Dave Clark Five	#7	
Gimme Some Lovin'	Spencer Davis Group	#7	
98.6	Keith	#7	
Funky Broadway	Wilson Pickett	#8	
Gimme Little Sign	Brenton Wood	#9	20 sec.
I'm a Man	Spencer Davis Group	#10	
Mirage	Tommy James & The Shondells	#10	
Brown Eyed Girl	Van Morrison	#10	
Green, Green Grass of Home	Tom Jones	#11	
Mercy, Mercy, Mercy	"Cannonball" Adderley	#11	
Let It Out (Let It All Hang Out)	The Hombres	#12	
Hey Baby (They're Playing Our Song)	The Buckinghams	#12	
I Take It Back	Sandy Posey	#12	
My Mammy	The Happenings	#13	
Lazy Day	Spanky & Our Gang	#14	
Keep the Ball Rollin'	Jay & The Techniques	#14	
Society's Child (Baby I've Been Thinking)	Janis Ian	#14	
The Return of the Red Baron	The Royal Guardsmen	#15	
Here We Go Again	Ray Charles	#15	
I've Been Lonely Too Long	The Young Rascals	#16	
I Had a Dream	Paul Revere & The Raiders	#17	
Getting' Together	Tommy James & The Shondells	#18	
I Was Kaiser Bill's Batman	Whistling Jack Smith	#20	
(I'm Not Your) Steppin' Stone	The Monkees	#20	
(I Wanna) Testify	The Parliaments	#20	
Groovin'	Booker T. & The MG's	#21	
For Your Precious Love	Oscar Toney, Jr.	#23	
Wear Your Love Like Heaven	Donovan	#23	
Fakin' It	Simon & Garfunkel	#23	
Step out of Your Mind	The American Breed	#24	
Neon Rainbow	The Box Tops	#24	
Yellow Balloon	The Yellow Balloon	#25	
Try a Little Tenderness	Otis Redding	#25	
I Like the Way	Tommy James	#25	
Shake a Tail Feather	James & Bobby Purify	#25	
Beg, Borrow and Steal	Ohio Express	#29	
My Back Pages	The Byrds	#30	
Watch the Flowers Grow	The Four Seasons	#30	
Pucker Up Buttercup	Jr. Walker/The All Stars	#31	
Wild Honey	The Beach Boys	#31	
I Found a Love - Part 1	Wilson Pickett	#32	

ORGAN (cont'd)

In the Heat of the Night	Ray Charles	#33	
Memphis Soul Stew	King Curtis	#33	
Indescribably Blue	Elvis Presley	#33	
Homburg	Procol Harum	#34	
Baby You Got It	Brenton Wood	#34	
Paper Cup	The 5th Dimension	#35	
Zip Code	The Five Americans	#36	
The Dis-Advantages of You	The Brass Ring	#36	
You Were on My Mind	Crispian St. Peters	#36	
Sound of Love	The Five Americans	#36	
Walkin' in the Sunshine	Roger Miller	#37	18 sec.
Hip Hug-Her	Booker T. & The MG's	#37	
Ride, Ride, Ride	Brenda Lee	#37	10 sec.
Beautiful People	Bobby Vee	#37	
Don't Let the Rain Fall down on Me	The Critters	#39	
When Something Is Wrong with My Baby	Sam & Dave	#42	
The Loser (With a Broken Heart)	Gary Lewis/Playboys	#43	
I've Got to Have a Reason	Dave Clark Five	#44	
Rock 'N' Roll Woman	Buffalo Springfield	#44	
Shoot Your Shot	Jr. Walker/The All Stars	#44	
Ha Ha Said the Clown	The Yardbirds	#45	
I (Who Have Nothing)	Terry Knight	#46	
Airplane Song (My Airplane)	The Royal Guardsmen	#46	
Put Your Mind at Ease	Every Mothers' Son	#46	
Somebody Help Me	Spencer Davis Group	#47	
Take Me (Just as I Am)	Solomon Burke	#49	
Dear Eloise	The Hollies	#50	
Nothing Takes the Place of You	Toussaint McCall	#52	
This Town	Frank Sinatra	#53	
I Want to Love You for What You Are	Ronnie Dove	#54	
Woman Like That, Yeah	Joe Tex	#54	
Shout Bamalama	Mickey Murray	#54	
Soul Dance Number Three	Wilson Pickett	#55	
Let's Spend the Night Together	The Rolling Stones	#55	
Karate	The Emperor's	#55	
Can't Get Enough of You, Baby	? & The Mysterians	#56	
Mercy, Mercy, Mercy	Marlena Shaw	#58	
Are You Never Coming Home	Sandy Posey	#59	
Pipe Dream	Blues Magoos	#60	
Live	Merry-Go-Round	#63	
Sunshine Games	The Music Explosion	#63	
It's Got to Be Mellow	Leon Haywood	#63	
Keep a Light in the Window Till I Come Home	Solomon Burke	#64	

ORGAN (cont'd)

Title	Artist	#	Notes
Funky Broadway Part 1	Dyke & The Blazers	#65	
Turn on Your Love Light	Oscar Toney, Jr.	#65	
The People in Me	The Music Machine	#66	
For He's a Jolly Good Fellow	Bobby Vinton	#66	
Just Out of Reach (Of My Two Empty Arms)	Percy Sledge	#66	
Stay Together Young Lovers	Brenda & The Tabulations	#66	
You Keep Me Hangin' On	The Vanilla Fudge	#67	
Dirty Man	Laura Lee	#68	
Black Sheep	Sam The Sham & The Pharaohs	#68	
My World Fell Down	Sagittarius	#70	
You Can't Stand Alone	Wilson Pickett	#70	10 sec.
Slim Jenkin's Place	Booker T. & The MG's	#70	
Nine Pound Steel	Joe Simon	#70	
That Acapulco Gold	The Rainy Daze	#70	
Sockin' 1-2-3-4	John Roberts	#71	
One by One	Blues Magoos	#71	
A Thousand Shadows	The Seeds	#72	
Whole Lotta Woman	Arthur Conley	#73	
Why? (Am I Treated So Bad)	"Cannonball" Adderley	#73	
Dancing in the Street	Mamas & Papas	#73	
Knucklehead	Bar-Kays	#76	
One Hurt Deserves Another	The Raeletts	#76	
You Got Me Hummin'	Sam & Dave	#77	
The Dark End of the Street	James Carr	#77	
They're Here	Boots Walker	#77	
I'll Do It for You	Toussaint McCall	#77	
Can't Stop Loving You	The Last Word	#78	
Go with Me	Gene & Debbe	#78	
Daylight Savin' Time	Keith	#79	
Raise Your Hand	Eddie Floyd	#79	
All Your Goodies are Gone (The Loser's Seat)	The Parliaments	#80	
There's a Chance We Can Make It	Blues Magoos	#81	
Leopard-Skin Pill-Box Hat	Bob Dylan	#81	
I Dig Girls	J.J. Jackson	#83	
I'll Always Have Faith in You	Carla Thomas	#85	
Nearer to You	Betty Harris	#85	20, 10 sec.
It Could Be We're in Love	The Cryan' Shames	#85	
Lovey Dovey/You're So Fine	Bunny Sigler	#86	
Full Measure	The Lovin' Spoonful	#87	
No Good to Cry	The Wildweeds	#88	
Heart Be Still	Lorraine Ellison	#89	
Red and Blue	Dave Clark Five	#89	

ORGAN (cont'd)

Sweet Soul Medley - Part 1	The Magnificent Men	#90	
Why Not Tonight	Jimmy Hughes	#90	
Mr. Bus Driver	Bruce Channel	#90	
Where Is the Party	Helena Ferguson	#90	
Sing Along with Me	Tommy Roe	#91	
What am I Living For	Percy Sledge	#91	
Why (Am I Treated so Bad)	Bobby Powell	#91	
Get the Message	Brian Hyland	#91	
Give Everybody Some	The Bar-Kays	#91	
Believe in Me - Part 1	Jesse James	#92	
On a Saturday Night	Eddie Floyd	#92	
Peas 'N' Rice	Freddie McCoy	#92	
Walk Tall	2 of Clubs	#92	
Temptation	Boots Randolph	#93	
A Letter to Dad	Every Father's Teenage Son	#93	
Alligator Bogaloo	Lou Donaldson	#93	
I Can't Help It (If I'm Still in Love with You)	B.J. Thomas	#94	
Let It Be Me	The Sweet Inspirations	#94	
The Jungle	B.B. King	#94	
Penny Arcade	The Cyrkle	#95	
Shake Hands and Walk Away Cryin'	Lou Christie	#95	
Who Do You Love	The Woolies	#95	
Different Strokes	Syl Johnson	#95	
Not So Sweet Martha Lorraine	Country Joe & The Fish	#95	
Make Love to Me	Johnny Thunder & Ruby Winters	#96	
No Time Like the Right Time	The Blues Project	#96	13 sec.
Slippin' & Slidin'	Willie Mitchell	#96	
96 Tears	Big Maybelle	#96	
Mercy, Mercy, Mercy	Larry Williams & Johnny Watson	#96	
The Jokers	Peter & Gordon	#97	
My Old Car	Lee Dorsey	#97	14 sec.
Devil's Angels	Davie Allan/The Arrows	#97	
Just Once in a Lifetime	Brenda & The Tabulations	#97	
I'm a Fool for You	James Carr	#97	
Girl (You Captivate Me)	? & The Mysterians	#98	
For Me	Sergio Mendes & Brasil '66	#98	
Mellow Yellow	Senator Bobby & Senator McKinley	#99	
Little Miss Sunshine	Tommy Roe	#99	
Drums	Jon & Robin	#100	
1968			
Tighten Up	Archie Bell & The Drells	#1	
People Got to Be Free	The Rascals	#1	
I Heart It Through the Grapevine	Marvin Gaye	#1	

ORGAN (cont'd)

Title	Artist	Chart	Duration
Fire	Arthur Brown	#2	
Cry Like a Baby	The Box Tops	#2	
Magic Carpet Ride	Steppenwolf	#3	
Hush	Deep Purple	#4	66 sec.
Simon Says	1910 Fruitgum Co.	#4	13 sec.
Midnight Confessions	The Grass Roots	#5	
Just Dropped In (To See What Condition My Condition Was In)	The First Edition/Kenny Rogers	#5	
1, 2, 3, Red Light	1910 Fruitgum Co.	#5	
Girl Watcher	The O'Kaysions	#5	
Slip Away	Clarence Carter	#6	
The House That Jack Built	Aretha Franklin	#6	
Think	Aretha Franklin	#7	
Dance to the Music	Sly & The Family Stone	#8	
Nobody but Me	The Human Beinz	#8	
I Can't Stop Dancing	Archie Bell & The Drells	#9	
Do You Know the Way to San Jose	Dionne Warwick	#10	
Take Time to Know Her	Percy Sledge	#11	
Chewy Chewy	Ohio Express	#15	
Scarborough Fair	Sergio Mendes & Brasil '66	#16	
Soul-Limbo	Booker T. & The MG's	#17	
My Baby Must Be a Magician	The Marvelettes	#17	
Bring It on Home to Me	Eddie Floyd	#17	
Playboy	Gene & Debbe	#17	
Too Much Talk	Paul Revere & The Raiders	#19	
Never Give You Up	Jerry Butler	#20	
Halfway to Paradise	Bobby Vinton	#23	
Tomorrow	Strawberry Alarm Clock	#23	
Soul Serenade	Willie Mitchell	#23	
Will You Love Me Tomorrow	The Four Seasons	#24	
Special Occasion	Smokey Robinson & The Miracles	#26	
Don't Take It so Hard	Paul Revere & The Raiders	#27	
In-A-Gadda-Da-Vida	Iron Butterfly	#30	
Goodbye My Love	James Brown	#31	
Hip City - Pt. 2	Jr. Walker	#31	
Explosion (In My Soul)	Soul Survivors	#33	
I Get the Sweetest Feeling	Jackie Wilson	#34	
I Met Her in Church	The Box Tops	#37	
Do Something to Me	Tommy James & The Shondells	#38	
Kentucky Woman	Deep Purple	#38	74 sec.
Take Me for a Little While	Vanilla Fudge	#38	
Paying the Cost to Be the Boss	B.B. King	#39	
The Funky Judge	Bull & The Matadors	#39	

ORGAN (cont'd)

Green Light	The American Breed	#39	
I've Got Dreams to Remember	Otis Redding	#41	
Back Up Train	Al Greene & The Soul Mate's *also listed as Soul Mates	#41	
Cover Me	Percy Sledge	#42	
A Man and a Half	Wilson Pickett	#42	
I Can't Dance to That Music You're Playin'	Martha & The Vandellas	#42	
Poor Baby	The Cowsills	#44	
Here I Am Baby	The Marvelettes	#44	
Suddenly You Love Me	The Tremeloes	#44	
And Suddenly	The Cherry People	#45	
Prayer Meetin'	Willie Mitchell	#45	
Shake	Shadows of Knight	#46	
Understanding	Ray Charles	#46	
Peace Brother Peace	Bill Medley	#48	
Get Out Now	Tommy James & The Shondells	#48	
Jealous Love	Wilson Pickett	#50	
For Your Precious Love	Jackie Wilson & Count Basie	#50	
Bring a Little Lovin'	Los Bravos	#51	
Sherry Don't Go	The Lettermen	#52	
Can't You See Me Cry	The New Colony Six	#52	
Unwind	Ray Stevens	#52	
Fire	Five by Five	#52	
Goodbye Baby (I Don't Want to See You Cry)	Tommy Boyce & Bobby Hart	#53	
Here Come the Judge	The Magistrates	#54	
Slow Drag	The Intruders	#54	
Peace of Mind	Nancy Wilson	#55	
Smell of Incense	Southwest F.O.B.	#56	
You Send Me	Aretha Franklin	#56	
Hey Hey Bunny	John Fred	#57	
I Ain't Got to Love Nobody Else	The Masqueraders	#57	
I'm Coming Home	Tom Jones	#57	
Cinderella Sunshine	Paul Revere & The Raiders	#58	
Back on My Feet Again	The Foundations	#59	
We're Rolling On (Part 1)	The Impressions	#59	
You've Still Got a Place in My Heart	Dean Martin	#60	
Looking for a Fox	Clarence Carter	#62	
Porpoise Song	The Monkees	#62	
May I Take a Giant Step (Into Your Heart)	1910 Fruitgum Co.	#63	12 sec.
Sudden Stop	Percy Sledge	#63	
A Man Needs a Woman	James Carr	#63	
Season of the Witch, Pt. 1	Vanilla Fudge	#65	
I Walk Alone	Marty Robbins	#65	11 sec.

ORGAN (cont'd)

Sit with the Guru	Strawberry Alarm Clock	#65	
Two-Bit Manchild	Neil Diamond	#66	
Cold Feet	Albert King	#67	
Barefoot in Baltimore	Strawberry Alarm Clock	#67	
With a Little Help from My Friends	Joe Cocker	#68	
I Wish I Knew (How It Would Feel to be Free)	Solomon Burke	#68	
I Got You Babe	Etta James	#69	
Mrs. Bluebird	Eternity's Children	#69	
Don't Cry My Love	The Impressions	#71	
I Say Love	The Royal Guardsmen	#72	
Funky Way	Calvin Arnold	#72	
Tin Soldier	Small Faces	#73	
Where Is My Mind	The Vanilla Fudge	#73	
Happy	Nancy Sinatra	#74	15 sec.
I'm Gonna Do What They Do to Me	B.B. King	#74	
You Ain't Going Nowhere	The Byrds	#74	
Night Fo' Last	Shorty Long	#75	
Message from Maria	Joe Simon	#75	
Love Machine	The O'Kaysions	#76	
Hitchcock Railway	Jose Feliciano	#77	
Mr. Bojangles	Jerry Jeff Walker	#77	
United (Part 1)	The Music Makers	#78	
Reach Out	Merrilee Rush	#79	
Don't Make the Good Girls Go Bad	Della Humphrey	#79	
A Voice in the Choir	Al Martino	#80	
Give Me One More Chance	Wilmer & The Dukes	#80	
Unchain My Heart	Herbie Mann	#81	
Lovin' Season	Gene & Debbe	#81	
Release Me	Johnny Adams	#82	
You Put It on Me	B.B. King	#82	
Turn On Your Love Light	Bill Black's Combo	#82	
Try It	Ohio Express	#83	
I Heard It Thru the Grapevine	King Curtis & Kingpins	#83	
Soulville	Aretha Franklin	#83	
Do What You Gotta Do	Nina Simone	#83	
Chain Gang	Jackie Wilson & Count Basie	#84	
In Another Land	Bill Wyman	#87	
Funky Fever	Clarence Carter	#88	
You Got the Love	Professor Morrison's Lollipop	#88	
Show Time	Detroit Emeralds	#89	
Nitty Gritty	Ricardo Ray	#90	
Without Love (There Is Nothing)	Oscar Toney, Jr.	#90	
Don't Pat Me on the Back and Call Me Brother	KaSandra	#91	

ORGAN (cont'd)

Up-Hard	Willie Mitchell	#91	
Love Explosion	Troy Keyes	#92	
Mellow Moonlight	Leon Haywood	#92	
M'Lady	Sly & The Family Stone	#93	
Up Tight, Good Man	Laura Lee	#93	
Harper Valley P.T.A.	King Curtis & Kingpins	#93	
Life	Sly & The Family Stone	#93	
Help Yourself (To All of My Lovin')	James & Bobby Purify	#94	
Sally Had a Party	Flavor	#95	
Golden Gate Park	Rejoice!	#96	
Driftin' Blues	Bobby Bland	#96	
The Worm	Jimmy McGriff	#97	
I Worry About You	Joe Simon	#98	
The B.B. Jones	B.B. King	#98	
Dear Delilah	Grapefruit	#98	
Chain of Fools (Part 1)	Jimmy Smith	#100	30, 29 sec.
A Whiter Shade of Pale	The Hesitations	#100	
1969			
Suspicious Minds	Elvis Presley	#1	
Na Na Hey Hey Kiss Him Goodbye	Steam	#1	
Come Together/Something	The Beatles	#1	
You've Made Me So Very Happy	Blood, Sweat & Tears	#2	
Crystal Blue Persuasion	Tommy James & The Shondells	#2	
Time of the Season	The Zombies	#3	49, 27 sec.
Worst That Could Happen	Brooklyn Bridge	#3	
Build Me Up Buttercup	The Foundations	#3	
What Does It Take (To Win Your Love)	Jr. Walker/The All Stars	#4	
Easy to Be Hard	Three Dog Night	#4	
Indian Giver	1910 Fruitgum Co.	#5	15 sec.
Baby It's You	Smith	#5	
Holly Holy	Neil Diamond	#6	
Time Is Tight	Booker T. & The MG's	#6	
Run Away Child, Running Wild	The Temptations	#6	
Sweet Cherry Wine	Tommy James & The Shondells	#7	
Lay Lady Lay	Bob Dylan	#7	
Hang 'Em High	Booker T. & The MG's	#9	
Tracy	The Cuff Links	#9	
Polk Salad Annie	Tony Joe White	#9	
Backfield in Motion	Mel & Tim	#10	
Eli's Coming	Three Dog Night	#10	
Gimme Gimme Good Lovin'	Crazy Elephant	#12	
Games People Play	Joe South	#12	
If I Can Dream	Elvis Presley	#12	

ORGAN (cont'd)

The Chokin' Kind	Joe Simon	#13	
Lo Mucho Que Te Quiero (The More I Love You)	Rene & Rene	#14	26 sec.
Cherry Hill Park	Billy Joe Royal	#15	
I'd Wait a Million Years	The Grass Roots	#15	
Keem-O-Sabe	The Electric Indian	#16	
Eleanor Rigby	Aretha Franklin	#17	
Ramblin' Gamblin' Man	Bob Seger System	#17	
When I Die	Motherlode	#18	
Ball of Fire	Tommy James & The Shondells	#19	
Don't Let the Joneses Get You Down	The Temptations	#20	
Stand	Sly & The Family Stone	#22	
Medicine Man (Part I)	Buchanan Brothers	#22	
Sugar on Sunday	The Clique	#22	
Brother Love's Travelling Salvation Show	Neil Diamond	#22	
Cissy Strut	The Meters	#23	
Hey Jude	Wilson Pickett	#23	
A Ray of Hope	The Rascals	#24	
Heaven Knows	The Grass Roots	#24	
Birthday	Underground Sunshine	#26	
See	The Rascals	#27	
Mendocino	Sir Douglas Quintet	#27	21 sec.
Marrakesh Express	Crosby, Stills & Nash	#28	
Jesus Is a Soul Man	Lawrence Reynolds	#28	
Try a Little Tenderness	Three Dog Night	#29	
Mercy	Ohio Express	#30	
The Popcorn	James Brown	#30	
Walk on By	Isaac Hayes	#30	
My Song	Aretha Franklin	#31	
In a Moment	The Intrigues	#31	
Move Over	Steppenwolf	#31	
Sophisticated Cissy	The Meters	#34	
Is It Something You've Got	Tyrone Davis	#34	
Don't Let Me Down	The Beatles	#35	
Baby Let's Wait	The Royal Guardsmen	#35	
Mrs. Robinson	Booker T. & The MG's	#37	
By the Time I Get to Phoenix	Isaac Hayes	#37	
May I	Bill Deal/The Rhondels	#39	
Heaven	The Rascals	#39	
Lowdown Popcorn	James Brown	#41	
Kozmic Blues	Janis Joplin	#41	
Muddy River	Johnny Rivers	#41	
Home Cookin'	Jr. Walker/The All Stars	#42	
Roosevelt and Ira Lee (Night of the Mossacin)	Tony Joe White	#44	

ORGAN (cont'd)

Don't Let Love Hang You Up	Jerry Butler	#44
Blessed Is the Rain	The Brooklyn Bridge	#45
Apricot Brandy	Rhinoceros	#46
Condition Red	The Goodees	#46
Welcome Me Love	The Brooklyn Bridge	#48
Rainbow Ride	Andy Kim	#49
When He Touches Me (Nothing Else Matters)	Peaches & Herb	#49
Lovin' Things	The Grassroots	#49
We Gotta All Get Together	Paul Revere & The Raiders	#50
You'll Never Walk Alone	The Brooklyn Bridge	#51
You Don't Have to Walk in the Rain	The Turtles	#51
Feelin' So Good (S.k.o.o.b.y.-D.o.o)	The Archies	#53
Love of the Common People	The Winstons	#54
Mah-Na-Mah-Na	Piero Umiliani	#55
Jingo	Santana	#56
Who's Making Love	Young-Holt Unlimited	#57
The Train	1910 Fruitgum Co.	#57
Turn On a Dream	The Box Tops	#58
Hey Joe	Wilson Pickett	#59
Ice Cream Song	The Dynamics	#59
Ease Back	The Meters	#61
Maybe the Rain Will Fall	The Cascades	#61
Son of a Lovin' Man	Buchanan Brothers	#61
That's the Way God Planned It	Billy Preston	#62
I Do	The Moments	#62
Listen to the Band	The Monkees	#63
I'll Bet You	Funkadelic	#63
Born to Be Wild	Wilson Pickett	#64
Runnin' Blue	The Doors	#64
Just Ain't No Love	Barbara Acklin	#67
Shotgun	Vanilla Fudge	#68
Witchi Tai To	Everything Is Everything	#69
30-60-90	Willie Mitchell	#69
Silver Threads and Golden Needles	The Cowsills	#74
The Prophecy of Daniel and John the Divine (Six-Six-Six)	The Cowsills	#75
Soul Experience	Iron Butterfly	#75
He Called Me Baby	Ella Washington	#77
Long Line Rider	Bobby Darin	#79
Almost Persuaded	Etta James	#79
The Grooviest Girl in the World	Fun & Games	#79
Mr. Walker, It's All Over	Billie Jo Spears	#80
Back in the U.S.S.R.	Chubby Checker	#82
She's Got Love	Thomas & Richard Frost	#83

ORGAN (cont'd)

Theme from "A Summer Place"	The Ventures	#83	
I Threw It All Away	Bob Dylan	#85	
No Not Much	The Smoke Ring	#85	18 sec.
Good Morning Starshine	Strawberry Alarm Clark	#87	
Slum Baby	Booker T. & The MG's	#88	
Wonderful	Blackwell	#89	
Sing a Simple Song	Sly & The Family Stone	#89	
Voodoo Woman	Simon Stokes	#90	
Love in the City	The Turtles	#91	
All I Have to Offer You (Is Me)	Charley Pride	#91	
You Keep Me Hanging On	Wilson Pickett	#92	
Let's Dance	Ola & The Janglers	#92	18 sec.
No One Better Than You	Petula Clark	#93	
How I Miss You Baby	Bobby Womack	#93	
That's the Way	Joe Tex	#94	
Ain't Got No; I Got Life	Nina Simone	#94	
All God's Children Got Soul	Dorothy Morrison	#95	
Everything I Do Gonh Be Funky (From Now On)	Lee Dorsey	#95	
Theme from Electric Surfboard	Brother Jack McDuff	#95	
In the Time of Our Lives	Iron Butterfly	#96	
Ivory	Bob Seger System	#97	
Just a Little Bit	Little Milton	#97	
Something's On her Mind	The Four Seasons	#98	
My Little Chickadee	The Foundations	#99	
Guess Who	Ruby Winters	#99	
Memphis Train	Buddy Miles	#100	
Camel Back	A.B. Skhy	#100	

PIANO

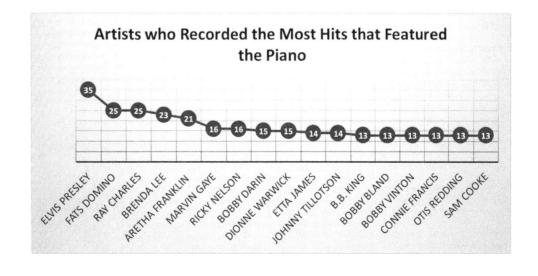

SONG	ARTIST	HOT 100	LENGTH OF SOLO
1960			
Georgia On My Mind	Ray Charles	#1	
I'm Sorry	Brenda Lee	#1	
Stuck on You	Elvis Presley	#1	
It's Now or Never	Elvis Presley	#1	
Theme from "A Summer Place"	Percy Faith	#1	
He'll Have to Go	Jim Reeves	#2	
Puppy Love	Paul Anka	#2	
Last Date	Floyd Cramer	#2	
Sixteen Reasons	Connie Stevens	#3	
Burning Bridges	Jack Scott	#3	
He'll Have to Stay	Jeanne Black	#4	
Walking to New Orleans	Fats Domino	#6	
Many Tears Ago	Connie Francis	#7	
Alone at Last	Jackie Wilson	#8	
Yogi	The Ivy Three	#8	
Please Help Me, I'm Falling	Hank Locklin	#8	16 sec.
I Love the Way You Love	Marv Johnson	#9	
Forever	The Little Dippers	#9	
Theme from "The Apartment"	Ferrante & Teicher	#10	
Summer's Gone	Paul Anka	#11	
Pineapple Princess	Annette	#11	
Young Emotions	Ricky Nelson	#12	
My Girl Josephine	Fats Domino	#14	
Three Nights a Week	Fats Domino	#15	
Doggin' Around	Jackie Wilson	#15	
Not One Minute More	Della Reese	#16	
Fame and Fortune	Elvis Presley	#17	
Smokie - Part 2	Bill Black's Combo	#17	
Diamonds and Pearls	The Paradons	#18	
Won't You Come Home Bill Bailey	Bobby Darin	#19	25 sec.
I Gotta Know	Elvis Presley	#20	
Last Date	Lawrence Welk	#21	
Lucille	The Everly Brothers	#21	
Clementine	Bobby Darin	#21	
Another Sleepless Night	Jimmy Clanton	#22	
Lonely Weekends	Charlie Rich	#22	
Rockin' Little Angel	Ray Smith	#22	
The Madison	Al Brown	#23	
Money (That's What I Want)	Barrett Strong	#23	
Hello Young Lovers	Paul Anka	#23	

PIANO (cont'd)

Got a Girl	The Four Preps	#24	
Am I That Easy to Forget	Debbie Reynolds	#25	
What Am I Living For	Conway Twitty	#26	
Mack the Knife	Ella Fitzgerald	#27	
Jump Over	Freddy Cannon	#28	
Ooh Poo Pah Doo Part II	Jessie Hill	#28	
The Twist	Hank Ballard & The Midnighters	#28	
Barbara	The Temptations	#29	
Sad Mood	Sam Cooke	#29	
When You Wish Upon a Star	Dion & The Belmonts	#30	
Time and the River	Nat "King" Cole	#30	
The Madison Time - Part 1	Ray Bryant Combo	#30	
Is There Any Chance	Marty Robbins	#31	
There's Something on Your Mind (Part 2)	Bobby Marchan	#31	
A Mess of Blues	Elvis Presley	#32	
All I Could Do Was Cry	Etta James	#33	
My Dearest Darling	Etta James	#34	
Yes Sir, That's My Baby	Ricky Nelson	#34	
Theme for Young Lovers	Percy Faith	#35	
Little Things Mean a Lot	Joni James	#35	
Don't Go to Strangers	Etta James	#36	
Run Red Run	The Coasters	#36	
Let's Have a Party	Wanda Jackson	#37	
Natural Born Lover	Fats Domino	#38	
(I Can't Help You) I'm Falling Too	Skeeter Davis	#39	20 sec.
Something Happened	Paul Anka	#41	
Whole Lotta Shakin' Goin' On	Chubby Checker	#42	
I Missed Me	Jim Reeves	#44	
Walking the Floor Over You	Pat Boone	#44	
Don't Fence Me In	Tommy Edwards	#45	
Clap Your Hands	The Beau-Marks	#45	
Paradise	Sammy Turner	#46	
(New In) The Ways of Love	Tommy Edwards	#47	
Walk Slow	Little Willie John	#48	
Teenage Sonata	Sam Cooke	#50	
Spring Rain	Pat Boone	#50	
Tell Me That You Love Me	Fats Domino	#51	
If I Can't Have You	Etta James & Harvey Fuqua	#52	
We Go Together	Jan and Dean	#53	
Honey Hush	Joe Turner	#53	
Please Help Me, I'm Falling	Rusty Draper	#54	18 sec.
Chattanooga Choo Choo	Ernie Fields	#54	
No Love Have I	Webb Pierce	#54	

PIANO (cont'd)

Title	Artist	Page	Time
Hardhearted Hannah	Ray Charles	#55	16, 22 sec.
Temptation	Roger Williams	#56	
Send Me the Pillow You Dream On	The Browns	#56	
Put Your Arms Around Me	Fats Domino	#58	
Alley-Oop	The Dyna-Sores	#59	
Humdinger	Freddy Cannon	#59	
Pink Chiffon	Mitchell Torok	#60	
A Cottage for Sale	Little Willie John	#63	
Come Back	Jimmy Clanton	#63	
Let It Rock	Chuck Berry	#64	17 sec.
Clementine	Jan & Dean	#65	
Have Mercy Baby	The Bobbettes	#66	
Is It Wrong (For Loving You)	Webb Pierce	#69	
And Now	Della Reese	#69	
Theme from "The Dark at the Top of the Stairs"	Ernie Freeman	#70	
Cry Cry Cry	Bobby Bland	#71	
Up Town	Roy Orbison	#72	
Teensville	Chet Atkins	#73	
The Old Oaken Bucket	Tommy Sands	#73	
No	Dodie Stevens	#73	
That's How Much	Brian Hyland	#74	
Mio Amore	The Flamingos	#74	
Gloria's Theme	Adam Wade	#74	26 sec.
The Big Time Spender (Parts I & II)	Cornbread & Biscuits	#75	
Night Theme	The Mark II	#75	
We Have Love	Dinah Washington	#76	
Tonight's the Night	The Chiffons	#76	
How High the Moon (Part 1)	Ella Fitzgerald	#76	
Second Honeymoon	Johnny Cash	#79	
The Christmas Song (Merry Christmas to You)	Nat "King" Cole	#80	14 sec.
Since I Met You Baby	Bobby Vee	#81	
In the Still of the Nite	The Five Satins	#81	
Journey of Love	The Crests	#81	
I Idolize You	Ike & Tina Turner	#82	
Shortnin' Bread	Paul Chaplain and His Emeralds	#82	
Forever	Billy Walker	#83	
Wheel of Fortune	LaVern Baker	#83	
Happy Shades of Love	Freddie Cannon	#83	
Down the Street to 301	Johnny Cash	#84	
Before I Grow Too Old	Fats Domino	#84	
Straight A's in Love	Johnny Cash	#84	
Blue Velvet	The Statues	#84	
My Little Marine	Jamie Horton	#84	

PIANO (cont'd)

The Lovin' Touch	Mark Dinning	#84	
Many a Wonderful Moment	Rosemary Clooney	#84	
Don't Let Love Pass Me By	Frankie Avalon	#85	
Rockin', Rollin' Ocean	Hank Snow	#87	
You Talk Too Much	Frankie Ford	#87	
I've Been Loved Before	Shirley & Lee	#88	
Over the Mountain; Across the Sea	Johnnie & Joe	#89	
I'll Take Care of You	Bobby Bland	#89	
Whip It On Me	Jessie Hill	#91	
Kissin' And Twistin'	Fabian	#91	
Harmony	Billy Bland	#91	
Wait	Jimmy Clanton	#91	
Honky-Tonk Girl	Johnny Cash	#92	
Watcha' Gonna Do	Nat "King" Cole	#92	
Talk to Me Baby	Annette	#92	
Nobody Knows You When You're Down and Out	Nina Simone	#93	
(Doin' The) Lovers Leap	Webb Pierce	#93	
Sweet Dreams	Don Gibson	#93	
A Closer Walk	Pete Fountain	#93	
Words	Pat Boone	#94	
Child of God	Bobby Darin	#95	
Don't Let the Sun Catch You Cryin'	Ray Charles	#95	33 sec.
Shortnin' Bread	The Bell Notes	#96	
Livin' Dangerously	The McGuire Sisters	#97	
Blue Christmas	The Browns	#97	
La Montana (If She Should Come to You)	Roger Williams	#98	
She's Mine	Conway Twitty	#98	11 sec.
If You Need Me	Fats Domino	#98	
She's Just A Whole Lot Like You	Hank Thompson	#99	
Let Them Talk	Little Willie John	#100	
Beachcomber	Bobby Darin	#100	
1961			
Mother-In-Law	Ernie K-Doe	#1	29 sec.
Moody River	Pat Boone	#1	
Mr. Postman	The Marvelettes	#1	
Surrender	Elvis Presley	#1	
Travelin' Man	Ricky Nelson	#1	
Runaway	Del Shannon	#1	
Exodus	Ferrante & Teicher	#2	
I Like It Like That (Part 1)	Chris Kenner	#2	
The Boll Weevil Song	Brook Benton	#2	
My True Story	The Jive Five	#3	
Fool 1	Brenda Lee	#3	

PIANO (cont'd)

Song	Artist	Rank	Time
Don't Worry	Marty Robbins	#3	
(Marie's the Name) His Latest Flame	Elvis Presley	#4	
Hurt	Timi Yuri	#4	
But I Do	Clarence Henry	#4	
Calendar Girl	Neil Sedaka	#4	14 sec.
Where the Boys Are	Connie Francis	#4	
On the Rebound	Floyd Cramer	#4	
I Feel So Bad	Elvis Presley	#5	
Angel Baby	Rosie & The Originals	#5	
The Writing on the Wall	Adam Wade	#5	
Every Beat of My Heart	Pips	#6	
This Time	Troy Shondell	#6	22 sec.
You Can Depend On Me	Brenda Lee	#6	
Heartaches	The Marcels	#7	
Without You	Johnny Tillotson	#7	
Ya Ya	Lee Dorsey	#7	
The Fly	Chubby Checker	#7	
Emotions	Brenda Lee	#7	
San Antonio Rose	Floyd Cramer	#8	
Tonight	Ferrante & Teicher	#8	
Asia Minor	Kokomo	#8	
Let's Get Together	Hayley Mills	#8	
Portrait of My Love	Steve Lawrence	#9	
Crazy	Patsy Cline	#9	
Those Oldies but Goodies (Remind Me of You)	Little Caesar & The Romans	#9	
Gee Whiz (Look at His Eyes)	Carla Thomas	#10	
As If I Didn't Know	Adam Wade	#10	
A Wonder Like You	Ricky Nelson	#11	
Think Twice	Brook Benton	#11	
You're the Reason	Bobby Edwards	#11	
I'm Gonna Knock on Your Door	Eddie Hodges	#12	
I Don't Know Why	Linda Scott	#12	
Please Love Me Forever	Cathy Jean/Roommates	#12	
I Fall to Pieces	Patsy Cline	#12	
Wings of a Dove	Ferlin Husky	#12	
Hello Walls	Faron Young	#12	
The Way You Look Tonight	The Lettermen	#13	
(He's My) Dreamboat	Connie Francis	#14	
Lazy River	Bobby Darin	#14	
Tonight I Fell in Love	The Tokens	#15	
Let the Four Winds Blow	Fats Domino	#15	
Sweets for My Sweets	The Drifters	#16	
Everlovin'	Ricky Nelson	#16	

PIANO (cont'd)

I Just Don't Understand	Ann-Margret	#17	
I'm Comin on Back to You	Jackie Wilson	#19	
Big Cold Wind	Pat Boone	#19	
Please Tell Me Why	Jackie Wilson	#20	
Let Me Belong to You	Brian Hyland	#20	
Peanut Butter	The Marathons	#20	
Frankie and Johnny	Brook Benton	#20	
Sea of Heartbreak	Don Gibson	#21	
Baby Oh Baby	The Shells	#21	
Bumble Boogie	B. Bumble and The Stingers	#21	
What a Party	Fats Domino	#22	
One Summer Night	The Diamonds	#22	
What a Price	Fats Domino	#22	
It's Keep Rainin'	Fats Domino	#23	
Little Egypt (Ying-Yang)	The Coasters	#23	
September in the Rain	Dinah Washington	#23	
I'm A Fool to Care	Joe Barry	#24	
Just Out of Reach (Of My Two Open Arms)	Solomon Burke	#24	
Heart and Soul	Jan & Dean	#25	
The Watusi	The Vibrations	#25	
You Are the Only One	Ricky Nelson	#25	
Jimmy's Girl	Johnny Tillotson	#25	
Take Five	Dave Brubeck Quartet	#25	
Foot Stomping - Part 1	The Flares	#25	
Funny	Maxine Brown	#25	
My Last Date (With You)	Skeeter Davis	#26	
I'm Hurtin'	Roy Orbison	#27	
For My Baby	Brook Benton	#28	
Missing You	Ray Peterson	#29	18 sec.
Princess	Frank Gari	#30	
What'd I Say	Jerry Lee Lewis	#30	
Trust in Me	Etta James	#30	
Lover's Island	The Blue Jays	#31	
Lonely Man	Elvis Presley	#32	
Fell in Love On Monday	Fats Domino	#32	
Shu Rah	Fats Domino	#32	
I Don't Want to Take a Chance	Mary Wells	#33	
Ain't That Just Like a Woman	Fats Domino	#33	
I'm Learning About Love	Brenda Lee	#33	
No One	Connie Francis	#34	
Lost Love	H.B. Barnum	#35	
Three Hearts in a Tangle	Roy Drusky	#35	
Count Every Star	Donnie & The Dreamers	#35	

PIANO (cont'd)

Title	Artist	Page
Exodus	Eddie Harris	#36
Love Theme from "One Eyed Jacks"	Ferrante & Teicher	#37
Jura (I Swear I Love You)	Les Paul & Mary Ford	#37
Rock-a-Bye Your Baby with a Dixie Melody	Aretha Franklin	#37
Like, Long Hair	Paul Revere & The Raiders	#38
My Last Date (With You)	Joni James	#38
I'm in the Mood for Love	The Chimes	#38
Better Tell Him No	The Starlets	#38
Please Don't Go	Ral Donner	#39
Don't Cry, Baby	Etta James	#39
Water Boy	Don Shirley Trio	#40
Don't Believe Him, Donna	Lenny Miles	#41
Movin'	Bill Black's Combo	#41
Soothe Me	Sims Twins	#42
Up A Lazy River	Si Zentner	#43
Underwater	The Frogmen	#44
It's Just a House Without You	Brook Benton	#45
Every Beat of My Heart	Gladys Knight & The Pips	#45
Under the Moon of Love	Curtis Lee	#46
(It Never Happens) In Real Life	Chuck Jackson	#46
San-Ho-Zay	Freddy King	#47
I Don't Mind	James Brown	#47
The Age for Love	Jimmy Charles	#47
Human	Tommy Hunt	#48
To Be Loved (Forever)	The Pentagons	#48
Baby, You're Right	James Brown	#49
Magic Moon (Clair de Lune)	The Rays	#49
Glory of Love	The Roommates	#49
Foolin' Around	Kay Starr	#49
You'd Better Come Home	Russel Byrd	#50
My Blue Heaven	Duane Eddy	#50
Fool That I Am	Etta James	#50
Baby You're So Fine	Mickey & Sylvia	#52
Te-Ta-Te-Ta-Te	Ernie K-Doe	#53
Sometime	Gene Thomas	#53
Cherie	Bobby Rydell	#54
Wizard of Love	The Ly-Dells	#54
It's Too Soon to Know	Etta James	#54
Hully Gully Again	Little Caesar and The Romans	#54
Eventually	Brenda Lee	#56
A Love of My Own	Carla Thomas	#56
Feel It	Sam Cooke	#56
Juke Box Saturday Night	Nino and The Ebb Tides	#57

PIANO (cont'd)

Title	Artist	#	Time
Lonely Street	Clarence Henry	#57	
Three Steps from the Altar	Shep & The Limelites	#58	
Mom and Dad's Waltz	Patti Page	#58	
Lonesome Number One	Don Gibson	#59	
Sweet Little You	Neil Sedaka	#59	15 sec.
Morning After	Mar-Keys	#60	
Pony Express	Danny & The Juniors	#60	
Nobody Cares (About Me)	Jeanette (Baby) Washington	#60	
More Than I Can Say	Bobby Vee	#61	12 sec.
Teardrops in My Heart	Joe Barry	#63	
Your Last Goodbye	Floyd Cramer	#63	
On Bended Knees	Clarence Henry	#64	
The Exodus Song (This Land Is Mine)	Pat Boone	#64	
Danny Boy	Andy Williams	#64	
You Don't Want My Love	Andy Williams	#64	
My Heart Belongs to Only You	Jackie Wilson	#65	
Ling-Ting-Tong	Buddy Knox	#65	
When I Fall in Love	Etta Jones	#65	
Lonely Blue Nights	Rosie	#66	
Young Boy Blues	Ben E. King	#66	
I Hear You Knocking	Fats Domino	#67	
The Most Beautiful Words	Della Reese	#67	
Somewhere Along the Way	Steve Lawrence	#67	
Miss Fine	The New Yorkers	#69	
It's Unbelievable	The Larks	#69	
Cinderella	Paul Anka	#70	
All of Everything	Frankie Avalon	#70	
A Certain Girl	Ernie K-Doe	#71	
(I've Got) Spring Fever	Little Willie John	#71	
For Me and My Gal	Freddy Cannon	#71	
Take a Fool's Advice	Nat "King" Cole	#71	
Don't Cry No More	Bobby Bland	#71	
Chills and Fever	Ronnie Love	#72	
I Don't Like It Like That	The Bobbettes	#72	
What Would You Do?	Jim Reeves	#73	
Where I Fell in Love	The Capris	#74	
Milord	Teresa Brewer	#74	
Never, Never	Jive Five	#74	
Please Come Home for Christmas	Charles Brown	#76	
Won't Be Long	Aretha Franklin	#76	
Tender Years	George Jones	#76	10 sec.
I Don't Want Nobody (To Have My Love but You)	Ella Johnson with Buddy Johnson	#78	
You Don't Know What It Means	Jackie Wilson	#79	

PIANO (cont'd)

Title	Artist	Page	Time
Son-In-Law	The Blossoms	#79	
You're Gonna Need Magic	Roy Hamilton	#80	
The Continental Walk	The Rollers	#80	
Back to the Hop	Danny & The Juniors	#80	
Ronnie	Marcy Joe	#81	
You're the Boss	LaVern Baker/Jimmy Ricks	#81	
La Dolce Vita	Ray Ellis	#81	
If	The Paragons	#82	
I'll Never Stop Wanting You	Brian Hyland	#83	
Rockin' Bicycle	Fats Domino	#83	
Come Along	Maurice Williams and The Zodiacs	#83	
And the Heavens Cried	Ronnie Savoy	#84	
Brother-in-Law (He's a Moocher)	Paul Peek	#84	11 sec.
I Wonder (If Your Love Will Ever Belong to Me)	The Pentagons	#84	
Blue Tomorrow	Billy Vaughn	#84	
Driving Wheel	Junior Parker	#85	
I Told You So	Jimmy Jones	#85	14 sec.
Theme from "Goodbye Again"	Ferrante & Teicher	#85	
If I Knew	Nat "King" Cole	#86	
Steps 1 and 2	Jack Scott	#86	
Drivin' Home	Duane Eddy	#87	
You're the Reason	Joe South	#87	
Milord	Edith Piaf	#88	
Lonesome Whistle Blues	Freddy King	#88	
Boogie Woogie	B. Bumble and The Stingers	#89	
The Mess Around	Bobby Freeman	#89	
Greetings (This Is Uncle Sam)	Valadiers	#89	
Dedicated (To the Songs I Love)	The 3 Friends	#89	
A City Girl Stole My Country Boy	Patti Page	#90	
Memphis	Donnie Brooks	#90	
My Heart's On Fire	Billy Bland	#90	
Canadian Sunset	Etta James	#91	
Mr. Pride	Chuck Jackson	#91	
Signed, Sealed and Deliverd	Rusty Draper	#91	
Gift of Love	Van Dykes	#91	
Wishin' on a Rainbow	Phill Wilson	#91	
Broken Heart and a Pillow Filled with Tears	Patti Page	#91	
Trouble in Mind	Nina Simone	#92	
I Can't Take It	Mary Ann Fisher	#92	
You're Following Me	Perry Como	#92	
It's All Right	Sam Cooke	#93	
She Really Loves You	Timi Yuri	#93	
You've Got to Love Her with a Feeling	Freddy King	#93	

PIANO (cont'd)

Oh Lonesome Me	Johnny Cash	#93	
For Your Love	The Wanderers	#93	
Now You Know	Little Willie John	#93	
Dooley	The Olympics	#94	
In Time	Steve Lawrence	#94	
I'm a Fool to Care	Oscar Black	#94	
I'll Never Be Free	Kay Starr	#94	
Dear Mr. D.J. Play It Again	Tina Robin	#95	
Tonite, Tonite	Mello-Kings	#95	
Hang On	Floyd Cramer	#95	
Impossible	Gloria Lynne	#95	
What Will I Tell My Heart	The Harptones	#96	
Don't Forget I Love You	The Butanes	#96	
Here's My Confession	Wyatt (Earp) McPherson	#97	
Lovedrops	Mickey & Sylvia	#97	
It Do Me So Good	Ann-Margret	#97	
Won'cha Come Home, Bill Bailey	Della Reese	#98	
Image - Part 1	Hank Levine	#98	
Cherry Berry Wine	Charlie McCoy	#99	
Panic	Otis Williams/Charms	#99	
Can't Help Lovin' That Girl of Mine	The Excels	#100	
Everybody's Cryin'	Jimmie Beaumont	#100	
What About Me	Don Gibson	#100	11 sec.
1962			
Don't Break the Heart That Loves You	Connie Francis	#1	
Monster Mash	Bobby "Boris" Pickett	#1	
He's a Rebel	The Crystals	#1	
Hey! Baby	Bruce Channel	#1	
Roses are Red (My Love)	Bobby Vinton	#1	
Big Girls Don't Cry	The Four Seasons	#1	
I Can't Stop Loving You	Ray Charles	#1	
Can't Help Falling in Love	Elvis Presley	#2	
The Wah Watusi	The Orlons	#2	
I Know (You Don't Love Me No More)	Barbara George	#3	
Sealed with a Kiss	Brian Hyland	#3	
Bobby's Girl	Marcie Blane	#3	
Dream Baby (How Long Must I Dream)	Roy Orbison	#4	
Break It to Me Gently	Brenda Lee	#4	
Party Lights	Claudine Clark	#5	
Love Letters	Ketty Lester	#5	
Old Rivers	Walter Brennan	#5	
She's Not You	Elvis Presley	#5	
Al Di La'	Emilio Pericoli	#6	

PIANO (cont'd)

Everybody Loves Me but You	Brenda Lee	#6	
You Belong to Me	The Duprees	#7	
Jonny Get Angry	Joanie Sommers	#7	
When I Fall in Love	The Lettermen	#7	
Alley Cat	Bent Fabric	#7	
Second Hand Love	Connie Francis	#7	
Lover Please	Clyde McPhatter	#7	10 sec.
You'll Lose a Good Thing	Barbara Lynn	#8	
Snap Your Fingers	Joe Henderson	#8	
Baby It's You	The Shirelles	#8	
Release Me	"Little Esther" Phillips	#8	
You Beat Me to the Punch	Mary Wells	#9	
Twistin' the Night Away	Sam Cooke	#9	
Gravy (For My Mashed Potatoes)	Dee Dee Sharp	#9	
Popeye (The Hitchhiker)	Chubby Checker	#10	
Dear One	Larry Finnegan	#11	19 sec.
Rumors	Johnny Crawford	#12	
Rain Rain Go Away	Bobby Vinton	#12	
Nothing Can Change This Love	Sam Cooke	#12	
Bring It on Home to Me	Sam Cooke & Lou Rawls	#13	
Dear Lonely Hearts	Nat "King" Cole	#13	
Town Without Pity	Gene Pitney	#13	
(Girls, Girls, Girls) Made to Love	Eddie Hodges	#14	
She's Got You	Patsy Cline	#14	
Sharing You	Bobby Vee	#15	
Heart in Hand	Brenda Lee	#15	
Cinderella	Jack Ross	#16	
I Wish That We Were Married	Ronnie & The Hi-Lites	#16	
Send Me the Pillow You Dream On	Johnny Tillotson	#17	
Call Me Mr. In-Between	Burl Ives	#19	
Shadrack	Brook Benton	#19	
I'm Blue (The Gong-Gong Song)	The Ikettes	#19	
I Left My Heart in San Francisco	Tony Bennett	#19	
Hide 'Nor Hair	Ray Charles	#20	
Punish Her	Bobby Vee	#20	
I Need Your Loving	Don Gardner/Dee Dee Ford	#20	
Johnny Jingo	Hayley Mills	#21	
You Win Again	Fats Domino	#22	
Funny How Time Slips Away	Jimmy Elledge	#22	
Nut Rocker	B. Bumble & The Stingers	#23	
Shame on Me	Bobby Bare	#23	
I Was Such a Fool (To Fall in Love with You)	Connie Francis	#24	
What'd I Say (Part 1)	Bobby Darin	#24	

PIANO (cont'd)

Song	Artist	#	Time
You Better Move On	Arthur Alexander	#24	
Dear Ivan	Jimmy Dean	#24	
Warmed Over Kisses (Left Over Love)	Brian Hyland	#25	
You are Mine	Frankie Avalon	#26	
Twist-Her	Bill Black's Combo	#26	
Do-Re-Mi	Lee Dorsey	#27	19 sec.
Turn on Your Love Light	Bobby Bland	#28	
That Stranger Used to Be My Girl	Trade Martin	#28	
Theme from Ben Casey	Valjean	#28	
Drums are My Beat	Sandy Nelson	#29	
Your Cheating Heart	Ray Charles	#29	
Jambalaya (On the Bayou)	Fats Domino	#30	
Route 66 Theme	Nelson Riddle	#30	
King of the Whole Wide World	Elvis Presley	#30	
Multiplication	Bobby Darin	#30	
Surfer's Stomp	The Mar-Kets	#31	
Anything That's Part of You	Elvis Presley	#31	
Have a Good Time	Sue Thompson	#31	
If a Man Answers	Bobby Darin	#32	
Twistin' Postman	The Marvelettes	#34	
Stop the Wedding	Etta James	#34	
The Greatest Hurt	Jackie Wilson	#34	
Dreamy Eyes	Johnny Tillotson	#35	
Chattanooga Choo Choo	Floyd Cramer	#36	
Where are You	Dinah Washington	#36	
Mama Sang a Song	Walter Brennan	#38	
Hey! Little Girl	Del Shannon	#38	
I Love You the Way You Are	Bobby Vinton	#38	
Poor Fool	Ike & Tina Turner	#38	
I'll Bring It Home to You	Carla Thomas	#41	
But Not for Me	Ketty Lester	#41	
Fortuneteller	Bobby Curtola	#41	17 sec.
Go on Home	Patti Page	#42	
Stormy Monday Blues	Bobby Bland	#43	
At the Club	Ray Charles	#44	
Swingin' Gently	Earl Grant	#44	
Ten Lonely Guys	Pat Boone	#45	
Hit Record	Brook Benton	#45	
You Talk About Love	Barbara George	#46	
I Will	Vic Dana	#47	
Papa-Oom-Mow-Mow	The Rivingtons	#48	
Maria	Roger Williams	#48	
Balboa Blue	The Mar-Kets	#48	

PIANO (cont'd)

Title	Artist	Ref	Time
The Boys' Night Out	Patti Page	#49	
Tra La La La La	Ike & Tina Turner	#50	
A Taste of Honey	Martin Denny	#50	
Annie Get Your Yo-Yo	Little Junior Parker	#51	
Number One Man	Bruce Channel	#52	
Walkin' with My Angel	Bobby Vee	#53	
Love Me as I Love You	George Maharis	#54	
Sweet Sixteen Bars	Earl Grant	#55	
He Thinks I Still Care	Connie Francis	#57	
Where Have You Been (All My Life)	Arthur Alexander	#58	15 sec.
Long as the Rose Is Red	Florraine Darlin	#62	
Rainbow at Midnight	Jimmie Rodgers	#62	
Second Fiddle Girl	Barbara Lynn	#63	14 sec.
Meet Me at the Twistin' Place	Johnnie Morisette	#63	
Just Got to Know	Jimmy McCracklin	#64	
Mr. Lonely	Buddy Greco	#64	
Anna (Go to Him)	Arthur Alexander	#68	
That's My Desire	The Sensations	#69	
Love Can't Wait	Marty Robbins	#69	
Somebody Have Mercy	Sam Cooke	#70	
Tears and Laughter	Dinah Washington	#71	
What's the Reason	Bobby Edwards	#71	
Don't Worry 'Bout Me	Vincent Edwards	#72	
But on the Other Hand Baby	Ray Charles	#72	
Heartaches	Patsy Cline	#73	
Big Love	Joe Henderson	#74	
The Rains Came	Big Sambo	#74	
Worried Mind	Ray Anthony	#74	
There'll Be No Next Time	Jackie Wilson	#75	
I Want to Be Loved	Dinah Washington	#76	
Midnight	Johnny Gibson	#76	
Who Will the Next Fool Be	Bobby Bland	#76	
The Alley Cat Song	David Thorne	#76	
Nothing New (Same Old Thing)	Fats Domino	#77	
So What	Bill Black's Combo	#78	
Did You Ever See a Dream Walking	Fats Domino	#79	
Lipstick Traces (On a Cigarette)	Benny Spellman	#80	
Silly Boy (She Doesn't Love You)	The Lettermen	#81	
I Told the Brook	Marty Robbins	#81	
The Jitterbug	The Dovells	#82	
Right String but the Wrong Yo-Yo	Dr. Feelgood & The Interns	#84	14 sec.
So Wrong	Patsy Cline	#85	
I'm Hanging Up My Heart for You	Solomon Burke	#85	

PIANO (cont'd)

Title	Artist	Rank	Time
Ain't That Loving You	Bobby Bland	#86	
You're Nobody 'Til Somebody Loves You	Dinah Washington	#87	
Life's Too Short	The Lafayettes	#87	
Lovesick Blues	Floyd Cramer	#87	
A Taste of Honey	Victor Feldman Quartet	#88	
There Is No Greater Love	The Wanderers	#88	
Amor	Roger Williams	#88	
Potato Peeler	Bobby Gregg	#89	
I Found a New Baby	Bobby Darin	#90	27 sec.
Imagine That	Patsy Cline	#90	
Baby It's Cold Outside	Ray Charles & Betty Carter	#91	
Oh! What It Seemed to Be	The Castells	#91	
Joey Baby	Anita & Th' So-And-So's	#91	
I Can't Say Goodbye	Bobby Vee	#92	
Don't Cry, Baby	Aretha Franklin	#92	
Dream	Dinah Washington	#92	
Four Walls	Kay Starr	#92	
I Wouldn't Know (What to Do)	Dinah Washington	#93	
The Waltz You Saved for Me	Ferlin Husky	#94	
Rough Lover	Aretha Franklin	#94	
What Did Daddy Do	Shep & The Limelites	#94	
The Basie Twist	Count Basie	#94	
When the Boys Get Together	Joanie Sommers	#94	
Smile	Ferrante & Teicher	#94	
You Don't Miss Your Water	William Bell	#95	
Dear Hearts and Gentle People	The Springfields	#95	
Your Heart Belongs to Me	The Supremes	#95	
Sweet Little Sixteen	Jerry Lee Lewis	#95	19 sec.
Let Me Entertain You	Ray Anthony	#96	
Cold, Cold Heart	Dinah Washington	#96	
Strange	Patsy Cline	#97	
Operator	Gladys Knight & The Pips	#97	
Does He Mean That Much to You?	Eddy Arnold	#98	
Lisa	Ferrante & Teicher	#98	
You're a Sweetheart	Dinah Washington	#98	
Portrait of a Fool	Conway Twitty	#98	
Where Do You Come From	Elvis Presley	#99	
Funny	Gene McDaniels	#99	
Popeye Joe	Ernie K-Doe	#99	40 sec.
Don't Stop the Wedding	Ann Cole	#99	
Mama (He Treats Your Daughter Mean)	Ruth Brown	#99	
Sugar Babe	Buster Brown	#99	
Till There Was You	Valjean	#100	

PIANO (cont'd)

Drown in My Own Tears	Don Shirley	#100	
Try a Little Tenderness	Aretha Franklin	#100	
Sweet Georgia Brown	Carroll Bros.	#100	
Houdini	Walter Brennan	#100	
1963			
It's My Party	Lesley Gore	#1	
Go Away Little Girl	Steve Lawrence	#1	
The End of the World	Skeeter Davis	#2	
Washington Square	The Village Stompers	#2	
Sally, Go 'Round the Roses	The Jaynetts	#2	
You're the Reason I'm Living	Bobby Darin	#3	
Cry Baby	Garnet Mimms & The Enchanters	#4	
Pipeline	Chantay's	#4	
Since I Fell for You	Lenny Welch	#4	
One Fine Day	The Chiffons	#5	
She's a Fool	Lesley Gore	#5	
Baby Workout	Jackie Wilson	#5	
Young Lovers	Paul & Paula	#6	
Losing You	Brenda Lee	#6	
Blame It on the Bossa Nova	Eydie Gorme	#7	
Take These Chains from My Heart	Ray Charles	#8	19 sec.
You've Really Got a Hold On Me	The Miracles	#8	
Still	Bill Anderson	#8	
(Down At) Papa Joe's	The Dixiebelles	#9	
Our Winter Love	Bill Pursell	#9	
Another Saturday Night	Sam Cooke	#10	
Pride and Joy	Marvin Gaye	#10	
Watermelon Man	Mongo Santamaria	#10	
Just One Look	Doris Troy	#10	
Little Red Rooster	Sam Cooke	#11	
Fools Rush In	Ricky Nelson	#12	
Danke Schoen	Wayne Newton	#13	
Send Me Some Lovin'	Sam Cooke	#13	
Hopeless	Andy Williams	#13	
Fly Me to the Moon - Bossa Nova	Joe Harnell	#14	
I Wanna Be Around	Tony Bennett	#14	
Frankie and Johnny	Sam Cooke	#14	
Pretty Paper	Roy Orbison	#15	
Laughing Boy	Mary Wells	#15	13 sec.
Painted, Tainted Rose	Al Martino	#15	
Mr. Bass Man	Johnny Cymbal	#16	
The Grass Is Greener	Brenda Lee	#17	
El Watusi	Ray Barretto	#17	

PIANO (cont'd)

Title	Artist	#	
Follow the Boys	Connie Francis	#17	
The Boy Next Door	The Secrets	#18	
The Good Life	Tony Bennett	#18	
Have You Heard	The Duprees	#18	
You Can Never Stop Me Loving You	Johnny Tillotson	#18	
Prisoner of Love	James Brown	#18	
Everybody Loves a Lover	The Shirelles	#19	
Misty	Lloyd Price	#21	
Over the Mountain (Across the Sea)	Bobby Vinton	#21	
The Love of My Man	Theola Kilgore	#21	
Living a Lie	Al Martino	#22	
Cast Your Fate to the Wind	Vince Guaraldi Trio	#22	
Can I Get a Witness	Marvin Gaye	#22	
Wiggle Wobble	Les Cooper	#22	
Ain't That a Shame!	The Four Seasons	#22	
If My Pillow Could Talk	Connie Francis	#23	
Cry to Me	Betty Harris	#23	
Make the World Go Away	Timi Yuro	#24	
My Whole World Is Falling Down	Brenda Lee	#24	
Out of My Mind	Johnny Tillotson	#24	
I Wonder	Brenda Lee	#25	
String Along	Ricky Nelson	#25	
The Cinnamon Cinder (It's a Very Nice Dance)	The Pastel Six	#25	
Wait Til' My Bobby Gets Home	Darlene Love	#26	
Days of Wine and Roses	Andy Williams	#26	
First Quarrel	Paul & Paula	#27	
Without Love (There Is Nothing)	Ray Charles	#29	
Proud	Johnny Crawford	#29	
Be Careful of Stones That You Throw	Dion	#31	
A Love She Can Count On	The Miracles	#31	
Witchcraft	Elvis Presley	#32	
Two Tickets to Paradise	Brook Benton	#32	
Red Sails in the Sunset	Fats Domino	#35	
Marlena	The Four Seasons	#36	
If You Need Me	Solomon Burke	#37	
Let's Kiss and Make Up	Bobby Vinton	#38	
Why Do Lovers Break Each Other's Heart?	Bob B. Soxx/Blue Jeans	#38	21 sec.
Your Old Stand By	Mary Wells	#40	
The Bounce	The Olympics	#40	
I'm Saving My Love	Skeeter Davis	#41	
Love for Sale	Arthur Lyman Group	#43	
Sweet Dreams (Of You)	Patsy Cline	#44	
Tips of My Fingers	Roy Clark	#45	

PIANO (cont'd)

She'll Never Know	Brenda Lee	#47	
You Don't Love Me Anymore (And I Can Tell)	Ricky Nelson	#47	
Rainbow	Gene Chandler	#47	
As Long as I Know He's Mine	The Marvelettes	#47	
I Got a Woman	Ricky Nelson	#49	
Java	Floyd Cramer	#49	
Strange I Know	The Marvelettes	#49	
You're Good for Me	Solomon Burke	#49	
Funny How Time Slips Away	Johnny Tillotson	#50	
Big Wide World	Teddy Randazzo	#51	
Do It - Rat Now	Bill Black's Combo	#51	
Long Tall Texan	Murry Kellum	#51	
Shake a Tail Feather	The Five Du-Tones	#51	
They Remind Me Too Much of You	Elvis Presley	#53	
8 X 10	Bill Anderson	#53	
Who Stole the Keeshka?	The Matys Bros.	#55	
Sometimes You Gotta Cry a Little	Bobby Bland	#56	
Night Life	Rusty Draper	#57	
Teenage Heaven	Johnny Cymbal	#58	
He's Mine (I Love Him, I Love Him, I Love Him)	Alice Wonder Land	#62	12 sec.
Gypsy Woman	Ricky Nelson	#62	
Memory Lane	The Hippies	#63	
Not Too Young to Get Married	Bob B. Soxx/Blue Jeans	#63	
Chicken Feed	Bent Fabric	#63	
Two Sides (To Every Story)	Etta James	#63	
Don't Let Her Be Your Baby	The Contours	#64	
If You Need Me	Wilson Pickett	#64	
Gravy Waltz	Steve Allen	#64	
Gotta Travel On	Timi Yuro	#64	
Would It Make Any Difference to You	Etta James	#64	
Be Mad Little Girl	Bobby Darin	#64	
You're Gonna Need Me	Barbara Lynn	#65	
The Jive Samba	Cannonball Adderley	#66	
This Is All I Ask	Burl Ives	#67	
I'm in Love Again	Ricky Nelson	#67	
Your Teenage Dreams	Johnny Mathis	#68	
I May Not Live to See Tomorrow	Brian Hyland	#69	
Bossa Nova U.S.A.	Dave Brubeck Quartet	#69	
This Is All I Ask	Tony Bennett	#70	
I Could Have Danced All Night	Ben E. King	#72	21 sec.
Ronnie, Call Me When You Get a Chance	Shelley Fabares	#72	
Will Power	The Cookies	#72	
Beggin to You	Marty Robbins	#74	

PIANO (cont'd)

Bill Bailey, Won't You Please Come Home	Ella Fitzgerald	#75	
Call Me Irresponsible	Jack Jones	#75	
Breath Taking Guy	The Supremes	#75	
I'm Crazy 'Bout My Baby	Marvin Gaye	#77	
Something Old, Something New	Paul & Paula	#77	
Land of 1000 Dances	Chris Kenner	#77	
I Can't Stop Loving You	Count Basie	#77	
Forever	The Marvelettes	#78	
Say Wonderful Things	Patti Page	#81	
What Does a Girl Do?	Marcie Blane	#82	10 sec.
Antony and Cleopatra Theme	Ferrante & Teicher	#83	
Leavin' on Your Mind	Patsy Cline	#83	
Thank You and Goodnight	The Angels	#84	
Theme from "Lawrence of Arabia"	Ferrante & Teicher	#84	
This Empty Place	Dionne Warwick	#84	
These Arms of Mine	Otis Redding	#85	
Cuando Calienta El Sol (When the Sun Is Hot)	Steve Allen (Copacabana Trio)	#85	
Trouble in Mind	Aretha Franklin	#86	
Don't Let Me Cross Over	Carl Butler & Pearl	#88	
That's the Only Way	The Four Seasons	#88	
Gone with the Wind	The Duprees	#89	
Did You Have a Happy Birthday?	Paul Anka	#89	
Detroit City No. 2	Ben Colder (Shep Wooley)	#90	
Al Di La	Connie Francis	#90	
Remember Baby	Shep & The Limelites	#91	
Guilty	Jim Reeves	#91	
The Same Old Hurt	Burl Ives	#91	
I'd Rather Be Here in Your Arms	The Duprees	#91	
Look at Me	Dobie Gray	#91	
Yeh-Yeh!	Mongo Santamaria	#92	
Now!	Lena Horne	#92	
Spring in Manhattan	Tony Bennett	#92	
Preacherman	Charlie Russo	#92	
Surfer Street	The Allisons	#93	
Cigarettes and Coffee Blues	Marty Robbins	#93	
Saturday Sunshine	Burt Bacharach	#93	
Don't Be Cruel	Barbara Lynn	#93	
Old Enough to Love	Ricky Nelson	#94	
Got You on My Mind	Cookie & His Cupcakes	#94	
Someone Somewhere	Junior Parker	#95	
The Minute You're Gone	Sonny James	#95	
My Foolish Heart	The Demensions	#95	
Faded Love	Patsy Cline	#96	

PIANO (cont'd)

Diane	Joe Harnell	#97	
At the Shore	Johnny Caswell	#97	
Pretty Boy Lonely	Patti Page	#98	
Black Cloud	Chubby Checker	#98	
Never Love a Robin	Bobby Vee	#99	
I Cried	Tammy Montgomery (Tammie Terrell)	#99	
The Last Minute (Pt. 1)	Jimmy McGriff	#99	
River's Invitation	Percy Mayfield	#99	
True Blue Lou	Tony Bennett	#99	
Breakwater	Lawrence Welk	#100	
Make the World Go Away	Ray Price	#100	
1964			
Everybody Loves Somebody	Dean Martin	#1	
Mr. Lonely	Bobby Vinton	#1	
Where Did Our Love Go	The Supremes	#1	
Oh, Pretty Woman	Roy Orbison w/The Candy Men	#1	
Baby Love	The Supremes	#1	
Last Kiss	J. Frank Wilson & The Cavaliers	#2	
She's a Woman	The Beatles	#4	
Java	Al Hirt	#4	
Let It Be Me	Betty Everett & Jerry Butler	#5	
People	Barbra Streisand	#5	
Um, Um, Um, Um, Um, Um	Major Lance	#5	
The Door Is Still Open to My Heart	Dean Martin	#6	
Ronnie	The Four Seasons	#6	
Walk on By	Dionne Warwick	#6	
Talk Back Trembling Lips	Johnny Tillotson	#7	
You Really Got Me	The Kinks	#7	
Quicksand	Martha & The Vandellas	#8	
Anyone Who Had a Heart	Dionne Warwick	#8	
Chug-A-Lug	Roger Miller	#9	
How Do You Do It?	Gerry & The Pacemakers	#9	10 sec.
My Heart Belongs to Only You	Bobby Vinton	#9	
I'm Gonna Be Strong	Gene Pitney	#9	
No Particular Place to Go	Chuck Berry	#10	
Save It for Me	The Four Seasons	#10	
(You Don't Know) How Glad I Am	Nancy Wilson	#11	
Baby I Need Your Loving	Four Tops	#11	
Selfish One	Jackie Ross	#11	
That's the Way Boys Are	Lesley Gore	#12	
As Usual	Brenda Lee	#12	
A Fool Never Learns	Andy Williams	#13	
Every Little Bit Hurts	Brenda Holloway	#13	

PIANO (cont'd)

I'm Into Something Good	Herman's Hermits	#13	
You Never Can Tell	Chuck Berry	#14	22 sec.
Tobacco Road	The Nashville Teens	#14	14 sec.
Southtown, U.S.A.	The Dixiebelles	#15	
Try It Baby	Marvin Gaye	#15	
Such a Night	Elvis Presley	#16	
I Like It	Gerry & The Pacemakers	#17	
What's the Matter with You Baby	Marvin Gaye & Mary Wells	#17	
Steal Away	Jimmy Hughes	#17	
Somewhere	The Tymes	#19	12 sec.
Just Be True	Gene Chandler	#19	
Reach out for Me	Dionne Warwick	#20	
Tears and Roses	Al Martino	#20	
The Matador	Major Lance	#20	
Ain't Nothing You Can Do	Bobby Bland	#20	
That Lucky Old Sun	Ray Charles	#20	
Yesterday's Gone	Chad & Jeremy	#21	
I Don't Want to Be Hurt Anymore	Nat "King" Cole	#22	
Nadine (Is It You?)	Chuck Berry	#23	
Blue Winter	Connie Francis	#24	
Letter from Sherry	Dale Ward	#25	
It's All in the Game	Cliff Richard	#25	
Think	Brenda Lee	#25	
Forever	Pete Drake	#25	
The Very Thought of You	Ricky Nelson	#26	
For Your Precious Love	Garnet Mimms & The Enchanters	#26	
Girl (Why You Wanna Make Me Blue)	The Temptations	#26	
I Wish You Love	Gloria Lynne	#28	
Viva Las Vegas	Elvis Presley	#29	
It Hurts Me	Elvis Presley	#29	
She Understands Me	Johnny Tillotson	#31	
I Believe	The Bachelors	#33	
Rock Me Baby	B.B. King	#34	
I Don't Want to See Tomorrow	Nat "King" Cole	#34	
Going Going Gone	Brook Benton	#35	
I Gotta Dance to Keep from Crying	The Miracles	#35	
I Rise, I Fall	Johnny Tillotson	#36	
Come On	Tommy Roe	#36	
I Don't Wanna Be a Loser	Lesley Gore	#37	
I'm Into Something Good	Earl-Jean	#38	
Tall Cool One	The Wailers	#38	
Giving Up	Gladys Knight & The Pips	#38	
Bless Our Love	Gene Chandler	#39	

PIANO (cont'd)

Title	Artist	#
Say You	Ronnie Dove	#40
I Had a Talk with My Man	Mitty Collier	#41
We Could	Al Martino	#41
Hey Girl Don't Bother Me	The Tams	#41
Share Your Love with Me	Bobby Bland	#42
Make Me Forget Her	Bobby Rydell	#43
Vaya Con Dios	The Drifters	#43
Too Late to Turn Back Now	Brook Benton	#43
I Still Get Jealous	Louis Armstrong	#45
Needle in a Haystack	The Velvelettes	#45
Milord	Bobby Darin	#45
Beg Me	Chuck Jackson	#45
Worry	Johnny Tillotson	#45
I Can't Stand It	Soul Sisters	#46
When You Loved Me	Brenda Lee	#47
He Says the Same Things to Me	Skeeter Davis	#47
Since I Don't Have You	Chuck Jackson	#47
Alone with You	Brenda Lee	#48
When You're Young and in Love	Ruby & The Romantics	#48
Can Your Monkey Do the Dog	Rufus Thomas	#48
Ain't Doing Too Bad (Part 1)	Bobby Bland	#49
That Girl Belongs to Yesterday	Gene Pitney	#49
A Tear Fell	Ray Charles	#50
You're No Good	Betty Everett	#51
Little Marie	Chuck Berry	#54
Just Ain't Enough Love	Eddie Holland	#54
No One to Cry To	Ray Charles	#55
The Price	Solomon Burke	#57
Invisible Tears	Ray Conniff	#57
Runnin' Out of Fools	Aretha Franklin	#57
Sole Sole Sole	Siw Malmkvist-Umberto Marcato	#58
(You Can't Let the Boy Overpower) The Man in You	The Miracles	#59
Carol	Tommy Roe	#61
What Good Am I Without You	Marvin Gaye & Kim Weston	#61
I Stand Accused	Jerry Butler	#61
Pain in My Heart	Otis Redding	#61
Listen Lonely Girl	Johnny Mathis	#62
Donnie	The Bermudas	#62
Congratulations	Ricky Nelson	#63
Something You Got	Ramsey Lewis Trio	#63
That's When It Hurts	Ben E. King	#63
I Should Care	Gloria Lynne	#64
That Boy John	The Raindrops	#64

PIANO (cont'd)

Title	Artist	#	Duration
Loving You More Every Day	Etta James	#65	
Try Me	Jimmy Hughes	#65	
He Walks Like a Man	Jody Miller	#66	
One Girl	Garnet Mimms	#67	
Almost There	Andy Williams	#67	
Come to Me	Otis Redding	#69	
I Wouldn't Trade You for the World	The Bachelors	#69	20 sec.
Hold Me	P.J. Proby	#70	
Chained and Bound	Otis Redding	#70	
A Woman's Love	Carla Thomas	#71	
Snap Your Fingers	Barbara Lewis	#71	
It's All Over	Ben E. King	#72	
Look Away	Garnet Mimms	#73	
Come See About Me	Nella Dodds	#74	
(It's No) Sin	The Duprees	#74	
If I'm a Fool for Loving You	Bobby Wood	#74	
Me Japanese Boy I Love You	Bobby Goldsboro	#74	
Do Anything You Wanna (Part I)	Harold Betters	#74	
Baby Come Home	Ruby & The Romantics	#75	
Don't Take Your Love from Me	Gloria Lynne	#76	
Leaving Here	Eddie Holland	#76	
Hey Now	Lesley Gore	#76	
Hey, Mr. Sax Man	Boots Randolph	#77	
A Quiet Place	Garnet Mimms & The Enchanters	#78	
I Don't Want to Walk Without You	Phyllis McGuire	#79	
It's for You	Cilla Black	#79	
Cold Cold Winter	The Pixies Three	#79	
It's All Right (You're Just in Love)	The Tams	#79	
To Each His Own	The Tymes	#79	
L-O-V-E	Nat "King" Cole	#81	
I'm the One	Gerry & The Pacemakers	#82	
I See You	Cathy & Joe	#82	
Baby Baby All the Time	The Superbs	#83	14 sec.
My Dreams	Brenda Lee	#85	
Silly Little Girl	The Tams	#87	
(The Story of) Woman, Love and a Man (Part 1)	Tony Clarke	#88	
Be Anything (But Be Mine)	Gloria Lynne	#88	
I've Got the Skill	Jackie Ross	#89	
Going Back to Louisiana	Bruce Channel	#89	
Lovers Always Forgive	Gladys Knight & The Pips	#89	
Never Trust a Woman	B.B. King	#90	
High Heel Sneakers	Jerry Lee Lewis	#91	32 sec.
Ask Me	Inez Foxx	#91	

PIANO (cont'd)

You're the Only World I Know	Sonny James	#91	
Yes I Do	Solomon Burke	#92	
That's Really Some Good	Rufus & Carla	#92	
All My Loving	The Hollyridge Strings	#93	
Run, Run, Run	The Supremes	#93	
I Wonder Who's Kissing Her Now	Bobby Darin	#93	
Don't Spread It Around	Barbara Lynn	#93	
Night Time Is the Right Time	Rufus & Carla	#94	
Talk to Me Baby	Barry Mann	#94	
When Joanna Loved Me	Tony Bennett	#94	
A Taste of Honey	Tony Bennett	#94	
I Don't Want to Hear Anymore	Jerry Butler	#95	
Please, Please, Please	James Brown	#95	
I Can't Believe What You Say (For Seeing What You Do)	Ike & Tina Turner	#95	
Lover's Prayer	Wallace Brothers	#97	
How Blue Can You Get	B.B. King	#97	
Good Time Tonight	The Soul Sisters	#98	
I'm on Fire	Jerry Lee Lewis	#98	
All Grown Up	The Crystals	#98	
Where or When	The Lettermen	#98	
Help the Poor	B.B. King	#98	
I'm Confessin' (That I Love You)	Nino Tempo & April Stevens	#99	
The Little White Cloud that Cried	Wayne Newton	#99	
Bachelor Boy	Cliff Richard w/The Shadows	#99	
The Things That I Used to Do	James Brown	#99	
It's a Sin to Tell a Lie	Tony Bennett	#99	30 sec.
Trouble I've Had	Clarence Ashe	#99	
Strange Things Happening	Little Junior Parker	#99	
Sally Was a Good Old Girl	Fats Domino	#99	
Heartbreak Hill	Fats Domino	#99	
Coming Back to You	Maxine Brown	#99	
You Were Wrong	Z.Z. Hill	#100	
1965			
Back in My Arms Again	The Supremes	#1	
Downtown	Petula Clark	#1	
I Got You Babe	Sonny & Cher	#1	
Count Me In	Gary Lewis/Playboys	#2	
Like a Rolling Stone	Bob Dylan	#2	
I Know a Place	Petula Clark	#3	
Crying in the Chapel	Elvis Presley	#3	
Rescue Me	Fontella Bass	#4	
King of the Road	Roger Miller	#4	

PIANO (cont'd)

Song	Artist	#	
Unchained Melody	The Righteous Brothers	#4	
The "In" Crowd	Ramsey Lewis Trio	#5	
Make the World Go Away	Eddy Arnold	#6	
How Sweet It Is to Be Loved by You	Marvin Gaye	#6	
I Can Never Go Home Anymore	The Shangri-Las	#6	
Engine Engine 9	Roger Miller	#7	
I'll Be Doggone	Marvin Gaye	#8	
The Boy from New York City	The Ad Libs	#8	
You Turn Me On (Turn On Song)	Ian Whitcomb & Bluesville	#8	
Don't Just Stand There	Patty Duke	#8	
Baby Don't Go	Sonny & Cher	#8	
Ain't That Peculiar	Marvin Gaye	#8	
Hurt So Bad	Little Anthony/Imperials	#10	
Go Now	The Moody Blues	#10	34 sec.
Cast Your Fate to the Wind	Sounds Orchestral	#10	
The Wedding	Julie Rogers	#10	
(Such An) Easy Question	Elvis Presley	#11	
Hang on Sloopy	Ramsey Lewis Trio	#11	
I'm Yours	Elvis Presley	#11	
Don't Think Twice	The Wonder Who (The Four Seasons)	#12	
A Walk in the Black Forest	Horst Jankowski	#12	
Action	Freddy Cannon	#13	
Sunshine, Lollipops and Rainbows	Lesley Gore	#13	
I'll Be There	Gerry & The Pacemakers	#14	
Puppet on a String	Elvis Presley	#14	
May the Bird of Paradise Fly Up Your Nose	"Little" Jimmy Dickens	#15	
Marie	The Bachelors	#15	
The Race Is On	Jack Jones	#15	
My Love, Forgive Me (Amore, Scusami)	Robert Goulet	#16	
Long Lonely Nights	Bobby Vinton	#17	
Give Him a Great Big Kiss	The Shangri-Las	#18	
Don't Forget I Still Love You	Bobbi Martin	#19	
I'll Make All Your Dreams Come True	Ronnie Dove	#21	
Agent Double-O-Soul	Edwin Starr	#21	
Mohair Sam	Charlie Rich	#21	
I've Been Loving You Too Long (To Stop Now)	Otis Redding	#21	
Send Me the Pillow You Dream On	Dean Martin	#22	
Got to Get You off My Mind	Solomon Burke	#22	
Shakin' All Over	Guess Who	#22	
Walk Away	Matt Monro	#23	
Oo Wee Baby, I Love You	Fred Hughes	#23	
Reelin' and Rockin'	Dave Clark Five	#23	
I Want To (Do Everything for You)	Joe Tex	#23	

PIANO (cont'd)

Sitting in the Park	Billy Stewart	#24	
Kiss Away	Ronnie Dove	#25	
Pretty Little Baby	Marvin Gaye	#25	
Home of the Brave	Jody Miller	#25	
Ride Away	Roy Orbison	#25	
Too Many Fish in the Sea	The Marvelettes	#25	
I Do Love You	Billy Stewart	#26	
No Arms Can Ever Hold You	The Bachelors	#27	
Sad, Sad Girl	Barbara Mason	#27	
With These Hands	Tom Jones	#27	
Hungry for Love	San Remo Golden Strings	#27	
Woman's Got Soul	The Impressions	#29	
Give Us Your Blessing	The Shangri-Las	#29	
You Were Only Fooling (While I Was Falling in Love)	Vic Damone	#30	
Dear Heart	Jack Jones	#30	
Chapel in the Moonlight	The Bachelors	#32	
Somewhere in Your Heart	Frank Sinatra	#32	
Bring It on Home to Me	The Animals	#32	
Rusty Bells	Brenda Lee	#33	
If I Ruled the World	Tony Bennett	#34	
Heartaches by the Number	Johnny Tillotson	#35	
You've Been in Love Too Long	Martha & The Vandellas	#36	
I Understand (Just How You Feel)	Freddie & The Dreamers	#36	
(All of a Sudden) My Heart Sings	Mel Carter	#38	
(Say) You're My Girl	Roy Orbison	#39	
Cara-Lin	The Strangeloves	#39	13 sec.
Ain't It True	Andy Williams	#40	
Break Away (From That Boy)	The Newbeats	#40	
Promised Land	Chuck Berry	#41	
Mr. Pitiful	Otis Redding	#41	
Smile	Betty Everett & Jerry Butler	#42	
At the Club	The Drifters	#43	
10 Little Bottles	Johnny Bond	#43	
Hole in the Wall	The Packers	#43	
Whose Heart Are You Breaking Tonight	Connie Francis	#43	
Seesaw	Don Covay/Goodtimers	#44	
Seven Letters	Ben E. King	#45	
Crawling Back	Roy Orbison	#46	
You Better Get It	Joe Tex	#46	
I Can't Stop Thinking of You	Bobbi Martin	#46	
Makin' Whoopee	Ray Charles	#46	
Boo-Ga-Loo	Tom & Jerrio	#47	
Fancy Pants	Al Hirt	#47	

PIANO (cont'd)

Title	Artist	Chart
You'll Never Walk Alone	Gerry & The Pacemakers	#48
Come Tomorrow	Manfred Mann	#50
(My Girl) Sloopy	Little Caesar & The Consuls	#50
Take Me in Your Arms (Rock Me a Little While)	Kim Weston	#50
You Got What It Takes	Joe Tex	#51
Moonlight and Roses (Bring Mem'ries of You)	Vic Dana	#51
Crystal Chandelier	Vic Dana	#51
My Heart Would Know	Al Martino	#52
Goodbye My Lover Goodbye	The Searchers	#52
(There's) Always Something There to Remind Me	Sandie Shaw	#52
Do What You Do Do Well	Ned Miller	#52
Mother Nature, Father Time	Brook Benton	#53
Now That You've Gone	Connie Stevens	#53
Don't Fight It	Wilson Pickett	#53
Somebody Else Is Taking My Place	Al Martino	#53
He Touched Me	Barbra Streisand	#53
Truly, Truly, True	Brenda Lee	#54
And I Love Him	Esther Phillips	#54
A Woman Can Change a Man	Joe Tex	#56
Tell Her (You Love Her Each Day)	Frank Sinatra	#57
Cry	Ray Charles	#58
I Can't Work No Longer	Billy Butler & The Chanters	#60
What's He Doing in My World	Eddy Arnold	#60
N-E-R-V-O-U-S	Ian Whitcomb	#60
Forgive Me	Al Martino	#61
Danger Heartbreak Dead Ahead	The Marvelettes	#61
Watermelon Man	Gloria Lynne	#62
Who Can I Turn To	Dionne Warwick	#62
Candy	The Astors	#63
Misty	The Vibrations	#63
Married Man	Richard Burton	#64
Looking with My Eyes	Dionne Warwick	#64
You'll Always Be the One I Love	Dean Martin	#64
Here I Am	Dionne Warwick	#65
One Monkey Don't Stop No Show	Joe Tex	#65
Bring a Little Sunshine (To My Heart)	Vic Dana	#66
Love Is a 5-Letter Word	James Phelps	#66
Like a Child	Julie Rogers	#67
I Found a Love Oh What a Love	Jo Ann & Troy	#67
Whipped Cream	Herb Alpert & The Tijuana Brass	#68
Our World	Johnny Tillotson	#70
I Love You So	Bobbi Martin	#70
Temptation 'Bout to Get Me	The Knight Bros.	#70

PIANO (cont'd)

All of My Life	Lesley Gore	#71	
Darling Take Me Back	Lenny Welch	#72	
The Man	Lorne Greene	#72	
Just Yesterday	Jack Jones	#73	
That's How Strong My Love Is	Otis Redding	#74	
Stand By Me	Earl Grant	#75	
Canadian Sunset	Sounds Orchestral	#76	
The World Through a Tear	Neil Sedaka	#76	
Real Live Girl	Steve Alaimo	#77	
Why Did I Choose You	Barbra Streisand	#77	
Gotta Have Your Love	The Sapphires	#77	
Funny Little Butterflies	Patty Duke	#77	
Dear Heart	Henry Mancini	#77	
Summer Wind	Wayne Newton	#78	
You Better Go	Derek Martin	#78	
Blind Man	Bobby Bland	#78	
I Gotta Woman (Part One)	Ray Charles	#79	
Hello, Dolly!	Bobby Darin	#79	
My Man	Barbra Streisand	#79	
Let the Good Times Roll	Roy Orbison	#81	
The Sidewinder, Part 1	Lee Morgan	#81	
Good Lovin'	The Olympics	#81	
Three O'Clock in the Morning	Lou Rawls	#83	
Fly Me to the Moon	LaVern Baker	#84	
I'm a Fool to Care	Ray Charles	#84	
Fly Me to the Moon	Tony Bennett	#84	
If You Don't (Love Me, Tell Me So)	Barbara Mason	#85	
Are You Sincere	Trini Lopez	#85	
Jerk and Twine	Jackie Ross	#85	
Keep on Trying	Bobby Vee	#85	
Then I'll Count Again	Johnny Tillotson	#86	
Blind Man	Little Milton	#86	
The Crying Game	Brenda Lee	#87	
The Way of Love	Kathy Kirby	#88	
Soul Sauce (Guacha Guaro)	Cal Tjader	#88	
Crying in the Chapel	Adam Wade	#88	
Cast Your Fate to the Wind	Steve Alaimo	#89	
I'm Satisfied	San Remo Golden Strings	#89	
Simpel Gimpel	Horst Jankowski	#91	
Maybe	The Shangri-Las	#91	
Somewhere	P.J. Proby	#91	
The First Thing Ev'ry Morning (And the Last Thing Ev'ry Night)	Jimmy Dean	#91	

PIANO (cont'd)

Are You Still My Baby	The Shirelles	#91	
No Faith, No Love	Mitty Collier	#91	
She's with Her Other Love	Leon Hayward (Leon Haywood)	#92	
Autumn Leaves - 1965	Roger Williams	#92	17, 17 sec.
For You	The Spellbinders	#93	
Ain't No Telling	Bobby Bland	#93	
I've Cried My Last Tear	The O'Jays	#94	
Danny Boy	Jackie Wilson	#94	
Don't Let Your Left Hand Know	Joe Tex	#95	
After Loving You	Della Reese	#95	
Welcome Home	Walter Jackson	#95	
Think	Jimmy McCracklin	#95	
For Your Love	Sam & Bill	#95	
The Shadow of Your Smile	Tony Bennett	#95	
It's Better to Have It	Barbara Lynn	#95	
Goldfinger	Jack LaForge	#96	
Girl on the Billboard	Del Reeves	#96	
Can't You Just See Me	Aretha Franklin	#96	
Tears Keep On Falling	Jerry Vale	#96	
Mean Old World	Ricky Nelson	#96	
Try to Remember	Roger Williams	#97	57 sec.
Blue Shadows	B.B. King	#97	
How Nice It Is	Billy Stewart	#97	
El Pussy Cat	Mongo Santamaria	#97	
No One	Brenda Lee	#98	
Yakety Axe	Chet Atkins	#98	
Where Were You When I Needed You	Jerry Vale	#99	
This Sporting Life	Ian Whitcomb	#100	26 sec.
Love Me as Though There Were No Tomorrow	Sonny Knight	#100	
He Ain't No Angel	The Ad Libs	#100	
1966			
Lightnin' Strikes	Lou Christie	#1	
Summer in the City	The Lovin' Spoonful	#1	
Daydream	The Lovin' Spoonful	#2	
Rainy Day Women 12 & 35	Bob Dylan	#3	
You Don't Have to Say You Love Me	Dusty Springfield	#4	
Ebb Tide	The Righteous Brothers	#5	
Cherry, Cherry	Neil Diamond	#6	
Crying Time	Ray Charles	#6	
Born Free	Roger Williams	#7	
Cool Jerk	The Capitols	#7	
What Becomes of the Brokenhearted	Jimmy Ruffin	#7	
Message to Michael	Dionne Warwick	#8	

PIANO (cont'd)

It's a Man's Man's Man's World	James Brown	#8	
I'm So Lonesome I Could Cry	B.J. Thomas	#8	
Sure Gonna Miss Her	Gary Lewis/Playboys	#9	
I've Got You Under My Skin	The Four Seasons	#9	
I Couldn't Live Without Your Love	Petula Clark	#9	
Jenny Take a Ride!	Mitch Ryder & The Detroit Wheels	#10	
Petula Clark	A Sign of the Times	#11	
Going to a Go-Go	The Miracles	#11	
Love Makes the World Go Round	Deon Jackson	#11	
Try Too Hard	Dave Clark Five	#12	
This Door Swings Both Ways	Herman's Hermits	#12	10 sec.
Don't Bring Me Down	The Animals	#12	
Oh How Happy	Shades of Blue	#12	
Born a Woman	Sandy Posey	#12	
Single Girl	Sandy Posey	#12	
634-5789 (Soulsville, U.S.A.)	Wilson Pickett	#13	
Love Is a Hurtin' Thing	Lou Rawls	#13	
Sunny Afternoon	The Kinks	#14	
Sweet Dreams	Tommy McLain	#15	
Turn-Down Day	The Cyrkle	#16	
The More I See You	Chris Montez	#16	
Little Latin Lupe Lu	Mitch Ryder & The Detroit Wheels	#17	
Together Again	Ray Charles	#19	
Love Letters	Elvis Presley	#19	
Wade in the Water	Ramsey Lewis	#19	
All I See Is You	Dusty Springfield	#20	
I Want You	Bob Dylan	#20	
(I'm A) Road Runner	Jr. Walker/The All Stars	#20	
Magic Town	The Vogues	#21	
I Really Don't Want to Know	Ronnie Dove	#22	
My Baby Loves Me	Martha & The Vandellas	#22	
Holy Cow	Lee Dorsey	#23	
Almost Persuaded	David Houston	#24	
Crying	Jay & The Americans	#25	
Frankie and Johnny	Elvis Presley	#25	
Husbands and Wives	Roger Miller	#26	
Somewhere	Len Barry	#26	
Like a Baby	Len Barry	#27	
A Hard Day's Night	Ramsey Lewis Trio	#29	
Fa-Fa-Fa-Fa-Fa (Sad Song)	Otis Redding	#29	
Help Me Girl	Eric Burdon/Animals	#29	
I'll Take Good Care of You	Garnet Mimms	#30	
Let's Go Get Stoned	Ray Charles	#31	

PIANO (cont'd)

I Love You 1000 Times	The Platters	#31
Second Hand Rose	Barbra Streisand	#32
There Will Never Be Another You	Chris Montez	#33
Just Like a Woman	Bob Dylan	#33
Tell Me Why	Elvis Presley	#33
Billy and Sue	B.J. Thomas	#34
Under Your Spell Again	Johnny Rivers	#35
The Impossible Dream (The Quest)	Jack Jones	#35
Dedicated Follower of Fashion	The Kinks	#36
Time After Time	Chris Montez	#36
I Want to Go with You	Eddy Arnold	#36
Are You There (With Another Girl)	Dionne Warwick	#39
The Last Word in Lonesome Is Me	Eddy Arnold	#40
Spinout	Elvis Presley	#40
A Million and One	Dean Martin	#41
Get Out of My Life, Woman	Lee Dorsey	#44
She Blew a Good Thing	The Poets	#45
Please Don't Stop Loving Me	Elvis Presley	#45
On This Side of Goodbye	The Righteous Brothers	#47
Little Darling, I Need You	Marvin Gaye	#47
Mas Que Nada	Sergio Mendes & Brasil '66	#47
Stop Her on Sight (S.O.S.)	Edwin Starr	#48
Please Mr. Sun	The Vogues	#48
Up Tight	Ramsey Lewis	#49
Wish You Were Here, Buddy	Pat Boone	#49
In the Arms of Love	Andy Williams	#49
Satisfied with You	Dave Clark Five	#50
Hurt	Little Anthony/Imperials	#51
A Young Girl	Noel Harrison	#51
A Symphony for Susan	The Arbors	#51
Somebody Like Me	Eddy Arnold	#53
Broomstick Cowboy	Bobby Goldsboro	#53
Bad Misunderstanding	The Critters	#55
Lullaby of Love	The Poppies	#56
Almost Persuaded No. 2	Ben Colder (Sheb Wooley)	#58
A Little Bit of Soap	The Exciters	#58
Wang Dang Doodle	Ko Ko Taylor	#58
Past, Present and Future	The Shangri-Las	#59
The Wheel of Hurt	Al Martino	#59
My Lover's Prayer	Otis Redding	#61
I Guess I'll Always Love You	Isley Brothers	#61
Georgia on My Mind	The Righteous Brothers	#62
In My Room (El Amore)	Verdelle Smith	#62

PIANO (cont'd)

Title	Artist	#
Cloudy Summer Afternoon (Raindrops)	Barry McGuire	#62
Let Me Be Good to You	Carla Thomas	#62
A Lover's Concerto	Sarah Vaughan	#63
Ain't Nobody Home	Howard Tate	#63
"Bang" "Bang"	The Joe Cuba Sextet	#63
Please Say You're Fooling	Ray Charles	#64
Lara's Theme from "Dr. Zhivago"	Roger Williams	#65
We Got a Thing That's in the Groove	The Capitols	#65
Snow Flake	Jim Reeves	#66
Take Some Time out for Love	Isley Brothers	#66
Too Soon to Know	Roy Orbison	#68
There's Something on Your Mind	Baby Ray	#69
Hi Heel Sneakers - Pt. 1	Ramsey Lewis Trio	#70
Love (Makes Me Do Foolish Things)	Martha & The Vandellas	#70
A Million and One	Vic Dana	#71
What Am I Going to Do Without Your Love	Martha & The Vandellas	#71
Winchester Cathedral	Dana Rollin	#71
Alvin's Boo-Ga-Loo	Alvin Cash & The Registers	#74
Bring Back the Time	B.J. Thomas	#75
Hey You! Little Boo-Ga-Loo	Chubby Checker	#76
Wait a Minute	Tim Tam & The Turn-Ons	#76
Smokey Joe's La La	Googie Rene Combo	#77
Love Takes a Long Time Growing	Deon Jackson	#77
Painter	Lou Christie	#81
Giddyup Go	Red Sovine	#82
Downtown	Mrs. Miller	#82
A Corner in the Sun	Walter Jackson	#83
Uptight (Everything's Alright)	Nancy Wilson	#84
Stop, Look and Listen	The Chiffons	#85
Just a Little Misunderstanding	The Contours	#85
My Sweet Potato	Booker T. & The MG's	#85
Don't Touch Me	Jeannie Seely	#85
Games That Lovers Play	Wayne Newton	#86
It's an Uphill Climb to the Bottom	Walter Jackson	#88
A Man and a Woman	Tamiko Jones w/Herbie Mann	#88
The Answer to My Prayer	Neil Sedaka	#89
La La La	Gerry & The Pacemakers	#90
Freddie Feelgood (And His Funky Little Five Piece Band)	Ray Stevens	#91
Goodnight My Love	Ben E. King	#91
Black Nights	Lowell Fulsom	#91
Too Slow	The Impressions	#91
So Much Love	Steve Alaimo	#92
Put Yourself in My Place	The Elgins	#92

PIANO (cont'd)

Still	The Sunrays	#93	
Fiddle Around	Jan & Dean	#93	
Can't You See (You're Losing Me)	Mary Wells	#94	
Where Am I Going?	Barbra Streisand	#94	
You Waited Too Long	The Five Stairsteps	#94	
Lookin' for Love	Ray Conniff	#94	
Blue River	Elvis Presley	#95	
Uptight (Everything's Alright)	The Jazz Crusaders	#95	
A Lover's Concerto	Mrs. Miller	#95	
Your Good Thing (Is About to End)	Mable John	#95	
Alfie	Cilla Black	#95	
Cry Softly	Nancy Ames	#95	
Baby Come On Home	Solomon Burke	#96	
Everybody Loves a Nut	Johnny Cash	#96	
Function at the Junction	Shorty Long	#97	
Let's Go Steady Again	Sam Cooke	#97	
Peak of Love	Bobby McClure	#97	
Is It Me?	Barbara Mason	#97	
Sharing You	Mitty Collier	#97	
Dommage, Dommage (Too Bad, Too Bad)	Paul Vance	#97	
Sam, You Made the Pants Too Long	Barbra Streisand	#98	
Fly Me to the Moon	Sam & Bill	#98	
I Need Love	Barbara Mason	#98	
Meditation (Meditacao)	Claudine Longet	#98	
For Your Precious Love	Jerry Butler	#99	
Takin' All I Can Get	Mitch Ryder & The Detroit Wheels	#100	
The Other Side of This Life	Peter, Paul & Mary	#100	
Greetings (This Is Uncle Sam)	The Monitors	#100	
1967			
Hello Goodbye	The Beatles	#1	
Ruby Tuesday	The Rolling Stones	#1	
Respect	Aretha Franklin	#1	
Groovin'	The Young Rascals	#1	
Daydream Believer	The Monkees	#1	
Penny Lane	The Beatles	#1	
Tell It Like It Is	Aaron Neville	#2	
Can't Take My Eyes Off You	Frankie Valli	#2	
Dedicated to the One I Love	Mamas & Papas	#2	13 sec.
I Heard It Through the Grapevine	Gladys Knight & The Pips	#2	
I Say a Little Prayer	Dionne Warwick	#4	
Expressway (To Your Heart)	Soul Survivors	#4	
How Can I Be Sure	The Young Rascals	#4	
Creeque Alley	Mamas & Papas	#5	

PIANO (cont'd)

Words of Love	Mamas & Papas	#5
98.6	Keith	#7
My Cup Runneth Over	Ed Ames	#8
(You Make Me Feel Like) A Natural Woman	Aretha Franklin	#8
Close Your Eyes	Peaches & Herb	#8
Tell It to the Rain	The Four Seasons	#10
Green, Green Grass of Home	Tom Jones	#11
Coming Home Soldier	Bobby Vinton	#11
People Are Strange	The Doors	#12
Pata Pata	Miriam Makeba	#12
Stand By Me	Spyder Turner	#12
Jackson	Nancy Sinatra & Lee Hazlewood	#14
Love Eyes	Nancy Sinatra	#15
Pretty Ballerina	The Left Banke	#15
Here We Go Again	Ray Charles	#15
I've Been Lonely Too Long	The Young Rascals	#16
Beggin'	The Four Seasons	#16
Lady Bird	Nancy Sinatra & Lee Hazlewood	#20
Twelve Thirty (Young Girls Are Coming to the Canyon)	Mamas & Papas	#20
Let's Fall in Love	Peaches & Herb	#21
Hypnotized	Linda Jones	#21
Groovin'	Booker T. & The MG's	#21
The Look of Love	Dusty Springfield	#22
When You're Young and in Love	The Marvelettes	#23
Too Many Fish in the Sea & Three Little Fishes	Mitch Ryder & The Detroit Wheels	#24
In the Chapel in the Moonlight	Dean Martin	#25
The Last Waltz	Engelbert Humperdinck	#25
Try a Little Tenderness	Otis Redding	#25
Yesterday	Ray Charles	#25
Love Bug Leave My Heart Alone	Martha & The Vandellas	#25
Hello Hello	The Sopwith "Camel"	#26
Tramp	Otis & Carla	#26
Detroit City	Tom Jones	#27
Dead End Street	Lou Rawls	#29
Hey, Leroy, Your Mama's Callin' You	Jimmy Castor	#31
Travlin' Man	Stevie Wonder	#32
Lovin' You	Bobby Darin	#32
Your Unchanging Love	Marvin Gaye	#33
Baby You're a Rich Man	The Beatles	#34
Homburg	Procol Harum	#34
Too Much of Nothing	Peter, Paul & Mary	#35
Making Memories	Frankie Laine	#35
Even the Bad Times are Good	The Tremeloes	#36

PIANO (cont'd)

Mr. Dream Merchant	Jerry Butler	#38
You've Made Me so Very Happy	Brenda Holloway	#39
Are You Lonely for Me	Freddy Scott	#39
I'll Take Care of Your Cares	Frankie Laine	#39
Wack Wack	The Young Holt Trio	#40
When Something Is Wrong with My Baby	Sam & Dave	#42
You Don't Know Me	Elvis Presley	#44
Show Business	Lou Rawls	#45
In the Misty Moonlight	Dean Martin	#46
You Wanted Someone to Play With (I Wanted Someone to Love)	Frankie Laine	#48
Together	The Intruders	#48
I'll Never Fall in Love Again	Tom Jones	#49
Soul Man	Ramsey Lewis	#49
We Love You	The Rolling Stones	#50
Nothing Takes the Place of You	Toussaint McCall	#52
A Beautiful Story	Sonny & Cher	#53
I Want to Love You for What You Are	Ronnie Dove	#54
Oh That's Good, No That's Bad	Sam The Sham & The Pharaohs	#54
Let's Spend the Night Together	The Rolling Stones	#55
I'm Gonna Miss You	The Artistics	#55
Lay Some Happiness On Me	Dean Martin	#55
I Could Be so Good to You	Don & The Goodtimes	#56
Take a Look	Aretha Franklin	#56
There's Always Me	Elvis Presley	#56
Tiny Bubbles	Don Ho	#57
Hung Up in Your Eyes	Brian Hyland	#58
Are You Never Coming Home	Sandy Posey	#59
Love Me Forever	Roger Williams	#60
Danny Boy	Ray Price	#60
Glory of Love	Otis Redding	#60
Communication Breakdown	Roy Orbison	#60
Piece of My Heart	Erma Franklin	#62
Oh Yeah!	The Joe Cuba Sextet	#62
A Woman's Hands	Joe Tex	#63
Just One Smile	Gene Pitney	#64
Just Out of Reach (Of My Two Empty Arms)	Percy Sledge	#66
One, Two, Three	Ramsey Lewis	#67
Look at Granny Run, Run	Howard Tate	#67
Sixteen Tons	Tom Jones	#68
If You Go Away	Damita Jo	#68
Slim Jenkin's Place	Booker T. & The MG's	#70
Nine Pound Steel	Joe Simon	#70

PIANO (cont'd)

That Acapulco Gold	The Rainy Daze	#70	
Cry to Me	Freddie Scott	#70	
Sweet, Sweet Lovin'	The Platters	#70	
Constant Rain (Chove Chuva)	Sergio Mendes & Brasil '66	#71	
Skate Now	Lou Courtney	#71	
Our Winter Love	The Lettermen	#72	
Deadend Street	The Kinks	#73	
Now I Know	Jack Jones	#73	
Spreadin' Honey	Watts 103rd St. Rhythm Band	#73	
Something Good (Is Going to Happent to You)	Carla Thomas	#74	
Day Tripper	Ramsey Lewis	#74	
You Mean the World to Me	David Houston	#75	
I'll Turn to Stone	Four Tops	#76	
One Hurt Deserves Another	The Raeletts	#76	
The Dark End of the Street	James Carr	#77	
Can't Help but Love You	The Standells	#78	
Judy	Elvis Presley	#78	19 sec.
Do the Thing	Lou Courtney	#80	
Mr. Pleasant	The Kinks	#80	
I'm Indestructible	Jack Jones	#81	
Night and Day	Sergio Mendes & Brasil '66	#82	
I've Lost You	Jackie Wilson	#82	
You, No One but You	Frankie Laine	#83	
Sunrise, Sunset	Roger Williams	#84	
Wanted: Lover, No Experience Necessary	Laura Lee	#84	
I'll Always Have Faith in You	Carla Thomas	#85	
Nearer to You	Betty Harris	#85	
Lovey Dovey/You're So Fine	Bunny Sigler	#86	
Funky Donkey	Pretty Purdie	#87	
Full Measure	The Lovin' Spoonful	#87	
My Special Prayer	Joe Simon	#87	
More and More	Andy Williams	#88	
Birds of Britain	Bob Crewe Generation	#89	
Heart Be Still	Lorraine Ellison	#89	
Ode to Billy Joe	Ray Bryant	#89	
Danger! She's a Stranger	The Five Stairsteps	#89	
Why Not Tonight	Jimmy Hughes	#90	
Hey Love	Stevie Wonder	#90	
Hello, Hello	Claudine Longet	#91	23, 12 sec.
Daddy's Home	Chuck Jackson & Maxine Brown	#91	
Here Comes Heaven	Eddy Arnold	#91	
When Love Slips Away	Dee Dee Warwick	#92	
It's Been a Long Long Time	The Elgins	#92	

PIANO (cont'd)

Trouble Down Here Below	Lou Rawls	#92
On a Saturday Night	Eddie Floyd	#92
Stout-Hearted Men	Barbra Streisand	#92
She Took You for a Ride	Aaron Neville	#92
Stop! And Think It Over	Perry Como	#92
There Must Be a Way	Jimmy Roselli	#93
Got to Have You Back	Isley Brothers	#93
I Can't Help It (If I'm Still in Love with You)	B.J. Thomas	#94
Penny Arcade	The Cyrkle	#95
Red Roses for Mom	Bobby Vinton	#95
Shake Hands and Walk Away Cryin'	Lou Christie	#95
Everybody Loves a Winner	William Bell	#95
Little Old Wine Drinker Me	Robert Mitchum	#96
Somebody's Sleeping in My Bed	Johnnie Taylor	#96
Hard Lovin' Loser	Judy Collins	#97
People Like You	Eddie Fisher	#97
Don't Rock the Boat	Eddie Floyd	#98
Walkin' Proud	The Pete Klint Quintet	#98
For Me	Sergio Mendes & Brasil '66	#98
When Tomorrow Comes	Carla Thomas	#99
Good Day Sunshine	Claudine Longet	#100
1968		
Grazing in the Grass	Hugh Masekela	#1
Judy in Disguise (With Glasses)	John Fred	#1
This Guy's in Love with You	Herb Alpert	#1
Hey Jude	The Beatles	#1
For Once in My Life	Stevie Wonder	#2
(Theme from) Valley of the Dolls	Dionne Warwick	#2
The Look of Love	Sergio Mendes & Brasil '66	#4
Lady Madonna	The Beatles	#4
I Wish It Would Rain	The Temptations	#4
(Sweet Sweet Baby) Since You've Been Gone	Aretha Franklin	#5
My Special Angel	The Vogues	#7
Think	Aretha Franklin	#7
Goin' Out of My Head/Can't Take My Eyes Off You	The Lettermen	#7
Turn Around, Look at Me	The Vogues	#7
The Ballad of Bonnie and Clyde	Georgie Fame	#7
I Can't Stop Dancing	Archie Bell & The Drells	#9
I Say a Little Prayer	Aretha Franklin	#10
If I Could Build My Whole World Around You	Marvin Gaye & Tammi Terrell	#10
Mighty Quinn (Quinn the Eskimo)	Manfred Mann	#10
Indian Lake	The Cowsills	#10
Susan	The Buckinghams	#11

PIANO (cont'd)

Revolution	The Beatles	#12	
Dream a Little Dream of Me	Mama Cass/Mamas & Papas	#12	23 sec.
Sweet Blindness	The 5th Dimension	#13	
Words	The Bee Gees	#15	
She's a Heartbreaker	Gene Pitney	#16	
Hey, Western Union Man	Jerry Butler	#16	
Ain't No Way	Aretha Franklin	#16	
Journey to the Center of the Mind	The Amboy Dukes	#16	
Soul-Limbo	Booker T. & The MG's	#17	
Am I That Easy to Forget	Engelbert Humperdinck	#18	24 sec.
Promises, Promises	Dionne Warwick	#19	
D.W. Washburn	The Monkees	#19	
Sealed with a Kiss	Gary Lewis/Playboys	#19	
I Will Always Think About You	The New Colony Six	#22	
Bang-Shang-A-Lang	The Archies	#22	
I Can Take or Leave Your Loving	Herman's Hermits	#22	
Cycles	Frank Sinatra	#23	
Cab Driver	The Mills Brothers	#23	
Just as Much as Ever	Bobby Vinton	#24	
Keep On Lovin' Me Honey	Marvin Gaye & Tammi Terrell	#24	
She's a Rainbow	The Rolling Stones	#25	40 sec.
Skip a Rope	Henson Cargill	#25	
(You Keep Me) Hangin' On	Joe Simon	#25	
Till	The Vogues	#27	
Mr. Businessman	Ray Stevens	#28	
Sunday Mornin'	Spanky & Our Gang	#30	
Two Little Kids	Peaches & Herb	#31	
Chained	Marvin Gaye	#32	
Down at Lulu's	The Ohio Express	#33	
Girls Can't Do What the Guys Do	Betty Wright	#33	
Men Are Getting' Scarce	Joe Tex	#33	
Explosion (In My Soul)	Soul Survivors	#33	
Take Good Care of My Baby	Bobby Vinton	#33	
You	Marvin Gaye	#34	
Country Girl - City Man	Billy Vera & Judy Clay	#36	
I Wanna Live	Glen Campbell	#36	
I Met Her in Church	The Box Tops	#37	
Don't Give Up	Petula Clark	#37	
A Question of Temperature	The Balloon Farm	#37	
Paying the Cost to Be the Boss	B.B. King	#39	
People	The Tymes	#39	
I've Never Found a Girl (To Love Me Like You Do)	Eddie Floyd	#40	
The Son of Hickory Holler's Tramp	O.C. Smith	#40	

PIANO (cont'd)

Title	Artist	#
Mission-Impossible	Lalo Schifrin	#41
I Wish It Would Rain	Gladys Knight & The Pips	#41
Brown Eyed Woman	Bill Medley	#43
Not Enough Indians	Dean Martin	#43
My Favorite Things	Herb Alpert & The Tijuana Brass	#45
In the Midnight Hour	The Mirettes	#45
Listen Here	Eddie Harris	#45
United	Peaches & Herb	#46
Understanding	Ray Charles	#46
Street Fighting Man	The Rolling Stones	#48
You Don't Know What You Mean to Me	Sam & Dave	#48
Hard to Handle	Otis Redding	#51
To Wait for Love	Herb Alpert	#51
It's Nice to Be with You	The Monkees	#51
Unwind	Ray Stevens	#52
New Orleans	Neil Diamond	#52
Can't You Find Another Way (Of Doing It)	Sam & Dave	#54
The Ten Commandments of Love	Peaches & Herb	#55
I Guess I'll Have to Cry, Cry, Cry	James Brown	#55
The Impossible Dream	Roger Williams	#55
The Weight	Jackie DeShannon	#55
Peace of Mind	Nancy Wilson	#55
You Send Me	Aretha Franklin	#56
Back in Love Again	The Buckinghams	#57
I'll Never Do You Wrong	Joe Tex	#59
Baby You Come Rollin' Across My Mind	The Peppermint Trolley Company	#59
I Can't Believe I'm Losing You	Frank Sinatra	#60
Dreams of the Everyday Housewife	Wayne Newton	#60
Love in Every Room	Paul Mauriat	#60
You've Still Got a Place in My Heart	Dean Martin	#60
Right Relations	Johnny Rivers	#61
I Loved and I Lost	The Impressions	#61
Lost	Jerry Butler	#62
The Weight	The Band	#63
A Man Needs a Woman	James Carr	#63
God Bless Our Love	The Ballads	#65
Stay Away	Elvis Presley	#67
Breaking up Is Hard to Do	The Happenings	#67
White Houses	Eric Burdon/Animals	#67
Cold Feet	Albert King	#67
California Earthquake	Mama Cass	#67
Mountains of Love	Ronnie Dove	#67
Sunday Sun	Neil Diamond	#68

PIANO (cont'd)

Title	Artist	Chart	Time
Impossible Mission (Mission Impossible)	Soul Survivors	#68	
Cinderella Rockefella	Esther & Abi Ofarim	#68	
100 Years	Nancy Sinatra	#69	
For Once in My Life	Jackie Wilson	#70	
Let Me Be Lonely	Dionne Warwick	#71	
Up-Up and Away	Hugh Masekela	#71	
I Got a Sure Thing	Ollie & The Nightingales	#73	
Here Comes the Rain, Baby	Eddy Arnold	#74	
I'm Gonna Do What They Do to Me	B.B. King	#74	
A Working Man's Prayer	Arthur Prysock	#74	
Let's Make a Promise	Peaches & Herb	#75	
Message from Maria	Joe Simon	#75	
Sweet Memories	Andy Williams	#75	
Private Number	Judy Clay & William Bell	#75	
That Kind of Woman	Merrilee Rush	#76	
Sweet Darlin'	Martha & The Vandellas	#80	
Vance	Roger Miller	#80	
You Put It on Me	B.B. King	#82	
Then You Can Tell Me Goodbye	Eddy Arnold	#84	
Soul Drippin'	The Mauds	#85	
Tit for Tat (Ain't No Talking Back)	James Brown	#86	
In Another Land	Bill Wyman	#87	
It's Crazy	Eddie Harris	#88	
You'll Never Walk Alone	Elvis Presley	#90	
Climb Every Mountain	The Hesitations	#90	
Georgia on My Mind	Wes Montgomery	#91	
Without Love (There Is Nothing)	Oscar Toney, Jr.	#91	
Billy You're My Friend	Gene Pitney	#92	19 sec.
Living in the U.S.A.	Steve Miller Band	#94	
The Shadow of Your Love	The 5 Stairsteps & Cubie	#94	
What's Made Milwaukee Famous (Has Made a Loser Out of Me)	Jerry Lee Lewis	#94	
Send My Baby Back	Freddie Hughes	#94	
The Woman I Love	B.B. King	#94	
Sally Had a Party	Flavor	#95	
Music Music Music	The Happenings	#96	
I Call It Love	The Manhattans	#96	
7:30 Guided Tour	The Five Americans	#96	
Another Place Another Time	Jerry Lee Lewis	#97	
In Some Time	Ronnie Dove	#98	
I Worry About You	Joe Simon	#98	
The B.B. Jones	B.B. King	#98	
Since You've Been Gone	Ramsey Lewis	#98	
Sally Was a Good Old Girl	Trini Lopez	#99	

PIANO (cont'd)

They Don't Make Love Like They Used To	Eddy Arnold	#99
Lady Madonna	Fats Domino	#100

1969

Love Theme from Romeo & Juliet	Henry Mancini	#1
I Can't Get Next to You	The Temptations	#1
Wedding Bell Blues	The 5th Dimension	#1
Everyday People	Sly & The Family Stone	#1
Come Together/Something	The Beatles	#1
And When I Die	Blood, Sweat & Tears	#2
It's Your Thing	The Isley Brothers	#2
Love (Can Make You Happy)	Mercy	#2
Hot Fun in the Summertime	Sly & The Family Stone	#2
Spinning Wheel	Blood, Sweat & Tears	#2
Soulful Strut	Young-Holt Unlimited	#3
Oh Happy Day	Edwin Hawkins Singers	#4
Sweet Caroline (Good Times Never Seemed So Good)	Neil Diamond	#4
One	Three Dog Night	#5
Donovan	Atlantis	#7
This Girl's in Love with You	Dionne Warwick	#7
Baby, Baby Don't Cry	Smokey Robinson & The Miracles	#8
Gitarzan	Ray Stevens	#8
This Girl Is a Woman Now	Gary Puckett & The Union Gap	#9
My Whole World Ended (The Moment You Left Me)	David Ruffin	#9
Backfield in Motion	Mel & Tim	#10
Oh, What a Night	The Dells	#10
Eli's Coming	Three Dog Night	#10
Is That All There Is	Peggy Lee	#11
The Chokin' Kind	Joe Simon	#13
Share Your Love with Me	Aretha Franklin	#13
Baby, I'm for Real	The Originals	#14
I'd Wait a Million Years	The Grass Roots	#15
Things I'd Like to Say	New Colony Six	#16
Eleanor Rigby	Aretha Franklin	#17
Your Good Thing (Is About to End)	Lou Rawls	#18
Soul Deep	The Box Tops	#18
Jealous Kind of Fella	Garland Green	#20
Don't Let the Joneses Get You Down	The Temptations	#20
What's the Use of Breaking Up	Jerry Butler	#20
Workin' On a Groovy Thing	The 5th Dimension	#20
Good Old Rock 'N Roll	Cat Mother & The All Night News Boys	#21
Brother Love's Travelling Salvation Show	Neil Diamond	#22
A Ray of Hope	The Rascals	#24

PIANO (cont'd)

California Soul	The 5th Dimension	#25	
Carry Me Back	The Rascals	#26	
Reuben James	Kenny Rogers & The First Edition	#26	
Mind, Body and Soul	The Flaming Ember	#26	
Goodnight My Love	Paul Anka	#27	
Along Came Jones	Ray Stevens	#27	
Mendocino	Sir Douglas Quintet	#27	
Bella Linda	The Grassroots	#28	
Jesus Is a Soul Man	Lawrence Reynolds	#28	
I Can't See Myself Leaving You	Aretha Franklin	#28	
My Song	Aretha Franklin	#31	
The River Is Wide	The Grassroots	#31	
Cloud Nine	Mongo Santamaria	#32	
To Know You Is to Love You	Bobby Vinton	#34	
Sunday Mornin'	Oliver	#35	
I've Been Hurt	Bill Deal/The Rhondels	#35	
With Pen in Hand	Vikki Carr	#35	
Memories	Elvis Presley	#35	
So Good Together	Andy Kim	#36	
Goo Goo Barabajagal (Love Is Hot)	Donovan w/The Jeff Beck Group	#36	
Something in the Air	Thunderclap Newman	#37	56 sec.
I'm Free	The Who	#37	
First of May	The Bee Gees	#37	
Heaven	The Rascals	#39	
Love Will Find a Way	Jackie DeShannon	#40	
Echo Park	Keith Barbour	#40	
Nobody but You Babe	Clarence Reid	#40	
Kozmic Blues	Janis Joplin	#41	
Earth Angel (Will You Be Mine)	The Vogues	#42	
On the Dock of the Bay	The Dells	#42	
Odds and Ends	Dionne Warwick	#43	
Don't Let Love Hang You Up	Jerry Butler	#44	
Blessed Is the Rain	The Brooklyn Bridge	#45	
And That Reminds Me (My Heart Reminds Me)	The Four Seasons	#45	
I'll Hold Out My Hand	The Clique	#45	
Abergavenny	Shannon (Marty Wilde)	#47	
Malinda	Bobby Taylor	#48	
Tonight I'll Be Staying Here with You	Bob Dylan	#50	
I Could Never Lie to You	The New Colony Six	#50	
Simple Song of Freedom	Tim Hardin	#50	
It's Never Too Late	Steppenwolf	#51	
The Girl I'll Never Know (Before You Loved Me)	Frankie Valli	#52	
Any Way That You Want Me	Evie Sands	#53	

PIANO (cont'd)

Tomorrow Tomorrow	The Bee Gees	#54	
Someday Soon	Judy Collins	#55	
These Are Not My People	Johnny Rivers	#55	
Riot	Hugh Masekela	#55	
Tragedy	Brian Hyland	#56	
Foolish Fool	Dee Dee Warwick	#57	
Who's Making Love	Young-Holt Unlimited	#57	
Tell All the People	The Doors	#57	
Say You Love Me	The Impressions	#58	
Back Door Man	Derek (Johnny Cymbal)	#59	
Ice Cream Song	The Dynamics	#59	
Badge	Cream	#60	
Electric Stories	The Four Seasons	#61	
Why I Sing the Blues	B.B. King	#61	
Glad She's a Woman	Bobby Goldsboro	#61	
Son of a Lovin' Man	Buchanan Brothers	#61	
Pretty World	Sergio Mendes & Brasil '66	#62	
Rain in My Heart	Frank Sinatra	#62	
I Do	The Moments	#62	
Didn't We	Richard Harris	#63	
I Can't Make It Alone	Lou Rawls	#63	
Without Her	Herb Alpert	#63	
Shangri-La	The Lettermen	#64	
In the Still of the Night	Paul Anka	#64	
Love Is All I Have to Give	The Checkmates, Ltd.	#65	
Volunteers	Jefferson Airplane	#65	
(Sittin' On) The Dock of the Bay	Sergio Mendes & Brasil '66	#66	
This Old Heart of Mine (Is Weak for You)	Tammi Terrell	#67	
I Shall Be Released	The Box Tops	#67	
The Young Folks	The Supremes	#69	
Delta Lady	Joe Cocker	#69	
Feeling Alright	Joe Cocker	#69	31 sec.
Marley Purt Drive	Jose Feliciano	#70	
When You Dance	Jay & The Americans	#70	
Looking Back	Joe Simon	#70	
Questions 67 and 68	Chicago	#71	
Truck Stop	Jerry Smith	#71	
Hello It's Me	Nazz	#71	
Love Man	Otis Redding	#72	
Baby, Don't Be Looking in My Mind	Joe Simon	#72	
We'll Cry Together	Maxine Brown	#73	
Don't Forget to Remember	Bee Gees	#73	
(I'm So) Afraid of Losing You Again	Charley Pride	#74	

PIANO (cont'd)

Title	Artist	Page	Time
Nothing Can Take the Place of You	Brook Benton	#74	
Get Off My Back Women	B.B. King	#74	
Singing My Song	Tammy Wynette	#75	
See Ruby Fall	Johnny Cash	#75	19 sec.
Poor Side of Town	Al Wilson	#75	
Just a Little Love	B.B. King	#76	
Julia	Ramsey Lewis	#76	
I'm Gonna Hold On Long as I Can	The Marvelettes	#76	
Gentle on My Mind	Aretha Franklin	#76	
Chelsea Morning	Judy Collins	#78	
Zazueira (Za-zoo-wher-a)	Herb Alpert & The Tijuana Brass	#78	
I Can't Say No to You	Betty Everett	#78	
San Francisco Is a Lonely Town	Joe Simon	#79	
Am I the Same Girl	Barbara Acklin	#79	
Eternity	Vikki Carr	#79	
Forever	Mercy	#79	
Almost Persuaded	Etta James	#79	
Mr. Walker, It's All Over	Billie Jo Spears	#80	
I'm Still a Struggling Man	Edwin Starr	#80	
Goodbye Columbus	The Association	#80	
Someday Man	The Monkees	#81	
Back in the U.S.S.R.	Chubby Checker	#82	
Stay and Love Me All Summer	Brian Hyland	#82	
Theme from "A Summer Place"	The Ventures	#83	
Kay	John Wesley Ryles I	#83	
By the Time I Get to Phoenix	The Mad Lads	#84	
Seven Years	The Impressions	#84	10 sec.
Great Balls of Fire	Tiny Tim	#85	
Love Is Just a Four-Letter Word	Joan Baez	#86	
It's Hard to Get Along	Joe Simon	#87	
Moonlight Sonata	Henry Mancini	#87	
Give It Away	Chi-Lites	#88	
I Can't Be All Bad	Johnny Adams	#89	
A Million to One	Brian Hyland	#90	
All I Have to Offer You (Is Me)	Charley Pride	#91	
From Both Sides Now	Dion	#91	
Brown Arms in Houston	Orpheus	#91	
(One of These Days) Sunday's Gonna' Come On Tuesday	New Establishment	#92	11 sec.
Born Again	Sam & Dave	#92	
Son of a Travelin' Man	Ed Ames	#92	
I'll Never Fall in Love Again	Burt Bacharach	#93	
That's the Way	Joe Tex	#94	
All God's Children Got Soul	Dorothy Morrison	#95	

PIANO (cont'd)

If I Only Had Time	Nick DeCaro	#95
Wichita Lineman	Sergio Mendes & Brasil '66	#95
Only You (And You Alone)	Bobby Hatfield	#95
It's Been a Long Time	Betty Everett	#96
I Don't Want to Cry	Ruby Winters	#97
It's a Groovy World	The Unifics	#97
Alice's Rock & Roll Restaurant	Arlo Guthrie	#97
I Can't Help It (If I'm Still in Love with You)	Al Martino	#97
Curly	Jimmy Clanton	#97
Something's On her Mind	The Four Seasons	#98
Drummer Man	Nancy Sinatra	#98
Why Is the Wine Sweeter (On the Other Side)	Eddie Floyd	#98
Galveston	Roger Williams	#99
Big in Vegas	Buck Owens	#100
July You're a Woman	Pat Boone	#100

SAXOPHONE

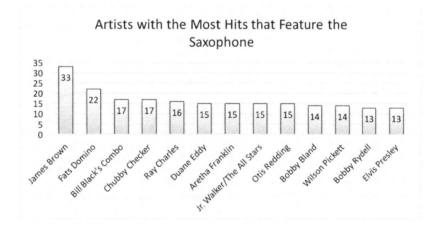

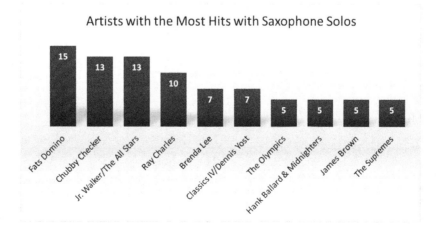

SONG	ARTIST	HOT 100	LENGTH OF SOLO
1960			
Twist	Chubby Checker	#1	14 sec.
Running Bear	Johnny Preston	#1	
Poetry in Motion	Johnny Tillotson	#2	
Wild One	Bobby Rydell	#2	
You Talk Too Much	Joe Jones	#3	
Where or When	Dion & The Belmonts	#3	
Sweet Nothin's	Brenda Lee	#4	30 sec.
Swingin' School	Bobby Rydell	#5	17 sec.
Go, Jimmy, Go	Jimmy Clanton	#5	12 sec.
A Million to One	Jimmy Charles	#5	
New Orleans	U.S. Bonds	#6	31 sec.
Let's Go, Let's Go, Let's Go	Hank Ballard & The Midnighters	#6	21 sec.
That's All You Gotta Do	Brenda Lee	#6	19, 16 sec.
Love You So	Ron Holden w/The Thunderbirds	#7	30 sec.
Let the Little Girl Dance	Billy Bland	#7	26 sec.
Finger Poppin' Time	Hank Ballard & The Midnighters	#7	19 sec.
Stairway to Heaven	Neil Sedaka	#9	15 sec.
White Silver Sands	Bill Black's Combo	#9	
Don't Be Cruel	Bill Black's Combo	#11	
Down By the Station	The Four Preps	#13	
Rockin' Around the Christmas Tree	Brenda Lee	#14	28 sec.
Feel so Fine	Johnny Preston	#14	12 sec.
The Hucklebuck	Chubby Checker	#14	18, 17 sec.
My Girl Josephine	Fats Domino	#14	
Beatnik Fly	Johnny & The Hurricanes	#15	
Blue Tango	Bill Black's Combo	#16	
Smokie - Part 2	Bill Black's Combo	#17	
Josephine	Bill Black's Combo	#18	
Ding-A-Ling	Bobby Rydell	#18	
(You've Got To) Move Two Mountains	Marv Johnson	#20	14 sec.
First Name Initial	Annette	#20	
Trouble in Paradise	The Crests	#20	
Rudolph the Red Nosed Reindeer	The Chipmunks	#21	
Don't Come Knockin'	Fats Domino	#21	22 sec.
To Each His Own	The Platters	#21	
Another Sleepless Night	Jimmy Clanton	#22	
Lonely Weekends	Charlie Rich	#22	22 sec.
The Madison	Al Brown	#23	
Hello Young Lovers	Paul Anka	#23	
Got a Girl	The Four Preps	#24	

SAXOPHONE (cont'd)

Shimmy, Shimmy, Ko-Ko-Bop	Little Anthony & The Imperials	#24	
Country Boy	Fats Domino	#25	36, 17 sec.
Bonnie Came Back	Duane Eddy	#26	
Twistin' U.S.A.	Danny & The Juniors	#27	17 sec.
Peter Gunn	Duane Eddy	#27	
Jump Over	Freddy Cannon	#28	
Ooh Poo Pah Doo Part II	Jessie Hill	#28	
The Twist	Hank Ballard & The Midnighters	#28	
Summer Set	Monte Kelly	#30	
Ruby Duby Du	Tobin Matthews	#30	
The Madison Time - Part 1	Ray Bryant Combo	#30	
Too Much Tequila	The Champs	#30	
There's Something on Your Mind (Part 2)	Bobby Marchan	#31	
Am I the Man	Jackie Wilson	#32	
Think	James Brown	#33	24 sec.
My Dearest Darling	Etta James	#34	
Yes Sir, That's My Baby	Ricky Nelson	#34	23 sec.
Little Things Mean a Lot	Joni James	#35	
Run Red Run	The Coasters	#36	20, 10 sec.
Little Coco Palm	Jerry Wallace	#36	27 sec.
(I Do The) Shimmy, Shimmy	Bobby Freeman	#37	16 sec.
In the Still of the Night	Dion & The Belmonts	#38	
Heartbreak (It's Hurtin' Me)	Little Willie John	#38	22 sec.
Natural Born Lover	Fats Domino	#38	65 sec.
Just a Little	Brenda Lee	#40	14 sec.
Ruby Duby Du from "Key Witness"	Charles Wolcott	#41	
Too Pooped to Pop "Casey"	Chuck Berry	#42	15 sec.
Whole Lotta Shakin' Goin' On	Chubby Checker	#42	17 sec.
Shimmy Like Kate	The Olympics	#42	27 sec.
For Love	Lloyd Price	#43	14 sec.
Shazam!	Duane Eddy	#45	15 sec.
My Love	Nat "King" Cole/Stan Kenton	#47	
Lawdy Miss Lawdy	Gary Stites	#47	15 sec.
What About Us	The Coasters	#47	26 sec.
Dance by the Light of the Moon	The Olympics	#47	12 sec.
Let the Good Times Roll	Shirley & Lee	#48	26 sec.
Down Yonder	Johnny & The Hurricanes	#48	
Heartbreak (It's Hurtin' Me)	Jon Thomas	#48	23 sec.
Wake Me, Shake Me	The Coasters	#51	
Tell Me That You Love Me	Fats Domino	#51	20 sec.
If I Can't Have You	Etta James & Harvey Fuqua	#52	
Harlem Nocturne	The Viscounts	#52	
I Shot Mr. Lee	The Bobbettes	#52	

SAXOPHONE (cont'd)

Title	Artist	#	Duration
Honey Hush	Joe Turner	#53	33 sec.
Chattanooga Choo Choo	Ernie Fields	#54	
At My Front Door	Dee Clark	#56	10 sec.
Alley-Oop	The Dyna-Sores	#59	12 sec.
Humdinger	Freddy Cannon	#59	
Right By My Side	Ricky Nelson	#59	25 sec.
The Urge	Freddy Cannon	#60	
Rocking Goose	Johnny & The Hurricanes	#60	
Amapola	Jacky Noguez	#63	20 sec.
Come Back	Jimmy Clanton	#63	
Rockin' Red Wing	Sammy Masters	#64	30 sec.
Just a Little Bit	Rosco Gordon	#64	22 sec.
Clementine	Jan & Dean	#65	11 sec.
(Let's Do) The Hully Gully Twist	Bill Doggett	#66	
The Bells	James Brown	#68	
Groovy Tonight	Bobby Rydell	#70	
Besame Mucho (Part One)	The Coasters	#70	
Easy Lovin'	Wade Flemons	#70	
Skokiaan (South African Song)	Bill Haley & His Comets	#70	
Cry Cry Cry	Bobby Bland	#71	
Ramona	The Blue Diamonds	#72	13 sec.
Up Town	Roy Orbison	#72	
Rambling	The Ramblers	#73	
No	Dodie Stevens	#73	14 sec.
Brontosaurus Stomp	The Piltdown Men	#75	
Time After Time	Frankie Ford	#75	13 sec.
Night Theme	The Mark II	#75	
Let the Good Times Roll	Ray Charles	#78	18 sec.
Kommotion	Duane Eddy	#78	
Swingin' Down the Lane	Jerry Wallace	#79	32 sec.
This Old Heart	James Brown	#79	16 sec.
In the Still of the Nite	The Five Satins	#81	28 sec.
Night Train	The Viscounts	#82	
One Mint Julep	Chet Atkins	#82	
Shadows of Love	LaVern Baker	#83	
Tuxedo Junction	Frankie Avalon	#83	32 sec.
Before I Grow Too Old	Fats Domino	#84	
(Do the) Mashed Potatoes (Part 1)	Nat Kendrick	#84	
Blue Velvet	The Statues	#84	
You Talk Too Much	Frankie Ford	#87	
Secret of Love	Elton Anderson	#88	
I've Been Loved Before	Shirley & Lee	#88	
House of Bamboo	Earl Grant	#88	22 sec.

SAXOPHONE (cont'd)

Song	Artist	Chart	Duration
Mojo Workout (Dance)	Larry Bright	#90	
Push Push	Austin Taylor	#90	12 sec.
Whip It On Me	Jessie Hill	#91	
Talk to Me Baby	Annette	#92	
How Deep Is the Ocean	Miss Toni Fisher	#93	51 sec.
Since I Made You Cry	The Rivieras	#93	18 sec.
You Were Born to Be Loved	Billy Bland	#94	26 sec.
Dance with Me Georgie	The Bobbettes	#95	22 sec.
Irresistible You	Bobby Peterson	#96	
Just Give Me A Ring	Clyde McPhatter	#96	15 sec.
Revival	Johnny & The Hurricanes	#97	
If You Need Me	Fats Domino	#98	24 sec.
The Old Payola Roll Blues (Side 1)	Stan Freberg/Jesse White	#99	11 sec.
This Is My Story	Mickey & Sylvia	#100	

1961

Song	Artist	Chart	Duration
Surrender	Elvis Presley	#1	
Hit the Road Jack	Ray Charles	#1	
Quarter to Three	Gary (U.S.) Bonds	#1	22 sec.
Runaround Sue	Dion	#1	
The Lion Sleeps Tonight	The Tokens	#1	14 sec.
Pony Time	Chubby Checker	#1	18 sec.
Runaway	Del Shannon	#1	
Tossin' and Turnin'	Bobby Lewis	#1	14 sec.
Daddy's Home	Shep & The Limelites	#2	
Shop Around	The Miracles	#2	18 sec.
Last Night	Mar-Keys	#3	
But I Do	Clarence Henry	#4	
Calendar Girl	Neil Sedaka	#4	
Dum Dum	Brenda Lee	#4	18 sec.
I Feel So Bad	Elvis Presley	#5	
You Must Have Been a Beautiful Baby	Bobby Darin	#5	
School Is Out	Gary (U.S.) Bonds	#5	
Angel Baby	Rosie & The Originals	#5	21 sec.
Hats off to Larry	Del Shannon	#5	
Baby Sittin' Boogie	Buzz Clifford	#6	10 sec.
Who Put the Bomp (In the Bomp, Bomp, Bomp)	Barry Mann	#7	
Ya Ya	Lee Dorsey	#7	
The Fly	Chubby Checker	#7	18 sec.
Pretty Little Angel Eyes	Curtis Lee	#7	19 sec.
Let's Twist Again	Chubby Checker	#8	11 sec.
One Track Mind	Bobby Lewis	#9	
Spanish Harlem	Ben E. King	#10	11 sec.
Good Time Baby	Bobby Rydell	#11	

SAXOPHONE (cont'd)

Title	Artist	#	Duration
Barbara-Ann	The Regents	#13	17 sec.
(He's My) Dreamboat	Connie Francis	#14	14 sec.
Let the Four Winds Blow	Fats Domino	#15	21 sec.
The Story of My Love	Paul Anka	#16	
"Pepe"	Duane Eddy	#18	
Tell Me Why	The Belmonts	#18	
I'm Comin on Back to You	Jackie Wilson	#19	
Hearts of Stone	Bill Black's Combo	#20	
Just for Old Time's Sake	The McGuire Sisters	#20	
Frankie and Johnny	Brook Benton	#20	
Jingle Bell Rock	Bobby Rydell & Chubby Checker	#21	
Baby Oh Baby	The Shells	#21	
That Old Black Magic	Bobby Rydell	#21	
Big John	The Shirelles	#21	
Rama Lama Ding Dong	The Edsels	#21	23 sec.
I Wanna Thank You	Bobby Rydell	#21	12 sec.
What a Party	Fats Domino	#22	
One Summer Night	The Diamonds	#22	
The Hoochi Coochi Coo	Hank Ballard & The Midnighters	#23	14 sec.
It's Keep Rainin'	Fats Domino	#23	30 sec.
Little Egypt (Ying-Yang)	The Coasters	#23	
Dance the Mess Around	Chubby Checker	#24	
I'm A Fool to Care	Joe Barry	#24	
Your Ma Said You Cried in Your Sleep Last Night	Kenny Dino	#24	
Heart and Soul	Jan & Dean	#25	
Ole Buttermilk Sky	Bill Black's Combo	#25	
The Watusi	The Vibrations	#25	19 sec.
The Fish	Bobby Rydell	#25	
Candy Man	Roy Orbison	#25	
Take Five	Dave Brubeck Quartet	#25	
Foot Stomping - Part 1	The Flares	#25	13 sec.
Funny	Maxine Brown	#25	
The Switch-A-Roo	Hank Ballard & The Midnighters	#26	
School Is In	Gary (U.S.) Bonds	#28	23 sec.
Wheels	Billy Vaughn	#28	
So Long Baby	Del Shannon	#28	
You Can't Sit Down (Part 2)	Philip Upchurch Combo	#29	
(Ghost) Riders in the Sky	Ramrods	#30	
Shu Rah	Fats Domino	#32	23 sec.
Ain't That Just Like a Woman	Fats Domino	#33	17 sec.
I'm Learning About Love	Brenda Lee	#33	20 sec.
Jeremiah Peabody's Poly Unsaturated Quick Dissolving Fast Acting Pleasant Tasting Green and Purple Pills	Ray Stevens	#35	

SAXOPHONE (cont'd)

Song	Artist	#	Duration
Kissin' on the Phone	Paul Anka	#35	
The Majestic	Dion	#36	
Exodus	Eddie Harris	#36	
Wait A Minute	The Coasters	#37	
Let's Go Again (Where We Went Last Night)	Hank Ballard & The Midnighters	#39	21 sec.
African Waltz	Cannonball Adderley	#41	
Movin'	Bill Black's Combo	#41	
Ready for Your Love	Shep & The Limelites	#42	
Hollywood	Connie Francis	#42	12 sec.
Good, Good Lovin'	Chubby Checker	#43	19 sec.
Underwater	The Frogmen	#44	
I Pity the Fool	Bobby Bland	#46	
Under the Moon of Love	Curtis Lee	#46	25 sec.
The Charleston	Ernie Fields	#47	
To Be Loved (Forever)	The Pentagons	#48	
Nothing but Good	Hank Ballard & The Midnighters	#49	
Baby, You're Right	James Brown	#49	21 sec.
Ain't It Baby	The Miracles	#49	14 sec.
My Blue Heaven	Duane Eddy	#50	
Watch Your Step	Bobby Parker	#51	14 sec.
Mighty Good Lovin'	The Miracles	#51	14 sec.
Sometime	Gene Thomas	#53	26 sec.
The Peppermint Twist	Danny Peppermint	#54	15 sec.
Music, Music, Music	The Sensations	#54	16 sec.
Mr. Happiness	Johnny Maestro	#57	
Lonely Street	Clarence Henry	#57	15 sec.
Honky Tonk (Part 2)	Bill Doggett	#57	
Three Steps from the Altar	Shep & The Limelites	#58	
Them That Got	Ray Charles	#58	19 sec.
The Way I Am	Jackie Wilson	#58	
For Sentimental Reasons	The Cleftones	#60	
Leave My Kitten Alone	Little Willie John	#60	28 sec.
Morning After	Mar-Keys	#60	
Pony Express	Danny & The Juniors	#60	17 sec.
On Bended Knees	Clarence Henry	#64	20 sec.
You Don't Want My Love	Andy Williams	#64	12 sec.
Lonely Blue Nights	Rosie	#66	27 sec.
Back Beat No. 1	The Rondels	#66	
Keep on Dancing	Hank Ballard & The Midnighters	#66	18 sec.
Young Boy Blues	Ben E. King	#66	
I Hear You Knocking	Fats Domino	#67	
Twistin' U.S.A.	Chubby Checker	#68	18 sec.
Miss Fine	The New Yorkers	#69	13 sec.

SAXOPHONE (cont'd)

Title	Artist	Page	Duration
It's Unbelievable	The Larks	#69	
Cinderella	Paul Anka	#70	
A Certain Girl	Ernie K-Doe	#71	26 sec.
(I've Got) Spring Fever	Little Willie John	#71	
For Me and My Gal	Freddy Cannon	#71	
Don't Cry No More	Bobby Bland	#71	22 sec.
Chills and Fever	Ronnie Love	#72	13 sec.
Leave My Kitten Alone	Johnny Preston	#73	24 sec.
Cerveza	Bert Kaempfert	#73	
Pitter-Patter	The Four Sportsmen	#76	
Little Pedro	The Olympics	#76	25 sec.
What a Walk	Bobby Lewis	#77	
Sound-Off	Titus Turner	#77	
Wabash Blues	The Viscounts	#77	
Summertime	The Marcels	#78	
Joanie	Frankie Calen	#78	
Son-In-Law	The Blossoms	#79	
My Memories of You	Donnie and The Dreamers	#79	
Flamingo Express	The Royaltones	#82	
If	The Paragons	#82	
Rockin' Bicycle	Fats Domino	#83	
Ring of Fire	Duane Eddy	#84	
Brother-in-Law (He's a Moocher)	Paul Peek	#84	
Charlena	The Sevilles	#84	25 sec.
Blue Tomorrow	Billy Vaughn	#84	
Ja-Da	Johnny & The Hurricanes	#86	
I Remember	Maurice Williams and The Zodiacs	#86	19 sec.
Dream Boy	Annette	#87	
Drivin' Home	Duane Eddy	#87	
Late Date	The Parkays	#89	
The Mess Around	Bobby Freeman	#89	17 sec.
California Sun	Joe Jones	#89	16 sec.
Hop Scotch	Santo and Johnny	#90	
My Heart's On Fire	Billy Bland	#90	
Come On Over	The Strollers	#91	
Don't Let Him Shop Around	Debbie Dean	#92	16 sec.
Honky Train	Bill Black's Combo	#92	
Kokomo	The Flamingos	#92	16 sec.
I Can't Take It	Mary Ann Fisher	#92	
Dear Mr. D.J. Play It Again	Tina Robin	#95	
Little Turtle Dove	Otis Williams/Charms	#95	
Girls Girls Girls (Part II)	The Coasters	#96	13 sec.
Don't Forget I Love You	The Butanes	#96	13 sec.

SAXOPHONE (cont'd)

Here's My Confession	Wyatt (Earp) McPherson	#97	
Won'cha Come Home, Bill Bailey	Della Reese	#98	
Image - Part 1	Hank Levine	#98	

1962

Loco-Motion	Little Eva	#1	12 sec.
He's a Rebel	The Crystals	#1	16 sec.
Duke of Earl	Gene Chandler	#1	
Soldier Boy	The Shirelles	#1	
Peppermint Twist - Part 1	Joey Dee & The Starliters	#1	
Wanderer	Dion	#2	20 sec.
The Wah Watusi	The Orlons	#2	13 sec.
Mashed Potato Time	Dee Dee Sharp	#2	16 sec.
Limbo Rock	Chubby Checker	#2	
Return to Sender	Elvis Presley	#2	
Lovers Who Wander	Dion	#3	
Slow Twistin'	Chubby Checker w/ Dee Dee Sharp	#3	14 sec.
Dream Baby (How Long Must I Dream)	Roy Orbison	#4	
Don't Hang Up	The Orlons	#4	
Let Me In	The Sensations	#4	21 sec.
Party Lights	Claudine Clark	#5	14 sec.
Ride!	Dee Dee Sharp	#5	12 sec.
Shout! Shout! (Knock Yourself Out)	Ernie Maresca	#6	
Lover Please	Clyde McPhatter	#7	11 sec.
You'll Lose a Good Thing	Barbara Lynn	#8	15 sec.
Vacation	Connie Francis	#9	14 sec.
Unchain My Heart	Ray Charles	#9	22 sec.
Twistin' the Night Away	Sam Cooke	#9	19 sec.
Twist, Twist Senora	Gary (U.S.) Bonds	#9	
Dear Lady Twist	Gary (U.S.) Bonds	#9	
Gravy (For my Mashed Potatoes)	Dee Dee Sharp	#9	
Love Came to Me	Dion	#10	
Popeye (The Hitchhiker)	Chubby Checker	#10	15 sec.
Rinky Dink	Baby Cortez	#10	
Conscience	James Darren	#11	
(Dance with the) Guitar Man	Duane Eddy	#12	
Dancin' Party	Chubby Checker	#12	10 sec.
Keep Your Hands off My Baby	Little Eva	#12	13 sec.
Town Without Pity	Gene Pitney	#13	
I'll Never Dance Again	Bobby Rydell	#14	
Irresistible You	Bobby Darin	#15	
Follow that Dream	Elvis Presley	#15	
Desafinado	Stan Getz/Charlie Byrd	#15	
Beechwood 4-5789	The Marvelettes	#17	

SAXOPHONE (cont'd)

Title	Artist	Rank	Duration
Chains	The Cookies	#17	
Having a Party	Sam Cooke	#17	
I've Got Bonnie	Bobby Rydell	#18	
Let's Go (Pony)	The Routers	#19	
Hey, Let's Twist	Joey Dee & The Starliters	#20	30 sec.
Hide 'Nor Hair	Ray Charles	#20	12 sec.
Walk on the Wild Side (Part 1)	Jimmy Smith	#21	
You Win Again	Fats Domino	#22	
A Wonderful Dream	The Majors	#22	14 sec.
Twistin' Matilda (And the Channel)	Jimmy Soul	#22	
Little Bitty Pretty One	Clyde McPhatter	#25	
Hully Gully Baby	The Dovells	#25	15 sec.
Twist-Her	Bill Black's Combo	#26	
Seven Day Weekend	Gary (U.S.) Bonds	#27	19 sec.
Do-Re-Mi	Lee Dorsey	#27	
Bristol Twistin' Annie	The Dovells	#27	15 sec.
Turn on Your Love Light	Bobby Bland	#28	19 sec.
It Started All Over Again	Brenda Lee	#29	
The Jam (Part 1)	Bobby Gregg	#29	
Jambalaya (On the Bayou)	Fats Domino	#30	27 sec.
King of the Whole Wide World	Elvis Presley	#30	14 sec.
Surfer's Stomp	The Mar-Kets	#31	
Have a Good Time	Sue Thompson	#31	
The Ballad of Paladin	Duane Eddy	#33	
Pop Pop Pop - Pie	The Sherrys	#35	16 sec.
Night Train	James Brown	#35	
Blues (Stay Away from Me)	Floyd Cramer	#36	
Do the New Continental	The Dovells	#37	16 sec.
Mary's Little Lamb	James Darren	#39	
The Alvin Twist	The Chipmunks	#40	
Limbo Rock	The Champs	#40	
(I Was) Born to Cry	Dion	#42	
Baby Face	Bobby Darin	#42	
Santa Claus Is Watching You	Ray Stevens	#45	
What's Gonna Happen When Summer's Done	Freddy Cannon	#45	
Flying Circle	Frank Slay	#45	
You Talk About Love	Barbara George	#46	
Stubborn Kind of Fellow	Marvin Gaye	#46	
Lost Someone	James Brown	#48	
Balboa Blue	The Mar-Kets	#48	
The Boys' Night Out	Patti Page	#49	17 sec.
Moments	Jennell Hawkins	#50	
Annie Get Your Yo-Yo	Little Junior Parker	#51	18 sec.

SAXOPHONE (cont'd)

Title	Artist	#	Duration
Pop-Eye	Huey Smith	#51	
So Deep	Brenda Lee	#52	14 sec.
Diddle-Dee-Dum (What Happens When Your Love Has Gone)	The Belmonts	#53	
Save All Your Lovin' for Me	Brenda Lee	#53	
Twistin' with Linda	The Isley Brothers	#54	
Yield Not to Temptation	Bobby Bland	#56	18 sec.
Above the Stars	Mr. Acker Bilk	#59	
My Real Name	Fats Domino	#59	19 sec.
Woman Is a Man's Best Friend	Teddy & The Twilights	#59	
Our Anniversary	Shep & The Limelites	#59	
Let's Go Trippin'	Dick Dale	#60	
Boom Boom	John Lee Hooker	#60	
Shout and Shimmy	James Brown	#61	
Oh My Angel	Bertha Tillman	#61	
It Will Stand	The Showmen	#61	
Second Fiddle Girl	Barbara Lynn	#63	
A Little Bit Now (A Little Bit Later)	The Majors	#63	11 sec.
Don't You Worry	Don Gardner/Dee Dee Ford	#66	
If You Were a Rock and Roll Record	Freddy Cannon	#67	
Happy Weekend	Dave "Baby" Cortez	#67	
Twistin' All Night Long	Danny & The Juniors w/Freddy Cannon	#68	
Lose Her	Bobby Rydell	#69	
That's My Desire	The Sensations	#69	
Tennessee	Jan & Dean	#69	
Midnight Special, Part 1	Jimmy Smith	#69	
Jivin' Around	Al Casey Combo	#71	
Don't Worry 'Bout Me	Vincent Edwards	#72	
La Paloma Twist	Chubby Checker	#72	
Roly Poly	Joey Dee & The Starliters	#74	
All Night Long	Sandy Nelson	#75	
Who Will the Next Fool Be	Bobby Bland	#76	
Oliver Twist	Rod McKuen	#76	
Sweet and Lovely	April Stevens & Nino Tempo	#77	
Deep in the Heart of Texas	Duane Eddy	#78	
So What	Bill Black's Combo	#78	
Did You Ever See a Dream Walking	Fats Domino	#79	
I'll Rmember Carol	Tommy Boyce	#80	12 sec.
Lipstick Traces (On a Cigarette)	Benny Spellman	#80	
Mashed Potatoes (Part 1)	Steve Alaimo	#81	
Broken Heart	The Fiestas	#81	
Mashed Potatoes U.S.A.	James Brown	#82	
Ol' Man River	Jimmy Smith	#82	

SAXOPHONE (cont'd)

Title	Artist	#	Duration
The Jitterbug	The Dovells	#82	14 sec.
She's a Troublemaker	The Majors	#83	12 sec.
Ain't That Loving You	Bobby Bland	#86	
Life's Too Short	The Lafayettes	#87	
Baby Elephant Walk	The Miniature Men	#87	
Heart Breaker	Dean Christie	#87	14 sec.
Do You Know How to Twist	Hank Ballard	#87	22 sec.
A Taste of Honey	Victor Feldman Quartet	#88	
March of the Siamese Children	Kenny Ball	#88	
Shimmy, Shimmy Walk, Part 1	The Megatons	#88	
Potato Peeler	Bobby Gregg	#89	
You Should'a Treated Me Right	Ike & Tina Turner	#89	19 sec.
Ida Jane	Fats Domino	#90	15 sec.
Walk on with the Duke	The Duke of Earl (Gene Chandler)	#91	
Oh! What It Seemed to Be	The Castells	#91	10 sec.
Dream	Dinah Washington	#92	
Cookin'	Al Casey Combo	#92	
Limelight	Mr. Acker Bilk	#92	
Pushin' Your Luck	Sleepy King	#92	
Copy Cat	Gary (U.S.) Bonds	#92	10 sec.
Teen Queen of the Week	Freddy Cannon	#92	
Doin' the Continental Walk	Danny & The Juniors	#93	18 sec.
I Really Don't Want to Know	Solomon Burke	#93	46 sec.
The Basie Twist	Count Basie	#94	
Rough Lover	Aretha Franklin	#94	18 sec.
What Did Daddy Do	Shep & The Limelites	#94	
Beach Party	Dave York	#95	16 sec.
Play the Thing	Marlowe Morris Quintet	#95	
Sugar Plum	Ike Clanton	#95	
Cold, Cold Heart	Dinah Washington	#96	13, 11 sec.
Send for Me (If You Need Some Lovin)	Barbara George	#96	15 sec.
Fiesta	Dave "Baby" Cortez	#96	
Duchess of Earl	Pearlettes	#96	
Limbo Dance	The Champs	#97	
Shake a Hand	Ruth Brown	#97	
I'm Tossin' and Turnin' Again	Bobby Lewis	#98	
Dance with Mr. Domino	Fats Domino	#98	14 sec.
My Time for Cryin'	Maxine Brown	#98	
Motorcycle	Tico & The Triumphs	#99	15 sec.
Cry Myself to Sleep	Del Shannon	#99	
Hully Gully Guitar	Jerry Reed	#99	
Tequila Twist	The Champs	#99	
Mama (He Treats Your Daughter Mean)	Ruth Brown	#99	

SAXOPHONE (cont'd)

Quarter to Four Stomp	The Stompers	#100	20 sec.
Sweet Georgia Brown	Carroll Bros.	#100	

1963

If You Wanna Be Happy	Jimmy Soul	#1	
Washington Square	The Village Stompers	#2	
Da Doo Ron Ron (When He Walked Me Home)	The Crystals	#3	11 sec.
South Street	The Orlons	#3	
You Can't Sit Down	The Dovells	#3	16 sec.
Heat Wave	Martha & The Vandellas	#4	
One Fine Day	The Chiffons	#5	10 sec.
Don't Say Nothin' Bad (About My Baby)	The Cookies	#7	24 sec.
Zip-A-Dee Doo-Dah	Bob B. Soxx/Blue Jeans	#8	
Wild Weekend	The Rebels	#8	
Mickey's Monkey	The Miracles	#8	10 sec.
You've Really Got a Hold On Me	The Miracles	#8	
Another Saturday Night	Sam Cooke	#10	
Hey, Girl	Freddie Scott	#10	
Do the Bird	Dee Dee Sharp	#10	12 sec.
Walking the Dog	Rufus Thomas	#10	
He's Sure the Boy I Love	The Crystals (Darlene Love)	#11	25 sec.
Birdland	Chubby Checker	#12	15 sec.
Not Me	The Orlons	#12	34 sec.
My Summer Love	Ruby & The Romantics	#16	
Mr. Bass Man	Johnny Cymbal	#16	
Wildwood Days	Bobby Rydell	#17	
The Boy Next Door	The Secrets	#18	16 sec.
Have You Heard	The Duprees	#18	
I'm Gonna Be Warm This Winter	Connie Francis	#18	10 sec.
Cross Fire!	The Orlons	#19	
Everybody Loves a Lover	The Shirelles	#19	28 sec.
Part Time Love	Little Johnny Taylor	#19	
Don't Set Me Free	Ray Charles	#20	20 sec.
Let's Turkey Trot	Little Eva	#20	17 sec.
Let's Limbo Some More	Chubby Checker	#20	
Misty	Lloyd Price	#21	
No One	Ray Charles	#21	20 sec.
Don't Make Me Over	Dionne Warwick	#21	
You Lost the Sweetest Boy	Mary Wells	#22	12 sec.
Wiggle Wobble	Les Cooper	#22	
Ain't That a Shame!	The Four Seasons	#22	
Shut Down	The Beach Boys	#23	
Wham!	Lonnie Mack	#24	
Twist It Up	Chubby Checker	#25	31 sec.

SAXOPHONE (cont'd)

Title	Artist	#	Duration
Bust Out	The Busters	#25	
The Cinnamon Cinder (It's a Very Nice Dance)	The Pastel Six	#25	11 sec.
Wait Til' My Bobby Gets Home	Darlene Love	#26	
Boss Guitar	Duane Eddy	#28	16 sec.
Without Love (There Is Nothing)	Ray Charles	#29	
Hitch Hike	Marvin Gaye	#30	
Baby Don't You Weep	Garnet Mimms & The Enchanters	#30	
A Love She Can Count On	The Miracles	#31	
Witchcraft	Elvis Presley	#32	29 sec.
See See Rider	LaVern Baker	#34	30 sec.
Why Don't You Believe Me	The Duprees	#37	
Why Do Lovers Break Each Other's Heart?	Bob B. Soxx/Blue Jeans	#38	
(Today I Met) The Boy I'm Gonna Marry	Darlene Love	#39	20 sec.
Your Old Stand By	Mary Wells	#40	
A Love So Fine	The Chiffons	#40	
Birthday Party	The Pixies Three	#40	10 sec.
The Bounce	The Olympics	#40	23 sec.
Shake a Hand	Jackie Wilson & Linda Hopkins	#42	
Rock Me in the Cradle of Love	Dee Dee Sharp	#43	11 sec.
Puddin N' Tain (Ask Me Again, I'll Tell You the Same)	The Alley Cats	#43	18 sec.
Shake Sherry	The Contours	#43	
Misery	The Dynamics	#44	24 sec.
Locking Up My Heart	The Marvelettes	#44	
Monkey-Shine	Bill Black's Combo	#47	
As Long as I Know He's Mine	The Marvelettes	#47	13 sec.
Come Go with Me	Dion	#48	15, 12 sec.
Old Smokey Locomotion	Little Eva	#48	14 sec.
I Got a Woman	Freddie Scott	#48	
Point Panic	The Surfaris	#49	
It's Too Late	Wilson Pickett	#49	
Strange I Know	The Marvelettes	#49	
Two Kinds of Teardrops	Del Shannon	#50	
Sting Ray	The Routers	#50	
Do It - Rat Now	Bill Black's Combo	#51	
Here I Stand	The Rip Chords	#51	
Long Tall Texan	Murry Kellum	#51	
Everybody Monkey	Freddy Cannon	#52	20 sec.
What Are Boys Made Of	The Percells	#53	
A Fine Fine Boy	Darlene Love	#53	12 sec.
Pin a Medal on Joey	James Darren	#54	
Who Stole the Keeshka?	The Matys Bros.	#55	21 sec.
Let's Stomp	Bobby Comstock	#57	12 sec.
Night Life	Rusty Draper	#57	

SAXOPHONE (cont'd)

Title	Artist	#	Duration
He's Got the Power	The Exciters	#57	
Not Too Young to Get Married	Bob B. Soxx/Blue Jeans	#63	10 sec.
Two Sides (To Every Story)	Etta James	#63	
Back at the Chicken Shack, Part 1	Jimmy Smith	#63	
Don't Let Her Be Your Baby	The Contours	#64	10 sec.
You're Gonna Need Me	Barbara Lynn	#65	
Sax Fifth Avenue	Johnny Beecher	#65	
Cottonfields	Ace Cannon	#67	
Bossa Nova U.S.A.	Dave Brubeck Quartet	#69	
How Much Is That Doggie in the Window	Baby Jane & The Rockabyes	#69	
I Am a Witness	Tommy Hunt	#71	
Ask Me	Maxine Brown	#75	
Breath Taking Guy	The Supremes	#75	
The Popeye Waddle	Don Covay	#75	
I'm Crazy 'Bout My Baby	Marvin Gaye	#77	
Signed, Sealed, and Delivered	James Brown	#77	
Red Pepper I	Roosevelt Fountain	#78	
Any Other Way	Chuck Jackson	#81	
Walk Right In	The Moments	#82	
Lonely Boy, Lonely Guitar	Duane Eddy	#82	
Thank You and Goodnight	The Angels	#84	
Tears of Joy	Chuck Jackson	#85	
Ann-Marie	The Belmonts	#86	
Dancin' Holiday	The Olympics	#86	13 sec.
Boss	The Rumblers	#87	
Rockin' Crickets	Rockin' Rebels	#87	
The Dog	Rufus Thomas	#87	
Mother, Please!	Jo Ann Campbell	#88	11 sec.
You Know It Ain't Right	Joe Hinton	#88	
Gone	The Rip Chords	#88	17 sec.
Better to Give than Receive	Joe Hinton	#89	21 sec.
It Won't Be This Way (Always)	The King Pins	#89	
Dance, Dance, Dance	Joey Dee	#89	
Remember Baby	Shep & The Limelites	#91	
Do the Monkey	King Curtis	#92	
Zing! Went the Strings of My Heart	The Furys	#92	
I'm Not a Fool Anymore	T.K. Hulin	#92	
Soulville	Dinah Washington	#92	
Preacherman	Charlie Russo	#92	
Crossfire Time	Dee Clark	#92	
Banzai Pipeline	Henry Mancini	#93	
Saltwater Taffy	Lonnie Mack	#93	
Surfer Street	The Allisons	#93	

SAXOPHONE (cont'd)

Your Baby's Gone Surfin'	Duane Eddy	#93	21 sec.
Stop Monkeyin' Aroun'	The Dovells	#94	
Spring	Birdlegs & Pauline	#94	36 sec.
Got You on My Mind	Cookie & His Cupcakes	#94	
When the Boy's Happy (The Girl's Happy Too)	The Four Pennies	#95	12 sec.
Little Star	Bobby Callender	#95	
Slop Time	The Sherrys	#97	20 sec.
Diane	Joe Harnell	#97	
At the Shore	Johnny Caswell	#97	11 sec.
The Scavenger	Dick Dale	#98	21 sec.
River's Invitation	Percy Mayfield	#99	
Every Beat of My Heart	James Brown	#99	
Please Don't Kiss Me Again	The Charmettes	#100	14 sec.

1964

Where Did Our Love Go	The Supremes	#1	13 sec.
Baby Love	The Supremes	#1	14 sec.
Can't You See That She's Mine	Dave Clark Five	#4	
Java	Al Hirt	#4	
Bits and Pieces	Dave Clark Five	#4	23 sec.
The Girl from Ipanema	Getz/Gilberto	#5	30 sec.
(Just Like) Romeo & Juliet	The Reflections	#6	
Quicksand	Martha & The Vandellas	#8	14 sec.
Anyone Who Had a Heart	Dionne Warwick	#8	19 sec.
I Wanna Love Him so Bad	The Jelly Beans	#9	14 sec.
The Way You Do the Things You Do	The Temptations	#11	15 sec.
Kissin' Cousins	Elvis Presley	#12	
People Say	The Dixie Cups	#12	
Talking About My Baby	The Impressions	#12	
Everybody Knows (I Still Love You)	Dave Clark Five	#15	
Shangri-La	Robert Maxwell	#15	
Such a Night	Elvis Presley	#16	
Farmer John	The Premiers	#19	
What'd I Say	Elvis Presley	#21	
Nadine (Is It You?)	Chuck Berry	#23	
When the Lovelight Starts Shining Through His Eyes	The Supremes	#23	
Out of Sight	James Brown	#24	
Sidewalk Surfin'	Jan & Dean	#25	
Baby Don't Do It	Marvin Gaye	#27	
What's Easy for Two Is so Hard for One	Mary Wells	#29	
20-75	Willie Mitchell	#31	
The Pink Panther Theme	Henry Mancini	#31	
I'll Be in Trouble	The Temptations	#33	
Girls Grow Up Faster Than Boys	The Cookies	#33	13 sec.

SAXOPHONE (cont'd)

Song	Artist	#	Time
You'll Never Walk Alone	Patti LaBelle & The Blue Belles	#34	
You'll Never Get to Heaven if You Break My Heart	Dionne Warwick	#34	
Tra La La La Suzy	Dean & Jean	#35	13 sec.
I Gotta Dance to Keep from Crying	The Miracles	#35	
Tennesse Waltz	Sam Cooke	#35	
Mixed-Up, Shook-Up, Girl	Patty & The Emblems	#37	
I'm Into Something Good	Earl-Jean	#38	14 sec.
Tall Cool One	The Wailers	#38	
Sweet William	Millie Small	#40	12 sec.
Do You Want to Dance	Del Shannon	#43	
I Want You to Meet My Baby	Eydie Gorme	#43	
In My Lonely Room	Martha & The Vandellas	#44	11 sec.
Looking for Love	Connie Francis	#45	
Needle in a Haystack	The Velvelettes	#45	12 sec.
You're My Remedy	The Marvelettes	#48	
Can Your Monkey Do the Dog	Rufus Thomas	#48	
Ain't Doing Too Bad (Part 1)	Bobby Bland	#49	50 sec.
Jump Back	Rufus Thomas	#49	
My One and Only, Jimmy Boy	The Girlfriends	#49	
Dumb Head	Ginny Arnell	#50	
My Baby Don't Dig Me	Ray Charles	#51	30 sec.
Soul Serenade	King Curtis	#51	
Smack Dab in the Middle	Ray Charles	#52	
Something You Got	Alvin Robinson	#52	21 sec.
I Knew It All the Time	Dave Clark Five	#53	
Bon-Doo-Wah	The Orlons	#55	10 sec.
He's a Good Guy (Yes He Is)	The Marvelettes	#55	12 sec.
Tea for Two	Nino Tempo & April Stevens	#56	
Everybody Needs Somebody to Love	Solomon Burke	#58	
Candy to Me	Eddie Holland	#58	
Kick That Little Foot Sally Ann	Round Robin	#61	
Who Cares	Fats Domino	#63	19 sec.
Yesterday's Hero	Gene Pitney	#64	
Knock! Knock! (Who's There?)	The Orlons	#64	
Peg O' My Heart	Robert Maxwell	#64	
That Boy John	The Raindrops	#64	
Try Me	Jimmy Hughes	#65	
Shimmy Shimmy	The Orlons	#66	13 sec.
I Can't Hear You	Betty Everett	#66	
Comin' On	Bill Black's Combo	#67	
Sha-La-La	The Shirelles	#69	
Tell Me Baby	Garnet Mimms	#69	
The Wonder of You	Ray Peterson	#70	11 sec.

SAXOPHONE (cont'd)

Title	Artist	#	Time
A Woman's Love	Carla Thomas	#71	
A House Is Not a Home	Dionne Warwick	#71	17, 12 sec.
Little Queenie	Bill Black's Combo	#73	
(It's No) Sin	The Duprees	#74	
A House Is Not a Home	Brook Benton	#75	
Hey, Mr. Sax Man	Boots Randolph	#77	27, 14, 15 sec.
Do-Wah-Diddy	The Exciters	#78	
Cold Cold Winter	The Pixies Three	#79	13 sec.
Kiko	Jimmy McGriff	#79	
Sailor Boy	The Chiffons	#81	18 sec.
From Russia with Love	The Village Stompers	#81	
Baby What You Want Me to Do	Etta James	#82	
Where Did I Go Wrong	Dee Dee Sharp	#82	
Where Does Love Go	Freddie Scott	#82	
The Dodo	Jumpin' Gene Simmons	#83	
Billie Baby	Lloyd Price	#84	
Searchin'	Ace Cannon	#84	
Hey Little One	J. Frank Wilson & The Cascades	#85	
Somebody Stole My Dog	Rufus Thomas	#86	
Can't Get Over (The Bossa Nova)	Eydie Gorme	#87	12 sec.
Gee	The Pixies Three	#87	10 sec.
Deep in the Heart of Harlem	Clyde McPhatter	#90	11 sec.
Ask Me	Inez Foxx	#91	
Tequila	Bill Black's Combo	#91	
Little Boy	The Crystals	#92	
Soul Hootenanny Pt. I	Gene Chandler	#92	28 sec.
Run, Run, Run	The Supremes	#93	12 sec.
Somebody New	Chuck Jackson	#93	
Night Time Is the Right Time	Rufus & Carla	#94	
Caldonia	James Brown	#95	19 sec.
I Can't Believe What You Say (For Seeing What You Do)	Ike & Tina Turner	#95	13 sec.
Gator Tails and Monkey Ribs	The Spats	#96	15 sec.
One Piece Topless Bathing Suit	The Rip Chords	#96	
Like Columbus Did	The Reflections	#96	
Long Tall Shorty	Tommy Tucker	#96	
The Son of Rebel Rouser	Duane Eddy	#97	
Lover's Prayer	Wallace Brothers	#97	
How Blue Can You Get	B.B. King	#97	
Good Time Tonight	The Soul Sisters	#98	
Trouble I've Had	Clarence Ashe	#99	
Heartbreak Hill	Fats Domino	#99	29 sec.
Just a Moment Ago	Soul Sisters	#100	

SAXOPHONE (cont'd)

You Were Wrong	Z.Z. Hill	#100	19 sec.
1965			
Back in My Arms Again	The Supremes	#1	
I Hear a Symphony	The Supremes	#1	13 sec.
I Can't Help Myself	Four Tops	#1	
1 2 3	Len Barry	#2	
Wooly Bully	Sam The Sham & The Pharaohs	#2	21 sec.
I Got You (I Feel Good)	James Brown	#3	
Rescue Me	Fontella Bass	#4	
Shotgun	Jr. Walker/The All Stars	#4	24, 15 sec.
Hold What You've Got	Joe Tex	#5	
It's the Same Old Song	Four Tops	#5	14 sec.
You've Got Your Troubles	The Fortunes	#7	
I Like It Like That	Dave Clark Five	#7	
Fever	The McCoys	#7	
Papa's Got a Brand New Bag (Part 1)	James Brown	#8	
It's Not Unusual	Tom Jones	#10	
I Want Candy	The Strangeloves	#11	
My Baby	The Temptations	#13	
Action	Freddy Cannon	#13	
Sunshine, Lollipops and Rainbows	Lesley Gore	#13	
Any Way You Want It	Dave Clark Five	#14	
Twine Time	Alvin Cash & The Crawlers	#14	
Something About You	Four Tops	#19	
Yeh, Yeh	Georgie Fame	#21	21 sec.
In the Midnight Hour	Wilson Pickett	#21	14 sec.
Mohair Sam	Charlie Rich	#21	
Do the Clam	Elvis Presley	#21	
Reelin' and Rockin'	Dave Clark Five	#23	
You're Nobody till Somebody Loves You	Dean Martin	#25	
Dream on Little Dreamer	Perry Como	#25	
Too Many Fish in the Sea	The Marvelettes	#25	
Ju Ju Hand	Sam The Sham & The Pharaohs	#26	21 sec.
Tonight's the Night	Solomon Burke	#28	
Shake and Fingerpop	Jr. Walker/The All Stars	#29	24, 22, 15, 14 sec.
You Were Only Fooling (While I Was Falling in Love)	Vic Damone	#30	
Sugar Dumpling	Sam Cooke	#32	
Ring Dang Doo	Sam The Sham & The Pharaohs	#33	19 sec.
Don't Mess up a Good Thing	Fontella Bass & Bobby McClure	#33	18 sec.
Use Your Head	Mary Wells	#34	15 sec.
Respect	Otis Redding	#35	
Do the Boomerang	Jr. Walker/The All Stars	#36	12 sec.

SAXOPHONE (cont'd)

Peaches "N" Cream	The Ikettes	#36	
Just a Little Bit	Roy Head	#39	15 sec.
It's Got the Whold World Shakin'	Sam Cooke	#41	
Mr. Pitiful	Otis Redding	#41	
Cleo's Back	Jr. Walker/The All Stars	#43	
Hole in the Wall	The Packers	#43	
New Orleans	Eddie Hodges	#44	27 sec.
Anytime at All	Frank Sinatra	#46	
Lipstick Traces (On a Cigarette)	The O'Jays	#48	14 sec.
Take Me in Your Arms (Rock Me a Little While)	Kim Weston	#50	
The 81	Candy & The Kisses	#51	
A Woman Can Change a Man	Joe Tex	#56	
It's Too Late, Baby Too Late	Arthur Prysock	#56	
First I Look at the Purse	The Contours	#57	18 sec.
Boot-Leg	Booker T. & The MG's	#58	
High Heel Sneakers	Stevie Wonder	#59	
The Barracuda	Alvin Cash & The Crawlers	#59	
N-E-R-V-O-U-S	Ian Whitcomb	#60	
Watermelon Man	Gloria Lynne	#62	
These Hands (Small but Mighty)	Bobby Bland	#63	
Try Me	James Brown	#63	
Candy	The Astors	#63	
Misty	The Vibrations	#63	
He Was Really Sayin' Something	The Velvelettes	#64	12 sec.
I Need You	The Impressions	#64	
Peanuts (La Cacahuata)	The Sunglows	#64	
The Climb	The Kingsmen	#65	
Bring a Little Sunshine (To My Heart)	Vic Dana	#66	
Love Is a 5-Letter Word	James Phelps	#66	
Land of a Thousand Dances (Part 1)	Thee Midniters	#67	
You Can Have Her	The Righteous Brothers	#67	
I'm so Thankful	The Ikettes	#74	
He's a Lover	Mary Wells	#74	19 sec.
That's How Strong My Love Is	Otis Redding	#74	
Stand By Me	Earl Grant	#75	
The Mouse	Soupy Sales	#76	
Blind Man	Bobby Bland	#78	
The Puzzle Song (A Puzzle in Song)	Shirley Ellis	#78	
I Gotta Woman (Part One)	Ray Charles	#79	31 sec.
Hello, Dolly!	Bobby Darin	#79	
Orange Blossom Special	Johnny Cash	#80	17 sec.
Let the Good Times Roll	Roy Orbison	#81	
The Sidewinder, Part 1	Lee Morgan	#81	

SAXOPHONE (cont'd)

Percolatin'	Willie Mitchell	#85	
Blind Man	Little Milton	#86	
Someone Is Watching	Solomon Burke	#89	19 sec.
Every Night, Every Day	Jimmy McCracklin	#91	
I Don't Know What You've Got but It's Got Me - Part 1	Little Richard	#92	
Have Mercy Baby	James Brown	#92	
Stop! Look What You're Doing	Carla Thomas	#92	
Tommy	Reparata & The Delrons	#92	
Think	Jimmy McCracklin	#95	30 sec.
Buster Browne	Willie Mitchell	#96	
Blue Shadows	B.B. King	#97	
In the Meantime	Georgia Fame	#97	11 sec.
I Want You to Be My Boy	The Exciters	#98	
Cross My Heart	Bobby Vee	#99	
Black Night	Bobby Bland	#99	
Stay Away from My Baby	Ted Taylor	#99	
Right Now and Not Later	Shangri-Las	#99	
Love Me Now	Brook Benton	#100	18 sec.
He Ain't No Angel	The Ad Libs	#100	
1966			
Time Won't Let Me	The Outsiders	#5	
Land of 1000 Dances	Wilson Pickett	#6	24 sec.
I'm Your Puppet	James & Bobby Purify	#6	
Don't Mess with Bill	The Marvelettes	#7	16 sec.
Wouldn't It Be Nice	The Beach Boys	#8	
Love Is like an Itching in My Heart	The Supremes	#9	12 sec.
Going to a Go-Go	The Miracles	#11	
This Old Heart of Mine (Is Weak for You)	Isley Brothers	#12	
Opus 17 (Don't You Worry 'Bout Me)	The Four Seasons	#13	
Ain't Too Proud to Beg	The Temptations	#13	14 sec.
B-A-B-Y	Carla Thomas	#14	
How Sweet It Is (To Be Loved By You)	Jr. Walker/The All Stars	#18	30, 22 sec.
(I'm A) Road Runner	Jr. Walker/The All Stars	#20	24, 14, 13 sec.
Hold On! I'm a Comin'	Sam & Dave	#21	
But It's Alright	J.J. Jackson	#22	
Mustang Sally	Wilson Pickett	#23	
Searching for My Love	Bobby Moore & The Rhythm Aces	#27	
Like a Baby	Len Barry	#27	
Get Ready	The Temptations	#29	
One More Heartache	Marvin Gaye	#29	16 sec.
Fa-Fa-Fa-Fa-Fa (Sad Song)	Otis Redding	#29	
Help Me Girl	Eric Burdon/Animals	#29	

SAXOPHONE (cont'd)

Title	Artist	Page	Duration
I Chose to Sing the Blues	Ray Charles/The Raeletts	#32	27 sec.
Somewhere There's a Someone	Dean Martin	#32	
The Phoenix Love Theme (Senza Fine)	The Brass Ring	#32	
(You're Gonna) Hurt Yourself	Frankie Valli	#39	
Ain't That a Groove (Part 1)	James Brown	#42	55 sec.
Get Out of My Life, Woman	Lee Dorsey	#44	
Whole Lot of Shakin' in My Heart (Since I Met You)	The Miracles	#46	
Little Darling, I Need You	Marvin Gaye	#47	
Stop Her on Sight (S.O.S.)	Edwin Starr	#48	
You're the One	The Marvelettes	#48	
The Philly Freeze	Alvin Cash & The Registers	#49	
Cleo's Mood	Jr. Walker/The All Stars	#50	
Money (That's What I Want) Part 1	Jr. Walker/The All Stars	#52	32 sec.
Money Won't Change You (Part 1)	James Brown	#53	
Somebody (Somewhere) Needs You	Darrell Banks	#55	
Helpless	Kim Weston	#56	
I Know You Better Than That	Bobby Goldsboro	#56	
Hide & Seek	The Sheep	#58	
Wang Dang Doodle	Ko Ko Taylor	#58	24 sec.
Nobody's Baby Again	Dean Martin	#60	
My Lover's Prayer	Otis Redding	#61	
I Guess I'll Always Love You	Isley Brothers	#61	13 sec.
Neighbor, Neighbor	Jimmy Hughes	#65	
Michelle	Bud Shank	#65	
Can't Satisfy	The Impressions	#65	15 sec.
There's Something on Your Mind	Baby Ray	#69	
I Don't Need No Doctor	Ray Charles	#72	
Darling Baby	The Elgins	#72	
Alvin's Boo-Ga-Loo	Alvin Cash & The Registers	#74	
Melody for an Unknown Girl	The Unknowns	#74	17, 17 sec.
Good Time Charlie	Bobby Bland	#75	
C.C. Rider	Bobby Powell	#76	
Killer Joe	The Kingsmen	#77	
Michelle	Billy Vaughn	#77	
Something I Want to Tell You	Johnny & The Expressions	#79	
I Put a Spell on You	Alan Price Set	#80	
Mame	Louis Armstrong	#81	
Headline News	Edwin Starr	#84	
Uptight (Everything's Alright)	Nancy Wilson	#84	
Pouring Water on a Drowning Man	James Carr	#85	
Hot Shot	The Buena Vistas	#87	
Spanish Harlem	King Curtis	#89	
Philly Dog	The Mar-Keys	#89	

SAXOPHONE (cont'd)

Since I Lost the One I Love	The Impressions	#90	16 sec.
Too Slow	The Impressions	#91	
Pin the Tail on the Donkey	Paul Peek	#91	
It's That Time of the Year	Len Barry	#91	10 sec.
Count Down	Dave "Baby" Cortez	#91	
Bad Eye	Willie Mitchell	#92	
Put Yourself in My Place	The Elgins	#92	
Think Twice	Jackie Wilson & LaVern Baker	#93	
Philly Dog	Herbie Mann	#93	
Rib Tip's (Part 1)	Andre Williams	#94	
Yesterday Man	Chris Andrews	#94	
Superman	Dino, Desi & Billy	#94	15 sec.
Can't You See (You're Losing Me)	Mary Wells	#94	11 sec.
I'm Your Hoochie Cooche Man (Part 1)	Jimmy Smith	#94	
Blue River	Elvis Presley	#95	
Uptight (Everything's Alright)	The Jazz Crusaders	#95	
Your Good Thing (Is About to End)	Mable John	#95	
Try My Love Again	Bobby Moore's Rhythm Aces	#97	
Baby I Love You	Jimmy Holiday	#98	
I Spy (For the FBI)	Jame Thomas	#98	
I Struck It Rich	Len Barry	#98	
Love Attack	James Carr	#99	
It Was a Very Good Year	Della Reese	#99	
Hand Jive	The Strangeloves	#100	
Help Me (Get Myself Back Together Again)	The Spellbinders	#100	
Safe and Sound	Fontella Bass	#100	

1967

Respect	Aretha Franklin	#1	16 sec.
Tell It Like It Is	Aaron Neville	#2	
I Heard It Through the Grapevine	Gladys Knight & The Pips	#2	12 sec.
Baby I Love You	Aretha Franklin	#4	
(Your Love Keeps Lifting Me) Higher and Higher	Jackie Wilson	#6	
Boogaloo Down Broadway	Fantastic Johnny C	#7	
Cold Sweat (Part 1)	James Brown	#7	
Funky Broadway	Wilson Pickett	#8	15 sec.
You Better Sit Down Kids	Cher	#9	13 sec.
I Never Loved a Man (The Way I Love You)	Aretha Franklin	#9	
Mercy, Mercy, Mercy	"Cannonball" Adderley	#11	
Music to Watch Girls By	Bob Crewe Generation	#15	
Let's Fall in Love	Peaches & Herb	#21	
Make Me Yours	Bettye Swann	#21	
Stag-O-Lee	Wilson Pickett	#22	
The Look of Love	Dusty Springfield	#22	

SAXOPHONE (cont'd)

Title	Artist	#	Duration
Let the Good Times Roll & Feel So Good	Bunny Sigler	#22	
Let Love Come Between Us	James & Bobby Purify	#23	11 sec.
Try a Little Tenderness	Otis Redding	#25	
Shake a Tail Feather	James & Bobby Purify	#25	
Tramp	Otis & Carla	#26	
Ode to Billy Joe	The Kingpins	#28	
Hey, Leroy, Your Mama's Callin' You	Jimmy Castor	#31	
Pucker Up Buttercup	Jr. Walker/The All Stars	#31	21, 19 sec.
In the Heat of the Night	Ray Charles	#33	49 sec.
Memphis Soul Stew	King Curtis	#33	
All	James Darren	#35	
The Dis-Advantages of You	The Brass Ring	#36	
You Were on My Mind	Crispian St. Peters	#36	
Come to the Sunshine	Harpers Bizarre	#37	
Wish You Didn't Have to Go	James & Bobby Purify	#38	
Big Boss Man	Elvis Presley	#38	
Are You Lonely for Me	Freddy Scott	#39	
Get It Together (Part 1)	James Brown	#40	
When Something Is Wrong with My Baby	Sam & Dave	#42	
It May Be Winter Outside (But in My Heart It's Spring)	Felice Taylor	#42	
Papa Was Too	Joe Tex	#44	
Shoot Your Shot	Jr. Walker/The All Stars	#44	27, 21, 16 sec.
Chattanooga Choo Choo	Harpers Bizarre	#45	
Show Business	Lou Rawls	#45	
Let Yourself Go	James Brown	#46	
Shake	Otis Redding	#47	
Soul Man	Ramsey Lewis	#49	
It's the Little Things	Sonny & Cher	#50	14 sec.
Karate-Boo-Ga-Loo	Jerryo	#51	
Woman Like That, Yeah	Joe Tex	#54	
Soul Dance Number Three	Wilson Pickett	#55	
(Open Up the Door) Let the Good Times In	Dean Martin	#55	
Soothe Me	Sam & Dave	#56	
Why (Am I Treated So Bad)	The Sweet Inspirations	#57	
Spooky	Mike Sharpe	#57	
Lonely Drifter	Pieces of Eight	#59	
Piece of My Heart	Erma Franklin	#62	
Jump Back	King Curtis	#63	
It's Got to Be Mellow	Leon Haywood	#63	
Turn on Your Love Light	Oscar Toney, Jr.	#65	
Look at Granny Run, Run	Howard Tate	#67	
Fall in Love with Me	Bettye Swann	#67	

SAXOPHONE (cont'd)

Title	Artist	#	Notes
Dirty Man	Laura Lee	#68	
Cry to Me	Freddie Scott	#70	
Sweet, Sweet Lovin'	The Platters	#70	
Am I Grooving You	Freddie Scott	#71	
Sockin' 1-2-3-4	John Roberts	#71	
Spreadin' Honey	Watts 103rd St. Rhythm Band	#73	
Something Good (Is Going to Happent to You)	Carla Thomas	#74	
I Stand Accused (Of Loving You)	The Glories	#74	
Every Day I Have the Blues	Billy Stewart	#74	
The Dark End of the Street	James Carr	#77	
Can't Help but Love You	The Standells	#78	
I Love You More Than Words Can Say	Otis Redding	#78	
Raise Your Hand	Eddie Floyd	#79	
Get Down	Harvey Scales	#79	
Eight Men, Four Women	O.V. Wright	#80	
I'm Indestructible	Jack Jones	#81	15 sec.
Ten Commandments	Prince Buster	#81	
I Dig Girls	J.J. Jackson	#83	
Wanted: Lover, No Experience Necessary	Laura Lee	#84	
Nearer to You	Betty Harris	#85	
Ain't Gonna Rest (Till I Get You)	The Five Stairsteps	#87	
Funky Donkey	Pretty Purdie	#87	
Ode to Billy Joe	Ray Bryant	#89	
Pearl Time	Andre Williams	#90	
Hold On I'm Coming	Chuck Jackson & Maxine Brown	#91	
Girls Are out to Get You	The Fascinations	#92	
On a Saturday Night	Eddie Floyd	#92	
Temptation	Boots Randolph	#93	
The Shadow of Your Smile	Boots Randolph	#93	
Alligator Bogaloo	Lou Donaldson	#93	
Why? (Am I Treated So Bad)	The Staple Singers	#95	
Only Love Can Break a Heart	Margaret Whiting	#96	
Slippin' & Slidin'	Willie Mitchell	#96	
96 Tears	Big Maybelle	#96	
Somebody's Sleeping in My Bed	Johnnie Taylor	#96	
I'm a Fool for You	James Carr	#97	
Come on Sock It to Me	Syl Johnson	#97	
Don't Rock the Boat	Eddie Floyd	#98	
Thread the Needle	Clarence Carter	#98	
When Tomorrow Comes	Carla Thomas	#99	
Think	Vicki Anderson & James Brown	#100	
Chain of Fools (Part 1)	Jimmy Smith	#100	

SAXOPHONE (cont'd)

1968			
(Sittin' On) The Dock of the Bay	Otis Redding	#1	
The Horse	Cliff Nobles & Co.	#2	
Spooky	Classics IV	#3	32 sec.
Lady Madonna	The Beatles	#4	12 sec.
Stormy	Classics IV/Dennis Yost	#5	19 sec.
Who's Making Love	Johnnie Taylor	#5	
(Sweet Sweet Baby) Since You've Been Gone	Aretha Franklin	#5	
Slip Away	Clarence Carter	#6	
The House That Jack Built	Aretha Franklin	#6	
I Got the Feelin'	James Brown	#6	
My Special Angel	The Vogues	#7	
I Thank You	Sam & Dave	#9	
I Can't Stop Dancing	Archie Bell & The Drells	#9	
If You Can Want	Smokey Robinson & The Miracles	#11	
Licking Stick - Licking Stick (Part 1)	James Brown	#14	
Funky Street	Arthur Conley	#14	
See Saw	Aretha Franklin	#14	
She's Lookin' Good	Wilson Pickett	#15	
Love Makes a Woman	Barbara Acklin	#15	15 sec.
The End of the Our Road	Gladys Knight & The Pips	#15	
Ain't No Way	Aretha Franklin	#16	
Bring It on Home to Me	Eddie Floyd	#17	
Fool for You	The Impressions	#22	
Soul Serenade	Willie Mitchell	#23	
I'm a Midnight Mover	Wilson Pickett	#24	
Come See About Me	Jr. Walker/The All Stars	#24	37, 21, 16 sec.
The Happy Song (Dum-Dum)	Otis Redding	#25	
Goodbye My Love	James Brown	#31	
Hip City - Pt. 2	Jr. Walker	#31	13 sec.
Lover's Holiday	Peggy Scott & Jo Jo Benson	#31	
Two Little Kids	Peaches & Herb	#31	
Chained	Marvin Gaye	#32	
Girls Can't Do What the Guys Do	Betty Wright	#33	
Men Are Getting' Scarce	Joe Tex	#33	
Hitch It to the Horse	Fantastic Johnny C	#34	
Security	Etta James	#35	
Amen	Otis Redding	#36	
There Was a Time	James Brown	#36	
I've Never Found a Girl (To Love Me Like You Do)	Eddie Floyd	#40	
The Son of Hickory Holler's Tramp	O.C. Smith	#40	
I've Got Dreams to Remember	Otis Redding	#41	

SAXOPHONE (cont'd)

Cover Me	Percy Sledge	#42	
I Can't Dance to That Music You're Playin'	Martha & The Vandellas	#42	
Prayer Meetin'	Willie Mitchell	#45	
Listen Here	Eddie Harris	#45	
Friends	The Beach Boys	#47	
The Story of Rock and Roll	The Turtles	#48	
You Don't Know What You Mean to Me	Sam & Dave	#48	
If You Don't Want My Love	Robert John	#49	
Jealous Love	Wilson Pickett	#50	
For Your Precious Love	Jackie Wilson & Count Basie	#50	
I Can Remember	James & Bobby Purify	#51	
America Is My Home - Pt. 1	James Brown	#52	
Morning Dew	Lulu	#52	
Fly Me to the Moon	Bobby Womack	#52	
Can't You Find Another Way (Of Doing It)	Sam & Dave	#54	
Peace of Mind	Nancy Wilson	#55	
You Send Me	Aretha Franklin	#56	
Good Combination	Sonny & Cher	#56	13 sec.
From the Teacher to the Preacher	Gene Chandler & Barbara Acklin	#57	
People Sure Act Funny	Arthur Conley	#58	
I'll Never Do You Wrong	Joe Tex	#59	
Don't Change Your Love	Five Stairsteps & Cubie	#59	
Talking About My Baby	Gloria Walker	#60	
I Loved and I Lost	The Impressions	#61	
I Promise to Wait My Love	Martha & The Vandellas	#62	
Looking for a Fox	Clarence Carter	#62	
Sudden Stop	Percy Sledge	#63	
A Man Needs a Woman	James Carr	#63	
That's a Lie	Ray Charles	#64	
The Doctor	Mary Wells	#65	
Keep On Dancing	Alvin Cash	#66	
Funky Walk Part I (East)	Dyke & The Blazers	#67	
Cold Feet	Albert King	#67	
Mountains of Love	Ronnie Dove	#67	20 sec.
Horse Fever	Cliff Nobles & Co.	#68	
I Got You Babe	Etta James	#69	
Up-Up and Away	Hugh Masekela	#71	
Unchained Melody	The Sweet Inspirations	#73	
I Got a Sure Thing	Ollie & The Nightingales	#73	
Do Unto Me	James & Bobby Purify	#73	
To Love Somebody	The Sweet Inspirations	#74	
Competition Ain't Nothin'	Little Carl Carlton	#75	
Private Number	Judy Clay & William Bell	#75	

SAXOPHONE (cont'd)

I Was Made to Love Her	Stevie Wonder	#76	
Stop	Howard Tate	#76	
Hitchcock Railway	Jose Feliciano	#77	
Mister Bo Jangles	Bobby Cole	#79	
Don't Make the Good Girls Go Bad	Della Humphrey	#79	
Sweet Darlin'	Martha & The Vandellas	#80	
You Need Me, Baby	Joe Tex	#81	
Release Me	Johnny Adams	#82	
There Was a Time	Gene Chandler	#82	
Turn On Your Love Light	Bill Black's Combo	#82	
The Mule	The James Boys	#82	
Valley of the Dolls	King Curtis	#83	
Sweet Young Thing Like You	Ray Charles	#83	
I Heard It Thru the Grapevine	King Curtis & Kingpins	#83	
Chain Gang	Jackie Wilson & Count Basie	#84	
Aunt Dora's Love Soul Shack	Arthur Conley	#85	
Soul Drippin'	The Mauds	#85	
Tit for Tat (Ain't No Talking Back)	James Brown	#86	
(She's) Some Kind of Wonderful	Fantastic Johnny C	#87	
A Little Rain Must Fall	The Epic Splendor	#87	
(You've Got) Personality and Chantilly Lace	Mitch Ryder	#87	
Here Come Da Judge	The Buena Vistas	#88	
It's Crazy	Eddie Harris	#88	
Funky Fever	Clarence Carter	#88	
You Don't Have to Say You Love Me	The Four Sonics	#89	
Show Time	Detroit Emeralds	#89	
Soul Train	Classics IV	#90	34 sec.
Don't Pat Me on the Back and Call Me Brother	KaSandra	#91	
Stay Close to Me	Five Stairsteps & Cubie	#91	
Up-Hard	Willie Mitchell	#91	
Funky North Philly	Bill Cosby	#91	12 sec.
Don't Be Afraid (Do as I Say)	Frankie Karl	#93	
Hard to Handle	Patti Drew	#93	
Up Tight, Good Man	Laura Lee	#93	
Harper Valley P.T.A.	King Curtis & Kingpins	#93	
The Woman I Love	B.B. King	#94	
Driftin' Blues	Bobby Bland	#96	
The Worm	Jimmy McGriff	#97	
She's About a Mover	Otis Clay	#97	
I Worry About You	Joe Simon	#98	
Chain of Fools (Part 1)	Jimmy Smith	#100	
1969			
Everyday People	Sly & The Family Stone	#1	

SAXOPHONE (cont'd)

Honky Tonk Women	The Rolling Stones	#1	
Traces	Classics IV/Dennis Yost	#2	16 sec.
It's Your Thing	The Isley Brothers	#2	
Touch Me	The Doors	#3	40 sec.
Build Me Up Buttercup	The Foundations	#3	
Put a Little Love in Your Heart	Jackie DeShannon	#4	
What Does It Take (To Win Your Love)	Jr. Walker/The All Stars	#4	30, 25, 29 sec.
Can I Change My Mind	Tyrone Davis	#5	
Color Him Father	The Winstons	#7	
Sweet Cherry Wine	Tommy James & The Shondells	#7	
Baby, Baby Don't Cry	Smokey Robinson & The Miracles	#8	
I'm Gonna Make You Mine	Lou Christie	#10	
Oh, What a Night	The Dells	#10	23 sec.
Son-Of-A Preacher Man	Dusty Springfield	#10	
Mother Popcorn (You Got to Have a Mother for Me) Part 1	James Brown	#11	
More Today Than Yesterday	Spiral Starecase	#12	
Too Weak to Fight	Clarence Carter	#13	
Share Your Love with Me	Aretha Franklin	#13	
Baby, I'm for Real	The Originals	#14	
Give It up or Turnit a Loose	James Brown	#15	
Cherry Hill Park	Billy Joe Royal	#15	
These Eyes	Jr. Walker/The All Stars	#16	18, 18 sec.
When I Die	Motherlode	#18	
The Weight	Aretha Franklin	#19	
The Nitty Gritty	Gladys Knight & The Pips	#19	
Everyday with You Girl	Classics IV/Dennis Yost	#19	20 sec.
I Don't Want Nobody to Give Me Nothing (Open Up the Door, I'll Get It Myself) (Part 1)	James Brown	#20	
Take Care of Your Homework	Johnnie Taylor	#20	
Papa's Got a Brand New Bag	Otis Redding	#21	
Let a Man Come in and Do the Popcorn (Part One)	James Brown	#21	
Stand	Sly & The Family Stone	#22	
Brother Love's Travelling Salvation Show	Neil Diamond	#22	
Hey Jude	Wilson Pickett	#23	
I Turned You On	The Isley Brothers	#23	19 sec.
Heaven Knows	The Grass Roots	#24	
California Soul	The 5th Dimension	#25	
Carry Me Back	The Rascals	#26	
Along Came Jones	Ray Stevens	#27	19 sec.
I Can't See Myself Leaving You	Aretha Franklin	#28	
The Popcorn	James Brown	#30	
My Song	Aretha Franklin	#31	
In a Moment	The Intrigues	#31	

SAXOPHONE (cont'd)

Title	Artist	Page	Duration
Snatching It Back	Clarence Carter	#31	
Cloud Nine	Mongo Santamaria	#32	
Is It Something You've Got	Tyrone Davis	#34	
Nothing but a Heartache	The Flirtations	#34	
We Got More Soul	Dyke & The Blazers	#35	
I've Been Hurt	Bill Deal/The Rhondels	#35	
Clean Up Your Own Back Yard	Elvis Presley	#35	
So Good Together	Andy Kim	#36	15 sec.
Let a Woman Be a Woman - Let a Man Be a Man	Dyke & The Blazers	#36	
Special Delivery	The Dells	#38	
Don't Touch Me	Bettye Swann	#38	
May I	Bill Deal/The Rhondels	#39	
So I Can Love You	The Emotions	#39	
Heaven	The Rascals	#39	
Nobody but You Babe	Clarence Reid	#40	
Lowdown Popcorn	James Brown	#41	
Kozmic Blues	Janis Joplin	#41	
Muddy River	Johnny Rivers	#41	
Soul Sister, Brown Sugar	Sam & Dave	#41	
Home Cookin	Jr. Walker/The All Stars	#42	25 sec.
California Dreamin'	Bobby Womack	#43	
Proud Mary	Solomon Burke	#45	
The Weight	Supremes & Temptations	#46	
Your Husband - My Wife	Brooklyn Bridge	#46	
Doin' Our Thing	Clarence Carter	#46	
I'd Rather Be An Old Man's Sweetheart (Than a Young Man's Fool)	Candi Station	#46	
Sad Girl	The Intruders	#47	
A Lover's Question	Otis Redding	#48	
Change of Heart	Dennis Yost/Classics IV	#49	18 sec.
When He Touches Me (Nothing Else Matters)	Peaches & Herb	#49	
I Like What You're Doing (To Me)	Carla Thomas	#49	
Mini-Skirt Minnie	Wilson Pickett	#50	
Ob-La-Di, Ob-La-Da	Arthur Conley	#51	
The Sweeter He Is - Part 1	The Soul Children	#52	
Jack and Jill	Tommy Roe	#53	
Love of the Common People	The Winstons	#54	
(We've Got) Honey Love	Martha & The Vandellas	#56	
Get It from the Bottom	The Steelers	#56	
Tell All the People	The Doors	#57	
The Train	1910 Fruitgum Co.	#57	
Midnight	Dennis Yost/Classics IV	#58	14 sec.
Rockin' in the Same Old Boat	Bobby Bland	#58	

SAXOPHONE (cont'd)

Song	Artist	#	Duration
Move in a Little Closer, Baby	Mama Cass	#58	
Crumbs Off the Table	The Glass House	#59	
Girl You're Too Young	Archie Bell & The Drells	#59	
Ice Cream Song	The Dynamics	#59	
Kool and the Gang	Kool & The Gang	#59	
While You're out Looking for Sugar?	The Honey Cone	#62	
Break Away	The Beach Boys	#63	
I Can't Make It Alone	Lou Rawls	#63	
Didn't You Know (You'd Have to Cry Sometime)	Gladys Knight & The Pips	#63	
Born to Be Wild	Wilson Pickett	#64	
Shangri-La	The Lettermen	#64	
Runnin' Blue	The Doors	#64	
Don't Forget About Me	Dusty Springfield	#64	
The Feeling Is Right	Clarence Carter	#65	
(Sittin' On) The Dock of the Bay	Sergio Mendes & Brasil '66	#66	
Till You Get Enough	Watts 103rd Street Rhythm Band	#67	
Just Ain't No Love	Barbara Acklin	#67	14 sec.
Lodi	Al Wilson	#67	
I've Been Loving You Too Long	Ike & Tina Turner	#68	
Proud Mary	The Checkmates, Ltd. feat. Sonny Charles	#69	
Witchi Tai To	Everything Is Everything	#69	
30-60-90	Willie Mitchell	#69	
When You Dance	Jay & The Americans	#70	11 sec.
Tracks of My Tears	Aretha Franklin	#71	
Love Man	Otis Redding	#72	
Baby, Don't Be Looking in My Mind	Joe Simon	#72	
Grits Ain't Groceries (All Around the World)	Little Milton	#73	
Bubble Gum Music	Rock & Roll Dubble Bubble	#74	
Get Off My Back Women	B.B. King	#74	
Poor Side of Town	Al Wilson	#75	
Getting the Corners	The T.S.U. Toronadoes	#75	
Just a Little Love	B.B. King	#76	
Gentle on My Mind	Aretha Franklin	#76	
He Called Me Baby	Ella Washington	#77	
Willie & Laura Mae Jones	Dusty Springfield	#78	
San Francisco Is a Lonely Town	Joe Simon	#79	
Black Berries - Pt 1	The Isley Brothers	#79	24 sec.
Sincerely	Paul Anka	#80	
Back in the U.S.S.R.	Chubby Checker	#82	
It's My Thing (You Can't Tell Me Who to Sock It To)	Marva Whitney	#82	
Was It Good to You	The Isley Brothers	#83	
Anything You Choose	Spanky & Our Gang	#86	

SAXOPHONE (cont'd)

Any Day Now	Percy Sledge	#86
That's Your Baby	Joe Tex	#88
Sing a Simple Song	Sly & The Family Stone	#89
Breakfast in Bed	Dusty Springfield	#91
My Wife, My Dog, My Cat	The Maskman & The Agents	#91
You Keep Me Hanging On	Wilson Pickett	#92
How I Miss You Baby	Bobby Womack	#93
I Love My Baby	Archie Bell & The Drells	#94
That's the Way	Joe Tex	#94
Ain't Got No; I Got Life	Nina Simone	#94
One Eye Open	The Maskman & The Agents	#95
Theme from Electric Surfboard	Brother Jack McDuff	#95
Feeling Alright	Mongo Santamaria	#96
It's Been a Long Time	Betty Everett	#96
Please Don't Desert Me Baby	Gloria Walker/Chevelles	#98
Guess Who	Ruby Winters	#99
Memphis Train	Buddy Miles	#100

SITAR

SONG	ARTIST	HOT 100
1966		
Paint It, Black	The Rolling Stones	#1
Grim Reaper of Love	The Turtles	#81
1967		
San Francisco (Be Sure to Wear Flowers in Your Hair)	Scott McKenzie	#4
Paper Sun	Traffic	#94
1968		
Carpet Man	The 5th Dimension	#29
Street Fighting Man	The Rolling Stones	#48
The Inner Light	The Beatles	#96
1969		
Hooked on a Feeling	B.J. Thomas	#5
Games People Play	Joe South	#12
What's the Use of Breaking Up	Jerry Butler	#20
No Matter What Sign You Are	The Supremes	#31
The Weight	Supremes & Temptations	#46
Love Is Just a Four-Letter Word	Joan Baez	#86

TUBULAR/CHURCH BELLS

SONG	ARTIST	HOT 100
1960		
Mission Bell	Donnie Brooks	#7
Where Are You	Frankie Avalon	#32
Rudolph the Red Nosed Reindeer	The Melodeers	#71
1961		
I Count the Tears	The Drifters	#17
Lullaby of Love	Frank Gari	#23
Little Altar Boy	Vic Dana	#45
Please Come Home for Christmas	Charles Brown	#76
Make Believe Wedding	The Castells	#98
1962		
Till Death Do Us Part	Bob Braun	#26
What Time Is It?	The Jive Five	#67
The Lost Penny	Brook Benton	#77
A Sunday Kind of Love	Jan & Dean	#95
Don't Stop the Wedding	Ann Cole	#99
1963		
Take These Chains from My Heart	Ray Charles	#8
Pretty Paper	Roy Orbison	#15
Marlena	The Four Seasons	#36
Whatever You Want	Jerry Butler	#68
Dum Dum Dee Dum	Johnny Cymbal	#77
Hear the Bells	The Tokens	#94
I Know I Know	Jimmy Smith	#96
1964		
Chapel of Love	The Dixie Cups	#1
I Wanna Love Him so Bad	The Jelly Beans	#9
People Say	The Dixie Cups	#12
The Shelter of Your Arms	Sammy Davis Jr.	#17
Big Man in Town	The Four Seasons	#20
Need to Belong	Jerry Butler	#31
I Have a Boyfriend	The Chiffons	#36
Do-Wah-Diddy	The Exciters	#78
Stay with Me	Frank Sinatra	#81
I Just Can't Say Goodbye	Bobby Rydell	#94
Rome Will Never Leave You	Richard Chamberlain	#99
1965		
Cara, Mia	Jay & The Americans	#4
Just a Little Bit Better	Herman's Hermits	#7
Laugh at Me	Sonny	#10
Some Enchanted Evening	Jay & The Americans	#13

TUBULAR/CHURCH BELLS (cont'd)

Here It Comes Again	The Fortunes	#27
Give Us Your Blessing	The Shangri-Las	#29
Rusty Bells	Brenda Lee	#33
The Dawn of Correction	The Spokesmen	#36
The Universal Soldier	Glen Campbell	#45
Little Bell	The Dixie Cups	#51
For Mama	Jerry Vale	#54
Wishing It Was You	Connie Francis	#57
The Man	Lorne Greene	#72
Crying in the Chapel	Adam Wade	#88
It's Almost Tomorrow	Jimmy Velvet	#93
Suddenly I'm All Alone	Walter Jackson	#96
You Can Have Him	Timi Yuro	#96
Diana	Bobby Rydell	#98
1966		
Lightnin' Strikes	Lou Christie	#1
Cherish	The Association	#1
Black Is Black	Los Bravos	#4
I've Got You Under My Skin	The Four Seasons	#9
Oh How Happy	Shades of Blue	#12
Rhapsody in the Rain	Lou Christie	#16
He	The Righteous Brothers	#18
Somewhere	Len Barry	#26
East West	Herman's Hermits	#27
Alfie	Cher	#32
Come Running Back	Dean Martin	#35
Past, Present and Future	The Shangri-Las	#59
Let's Call It a Day Girl	The Razor's Edge	#77
Happiness	Shades of Blue	#78
3000 Miles	Brian Hyland	#99
1967		
The Love I Saw in You Was Just a Mirage	Smokey Robinson & The Miracles	#20
Pay You Back with Interest	The Hollies	#28
No Milk Today	Herman's Hermits	#35
Out of the Blue	Tommy James & The Shondells	#43
You Gave Me Something (And Everything's Alright)	The Fantastic Four	#55
Graduation Day	The Arbors	#59
Keep a Light in the Window Till I Come Home	Solomon Burke	#64
For He's a Jolly Good Fellow	Bobby Vinton	#66
Precious Memories	The Romeos	#67
Walk with Faith in Your Heart	The Bachelors	#83
Shake Hands and Walk Away Cryin'	Lou Christie	#95

TUBULAR/CHURCH BELLS (cont'd)

1968

Love Power	The Sandpebbles	#22
The Ten Commandments of Love	Peaches & Herb	#55
Be Young, Be Foolish, Be Happy	The Tams	#61
Porpoise Song	The Monkees	#62
If This World Were Mine	Marvin Gaye & Tammi Terrell	#68
A Voice in the Choir	Al Martino	#80
Never My Love	The Sandpebbles	#98

1969

Sweet Cherry Wine	Tommy James & The Shondells	#7
Baby, I'm for Real	The Originals	#14
Make Believe	Wind (Tony Orlando)	#28
Does Anybody Know I'm Here	The Dells	#38
Moments to Remember	The Vogues	#47
Kay	John Wesley Ryles I	#83
Let's Call It a Day Girl	Bobby Vee	#92

UKULELE

YEAR	SONG	ARTIST	HOT 100
1963	Those Lazy-Hazy-Crazy Days of Summer	Nat "King" Cole	#6
1963	(Down At) Papa Joe's	The Dixiebelles	#9
1963	That Sunday, That Summer	Nat "King" Cole	#12
1964	Silly Ol' Summertime	New Christy Minstrels	#92
1968	Tip-Toe Thru' the Tulips with Me	Tiny Tim	#17
1968	D.W. Washburn	The Monkees	#19

VIBRASLAP

YEAR	SONG	ARTIST	HOT 100
1967	Little Ole Wine Drinker, Me	Dean Martin	#38
1968	Green Tambourine	The Lemon Pipers	#1
1968	Don't Take It so Hard	Paul Revere & The Raiders	#27
1968	Give a Damn	Spanky & Our Gang	#43
1968	Jelly Jungle (Of Orange Marmalada)	Lemon Pipers	#51
1969	Hawaii Five-O	The Ventures	#4
1969	I'm Gonna Make You Mine	Lou Christie	#10
1969	Don't Wake Me Up in the Morning, Michael	Pepperment Rainbow	#54
1969	Feeling Alright	Joe Cocker	#69

The 60s Music Compendium
VIOLIN

For songs that feature an entire orchestra- not just the string section- check out the "orchestra" list.

SONG	ARTIST	HOT 100
1960		
Georgia On My Mind	Ray Charles	#1
Save the Last Dance for Me	The Drifters	#1
I'm Sorry	Brenda Lee	#1
Only the Lonely (Know the Way I Feel)	Roy Orbison	#2
Puppy Love	Paul Anka	#2
Chain Gang	Sam Cooke	#2
Last Date	Floyd Cramer	#2
Sixteen Reasons	Connie Stevens	#3
Good Timin'	Jimmy Jones	#3
Volare	Bobby Rydell	#4
Because They're Young	Duane Eddy	#4
He'll Have to Stay	Jeanne Black	#4
Baby (You've Got What It Takes)	Dinah Washington & Brook Benton	#5
Paper Roses	Anita Bryant	#5
Walking to New Orleans	Fats Domino	#6
That's All You Gotta Do	Brenda Lee	#6
Devil of Angel	Bobby Vee	#6
Footsteps	Steve Lawrence	#7
A Rockin' Good Way (To Mess Around and Fall in Love)	Dinah Washington & Brook Benton	#7
Let It Be Me	The Everly Brothers	#7
Kiddio	Brook Benton	#7
Mission Bell	Donnie Brooks	#7
Mama	Connie Francis	#8
You're Sixteen	Johnny Burnette	#8
Blue Angel	Roy Orbison	#9
Pretty Blue Eyes	Steve Lawrence	#9
O Dio Mio	Annette	#10
Summer's Gone	Paul Anka	#11
Cherry Pie	Skip & Flip	#11
Dreamin'	Johnny Burnette	#11
(You Were Made For) All My Love	Jackie Wilson	#12
Young Emotions	Ricky Nelson	#12
Sleep	Little Willie John	#13
Step by Step	The Crests	#14
Sway	Bobby Rydell	#14
Three Nights a Week	Fats Domino	#15
This Magic Moment	The Drifters	#16
Over the Rainbow	The Demensions	#16
The Same One	Brook Benton	#16

VIOLIN (cont'd)

Teddy	Connie Francis	#17
You Mean Everything to Me	Neil Sedaka	#17
I Really Don't Want to Know	Tommy Edwards	#18
Jealous of You (Tango Della Gelosia)	Connie Francis	#19
Last Date	Lawrence Welk	#21
Don't Come Knockin'	Fats Domino	#21
Mountain of Love	Harold Dorman	#21
I'll Save the Last Dance for You	Damita Jo	#22
Ta Ta	Clyde McPhatter	#23
(There Was A) Tall Oak Tree	Dorsey Burnette	#23
This Bitter Earth	Dinah Washington	#24
Fools Rush In (Where Angels Fear to Tread)	Brook Benton	#24
Am I That Easy to Forget	Debbie Reynolds	#25
What Am I Living For	Conway Twitty	#26
Sad Mood	Sam Cooke	#29
Apple Green	June Valli	#29
Love Walked In	Dinah Washington	#30
Nobody Loves Me Like You	The Flamingos	#30
Am I Losing You	Jim Reeves	#31
Doll House	Donnie Brooks	#31
Is There Any Chance	Marty Robbins	#31
Anymore	Teresa Brewer	#31
If I Had a Girl	Rod Lauren	#31
Am I the Man	Jackie Wilson	#32
My Dearest Darling	Etta James	#34
Little Things Mean a Lot	Joni James	#35
Is a Blue Bird Blue	Conway Twitty	#35
Little Coco Palm	Jerry Wallace	#36
The Ties That Bind	Brook Benton	#37
It Only Happened Yesterday	Jack Scott	#38
Natural Born Lover	Fats Domino	#38
Tonight's the Night	The Shirelles	#39
Eternally	Sarah Vaughan	#41
Something Happened	Paul Anka	#41
Malaguena	Connie Francis	#42
You're Looking Good	Dee Clark	#43
Lisa	Jeanne Black	#43
The Way of a Clown	Teddy Randazzo	#44
You Don't Know Me	Lenny Welch	#45
Somebody to Love	Bobby Darin	#45
(New In) The Ways of Love	Tommy Edwards	#47
Dance by the Light of the Moon	The Olympics	#47
Walk Slow	Little Willie John	#48

VIOLIN (cont'd)

Teenage Sonata	Sam Cooke	#50
I Wish I'd Never Been Born	Patti Page	#52
It Could Happent to You	Dinah Washington	#53
We Go Together	Jan and Dean	#53
Silent Night	Bing Crosby	#54
Lonely Wind	The Drifters	#54
That Old Feeling	Kitty Kallen	#55
Send Me the Pillow You Dream On	The Browns	#56
The Puppet Song	Frankie Avalon	#56
Earth Angel	Johnny Tillotson	#57
Put Your Arms Around Me	Fats Domino	#58
Hither and Thither and Yon	Brook Benton	#58
Ruby	Adam Wade	#58
I Don't Know What It Is	The Bluenotes	#61
One of the Lucky Ones	Anita Bryant	#62
Don't Deceive Me	Ruth Brown	#62
A Cottage for Sale	Little Willie John	#63
Pledging my Love	Johnny Tillotson	#63
I Can't Help It	Adam Wade	#64
Ballad of the Alamo	Bud & Travis	#64
Patsy	Jack Scott	#65
I Walk the Line	Jaye P. Morgan	#66
Tell Her for Me	Adam Wade	#66
She Should Come to You (La Montana)	Anthony Newley	#67
Do You Mind	Andy Williams	#70
Too Young to Go Steady	Connie Stevens	#71
I Was Such a Fool (To Fall in Love with You)	The Flamingos	#71
Up Town	Roy Orbison	#72
Time Machine	Dante & The Evergreens	#73
Climb Every Mountain	Tony Bennett	#74
We Have Love	Dinah Washington	#76
La Montana (If She Should Come to You)	Frank De Vol	#77
It's Not the End of Everything	Tommy Edwards	#78
My Hero	The Blue Notes	#78
Kommotion	Duane Eddy	#78
I'll Be There	Bobby Darin	#79
I'll Be Seeing You	The Five Satins	#79
The Christmas Song (Merry Christmas to You)	Nat "King" Cole	#80
Since I Met You Baby	Bobby Vee	#81
Journey of Love	The Crests	#81
That's When I Cried	Jimmy Jones	#83
Midnight Lace	Ray Ellis	#84
The Lovin' Touch	Mark Dinning	#84

VIOLIN (cont'd)

Have You Ever Been Lonely (Have You Ever Been Blue)	Teresa Brewer	#84
Side Car Cycle	Charlie Ryan	#84
Many a Wonderful Moment	Rosemary Clooney	#84
Don't Let Love Pass Me By	Frankie Avalon	#85
Cool Water	Jack Scott	#85
The Girl with the Story in Her Eyes	Safaris	#85
My Empty Room	Little Anthony & The Imperials	#86
You're My Baby	Sarah Vaughan	#87
Suddenly	Nickey DeMatteo	#90
Stranger from Durango	Richie Allen	#90
Jambalaya	Bobby Comstock	#90
Talk to Me Baby	Annette	#92
Honky-Tonk Girl	Johnny Cash	#92
Someday You'll Want Me to Want You	Brook Benton	#93
Since I Made You Cry	The Rivieras	#93
Don't Let the Sun Catch You Cryin'	Ray Charles	#95
The Whiffenpoof Song	Bob Crewe	#96
La Montana (If She Should Come to You)	Roger Williams	#98
I Need You Now	100 Strings & Joni James	#98
She's Just A Whole Lot Like You	Hank Thompson	#99
The Last Dance	The McGuire Sisters	#99
Fallen Angel	Webb Pierce	#99
Let Them Talk	Little Willie John	#100
Beachcomber	Bobby Darin	#100
1961		
Mother-In-Law	Ernie K-Doe	#1
Will You Love Me Tomorrow	The Shirelles	#1
Take Good Care of My Baby	Bobby Vee	#1
Crying	Roy Orbison	#2
Run to Him	Bobby Vee	#2
Raindrops	Dee Clark	#2
The Boll Weevil Song	Brook Benton	#2
I've Told Every Little Star	Linda Scott	#3
Fool 1	Brenda Lee	#3
A Hundred Pounds of Clay	James Darren	#3
Hurt	Timi Yuri	#4
Where the Boys Are	Connie Francis	#4
Mama Said	The Shirelles	#4
Stand By Me	Ben E. King	#4
I Love How You Love Me	The Paris Sisters	#5
Sad Movies (Make Me Cry)	Sue Thompson	#5
The Writing on the Wall	Adam Wade	#5
Baby Sittin' Boogie	Buzz Clifford	#6

VIOLIN (cont'd)

Together	Connie Francis	#6
Rubber Ball	Bobby Vee	#6
You Can Depend On Me	Brenda Lee	#6
Without You	Johnny Tillotson	#7
Breakin' in a Brand New Broken Heart	Connie Francis	#7
Emotions	Brenda Lee	#7
Take Good Care of Her	Adam Wade	#7
Tonight	Ferrante & Teicher	#8
Asia Minor	Kokomo	#8
My Empty Arms	Jackie Wilson	#9
I Understand (Just How You Feel)	The G-Clefs	#9
Corinna, Corinna	Ray Peterson	#9
Dance On Little Girl	Paul Anka	#10
Gee Whiz (Look at His Eyes)	Carla Thomas	#10
Spanish Harlem	Ben E. King	#10
Little Devil	Neil Sedaka	#11
Think Twice	Brook Benton	#11
Moon River	Jerry Butler	#11
A Little Bit of Soap	The Jarmels	#12
I'll Be There	Damito Jo	#12
You Can Have Her	Roy Hamilton	#12
Tonight My Love, Tonight	Paul Anka	#13
The Way You Look Tonight	The Lettermen	#13
Never on Sunday	The Chordettes	#13
Please Stay	The Drifters	#14
Look in My Eyes	The Chantels	#14
Tonight I Fell in Love	The Tokens	#15
Bless You	Tony Orlando	#15
Little Boy Sad	Johnny Burnette	#17
I Count the Tears	The Drifters	#17
God, Country and My Baby	Johnny Burnette	#18
Amor	Ben E. King	#18
Let Me Belong to You	Brian Hyland	#20
Model Girl	Johnny Maestro	#20
Sacred	The Castells	#20
That Old Black Magic	Bobby Rydell	#21
C'est Si Bon (It's So Good)	Conway Twitty	#22
Angel on My Shoulder	Shelby Flint	#22
Lullaby of Love	Frank Gari	#23
September in the Rain	Dinah Washington	#23
Lovey Dovey	Buddy Know	#25
"Nag"	The Halos	#25
Baby's First Christmas	Connie Francis	#26

VIOLIN (cont'd)

My Last Date (With You)	Skeeter Davis	#26
Tonight (Could Be the Night)	The Velvets	#26
There She Goes	Jerry Wallace	#26
I'm Hurtin'	Roy Orbison	#27
Utopia	Frank Gari	#27
For My Baby	Brook Benton	#28
Well, I Told You	The Chantels	#29
If I Didn't Care	The Platters	#30
Princess	Frank Gari	#30
(He's) The Great Imposter	The Fleetwoods	#30
Trust in Me	Etta James	#30
A Tear	Gene McDaniels	#31
Some Kind of Wonderful	The Drifters	#32
Stayin' In	Bobby Vee	#33
I Don't Want to Take a Chance	Mary Wells	#33
Kissin' on the Phone	Paul Anka	#35
Lost Love	H.B. Barnum	#35
I Don't Want to Cry	Chuck Jackson	#36
Years from Now	Jackie Wilson	#37
My Last Date (With You)	Joni James	#38
Halfway to Paradise	Tony Orlando	#39
Don't Cry, Baby	Etta James	#39
Your One and Only Love	Jackie Wilson	#40
Nature Boy	Bobby Darin	#40
Don't Believe Him, Donna	Lenny Miles	#41
A Thing of the Past	The Shirelles	#41
Smile	Timi Yuri	#42
Every Breath I Take	Gene Pitney	#42
Starlight, Starbright	Linda Scott	#44
The Tear of the Year	Jackie Wilson	#44
It's Just a House Without You	Brook Benton	#45
Little Altar Boy	Vic Dana	#45
(It Never Happens) In Real Life	Chuck Jackson	#46
What Would I Do	Mickey & Sylvia	#46
You'll Answer to Me	Patti Page	#46
At Last	Etta James	#47
The Age for Love	Jimmy Charles	#47
Magic Moon (Clair de Lune)	The Rays	#49
You'd Better Come Home	Russel Byrd	#50
What Am I Gonna Do	Jimmy Clanton	#50
Fool That I Am	Etta James	#50
Everybody's Gotta Pay Some Dues	The Miracles	#52
First Taste of Love	Ben E. King	#53

VIOLIN (cont'd)

Your Other Love	The Flamingos	#54
It's Too Soon to Know	Etta James	#54
What a Sweet Thing That Was	The Shirelles	#54
Dream	Etta James	#55
Eventually	Brenda Lee	#56
Be My Boy	Paris Sisters	#56
A Love of My Own	Carla Thomas	#56
Sad Movies (Make Me Cry)	The Lennon Sisters	#56
Happy Days	Marv Johnson	#58
Big Big World	Johnny Burnette	#58
The Way I Am	Jackie Wilson	#58
I Wake Up Crying	Chuck Jackson	#59
More Than I Can Say	Bobby Vee	#61
The Very Thought of You	Little Willie John	#61
Merry-Go-Round	Marv Johnson	#61
Tonight I Won't Be There	Adam Wade	#61
Turn Around, Look at Me	Glen Campbell	#62
Oh, How I Miss You Tonight	Jeanne Black	#63
Orange Blossom Special	Billy Vaughn	#63
Your Last Goodbye	Floyd Cramer	#63
Danny Boy	Andy Williams	#64
Don't Read the Letter	Patti Page	#65
My Heart Belongs to Only You	Jackie Wilson	#65
Ling-Ting-Tong	Buddy Knox	#65
Young Boy Blues	Ben E. King	#66
The Most Beautiful Words	Della Reese	#67
My Claire de Lune	Steve Lawrence	#68
A Scottish Soldier (Green Hills of Tyrol)	Andy Stewart	#69
Cinderella	Paul Anka	#70
Daydreams	Johnny Crawford	#70
All of Everything	Frankie Avalon	#70
Shy Away	Jerry Fuller	#71
Take a Fool's Advice	Nat "King" Cole	#71
Too Many Rules	Connie Francis	#72
I Apologize	Timi Yuri	#72
The Next Kiss (Is the Last Goodbye)	Conway Twitty	#72
Room Full of Tears	The Drifters	#72
Let True Love Begin	Nat "King" Cole	#73
Run, Run, Run	Ronny Douglas	#75
Keep Your Hands Off of Him	Damita Jo	#75
The Lonely Crowd	Teddy Vann	#76
Little Pedro	The Olympics	#76
Well-A, Well-A	Shirley & Lee	#77

VIOLIN (cont'd)

Title	Artist	Chart
You Don't Know What It Means	Jackie Wilson	#79
Lonely Life	Jackie Wilson	#80
You're Gonna Need Magic	Roy Hamilton	#80
Here Comes the Night	Ben E. King	#81
Top Forty, News, Weather and Sports	Mark Dinning	#81
Who Else but You	Frankie Avalon	#82
Kissin Game	Dion	#82
Happy Times (Are Here to Stay)	Tony Orlando	#82
I'll Never Stop Wanting You	Brian Hyland	#83
And the Heavens Cried	Ronnie Savoy	#84
In Between Tears	Lenny Miles	#84
Ring of Fire	Duane Eddy	#84
I Wonder (If Your Love Will Ever Belong to Me)	The Pentagons	#84
Blue Tomorrow	Billy Vaughn	#84
The Door to Paradise	Bobby Rydell	#85
A Texan and a Girl from Mexico	Anita Bryant	#85
Sad Eyes (Don't You Cry)	The Echoes	#88
Laugh	The Velvets	#90
A City Girl Stole My Country Boy	Patti Page	#90
This World We Love In (Il Cielo In Una Stanza)	Mina	#90
Theme from "The Great Imposter"	Henry Mancini	#90
Faraway Star	The Chordettes	#90
Hop Scotch	Santo and Johnny	#90
Memphis	Donnie Brooks	#90
Life's a Holiday	Jerry Wallace	#91
A Little Feeling (Called Love)	Jack Scott	#91
(How Can I Write on Paper) What I Feel in My Heart	Jim Reeves	#92
Kokomo	The Flamingos	#92
It's All Right	Sam Cooke	#93
She Really Loves You	Timi Yuri	#93
For Your Love	The Wanderers	#93
Guilty of Loving You	Jerry Fuller	#94
Early Every Morning (Early Every Evening Too)	Dinah Washington	#95
Seven Day Fool	Etta James	#95
Hang On	Floyd Cramer	#95
I Lied to My Heart	The Enchanters	#96
What Will I Tell My Heart	The Harptones	#96
Free Me	Johnny Preston	#97
Broken Hearted	The Miracles	#97
Walkin' Back to Happiness	Helen Shapiro	#100
Sweet Little Kathy	Ray Peterson	#100
You Don't Have to Be a Tower of Strength	Gloria Lynne	#100

VIOLIN (cont'd)

1962

Don't Break the Heart That Loves You	Connie Francis	#1
Breaking Up Is Hard to Do	Neil Sedaka	#1
Johnny Angel	Shelley Fabares	#1
Roses are Red (My Love)	Bobby Vinton	#1
I Can't Stop Loving You	Ray Charles	#1
You Don't Know Me	Ray Charles	#2
Ramblin' Rose	Nat "King" Cole	#2
It Keeps Right on A-hurtin'	Johnny Tillotson	#3
All Alone Am I	Brenda Lee	#3
(The Man Who Shot) Liberty Valance	Gene Pitney	#4
Break It to Me Gently	Brenda Lee	#4
Happy Birthday, Sweet Sixteen	Neil Sedaka	#5
Love Letters	Ketty Lester	#5
She Cried	Jay & The Americans	#5
Old Rivers	Walter Brennan	#5
Al Di La'	Emilio Pericoli	#6
Gina	Johnny Mathis	#6
Everybody Loves Me but You	Brenda Lee	#6
Patches	Dickey Lee	#6
You Belong to Me	The Duprees	#7
When I Fall in Love	The Lettermen	#7
Second Hand Love	Connie Francis	#7
What's Your Name	Don & Juan	#7
Playboy	The Marvelettes	#7
When the Boy in Your Arms (Is the Boy in Your Heart)	Connie Francis	#10
Don't Play That Song (You Lied)	Ben E. King	#11
What's a Matter Baby (Is It Hurting You)	Timi Yuro	#12
Rumors	Johnny Crawford	#12
Rain Rain Go Away	Bobby Vinton	#12
Nothing Can Change This Love	Sam Cooke	#12
Smoky Places	The Corsairs	#12
Bring It on Home to Me	Sam Cooke & Lou Rawls	#13
Dear Lonely Hearts	Nat "King" Cole	#13
Uptown	The Crystals	#13
Your Nose Is Gonna Grow	Johnny Crawford	#14
Revenge	Brook Benton	#15
Sharing You	Bobby Vee	#15
Please Don't Ask About Barbara	Bobby Vee	#15
I Sold My Heart to the Junkman	The Blue-Belles	#15
I Wish That We Were Married	Ronnie & The Hi-Lites	#16
Send Me the Pillow You Dream On	Johnny Tillotson	#17
Come Back Silly Girl	The Lettermen	#17

VIOLIN (cont'd)

Having a Party	Sam Cooke	#17
Eso Beso (That Kiss!)	Paul Anka	#19
Letter Full of Tears	Gladys Knight & The Pips	#19
I Left My Heart in San Francisco	Tony Bennett	#19
Make It Easy on Yourself	Jerry Butler	#20
Punish Her	Bobby Vee	#20
There's No Other (Like My Baby)	The Crystals	#20
Silver Threads and Golden Needles	The Springfields	#20
Love Me Tender	Richard Chamberlain	#21
Point of No Return	Gene McDaniels	#21
So This Is Love	The Castells	#21
Johnny Loves Me	Shelley Fabares	#21
Ginny Come Lately	Brian Hyland	#21
Tell Me	Dick & DeeDee	#22
Funny How Time Slips Away	Jimmy Elledge	#22
It Might as Well Rain Until September	Carole King	#22
Little Red Rented Rowboat	Joe Dowell	#23
Any Day Now (My Wild Beautiful Bird)	Chuck Jackson	#23
I Was Such a Fool (To Fall in Love with You)	Connie Francis	#24
I Can't Help It (If I'm Still in Love with You)	Johnny Tillotson	#24
Leah	Roy Orbison	#25
Till Death Do Us Part	Bob Braun	#26
You are Mine	Frankie Avalon	#26
The Crowd	Roy Orbison	#26
Theme from Ben Casey	Valjean	#28
When My Little Girl Is Smiling	The Drifters	#28
Your Cheating Heart	Ray Charles	#29
Jamie	Eddie Holland	#30
Workin' for the Man	Roy Orbison	#33
He Knows I Love Him Too Much	The Paris Sisters	#34
The Greatest Hurt	Jackie Wilson	#34
What's So Good About Goodbye	The Miracles	#35
Johnny Will	Pat Boone	#35
Chattanooga Choo Choo	Floyd Cramer	#36
Stop the Music	The Shirelles	#36
Where are You	Dinah Washington	#36
Mama Sang a Song	Walter Brennan	#38
Hey! Little Girl	Del Shannon	#38
I Love You the Way You Are	Bobby Vinton	#38
I'll Try Something New	The Miracles	#39
I'll Bring It Home to You	Carla Thomas	#41
Born to Lose	Ray Charles	#41
How Is Julie?	The Lettermen	#42

VIOLIN (cont'd)

Mr. Songwriter	Connie Stevens	#43
Patti Ann	Johnny Crawford	#43
No One Will Ever Know	Jimmie Rodgers	#43
Ten Lonely Guys	Pat Boone	#45
Hit Record	Brook Benton	#45
King of Clowns	Neil Sedaka	#45
The Things We Did Last Summer	Shelley Fabares	#46
I Will	Vic Dana	#47
Don't Ask Me to Be Friends	The Everly Brothers	#48
You Threw a Lucky Punch	Gene Chandler	#49
Why'd You Wanna Make Me Cry	Connie Stevens	#52
When I Get Thru with You (You'll Love Me Too)	Patsy Cline	#53
Walkin' with My Angel	Bobby Vee	#53
Love Me as I Love You	George Maharis	#54
Ecstasy	Ben E. King	#56
Runaway	Lawrence Welk	#56
Never in a Million Years	Linda Scott	#56
I Could Have Loved You so Well	Ray Peterson	#57
He Thinks I Still Care	Connie Francis	#57
Hearts	Jackie Wilson	#58
If I Didn't Have a Dime (To Play the Jukebox)	Gene Pitney	#58
If I Cried Every Time You Hurt Me	Wanda Jackson	#58
Yessiree	Linda Scott	#60
Untie Me	The Tams	#60
Baby Has Gone Bye Bye	George Maharis	#62
Long as the Rose Is Red	Florraine Darlin	#62
You Can Run (But You Can't Hide)	Jerry Butler	#63
Anna (Go to Him)	Arthur Alexander	#68
Stranger on the Shore	The Drifters	#73
Worried Mind	Ray Anthony	#74
Memories of Maria	Jerry Byrd	#74
There'll Be No Next Time	Jackie Wilson	#75
A Miracle	Frankie Avalon	#75
Too Late to Worry- Too Blue to Cry	Glen Campbell	#76
I Want to Be Loved	Dinah Washington	#76
Midnight	Johnny Gibson	#76
The Alley Cat Song	David Thorne	#76
Pictures in the Fire	Pat Boone	#77
Desafinado (Slightly Out of Tune)	Pat Thomas	#78
Silly Boy (She Doesn't Love You)	The Lettermen	#81
A Girl Has to Know	The G-Clefs	#81
Forever and a Day	Jackie Wilson	#82
A Little Bitty Tear	Wanda Jackson	#84

VIOLIN (cont'd)

Twilight Time	Andy Williams	#86
Let Me Be the One	The Paris Sisters	#87
Lovesick Blues	Floyd Cramer	#87
Too Bad	Ben E. King	#88
There Is No Greater Love	The Wanderers	#88
Here Comes That Feelin'	Brenda Lee	#89
You Can't Lie to a Liar	Ketty Lester	#90
Imagine That	Patsy Cline	#90
Adios Amigo	Jim Reeves	#90
It's Magic	The Platters	#91
Oh! What It Seemed to Be	The Castells	#91
Magic Wand	Don & Juan	#91
I Can't Say Goodbye	Bobby Vee	#92
The Door Is Open	Tommy Hunt	#92
Aladdin	Bobby Curtola	#92
Four Walls	Kay Starr	#92
I Wouldn't Know (What to Do)	Dinah Washington	#93
Jane, Jane, Jane	The Kingston Trio	#93
When the Boys Get Together	Joanie Sommers	#94
Smile	Ferrante & Teicher	#94
Way Over There	The Miracles	#94
Quando, Quando, Quando (Tell Me When)	Pat Boone	#95
Dear Hearts and Gentle People	The Springfields	#95
Operator	Gladys Knight & The Pips	#97
One More Town	The Kingston trio	#97
Lover Come Back	Doris Day	#98
The Wonderful World of the Young	Andy Williams	#99
The Moon Was Yellow	Frank Sinatra	#99
Funny	Gene McDaniels	#99
Don't Stop the Wedding	Ann Cole	#99
Father Knows Best	The Radiants	#100
Try a Little Tenderness	Aretha Franklin	#100
Goodbye Dad	The Castle Sisters	#100
Houdini	Walter Brennan	#100
1963		
I'm Leaving It up to You	Dale & Grace	#1
Go Away Little Girl	Steve Lawrence	#1
I Will Follow Him	Little Peggy March	#1
The End of the World	Skeeter Davis	#2
Be My Baby	The Ronettes	#2
Can't Get Used to Losing You	Andy Williams	#2
I Love You Because	Al Martino	#3
The Night Has a Thousand Eyes	Bobby Vee	#3

VIOLIN (cont'd)

Song	Artist	Rank
You're the Reason I'm Living	Bobby Darin	#3
Since I Fell for You	Lenny Welch	#4
Those Lazy-Hazy-Crazy Days of Summer	Nat "King" Cole	#6
Then He Kissed Me	The Crystals	#6
I Can't Stay Mad at You	Skeeter Davis	#7
In Dreams	Roy Orbison	#7
Take These Chains from My Heart	Ray Charles	#8
Still	Bill Anderson	#8
Our Winter Love	Bill Pursell	#9
18 Yellow Roses	Bobby Darin	#10
500 Miles Away from Home	Bobby Bare	#10
Hey, Girl	Freddie Scott	#10
Talk to Me	Sunny & The Sunglows	#11
Half Heaven- Half Heartache	Gene Pitney	#12
That Sunday, That Summer	Nat "King" Cole	#12
Charms	Bobby Vee	#13
Hopeless	Andy Williams	#13
All I Have to Do Is Dream	Richard Chamberlain	#14
Detroit City	Bobby Bare	#16
Young and in Love	Dick & DeeDee	#17
El Watusi	Ray Barretto	#17
Alice in Wonderland	Neil Sedaka	#17
I'm Gonna Be Warm This Winter	Connie Francis	#18
You Can Never Stop Me Loving You	Johnny Tillotson	#18
My Coloring Book	Sandy Stewart	#20
True Love Never Runs Smooth	Gene Pitney	#21
The Love of My Man	Theola Kilgore	#21
Don't Make Me Over	Dionne Warwick	#21
Falling	Roy Orbison	#22
Living a Lie	Al Martino	#22
Make the World Go Away	Timi Yuro	#24
Out of My Mind	Johnny Tillotson	#24
Shutters and Boards	Jerry Wallace	#24
I Wonder	Brenda Lee	#25
Don't Say Goodnight and Mean Goodbye	The Shirelles	#26
Hello Heartache, Goodbye Love	Little Peggy March	#26
Walking Proud	Steve Lawrence	#26
Let's Got Steady Again	Neil Sedaka	#26
Don't Be Afraid, Little Darlin'	Steve Lawrence	#26
Poor Little Rich Girl	Steve Lawrence	#27
Your Other Love	Connie Francis	#28
I Got What I Wanted	Brook Benton	#28
I Want to Stay Here	Steve & Eydie	#28

VIOLIN (cont'd)

Proud	Johnny Crawford	#29
Be Careful of Stones That You Throw	Dion	#31
I Wish I Were a Princess	Little Peggy March	#32
Trouble Is My Middle Name	Bobby Vinton	#33
Let's Kiss and Make Up	Bobby Vinton	#38
Remember Diana	Paul Anka	#39
(I Love You) Don't You Forget It	Perry Como	#39
That's How Heartaches Are Made	Baby Washington	#40
I'm Saving My Love	Skeeter Davis	#41
Blue Guitar	Richard Chamberlain	#42
Shake Me I Rattle (Squeeze Me I Cry)	Marion Worth	#42
All Over the World	Nat "King" Cole	#42
Tell Him I'm Not Home	Chuck Jackson	#42
More	Vic Dana	#42
Treat My Baby Good	Bobby Darin	#43
Sweet Dreams (Of You)	Patsy Cline	#44
When a Boy Falls in Love	The Dynamics	#44
The Ballad of Jed Clampett	Lester Flatt/Earl Scruggs	#44
Rags to Riches	Sunny & The Sunliners	#45
Tips of My Fingers	Roy Clark	#45
She'll Never Know	Brenda Lee	#47
The Dreamer	Neil Sedaka	#47
Young Wings Can Fly (Higher Than You Know)	Ruby & The Romantics	#47
Funny How Time Slips Away	Johnny Tillotson	#50
Big Wide World	Teddy Randazzo	#51
8 X 10	Bill Anderson	#53
What Does a Girl Do?	The Shirelles	#53
Don't Try to Fight It, Baby	Eydie Gorme	#53
These Foolish Things	James Brown	#55
I'm Just a Country Boy	George McCurn	#55
The Impossible Happened	Little Peggy March	#57
How Can I Forget	Jimmy Holiday	#57
Shirl Girl	Wayne Newton	#58
Dearer Than Life	Brook Benton	#59
This Is My Prayer	Theola Kilgore	#60
Come Back	Johnny Mathis	#61
Daughter	The Blenders	#61
Leave Me Alone	Baby Washington	#62
Gotta Travel On	Timi Yuro	#64
It's A Lonely Town (Lonely Without You)	Gene McDaniels	#64
Would It Make Any Difference to You	Etta James	#64
Baby, Baby, Baby	Sam Cooke	#66
Meditation (Meditacao)	Charlie Byrd	#66

VIOLIN (cont'd)

This Is All I Ask	Burl Ives	#67
My Block	The Four Pennies	#67
Don't Wanna Think About Paula	Dickey Lee	#68
What to Do with Laurie	Mike Clifford	#68
Your Teenage Dreams	Johnny Mathis	#68
Whatever You Want	Jerry Butler	#68
Give Us Your Blessing	Ray Peterson	#70
Ronnie, Call Me When You Get a Chance	Shelley Fabares	#72
Reach Out for Me	Lou Johnson	#74
Ask Me	Maxine Brown	#75
Get Him	The Exciters	#76
Eternally	The Chantels	#77
Two-Ten, Six-Eighteen (Doesn't Anybody Know My Name)	Jimmie Rodgers	#78
Everybody Go Home	Eydie Gorme	#80
Insult to Injury	Timi Yuro	#81
Make the Music Play	Dionne Warwick	#81
Ain't Gonna Kiss Ya	The Ribbons	#81
Say Wonderful Things	Patti Page	#81
Heart! (I Hear You Beating)	Wayne Newton	#82
Leavin' on Your Mind	Patsy Cline	#83
Thank You and Goodnight	The Angels	#84
A Letter from Betty	Bobby Vee	#85
How Can I Forget	Ben E. King	#85
Cuando Calienta El Sol (When the Sun Is Hot)	Steve Allen (Copacabana Trio)	#85
Nothing Goes Up (Without Coming Down)	Nat "King" Cole	#87
If Mary's There	Brian Hyland	#88
That's How It Goes	George Maharis	#88
Did You Have a Happy Birthday?	Paul Anka	#89
Detroit City No. 2	Ben Colder (Shep Wooley)	#90
Meditation (Meditacao)	Pat Boone	#91
Guilty	Jim Reeves	#91
Shy Girl	The Cascades	#91
Say Wonderful Things	Ronnie Carroll	#91
Toys in the Attic	Jack Jones	#92
Spring in Manhattan	Tony Bennett	#92
Mr. Wishing Well	Nat "King" Cole	#92
Where Did the Good Times Go	Dick & DeeDee	#93
What a Fool I've Been	Carla Thomas	#93
Here Comes the Boy	Tracey Dey	#93
Lonely Drifter	The O'Jays	#93
The Ten Commandments of Love	James MacArthur	#94
Hear the Bells	The Tokens	#94
My Foolish Heart	The Demensions	#95

VIOLIN (cont'd)

I Know I Know	Jimmy Smith	#96
One Boy Too Late	Mike Clifford	#96
Danger	Vic Dana	#96
Faded Love	Patsy Cline	#96
Faded Love	Jackie DeShannon	#97
Still No. 2	Ben Colder (Sheb Wooley)	#98
Never Love a Robin	Bobby Vee	#99
Hey Lonely One	Baby Washington	#100
Not For All the Money in the World	The Shirelles	#100
Make the World Go Away	Ray Price	#100
1964		
Everybody Loves Somebody	Dean Martin	#1
You Don't Own Me	Lesley Gore	#2
Under the Boardwalk	The Drifters	#4
Forget Him	Bobby Rydell	#4
Let It Be Me	Betty Everett & Jerry Butler	#5
The Door Is Still Open to My Heart	Dean Martin	#6
Talk Back Trembling Lips	Johnny Tillotson	#7
Stop and Think It Over	Dale & Grace	#8
Anyone Who Had a Heart	Dionne Warwick	#8
White on White	Danny Williams	#9
My Heart Belongs to Only You	Bobby Vinton	#9
It's Over	Roy Orbison	#9
I'm Gonna Be Strong	Gene Pitney	#9
The Bachelors	Diane	#10
Baby I Need Your Loving	Four Tops	#11
As Usual	Brenda Lee	#12
Every Little Bit Hurts	Brenda Holloway	#13
Right or Wrong	Ronnie Dove	#14
I Don't Want to See You Again	Peter & Gordon	#16
The Shelter of Your Arms	Sammy Davis Jr.	#17
In the Misty Moonlight	Jerry Wallace	#19
Reach out for Me	Dionne Warwick	#20
Tears and Roses	Al Martino	#20
That Lucky Old Sun	Ray Charles	#20
Yesterday's Gone	Chad & Jeremy	#21
I Don't Want to Be Hurt Anymore	Nat "King" Cole	#22
Baby, I Love You	The Ronettes	#24
Ebb Tide	Lenny Welch	#25
Letter from Sherry	Dale Ward	#25
It's All in the Game	Cliff Richard	#25
Think	Brenda Lee	#25
Turn Around	Dick & DeeDee	#27

VIOLIN (cont'd)

Softly, As I Leave You	Frank Sinatra	#27
She Understands Me	Johnny Tillotson	#31
Miller's Cave	Bobby Bare	#33
I Believe	The Bachelors	#33
I've Got Sand in My Shoes	The Drifters	#33
You'll Never Get to Heaven if You Break My Heart	Dionne Warwick	#34
I Don't Want to See Tomorrow	Nat "King" Cole	#34
Wrong for Each Other	Andy Williams	#34
Going Going Gone	Brook Benton	#35
I Can't Stop Talking About You	Steve & Eydie	#35
I Rise, I Fall	Johnny Tillotson	#36
Worried Guy	Johnny Tillotson	#37
My Heart Cries for You	Ray Charles	#38
Say You	Ronnie Dove	#40
All Cried Out	Dusty Springfield	#41
We Could	Al Martino	#41
Share Your Love with Me	Bobby Bland	#42
Without the One You Love (Life's Not Worth While)	Four Tops	#43
Too Late to Turn Back Now	Brook Benton	#43
Worry	Johnny Tillotson	#45
When You Loved Me	Brenda Lee	#47
Another Cup of Coffee	Brook Benton	#47
He Says the Same Things to Me	Skeeter Davis	#47
Alone with You	Brenda Lee	#48
Gonna Get Along Without You Now	Skeeter Davis	#48
When You're Young and in Love	Ruby & The Romantics	#48
My True Carrie, Love	Nat "King" Cole	#49
A Tear Fell	Ray Charles	#50
The World I Used to Know	Jimmie Rodgers	#51
Smack Dab in the Middle	Ray Charles	#52
Castles in the Sand	Little Stevie Wonder	#52
Bye Bye Barbara	Johnny Mathis	#53
The French Song	Lucille Starr	#54
No One to Cry To	Ray Charles	#55
I Wanna Be with You	Nancy Wilson	#57
Runnin' Out of Fools	Aretha Franklin	#57
Watch Your Step	Brooks O'Dell	#58
(You Can't Let the Boy Overpower) The Man in You	The Miracles	#59
The First Night of the Full Moon	Jack Jones	#59
The World of Lonely People	Anita Bryant	#59
I'll Always Love You	Brenda Holloway	#60
I Stand Accused	Jerry Butler	#61
Listen Lonely Girl	Johnny Mathis	#62

VIOLIN (cont'd)

Song	Artist	#
Something You Got	Ramsey Lewis Trio	#63
That's When It Hurts	Ben E. King	#63
Hickory, Dick and Doc	Bobby Vee	#63
Sometimes I Wonder	Major Lance	#64
The Loneliest Night	Dale & Grace	#65
He Walks Like a Man	Jody Miller	#66
True Love Goes On and On	Burl Ives	#66
Long Gone Lonesome Blues	Hank Williams, Jr.	#67
I Wouldn't Trade You for the World	The Bachelors	#69
The Wonder of You	Ray Peterson	#70
Out of Sight - Out of Mind	Sunny & The Sunliners	#71
If You Want This Love	Sonny Knight	#71
If I'm a Fool for Loving You	Bobby Wood	#74
A House Is Not a Home	Brook Benton	#75
We Belong Together	Jimmy Velvet	#75
Be My Girl	The Four-Evers	#75
Yet… I Know (Et Pourtant)	Steve Lawrence	#77
A Quiet Place	Garnet Mimms & The Enchanters	#78
I Don't Want to Walk Without You	Phyllis McGuire	#79
It's for You	Cilla Black	#79
To Each His Own	The Tymes	#79
Where Did I Go Wrong	Dee Dee Sharp	#82
I Guess I'm Crazy	Jim Reeves	#82
Baby Baby All the Time	The Superbs	#83
Baby's Gone	Gene Thomas	#84
Tell Me Mama	Christine Quaite	#85
The Things in This House	Bobby Darin	#86
Father Sebastian	The Ramblers	#86
Can't Get Over (The Bossa Nova)	Eydie Gorme	#87
All My Trials	Dick & DeeDee	#89
Deep in the Heart of Harlem	Clyde McPhatter	#90
Dream Lover	The Paris Sisters	#91
Stockholm	Lawrence Welk	#91
How Much Can a Lonely Heart Stand	Skeeter Davis	#92
If You See My Love	Lenny Welch	#92
Little Boy	The Crystals	#92
Yes I Do	Solomon Burke	#92
I Wonder Who's Kissing Her Now	Bobby Darin	#93
Don't Spread It Around	Barbara Lynn	#93
I Just Can't Say Goodbye	Bobby Rydell	#94
Have I Stayed Away Too Long	Bobby Bare	#94
Caldonia	James Brown	#95
Willyam, Willyam	Dee Dee Sharp	#97

VIOLIN (cont'd)

Where or When	The Lettermen	#98
The Little White Cloud that Cried	Wayne Newton	#99
Rome Will Never Leave You	Richard Chamberlain	#99
When You Walk in the Room	Jackie DeShannon	#99
I Can't Get You Out of My Heart	Al Martino	#99
Who's Been Sleeping in My Bed	Linda Scott	#100
1965		
You've Lost That Lovin' Feelin'	The Righteous Brothers	#1
I Can't Help Myself	The Four Tops	#1
Yesterday	The Beatles	#1
Cara, Mia	Jay & The Americans	#4
Yes, I'm Ready	Barbara Mason	#5
It's the Same Old Song	Four Tops	#5
Make the World Go Away	Eddy Arnold	#6
I'll Be Doggone	Marvin Gaye	#8
Hush, Hush, Sweet Charlotte	Patti Page	#8
Hold Me, Thrill Me, Kiss Me	Mel Carter	#8
Don't Just Stand There	Patty Duke	#8
Just Once in My Life	The Righteous Brothers	#9
Cast Your Fate to the Wind	Sounds Orchestral	#10
The Wedding	Julie Rogers	#10
Make Me Your Baby	Barbara Lewis	#11
Baby, I'm Yours	Barbara Lewis	#11
A Walk in the Black Forest	Horst Jankowski	#12
Bye, Bye, Baby (Baby, Goodbye)	The Four Seasons	#12
Too Many Rivers	Brenda Lee	#13
One Kiss for Old Times' Sake	Ronnie Dove	#14
The Race Is On	Jack Jones	#15
Take Me Back	Little Anthony/Imperials	#16
A Little Bit of Heaven	Ronnie Dove	#16
Ooo Baby Baby	The Miracles	#16
Long Lonely Nights	Bobby Vinton	#17
Everyone's Gone to the Moon	Jonathan King	#17
Before and After	Chad & Jeremy	#17
Don't Forget I Still Love You	Bobbi Martin	#19
Just You	Sonny & Cher	#20
I'll Make All Your Dreams Come True	Ronnie Dove	#21
Round Every Corner	Petula Clark	#21
L-O-N-E-L-Y	Bobby Vinton	#22
If I Loved You	Chad & Jeremy	#23
Summer Nights	Marianne Faithfull	#24
Ask the Lonely	The Four Tops	#24
Oh No Not My Baby	Maxine Brown	#24

VIOLIN (cont'd)

Kiss Away	Ronnie Dove	#25
When I'm Gone	Brenda Holloway	#25
Ride Away	Roy Orbison	#25
Come and Stay with Me	Marianne Faithfull	#26
No Arms Can Ever Hold You	The Bachelors	#27
Sad, Sad Girl	Barbara Mason	#27
With These Hands	Tom Jones	#27
What Have They Done to the Rain	The Searchers	#29
Chapel in the Moonlight	The Bachelors	#32
Somewhere in Your Heart	Frank Sinatra	#32
Rusty Bells	Brenda Lee	#33
Concrete and Clay	Eddie Rambeau	#35
I Understand (Just How You Feel)	Freddie & The Dreamers	#36
…And Roses and Roses	Andy Williams	#36
(All of a Sudden) My Heart Sings	Mel Carter	#38
Little Lonely One	Tom Jones	#42
Whose Heart Are You Breaking Tonight	Connie Francis	#43
Seven Letters	Ben E. King	#45
Crawling Back	Roy Orbison	#46
I Can't Stop Thinking of You	Bobbi Martin	#46
Seein' the Right Love Go Wrong	Jack Jones	#46
Trains and Boats and Planes	Billy J. Kramer	#47
Jealous Heart	Connie Francis	#47
You'll Never Walk Alone	Gerry & The Pacemakers	#48
For Mama (La Mamma)	Connie Francis	#48
Angel	Johnny Tillotson	#51
Crystal Chandelier	Vic Dana	#51
Born to Be Together	The Ronettes	#52
My Heart Would Know	Al Martino	#52
Out in the Streets	The Shangri-Las	#53
Mother Nature, Father Time	Brook Benton	#53
Somebody Else Is Taking My Place	Al Martino	#53
It's Gonna Be Fine	Glenn Yarbrough	#54
Truly, Truly, True	Brenda Lee	#54
For Mama	Jerry Vale	#54
It's Gonna Be Alright	Maxine Brown	#56
It's Too Late, Baby Too Late	Arthur Prysock	#56
Wishing It Was You	Connie Francis	#57
Think of the Good Times	Jay & The Americans	#57
Cry	Ray Charles	#58
What's He Doing in My World	Eddy Arnold	#60
Theme from "Harlow" (Lonely Girl)	Bobby Vinton	#61
Forgive Me	Al Martino	#61

VIOLIN (cont'd)

You'll Always Be the One I Love	Dean Martin	#64
Give All Your Love to Me	Gerry & The Pacemakers	#68
I Love You So	Bobbi Martin	#70
The Loser	The Skyliners	#72
The Girl from Peyton Place	Dickey Lee	#73
Roses and Rainbows	Danny Hutton	#73
Only Those in Love	Baby Washington	#73
Apples and Bananas	Lawrence Welk	#75
I Need You	Chuck Jackson	#75
Canadian Sunset	Sounds Orchestral	#76
Danny Boy	Patti LaBelle & The Bluebells	#76
Real Live Girl	Steve Alaimo	#77
Funny Little Butterflies	Patty Duke	#77
Operator	Brenda Holloway	#78
I Really Love You	Dee Dee Sharp	#78
Is It Really Over?	Jim Reeves	#79
I Won't Love You Anymore (Sorry)	Lesley Gore	#80
Roundabout	Connie Francis	#80
Three O'Clock in the Morning	Lou Rawls	#83
Fly Me to the Moon	LaVern Baker	#84
I'm a Fool to Care	Ray Charles	#84
(There'll Come a Day When) Ev'ry Little Bit Hurts	Bobby Vee	#84
So Long Babe	Nancy Sinatra	#86
Then I'll Count Again	Johnny Tillotson	#86
The Crying Game	Brenda Lee	#87
This Is It	Jim Reeves	#88
The Way of Love	Kathy Kirby	#88
My Cherie	Al Martino	#88
Oowee, Oowee	Perry Como	#88
Let's Move & Groove (Together)	Johnny Nash	#88
Cast Your Fate to the Wind	Steve Alaimo	#89
Go Away from My World	Marianne Faithfull	#89
I Have Dreamed	Chad & Jeremy	#91
Try to Remember	The Brothers Four	#91
Are You Still My Baby	The Shirelles	#91
Autumn Leaves - 1965	Roger Williams	#92
It's Almost Tomorrow	Jimmy Velvet	#93
I'm Over You	Jan Bradley	#93
After Loving You	Della Reese	#95
Welcome Home	Walter Jackson	#95
You Can Have Him	Timi Yuro	#96
From a Window	Chad & Jeremy	#97
You're Next	Jimmy Witherspoon	#98

VIOLIN (cont'd)

No One	Brenda Lee	#98
Where Were You When I Needed You	Jerry Vale	#99
I've Got Five Dollars and It's Saturday Night	George Jones & Gene Pitney	#99
Love Me as Though There Were No Tomorrow	Sonny Knight	#100
1966		
Poor Side of Town	Johnny Rivers	#1
Monday, Monday	Mamas & Papas	#1
(You're My) Soul and Inspiration	The Righteous Brothers	#1
Bang Bang (My Baby Shot Me Down)	Cher	#2
I Saw Her Again	Mamas & Papas	#5
Walk Away Renee	The Left Banke	#5
Ebb Tide	The Righteous Brothers	#5
Dandy	Herman's Hermits	#5
Elusive Butterfly	Bob Lind	#5
As Tears Go By	The Rolling Stones	#6
Crying Time	Ray Charles	#6
Message to Michael	Dionne Warwick	#8
If I Were a Carpenter	Bobby Darin	#8
I'm Ready for Love	Martha & The Vandellas	#9
Eleanor Rigby	The Beatles	#11
My Heart's Symphony	Gary Lewis/Playboys	#13
One Has My Name (The Other Has My Heart)	Barry Young	#13
He	The Righteous Brothers	#18
When Liking Turns to Loving	Ronnie Dove	#18
Together Again	Ray Charles	#19
Let's Start All Over Again	Ronnie Dove	#20
Girl in Love	The Outsiders	#21
Trains and Boats and Planes	Dionne Warwick	#22
I Really Don't Want to Know	Ronnie Dove	#22
Look Through My Window	Mamas & Papas	#24
The Dangling Conversation	Simon & Garfunkel	#25
I Just Don't Know What to do with Myself	Dionne Warwick	#26
Somewhere	Len Barry	#26
Happy Summer Days	Ronnie Dove	#27
Sandy	Ronny & The Daytonas	#27
East West	Herman's Hermits	#27
I Love You Drops	Vic Dana	#30
Think I'll Go Somewhere and Cry Myself to Sleep	Al Martino	#30
Breakin' up Is Breakin' up My Heart	Roy Orbison	#31
Friday's Child	Nancy Sinatra	#36
Time After Time	Chris Montez	#36
I Want to Go with You	Eddy Arnold	#36
I've Got to Be Somebody	Billy Joe Royal	#38

VIOLIN (cont'd)

Dum-De-Da	Bobby Vinton	#40
All That I Am	Elvis Presley	#41
A Million and One	Dean Martin	#41
The Tip of My Fingers	Eddy Arnold	#43
Little Darling, I Need You	Marvin Gaye	#47
It's Good News Week	Hedgehoppers Anonymous	#48
Heaven Must Have Sent You	The Elgins	#50
Broomstick Cowboy	Bobby Goldsboro	#53
Suspicions	The Sidekicks	#55
Helpless	Kim Weston	#56
A Little Bit of Soap	The Exciters	#58
Tears	Bobby Vinton	#59
Past, Present and Future	The Shangri-Las	#59
Blue Side of Lonesome	Jim Reeves	#59
Nobody's Baby Again	Dean Martin	#60
I Guess I'll Always Love You	Isley Brothers	#61
Georgia on My Mind	The Righteous Brothers	#62
A Day in the Life of a Fool	Jack Jones	#62
A Lover's Concerto	Sarah Vaughan	#63
If You Gotta Make a Fool of Somebody	Maxine Brown	#63
I'll Love You Forever	The Holidays	#63
I've Got to Do a Little Bit Better	Joe Tex	#64
Please Say You're Fooling	Ray Charles	#64
Remember the Rain	Bob Lind	#64
Truly Julie's Blues (I'll Be There)	Bob Lind	#65
Teenager's Prayer	Joe Simon	#66
Too Soon to Know	Roy Orbison	#68
A Million and One	Vic Dana	#71
I Can't Believe You Love Me	Tammie Terrell	#72
I Only Have Eyes for You	The Lettermen	#72
When a Woman Loves a Man	Esther Phillips	#73
Melody for an Unknown Girl	The Unknowns	#74
Baby Toys	The Toys	#76
(We'll Be) United	The Intruders	#78
Petticoat White (Summer Sky Blue)	Bobby Vinton	#81
Giddyup Go	Red Sovine	#82
Games That Lovers Play	Wayne Newton	#86
Goodnight My Love	Ben E. King	#91
Dommage, Dommage (Too Bad, Too Bad)	Jerry Vale	#93
Fiddle Around	Jan & Dean	#93
You Waited Too Long	The Five Stairsteps	#94
Off to Dublin in the Green	Abbey Tavern Singers	#94
Baby I Need You	The Manhattans	#96

VIOLIN (cont'd)

Come Share the Good Times with Me	Julie Monday	#96
Where the Sun Has Never Shone	Jonathan King	#97
Is It Me?	Barbara Mason	#97
Sharing You	Mitty Collier	#97
Dommage, Dommage (Too Bad, Too Bad)	Paul Vance	#97
I Need Love	Barbara Mason	#98
To Show I Love You	Peter & Gordon	#98
Spanish Night and You	Connie Francis	#99
Help Me (Get Myself Back Together Again)	The Spellbinders	#100
1967		
Hello Goodbye	The Beatles	#1
Ruby Tuesday	The Rolling Stones	#1
Love Is Here and Now You're Gone	The Supremes	#1
Ode to Billy Joe	Bobbie Gentry	#1
To Sir with Love	Lulu	#1
Reflections	The Supremes	#2
I Was Made to Love Her	Stevie Wonder	#2
Baby I Need Your Lovin'	Johnny Rivers	#3
Don't Sleep in the Subway	Petula Clark	#5
Your Precious Love	Marvin Gaye & Tammi Terrell	#5
You're My Everything	The Temptations	#6
Up - Up and Away	The 5th Dimension	#7
All I Need	The Temptations	#8
My Cup Runneth Over	Ed Ames	#8
Close Your Eyes	Peaches & Herb	#8
Sunday Will Never Be the Same	Spanky & Our Gang	#9
In and Out of Love	The Supremes	#9
C'mon Marianne	The Four Seasons	#9
The Tracks of My Tears	Johnny Rivers	#10
Tell It to the Rain	The Four Seasons	#10
Girl, You'll Be a Woman Soon	Neil Diamond	#10
Green, Green Grass of Home	Tom Jones	#11
(The Lights Went Out In) Massachusetts	The Bee Gees	#11
Coming Home Soldier	Bobby Vinton	#11
I'm Wondering	Stevie Wonder	#12
I Take It Back	Sandy Posey	#12
New York Mining Disaster 1941 Have You Seen My Wife, Mr. Jones	The Bee Gees	#14
With This Ring	The Platters	#14
Lazy Day	Spanky & Our Gang	#14
Society's Child (Baby I've Been Thinking)	Janis Ian	#14
(Loneliness Made Me Realize) It's You That I Need	The Temptations	#14
Pretty Ballerina	The Left Banke	#15

VIOLIN (cont'd)

Title	Artist	Page
Alfie	Dionne Warwick	#15
Beggin'	The Four Seasons	#16
Go Where You Wanna Go	The 5th Dimension	#16
Don't Go Out into the Rain (You're Going to Melt)	Herman's Hermits	#18
Epistle to Dippy	Donovan	#19
Ain't No Mountain High Enough	Marvin Gaye & Tammi Terrell	#19
The Love I Saw in You Was Just a Mirage	Smokey Robinson & The Miracles	#20
Twelve Thirty (Young Girls Are Coming to the Canyon)	Mamas & Papas	#20
Dry Your Eyes	Brenda & The Tabulations	#20
Where Will the Words Come From	Gary Lewis/Playboys	#21
The Look of Love	Dusty Springfield	#22
For Your Precious Love	Oscar Toney, Jr.	#23
When You're Young and in Love	The Marvelettes	#23
Lightning's Girl	Nancy Sinatra	#24
The Last Waltz	Engelbert Humperdinck	#25
By the Time I Get to Phoenix	Glen Campbell	#26
Detroit City	Tom Jones	#27
Mary in the Morning	Al Martino	#27
Ode to Billy Joe	The Kingpins	#28
Gonna Give Her All the Love I've Got	Jimmy Ruffin	#29
Watch the Flowers Grow	The Four Seasons	#30
Sunday for Tea	Peter & Gordon	#31
Making Every Minute Count	Spanky & Our Gang	#31
Your Unchanging Love	Marvin Gaye	#33
There's Got to Be a Word!	The Innocence	#34
Blue Autumn	Bobby Goldsboro	#35
No Milk Today	Herman's Hermits	#35
Back on the Street Again	The Sunshine Company	#36
Little Ole Wine Drinker, Me	Dean Martin	#38
Everybody Needs Love	Gladys Knight & The Pips	#39
I'll Take Care of Your Cares	Frankie Laine	#39
Why Do Fools Fall in Love	The Happenings	#41
It May Be Winter Outside (But in My Heart It's Spring)	Felice Taylor	#42
The Loser (With a Broken Heart)	Gary Lewis/Playboys	#43
You Only Live Twice	Nancy Sinatra	#44
One More Mountain to Climb	Ronnie Dove	#45
Buy for Me the Rain	Nitty Gritty Dirt Band	#45
I (Who Have Nothing)	Terry Knight	#46
Funny Familiar Forgotten Feelings	Tom Jones	#49
I'll Never Fall in Love Again	Tom Jones	#49
What's It Gonna Be	Dusty Springfield	#49
Summer Wine	Nancy Sinatra & Lee Hazlewood	#49
Happy	The Sunshine Company	#50

VIOLIN (cont'd)

Casanova (Your Playing Days are Over)	Ruby Andrews	#51
Jill	Gary Lewis/Playboys	#52
Cry Softly Lonely One	Roy Orbison	#52
Take a Look	Aretha Franklin	#56
There's Always Me	Elvis Presley	#56
Hung Up in Your Eyes	Brian Hyland	#58
When You're Gone	Brenda & The Tabulations	#58
Danny Boy	Ray Price	#60
If This Is Love (I'd Rather Be Lonely)	The Precisions	#60
Baby Please Come Back Home	J.J. Barnes	#61
The Lady Came from Baltimore	Bobby Darin	#62
Oooh, Baby Baby	The Five Stairsteps	#63
A Woman's Hands	Joe Tex	#63
Wish Me a Rainbow	The Gunter Kallmann Chorus	#63
Laura, What's He Got That I Ain't Got	Frankie Laine	#66
Who's Lovin' You	Brenda & The Tabulations	#66
For He's a Jolly Good Fellow	Bobby Vinton	#66
Stay Together Young Lovers	Brenda & The Tabulations	#66
Don't You Miss Me a Little Bit Baby	Jimmy Ruffin	#68
If You Go Away	Damita Jo	#68
Girl I Need You	The Artistics	#69
I Wish You Could Be Here	The Cyrkle	#70
My World Fell Down	Sagittarius	#70
Our Winter Love	The Lettermen	#72
Shame on Me	Chuck Jackson	#76
It's So Hard Being a Loser	The Contours	#79
Georgia Pines	The Candymen	#81
Walk with Faith in Your Heart	The Bachelors	#83
I'll Always Have Faith in You	Carla Thomas	#85
Ain't Gonna Rest (Till I Get You)	The Five Stairsteps	#87
Lonely Again	Eddy Arnold	#87
Happy	The Blades of Grass	#87
More and More	Andy Williams	#88
Take Me for a Little While	Patti LaBelle & The Bluebelles	#89
Red and Blue	Dave Clark Five	#89
Mr. Bus Driver	Bruce Channel	#90
Hello, Hello	Claudine Longet	#91
It's Been a Long Long Time	The Elgins	#92
Our Song	Jack Jones	#92
The Shadow of Your Smile	Boots Randolph	#93
Darling Be Home Soon	Bobby Darin	#93
I Can't Help It (If I'm Still in Love with You)	B.J. Thomas	#94
Time Alone Will Tell	Connie Francis	#94

VIOLIN (cont'd)

Let It Be Me	The Sweet Inspirations	#94
You're a Very Lovely Woman	The Merry-Go-Round	#94
Felicidad	Sally Field	#94
Hey Joe	Cher	#94
Red Roses for Mom	Bobby Vinton	#95
Shake Hands and Walk Away Cryin'	Lou Christie	#95
Everybody Loves a Winner	William Bell	#95
Only Love Can Break a Heart	Margaret Whiting	#96
I Believed It All	Pozo Seco Singers	#96
Little Old Wine Drinker Me	Robert Mitchum	#96
Just Once in a Lifetime	Brenda & The Tabulations	#97
I Want to Talk About You	Ray Charles	#98
Take Me in Your Arms and Love Me	Gladys Knight & The Pips	#98
Live for Life	Jack Jones	#99
Time Seller	Spencer Davis Group	#100
1968		
Green Tambourine	The Lemon Pipers	#1
Love Child	The Supremes	#1
Honey	Bobby Goldsboro	#1
For Once in My Life	Stevie Wonder	#2
La-La Means I Love You	The Delfonics	#4
I Wish It Would Rain	The Temptations	#4
Love Is All Around	The Troggs	#7
You're All I Need to get By	Marvin Gaye & Tammi Terrell	#7
Shoo-Be-Doo-Be-Doo-Da-Day	Stevie Wonder	#9
I Love How You Love Me	Bobby Vinton	#9
Different Drum	Stone Poneys feat. Linda Ronstadt	#13
I Could Never Love Another (After Loving You)	The Temptations	#13
Hey, Western Union Man	Jerry Butler	#16
Scarborough Fair	Sergio Mendes & Brasil '66	#16
Tip-Toe Thru' the Tulips with Me	Tiny Tim	#17
My Baby Must Be a Magician	The Marvelettes	#17
Am I That Easy to Forget	Engelbert Humperdinck	#18
Sealed with a Kiss	Gary Lewis/Playboys	#19
If I Were a Carpenter	Four Tops	#20
There Is	The Dells	#20
I Can Take or Leave Your Loving	Herman's Hermits	#22
Cycles	Frank Sinatra	#23
Tuesday Afternoon (Forever Afternoon)	The Moody Blues	#24
She's a Rainbow	The Rolling Stones	#25
(You Keep Me) Hangin' On	Joe Simon	#25
Please Return Your Love to Me	The Temptations	#26
Forever Came Today	The Supremes	#28

VIOLIN (cont'd)

Song	Artist	#
Break Your Promise	The Delfonics	#35
Eleanor Rigby	Ray Charles	#35
I Wanna Live	Glen Campbell	#36
Ame Caline (Soul Coaxing)	Raymond Lefevre	#37
Born Free	The Hesitations	#38
People	The Tymes	#39
Naturally Stoned	The Avant-Garde	#40
Back Up Train	Al Greene & The Soul Mate's *also listed as Soul Mates	#41
Everybody Knows	Dave Clark Five	#43
And Suddenly	The Cherry People	#45
Rice Is Nice	The Lemon Pipers	#46
Jealous Love	Wilson Pickett	#50
I'm in a Different World	Four Tops	#51
Sherry Don't Go	The Lettermen	#52
Zabadak	Dave Dee, Dozy, Beaky, Mick & Tich	#52
Safe in My Garden	Mamas & Papas	#53
Hey Little One	Glen Campbell	#54
Slow Drag	The Intruders	#54
Foggy Mountain Breakdown (Theme from Bonnie & Clyde)	Flatt & Scruggs	#55
From the Teacher to the Preacher	Gene Chandler & Barbara Acklin	#57
Oh, How It Hurts	Barbara Mason	#59
Baby You Come Rollin' Across My Mind	The Peppermint Trolley Company	#59
Love in Every Room	Paul Mauriat	#60
Red Red Wine	Neil Diamond	#62
Workin' on a Groovy Thing	Patti Drew	#62
Destination: Anywhere	The Marvelettes	#63
Anyone for Tennis	Cream	#64
Burning Spear	The Soulful Strings	#64
God Bless Our Love	The Ballads	#65
Gentle on My Mind	Patti Page	#66
Sunday Sun	Neil Diamond	#68
If This World Were Mine	Marvin Gaye & Tammi Terrell	#68
Impossible Mission (Mission Impossible)	Soul Survivors	#68
100 Years	Nancy Sinatra	#69
Unchained Melody	The Sweet Inspirations	#73
I Got a Sure Thing	Ollie & The Nightingales	#73
A Working Man's Prayer	Arthur Prysock	#74
Sweet Memories	Andy Williams	#75
Private Number	Judy Clay & William Bell	#75
Do You Wanna Dance	Mamas & Papas	#76
Here's to You	Hamilton Camp	#76
I'll Say Forever My Love	Jimmy Ruffin	#77

VIOLIN (cont'd)

Oh Lord, Why Lord	Los Pop Tops	#78
Mister Bo Jangles	Bobby Cole	#79
Goin' Away	The Fireballs	#79
A Voice in the Choir	Al Martino	#80
Anything	Eric Burdon/Animals	#80
Vance	Roger Miller	#80
To Each His Own	Frankie Laine	#82
Valley of the Dolls	King Curtis	#83
I Am Your Man	Bobby Taylor	#85
If Love Is in Your Heart	Friend & Lover	#86
Cross My Heart	Billy Stewart	#86
A Tribute to a King	William Bell	#86
Let the Heartaches Begin	Long John Baldry	#88
Georgia on My Mind	Wes Montgomery	#91
Without Love (There Is Nothing)	Oscar Toney, Jr.	#91
The Father of Girls	Perry Como	#92
Up to My Neck in High Muddy Water	Linda Ronstadt/Stone Poneys	#93
What's Made Milwaukee Famous (Has Made a Loser Out of Me)	Jerry Lee Lewis	#94
People World	Jim & Jean	#94
I Can't Make It Alone	Bill Medley	#95
Never Get Enough of Your Love	Oscar Toney, Jr.	#95
Little Green Apples	Patti Page	#96
Mister Nico	Four Jacks & A Jill	#96
Tomboy	Ronnie Dove	#96
I Call It Love	The Manhattans	#96
Baroque-A-Nova	Mason Williams	#96
(I Can Feel Your Love) Slipping Away	Barbara Mason	#97
Another Place Another Time	Jerry Lee Lewis	#97
In Some Time	Ronnie Dove	#98
Never My Love	The Sandpebbles	#98
Since You've Been Gone	Ramsey Lewis	#98
I'm into Lookin' for Someone to Love Me	Bobby Vee	#98
She'll Be There	Vikki Carr	#99
Congratulations	Cliff Richard	#99
1969		
Someday We'll Be Together	The Supremes	#1
Dizzy	Tommy Roe	#1
Come Together/Something	The Beatles	#1
Jean	Oliver	#2
Good Morning Starshine	Oliver	#3
Too Busy Thinking About My Baby	Marvin Gaye	#4
Only the Strong Survive	Jerry Butler	#4
Everybody's Talkin'	Nilsson	#6

VIOLIN (cont'd)

I Started a Joke	The Bee Gees	#6
You Showed Me	The Turtles	#6
Holly Holy	Neil Diamond	#6
That's the Way Love Is	Marvin Gaye	#7
The Boxer	Simon & Garfunkel	#7
Yester-Me, Yester-You, Yesterday	Stevie Wonder	#7
I'm Livin' in Shame	The Supremes	#10
Games People Play	Joe South	#12
Quentin's Theme	The Charles Randolph Grean Sounde	#13
These Eyes	Jr. Walker/The All Stars	#16
Things I'd Like to Say	New Colony Six	#16
Yesterday, When I Was Young	Roy Clark	#19
Jealous Kind of Fella	Garland Green	#20
The Letter	The Arbors	#20
Moody Woman	Jerry Butler	#24
California Soul	The 5th Dimension	#25
Mind, Body and Soul	The Flaming Ember	#26
The Composer	The Supremes	#27
Bella Linda	The Grassroots	#28
Make Believe	Wind (Tony Orlando)	#28
Heather Honey	Tommy Roe	#29
Good Lovin' Ain't Easy to Come By	Marvin Gaye & Tammi Terrell	#30
No Matter What Sign You Are	The Supremes	#31
The Windmills of Your Mind	Dusty Springfield	#31
Doggone Right	Smokey Robinson & The Miracles	#32
I Guess the Lord Must Be in New York City	Nilsson	#34
To Know You Is to Love You	Bobby Vinton	#34
The Days of Sand and Shovels	Bobby Vinton	#34
With Pen in Hand	Vikki Carr	#35
Here I Go Again	Smokey Robinson & The Miracles	#37
First of May	The Bee Gees	#37
Are You Happy	Jerry Butler	#39
Echo Park	Keith Barbour	#40
Johnny One Time	Brenda Lee	#41
We Love You, Call Collect	Art Linkletter	#42
On the Dock of the Bay	The Dells	#42
And That Reminds Me (My Heart Reminds Me)	The Four Seasons	#45
It's Only Love	B.J. Thomas	#45
I Forgot to Be Your Lover	William Bell	#45
I'm a Drifter	Bobby Goldsboro	#46
Condition Red	The Goodees	#46
Malinda	Bobby Taylor	#48
A Minute of Your Time	Tom Jones	#48

VIOLIN (cont'd)

Everybody Knows Matilda	Duke Baxter	#52
The Girl I'll Never Know (Before You Loved Me)	Frankie Valli	#52
Not on the Outside	The Moments	#57
You Got Soul	Johnny Nash	#58
Midnight	Dennis Yost/Classics IV	#58
Say You Love Me	The Impressions	#58
Girl You're Too Young	Archie Bell & The Drells	#59
Hushabye	Jay & The Americans	#62
Rhythm of the Rain	Gary Lewis/Playboys	#63
Ballad of Easy Rider	The Byrds	#65
Love Is All I Have to Give	The Checkmates, Ltd.	#65
I Can't Quit Her	The Arbors	#67
Maybe Tomorrow	The Iveys (Badfinger)	#67
This Old Heart of Mine (Is Weak for You)	Tammi Terrell	#67
Where Do You Go To (My Lovely)	Peter Sarstedt	#70
Don't Tell Your Mama (Where You've Been)	Eddie Floyd	#73
We'll Cry Together	Maxine Brown	#73
Don't Forget to Remember	Bee Gees	#73
Armstrong	John Stewart	#74
Let Me Be the One	Peaches & Herb	#74
(I'm So) Afraid of Losing You Again	Charley Pride	#74
Nothing Can Take the Place of You	Brook Benton	#74
Julia	Ramsey Lewis	#76
Rain	Jose Feliciano	#76
Chelsea Morning	Judy Collins	#78
Lady-O	The Turtles	#78
Sunday Mornin' Comin' Down	Ray Stevens	#81
The Ten Commandments of Love	Little Anthony/Imperials	#82
Good Clean Fun	The Monkees	#82
Stay and Love Me All Summer	Brian Hyland	#82
Dynamite Woman	Sir Douglas Quintet	#83
Kay	John Wesley Ryles I	#83
Farewell Love Scene	Romeo & Juliet Soundtrack	#86
A Million to One	Brian Hyland	#90
Never Comes the Day	The Moody Blues	#91
Oh How Happy	Blinky & Edwin Starr	#92
If I Only Had Time	Nick DeCaro	#95
Wichita Lineman	Sergio Mendes & Brasil '66	#95
That's How Heartaches Are Made	The Marvelettes	#97
I Can't Help It (If I'm Still in Love with You)	Al Martino	#97
Pass the Apple Eve	B.J. Thomas	#97
Curly	Jimmy Clanton	#97
I'm Gonna Do All I Can (To Do Right By My Man)	Ike & Tina Turner	#98

VIOLIN (cont'd)

I Can't Do Enough	The Dells	#98
Here We Go Again	Nancy Sinatra	#98

MISCELLANEOUS INSTRUMENTS

If a notable instrument was featured on three or fewer songs, it will be listed here. Note the many Indian instruments used by the Beatles towards the end of the decade.

YEAR	SONGS	ARTIST	HOT 100	INSTRUMENT
1966	Barbara Ann	The Beach Boys	#2	Ash Tray
1961	Theme from "Tunes of Glory"	The Cambridge Strings	#60	Bagpipes
1961	Tunes of Glory	Mitch Miller	#88	Bagpipes
1968	Those Were the Days	Mary Hopkins	#2	Balalaika
1967	The 59th Street Bridge Song (Feelin' Groovy)	Harpers Bizarre	#13	Bassoon
1968	Jennifer Juniper	Donovan	#26	Bassoon
1968	Dancing Bear	Mamas & Papas	#51	Bassoon
1960	Banjo Boy	Art Mooney	#100	Bells
1961	Baby's First Christmas	Connie Francis	#26	Bells
1961	The Bells are Ringing	The Van Dykes	#99	Bells
1961	Merry-Go-Round	Marv Johnson	#61	Calliope
1963	Be My Baby	The Ronettes	#2	Castinets
1966	Good Vibrations	The Beach Boys	#1	Cello
1969	Camel Back	A.B. Skhy	#100	Clavinet
1967	Sit Down, I Think I Love You	The Mojo Men	#36	Dobro
1966	Little Man	Sonny & Cher	#21	Dulcimer
1966	Lady Jane	The Rolling Stones	#24	Dulcimer
1968	Those Were the Days	Mary Hopkins	#2	Dulcimer
1964	Big Man in Town	The Four Seasons	#20	English Horn
1968	The Inner Light	The Beatles	#96	Harmonium
1967	Strawberry Fields Forever	The Beatles	#8	Mellotron
1967	I Am the Walrus	The Beatles	#56	Mellotron
1969	To Susan on the West Coast Waiting	Donovan	#35	Melodica
1961	Sleepy-Eyed John	Johnny Horton	#54	Mouth Harp
1966	Good Vibrations	The Beach Boys	#1	Mouth Harp
1963	Shake Me I Rattle (Squeeze Me I Cry)	Marion Worth	#42	Music Box
1966	Wild Thing	The Troggs	#1	Ocarina
1967	Wild Thing	Senator Bobby	#20	Ocarina
1968	The Good, the Bad and the Ugly	Hugo Montenegro	#2	Ocarina
1967	Penny Lane	The Beatles	#1	Piccolo Trumpet
1967	Ruby Tuesday	The Rolling Stones	#1	Recorder
1967	Windy	The Association	#1	Recorder
1968	Anyone for Tennis	Cream	#64	Recorder

MISCELLANEOUS INSTRUMENTS (cont'd)

1967	Carrie-Anne	The Hollies	#9	Steel Drums
1969	Day After Day (It's Slippin' Away)	Shango	#57	Steel Drums
1968	The Inner Light	The Beatles	#96	Santoor
1968	The Inner Light	The Beatles	#96	Sarod
1968	The Inner Light	The Beatles	#96	Shanhais
1964	Forever	Pete Drake	#25	Steel Guitar (Talking)
1968	The Inner Light	The Beatles	#96	Sur-Bahar
1967	Strawberry Fields Forever	The Beatles	#8	Swarmandal
1968	The Inner Light	The Beatles	#96	Thar-Shanhai
1966	Good Vibrations	The Beach Boys	#1	Theremin

TOP ARTISTS OF THE 1960s

To make it onto the "Top Groups" chart, a group had to have at least 18 Hot 100 hits. Any 60s music fan will know which group had the most hits of the sixties, but I bet the group in second place will surprise people.

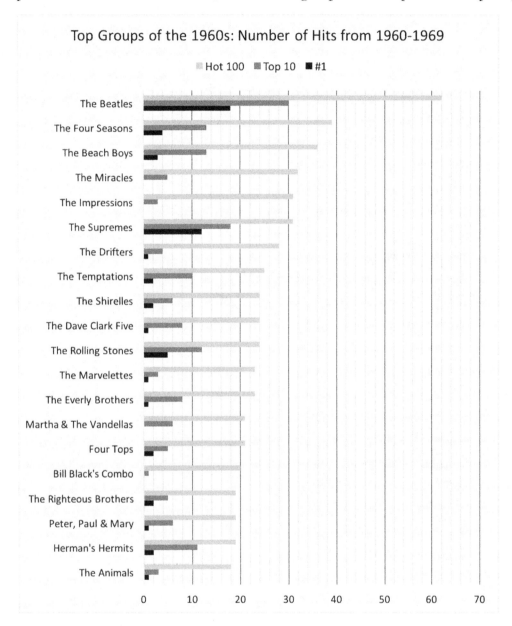

To appear on the "Solo Artists" chart, an artist had to have at least 22 Hot 100 hits, with a few exceptions. I included Chuck Berry, Bob Dylan, and Jimi Hendrix, even though they didn't come close to having 22 Hot 100 hits in the 60s. While no one would question their impact and influence on popular music, it's interesting to note that they had very few songs on the charts in the 60s.

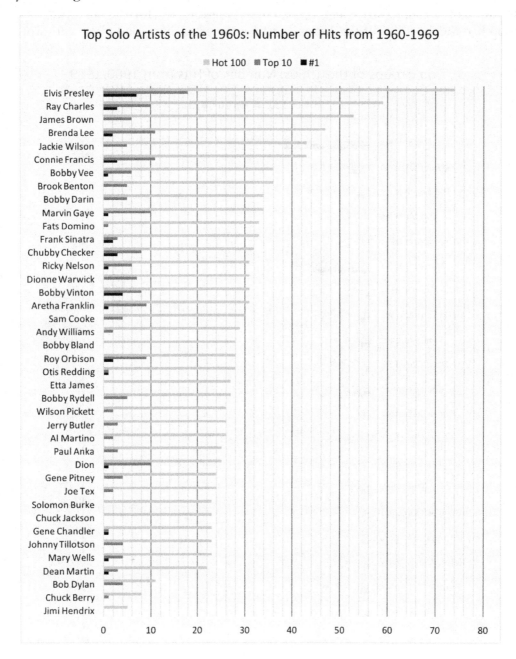

The Beach Boys

Illustration by Kelsey Graham

"Brian Wilson is, without a doubt, a pop genius."[1] -Eric Clapton

"Without 'Pet Sounds', 'Sgt. Pepper' never would have happened. 'Pepper' was an attempt to equal 'Pet Sounds'."[2] -Beatles' producer George Martin

"Brian showed us all the endless possibilities in what's been recorded and how it can be layered and combined or subtracted to create something that certainly came from his California roots, which to me, has always represented the promise and sweetness in America. With that joyousness, he became our Mozart of Rock 'N Roll."[3] -Art Garfunkel

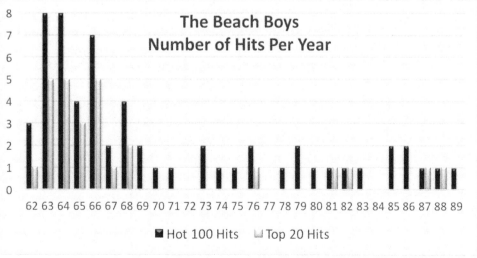

The Beatles

Illustration by Matt Cleveland

"They were a great influence to us because they were songwriters, they broke a lot of rules and they created an artistic credibility in the pop music business, which was never there before."[4] -Robin Gibb of the Bee Gees

"They were doing things nobody was doing. Their chords were outrageous, just outrageous, and their harmonies made it all valid... I knew they were pointing the direction of where music had to go."[5] -Bob Dylan

"We reckoned we could make it because there were four of us. None of us would've made it alone, because Paul wasn't quite strong enough, I didn't have enough girl-appeal, George was too quiet, and Ringo was the drummer. But we thought that everyone would be able to dig at least one of us, and that's how it turned out."[6] -John Lennon

"There's no outdoing the Beatles".[7] -Brian Wilson of the Beach Boys

It would be hard to overstate the Beatles' impact on America when they arrived in 1964. It wouldn't be out of line to say that they influenced nearly every part of American culture. The following charts illustrate the popularity their music attained in America.

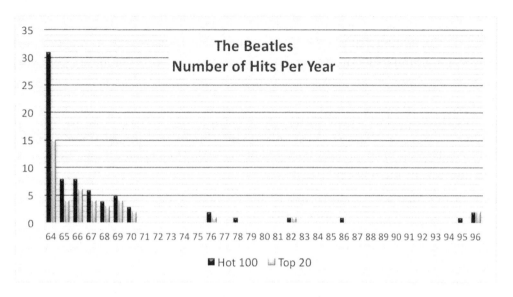

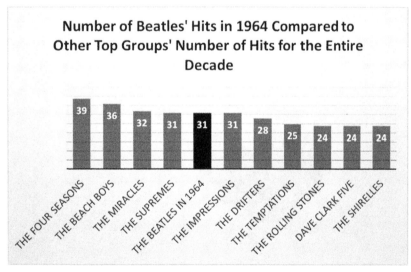

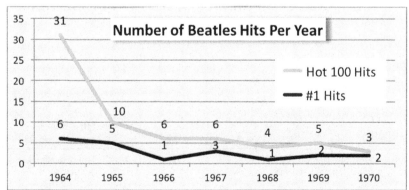

I wanted to see if there was a way to objectively measure the Beatles' influence and impact on popular American music, using data gathered from the Hot 100 chart. Specifically, I wondered if the Beatles had a negative impact on certain artists' careers. Did some artists' career come to a premature end because they weren't cool enough, or "hip" enough to compete with the Beatles? I was thinking especially of artists like Frank Sinatra and Perry Como- older singers whose appeal was quickly vanishing in the face of the Beatles and the British Invasion. I also thought of artists like Connie Francis, Bobby Rydell, and Bobby Darin. These artists weren't old by any means in 1964: Darin was 28, Francis was 26, and Rydell was 22. Though they were considerably younger than artists like Sinatra and Como, their music was nothing like the Beatles' style of rock 'n roll. It just couldn't compare. Could it compete?

To determine if the Beatles' success had a negative effect on other artists' careers, I compared the number of hits artists had pre and post-Beatles-debut, as well as the average chart position of each of their hits pre and post-Beatles-debut. To filter out any small sample sizes, only artists who had accumulated ten or more Hot 100 hits before 1964, and were still active in 1963, were included in the data. If an artist's appearances on the Hot 100 ended in 1962, I did not include them in the data.

Dinah Washington is not included. Though she had 21 hits through 1963, she died in December of that year. I think her death had more to do with her disappearance on the charts than the Beatles' debut. I did include Sam Cooke, however. Although he died in December of 1964, he had enough songs in the vault that he had seven more hits after he died. His last hit charted in 1966.

The data is rather startling, overall. Out of 59 artists who had at least ten hits prior to the Beatles' debut and were still active in 1963, only 11 had at least as many hits after the Beatles' debut. To be sure, the Beatles were not to blame for the decline of every artist's career, but way too many artists performed worse on the Hot 100 after their debut for it to be a coincidence in each and every instance.

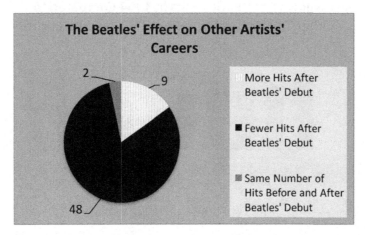

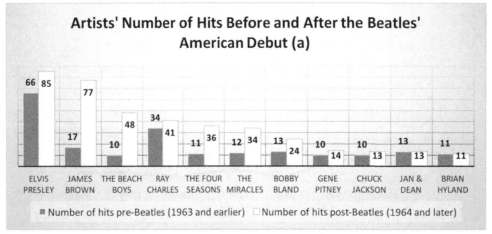

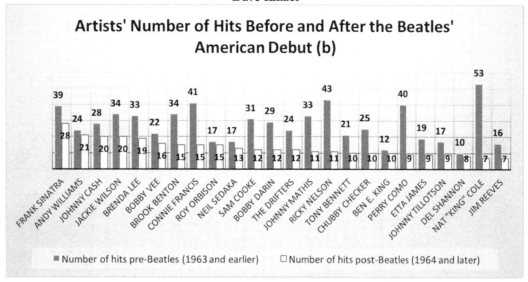

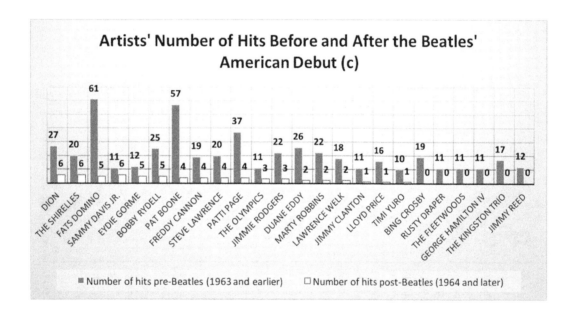

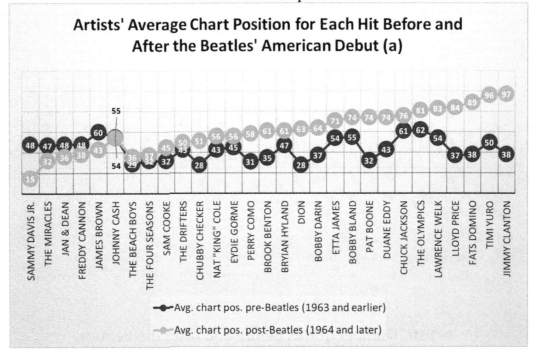

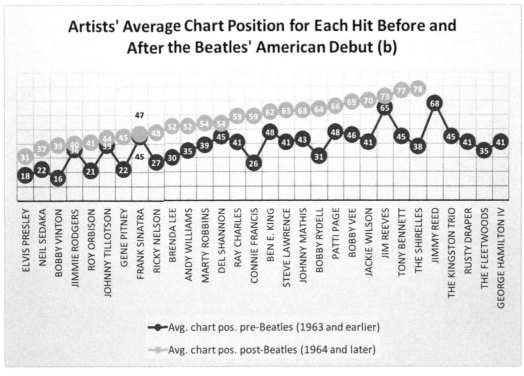

This next chart helps illustrates why the Beatles were so popular- they were all terrific individual musicians. Not only did they all have at least five solo top ten hits, each of them also had at least two #1 hits. Of course, if John Lennon hadn't taken a break in the last half of the 1970s, he would've had even more hits. For each of them to have a tremendously successful solo career *and* be a member of the most popular group of all-time? That's impressive.

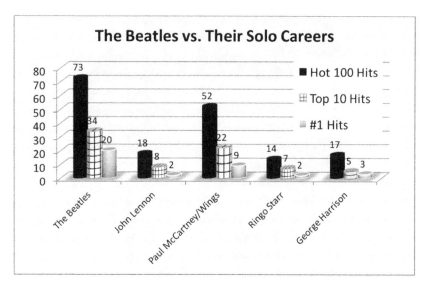

The 60s Music Compendium
Chuck Berry

Illustration by David Perez

"I grew up thinking art was pictures until I got into music and found I was an artist and didn't paint."[8] -Chuck Berry

"If you tried to give rock and roll another name, you might call it 'Chuck Berry.'"[9] -John Lennon

"Now you and Elvis are pretty good, but you ain't Chuck Berry."[10] -Mamie Lewis to her son, Jerry Lee Lewis

"The idea of intelligent rock 'n' roll probably starts with Chuck Berry."[11] -Donald Fagen of Steely Dan

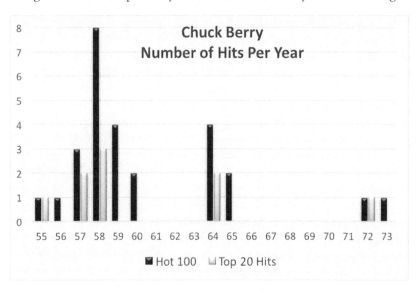

James Brown

Illustration by Daniel Rude

"When I'm on stage, I'm trying to do one thing: bring people joy."[12] -James Brown

"Of course. I copied all his moves."[13] -Mick Jagger, of the Rolling Stones, on whether or not Brown's stage moves influenced him

"James Brown, Ray Charles, Jackie Wilson, Chuck Berry and Little Richard - I think they had strong influences on a lot of people, because there were the guys who really got rock and roll going. I like to start with the origin of things, because once it gets along it changes. It's so interesting to see how it really was in the beginning."[14] -Michael Jackson

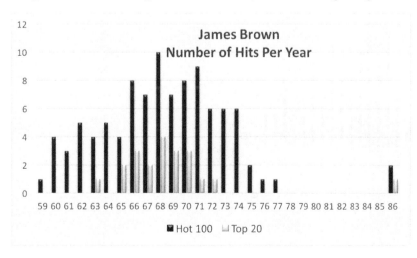

Ray Charles

Illustration by Eric Eckert

"There's a reason they called Ray Charles 'The Genius.' Think of how he reinvented country music in a way that worked for him. He showed there are no limitations, not for someone as good as he is. Whatever Ray Charles did, whatever he touched, he made it his own. He's his own genre. It's all Ray Charles music now."[15] -Van Morrison

"This may sound like sacrilege but I think Ray Charles was more important than Elvis Presley."[16] -Billy Joel

"Before I started being myself, I tried 1,000 percent to sound like Nat "King" Cole. I could get hired, but nobody knew what my name was. So one day I decided to be myself."[17] -Ray Charles

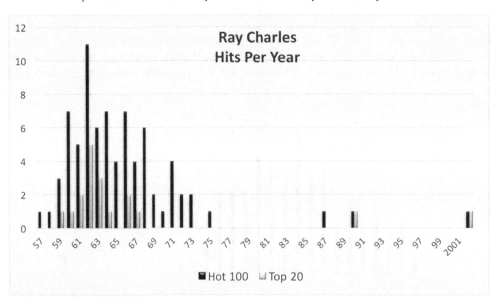

Sam Cooke

Illustration by Charlotte Sze Nok Ng

"I think the secret is observation. If you observe what's going on and try to figure out how people are thinking and determine the times of your day, I think you can always write something that people will understand."[18] -Sam Cooke, to Dick Clark, on the secret to writing hit songs

"Sam opened the door for more singers than you'd ever dream of, because it was an approach to music that we didn't ever think the public would accept from blacks anyhow. He influenced most of us."[19] -Ben E. King

"Sam was a prince of a man… Sam had the looks, he had the voice, he had the manner, he had the charm and he had the savoir faire."[20] -Aretha Franklin

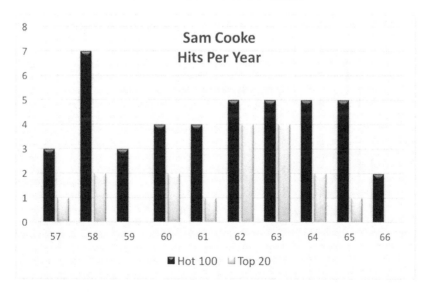

The Four Seasons

Illustration by Julia O'Malley

"I didn't go to any professional school to learn how to sing. I bought people's records, listened to them, tried to do what the singer did by imitating them, as close as I could possibly get."[21] -Frankie Valli

"Frankie Valli has become one of the hallmark voices of our generation. He created a style that we all still strive to emulate."[22] -Barry Gibb of the Bee Gees

"Frankie Valli is not only one of the more influential and recognizable voices of the 60's, but also of the Vietnam era and beyond. His shows were always a joy for me to play. It was a thrill to see the smiles on the faces of the audience night after night as they recognized yet another song from their lives."[23] -Lynn Hammann, drummer for the Four Seasons

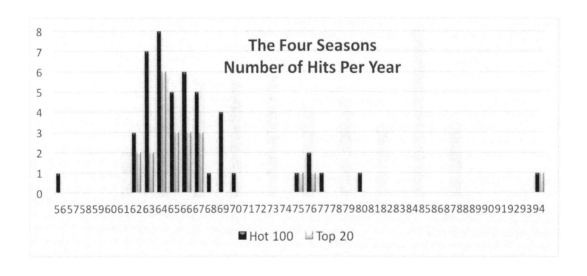

Connie Francis

Illustration by Melissa N. Van

"I was very in awe of her."[24] -Neil Sedaka, on meeting Francis for the first time

"She could get more out of a song with her interpretation, her warmth, her belief, than almost anybody. I've always felt that Connie had the best pipes in the business."[25] -Don Kirshner, music publisher, producer, songwriter, and manager

"She could play a night club engagement and appeal to people who were old enough to smoke and drink and go out at night, and at the same time appear at a sock hop and turn little girls and boys upside down in their admiration for her. It's a very unique talent."[26] -Dick Clark

"The best female vocalist ever to come out of America."[27] -Chris Isaak

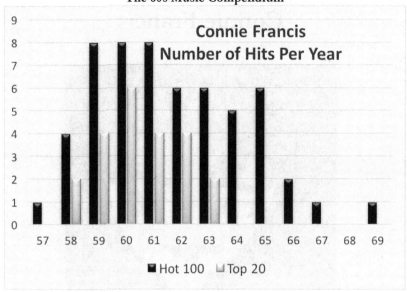

Aretha Franklin

Illustration by Matt Cleveland

"Aretha Franklin, Billie Holiday....They are so subtle, they can milk you with two notes. They can go no farther than from A to B, and they can make you feel like they told you the whole universe."[28] -Janis Joplin

"We all felt we were onto something new, from the perspective that she was bridging a gap in a way that hadn't been done before, bringing rhythm and blues into pop and into the mainstream."[29] -Keyboardist Spooner Oldham, played organ on "Respect"

"Her voice is one of the great natural instruments that I've ever heard, and the way she uses it is just so instinctive, she knows exactly what she wants."[30] -Keith Richards of the Rolling Stones

"When Aretha came on the scene, as far as how I would rank her- I would certainly have to put her among the creators. You know, people who genuinly create the sound that other people wish they could do."[31] -Ray Charles

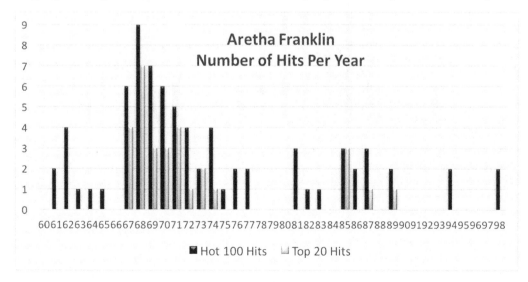

Brenda Lee

Illustration by Margee Bright-Ragland

"If anybody influenced me in my style of singing, he probably did more than anybody…"[32] -Brenda Lee on Frank Sinatra

"She has the greatest rock and roll voice of them all."[33] -John Lennon

"There are artists who sing songs, and artists who own the songs they sing. Brenda owns her songs. She pours real life experience into every note, every phrase, every lyric. She brings passion and soul into everything she does."[34] -Jewel

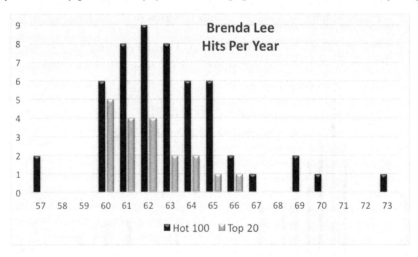

Elvis Presley

Illustration by Matt Cleveland

"Elvis didn't know how great he was. He never came off like, 'I'm the king of rock 'n' roll.' As a matter of fact, there were many times on stage when people yelled out, 'Elvis, you're the king!' And Elvis would say, 'No, I'm not the king. God's the king.'"[35] James Burton, guitar player for Presley

"There are several unbelievable things about Elvis, but the most incredible is his staying power in a world where meteoric careers fade like shooting stars."[36] -"Newsweek," August 11, 1969

"You have no idea how great he is, really you don't. You have no comprehension - it's absolutely impossible. I can't tell you why he's so great, but he is. He's sensational."[37] -Phil Spector, producer and songwriter

"This boy had everything. He had the looks, the moves, the manager, and the talent. And he didn't look like Mr. Ed like a lot of the rest of us did. In the way he looked, way he talked, way he acted - he really was different."[38] -Carl Perkins

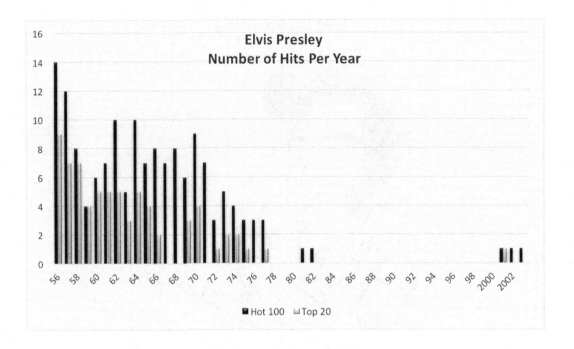

The Rolling Stones

Illustration by Lindell Connor

"The only things Mick and I disagree about is the band, the music, and what we do."[39] -Keith Richards

"I'd rather be dead than singing 'Satisfaction' when I'm forty-five."[40] -Mick Jagger (b. 1943)

"By actually starting to peak after the (British) Invasion, they transcended it. The Beatles didn't live past the end of the sixties. The Rolling Stones were actually just getting going."[41] -Lenny Kaye of the Patti Smith Group

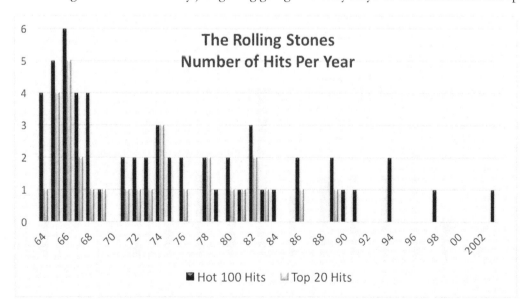

The Supremes

Illustration by Kelsey Cleary

"I'm not really a songwriter- I'm an interpreter. So in a sense I am an actress first and foremost. I act out the songs, and I lead with my heart."[42] -Diana Ross

"The main reason is that we truly loved each other, and when we came together it was a perfect union of people, because we were so compatible."[43] -Mary Wilson, on why the Supremes had such a successful career

"I'm very grateful for groups like the Supremes that have gone on ahead of us because they've helped pave the road and make it easier for female artists today."[44] -Cindy Herron of En Vogue

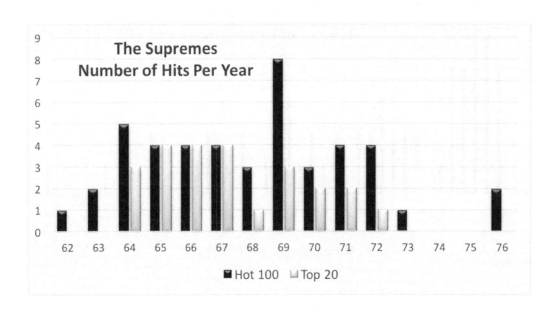

Diana Ross left the Supremes in late 1969. While she went on to have an extremely successful solo career, as the next chart shows, the Supremes struggled to continue their run of success without Ross.

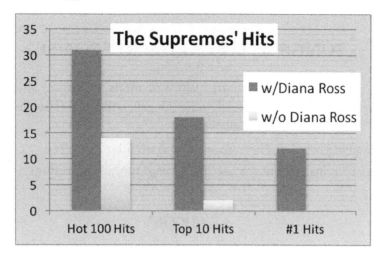

MUSIC THEORY

SONGS WITH CALL & RESPONSE

Call and response is when a vocalist sings a phrase (the call), and another singer or choir answers with a phrase (response). It is usually associated with a solo singer issuing the call, and a choir singing a response, but either part (or both parts) may be voiced with an instrument instead.

Call and response is often used in gospel or blues music, and is used far less often in pop music.

The notes column indicates which instrument (or voice) is doing the call and response for selected songs.

SONG	ARTIST	NOTES	HOT 100
1960			
Walking to New Orleans	Fats Domino	Voice and strings	#6
New Orleans	U.S. Bonds		#6
Theme for Young Lovers	Percy Faith	Strings and piano	#35
Rocking Goose	Johnny & The Hurricanes	Guitar and sax	#60
Easy Lovin'	Wade Flemons	Vocals and instruments	#70
Let the Good Times Roll	Ray Charles	Lead vocal and instruments	#78
Have You Ever Been Lonely (Have You Ever Been Blue)	Teresa Brewer	Vocals and instruments	#84
The Yen Yet Song	Gary Cane		#99
1961			
School is Out	Gary (U.S.) Bonds	Voices in chorus	#5
I Wanna Thank You	Bobby Rydell	Voices in chorus	#21
California Sun	Joe Jones	Voice and horns	#89
A Cross Stands Alone	Jimmy Witter	Voice and organ	#89
Here's My Confession	Wyatt (Earp) McPherson	Voice and instruments	#97
1962			
I Can't Stop Loving You	Ray Charles		#1
Johnny Will	Pat Boone	Voice and harmonica	#35
I'm Going Back to School	Dee Clark	Voices on verses	#52
Just Tell Her Jim Said Hello	Elvis Presley		#55
Yield Not to Temptation	Bobby Bland	Voices	#56
Boom Boom	John Lee Hooker	Voice and instruments	#60
Meet Me at the Twistin' Place	Johnnie Morisette	Voices	#63
Yes Indeed	Pete Fountain	Clarinet and voices	#69
Next Door to the Blues	Etta James	Voices	#71
Gonna Raise a Rukus Tonight	Jimmy Dean		#73
1963			
My Boyfriend's Back	The Angels	Lead and backup singers	#1
He's So Fine	The Chiffons	Lead and backup singers	#1
Sally, Go 'Round the Roses	The Jaynetts	Lead and backup singers	#2
Blame It on the Bossa Nova	Eydie Gorme	Lead and backup singers	#7

SONGS WITH CALL & RESPONSE (cont'd)

Mickey's Monkey	The Miracles	Lead and backup singers	#8
The Monkey Time	Major Lance	Lead and backup singers	#8
Not Me	The Orlons	Lead and backup singers	#12
Send Me Some Lovin'	Sam Cooke	Lead and backup singers	#13
On Top of Spaghetti	Tom Glazer	Lead and children's chorus	#14
Mr. Bass Man	Johnny Cymbal	Lead and backup singers	#16
Don't Set Me Free	Ray Charles	Lead and backup singers	#20
Twist It Up	Chubby Checker	Lead and backup singers	#25
Hitch Hike	Marvin Gaye	Lead and backup singers	#30
A Love She Can Count On	The Miracles	Lead and backup singers	#31
Java	Floyd Cramer	Piano and horns	#49
I'm a Woman	Peggy Lee	Voice and instruments	#54
Groovy Baby	Billy Abbott	Lead and backup singers	#55
You Know It Ain't Right	Joe Hinton	Voice and sax	#88
Crossfire Time	Dee Clark	Voices	#92
Spring	Birdlegs & Pauline	Voice and sax	#94

1964

Do Wah Diddy Diddy	Manfred Mann	Lead and backup singers	#1
Twist and Shout	The Beatles	Lead and backup singers	#2
Bits and Pieces	Dave Clark Five	Lead and backup singers	#4
California Sun	The Rivieras		#5
No Particular Place to Go	Chuck Berry	Lead singer and instruments	#10
Do You Love Me	Dave Clark Five	Lead and backup singers	#11
Farmer John	The Premiers	Lead and backup singers	#19
What'd I Say	Elvis Presley	Lead and backup singers	#21
Oh Baby Don't You Weep (Part 1)	James Brown	Lead and backup singers	#23
Out of Sight	James Brown	Lead and instruments	#24
Forever	Pete Drake	Lead and backup singers	#25
Hey Harmonica Man	Stevie Wonder	Lead and backup singers	#29
That's What Love is Made Of	The Miracles	Lead and backup singers	#35
Tra La La La Suzy	Dean & Jean	Lead and backup singers	#35
You're My Remedy	The Marvelettes	Lead and backup singers	#48
Jump Back	Rufus Thomas		#49
Smack Dab in the Middle	Ray Charles	Lead and backup singers	#52
Sole Sole Sole	Siw Malmkvist-Umberto Marcato		#58
Pearly Shells (Popo O Ewa)	Burl Ives		#60
Kick That Little Foot Sally Ann	Round Robin	Lead and backup singers	#61
Leaving Here	Eddie Holland		#76
Saginaw, Michigan	Lefty Frizzell	Lead and backup singers	#85
Up Above My Head (I Hear Music in the Air)	Al Hirt	Lead and backup singers	#85
Night Time is the Right Time	Rufus & Carla	Voices	#94
Sally Was a Good Old Girl	Fats Domino	Lead and backup singers	#99

SONGS WITH CALL & RESPONSE (cont'd)

Just a Moment Ago	Soul Sisters	Voices and instruments	#100
1965			
Yes, I'm Ready	Barbara Mason	Lead and backup singers	#5
I Like It Like That	Dave Clark Five		#7
Since I Lost My Baby	The Temptations	Lead and backup singers	#17
Iko Iko	The Dixie Cups	Lead and backup singers	#20
Round Every Corner	Petula Clark	Lead and backup singers	#21
Do the Clam	Elvis Presley	Sax and guitar	#21
Too Many Fish in the Sea	The Marvelettes	Lead and backup singers	#25
Apple of My Eye	Roy Head & The Traits	Lead and backup singers	#32
Boom Boom	The Animals	Lead singer and instruments	#43
New Orleans	Eddie Hodges	Lead and backup singers	#44
Annie Fanny	The Kingsmen		#47
Come On Do the Jerk	The Miracles	Lead singer and backup singers	#50
The Climb	The Kingsmen	Lead singer and backup singers	#65
Land of a Thousand Dances (Part 1)	Thee Midniters	Lead singer and horns	#67
Lip Sync (To the Tongue Twisters)	Len Barry		#84
He Ain't No Angel	The Ad Libs	Lead and backup singers	#100
1966			
Good Lovin'	The Young Rascals	Lead and backup singers	#1
I'm Your Puppet	James & Bobby Purify	Lead singers and instruments	#6
Mother's Little Helper	The Rolling Stones	Lead singer and instruments	#8
Gloria	Shadows of Knight	Lead and backup singers	#10
Going to a Go-Go	The Miracles	Lead and backup singers	#11
Respectable	The Outsiders	Lead and backup singers	#15
Lady Jane	The Rolling Stones	Lead singer and dulcimer	#24
Fa-Fa-Fa-Fa-Fa (Sad Song)	Otis Redding	Lead singer and horns	#29
The Rains Came	Sir Douglas Quintet	Lead and backup singers	#31
I Want to Be with You	Dee Dee Warwick	Lead and backup singers	#41
I Can't Let Go	The Hollies	Lead and backup singers	#42
We Got a Thing That's in the Groove	The Capitols	Lead and backup singers	#65
My Generation	The Who	Lead and backup singers	#74
Every Day and Every Night	The Trolls	Lead and backup singers	#96
1967			
You Got to Me	Neil Diamond	Lead and backup singers	#18
Somebody Help Me	Spencer Davis Group	Lead and backup singers	#47
Oh That's Good, No That's Bad	Sam The Sham & The Pharaohs	Lead and backup singers	#54
Lonely Drifter	Pieces of Eight	Lead and backup singers	#59
It's Got to Be Mellow	Leon Haywood	Lead and backup singers	#63
Deadend Street	The Kinks	Lead and backup singers	#73
Raise Your Hand	Eddie Floyd	Lead and backup singers	#79
I Want You to Be My Baby	Ellie Greenwich	Lead and backup singers	#83
Tip Toe	Robert Parker		#83

SONGS WITH CALL & RESPONSE (cont'd)

Omaha	Moby Grape	Lead and backup singers	#88
Heart Be Still	Lorraine Ellison	Lead and backup singers	#89
1968			
Born to Be Wild	Steppenwolf	Lead singer and guitar	#2
Mony Mony	Tommy James & The Shondells	Lead and backup singers	#3
Simon Says	1910 Fruitgum Co.	Lead and backup singers	#4
Say It Loud - I'm Black and I'm Proud (Part 1)	James Brown	Lead and backup singers	#10
Time Has Come Today	The Chambers Brothers	Lead and backup singers	#11
Bang-Shang-A-Lang	The Archies	Lead and backup singers	#22
Magic Bus	The Who	Lead and backup singers	#25
New Orleans	Neil Diamond	Lead and backup singers	#52
The Ten Commandments of Love	Peaches & Herb		#55
That's a Lie	Ray Charles	Lead and backup singers	#64
Cinderella Rockefella	Esther & Abi Ofarim	Lead singers	#68
Ain't Nothin' but a House Party	The Show Stoppers		#87
1969			
Time of the Season	The Zombies	Lead and backup singers	#3
Color Him Father	The Winstons	Lead and backup singers	#7
Birthday	Underground Sunshine		#26
Love Is All I Have to Give	The Checkmates, Ltd.	Lead and backup singers	#65
Just a Little Love	B.B. King	Lead singer and audience	#76
Shout! - Part 1	Chambers Brothers	Lead and backup singers	#83
Good Morning Starshine	Strawberry Alarm Clark	Lead and backup singers	#87
That's Your Baby	Joe Tex	Lead and backup singers	#88

SONGS THAT MODULATE

Modulation is when a song modulates, or changes keys. Usually, this will happen towards the end of a song when the artist wants the song's intensity or level of excitement to increase. Almost all songs that modulate do it only once, but a few songs will modulate two or more times.

The ten highest charting songs from each year that used modulation are listed below.

SONG	ARTIST	HOT 100
1960		
Itsy Bitsy Teenie Weenie Yellow Polka Dot Bikini	Brian Hyland	#1
Everybody's Somebody's Fool	Connie Francis	#1
Beyond the Sea	Bobby Darin	#6
Forever	The Little Dippers	#9
Sleep	Little Willie John	#13
Sway	Bobby Rydell	#14
Perfidia	The Ventures	#15
Teddy	Connie Francis	#17

SONGS WITH MODULATION (cont'd)

| First Name Initial | Annette | #20 |
| Clementine | Bobby Darin | #21 |

1961

The Mountain's High	Dick & DeeDee	#2
Little Devil	Neil Sedaka	#11
Please Love Me Forever	Cathy Jean/Roommates	#12
Tonight I Fell in Love	The Tokens	#15
Just for Old Time's Sake	The McGuire Sisters	#20
Frankie and Johnny	Brook Benton	#20
Just Out of Reach (Of My Two Open Arms)	Solomon Burke	#24
Baby's First Christmas	Connie Francis	#26
Ram-Bunk-Shush	The Ventures	#29
(Ghost) Riders in the Sky	Ramrods	#30

1962

Lovers Who Wander	Dion	#3
Sealed with a Kiss	Brian Hyland	#3
Happy Birthday, Sweet Sixteen	Neil Sedaka	#5
Old Rivers	Walter Brennan	#5
Wolverton Mountain	Claude King	#6
P.T. 109	Jimmy Dean	#8
Cindy's Birthday	Johnny Crawford	#8
Come Back Silly Girl	The Lettermen	#17
I've Got Bonnie	Bobby Rydell	#18
Cajun Queen	Jimmy Dean	#22

1963

Washington Square	The Village Stompers	#2
She's a Fool	Lesley Gore	#5
Still	Bill Anderson	#8
Denise	Randy & The Rainbows	#10
Martian Hop	The Ran-Dells	#16
Alice in Wonderland	Neil Sedaka	#17
You Can Never Stop Me Loving You	Johnny Tillotson	#18
I Adore Him	The Angels	#25
Walking Proud	Steve Lawrence	#26
Don't Be Afraid, Little Darlin'	Steve Lawrence	#26

1964

Ringo	Lorne Greene	#1
G.T.O.	Ronny & The Daytonas	#4
Hey Little Cobra	The Rip Chords	#4
Don't Let the Rain Come Down (Crooked Little Man)	The Serendipity Singers	#6
Dance, Dance, Dance	The Beach Boys	#8
Chug-A-Lug	Roger Miller	#9
When I Grow Up (To Be a Man)	The Beach Boys	#9

SONGS WITH MODULATION (cont'd)

Drag City	Jan & Dean	#10
Al-Di-La	Ray Charles Singers	#29
Beans in My Ears	The Serendipity Singers	#30
1965		
I'm Telling You Now	Freddie & The Dreamers	#1
I Hear a Symphony	The Supremes	#1
Downtown	Petula Clark	#1
A Lover's Concerto	The Toys	#2
I Know a Place	Petula Clark	#3
Everybody Loves a Clown	Gary Lewis/Playboys	#4
Silhouettes	Herman's Hermits	#5
Amen	The Impressions	#7
Down in the Boondocks	Billy Joe Royal	#9
Sunshine, Lollipops and Rainbows	Lesley Gore	#13
1966		
My Love	Petula Clark	#1
Cherish	The Association	#1
A Groovy Kind of Love	The Mindbenders	#2
Sunny	Bobby Hebb	#2
Snoopy vs. the Red Baron	The Royal Guardsmen	#2
No Matter What Shape (Your Stomach's In)	The T-Bones	#3
See You in September	The Happenings	#3
What Becomes of the Brokenhearted	Jimmy Ruffin	#7
A Must to Avoid	Herman's Hermits	#8
Sweet Pea	Tommy Roe	#8
1967		
The Happening	The Supremes	#1
Dedicated to the One I Love	Mamas & Papas	#2
My Cup Runneth Over	Ed Ames	#8
Sunday Will Never Be the Same	Spanky & Our Gang	#9
Lazy Day	Spanky & Our Gang	#14
The Return of the Red Baron	The Royal Guardsmen	#15
Go Where You Wanna Go	The 5th Dimension	#16
I've Passed This Way Before	Jimmy Ruffin	#17
I Was Kaiser Bill's Batman	Whistling Jack Smith	#20
Yellow Balloon	The Yellow Balloon	#25
1968		
Harper Valley P.T.A.	Jeannie C. Riley	#1
Young Girl	Gary Puckett & The Union Gap	#2
Woman, Woman	Gary Puckett & The Union Gap	#4
Think	Aretha Franklin	#7
Chewy Chewy	Ohio Express	#15
My Baby Must Be a Magician	The Marvelettes	#17

SONGS WITH MODULATION (cont'd)

Am I That Easy to Forget	Engelbert Humperdinck	#18
A Man Without Love	Engelbert Humperdinck	#19
Will You Love Me Tomorrow	The Four Seasons	#24
The Snake	Al Wilson	#27
1969		
Dizzy	Tommy Roe	#1
In the Year 2525	Zager & Evans	#1
My Cherie Amour	Stevie Wonder	#4
My Whole World Ended (The Moment You Left Me)	David Ruffin	#9
I've Gotta Be Me	Sammy Davis Jr.	#11
The Weight	Aretha Franklin	#19
Everyday with You Girl	Classics IV/Dennis Yost	#19
Heather Honey	Tommy Roe	#29
Don't It Make You Want to Go Home	Joe South & The Believers	#41
Honey (I Miss You)	O.C. Smith	#44

SONGS WITH OSTINATOS

An ostinato is a short, repetitive rhythmic or melodic phrase. An ostinato can be an instrument or a vocal part. The key, though, is that it is a short phrase that repeats. I only included songs that had distinctive or especially important ostinatos, or ostinatos that dominated the music.

For a great example of a song filled with ostinatos, listen to "I Can't Stand Myself (When You Touch Me)" by James Brown, from 1968. It has both instrumental and vocal ostinatos.

SONG	ARTIST	HOT 100
1960		
Stuck on You	Elvis Presley	#1
Swingin' School	Bobby Rydell	#5
Baby (You've Got What It Takes)	Dinah Washington & Brook Benton	#5
Kiddio	Brook Benton	#7
Pineapple Princess	Annette	#11
Feel so Fine	Johnny Preston	#14
Look for a Star	Billy Vaughn	#19
Lucille	The Everly Brothers	#21
Lonely Weekends	Charlie Rich	#22
The Madison	Al Brown	#23
The Little Drummer Boy	Harry Simeone	#24
T.L.C. Tender Love and Care	Jimmie Rodgers	#24
Shimmy, Shimmy, Ko-Ko-Bop	Little Anthony & The Imperials	#24
Hot Rod Lincoln	Johnny Bond	#26
Peter Gunn	Duane Eddy	#27
Ooh Poo Pah Doo Part II	Jessie Hill	#28
Love Walked In	Dinah Washington	#30

SONGS WITH OSTINATOS (cont'd)

Nobody Loves Me Like You	The Flamingos	#30
Too Much Tequila	The Champs	#30
A Mess of Blues	Elvis Presley	#32
Think	James Brown	#33
Heartbreak (It's Hurtin' Me)	Little Willie John	#38
Natural Born Lover	Fats Domino	#38
Fannie Mae	Buster Brown	#38
Alley-Oop	The Dyna-Sores	#59
Just a Little Bit	Rosco Gordon	#64
Is It Wrong (For Loving You)	Webb Pierce	#69
Besame Mucho (Part One)	The Coasters	#70
Skokiaan (South African Song)	Bill Haley & His Comets	#70
Up Town	Roy Orbison	#72
Teensville	Chet Atkins	#73
Psycho	Bobby Hendricks	#73
Roadrunner	Bo Diddley	#75
I Idolize You	Ike & Tina Turner	#82
Wheel of Fortune	LaVern Baker	#83
(Do the) Mashed Potatoes (Part 1)	Nat Kendrick	#84
You've Got the Power	James Brown w/Bea Ford	#86
Smokie- Part 2	Bill Doggett	#95
1961		
Running Scared	Roy Orbison	#1
Moody River	Pat Boone	#1
Mother-In-Law	Ernie K-Doe	#1
Runaround Sue	Dion	#1
The Lion Sleeps Tonight	The Tokens	#1
The Boll Weevil Song	Brook Benton	#2
(Marie's the Name) His Latest Flame	Elvis Presley	#4
Tonight I Fell in Love	The Tokens	#15
Little Boy Sad	Johnny Burnette	#17
Amor	Ben E. King	#18
My Kind of Girl	Matt Monro	#18
Peanut Butter	The Marathons	#20
That Old Black Magic	Bobby Rydell	#21
What a Price	Fats Domino	#22
The Hoochi Coochi Coo	Hank Ballard & The Midnighters	#23
Your Ma Said You Cried in Your Sleep Last Night	Kenny Dino	#24
Take Five	Dave Brubeck Quartet	#25
The Switch-A-Roo	Hank Ballard & The Midnighters	#26
Tonight (Could Be the Night)	The Velvets	#26
If I Didn't Care	The Platters	#30
Anybody but Me	Brenda Lee	#31

SONGS WITH OSTINATOS (cont'd)

Ain't That Just Like a Woman	Fats Domino	#33
Ginnie Bell	Paul Dino	#38
Let's Go Again (Where We Went Last Night)	Hank Ballard & The Midnighters	#39
Nature Boy	Bobby Darin	#40
Don't Believe Him, Donna	Lenny Miles	#41
Every Breath I Take	Gene Pitney	#42
I Pity the Fool	Bobby Bland	#46
Watch Your Step	Bobby Parker	#51
Mighty Good Lovin'	The Miracles	#51
Lonesome Number One	Don Gibson	#59
Turn Around, Look at Me	Glen Campbell	#62
Cerveza	Bert Kaempfert	#73
Brother-in-Law (He's a Moocher)	Paul Peek	#84
Blue Tomorrow	Billy Vaughn	#84
Driving Wheel	Junior Parker	#85
The Door to Paradise	Bobby Rydell	#85
California Sun	Joe Jones	#89
True, True Love	Frankie Avalon	#90
The Float	Hank Ballard & The Midnighters	#92
Kokomo	The Flamingos	#92
Pocketful of Rainbows	Deane Hawley	#93
Little Turtle Dove	Otis Williams/Charms	#95
Here's My Confession	Wyatt (Earp) McPherson	#97
A Lover's Question	Ernestine Anderson	#98
The Bells are Ringing	The Van Dykes	#99
1962		
Dear Lady Twist	Gary (U.S.) Bonds	#9
The Cha-Cha-Cha	Bobby Rydell	#10
Love Came to Me	Dion	#10
Irresistible You	Bobby Darin	#15
Shadrack	Brook Benton	#19
I Need Your Loving	Don Gardner/Dee Dee Ford	#20
Small Sad Sam	Phil McLean	#21
Cajun Queen	Jimmy Dean	#22
Village of Love	Nathaniel Mayer & The Fabulous Twilights	#22
When My Little Girl is Smiling	The Drifters	#28
Drums are My Beat	Sandy Nelson	#29
Night Train	James Brown	#35
Papa-Oom-Mow-Mow	The Rivingtons	#48
You Can't Judge a Book by the Cover	Bo Diddley	#48
Baby Elephant Walk	Lawrence Welk	#48
Just Tell Her Jim Said Hello	Elvis Presley	#55

SONGS WITH OSTINATOS (cont'd)

Patricia- Twist	Perez Prado	#65
Don't You Worry	Don Gardner/Dee Dee Ford	#66
What Time is It?	The Jive Five	#67
Somebody Have Mercy	Sam Cooke	#70
Stranger on the Shore	The Drifters	#73
All Night Long	Sandy Nelson	#75
Mashed Potatoes (Part 1)	Steve Alaimo	#81
Keep Your Hands in Your Pockets	The Playmates	#88
Amor	Roger Williams	#88
Summertime	Ricky Nelson	#89
Ida Jane	Fats Domino	#90
I Found Love	Jackie Wilson & Linda Hopkins	#93
The Searching is Over	Joe Henderson	#94
Play the Thing	Marlowe Morris Quintet	#95
Little Young Lover	The Impressions	#96
Lisa	Ferrante & Teicher	#98
1963		
Louie Louie	The Kingsmen	#2
Then He Kissed Me	The Crystals	#6
Wild Weekend	The Rebels	#8
The Monkey Time	Major Lance	#8
El Watusi	Ray Barretto	#17
Let's Turkey Trot	Little Eva	#20
Call On Me	Bobby Bland	#22
Blue Guitar	Richard Chamberlain	#42
Monkey-Shine	Bill Black's Combo	#47
Speed Ball	Ray Stevens	#59
Heart	Kenny Chandler	#64
Jack the Ripper	Link Wray	#64
Signed, Sealed, and Delivered	James Brown	#77
Land of 1000 Dances	Chris Kenner	#77
How Can I Forget	Ben E. King	#85
I'm Down to My Last Heartbreak	Wilson Pickett	#95
River's Invitation	Percy Mayfield	#99
1964		
Haunted House	Gene Simmons	#11
You're a Wonderful One	Marvin Gaye	#15
Ain't Nothing You Can Do	Bobby Bland	#20
Sugar Lips	Al Hirt	#30
Rock Me Baby	B.B. King	#34
I Can't Stand It	Soul Sisters	#46
Ain't Doing Too Bad (Part 1)	Bobby Bland	#49

SONGS WITH OSTINATOS (cont'd)

That Girl Belongs to Yesterday	Gene Pitney	#49
Anyone Who Knows What Love Is (Will Understand)	Irma Thomas	#52
Everybody Needs Somebody to Love	Solomon Burke	#58
Candy to Me	Eddie Holland	#58
The Dodo	Jumpin' Gene Simmons	#83
Big Boss Line	Jackie Wilson	#94
The Son of Rebel Rouser	Duane Eddy	#97
Trouble I've Had	Clarence Ashe	#99
1965		
Hang on Sloopy	The McCoys	#1
(I Can't Get No) Satisfaction	The Rolling Stones	#1
I'll Be Doggone	Marvin Gaye	#8
The Boy from New York City	The Ad Libs	#8
I Will	Dean Martin	#10
I Want Candy	The Strangeloves	#11
We Gotta Get Out of This Place	The Animals	#13
Something About You	Four Tops	#19
Who'll Be the Next in Line	The Kinks	#34
Just a Little Bit	Roy Head	#39
Seein' the Right Love Go Wrong	Jack Jones	#46
Dance with Me	The Mojo Men	#61
Land of a Thousand Dances (Part 1)	Thee Midniters	#67
Canadian Sunset	Sounds Orchestral	#76
Every Night, Every Day	Jimmy McCracklin	#91
Gloria	Them	#93
Teasin' You	Willie Tee	#97
Stay Away from My Baby	Ted Taylor	#99
1966		
No Matter What Shape (Your Stomach's In)	The T-Bones	#3
Day Tripper	The Beatles	#5
Hooray for Hazel	Tommy Roe	#6
Cherry, Cherry	Neil Diamond	#6
Working in the Coal Mine	Lee Dorsey	#8
Hold On! I'm a Comin'	Sam & Dave	#21
But It's Alright	J.J. Jackson	#22
I Need Somebody	? & The Mysterians	#22
One More Heartache	Marvin Gaye	#29
Night Time	The Strangeloves	#30
Happenings Ten Years Time Ago	The Yardbirds	#30
Batman Theme	Neal Hefti	#35
One Track Mind	The Knickerbockers	#46
Look at Me Girl	Bobby Vee	#52
Helpless	Kim Weston	#56

SONGS WITH OSTINATOS (cont'd)

Song	Artist	Chart
There's Something on Your Mind	Baby Ray	#69
Lonely Summer	The Shades of Blue	#72
My Sweet Potato	Booker T. & The MG's	#85
Follow Your Heart	The Manhattans	#92
Mine Exclusively	The Olympics	#99
Day Tripper	The Vontastics	#100
1967		
Expressway (To Your Heart)	Soul Survivors	#4
Cold Sweat (Part 1)	James Brown	#7
Gimme Some Lovin'	Spencer Davis Group	#7
Soul Finger	Bar-Kays	#17
And Get Away	The Esquires	#22
Blues' Theme	Davie Allan/The Arrows	#37
Museum	Herman's Hermits	#39
Wack Wack	The Young Holt Trio	#40
I Take What I Want	James & Bobby Purify	#41
Shoot Your Shot	Jr. Walker/The All Stars	#44
Funky Broadway Part 1	Dyke & The Blazers	#65
Slim Jenkin's Place	Booker T. & The MG's	#70
Knucklehead	Bar-Kays	#76
Ten Commandments	Prince Buster	#81
Lovey Dovey/You're So Fine	Bunny Sigler	#86
Hey Love	Stevie Wonder	#90
Why (Am I Treated so Bad)	Bobby Powell	#91
Feel so Bad	Little Milton	#91
Hold On I'm Coming	Chuck Jackson & Maxine Brown	#91
Make a Little Love	Lowell Fulsom	#97
1968		
Spooky	Classics IV	#3
(The Lament of the Cherokee) Indian Reservation	Don Fardon	#20
There Is	The Dells	#20
The Happy Song (Dum-Dum)	Otis Redding	#25
I Can't Stand Myself (When You Touch Me)	James Brown	#28
Goodbye My Love	James Brown	#31
Explosion (In My Soul)	Soul Survivors	#33
Call Me Lightning	The Who	#40
In the Midnight Hour	The Mirettes	#45
Two-Bit Manchild	Neil Diamond	#66
Impossible Mission (Mission Impossible)	Soul Survivors	#68
I Got You Babe	Etta James	#69
You Got the Love	Professor Morrison's Lollipop	#88
1969		
In the Ghetto	Elvis Presley	#3

SONGS WITH OSTINATOS (cont'd)

Can I Change My Mind	Tyrone Davis	#5
I'm Livin' in Shame	The Supremes	#10
Give It up or Turnit a Loose	James Brown	#15
I Don't Want Nobody to Give Me Nothing (Open Up the Door, I'll Get It Myself) (Part 1)	James Brown	#20
Let a Man Come in and Do the Popcorn (Part One)	James Brown	#21
I Turned You On	The Isley Brothers	#23
Let a Woman Be a Woman - Let a Man Be a Man	Dyke & The Blazers	#36
The Minotaur	Dick Hyman	#38
Lowdown Popcorn	James Brown	#41
Time Machine	The Grand Funk Railroad	#48
(We've Got) Honey Love	Martha & The Vandellas	#56
Feeling Alright	Joe Cocker	#69
It's My Thing (You Can't Tell Me Who to Sock It To)	Marva Whitney	#82
I Can't Be All Bad	Johnny Adams	#89
Let Me Love You	Ray Charles	#94
Theme from Electric Surfboard	Brother Jack McDuff	#95
Ivory	Bob Seger System	#97

SONGS WITH A COUNTERMELODY

A countermelody is when two different melodies are sung or played at the same time. One of the melodies will usually be more important, or featured, while the other melody is usually in the background. Another characteristic of countermelodies is that both of the melodies can be sung separately, and they'll sound just fine. If each part sounds boring or weird by itself, then it probably isn't a countermelody- it's most likely simply a harmony part.

If you're still not sure exactly what a countermelody is, listen to "I Understand (Just How You Feel)" by Freddie & The Dreamers from 1965. The countermelody starts when they start singing. You'll hear an original melody while the countermelody (in this case, another song- "Auld Lang Syne") is sung a bit quieter than the main melody.

SONG	ARTIST	HOT 100
1960		
Anyway the Wind Blows	Doris Day	#50
1961		
I Understand (Just How You Feel)	The G-Clefs	#9
The Gypsy Rover	The Highwaymen	#42
Laugh	The Velvets	#90
Faraway Star	The Chordettes	#90
1962		
Next Door to an Angel	Neil Sedaka	#5
Me and My Shadow	Frank Sinatra & Sammy Davis Jr.	#64
1963		
Mockingbird	Inez Foxx w/Charlie Foxx	#7
Blue Bayou	Roy Orbison	#29

SONGS WITH A COUNTERMELODY (cont'd)

Song	Artist	Chart
All Over the World	Nat "King" Cole	#42
A Stranger in Your Town	The Shacklefords	#70
Hi Diddle Diddle	Inez Foxx	#98
1964		
Tea for Two	Nino Tempo & April Stevens	#56
Silly Ol' Summertime	New Christy Minstrels	#92
Oh, Rock My Soul (Part I)	Peter, Paul & Mary	#93
1965		
I Hear a Symphony	The Supremes	#1
Help!	The Beatles	#1
You've Got Your Troubles	The Fortunes	#7
Here It Comes Again	The Fortunes	#27
I Understand (Just How You Feel)	Freddie & The Dreamers	#36
1966		
I'm Ready for Love	Martha & The Vandellas	#9
God Only Knows	The Beach Boys	#39
Follow Me	Lyme & Cybelle	#65
Follow Your Heart	The Manhattans	#92
1967		
Hello Goodbye	The Beatles	#1
I Was Kaiser Bill's Batman	Whistling Jack Smith	#20
Anything Goes	Harpers Bizarre	#43
Goodnight My Love	The Happenings	#51
What've I Done (To Make You Mad)	Linda Jones	#61
1968		
You're All I Need to get By	Marvin Gaye & Tammi Terrell	#7
Scarborough Fair/Canticle	Simon & Garfunkel	#11
Dancing Bear	Mamas & Papas	#51
Zabadak	Dave Dee, Dozy, Beaky, Mick & Tich	#52
Safe in My Garden	Mamas & Papas	#53
Hey Boy Take a Chance on Love	Ruby Andrews	#92
Battle of New Orleans	Harpers Bizarre	#95
1969		
Grazing in the Grass	Friends of Distinction	#3
Donovan	Atlantis	#7
Tracy	The Cuff Links	#9
And That Reminds Me (My Heart Reminds Me)	The Four Seasons	#45

SONGS WITH UNUSUAL TIME SIGNATURES

Every song has a time signature. The time signature indicates which kind of note gets the beat (for example, the quarter note), and it tells how many beats there will be in each measure. By far, the most common time signature used will indicate four beats per measure.

The five songs below, however, used time signatures that sound and feel significantly different from the standard 4/4 time. Having an odd number of beats per measure, as opposed to the standard four, creates significant challenges for both the musicians and listeners. It makes the music more interesting and much less predictable. "Take Five" is perhaps the most famous pop song of all time with an unusual time signature.

YEAR	SONG	ARTIST	HOT 100	TIME SIGNATURE(S)
1961	Take Five	Dave Brubeck Quartet	#25	5 / 4
1962	Unsquare Dance	Dave Brubeck Quartet	#74	7 / 4
1967	I Say a Little Prayer for You	Dionne Warwick	#4	4 / 4, 10 / 4, 11 / 4
1967	Glad to Be Unhappy	Mamas & Papas	#26	4 / 4, 5 / 4
1968	Mission-Impossible	Lalo Schifrin	#41	5 / 4

VOICE

SONGS WITH FALSETTO

Falsetto is a singing technique unique to the male singer that allows him to sing notes that sound impossibly high. Two of the most famous falsetto singers in pop history came from the 1960s: Brian Wilson of the Beach Boys and Frankie Valli of the Four Seasons. Lou Christie and Dick (from "Dick & Deedee") also used their falsetto voice frequently. Every song listed here has a section (if not the whole song) where a falsetto voice is featured. Songs that only have a falsetto voice for a few seconds are not included.

SONG	ARTIST	HOT 100
1960		
Stay	Maurice Williams & The Zodiacs	#1
Handy Man	Jimmie Jones	#2
Good Timin'	Jimmy Jones	#3
Feel so Fine	Johnny Preston	#14
Why Do I Love You So	Johnny Tillotson	#42
Paradise	Sammy Turner	#46
My Hero	The Blue Notes	#78
1961		
The Lion Sleeps Tonight	The Tokens	#1
Runaway	Del Shannon	#1
The Mountain's High	Dick & Deedee	#2
Who Put the Bomp (In the Bomp, Bomp, Bomp)	Barry Mann	#7
Pretty Little Angel Eyes	Curtis Lee	#7
Barbara-Ann	The Regents	#13

SONGS WITH FALSETTO (cont'd)

Tonight I Fell in Love	The Tokens	#15
Heart and Soul	Jan & Dean	#25
Once Upon a Time	Rochell & The Candles	#26
Runaround	The Regents	#28
Lover's Island	The Blue Jays	#31
Count Every Star	Donnie & The Dreamers	#35
In My Heart	The Timetones	#51
Peanuts	Rick and The Keens	#60
It's Unbelievable	The Larks	#69
My Memories of You	Donnie and The Dreamers	#79
If	The Paragons	#82
Come Along	Maurice Williams and The Zodiacs	#83
I Told You So	Jimmy Jones	#85
Anniversary of Love	The Caslons	#89
Love (I'm So Glad) I Found You	The Spinners	#91
I Lied to My Heart	The Enchanters	#96
1962		
Duke of Earl	Gene Chandler	#1
Sherry	The Four Seasons	#1
Big Girls Don't Cry	The Four Seasons	#1
I Love You	The Volumes	#22
Santa Claus is Coming to Town	The Four Seasons	#23
That's My Pa	Sheb Wooley	#51
B'wa Nina (Pretty Girl)	The Tokens	#55
A Little Bit Now (A Little Bit Later)	The Majors	#63
Cry Myself to Sleep	Del Shannon	#99
1963		
Surf City	Jan & Dean	#1
Walk Like a Man	The Four Seasons	#1
Candy Girl	Four Seasons	#3
Two Faces Have I	Lou Christie	#6
Denise	Randy & The Rainbows	#10
Little Town Flirt	Del Shannon	#12
Young and in Love	Dick & Deedee	#17
Ain't That a Shame!	The Four Seasons	#22
The Gypsy Cried	Lou Christie	#24
New Mexican Rose	The Four Seasons	#36
Marlena	The Four Seasons	#36
How Many Teardrops	Lou Christie	#46
Brenda	The Cupids	#57
Sue's Gotta Be Mine	Del Shannon	#71
Soon (I'll Be Home Again)	The Four Seasons	#77
That's the Only Way	The Four Seasons	#88

SONGS WITH FALSETTO (cont'd)

You Know It Ain't Right	Joe Hinton	#88
Where Did the Good Times Go	Dick & Deedee	#93
Hear the Bells	The Tokens	#94
1964		
Rag Doll	The Four Seasons	#1
I Get Around	The Beach Boys	#1
The Little Old Lady (From Pasadena)	Jan & Dean	#3
Dawn (Go Away)	The Four Seasons	#3
G.T.O.	Ronny & The Daytonas	#4
Fun, Fun, Fun	The Beach Boys	#5
Ronnie	The Four Seasons	#6
Dance, Dance, Dance	The Beach Boys	#8
Dead Man's Curve	Jan & Dean	#8
Save It for Me	The Four Seasons	#10
Drag City	Jan & Dean	#10
Keep On Pushing	The Impressions	#10
Funny (How Time Slips Away)	Joe Hinton	#13
Everything's Alright	The Newbeats	#16
Stay	The Four Seasons	#16
Big Man in Town	The Four Seasons	#20
Handy Man	Del Shannon	#22
Don't Worry Baby	The Beach Boys	#24
Girl (Why You Wanna Make Me Blue)	The Temptations	#26
Alone	The Four Seasons	#28
The New Girl in School	Jan & Dean	#37
Wendy	The Beach Boys	#44
Summer Means Fun	Bruce & Terry	#72
Sincerely	The Four Seasons	#75
The Anaheim, Azusa & Cucamonga Sewing Circle, Book Review and Timing Association	Jan & Dean	#77
High on a Hill	Scott English	#77
All My Trials	Dick & Deedee	#89
1965		
Let's Hang On	The Four Seasons	#3
California Girls	The Beach Boys	#3
The Jerk	The Larks	#7
Do You Wanna Dance?	The Beach Boys	#12
Don't Think Twice	The Wonder Who (The Four Seasons)	#12
Run, Baby Run (Baby, Goodbye)	The Newbeats	#12
Liar, Liar	The Castaways	#12
Thou Shalt Not Steal	Dick & Dee Dee	#13
Ooo Baby Baby	The Miracles	#16
Girl Come Running	The Four Seasons	#30

SONGS WITH FALSETTO (cont'd)

Title	Artist	Chart
New York's a Lonely Town	The Trade Winds	#32
Ain't It True	Andy Williams	#40
Break Away (from That Boy)	The Newbeats	#40
(The Bees Are for the Birds) The Birds Are for the Bees	The Newbeats	#50
I Live for the Sun	The Sunrays	#51
Toy Soldier	The Four Seasons	#64
I Need You	The Impressions	#64
Be My Baby	Dick & Deedee	#87
My Buddy Seat	The Hondells	#87
Stay Away from My Baby	Ted Taylor	#99

1966

Title	Artist	Chart
Lightnin' Strikes	Lou Christie	#1
Barbara Ann	The Beach Boys	#2
Sloop John B.	The Beach Boys	#3
See You in September	The Happenings	#3
I've Got You Under My Skin	The Four Seasons	#9
Go Away Little Girl	The Happenings	#12
Opus 17 (Don't You Worry 'Bout Me)	The Four Seasons	#13
Rhapsody in the Rain	Lou Christie	#16
Andrea	The Sunrays	#41
Outside the Gates of Heaven	Lou Christie	#45
I'm a Nut	Leroy Pullins	#57
This Can't Be True	Eddie Holman	#57
Little Boy (In Grown Up Clothes)	The Four Seasons	#60
The Proud One	Frankie Vallie	#68
Wait a Minute	Tim Tam & The Turn-Ons	#76
Painter	Lou Christie	#81
On the Good Ship Lollipop	The Wonder Who (The Four Seasons)	#87
Since I Lost the One I Love	The Impressions	#90
Too Slow	The Impressions	#91
Shake Hands (And Come Out Crying)	The Newbeats	#92
No Man is an Island	The Van Dykes	#94
Big Time	Lou Christie	#95
You're Nobody Till Somebody Loves You	The Wonder Who? (The Four Seasons)	#96
Because I Love You	Billy Stewart	#96

1967

Title	Artist	Chart
I Got Rhythm	The Happenings	#3
You're My Everything	The Temptations	#6
(Your Love Keeps Lifting Me) Higher and Higher	Jackie Wilson	#6
C'mon Marianne	The Four Seasons	#9
Tell It to the Rain	The Four Seasons	#10
Silence is Golden	The Tremeloes	#11
Get on Up	The Esquires	#11

SONGS WITH FALSETTO (cont'd)

Song	Artist	Hot 100
My Mammy	The Happenings	#13
For Your Love	Peaches & Herb	#20
Watch the Flowers Grow	The Four Seasons	#30
Why Do Fools Fall in Love	The Happenings	#41
Goodnight My Love	The Happenings	#51
Cry Softly Lonely One	Roy Orbison	#52
I Can't Stay Away from You	The Impressions	#80
Lonesome Road	The Wonder Who?	#89
I Could Be So Happy	The Magnificent Men	#93
Shake Hands and Walk Away Cryin'	Lou Christie	#95
1968		
We're a Winner	The Impressions	#14
Chewy Chewy	Ohio Express	#15
Tip-Toe Thru' the Tulips with Me	Tiny Tim	#17
Will You Love Me Tomorrow	The Four Seasons	#24
Please Return Your Love to Me	The Temptations	#26
Breaking up Is Hard to Do	The Happenings	#67
Release Me	Johnny Adams	#82
You Don't Have to Say You Love Me	The Four Sonics	#89
Don't Be Afraid (Do as I Say)	Frankie Karl	#93
I've Got Love for My Baby	Young Hearts	#94
1969		
A Ray of Hope	The Rascals	#24
Make Believe	Wind (Tony Orlando)	#28
Reconsider Me	Johnny Adams	#28
You Got Yours and I'll Get Mine	The Delfonics	#40
I Do	The Moments	#62
Somebody Loves You	The Delfonics	#72
Seven Years	The Impressions	#84
You've Got the Power	The Esquires	#91

SONGS WITH CHIPMUNK VOICES

SONG	ARTIST	HOT 100
1960		
Rudolph the Red Nosed Reindeer	The Chipmunks	#21
Alvin's Orchestra	The Chipmunks	#33
The Chipmunk Song (Christmas Don't Be Late)	The Chipmunks	#45
The Puppet Song	Frankie Avalon	#56
Alvin for President	The Chipmunks	#95

SONGS WITH CHIPMUNK VOICES (cont'd)

1961		
Alvin's Harmonica	The Chipmunks	#73
1962		
The Alvin Twist	The Chipmunks	#40
Lose Her	Bobby Rydell	#69
1963		
Pepino the Italian Mouse	Lou Monte	#5
Pepino's Friend Pasqual (The Italian Pussy-Cat)	Lou Monte	#78
1964		
Rip Van Winkle	The Devotions	#36

SONGS WITH WHISTLING

SONG	ARTIST	HOT 100
1960		
Handy Man	Jimmie Jones	#2
Many Tears Ago	Connie Francis	#7
Delaware	Perry Como	#22
White Christmas	Bing Crosby	#27
Baciare Baciare (Kissing Kissing)	Dorothy Collins	#43
The Same Old Me	Guy Mitchell	#51
I Don't Know What It Is	The Bluenotes	#61
The Brigade of Broken Hearts	Paul Evans	#81
1961		
Michael	The Highwaymen	#1
The Gypsy Rover	The Highwaymen	#42
The Guns of Navarone	Joe Reisman	#74
1962		
Only Love Can Break a Heart	Gene Pitney	#2
Limbo Rock	Chubby Checker	#2
I'll See You in My Dreams	Pat Boone	#32
Pop-Eye	Huey Smith	#51
Happy Jose (Ching-Ching)	Jack Ross	#57
Baby Has Gone Bye Bye	George Maharis	#62
The Alley Cat Song	David Thorne	#76
Adios Amigo	Jim Reeves	#90
Zero-Zero	Lawrence Welk	#98
Sweet Georgia Brown	Carroll Bros.	#100
1963		
Sukiyaki	Kyu Sakamoto	#1
Twenty Miles	Chubby Checker	#15

SONGS WITH WHISTLING (cont'd)

Ally Ally Oxen Free	The Kingston Trio	#61
1964		
Turn Around	Dick & DeeDee	#27
Alone	The Four Seasons	#28
Lazy Elsie Molly	Chubby Checker	#40
Who Cares	Fats Domino	#63
T'ain't Nothin' to Me	The Coasters	#64
A Happy Guy	Ricky Nelson	#82
I'm Confessin' (That I Love You)	Nino Tempo & April Stevens	#99
1965		
Save Your Heart for Me	Gary Lewis/Playboys	#2
England Swings	Roger Miller	#8
Cast Your Fate to the Wind	Steve Alaimo	#89
1966		
Winchester Cathedral	New Vaudeville Band	#1
Daydream	The Lovin' Spoonful	#2
1967		
Here Comes My Baby	The Tremeloes	#13
I Was Kaiser Bill's Batman	Whistling Jack Smith	#20
Peek-A-Boo	New Vaudeville Band	#72
Only Love Can Break a Heart	Margaret Whiting	#96
1968		
(Sittin' On) The Dock of the Bay	Otis Redding	#1
The Good, the Bad and the Ugly	Hugo Montenegro	#2
Dream a Little Dream of Me	Mama Cass/Mamas & Papas	#12
It's Wonderful	The Young Rascals	#20
Tapioca Tundra	The Monkees	#34
Hang 'Em High	Hugo Montenegro	#82
(Sittin' On) The Dock of the Bay	King Curtis & Kingpins	#84
Lili Marlene	Al Martino	#87
1969		
Everyday with You Girl	Classics IV/Dennis Yost	#19
Odds and Ends	Dionne Warwick	#43
Day After Day (It's Slippin' Away)	Shango	#57

SONGS WITH 100% SPEAKING

There are quite a few songs from the 60s that had speaking in them. Usually, it would be the lead singer speaking to his/her lost love, or maybe reciting some patriotic poem, or telling some old story. The songs below only include those in which the lead singer (speaker?) speaks for the entire time. In other words, he/she does not sing at all, though there may be a choir singing in the background.

SONG	ARTIST	HOT 100
1960		
Hot Rod Lincoln	Charlie Ryan	#33
Shoppin' for Clothes	The Coasters	#83
Side Car Cycle	Charlie Ryan	#84
1961		
Big Bad John	Jimmy Dean	#1
The Astronaut (Parts 1 & 2)	Jose Jimenez	#19
A Little Dog Cried	Jimmie Rodgers	#71
Battle of Gettysburg	Fred Darian	#100
1962		
Old Rivers	Walter Brennan	#5
Small Sad Sam	Phil McLean	#21
Cajun Queen	Jimmy Dean	#22
Dear Ivan	Jimmy Dean	#24
To a Sleeping Beauty	Jimmy Dean	#26
Mama Sang a Song	Stan Kenton	#32
Mama Sang a Song	Walter Brennan	#38
Mama Sang a Song	Bill Anderson	#89
Houdini	Walter Brennan	#100
1963		
El Watusi	Ray Barretto	#17
This Is All I Ask	Burl Ives	#67
1965		
10 Little Bottles	Johnny Bond	#43
Married Man	Richard Burton	#64
1966		
They're Coming to Take Me Away, Ha-Haaa!	Napoleon XIV	#3
The Ballad of Irving	Frank Gallop	#34
Day for Decision	Johnny Sea	#35
History Repeats Itself	Buddy Starcher	#39
Past, Present and Future	The Shangri-Las	#59
Giddyup Go	Red Sovine	#82
History Repeats Itself	Cab Calloway	#89
1967		
Little Ole Man (Uptight-Everything's Alright)	Bill Cosby	#4

SONGS WITH 100% SPEAKING (cont'd)

An Open Letter to My Teenage Son	Victor Lundberg	#10
Gallant Men	Senator Everett McKinley Dirksen	#29
Don't Blame the Children	Sammy Davis, Jr.	#37
Ten Commandments	Prince Buster	#81
A Letter to Dad	Every Father's Teenage Son	#93
1968		
Here Comes the Judge	Pigmeat Markham	#19
Ballad of Two Brothers	Autry Inman	#48
America Is My Home - Pt. 1	James Brown	#52
Keep On Dancing	Alvin Cash	#66
Don't Pat Me on the Back and Call Me Brother	KaSandra	#91
1969		
A Boy Named Sue	Johnny Cash	#2
We Love You, Call Collect	Art Linkletter	#42
The Pledge of Allegiance	Red Skelton	#44
Hook and Sling - Part 1	Eddie Bo	#73

SONGS WITH YODELING

Okay, so the "yodeling" in these two songs might not pass muster in Switzerland, but it's the closest thing to yodeling you'll find in popular music!

YEAR	SONG	ARTIST	HOT 100
1962	The Swiss Maid	Del Shannon	#64
1963	Lovesick Blues	Frank Ifield	#44

SINGERS

SONGS WITH AN ADULT CHOIR

SONG	ARTIST	HOT 100
1960		
Theme from "The Unforgiven" (The Need for Love)	Don Costa	#27
White Christmas	Bing Crosby	#27
Dutchman's Gold	Walter Brennan w/Billy Vaughn	#30
Talk That Talk	Jackie Wilson	#34
Just Come Home	Hugo & Luigi	#35
Just a Closer Walk with Thee	Jimmie Rodgers	#44
The Way of a Clown	Teddy Randazzo	#44
Adeste Fideles (Oh, Come, All Ye Faithful)	Bing Crosby	#45
Christmas Auld Lang Syne	Bobby Darin	#51
Someone Love You, Joe	The Singing Belles	#91

SONGS WITH AN ADULT CHOIR (cont'd)

Child of God	Bobby Darin	#95
I Need You Now	100 Strings & Joni James	#98

1961

Tonight	Ferrante & Teicher	#8
Moon River	Henry Mancini	#11
Oh Mein Papa	Dick Lee	#94
The Little Drummer Boy	Jack Halloran Singers	#96

1962

I Can't Stop Loving You	Ray Charles	#1
You Don't Know Me	Ray Charles	#2
Ramblin' Rose	Nat "King" Cole	#2
Release Me	"Little Esther" Phillips	#8
Dear Lonely Hearts	Nat "King" Cole	#13
Shadrack	Brook Benton	#19
Mama Sang a Song	Stan Kenton	#32
Mama Sang a Song	Walter Brennan	#38
Born to Lose	Ray Charles	#41
Yes Indeed	Pete Fountain	#69
The Lost Penny	Brook Benton	#77
Marianna	Johnny Mathis	#86
Mama Sang a Song	Bill Anderson	#89

1963

That Sunday, That Summer	Nat "King" Cole	#12
Make the World Go Away	Timi Yuro	#24
Days of Wine and Roses	Henry Mancini	#33
Toys in the Attic	Joe Sherman	#85
Say Wonderful Things	Ronnie Carroll	#91

1964

Everybody Loves Somebody	Dean Martin	#1
Love Me with All of Your Heart	Ray Charles Singers	#3
That Lucky Old Sun	Ray Charles	#20
I Don't Want to Be Hurt Anymore	Nat "King" Cole	#22
Softly, As I Leave You	Frank Sinatra	#27
Al-Di-La	Ray Charles Singers	#29
Always Together	Al Martino	#33
I Don't Want to See Tomorrow	Nat "King" Cole	#34
My Heart Cries for You	Ray Charles	#38
Love is All We Need	Vic Dana	#53
Invisible Tears	Ray Conniff	#57
Till the End of Time	Ray Charles Singers	#83
I Wonder Who's Kissing Her Now	Bobby Darin	#93
Pretend You Don't See Her	Bobby Vee	#97
It's a Cotton Candy World	Jerry Wallace	#99

SONGS WITH AN ADULT CHOIR (cont'd)

1965

One More Time	Ray Charles Singers	#32
Tell Her (You Love Her Each Day)	Frank Sinatra	#57
You'll Always Be the One I Love	Dean Martin	#64
Bring a Little Sunshine (To My Heart)	Vic Dana	#66
This is My Prayer	Ray Charlse Singers	#72
Dear Heart	Henry Mancini	#77
I'm a Fool to Care	Ray Charles	#84
My Cherie	Al Martino	#88
It's Almost Tomorrow	Jimmy Velvet	#93
Tears Keep On Falling	Jerry Vale	#96

1966

Somewhere, My Love	Ray Conniff	#9
One Has My Name (The Other Has My Heart)	Barry Young	#13
Spanish Eyes	Al Martino	#15
Happy Summer Days	Ronnie Dove	#27
Go Ahead and Cry	The Righteous Brothers	#30
History Repeats Itself	Cab Calloway	#89
Lookin' for Love	Ray Conniff	#94

1967

In the Chapel in the Moonlight	Dean Martin	#25
Gallant Men	Senator Everett McKinley Dirksen	#29
Making Memories	Frankie Laine	#35
Don't Blame the Children	Sammy Davis, Jr.	#37
I'll Take Care of Your Cares	Frankie Laine	#39
Daddys Little Girl	Al Martino	#42
In the Misty Moonlight	Dean Martin	#46
Wish Me a Rainbow	The Gunter Kallmann Chorus	#63
You, No One but You	Frankie Laine	#83
More and More	Andy Williams	#88
Up-Up and Away	Johnny Mann Singers	#91
There Must Be a Way	Jimmy Roselli	#93

1968

Battle Hymn of the Republic	Andy Williams	#33
My Favorite Things	Herb Alpert & The Tijuana Brass	#45
Love is Blue (L'Amour Est Bleu)	Manny Kellem	#96

1969

Oh Happy Day	Edwin Hawkins Singers	#4
Holly Holy	Neil Diamond	#6
Love Me Tonight	Tom Jones	#13
Give Peace a Chance	John Lennon	#14
Day Is Done	Peter, Paul & Mary	#21
Dammit Isn't God's Last Name	Frankie Laine	#86

SONGS WITH AN ADULT CHOIR (cont'd)

I Can't Help It (If I'm Still in Love with You)	Al Martino	#97

SONGS WITH A CHILDREN'S CHOIR

YEAR	SONG	ARTIST	HOT 100
1960	Banjo Boy	Dorothy Collins	#79
1960	The Yen Yet Song	Gary Cane	#99
1963	On Top of Spaghetti	Tom Glazer	#14
1967	I Am the Walrus	The Beatles	#56
1968	Those Were the Days	Mary Hopkins	#2
1968	The Yard Went on Forever	Richard Harris	#64

MALE/FEMALE DUETS

SONG	ARTIST	HOT 100
1960		
Baby (You've Got What It Takes)	Dinah Washington & Brook Benton	#5
A Rockin' Good Way (To Mess Around and Fall in Love)	Dinah Washington & Brook Benton	#7
Let the Good Times Roll	Shirley & Lee	#48
If I Can't Have You	Etta James & Harvey Fuqua	#52
Pink Chiffon	Mitchell Torok	#60
Spoonful	Etta James & Harvey Fuqua	#78
You've Got the Power	James Brown w/Bea Ford	#86
I've Been Loved Before	Shirley & Lee	#88
1961		
The Mountain's High	Dick & DeeDee	#2
What Would I Do	Mickey & Sylvia	#46
Well-A, Well-A	Shirley & Lee	#77
You're the Boss	LaVern Baker/Jimmy Ricks	#81
I'll Never Be Free	Kay Starr	#94
Lovedrops	Mickey & Sylvia	#97
1962		
Slow Twistin'	Chubby Checker w/Dee Dee Sharp	#3
You Are My Sunshine	Ray Charles	#7
Don't You Worry	Don Gardner/Dee Dee Ford	#66
Sweet and Lovely	April Stevens & Nino Tempo	#77
Baby It's Cold Outside	Ray Charles & Betty Carter	#91
I Found Love	Jackie Wilson & Linda Hopkins	#93
1963		
Deep Purple	Nino Tempo & April Stevens	#1
I'm Leaving It up to You	Dale & Grace	#1
Hey Paula	Paul & Paula	#1

MALE/FEMALE DUETS (cont'd)

Song	Artist	Chart
Young Lovers	Paul & Paula	#6
Mockingbird	Inez Foxx w/Charlie Foxx	#7
Young and in Love	Dick & DeeDee	#17
Follow the Boys	Connie Francis	#17
First Quarrel	Paul & Paula	#27
I Want to Stay Here	Steve & Eydie	#28
Swinging on a Star	Big Dee Irwin w/Little Eva	#38
What a Guy	The Raindrops	#41
Shake a Hand	Jackie Wilson & Linda Hopkins	#42
First Day Back at School	Paul & Paula	#60
You Never Miss Your Water (Till the Well Runs Dry)	"Little Esther" Phillips & "Big Al" Downing	#73
Something Old, Something New	Paul & Paula	#77
Don't Let Me Cross Over	Carl Butler & Pearl	#88
Where Did the Good Times Go	Dick & DeeDee	#93
Hi Diddle Diddle	Inez Foxx	#98

1964

Song	Artist	Chart
Let It Be Me	Betty Everett & Jerry Butler	#5
Stop and Think It Over	Dale & Grace	#8
Whispering	Nino Tempo & April Stevens	#11
What's the Matter with You Baby	Marvin Gaye & Mary Wells	#17
Once Upon a Time	Marvin Gaye & Mary Wells	#19
Turn Around	Dick & DeeDee	#27
Stardust	Nino Tempo & April Stevens	#32
Hey Jean, Hey Dean	Dean & Jean	#32
Tra La La La Suzy	Dean & Jean	#35
I Can't Stop Talking About You	Steve & Eydie	#35
Baby Baby Baby	Anna King-Bobby Byrd	#52
Hurt by Love	Inez Foxx	#54
Tea for Two	Nino Tempo & April Stevens	#56
Sole Sole Sole	Siw Malmkvist-Umberto Marcato	#58
It Ain't Me, Babe	Johnny Cash	#58
What Good Am I Without You	Marvin Gaye & Kim Weston	#61
The Loneliest Night	Dale & Grace	#65
I See You	Cathy & Joe	#82
All My Trials	Dick & DeeDee	#89
That's Really Some Good	Rufus & Carla	#92
Night Time Is the Right Time	Rufus & Carla	#94
Slipin' and Slidin'	Jim & Monica	#96
I'm Confessin' (That I Love You)	Nino Tempo & April Stevens	#99

1965

Song	Artist	Chart
I Got You Babe	Sonny & Cher	#1
Baby Don't Go	Sonny & Cher	#8
Thou Shalt Not Steal	Dick & Dee Dee	#13

MALE/FEMALE DUETS (cont'd)

But You're Mine	Sonny & Cher	#15
Just You	Sonny & Cher	#20
Don't Mess up a Good Thing	Fontella Bass & Bobby McClure	#33
Smile	Betty Everett & Jerry Butler	#42
Something You Got	Chuck Jackson & Maxine Brown	#55
Super-cali-fragil-istic-expi-ali-docious	Julie Andrews-Dick Van Dyke	#66
I Found a Love Oh What a Love	Jo Ann & Troy	#67
The Letter	Sonny & Cher	#75
Be My Baby	Dick & Dee Dee	#87
You'll Miss Me (When I'm Gone)	Fontella Bass & Bobby McClure	#91
Can't Let You Out of My Sight	Chuck Jackson & Maxine Brown	#91
I Need You So	Chuck Jackson & Maxine Brown	#98
1966		
What Now My Love	Sonny & Cher	#14
Little Man	Sonny & Cher	#21
All Strung Out	Nino Tempo & April Stevens	#26
Have I Stayed Too Long	Sonny & Cher	#49
Wang Dang Doodle	Ko Ko Taylor	#58
Follow Me	Lyme & Cybelle	#65
Living for You	Sonny & Cher	#87
Think Twice	Jackie Wilson & LaVern Baker	#93
1967		
Somethin' Stupid	Nancy & Frank Sinatra	#1
Your Precious Love	Marvin Gaye & Tammi Terrell	#5
The Beat Goes On	Sonny & Cher	#6
Close Your Eyes	Peaches & Herb	#8
Love Is Strange	Peaches & Herb	#13
It Takes Two	Marvin Gaye and Kim Weston	#14
Jackson	Nancy Sinatra & Lee Hazlewood	#14
Do It Again a Little Bit Slower	Jon & Robin	#18
Ain't No Mountain High Enough	Marvin Gaye & Tammi Terrell	#19
Lady Bird	Nancy Sinatra & Lee Hazlewood	#20
For Your Love	Peaches & Herb	#20
Let's Fall in Love	Peaches & Herb	#21
Tramp	Otis & Carla	#26
Knock on Wood	Otis & Carla	#30
Summer Wine	Nancy Sinatra & Lee Hazlewood	#49
It's the Little Things	Sonny & Cher	#50
A Beautiful Story	Sonny & Cher	#53
Plastic Man	Sonny & Cher	#74
Go with Me	Gene & Debbe	#78
I Can't Go On Livin' Baby Without You	Nino Tempo & April Stevens	#86
My Elusive Dreams	David Houston & Tammy Wynette	#89

MALE/FEMALE DUETS (cont'd)

Daddy's Home	Chuck Jackson & Maxine Brown	#91
Hold On I'm Coming	Chuck Jackson & Maxine Brown	#91
Mockingbird	Aretha Franklin	#94
Make Love to Me	Johnny Thunder & Ruby Winters	#96
I'm a Fool for You	James Carr	#97
Think	Vicki Anderson & James Brown	#100
Drums	Jon & Robin	#100
1968		
You're All I Need to Get By	Marvin Gaye & Tammi Terrell	#7
Ain't Nothing Like the Real Thing	Marvin Gaye & Tammi Terrell	#8
If I Could Build My Whole World Around You	Marvin Gaye & Tammi Terrell	#10
Reach Out of the Darkness	Friend & Lover	#10
Scarborough Fair	Sergio Mendes & Brasil '66	#16
Playboy	Gene & Debbe	#17
Keep On Lovin' Me Honey	Marvin Gaye & Tammi Terrell	#24
Some Velvet Morning	Nancy Sinatra & Lee Hazlewood	#26
Pickin' Wild Mountain Berries	Peggy Scott & Jo Jo Benson	#27
Lover's Holiday	Peggy Scott & Jo Jo Benson	#31
Two Little Kids	Peaches & Herb	#31
Country Girl - City Man	Billy Vera & Judy Clay	#36
United	Peaches & Herb	#46
Storybook Children	Billy Vera & Judy Clay	#54
The Ten Commandments of Love	Peaches & Herb	#55
Good Combination	Sonny & Cher	#56
From the Teacher to the Preacher	Gene Chandler & Barbara Acklin	#57
Lovey Dovey	Otis & Carla	#60
If This World Were Mine	Marvin Gaye & Tammi Terrell	#68
Cinderella Rockefella	Esther & Abi Ofarim	#68
Mornin' Glory	Bobbie Gentry & Glen Campbell	#74
Let's Make a Promise	Peaches & Herb	#75
Private Number	Judy Clay & William Bell	#75
(1-2-3-4-5-6-7) Count the Days	Inez & Charlie Foxx	#76
Lovin' Season	Gene & Debbe	#81
If Love Is in Your Heart	Friend & Lover	#86
Dr. Jon (The Medicine Man)	Jon & Robin	#87
People World	Jim & Jean	#94
1969		
Good Lovin' Ain't Easy to Come By	Marvin Gaye & Tammi Terrell	#30
Let It Be Me	Glen Campbell & Bobbie Gentry	#36
Soulshake	Peggy Scott & Jo Jo Benson	#37
When He Touches Me (Nothing Else Matters)	Peaches & Herb	#49
What You Gave Me	Marvin Gaye & Tammi Terrell	#49
I Still Believe in Tomorrow	John & Anne Ryder	#70

MALE/FEMALE DUETS (cont'd)

Let Me Be the One	Peaches & Herb	#74
I Want to Love You Baby	Peggy Scott & Jo Jo Benson	#81
Oh How Happy	Blinky & Edwin Starr	#92
I'm Gonna Do All I Can (To Do Right By My Man)	Ike & Tina Turner	#98

MALE/MALE DUETS

SONG	ARTIST	HOT 100
1960		
Cathy's Clown	The Everly Brothers	#1
Let It Be Me	The Everly Brothers	#7
So Sad (To Watch Good Love Go Bad)	The Everly Brothers	#7
When Will I Be Loved	The Everly Brothers	#8
Always It's You	The Everly Brothers	#56
Ballad of the Alamo	Bud & Travis	#64
Gee	Jan and Dean	#81
1961		
Walk Right Back	The Everly Brothers	#7
Ebony Eyes	The Everly Brothers	#8
Don't Blame Me	The Everly Brothers	#20
Jingle Bell Rock	Bobby Rydell & Chubby Checker	#21
Heart and Soul	Jan & Dean	#25
Temptation	The Everly Brothers	#27
Stick with Me Baby	The Everly Brothers	#41
All I Have to Do Is Dream	The Everly Brothers	#96
1962		
Next Door to an Angel	Neil Sedaka	#5
Crying in the Rain	The Everly Brothers	#6
That's Old Fashioned (That's the Way Love Should Be)	The Everly Brothers	#9
Bring It on Home to Me	Sam Cooke & Lou Rawls	#13
Don't Ask Me to Be Friends	The Everly Brothers	#48
Me and My Shadow	Frank Sinatra & Sammy Davis Jr.	#64
Tennessee	Jan & Dean	#69
How Can I Meet Her?	The Everly Brothers	#75
I'm Here to Get My Baby Out of Jail	The Everly Brothers	#76
Sam's Song	Dean Martin & Sammy Davis Jr.	#94
1963		
Surf City	Jan & Dean	#1
Honolulu Lulu	Jan & Dean	#11
Linda	Jan & Dean	#28
My Babe	The Righteous Brothers	#75

MALE/MALE DUETS (cont'd)

1964

A World Without Love	Peter & Gordon	#1
The Little Old Lady (From Pasadena)	Jan & Dean	#3
A Summer Song	Chad & Jeremy	#7
Dead Man's Curve	Jan & Dean	#8
Drag City	Jan & Dean	#10
Nobody I Know	Peter & Gordon	#12
I Don't Want to See You Again	Peter & Gordon	#16
Yesterday's Gone	Chad & Jeremy	#21
Sidewalk Surfin'	Jan & Dean	#25
Gone, Gone, Gone	The Everly Brothers	#31
The New Girl in School	Jan & Dean	#37
Angelito	Rene & Rene	#43
Summer Means Fun	Bruce & Terry	#72
The Ferris Wheel	The Everly Brothers	#72
The Anaheim, Azusa & Cucamonga Sewing Circle, Book Review and Timing Association	Jan & Dean	#77

1965

You've Lost That Lovin' Feelin'	The Righteous Brothers	#1
Just Once in My Life	The Righteous Brothers	#9
I Go to Pieces	Peter & Gordon	#9
True Love Ways	Peter & Gordon	#14
Willow Weep for Me	Chad & Jeremy	#15
Everyone's Gone to the Moon	Jonathan King	#17
If I Loved You	Chad & Jeremy	#23
To Know You Is to Love You	Peter & Gordon	#24
You Really Know How to Hurt a Guy	Jan & Dean	#27
I Found a Girl	Jan & Dean	#30
Hung on You	The Righteous Brothers	#47
What Do You Want with Me	Chad & Jeremy	#51
(Here They Come) From All Over the World	Jan & Dean	#56
You Can Have Her	The Righteous Brothers	#67
Before You Go	Buck Owens	#83
Don't Pity Me	Peter & Gordon	#83
Justine	The Righteous Brothers	#85
I Have Dreamed	Chad & Jeremy	#91
For Your Love	Sam & Bill	#95
From a Window	Chad & Jeremy	#97
I've Got Five Dollars and It's Saturday Night	George Jones & Gene Pitney	#99

1966

The Sound of Silence	Simon & Garfunkel	#1
(You're My) Soul and Inspiration	The Righteous Brothers	#1
I Am a Rock	Simon & Garfunkel	#3

MALE/MALE DUETS (cont'd)

Ebb Tide	The Righteous Brothers	#5
Homeward Bound	Simon & Garfunkel	#5
Lady Godiva	Peter & Gordon	#6
I'm Your Puppet	James & Bobby Purify	#6
A Hazy Shade of Winter	Simon & Garfunkel	#13
Woman	Peter & Gordon	#14
He	The Righteous Brothers	#18
Michelle	David & Jonathan	#18
Popsicle	Jan & Dean	#21
Hold On! I'm a Comin'	Sam & Dave	#21
The Dangling Conversation	Simon & Garfunkel	#25
Distant Shores	Chad & Jeremy	#30
Go Ahead and Cry	The Righteous Brothers	#30
I Can't Grow Peaches on a Cherry Tree	Just Us	#34
On This Side of Goodbye	The Righteous Brothers	#47
There's No Living Without Your Loving	Peter & Gordon	#50
Georgia on My Mind	The Righteous Brothers	#62
Said I Wasn't Gonna Tell Nobody	Sam & Dave	#64
Take Some Time out for Love	Isley Brothers	#66
Batman	Jan & Dean	#66
You Are She	Chad & Jeremy	#87
You Don't Know Like I Know	Sam & Dave	#90
Fiddle Around	Jan & Dean	#93
Fly Me to the Moon	Sam & Bill	#98
To Show I Love You	Peter & Gordon	#98
1967		
Soul Man	Sam & Dave	#2
Knight in Rusty Armour	Peter & Gordon	#15
At the Zoo	Simon & Garfunkel	#16
Fakin' It	Simon & Garfunkel	#23
Let Love Come Between Us	James & Bobby Purify	#23
Shake a Tail Feather	James & Bobby Purify	#25
Sunday for Tea	Peter & Gordon	#31
Wish You Didn't Have to Go	James & Bobby Purify	#38
Out & About	Tommy Boyce & Bobby Hart	#39
Bowling Green	The Everly Brothers	#40
When Something Is Wrong with My Baby	Sam & Dave	#42
Melancholy Music Man	The Righteous Brothers	#43
Soothe Me	Sam & Dave	#56
Stranded in the Middle of No Place	The Righteous Brothers	#72
You Got Me Hummin'	Sam & Dave	#77
Mercy, Mercy, Mercy	Larry Williams & Johnny Watson	#96
The Jokers	Peter & Gordon	#97

MALE/MALE DUETS (cont'd)

Song	Artist	Hot 100
When the Good Sun Shines	Elmo & Almo	#98
1968		
Mrs. Robinson	Simon & Garfunkel	#1
I Wonder What She's Doing Tonite	Tommy Boyce & Bobby Hart	#8
I Thank You	Sam & Dave	#9
Scarborough Fair/Canticle	Simon & Garfunkel	#11
Alice Long (You're Still My Favorite Girlfriend)	Tommy Boyce & Bobby Hart	#27
You Don't Know What You Mean to Me	Sam & Dave	#48
I Can Remember	James & Bobby Purify	#51
Goodbye Baby (I Don't Want to See You Cry)	Tommy Boyce & Bobby Hart	#53
Can't You Find Another Way (Of Doing It)	Sam & Dave	#54
Everybody Got to Believe in Somebody	Sam & Dave	#73
Help Yourself (To All of My Lovin')	James & Bobby Purify	#94
1969		
In the Year 2525	Zager & Evans	#1
The Boxer	Simon & Garfunkel	#7
Backfield in Motion	Mel & Tim	#10
Lo Mucho Que Te Quiero (The More I Love You)	Rene & Rene	#14
Soul Sister, Brown Sugar	Sam & Dave	#41
If It Wasn't for Bad Luck	Ray Charles & Jimmy Lewis	#77
She's Got Love	Thomas & Richard Frost	#83
Born Again	Sam & Dave	#92

FEMALE/FEMALE DUETS

YEAR	SONG	ARTIST	HOT 100
1964	Have You Ever Been Lonely (Have You Ever Been Blue)	The Caravelles	#94
1966	In the Basement - Part 1	Etta James & Sugar Pie DeSanto	#97
1967	Walk Tall	2 of Clubs	#92

MISCELLANEOUS

SONGS WITH SOUND EFFECTS

SONG	ARTIST	SOUND EFFECT	HOT 100
1960			
Mr. Custer	Larry Verne		#1
Hot Rod Lincoln	Johnny Bond		#26
Hot Rod Lincoln	Charlie Ryan	car horns	#33
Alley-Oop	The Dyna-Sores	jungle noises	#59

SONGS WITH SOUND EFFECTS (cont'd)

Kookie Little Paradise	Jo Ann Campbell	Tarzan and bird noises	#61
Kookie Little Paradise	The Tree Swingers	Tarzan and bird noises	#73
Mister Livingston	Larry Verne		#75
1961			
I'm Gonna Knock on Your Door	Eddie Hodges		#12
(Ghost) Riders in the Sky	Ramrods	cowboy noises	#30
The Blizzard	Jim Reeves	wind	#62
1962			
Monster Mash	Bobby "Boris" Pickett		#1
My Boomerang Won't Come Back	Charlie Drake		#21
Monsters' Holiday	Bobby "Boris" Pickett		#30
Walkin' with My Angel	Bobby Vee	footsteps	#53
Road Hog	John D. Loudermilk	car horn	#65
409	Beach Boys		#76
Beach Party	Dave York	party sounds	#95
Motorcycle	Tico & The Triumphs	motorcycle sounds	#99
1963			
Rhythm of the Rain	The Cascades	thunderstorm sounds	#3
Martian Hop	The Ran-Dells	space noises	#16
Harry the Hairy Ape	Ray Stevens	ape noises	#17
The Last Leaf	The Cascades	wind sounds	#60
Two-Ten, Six-Eighteen (Doesn't Anybody Know My Name)	Jimmie Rodgers	train whistle	#78
The Dog	Rufus Thomas	dog sounds	#87
The Lone Teen Ranger	Jerry Landis		#97
1964			
Remember (Walkin' in the Sand)	The Shangri-Las	beach sounds	#5
Dead Man's Curve	Jan & Dean	car sounds	#8
Walking in the Rain	The Ronettes	rain sounds	#23
Rip Van Winkle	The Devotions		#36
Lumberjack	Brook Benton	sawing wood	#53
Custom Machine	Bruce & Terry	car noises	#85
1965			
Leader of the Laundromat	The Detergents	laundromat and car sounds	#19
Ride Your Pony	Lee Dorsey	gun shot	#28
Inky Dinky Spider (The Spider Song)	The Kids Next Door		#84
I Want My Baby Back	Jimmy Cross	car cash, graveyard noises	#92
El Pussy Cat	Mongo Santamaria	cat noises	#97
1966			
Summer in the City	The Lovin' Spoonful	traffic noises	#1
Snoopy vs. the Red Baron	The Royal Guardsmen		#2
Downtown	Mrs. Miller	birds chirping	#82

SONGS WITH SOUND EFFECTS (cont'd)

1967			
Groovin'	The Young Rascals	bird noises	#1
Daydream Believer	The Monkees	alarm clock	#1
So You Want to Be a Rock 'N' Roll Star	The Byrds	cheering crowd noises	#29
Chattanooga Choo Choo	Harpers Bizarre	train sounds	#45
My World Fell Down	Sagittarius	alarm clock	#70
They're Here	Boots Walker		#77
1968			
The Ballad of Bonnie and Clyde	Georgie Fame	police sirens, gunshots	#7
Summer Rain	Johnny Rivers	rain sounds	#14
Explosion (In My Soul)	Soul Survivors	explosion	#33
The Unknown Soldier	The Doors	soldier noises	#39
Zabadak	Dave Dee, Dozy, Beaky, Mick & Tich	bird sounds	#52
Porpoise Song	The Monkees	porpoise noises	#62
Mrs. Bluebird	Eternity's Children	bird sounds	#69
(Sittin' On) The Dock of the Bay	King Curtis & Kingpins	ocean noises	#84
The Biplane, Ever More	The Irish Rovers	plane noises	#91
Living in the U.S.A.	Steve Miller Band	car noises	#94
Yesterday's Rain	Spanky & Our Gang	thunderstorm noises	#94
Never Get Enough of Your Love	Oscar Toney, Jr.	train noises	#95
1969			
Gitarzan	Ray Stevens	jungle noises	#8
Condition Red	The Goodees	car accident, siren	#46
Maybe the Rain Will Fall	The Cascades	thunderstorm	#61
The Prophecy of Daniel and John the Divine (Six-Six-Six)	The Cowsills	thunderstorm	#75
Theme from Electric Surfboard	Brother Jack McDuff	car crash	#95

ANSWER SONGS

Answer songs are songs that are written and recorded in response to another song.

ANSWER SONG	ARTIST	HOT 100	SONG THAT INSPIRED ANSWER SONG
1960			
He'll Have to Stay	Jeanne Black	#4	Jim Reeves' "He'll Have to Go"
I'll Save the Last Dance for You	Damita Jo	#22	The Drifters' "Save the Last Dance for Me"
(I Can't Help You) I'm Falling Too	Skeeter Davis	#39	Hank Locklin's "Please Help Me I'm Falling"
I Shot Mr. Lee	The Bobbettes	#52	Their previous hit "Mr. Lee"
1961			
Daddy's Home	Shep & The Limelites	#2	The Heartbeats' "A Thousand Miles Away"
I'll Be There	Damita Jo	#12	Ben E. King's "Stand By Me"
Well, I Told You	The Chantels	#29	Ray Charles' "Hit the Road, Jack"

ANSWER SONGS (cont'd)

Yes, I'm Lonesome Tonight	Dodie Stevens	#60	Elvis Presley's "Are You Lonesome Tonight"
I Don't like It like That	The Bobbettes	#72	Chris Kenner's "I Like It Like That"
Son-In-Law	Louise Brown	#76	Ernie K-Doe's "Mother-In-Law"
Son-In-Law	The Blossoms	#79	Ernie K-Doe's "Mother-In-Law"
Don't Let Him Shop Around	Debbie Dean	#92	The Miracles' "Shop Around"
You Don't Have to Be a Tower of Strength	Gloria Lynne	#100	Gene McDaniel's "Tower of Strength"
1962			
Gravy (For My Mashed Potatoes)	Dee Dee Sharp	#9	Sharp's previous hit "Mashed Potato Time"
Johnny Loves Me	Shelley Fabares	#21	Fabares' previous hit "Johnny Angel"
Small Sad Sam	Phil McLean	#21	Jimmy Dean's "Big Bad John"
Monster's Holiday	Bobby "Boris" Pickett and The Crypt Kickers	#30	their previous hit "Monster Mash"
I'm the Girl from Wolverton Mountain	Jo Ann Campbell	#38	Claude King's "Wolverton Mountain"
I'll Bring It Home to You	Carla Thomas	#41	Sam Cooke's "Bring It on Home to Me"
You Threw a Lucky Punch	Gene Chandler	#49	Mary Wells' "You Beat Me to the Punch"
Long as the Rose Is Red	Florraine Darlin	#62	Bobby Vinton's "Roses are Red"
Walk on with the Duke	Gene Chandler	#91	His previous hit "Duke of Earl"
Don't Stop the Wedding	Ann Cole	#99	Etta James' "Stop the Wedding"
1963			
Judy's Turn to Cry	Lesley Gore	#5	Gore's previous hit "It's My Party"
Your Boyfriend's Back	Bobby Comstock	#98	Angels' "My Boyfriends Back"
1964			
Slip-In Mules (No High Heel Sneakers)	Sugar Pie DeSanto	#48	Tommy Tucker's "Hi-Heel Sneakers"
Little Marie	Chuck Berry	#54	Johnny River's hit "Memphis" (Berry also recorded it)
Society Girl	The Rag Dolls	#91	The Four Seasons' "Rag Doll"
Mo-Onions	Booker T. & The MG's	#97	Their previous hit "Green Onions"
1965			
My Girl	The Temptations	#1	Mary Wells' "My Guy"
Queen of the House	Jody Miller	#12	Roger Miller's "King of the Road"
A Change Is Gonna Come	Sam Cooke	#31	Bob Dylan's "Blowin' in the Wind"
Dawn of Correction	The Spokesmen	#36	Barry McGuire's "Eve of Destruction"

SONGS ABOUT DANCES

The 60s Music Compendium

Songs about dances were popular in the early 60s. Quite a few artists had two or three hits about dances. Only one singer had more than three- Chubby Checker made a career out of singing about dances.

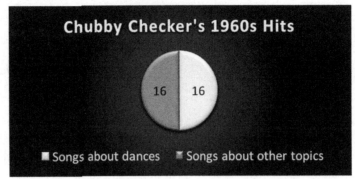

SONG	ARTIST	HOT 100
1960		
Twist	Chubby Checker	#1
The Hucklebuck	Chubby Checker	#14
The Madison	Al Brown	#23
The Madison Time - Part 1	Ray Bryant	#30
1961		
Pony Time	Chubby Checker	#1
Bristol Stomp	The Dovells	#2
The Fly	Chubby Checker	#7
The Hoochi Coochi Coo	Hank Ballard & The Midnighters	#23
Dance the Mess Around	Chubby Checker	#24
The Watusi	The Vibrations	#25
The Fish	Bobby Rydell	#25
The Switch-A-Roo	Hank Ballard & The Midnighters	#26
The Continental Walk	Hank Ballard & The Midnighters	#33
The Majestic	Dion	#36
The Peppermint Twist	Danny Peppermint	#54
Hully Gully Again	Little Caesar and The Romans	#54
Twistin' U.S.A.	Chubby Checker	#68
The Charanga	Merv Griffin	#69
Back to the Hop	Danny & The Juniors	#80
The Mess Around	Bobby Freeman	#89
1962		
Loco-Motion	Little Eva	#1
Monster Mash	Bobby "Boris" Pickett	#1
Twist	Chubby Checker	#1
Peppermint Twist - Part 1	Joey Dee & The Starliters	#1
The Wah Watusi	The Orlons	#2
Mashed Potato Time	Dee Dee Sharp	#2
Limbo Rock	Chubby Checker	#2

SONGS ABOUT DANCES (cont'd)

Slow Twistin'	Chubby Checker w/ Dee Dee Sharp	#3
Twistin' the Night Away	Sam Cooke	#9
Twist, Twist Senora	Gary (U.S.) Bonds	#9
Dear Lady Twist	Gary (U.S.) Bonds	#9
Popeye (The Hitchhiker)	Chubby Checker	#10
Dancin' Party	Chubby Checker	#12
Hey, Let's Twist	Joey Dee & The Starliters	#20
The Push and Kick	Mark Valentino	#27
Pop Pop Pop - Pie	The Sherrys	#35
Do the New Continental	The Dovells	#37
The Alvin Twist	The Chipmunks	#40
Pop-Eye	Huey Smith	#51
Twistin' with Linda	The Isley Brothers	#54
La Paloma Twist	Chubby Checker	#72
Ev'rybody's Twistin'	Frank Sinatra	#75
Oliver Twist	Rod McKuen	#76
Mashed Potatoes (Part 1)	Steve Alaimo	#81
Mashed Potatoes U.S.A.	James Brown	#82
The Jitterbug	The Dovells	#82
Do You Know How to Twist	Hank Ballard	#87
Dancin' the Strand	Maureen Gray	#91
Doin' the Continental Walk	Danny & The Juniors	#93
The (Bossa Nova) Bird	The Dells	#97
Limbo Dance	The Champs	#97
Popeye Joe	Ernie K-Doe	#99
Limbo	The Capris	#99
Quarter to Four Stomp	The Stompers	#100
1963		
Loop de Loop	Johnny Thunder	#4
Baby Workout	Jackie Wilson	#5
The Monkey Time	Major Lance	#8
Do the Bird	Dee Dee Sharp	#10
Let's Turkey Trot	Little Eva	#20
Let's Limbo Some More	Chubby Checker	#20
Twist It Up	Chubby Checker	#25
The Cinnamon Cinder (It's a Very Nice Dance)	The Pastel Six	#25
The Bounce	The Olympics	#40
Some Kinda Fun	Chris Montez	#43
Everybody Monkey	Freddy Cannon	#52
Let's Stomp	Bobby Comstock	#57
The Popeye Waddle	Don Covay	#75
Land of 1000 Dances	Chris Kenner	#77
The Dog	Rufus Thomas	#87

SONGS ABOUT DANCES (cont'd)

Do the Monkey	King Curtis	#92
Slop Time	The Sherrys	#97
Oo-La-La-Limbo	Danny & The Juniors	#99
1964		
C'mon and Swim	Bobby Freeman	#5
Hippy Hippy Shake	Swinging Blue Jeans	#24
Bird Dance Beat	The Trashmen	#30
Can You Do It	The Contours	#41
Harlem Shuffle	Bob & Earl	#44
Can Your Monkey Do the Dog	Rufus Thomas	#48
She Want T' Swim	Chubby Checker	#50
S-W-I-M	Bobby Freeman	#56
Shimmy Shimmy	The Orlons	#66
Can't Get Over (The Bossa Nova)	Eydie Gorme	#87
Big Boss Line	Jackie Wilson	#94
1965		
Keep On Dancing	The Gentrys	#4
Shotgun	Jr. Walker/The All Stars	#4
Shake	Sam Cooke	#7
Papa's Got a Brand New Bag (Part 1)	James Brown	#8
Do the Freddie	Freddie & The Dreamers	#18
Shake and Fingerpop	Jr. Walker/The All Stars	#29
Land of 1000 Dances	Cannibal & The Headhunters	#30
Do the Boomerang	Jr. Walker/The All Stars	#36
Let's Do the Freddie	Chubby Checker	#40
Can You Jerk Like Me	The Contours	#47
Come On Do the Jerk	The Miracles	#50
The 81	Candy & The Kisses	#51
The Barracuda	Alvin Cash & The Crawlers	#59
Land of a Thousand Dances (Part 1)	Thee Midniters	#67
Everybody Do the Sloopy	Johnny Thunder	#67
The Mouse	Soupy Sales	#76
1966		
Land of 1000 Dances	Wilson Pickett	#6
Barefootin'	Robert Parker	#7
Cool Jerk	The Capitols	#7
The Duck	Jackie Lee	#14
Baby, Do the Philly Dog	The Olympics	#63
We Got a Thing That's in the Groove	The Capitols	#65
Alvin's Boo-Ga-Loo	Alvin Cash & The Registers	#74
1967		
Pata Pata	Miriam Makeba	#12
Shake a Tail Feather	James & Bobby Purify	#25

SONGS ABOUT DANCES (cont'd)

Soul Dance Number Three	Wilson Pickett	#55
Karate	The Emperor's	#55
Skate Now	Lou Courtney	#71
Get Down	Harvey Scales	#79
Pearl Time	Andre Williams	#90
1968		
Tighten Up	Archie Bell & The Drells	#1
Nobody but Me	The Human Beinz	#8
Funky Street	Arthur Conley	#14
Hitch It to the Horse	Fantastic Johnny C	#34
Do the Choo Choo	Archie Bell & The Drells	#44
Slow Drag	The Intruders	#54
Keep On Dancing	Alvin Cash	#66
Funky Walk Part I (East)	Dyke & The Blazers	#67
There Was a Time	Gene Chandler	#82
Funky Fever	Clarence Carter	#88
1969		
Papa's Got a Brand New Bag	James Brown	#21
Let's Dance	Ola & The Janglers	#92

SONGS WITH DEATHS

Over 4,000 people died in the songs of the 1960s! They are listed below, arranged from the songs with the most deaths to the songs with the fewest deaths.

YEAR	SONG	ARTIST	HOT 100	NUMBER OF DEATHS
1960	Sink the Bismark	Johnny Horton	#3	app. 3500
1960	Ballad of the Alamo	Bud & Travis	#64	189
1960	Ballad of the Alamo	Marty Robbins	#34	185
1966	Snoopy vs. the Red Baron	The Royal Guardsmen	#2	80
1961	The Touchables	Dickie Goodman	#60	28
1962	Steel Men	Jimmy Dean	#41	18
1961	The Touchables in Brooklyn	Dickie Goodman	#42	3
1968	The Ballad of Bonnie and Clyde	Georgie Fame	#7	3
1960	Running Bear	Johnny Preston	#1	2
1962	P.T. 109	Jimmy Dean	#8	2
1963	Give Us Your Blessing	Ray Peterson	#70	2
1964	Miller's Cave	Bobby Bare	#33	2
1965	Give Us Your Blessing	The Shangri-Las	#29	2
1966	There's Something on Your Mind	Baby Ray	#69	2
1969	Running Bear	Sonny James	#94	2
1960	Mr. Custer	Larry Verne	#1	1

SONGS WITH DEATHS (cont'd)

1960	Teen Angel	Mark Dinning	#1	1
1960	Tell Laura I Love Her	Ray Peterson	#7	1
1960	There's Something on Your Mind (Part 2)	Bobby Marchan	#31	1
1960	Bad Man's Blunder	The Kingston Trio	#37	1
1960	I Shot Mr. Lee	The Bobbettes	#52	1
1960	Clementine	Jan & Dean	#65	1
1960	Delia Gone	Pat Boone	#66	1
1961	Moody River	Pat Boone	#1	1
1961	Big Bad John	Jimmy Dean	#1	1
1961	Frankie and Johnny	Brook Benton	#20	1
1961	Jimmy Martinez	Marty Robbins	#51	1
1961	The Blizzard	Jim Reeves	#62	1
1961	A Scottish Soldier (Green Hills of Tyrol)	Andy Stewart	#69	1
1961	The Comancheros	Claude King	#71	1
1961	Apache	Sonny James	#87	1
1961	A Cross Stands Alone	Jimmy Witter	#89	1
1961	The Battle of Gettysburg	Fred Darian	#100	1
1962	(The Man Who Shot) Liberty Valance	Gene Pitney	#4	1
1962	Old Rivers	Walter Brennan	#5	1
1962	I've Got Bonnie	Bobby Rydell	#18	1
1962	Mary Ann Regrets	Burl Ives	#39	1
1962	The Ballad of Thunder Road	Robert Mitchum	#65	1
1962	I'm Here to Get My Baby Out of Jail	The Everly Brothers	#76	1
1963	Harry the Hairy Ape	Ray Stevens	#17	1
1963	Be Careful of Stones That You Throw	Dion	#31	1
1964	Leader of the Pack	The Shangri-Las	#1	1
1964	Ringo	Lorne Greene	#1	1
1964	Last Kiss	J. Frank Wilson & The Cavaliers	#2	1
1964	In the Summer of His Years	Connie Francis	#46	1
1964	Frankie and Johnny	Greenwood County Singers	#75	1
1965	I Want My Baby Back	Jimmy Cross	#92	1
1966	The Ballad of the Green Berets	SSgt. Barry Sadler	#1	1
1966	The Ballad of Irving	Frank Gallop	#34	1
1966	Billy and Sue	B.J. Thomas	#34	1
1966	A Young Girl	Noel Harrison	#51	1
1966	He Wore the Green Beret	Nancy Ames	#89	1
1967	Ode to Billy Joe	Bobbie Gentry	#1	1
1967	My Elusive Dreams	David Houston & Tammy Wynette	#89	1
1968	Honey	Bobby Goldsboro	#1	1
1968	Delilah	Tom Jones	#15	1
1968	The Son of Hickory Holler's Tramp	O.C. Smith	#40	1
1969	In the Ghetto	Elvis Presley	#3	1
1969	I Started a Joke	The Bee Gees	#6	1

SONGS WITH DEATHS (cont'd)

1969	Color Him Father	The Winstons	#7	1
1969	The Beginning of My End	The Unifics	#36	1
1969	Honey (I Miss You)	O.C. Smith	#44	1
1969	Condition Red	The Goodees	#46	1
1969	The Carroll County Accident	Porter Wagoner	#92	1
1969	Big Bruce	Steve Greenberg	#97	1
1961	Ebony Eyes	The Everly Brothers	#8	? (plane crash)
1962	Shadrack	Brook Benton	#19	Unknown number of soldiers

SONGS WITH FALSE ENDINGS

These are the songs that you think are over… but then they're not. Usually, these songs will just come to a sudden halt, only to continue a couple seconds later, but sometimes they fool you with a fadeout that doesn't totally… fadeout.

SONG	ARTIST	HOT 100
1960		
Let's Go, Let's Go, Let's Go	Hank Ballard & The Midnighters	#6
The Little Drummer Boy	Harry Simeone	#24
Clap Your Hands	The Beau-Marks	#45
This Old Heart	James Brown	#79
1962		
Do You Love Me	The Contours	#3
I Need Your Loving	Don Gardner/Dee Dee Ford	#20
1963		
(I Love You) Don't You Forget It	Perry Como	#39
The Bounce	The Olympics	#40
Shake Sherry	The Contours	#43
All About My Girl	Jimmy McGriff	#50
Red Pepper I	Roosevelt Fountain	#78
Dance, Everybody, Dance	The Dartells	#99
1964		
She's the One	The Chartbusters	#33
The World I Used to Know	Jimmie Rodgers	#51
Please, Please, Please	James Brown	#95
1965		
Keep On Dancing	The Gentrys	#4
The Organ Grinder's Swing	Jimmy Smith w/ Kenny Burrell & Grady Tate	#92
1966		
Good Lovin'	The Young Rascals	#1

SONGS WITH FALSE ENDINGS (cont'd)

Monday, Monday	Mamas & Papas	#1
Listen People	Herman's Hermits	#3
Shapes of Things	The Yardbirds	#11
The Little Girl I Once Knew	The Beach Boys	#20
Come On Let's Go	The McCoys	#22
1967		
Hello Goodbye	The Beatles	#1
Bernadette	Four Tops	#4
I Was Kaiser Bill's Batman	Whistling Jack Smith	#20
The Happening	Herb Alpert & The Tijuana Brass	#32
Girls in Love	Gary Lewis/Playboys	#39
Little Games	The Yardbirds	#51
My World Fell Down	Sagittarius	#70
It Could Be We're in Love	The Cryan' Shames	#85
Shake Hands and Walk Away Cryin'	Lou Christie	#95
1968		
This Guy's in Love with You	Herb Alpert	#1
Face It Girl, It's Over	Nancy Wilson	#29
Sunday Mornin'	Spanky & Our Gang	#30
My Favorite Things	Herb Alpert & The Tijuana Brass	#45
Zabadak	Dave Dee, Dozy, Beaky, Mick & Tich	#52
Down Here on the Ground	Lou Rawls	#69
Reach Out	Merrilee Rush	#79
1969		
Suspicious Minds	Elvis Presley	#1
And When I Die	Blood, Sweat & Tears	#2
First of May	The Bee Gees	#37
Listen to the Band	The Monkees	#63
Something's On her Mind	The Four Seasons	#98

SONGS WITH MISTAKES

I stayed away from including songs where the error is simply someone coughing while they were recording, and other similar mistakes. I find the mistakes listed below far more interesting than those types of errors. What's interesting is almost all of these songs were huge hits. Even Ella Fitzgerald's song, while not a big hit, won a Grammy!

YEAR	SONG	ARTIST	HOT 100	MISTAKE(S)
1960	Baby (You've Got What It Takes)	Dinah Washington & Brook Benton	#5	Towards the end of the song, you can hear Benton sing at the wrong time. Washington tells him, "You're in my spot again, honey." He replies, "I like your spot."
1960	Mack the Knife	Ella Fitzgerald	#27	In this live recording, Fitzgerald completely forgot the lyrics at one point. She ad libbed beautifully, and consequently won a Grammy for the performance.

SONGS WITH MISTAKES (cont'd)

Year	Song	Artist	Hot 100	Notes
1963	Louie Louie	The Kingsmen	#2	This entire recording is a trainwreck: garbled lyrics, singer comes in at wrong time, dropped drum stick, band plays chorus-part at wrong time, obscenity shouted, etc. Apparently, no one suggested that they do a second take.
1966	Barbara Ann	The Beach Boys	#2	After the break, several singers mess up the words to the verses and laugh about it.
1966	I Saw Her Again	Mamas & Papas	#5	Near the end of the song, Denny Doherty sings "I saw her-" a full measure early. He stops, then continues at the correct time with "I saw her again…"
1968	Hey Jude	The Beatles	#1	Just before the three minute mark, one of the Beatles makes a mistake and swears. If you're not listening for it, you'll probably miss it, as it's almost buried beneath all the instruments.
1969	I've Been Loving You Too Long	Ike & Tina Turner	#68	Ike can be heard telling Tina the lyrics in the background.

SONGS RECORDED BY MORE THAN ONE ARTIST THAT DEBUTED IN THE HOT 100 IN THE SAME YEAR

SONG	ARTIST	HOT 100	ARTIST	HOT 100
1960				
The Twist	Chubby Checker	#1	Hank Ballard & The Midnighters	#28
He'll Have to Go (Stay)	Jim Reeves	#2	Jeanne Black	#4
Last Date	Floyd Cramer	#2	Lawrence Welk	#21
You Talk Too Much	Joe Jones	#3	Frankie Ford	#87
Please Help Me, I'm Falling	Hank Locklin	#8	Rusty Draper	#54
Forever	The Little Dippers	#9	Billy Walker	#83
Look for a Star	Garry Miles	#16	Billy Vaughn	#19
	Garry Mills	#26	Deane Hawley	#29
Smokie	Bill Black's Combo	#17	Bill Doggett	#95
Clementine	Bobby Darin	#21	Jan & Dean	#65
Hot Rod Lincoln	Johnny Bond	#26	Charlie Ryan	#33
Ruby	Ray Charles	#28	Adam Wade	#58
Ruby Duby Du	Tobin Mathews	#30	Charles Wolcott	#41
Ballad of the Alamo	Marty Robbins	#34	Bud & Travis	#64
Heartbreak (It's Hurtin' Me)	Little Willie John	#38	Jon Thomas	#48
Tonight's the Night	The Shirelles	#39	The Chiffons	#76
Alabam	Pat Boone	#47	Cowboy Copas	#63
Banjo Boy	Jan & Kjeld	#48	Dorothy Collins	#79
	Art Mooney	#100		
Theme from "The Sundowners"	Billy Vaughn	#51	Felix Slatkin	#70
	Leroy Holmes	#95		

SONGS RECORDED BY MORE THAN ONE ARTIST THAT DEBUTED… (cont'd)

Put Your Arms Around Me Honey	Fats Domino	#58	Ray Smith	#91
Kookie Little Paradise	Jo Ann Campbell	#61	The Tree Swingers	#73
If She Should Come to You (La Montana)	Anthony Newley	#67	Frank DeVol	#77
	Roger Williams	#98		
Do You Mind?	Andy Williams	#70	Anthony Newley	#91
Shortnin' Bread	Paul Chaplain	#82	David Carroll	#96
Midnight Lace	Ray Ellis	#84	Ray Conniff	#92
1961				
Calcutta	Lawrence Welk	#1	The Four Preps	#96
Wonderland by Night	Bert Kaempfert	#1	Louis Prima	#15
	Anita Bryant	#18		
Pony Time	Chubby Checker	#1	The Goodtimers	#60
	The Bell Notes	#96		
Exodus	Ferrante & Teicher	#2	Mantovani and His Orchestra	#31
	Eddie Harris	#36	Pat Boone	#64
Apache	Jorgen Ingmann	#2	Sonny James	#87
Wheels	The String-A-Longs	#3	Billy Vaughn	#28
Sad Movies (Make Me Cry)	Sue Thompson	#5	The Lennon Sisters	#56
Every Beat of My Heart	The Pips	#6	Gladys Knight & The Pips	#45
Tonight	Ferrante & Teicher	#8	Eddie Fisher	#44
Gee Whiz (Look at His Eyes)	Carla Thomas	#10	The Innocents	#28
Moon River	Jerry Butler	#11	Henry Mancini	#11
You're the Reason	Bobby Edwards	#11	Joe South	#87
I'm a Fool to Care	Joe Barry	#24	Oscar Black	#94
My Last Date (With You)	Skeeter Davis	#26	Joni James	#38
Wayward Wind	Tex Ritter	#28	Gogi Grant	#50
(Ghost) Riders in the Sky	The Ramrods	#30	Lawrence Welk	#87
The Continental Walk	Hank Ballard & The Midnighters	#33	The Rollers	#80
Yes, I'm Lonesome Tonight	Thelma Carpenter	#55	Dodie Stevens	#60
Theme from "Tunes of Glory"	Cambridge Strings & Singers	#60	Mitch Miller	#88
Milord	Teresa Brewer	#74	Edith Piaf	#88
Black Land Farmer	Frankie Miller	#82	Wink Martindale	#85
1962				
Stranger on the Shore	Mr. Acker Bilk	#1	Andy Williams	#38
	The Drifters	#73		
Limbo Rock	Chubby Checker	#2	The Champs	#40
Alley Cat	Bent Fabric	#7	David Thorne	#76
Little Bitty Tear	Burl Ives	#9	Wanda Jackson	#84
Desafinado	Stan Getz/Charlie Byrd	#15	Pat Thomas	#78
What Kind of Fool am I	Sammy Davis, Jr.	#17	Anthony Newley	#85
	Robert Goulet	#89		
Walk on the Wild Side	Jimmy Smith	#21	Brook Benton	#43

SONGS RECORDED BY MORE THAN ONE ARTIST THAT DEBUTED… (cont'd)

Mama Sang a Song	Stan Kenton	#32	Walter Brennan	#38
	Bill Anderson	#89		
Ben Crazy/Dr. Ben Basey	Dickie Goodman	#44	Mickey Shorr & the Cutups	#60
Baby Elephant Walk	Lawrence Welk	#48	Miniature Men	#87
Taste of Honey	Martin Denny	#50	Victor Feldman Quartet	#88
Lollipops and Roses	Paul Petersen	#54	Jack Jones	#66
This Land Is Your Land	The New Christy Minstrels	#93	Ketty Lester	#97
1963				
Walk Right In	The Rooftop Singers	#1	The Moments	#82
Still	Bill Anderson	#8	Ben Colder	#98
More	Kai Winding	#8	Vic Dana	#42
My Coloring Book	Kitty Kallen	#18	Sandy Stewart	#20
Days of Wine and Roses	Andy Williams	#26	Henry Mancini	#33
If You Need Me	Solomon Burke	#37	Wilson Pickett	#64
How Can I Forget	Jimmy Holiday	#57	Ben E. King	#85
Heart	Kenny Chandler	#64	Wayne Newton	#82
Meditation (Meditacao)	Charlie Byrd	#66	Pat Boone	#91
This Is All I Ask	Burl Ives	#67	Tony Bennett	#70
Call Me Irresponsible	Jack Jones	#75	Frank Sinatra	#78
Say Wonderful Things	Patti Page	#81	Ronnie Carroll	#91
Toys in the Attic	Joe Sherman	#85	Jack Jones	#92
Faded Love	Patsy Cline	#96	Jackie DeShannon	#97
1964				
Come See About Me	The Supremes	#1	Nella Dodds	#74
Kansas City	Wilbert Harrison	#1	Trini Lopez	#23
Do Wah Diddy Diddy	Manfred Mann	#1	The Exciters	#78
World Without Love	Peter & Gordon	#1	Bobby Rydell	#80
I Want to Hold Your Hand	The Beatles	#1	Boston Pops Orchestra	#55
She Loves You	The Beatles	#1	Die Beatles (Sie Liebt Dich)	#97
People	Barbra Streisand	#5	Nat "King" Cole	#100
Little Honda	The Hondells	#9	The Beach Boys	#65
Hi-Heel Sneakers	Tommy Tucker	#11	Jerry Lee Lewis	#91
I'm Into Something Good	Herman's Hermits	#13	Earl-Jean	#38
Yesterday's Gone	Chad & Jeremy	#21	The Overlanders	#75
Be Anything (But Be Mine)	Connie Francis	#25	Gloria Lynne	#88
It's All Over Now	The Rolling Stones	#26	The Valentinos	#94
When You Walk in the Room	The Searchers	#35	Jackie DeShannon	#99
Charade	Samy Kaye	#36	Henry Mancini	#36
	Andy Williams	#100		
Gonna Send You Back to Georgia	Timmy Shaw	#41	The Animals	#57
All My Loving	Beatles	#45	Hollyridge Strings	#93
You're No Good	Betty Everett	#51	Swinging Blue Jeans	#97

SONGS RECORDED BY MORE THAN ONE ARTIST THAT DEBUTED... (cont'd)

Something You Got	Alvin Robinson	#52	Ramsey Lewis Trio	#63
Little Boxes	Pete Seeger	#70	Womenfolk	#83
A House Is Not a Home	Dionne Warwick	#71	Brook Benton	#75
All My Loving	Hollyridge Strings	#93	Beatles	#45

1965

Downtown	Petula Clark	#1	Allan Sherman (Crazy Downtown)	#40
"In" Crowd	Ramsey Lewis	#5	Dobie Gray	#13
Goldfinger	Shirley Bassey	#8	Billy Strange	#55
	John Barry	#72	Jack LaForge	#96
Red Roses for a Blue Lady	Vic Dana	#10	Bert Kaempfert	#11
	Wayne Newton	#23		
Race Is On	Jack Jones	#15	George Jones	#96
All I Really Want to Do	Cher	#15	The Byrds	#40
Dear Heart	Andy Williams	#24	Jack Jones	#30
	Henry Mancini	#77		
Home of the Brave	Jody Miller	#25	Bonnie & The Treasures	#77
Concrete and Clay	Unit Four Plus Two	#28	Eddie Rambeau	#35
Three O'Clock in the Morning	Bert Kaempfert	#33	Lou Rawls	#83
Universal Soldier	Glen Campbell	#45	Donovan	#53
For Mama	Connie Francis	#48	Jerry Vale	#54
Try to Remember	Ed Ames	#73	The Brothers Four	#91
	Roger Williams	#97		
Blind Man	Bobby Bland	#78	Little Milton	#86
Forget Domani	Frank Sinatra	#78	Connie Francis	#79

1966

Winchester Cathedral	New Vaudeville Band	#1	Dana Rollin	#71
When a Man (Woman) Loves a Woman (Man)	Percy Sledge	#1	Esther Phillips	#73
Uptight (Everything's Alright)	Stevie Wonder	#3	Ramsey Lewis	#49
	Nancy Wilson	#84	The Jazz Crusaders	#95
Secret Agent Man	Johnny Rivers	#3	The Ventures	#54
Somewhere, My Love	Ray Conniff	#9	Roger Williams (Lara's Theme)	#65
What Now My Love	Sonny & Cher	#14	Herb Alpert	#24
	"Groove" Holmes	#96		
Batman Theme	The Marketts	#17	Neal Hefti	#35
Michelle	David & Jonathan	#18	Bud Shank	#65
	Billy Vaughn	#77		
Mame	Herb Alpert	#19	Bobby Darin	#53
	Louis Armstrong	#81		
Almost Persuaded (No. 2)	David Houston	#24	Ben Colder (Sheb Wooley)	#58
Wheel of Hurt	Margaret Whiting	#26	Al Martino	#59
It was a Very Good Year	Frank Sinatra	#28	Della Reese	#99

SONGS RECORDED BY MORE THAN ONE ARTIST THAT DEBUTED... (cont'd)

Secret Love	Billy Stewart	#29	Richard "Groove" Holmes	#99
Help Me Girl	The Animals	#29	The Outsiders	#37
I Can Make It with You	Pozo-Seco Singers	#32	Jackie DeShannon	#68
Alfie	Cher	#32	Cilla Black	#95
History Repeats Itself	Buddy Starcher	#39	Cab Calloway	#89
Million and One	Dean Martin	#41	Vic Dana	#71
Younger Girl	The Critters	#42	The Hondells	#52
Games That Lovers Play	Eddie Fisher	#45	Wayne Newton	#86
Almost Persuaded (No. 2)	Ben Colder (Sheb Wooley)	#58	David Houston	#24
Philly Dog	The Mar-Keys	#89	Herbie Mann	#93
So Much Love	Steve Alaimo	#92	Ben E. King	#96
Dommage, Dommage (Too Bad, Too Bad)	Jerry Vale	#93	Paul Vance	#97
Alfie	Cilla Black	#95	Cher	#32

1967

The Happening	The Supremes	#1	Herb Alpert	#32
Groovin'	The Young Rascals	#1	Booker T. & The MG's	#21
Windy	The Association	#1	Wes Montgomery	#44
To Sir with Love	Lulu	#1	Herbie Mann	#93
Ode to Billie Joe	Bobbie Gentry	#1	The Kingpins	#28
	Ray Bryant	#89		
Georgy Girl	The Seekers	#2	The Baja Marimba Band	#98
Sweet Soul Music	Arthur Conley	#2	Magnificent Men (medley)	#90
Soul Man	Sam & Dave	#2	Ramsey Lewis	#49
Mercy, Mercy, Mercy	The Buckinghams	#5	"Cannonball" Adderley	#11
	Marlena Shaw	#58	Larry Williams & Johnny Watson	#96
Up-Up and Away	The 5th Dimension	#7	The Johnny Mann Singers	#91
For What It's Worth	Buffalo Springfield	#7	The Staple Singers	#66
	King Curtis	#87		
Funky Broadway	Wilson Pickett	#8	Dyke & The Blazers	#65
Darling Be Home Soon	Lovin' Spoonful	#15	Bobby Darin	#93
There Goes My Everything	Engelbert Humperdinck	#20	Jack Greene	#65
Tramp	Otis Redding & Carla Thomas	#26	Lowell Fusion	#52
Hello Hello	Sopwith "Camel"	#26	Claudine Longet	#91
Music to Watch Girls By	Bob Crewe Generation	#34	Andy Williams	#34
Beautiful People	Bobby Vee	#37	Kenny O'Dell	#38
Little Old Wine Drinker, Me	Dean Martin	#38	Robert Mitchum	#96
Happy	The Sunshine Company	#50	Blades of Grass	#87
Why (Am I Treated So Bad)	The Sweet Inspirations	#57	"Cannonball" Adderley	#73
	Bobby Powell	#91	The Staple Singers	#95
Laura, What's He Got That I Ain't Got	Frankie Laine	#66	Brook Benton	#78

1968

Harper Valley P.T.A.	Jeannie C. Riley	#1	Ben Colder (Sheb Wooley)	#67

SONGS RECORDED BY MORE THAN ONE ARTIST THAT DEBUTED... (cont'd)

	King Curtis	#93		
(Sittin' On) The Dock of the Bay	Otis Redding	#1	King Curtis	#84
Love Is Blue	Paul Mauriat	#1	Al Martino	#57
	Claudine Longet	#71	Manny Kellem	#96
Theme from "Valley of the Dolls"	Dionne Warwick	#2	King Curtis	#83
Little Green Apples	O.C. Smith	#2	Roger Miller	#39
	Patti Page	#96		
I Wish It Would Rain	The Temptations	#4	Gladys Knight & The Pips	#41
(Sweet Sweet Baby) Since You've Been Gone	Aretha Franklin	#5	Ramsey Lewis	#98
Scarborough Fair	Simon & Garfunkel	#11	Sergio Mendes	#16
Dreams of the Everyday Housewife	Glen Campbell	#32	Wayne Newton	#60
There was a Time	James Brown	#36	Gene Chandler	#82
Hard to Handle	Otis Redding	#51	Patti Drew	#93
The Weight	Jackie DeShannon	#55	The Band	#63
Isn't It Lonely Together	O.C. Smith	#63	Robert Knight	#97
Mr. Bojangles	Jerry Jeff Walker	#77	Bobby Cole	#79
Do What You Gotta Do	Nina Simone	#83	Bobby Vee	#83
1969				
Love Theme from Romeo & Juliet	Henry Mancini	#1	Johnny Mathis	#96
Proud Mary	Creedence Clearwater Revival	#2	Solomon Burke	#45
	The Checkmates, Ltd. feat. Sonny Charles	#69		
Wichita Lineman	Glen Campbell	#3	Sergio Mendes	#95
These Eyes	Guess Who?	#6	Jr. Walker	#16
Cloud Nine	The Temptations	#6	Mongo Santamaria	#32
Happy Heart	Andy Williams	#22	Petula Clark	#62
Lodi	Creedence Clearwater Revival	#52	Al Wilson	#67
Sausalito	The Ohio Express	#86	Al Martino	#99

SONGS THAT BORROW FROM OTHER CREATIVE WORKS

This section lists songs that sampled or borrowed lyrics or a melody from another work of art. Usually, the work of art was another song, but a few songs borrowed lyrics from a poem or some other source. Songs that borrow from classical pieces of music, like those of Mozart and Beethoven, are listed in the section following this one.

SONG	ARTIST	HOT 100	SOURCE OF BORROWED LYRICS/MELODY
1960			
The Twist	Chubby Checker	#1	Clyde McPhatter & The Drifters' "What'cha Gonna Do"
Cradle of Love	Johnny Preston	#7	Uses lyrics from nursery rhymes
Eternally	Sarah Vaughan	#8	Charlie Chaplin's "Terry's Theme"
Beatnik Fly	Johnny & The Hurricanes	#15	Children's song "Jimmy Crack Corn"
Rockin' Little Angel	Ray Smith	#22	"Buffalo Girls"
Ol' Mac Donald	Frank Sinatra	#25	Children's song "Old MacDonald"
Bonnie Came Back	Duane Eddy	#26	Cover of "My Bonnie Lies Over the Ocean"
Shimmy Like Kate	The Olympics	#42	"I Wish I Could Shimmy Like My Sister Kate"
Dance By the Light of the Moon	The Olympics	#47	"Buffalo Girls" and "Dance with a Dolly"
Big Boy Pete	The Olympics	#50	The Kingsmen's "The Jolly Green Giant"
Christmas Auld Lang Syne	Bobby Darin	#51	Vocal melody is "Auld Lang Syne", flute plays snippet of "Deck the Halls" at end
Johnny Freedom	Johnny Horton	#69	American patriotic song "America"
The Christmas Song (Merry Christmas to You)	Nat "King" Cole	#80	"Jingle Bells"
Shortnin' Bread	Paul Chaplain and his Emeralds	#82	American folk song of same name
Night Train	The Viscounts	#82	Duke Ellington's "Happy-Go-Lucky Local"
Shoppin' for Clothes	The Coasters	#83	Cover of "Clothes Line (Wrap It Up)" by Boogaloo and His Gallant Crew
My Little Marine	Jamie Horton	#84	American song "Marine's Hymn"
Someone Love You, Joe	The Singing Belles	#91	Spiritual "Kumbaya"
Teenage Hayride	Tender Slim	#93	Children's song "Three Blind Mice" & "Pop Goes the Weasel"
A Closer Walk	Pete Fountain	#93	Hymn "Just A Closer Walk with Thee"
Words	Pat Boone	#94	"Silver Threads Among the Gold"
Shortnin' Bread	The Bell Notes	#96	American folk song of same name
Revival	Johnny & The Hurricanes	#97	"When the Saints Go Marching In"
1961			
Wooden Heart	Joe Dowell	#1	German folk song "Muss I Denn"
Pony Time	Chubby Checker	#1	The Midnighters' "Sexy Ways"
Quarter to Three	Gary (U.S.) Bonds	#1	The Church Street Five's "A Night with Daddy G"
Yellow Bird	Arthur Lyman Group	#4	Haitian song "Choucoune"
I Understand (Just How You Feel)	The G-Clefs	#9	"Auld Lang Syne"

SONGS THAT BORROW FROM OTHER CREATIVE WORKS (cont'd)

I'll Be There	Damito Jo	#12	Same music as "Stand By Me", different lyrics
Peanut Butter	The Vibrations/The Marathons	#20	The Olympics' "(Baby) Hully Gully"
The Watusi	The Vibrations	#25	Hank Ballard & The Midnighters' "Let's Go, Let's Go, Let's Go"
Frogg	The Brothers Four	#32	Old children's song "Frog Went A Courtin'"
Juke Box Saturday Night	Nino and The Ebb Tides	#57	Uses excerpts of various hit songs
Theme from "Tunes of Glory"	The Cambridge Strings	#60	"Scotland the Brave"
Trees	The Platters	#62	Words from Joyce Kilmer's poem "Trees"
Danny Boy	Andy Williams	#64	Irish song "Londonderry Air"
Yellow Bird	Lawrence Welk and His Orchestra	#71	Haitian song "Choucoune"
Come Along	Maurice Williams and The Zodiacs	#83	Very similar to "Stay"
Tunes of Glory	Mitch Miller	#88	"Scotland the Brave"
Dedicated (To the Songs I Love)	The 3 Friends	#89	Samples many lyrics and some melodies from earlier hits
A Cross Stands Alone	Jimmy Witter	#89	"Taps"
Why Not Now	Matt Monro	#92	"Ay, Ay, Ay"
Dear Mr. D.J. Play It Again	Tina Robin	#95	Samples "Goodnight Sweetheart" & "Earth Angel"
1962			
Can't Help Falling in Love	Elvis Presley	#2	French song "Plasir d'Amour"
Percolator (Twist)	Billy Joe & The Checkmates	#10	Maxwell House Coffee commercial
My Own True Love	The Duprees	#13	"Tara's Theme" (from movie "Gone with the Wind")
Love Me Tender	Richard Chamberlain	#21	"Aura Lee"
Dear Ivan	Jimmy Dean	#24	"The Battle Hymn of the Republic"
To a Sleeping Beauty	Jimmy Dean	#26	"Memories"
Monsters' Holiday	Bobby "Boris" Pickett	#30	"Jingle Bells"
Mary's Little Lamb	James Darren	#39	"Mary Had a Little Lamb"
Flying Circle	Frank Slay	#45	Israeli folk song "Hava Nagila"
The Burning of Atlanta	Claude King	#53	Confederate song "Dixie"
The Big Draft	The Four Preps	#61	"Heartache", "Anchors Aweigh", "Michael, Row Your Boat Ashore", "Runaround Sue",
Road Hog	John D. Loudermilk	#65	The Browns' "Ground Hog"
My Daddy Is President	Little Jo Ann	#67	"Hail to the Chief" and "Twinkle Twinkle Little Star"
Twistin' All Night Long	Danny & The Juniors w/Freddy Cannon	#68	Includes snippets of several other singers/songs
Do You Know How to Twist	Hank Ballard and the Midnighters	#87	Ballard's earlier hit ""Let's Go, Let's Go, Let's Go"
Walk on with the Duke	The Duke of Earl (Gene Chandler)	#91	"Duke of Earl"
Magic Wand	Don & Juan	#91	Melody similar to "Dedicated to the One I Love"
Duchess of Earl	Pearlettes	#96	"Duke of Earl"
The John Birch Society	Chad Mitchell Trio	#99	"America the Beautiful"
1963			
Fingertips - Pt. 2	Little Stevie Wonder	#1	"Mary Had a Little Lamb"

SONGS THAT BORROW FROM OTHER CREATIVE WORKS (cont'd)

If You Wanna Be Happy	Jimmy Soul	#1	"Ugly Woman"
I Will Follow Him	Little Peggy March	#1	French song "Chariot"
Surfin' U.S.A.	The Beach Boys	#3	Chuck Berry's "Sweet Little Sixteen"
Loop de Loop	Johnny Thunder	#4	Children's song "Looby Loo"
Mockingbird	Inez Foxx w/Charlie Foxx	#7	Children's song "Hush Little Baby"
Reverend Mr. Black	Kingston Trio	#8	American folk song "Lonesome Valley"
Loddy Lo	Chubby Checker	#12	Bahamian folk song "Hey Li-Lee, Hey Li-Lee Lo"
Let's Turkey Trot	Little Eva	#20	The Cleftones' "Little Girl of Mine"
My Boyfriend's Coming Home for Christmas	Toni Wine	#22	"The First Noel"
My Whole World Is Falling Down	Brenda Lee	#24	Children's song "London Bridge Is Falling Down"
Stewball	Peter, Paul & Mary	#35	"Skewbald"
Drownin' My Sorrows	Connie Francis	#36	"Red River Valley"
Old Smokey Locomotion	Little Eva	#48	"On Top of Old Smokey"
Baby I Do Love You	The Galens	#70	German folk song "Du Du Liegst Mir Im Herzen"
We Shall Overcome	Joan Baez	#90	Hymn "I'll Overcome Some Day"
Remember Baby	Shep & The Limelites	#91	"Auld Lang Syne"
Now!	Lena Horne	#92	Israeli folk song "Hava Nagila"
Why Do Kids Grow Up	Randy & The Rainbows	#97	Borrows heavily from their earlier hit "Denise"
1964			
Hello, Dolly!	Louis Armstrong	#1	"Sunflower" (state song of Kansas)
Fun, Fun, Fun	The Beach Boys	#5	Opening guitar riff from Chuck Berry's "Johnny B. Goode"
Sidewalk Surfin'	Jan & Dean	#25	The Beach Boys' "Catch a Wave"
Understand Your Man	Johnny Cash	#35	"Don't Think Twice, It's All Right"
We Love You Beatles	The Carefrees	#39	"We Love You Conrad" from musical "Bye, Bye, Birdie"
He's a Good Guy (Yes He Is)	The Marvelettes	#55	Viennese song "Oh du lieber Augustin"
Ain't That Just Like Me	The Searchers	#61	Uses lyrics from several children's songs and nursery rhymes
Hickory, Dick and Doc	Bobby Vee	#63	Children's song "Three Blind Mice"
Winkin', Blinkin' and Nod	Carly Simon	#73	Children's poem by Eugene Field
Frankie and Johnny	The Greenwood County Singers	#75	American folk song
The Anaheim, Azusa & Cucamonga Sewing Circle, Book Review and Timing Association	Jan & Dean	#77	Contains "Go, grannies…" lyric from earlier hit "Little Old Lady from Pasadena"
A Letter to the Beatles	The Four Preps	#85	The Beatles' "I Want to Hold Your Hand"
I've Got the Skill	Jackie Ross	#89	"The Streets of Cairo"
That's Really Some Good	Rufus & Carla	#92	"Yankee Doodle"
Oh, Rock My Soul (Part I)	Peter, Paul & Mary	#93	Spiritual "Bosom of Abraham"
Little Donna	The Rivieras	#93	Chuck Berry's "Rock and Roll Music"
Jailer, Bring Me Water	Trini Lopez	#94	"Go Tell Aunt Rhoda"
1965			
The Clapping Song (Clap Pat Clap Slap)	Shirley Ellis	#8	1930s hit "Little Rubber Dolly"

SONGS THAT BORROW FROM OTHER CREATIVE WORKS (cont'd)

Song	Artist	Chart	Borrowed From
Leader of the Laundromat	The Detergents	#19	Parody of "Leader of the Pack"
My Mom and Santa Claus	George Jones	#23	"I Saw Mommy Kissing Santa Claus"
May You Always	Harry Harrison	#26	"Auld Lang Syne"
I Understand (Just How You Feel)	Freddie & The Dreamers	#36	Countermelody is "Auld Lange Syne"
Crazy Downtown	Allan Sherman	#40	Parody of Petula Clark's "Downtown"
Annie Fanny	The Kingsmen	#47	The Hollywood Argyle's "Alley Oop" (example of rip-off)
(Here They Come) From All Over the World	Jan & Dean	#56	Beach Boys' "I Get Around"
Everybody Do the Sloopy	Johnny Thunder	#67	Children's song "Looby Loo"
Danny Boy	Patti LaBelle	#76	Irish song "Londonberry Air"
The Puzzle Song (A Puzzle in Song)	Shirley Ellis	#78	Tongue twister "Peter Piper"
Hello, Dolly!	Bobby Darin	#79	"Sunflower"
Lip Sync (To the Tongue Twisters)	Len Barry	#84	Several famous tongue twisters
The Organ Grinder's Swing	Jimmy Smith w/ Kenny Burrell & Grady Tate	#92	Children's song "Great Big House in New Orleans"
She's with Her Other Love	Leon Hayward (Leon Haywood)	#92	The Supremes' "Baby Baby"
Danny Boy	Jackie Wilson	#94	Irish song "Londonberry Air"
Yakety Axe	Chet Atkins	#98	Melodies from several fiddle tunes and Boots Randolph's "Yakety Sax"
1966			
Paperback Writer	The Beatles	#1	Background vocals sing 1st phrase of French nursery rhyme "Frere Jacques"
No Matter What Shape (Your Stomach's In)	The T-Bones	#3	Alka Seltzer commercial
Sloop John B.	The Beach Boys	#3	West Indies folk song "The Wreck of the John B. Sails"
Guantanamera	The Sandpipers	#9	Poem by Cuban Jose Marti
I Need Somebody	? & The Mysterians	#22	"Mary Had a Little Lamb"
Thunderball	Tom Jones	#25	Original James Bond theme
Somewhere	Len Barry	#26	"Maria" from Musical "West Side Story"
It's Only Love	Tommy James and The Shondells	#31	Children's song "This Old Man"
Day for Decision	Johnny Sea	#35	"America the Beautiful"
History Repeats Itself	Buddy Starcher	#39	"Battle Hymn of the Republic"
Sippin' 'N Chippin'	The T-Bones	#62	"Hail, Hail, the Gang's All Here" & Nabisco commercial
Batman	Jan & Dean	#66	Includes some text from Batman comic books
History Repeats Itself	Cab Calloway	#89	"Battle Hymn of the Republic"
I'll Be Home	The Platters	#97	"Taps"
Hand Jive	The Strangeloves	#100	Same melody as their previous hit "I Want Candy"
1967			
All You Need Is Love	The Beatles	#1	Intro is from the French National Anthem, part of "She Loves You" is sung at end
An Open Letter to My Teenage Son	Victor Lundberg	#10	American patriotic song "America"
Let It Out (Let It All Hang Out)	The Hombres	#12	"Cigareetes, Whuskey, and Wild, Wild Women"
Stand By Me	Spyder Turner	#12	Includes parts of several hits by other artists

SONGS THAT BORROW FROM OTHER CREATIVE WORKS (cont'd)

Happy Birthday, Jesus (A Child's Prayer)	Patti Page	#15	"Silent Night"
Stag-O-Lee	Wilson Pickett	#22	"Stack-O-Lee"
Love Me Tender	Percy Sledge	#40	"Aura Lee"
I Am the Walrus	The Beatles	#56	Shakespeare's "King Lear" read in background
Danny Boy	Ray Price	#60	Irish song "Londonderry Air"
Hooray for the Salvation Army Band	Bill Cosby	#71	Gospel song "Bringing in the Sheaves"
A Letter to Dad	Every Father's Teenage Son	#93	American patriotic song "America"
1968			
Ballad of Two Brothers	Autry Inman	#48	"Battle Hymn of the Republic"
Here Come the Judge	The Magistrates	#54	"Ding-Dong! The Witch is Dead" from musical "The Wizard of Oz"
Stay Away	Elvis Presley	#67	"Greensleeves"
The Ol' Race Track	The Mills Brothers	#83	U.S. Army bugle call "First Call"
Forget Me Not	Martha & The Vandellas	#93	Confederate song "Dixie"
Battle of New Orleans	Harpers Bizarre	#95	Confederate song "Dixie"
1969			
Spinning Wheel	Blood, Sweat & Tears	#2	Austrian song "O Du Lieber Augustin" ("Did You Ever See a Lassie")
Touch Me	The Doors	#3	Used "Stronger than dirt" line from Ajax commercial
Good Old Rock 'N Roll	Cat Mother & The All Night News Boys	#21	Includes parts of many classic hits
A Ray of Hope	The Rascals	#24	"Battle Hymn of the Republic"
Rain	Jose Feliciano	#76	Children's song "It's Raining, It's Pouring"
Sunday Mornin' Comin' Down	Ray Stevens	#81	Gospel song "Bringing in the Sheaves"

SONGS THAT BORROW FROM CLASSICAL WORKS

Several songwriters of the 60s turned to classical music for help. And why not? If you need assistance when writing a new song, who better to turn to then the greatest composers of all time?

Somewhat surprisingly, the composer whose melodies were used the most often was not Mozart, Beethoven, or J.S. Bach- the three composers generally agreed to be the top three composers in history- it was the Russian composer Tchaikovsky. His works were used in six 60s songs. One note about the German composer Christian Petzold: It is now believed that he, not J.S. Bach, composed the "Minuet in G Major".

A song will be listed below even if it only used a short snippet of a classical work. For example, "Cindy's Birthday", from 1962, uses a very short excerpt from the "William Tell Overture". If you're not paying close attention, you might miss it. Some songs, however, used a melody from a classical work for nearly the entire song. The best example of this might be "A Lover's Concerto", by The Toys. Almost the entire melody is taken from Petzold's "Minuet in G Major".

SONG	ARTIST	HOT 100	SOURCE OF BORROWED MELODY
1960			
It's Now or Never	Elvis Presley	#1	Italian song "O Sole Mio"
Night	Jackie Wilson	#4	Saint-Saëns' aria "My Heart at Thy Sweet Voice"
Alone at Last	Jackie Wilson	#8	Tchaikovsky's "Piano Concerto in B Flat"

SONGS THAT BORROW FROM CLASSICAL WORKS (cont'd)

The Way of a Clown	Teddy Randazzo	#44	Leoncavallo's "Vesti La Giubba" (aria from 1892 opera, "Pagliacci")
Anyway the Wind Blows	Doris Day	#50	Fučík's "Entrance of the Gladiators"
Put Your Arms Around Me	Fats Domino	#58	Mendelssohn's "Wedding March"
1961			
Surrender	Elvis Presley	#1	Italian song "Torna a Surriento"
Asia Minor	Kokomo	#8	Grieg's "Piano Concerto in A Minor"
My Empty Arms	Jackie Wilson	#9	"Vesti la Giubba", from Leoncavallo's opera "I Pagliacci"
Tonight My Love, Tonight	Paul Anka	#13	Verdi's "Rigoletto"
Bumble Boogie	B. Bumble & The Stingers	#21	Rimsky-Korsakov's "Flight of the Bumblebee"
The Graduation Song… Pomp and Circumstance	Adriam Kimberly	#34	Elgar's "Pomp and Circumstance"
Like, Long Hair	Paul Revere & The Raiders	#38	Rachmaninoff's "Prelude in C-Sharp Minor"
Magic Moon (Clair de Lune)	The Rays	#49	Debussy's "Suite Bergamesque"
My Claire de Lune	Steve Lawrence	#68	Debussy's "Suite Bergamesque"
Dream Boy	Annette	#87	Denza's "Funiculì, Funiculà"
In Time	Steve Lawrence	#94	Tchaikovsky's "Pathetique Symphony"
Make Believe Wedding	The Castells	#98	"Bridal Chorus" from Wagner's opera "Lohengrin"
1962			
Cindy's Birthday	Johnny Crawford	#8	Rossini's "William Tell Overture"
Nut Rocker	B. Bumble & The Stingers	#23	Tchaikovsky's "March of the Toy Soldiers" from "The Nutcracker"
Santa Claus Is Watching You	Ray Stevens	#45	Rossini's "William Tell Overture"
1963			
Hello Mudduh, Hello Fadduh! (A Letter from Camp)	Allan Sherman	#2	Ponchielli's "Dance of the Hours"
Dum Dum Dee Dum	Johnny Cymbal	#77	"Bridal Chorus" from Wagner's opera "Lohengrin"
Dancin' Holiday	The Olympics	#86	Liszt's "Hungarian Rhapsody No. 2"
The Lone Teen Ranger	Jerry Landis	#97	Rossini's "William Tell Overture"
1964			
Somewhere	The Tymes	#19	Mozart's "Piano Sonata No. 15 in C Major"
Hello Mudduh, Hello Fadduh! (A Letter from Camp) (New 1964 version)	Allan Sherman	#59	Ponchielli's "Dance of the Hours"
Til the End of Time	Ray Charles Singers	#83	Chopin's "Polonaise"
1965			
A Lover's Concerto	The Toys	#2	Petzold's "Minuet in G Major"
Hawaii Honeymoon	The Waikikis	#91	"Bridal Chorus" from Wagner's opera "Lohengrin"
The Silence (Il Silenzio)	Al Hirt	#96	Tchaikovsky's "Capriccio Italien"
1966			
Summertime	Billy Stewart	#10	Gershwin's opera "Porgy and Bess"
Rhapsody in the Rain	Lou Christie	#16	Tchaikovsky's "Romeo and Juliet"
Attack	The Toys	#18	"March" from Tchaikovsky's "Nutcracker"
Can I Trust You?	The Bachelors	#49	Italian song "Lo Ti Darò Di Più" by Orietta Berti and Ornella Vanoni
Lullaby of Love	The Poppies	#56	Brahms' "Lullaby"

SONGS THAT BORROW FROM CLASSICAL WORKS (cont'd)

Past, Present and Future	The Shangri-Las	#59	Beethoven's "Moonlight Sonata"
In My Room (El Amore)	Verdelle Smith	#62	Bach's "Toccata in D Minor"
A Lover's Concerto	Sarah Vaughan	#63	Petzold's "Minuet in G Major"
Cry Softly	Nancy Ames	#95	Liszt's "Liebestraum No. 3"
A Lover's Concerto	Mrs. Miller	#95	Petzold's "Minuet in G Major" (previously attributed to J.S. Bach)
1967			
A Whiter Shade of Pale	Procol Harum	#5	Bach's "Sleepers Awake"
1968			
Carmen	Herb Alpert & The Tijuana Brass	#51	Bizet's opera "Carmen", also plays parts of earlier hits by The Tijuana Brass
Oh Lord, Why Lord	Los Pop Tops	#78	Pachelbel's "Canon in D Major"
1941	Tom Northcott	#88	Fučík's "Entrance of the Gladiators"
A Whiter Shade of Pale	The Hesitations	#100	Bach's "Sleepers Awake"
1969			
Eternity	Vikki Carr	#79	Mozart's "Symphony #40"

SONGS WITH FOREIGN LANGUAGES

A song will be listed here even if it only has one word in a foreign language.

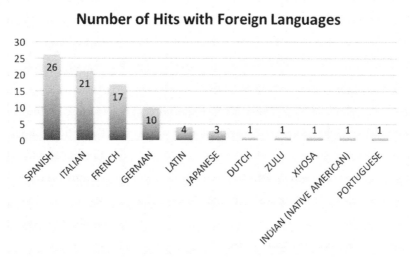

Number of Hits with Foreign Languages

LANGUAGE	YEAR	SONG	ARTIST	HOT 100
Dutch	1960	Banjo Boy	Jan & Kjeld	#58
French	1960	Delaware	Perry Como	#22
French	1960	Down by the Riverside	Les Compagnons de la Chanson	#60
French	1961	Milord	Edith Piaf	#88
French	1963	Dominique	The Singing Nun	#1
French	1963	Love (Makes the World Go 'Round)	Paul Anka	#26
French	1963	It's a Mad, Mad, Mad, Mad World	The Shirelles	#92
French	1964	You Never Can Tell	Chuck Berry	#14
French	1964	Milord	Bobby Darin	#45

SONGS WITH FOREIGN LANGUAGES (cont'd)

Language	Year	Title	Artist	Chart
French	1964	The French Song	Lucille Starr	#54
French	1966	Michelle	David & Jonathan	#18
French	1966	Dommage, Dommage (Too Bad, Too Bad)	Jerry Vale	#93
French	1966	Dommage, Dommage (Too Bad, Too Bad)	Paul Vance	#97
French	1966	Meditation (Meditacao)	Claudine Longet	#98
French	1968	Jennifer Juniper	Donovan	#26
French	1968	Les Bicyclettes de Belsize	Engelbert Humperdinck	#31
French	1968	Love Is Blue (L'Amour Est Bleu)	Claudine Longet	#71
French	1969	My Cherie Amour	Stevie Wonder	#4
German	1960	Sailor (Your Home Is the Sea)	Lolita	#5
German	1960	Delaware	Perry Como	#22
German	1961	Wooden Heart	Joe Dowell	#1
German	1961	La Pachanga	Audrey Arno	#87
German	1961	(A Ship Will Come) Ein Schiff Wird Kommen	Lale Anderson	#88
German	1961	Cowboy Jimmy Joe (Die Sterne Der Prarie)	Lolita	#94
German	1962	Marianna	Johnny Mathis	#86
German	1963	Danke Schoen	Wayne Newton	#13
German	1964	Sie Liebt Dich (She Loves You)	Die Beatles	#97
German	1966	Wiederseh'n	Al Martino	#57
Indian (Native American)	1969	Witchi Tai To	Everything Is Everything	#69
Italian	1960	Volare	Bobby Rydell	#4
Italian	1960	Mama	Connie Francis	#8
Italian	1960	O Dio Mio	Annette	#10
Italian	1960	Jealous of You (Tango Della Gelosia)	Connie Francis	#19
Italian	1960	Baciare Baciare (Kissing Kissing)	Dorothy Collins	#43
Italian	1960	Mio Amore	The Flamingos	#74
Italian	1960	Senza Mamma (With No One)	Connie Francis	#87
Italian	1961	This World We Love In (Il Cielo In Una Stanza)	Mina	#90
Italian	1962	Al Di La'	Emilio Pericoli	#6
Italian	1963	Pepino the Italian Mouse	Lou Monte	#5
Italian	1963	Love (Makes the World Go 'Round)	Paul Anka	#26
Italian	1963	Pepin's Friend Pasqual (The Italian Pussy-Cat)	Lou Monte	#78
Italian	1963	Al Di La	Connie Francis	#90
Italian	1963	From the Bottom of My Heart (Dammi, Dammi, Dammi)	Dean Martin	#91
Italian	1963	It's a Mad, Mad, Mad, Mad World	The Shirelles	#92
Italian	1964	Sole Sole Sole	Siw Malmkvist-Umberto Marcato	#58
Italian	1964	I Can't Get You Out of My Heart	Al Martino	#99
Italian	1965	Cara, Mia	Jay & The Americans	#4
Italian	1965	My Love, Forgive Me (Amore, Scusami)	Robert Goulet	#16
Italian	1965	For Mama (La Mamma)	Connie Francis	#48
Italian	1965	For Mama	Jerry Vale	#54
Japanese	1963	Sukiyaki	Kyu Sakamoto	#1

SONGS WITH FOREIGN LANGUAGES (cont'd)

Japanese	1963	China Nights (Shina No Yoru)	Kyu Sakamoto	#58
Japanese	1963	It's a Mad, Mad, Mad, Mad World	The Shirelles	#92
Latin	1960	The Village of St. Bernadette	Andy Williams	#7
Latin	1960	Adeste Fideles (Oh, Come, All Ye Faithful)	Bing Crosby	#45
Latin	1965	The Wedding	Julie Rogers	#10
Latin	1968	A Voice in the Choir	Al Martino	#80
Nonsense	1968	Zabadak	Dave Dee, Dozy, Beaky, Mick & Tich	#52
Portuguese	1967	Constant Rain (Chove Chuva)	Sergio Mendes & Brasil '66	#71
Spanish	1960	Delaware	Perry Como	#22
Spanish	1960	El Matador	The Kingston Trio	#32
Spanish	1960	Malaguena	Connie Francis	#42
Spanish	1960	Besame Mucho (Part One)	The Coasters	#70
Spanish	1962	Eso Beso (That Kiss!)	Paul Anka	#19
Spanish	1962	La Paloma Twist	Chubby Checker	#72
Spanish	1962	La Bamba	The Tokens	#85
Spanish	1962	Adios Amigo	Jim Reeves	#90
Spanish	1962	Quando, Quando, Quando (Tell Me When)	Pat Boone	#95
Spanish	1963	El Watusi	Ray Barretto	#17
Spanish	1963	New Mexican Rose	The Four Seasons	#36
Spanish	1963	Que Sera, Sera (Whatever Will Be, Will Be)	The High Keyes	#47
Spanish	1963	Enamorado	Keith Colley	#66
Spanish	1963	Cuando Calienta El Sol (When the Sun Is Hot)	Steve Allen (Copacabana Trio)	#85
Spanish	1963	It's a Mad, Mad, Mad, Mad World	The Shirelles	#92
Spanish	1964	Vaya Con Dios	The Drifters	#43
Spanish	1964	Angelito	Rene & Rene	#43
Spanish	1965	Wooly Bully	Sam The Sham & The Pharaohs	#2
Spanish	1966	Guantanamera	The Sandpipers	#9
Spanish	1966	Louie, Louie	The Sandpipers	#30
Spanish	1966	Mas Que Nada	Sergio Mendes & Brasil '66	#47
Spanish	1966	"Bang" "Bang"	The Joe Cuba Sextet	#63
Spanish	1966	La Bamba - Part 1	Trini Lopez	#86
Spanish	1966	Spanish Night and You	Connie Francis	#99
Spanish	1967	Felicidad	Sally Field	#94
Spanish	1969	Lo Mucho Que Te Quiero (The More I Love You)	Rene & Rene	#14
Xhosa	1967	Pata Pata	Miriam Makeba	#12
Zulu	1968	Malayisha	Miriam Makeba	#85
Unknown*	1965	Iko Iko	The Dixie Cups	#20
	*Possibly Haitian, West African, or Creole French			

SONGS OF EXTREME DURATION

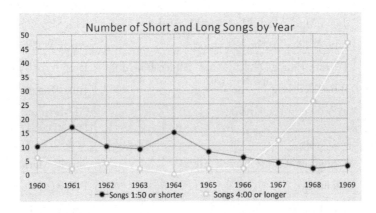

THE LONGESTS SONGS OF THE 1960s

(4:00 or longer)

YEAR	SONG	ARTIST	HOT 100	LENGTH OF SONG
1961	The Astronaut (Parts 1 & 2)	Jose Jimenez	#19	8:15
1969	The Minotaur	Dick Hyman	#38	7:21
1968	MacArthur Park	Richard Harris	#2	7:20
1968	Hey Jude	The Beatles	#1	7:11
1969	By the Time I Get to Phoenix	Isaac Hayes	#37	6:45
1968	Stay in My Corner	The Dells	#10	6:10
1965	Like a Rolling Stone	Bob Dylan	#2	6:00
1962	Midnight Special, Part 1	Jimmy Smith	#69	5:54
1960	The Big Time Spender (Parts I & II)	Cornbread & Biscuits	#75	5:50
1966	Day for Decision	Johnny Sea	#35	5:37
1968	Goodbye My Love	James Brown	#31	5:33
1969	Eloise	Barry Ryan	#86	5:26
1962	To a Sleeping Beauty	Jimmy Dean	#26	5:12
1969	The Boxer	Simon & Garfunkel	#7	5:10
1969	Oh Happy Day	Edwin Hawkins Singers	#4	5:08
1969	We Love You, Call Collect	Art Linkletter	#42	5:07
1968	Those Were the Days	Mary Hopkin	#2	5:05
1969	Camel Back	A.B. Skhy	#100	5:05
1969	MacArthur Park	Waylon Jennings & The Kimberlys	#93	5:04
1968	Right Relations	Johnny Rivers	#61	5:00
1968	The Yard Went on Forever	Richard Harris	#64	5:00
1967	Danny Boy	Ray Price	#60	4:58
1969	Atlantis	Donovan	#7	4:57
1968	With a Little Help from My Friends	Joe Cocker	#68	4:55
1968	I Can't Turn You Loose	The Chambers Brothers	#37	4:50
1962	The Big Draft	The Four Preps	#61	4:49

THE LONGEST SONGS OF THE 1960s (cont'd)

1969	Aquarius/Let the Sunshine In	The 5th Dimension	#1	4:49
1969	Give Peace a Chance	John Lennon	#14	4:49
1969	Run Away Child, Running Wild	The Temptations	#6	4:46
1969	In the Time of Our Lives	Iron Butterfly	#96	4:46
1961	More Money for You and Me	The Four Preps	#17	4:45
1968	Time Has Come Today	The Chambers Brothers	#11	4:45
1969	Questions 67 and 68	Chicago	#71	4:45
1969	Alice's Rock & Roll Restaurant	Arlo Guthrie	#97	4:44
1969	You Keep Me Hanging On	Wilson Pickett	#92	4:43
1960	Mack the Knife	Ella Fitzgerald	#27	4:42
1967	Ballad of You & Me & Pooneil	Jefferson Airplane	#42	4:42
1968	Reach Out	Merrilee Rush	#79	4:42
1969	Where Do You Go To (My Lovely)	Peter Sarstedt	#70	4:42
1960	El Paso	Marty Robbins	#1	4:40
1968	The Weight	The Band	#63	4:40
1967	We Love You	The Rolling Stones	#50	4:39
1967	Get Together	The Youngbloods	#62	4:37
1969	Get Together	The Youngbloods	#5	4:37
1969	Don't Let the Joneses Get You Down	The Temptations	#20	4:37
1967	I am the Walrus	The Beatles	#56	4:35
1968	Vance	Roger Miller	#80	4:35
1969	Suite: Judy Blue Eyes	Crosby, Stills & Nash	#21	4:35
1969	My Way	Frank Sinatra	#27	4:35
1969	See	The Rascals	#27	4:34
1968	Suzie Q. (Part One)	Creedence Clearwater Revival	#11	4:33
1963	I Can't Stop Loving You	Count Basie	#77	4:31
1968	I Love You	People	#14	4:31
1966	Misty	"Groove" Holmes	#44	4:30
1969	Holly Holy	Neil Diamond	#6	4:30
1969	Proud Mary	The Checkmates, Ltd. feat. Sonny Charles	#69	4:30
1968	I Put a Spell on You	Creedence Clearwater Revival	#58	4:26
1969	Going in Circles	The Friends of Distinction	#15	4:25
1969	Sunday Mornin' Comin' Down	Ray Stevens	#81	4:25
1969	Try a Little Tenderness	Three Dog Night	#29	4:23
1967	An Open Letter to My Teenage Son	Victor Lundberg	#10	4:22
1960	The Old Payola Roll Blues (Side I)	Stan Freberg/Jesse White	#99	4:21
1968	Monterey	Eric Burdon/Animals	#15	4:21
1969	Farewell Love Scene	Romeo & Juliet Soundtrack	#86	4:21
1969	Suspicious Minds	Elvis Presley	#1	4:20
1969	Walk on By	Isaac Hayes	#30	4:20
1969	Is That All There Is	Peggy Lee	#11	4:19
1969	This Girl's in Love with You	Dionne Warwick	#7	4:18
1968	Hush	Deep Purple	#4	4:17

THE LONGEST SONGS OF THE 1960s (cont'd)

Year	Song	Artist	Hot 100	Length
1969	Julia	Ramsey Lewis	#76	4:17
1969	Come Together	The Beatles	#1	4:16
1969	Crossroads	Cream	#28	4:16
1968	Peace Brother Peace	Bill Medley	#48	4:15
1969	You'll Never Walk Alone	The Brooklyn Bridge	#51	4:15
1967	What Now My Love	Mitch Ryder	#30	4:14
1969	Sweet Cherry Wine	Tommy James & The Shondells	#7	4:14
1967	Ode to Billy Joe	Bobbie Gentry	#1	4:13
1969	You've Lost That Lovin' Feeling	Dionne Warwick	#16	4:13
1969	The Pledge of Allegiance	Red Skelton	#44	4:13
1969	Love Is All I Have to Give	The Checkmates, Ltd.	#65	4:13
1967	Little Ole Man (Uptight-Everthing's Alright)	Bill Cosby	#4	4:12
1968	Ain't No Way	Aretha Franklin	#16	4:12
1969	Feeling Alright	Joe Cocker	#69	4:12
1967	Child of Clay	Jimmie Rodgers	#31	4:11
1968	She's a Rainbow	The Rolling Stones	#25	4:10
1965	Danny Boy	Jackie Wilson	#94	4:08
1960	Someday (You'll Want Me to Want You)	Della Reese	#56	4:07
1962	Baby It's Cold Outside	Ray Charles & Betty Carter	#91	4:05
1967	Strawberry Fields Forever	The Beatles	#8	4:05
1969	Daddy's Little Man	O.C. Smith	#34	4:05
1967	A Whiter Shade of Pale	Procol Harum	#5	4:04
1968	Living in the U.S.A.	Steve Miller Band	#94	4:03
1963	This Is All I Ask	Burl Ives	#67	4:02
1968	This Guy's in Love with You	Herb Alpert	#1	4:02
1969	Oh, What a Night	The Dells	#10	4:02
1969	Hey Jude	Wilson Pickett	#23	4:02
1969	Tomorrow Tomorrow	The Bee Gees	#54	4:02
1960	Senza Mamma (With No One)	Connie Francis	#87	4:01
1968	All Along the Watchtower	Jimi Hendrix	#20	4:01
1969	Testify (I Wonna)	Johnnie Taylor	#36	4:01
1968	Mrs. Robinson	Simon & Garfunkel	#1	4:00
1968	Porpoise Song	The Monkees	#62	4:00
1969	Hello It's Me	Nazz	#71	4:00

THE SHORTEST SONGS OF THE 1960s

(1:50 or shorter)

YEAR	SONG	ARTIST	HOT 100	LENGTH OF SONG
1964	Little Boxes	The Womenfolk	#83	1:02

THE SHORTEST SONGS OF THE 1960s (cont'd)

1963	Ten Little Indians	The Beach Boys	#49	1:25
1967	Long Legged Girl (With the Short Dress On)	Elvis Presley	#63	1:26
1961	Let's Get Together	Hayley Mills	#8	1:28
1962	Sugar Blues	Ace Cannon	#92	1:30
1966	Please Tell Me Why	Dave Clark Five	#28	1:30
1960	At My Front Door	Dee Clark	#56	1:32
1960	What Do You Want?	Bobby Vee	#93	1:34
1963	One Broken Heart for Sale	Elvis Presley	#11	1:34
1962	Follow That Dream	Elvis Presley	#15	1:35
1964	Custom Machine	Bruce & Terry	#85	1:36
1965	Sunshine, Lollipops and Rainbows	Lesley Gore	#13	1:37
1960	Stay	Maurice Williams & The Zodiacs	#1	1:38
1962	Johnny Jingo	Hayley Mills	#21	1:38
1964	Peg O' My Heart	Robert Maxwell	#64	1:38
1965	I Like It Like That	Dave Clark Five	#7	1:38
1969	Ballad of Easy Rider	The Byrds	#65	1:39
1960	Three Nights a Week	Fats Domino	#15	1:40
1966	Theme from the Wild Angels	Davie Allan/The Arrows	#99	1:40
1967	Glad to Be Unhappy	Mamas & Papas	#26	1:40
1967	Mairzy Doats	The Innocence	#75	1:40
1962	Oliver Twist	Rod McKuen	#76	1:41
1964	Everybody Knows (I Still Love You)	Dave Clark Five	#15	1:41
1965	Do-Wacka-Do	Roger Miller	#31	1:41
1961	Ram-Bunk-Shush	The Ventures	#29	1:42
1961	Frogg	Fats Domino	#32	1:42
1963	Please Don't Talk to the Lifeguard	Diane Ray	#31	1:42
1964	Sweet William	Millie Small	#40	1:42
1961	Tonight I Fell in Love	The Tokens	#15	1:43
1965	The Race Is On	Jack Jones	#15	1:43
1961	Cherry Pink and Apple Blossom White	Jerry Murad's Harmonicats	#56	1:44
1962	A Little Too Much	Clarence Henry	#77	1:44
1962	Did You Ever See a Dream Walking	Fats Domino	#79	1:44
1961	Language of Love	John D. Loudermilk	#32	1:45
1961	Come Along	Maurice Williams & The Zodiacs	#83	1:45
1961	Hang On	Floyd Cramer	#95	1:45
1962	Santa Claus Is Coming to Town	The Four Seasons	#23	1:45
1965	Just a Little Bit	Roy Head	#39	1:45
1969	She's a Lady	John Sebastian	#84	1:45
1960	Ruby Duby Du from Key Witness	Charles Wolcott	#41	1:46
1960	Tonight's the Night	The Chiffons	#76	1:46
1961	Quite a Party	The Fireballs	#27	1:46
1964	Have You Ever Been Lonely (Have You Ever Been Blue)	The Caravelles	#94	1:46

THE SHORTEST SONGS OF THE 1960s (cont'd)

1960	Rocking Goose	Johnny & The Hurricanes	#60	1:47
1961	Well-A, Well-A	Shirley & Lee	#77	1:47
1962	My Daddy Is President	Little Jo Ann	#67	1:47
1963	Little Deuce Coup	The Beach Boys	#15	1:47
1963	Why Do Kids Grow Up	Randy & The Rainbows	#97	1:47
1964	Dang Me	Roger Miller	#7	1:47
1965	Summer Nights	Marianne Faithfull	#24	1:47
1966	Rib Tip's (Part 1)	Andre Williams	#94	1:47
1960	Let It Rock	Chuck Berry	#64	1:48
1961	Should I	The String-A-Longs	#42	1:48
1962	How Can I Meet Her?	The Everly Brothers	#75	1:48
1963	Jenny Brown	The Smothers Brothers	#84	1:48
1967	Devil's Angels	Davie Allan/The Arrows	#97	1:48
1968	Tip-Toe Thru' the Tulips with Me	Tiny Tim	#17	1:48
1964	From Me to You	The Beatles	#41	1:49
1964	There's a Place	The Beatles	#74	1:49
1964	I'm Just Happy to Dance with You	The Beatles	#95	1:49
1965	I'm Henry VIII, I Am	Herman's Hermits	#1	1:49
1966	Love Is All We Need	Mel Carter	#50	1:49
1968	Your Time Hasn't Come Yet, Baby	Elvis Presley	#72	1:49
1960	If You Need Me	Fats Domino	#98	1:50
1960	She's Mine	Conway Twitty	#98	1:50
1961	What a Party	Fats Domino	#22	1:50
1961	Wild in the Country	Elvis Presley	#26	1:50
1961	Be My Boy	Paris Sisters	#56	1:50
1961	On Bended Knees	Clarence Henry	#64	1:50
1961	I Don't Like It Like That	The Bobbettes	#72	1:50
1961	Anniversary of Love	The Caslons	#89	1:50
1962	The Boys' Night Out	Patti Page	#49	1:50
1963	I Wonder What She's Doing Tonight	Barry & The Tamerlanes	#21	1:50
1963	Shut Down	The Beach Boys	#23	1:50
1963	Who Stole the Keeshka?	The Matys Bros.	#55	1:50
1964	Penetration	The Pyramids	#18	1:50
1964	Hippy Hippy Shake	Swinging Blue Jeans	#24	1:50
1964	Not Fade Away	The Rolling Stones	#48	1:50
1964	Little Honda	The Beach Boys	#65	1:50
1964	L-O-V-E	Nat "King" Cole	#81	1:50
1965	Dear Dad	Chuck Berry	#95	1:50
1966	At the Scene	Dave Clark Five	#18	1:50
1966	Lookin' for Love	Ray Conniff	#94	1:50
1969	Hawaii Five-O	The Ventures	#4	1:50

BEST/WORST LISTS

SONGS THAT DESERVED TO MAKE THE TOP 40

These are very good songs that I feel deserved a better fate on the charts. I'm not necessarily saying they are the best songs of the decade, just that they should've made the top 40. If you're interested in finding some overlooked gems from the 60s that don't get much radio play today, this would be a great list to peruse.

SONG	ARTIST	HOT 100
1960		
Mary Don't You Weep	Stonewall Jackson	#41
Malaguena	Connie Francis	#42
Tell Me That You Love Me	Fats Domino	#51
I Wish I'd Never Been Born	Patti Page	#52
If I Can't Have You	Etta James & Harvey Fuqua	#52
I Shot Mr. Lee	The Bobbettes	#52
No Love Have I	Webb Pierce	#54
Let It Rock	Chuck Berry	#64
Ramona	The Blue Diamonds	#72
No	Dodie Stevens	#73
Let the Good Times Roll	Ray Charles	#78
Nobody Knows You When You're Down and Out	Nina Simone	#93
Since I Made You Cry	The Rivieras	#93
The Whiffenpoof Song	Bob Crewe	#96
She's Mine	Conway Twitty	#98
If You Need Me	Fats Domino	#98
1961		
Every Breath I Take	Gene Pitney	#42
Good, Good Lovin'	Chubby Checker	#43
In My Heart	The Timetones	#51
First Taste of Love	Ben E. King	#53
I Never Knew	Clyde McPhatter	#56
Don't Get Around Much Anymore	The Belmonts	#57
Let True Love Begin	Nat "King" Cole	#73
Summertime	The Marcels	#78
You Don't Know What It Means	Jackie Wilson	#79
You're the Boss	LaVern Baker/Jimmy Ricks	#81
Tennessee Flat-Top Box	Johnny Cash	#84
Driving Wheel	Junior Parker	#85
Laugh	The Velvets	#90
1962		
But Not for Me	Ketty Lester	#41

SONGS THAT DESERVED TO MAKE THE TOP 40 (cont'd)

Afrikaan Beat	Bert Kaempfert	#42
Papa-Oom-Mow-Mow	The Rivingtons	#48
You Can't Judge a Book by the Cover	Bo Diddley	#48
Swiss Maid	Del Shannon	#64
I've Been Everywhere	Hank Snow	#68
Down in the Valley	Solomon Burke	#71
Big Love	Joe Henderson	#74
How Can I Meet Her?	The Everly Brothers	#75
Nothing New (Same Old Thing)	Fats Domino	#77
La Bomba	The Tokens	#85
You're Nobody 'Til Somebody Loves You	Dinah Washington	#87
Here Comes That Feelin'	Brenda Lee	#89
Mama Sang a Song	Bill Anderson	#89
Sweet Little Sixteen	Jerry Lee Lewis	#95
The (Bossa Nova) Bird	The Dells	#97
1963		
Tell Him I'm Not Home	Chuck Jackson	#42
The Dreamer	Neil Sedaka	#47
Pin a Medal on Joey	James Darren	#54
The Last Leaf	The Cascades	#60
Two Sides (To Every Story)	Etta James	#63
Ronnie, Call Me When You Get a Chance	Shelley Fabares	#72
Get Him	The Exciters	#76
Come Dance with Me	Jay & The Americans	#76
Any Other Way	Chuck Jackson	#81
Trouble in Mind	Aretha Franklin	#86
Now!	Lena Horne	#92
Baby, What's Wrong	Lonnie Mack	#93
Hear the Bells	The Tokens	#94
Why Do Kids Grow Up	Randy & The Rainbows	#97
1964		
From Me to You	The Beatles	#41
I Want You to Meet My Baby	Eydie Gorme	#43
Wendy	The Beach Boys	#44
Run, Run, Run	The Gestures	#44
All My Loving	The Beatles	#45
My True Carrie, Love	Nat "King" Cole	#49
Good Night Baby	The Butterflys	#51
I Should Have Known Better	The Beatles	#53
If I Fell	The Beatles	#53
So Long Dearie	Louis Armstrong	#56
Tonight You're Gonna Fall in Love with Me	The Shirelles	#57
Sole Sole Sole	Siw Malmkvist-Umberto Marcato	#58

SONGS THAT DESERVED TO MAKE THE TOP 40 (cont'd)

Book of Love	The Raindrops	#62
Who Cares	Fats Domino	#63
Little Honda	The Beach Boys	#65
I Can't Hear You	Betty Everett	#66
Come See About Me	Nella Dodds	#74
Hey Now	Lesley Gore	#76
The Anaheim, Azusa & Cucamonga Sewing Circle, Book Review and Timing Association	Jan & Dean	#77
Mexican Drummer Man	Herb Alpert & The Tijuana Brass	#77
Hey, Mr. Sax Man	Boots Randolph	#77
Yet… I Know (Et Pourtant)	Steve Lawrence	#77
Cold Cold Winter	The Pixies Three	#79
Beautician Blues	B.B. King	#82
Up Above My Head (I Hear Music in the Air)	Al Hirt	#85
Gee	The Pixies Three	#87
Maybe Tonight	The Shirelles	#88
Shout	Lulu & The Luvers	#94
I'm on Fire	Jerry Lee Lewis	#98
I'm Confessin' (That I Love You)	Nino Tempo & April Stevens	#99
1965		
Promised Land	Chuck Berry	#41
Act Naturally	The Beatles	#47
A Time to Love - A Time to Cry (Petite Fleur)	Lou Johnson	#59
Watermelon Man	Gloria Lynne	#62
Remember When	Wayne Newton	#69
Lovely, Lovely (Loverly, Loverly)	Chubby Checker	#70
I Gotta Woman (Part One)	Ray Charles	#79
Hello, Dolly!	Bobby Darin	#79
Good Lovin'	The Olympics	#81
Blind Man	Little Milton	#86
Pied Piper	The Changin' Times	#87
Gloria	Them	#93
I Can't Explain	The Who	#93
A Little Bit of Soap	Garnet Mimms	#95
Think	Jimmy McCracklin	#95
Girl on the Billboard	Del Reeves	#96
You Can Have Him	Timi Yuro	#96
If You Really Want Me to, I'll Go	The Ron-Dels	#97
He Ain't No Angel	The Ad Libs	#100
1966		
Get Out of My Life, Woman	Lee Dorsey	#44
The One on the Right Is on the Left	Johnny Cash	#46
Memories are Made of This	The Drifters	#48

SONGS THAT DESERVED TO MAKE THE TOP 40 (cont'd)

Please Don't Ever Leave Me	The Cyrkle	#59
Neighbor, Neighbor	Jimmy Hughes	#65
We Got a Thing That's in the Groove	The Capitols	#65
Out of This World	The Chiffons	#67
The Proud One	Frankie Vallie	#68
Mame	Louis Armstrong	#81
River Deep-Mountain High	Ike & Tina Turner	#88
Can I Get to Know You Better	The Turtles	#89
Put Yourself in My Place	The Elgins	#92
One Too Many Mornings	Beau Brummels	#95
Cry Softly	Nancy Ames	#95
1967		
Anything Goes	Harpers Bizarre	#43
Summer Wine	Nancy Sinatra & Lee Hazlewood	#49
Pictures of Lily	The Who	#51
Cry Softly Lonely One	Roy Orbison	#52
I Could Be so Good to You	Don & The Goodtimes	#56
Communication Breakdown	Roy Orbison	#60
Get Together	The Youngbloods	#62
I Feel Good (I Feel Bad)	Lewis & Clarke Expedition	#64
It's a Happening World	The Tokens	#69
I Wish You Could Be Here	The Cyrkle	#70
Am I Grooving You	Freddie Scott	#71
They're Here	Boots Walker	#77
I Want You to Be My Baby	Ellie Greenwich	#83
Full Measure	The Lovin' Spoonful	#87
Postcard from Jamaica	The Sopwith "Camel"	#88
Heart Be Still	Lorraine Ellison	#89
Hold On I'm Coming	Chuck Jackson & Maxine Brown	#91
Got to Have You Back	Isley Brothers	#93
Gonna Get Along Without Ya' Now	Trini Lopez	#93
Shake Hands and Walk Away Cryin'	Lou Christie	#95
1968		
Mission-Impossible	Lalo Schifrin	#41
Guitar Man	Elvis Presley	#43
In the Midnight Hour	The Mirettes	#45
Street Fighting Man	The Rolling Stones	#48
Dancing Bear	Mamas & Papas	#51
Hard to Handle	Otis Redding	#51
Zabadak	Dave Dee, Dozy, Beaky, Mick & Tich	#52
In Need of a Friend	The Cowsills	#54
You Send Me	Aretha Franklin	#56
Love Is Blue	Al Martino	#57

SONGS THAT DESERVED TO MAKE THE TOP 40 (cont'd)

My Way of Life	Frank Sinatra	#64
Foxey Lady	Jimi Hendrix	#67
I Got You Babe	Etta James	#69
Love Is Blue (L'Amour Est Bleu)	Claudine Longet	#71
I'm Gonna Do What They Do to Me	B.B. King	#74
Sweet Memories	Andy Williams	#75
Oh Lord, Why Lord	Los Pop Tops	#78
Malayisha	Miriam Makeba	#85
Love Is Blue (L'Amour Est Bleu)	Manny Kellem	#96
Lady Madonna	Fats Domino	#100
1969		
Earth Angel (Will You Be Mine)	The Vogues	#42
Ob-La-Di, Ob-La-Da	Arthur Conley	#51
Jack and Jill	Tommy Roe	#53
River Deep-Mountain High	Deep Purple	#53
Day After Day (It's Slippin' Away)	Shango	#57
I Want to Take You Higher	Sly & The Family Stone	#60
Break Away	The Beach Boys	#63
Rhythm of the Rain	Gary Lewis/Playboys	#63
Proud Mary	The Checkmates, Ltd. feat. Sonny Charles	#69
Feeling Alright	Joe Cocker	#69
Am I the Same Girl	Barbara Acklin	#79
Almost Persuaded	Etta James	#79
Don't Waste My Time	John Mayall	#81
Dynamite Woman	Sir Douglas Quintet	#83
Love Is Just a Four-Letter Word	Joan Baez	#86
It's Hard to Get Along	Joe Simon	#87
Moonlight Sonata	Henry Mancini	#87
Never Comes the Day	The Moody Blues	#91
The Carroll County Accident	Porter Wagoner	#92
Only You (And You Alone)	Bobby Hatfield	#95

THE BEST INSTRUMENTAL SONGS OF THE 1960s

SONG	ARTIST	HOT 100
1960		
Theme from "A Summer Place"	Percy Faith	#1
Walk - Don't Run	The Ventures	#2
Peter Gunn	Duane Eddy	#27
The Sundowners	Billy Vaughn	#51
Skokiaan (South African Song)	Bill Haley & His Comets	#70
A Closer Walk	Pete Fountain	#93

THE BEST INSTRUMENTAL SONGS OF THE 1960s (cont'd)

1961		
Exodus	Ferrante & Teicher	#2
Bonanza	Al Caiola	#19
Bumble Boogie	B. Bumble and The Stingers	#21
Take Five	Dave Brubeck Quartet	#25
The Magnificent Seven	Al Caiola	#35
Riders in the Sky	Lawrence Welk	#87
Boogie Woogie	B. Bumble and The Stingers	#89
Hang On	Floyd Cramer	#95
1962		
Midnight in Moscow	Kenny Ball	#2
Green Onions	Booker T. & The MG's	#3
The Lonely Bull	Herb Alpert & The Tijuana Brass	#6
Afrikaan Beat	Bert Kaempfert	#42
Baby Elephant Walk	Lawrence Welk	#48
Patricia- Twist	Perez Prado	#65
Unsquare Dance	Dave Brubeck Quartet	#74
Ol' Man River	Jimmy Smith	#82
The Green Leaves of Summer	Kenny Ball	#87
Lovesick Blues	Floyd Cramer	#87
Lisa	Ferrante & Teicher	#98
1963		
Wipe Out	The Surfaris	#2
Memphis	Lonnie Mack	#5
Cast Your Fate to the Wind	Vince Guaraldi Trio	#22
The Lonely Surfer	Jack Nitzsche	#39
Java	Floyd Cramer	#49
Jellybread	Booker T. & The MG's	#82
Theme from "Lawrence of Arabia"	Ferrante & Teicher	#84
Banzai Pipeline	Henry Mancini	#93
1964		
The Pink Panther Theme	Henry Mancini	#31
The James Bond Theme	Billy Strange	#58
A Shot in the Dark	Henry Mancini	#97
1965		
3rd Man Theme	Herb Alpert & The Tijuana Brass	#47
Fancy Pants	Al Hirt	#47
Al's Place	Al Hirt	#57
Whipped Cream	Herb Alpert & The Tijuana Brass	#68
Soul Sauce (Guacha Guaro)	Cal Tjader	#88
Yakety Axe	Chet Atkins	#98
1966		
The Work Song	Herb Alpert & The Tijuana Brass	#18

THE BEST INSTRUMENTAL SONGS OF THE 1960s (cont'd)

What Now My Love	Herb Alpert & The Tijuana Brass	#24
Tijuana Taxi	Herb Alpert & The Tijuana Brass	#38
Michelle	Bud Shank	#65
1967		
Music to Watch Girls By	Bob Crewe Generation	#15
I Was Kaiser Bill's Batman	Whistling Jack Smith	#20
A Banda (Ah Bahn-da)	Herb Alpert & The Tijuana Brass	#35
1968		
Love Is Blue	Paul Mauriat	#1
Classical Gas	Mason Williams	#2
Mission-Impossible	Lalo Schifrin	#41
Horse Fever	Cliff Nobles & Co.	#68
1969		
Hawaii Five-O	The Ventures	#4
Chitty Chitty Bang Bang	Paul Mauriat	#76
Moonlight Sonata	Henry Mancini	#87

THE BEST 241 SONGS OF THE 1960s

Here we go. The best songs of the 1960s coming from someone who has listened to all 6,886 of them. And they're ranked. It would've been far easier to simply list them in alphabetical order, but what fun is that?

You'll find quite a few songs from the Beach Boys, Four Seasons, and the Beatles. And although you'll find several songs by the Rolling Stones, you won't find "Satisfaction". It has to be the most overrated song in history. I'm not saying it's a bad song, but I simply don't think that it is one of the best songs of all time.

So check out the list, see what you think. If you see a song you don't recognize, go to YouTube and listen to it! Hopefully, you'll discover some great old songs for the first time.

RANK	YEAR	SONG	ARTIST	HOT 100
#1	1966	Good Vibrations	The Beach Boys	#1
#2	1967	Respect	Aretha Franklin	#1
#3	1963	Be My Baby	The Ronettes	#2
#4	1961	Runaway	Del Shannon	#1
#5	1965	California Girls	The Beach Boys	#3
#6	1961	Blue Moon	The Marcels	#1
#7	1962	What's a Matter Baby (Is it Hurting You)	Timi Yuro	#12
#8	1966	God Only Knows	The Beach Boys	#39
#9	1969	The Boxer	Simon & Garfunkel	#7
#10	1965	Unchained Melody	The Righteous Brothers	#4
#11	1964	Dawn (Go Away)	The Four Seasons	#3
#12	1964	Don't Worry Baby	The Beach Boys	#24
#13	1969	Suspicious Minds	Elvis Presley	#1
#14	1967	A Whiter Shade of Pale	Procol Harum	#5
#15	1964	Fun, Fun, Fun	The Beach Boys	#5

THE BEST 241 SONGS OF THE 1960s (cont'd)

#16	1964	I Want to Hold Your Hand	The Beatles	#1
#17	1966	California Dreamin'	Mamas & Papas	#4
#18	1966	Wouldn't It Be Nice	The Beach Boys	#8
#19	1964	Rag Doll	The Four Seasons	#1
#20	1968	Dancing Bear	Mamas & Papas	#51
#21	1966	I Am a Rock	Simon & Garfunkel	#3
#22	1968	Lady Madonna	The Beatles	#4
#23	1964	A Hard Day's Night	The Beatles	#1
#24	1967	Creeque Alley	Mamas & Papas	#5
#25	1964	Twist and Shout	The Beatles	#2
#26	1964	The House of the Rising Sun	The Animals	#1
#27	1965	Like a Rolling Stone	Bob Dylan	#2
#28	1968	Hey Jude	The Beatles	#1
#29	1964	Oh, Pretty Woman	Roy Orbison w/The Candy Men	#1
#30	1963	Ring of Fire	Johnny Cash	#17
#31	1962	Big Girls Don't Cry	The Four Seasons	#1
#32	1968	Young Girl	Gary Puckett & The Union Gap	#2
#33	1962	Sherry	The Four Seasons	#1
#34	1964	When I Grow Up (To Be a Man)	The Beach Boys	#9
#35	1964	The New Girl in School	Jan & Dean	#37
#36	1964	Mexican Drummer Man	Herb Alpert & The Tijuana Brass	#77
#37	1963	Walk Like a Man	The Four Seasons	#1
#38	1964	You Don't Own Me	Lesley Gore	#2
#39	1968	Woman, Woman	Gary Puckett & The Union Gap	#4
#40	1969	Aquarius/Let the Sunshine In	The 5th Dimension	#1
#41	1964	You Never Can Tell	Chuck Berry	#14
#42	1964	Ronnie	The Four Seasons	#6
#43	1964	Big Man in Town	The Four Seasons	#20
#44	1960	It's Now or Never	Elvis Presley	#1
#45	1963	Surfer Girl	The Beach Boys	#7
#46	1964	Where Did Our Love Go	The Supremes	#1
#47	1966	Sloop John B.	The Beach Boys	#3
#48	1967	(Your Love Keeps Lifting Me) Higher and Higher	Jackie Wilson	#6
#49	1966	I Saw Her Again	Mamas & Papas	#5
#50	1969	Everyday People	Sly & The Family Stone	#1
#51	1967	Heroes and Villains	The Beach Boys	#12
#52	1969	Hair	The Cowsills	#2
#53	1960	Mule Skinner Blues	The Fendermen	#5
#54	1967	Brown Eyed Girl	Van Morrison	#10
#55	1961	Crazy	Patsy Cline	#9
#56	1966	The Sound of Silence	Simon & Garfunkel	#1
#57	1967	Somebody to Love	Jefferson Airplane	#5
#58	1961	Heartaches	The Marcels	#7

THE BEST 241 SONGS OF THE 1960s (cont'd)

#	Year	Title	Artist	Chart
#59	1960	Malaguena	Connie Francis	#42
#60	1968	Classical Gas	Mason Williams	#2
#61	1961	The Lion Sleeps Tonight	The Tokens	#1
#62	1966	Working My Way Back to You	The Four Seasons	#9
#63	1966	Five O'Clock World	The Vogues	#4
#64	1966	I Fought the Law	Bobby Fuller Four	#9
#65	1966	Barbara Ann	The Beach Boys	#2
#66	1969	A Boy Named Sue	Johnny Cash	#2
#67	1960	Wonderful World	Sam Cooke	#12
#68	1968	Scarborough Fair/Canticle	Simon & Garfunkel	#11
#69	1967	Soul Man	Sam & Dave	#2
#70	1962	Do You Love Me	The Contours	#3
#71	1967	Dedicated to the One I Love	Mamas & Papas	#2
#72	1968	Judy in Disguise (With Glasses)	John Fred	#1
#73	1967	Incense and Peppermints	Strawberry Alarm Clark	#1
#74	1963	Surfin' U.S.A.	The Beach Boys	#3
#75	1965	Turn! Turn! Turn! (To Everything There is a Season)	The Byrds	#1
#76	1965	Help!	The Beatles	#1
#77	1964	The Anaheim, Azusa & Cucamonga Sewing Circle, Book Review and Timing Association	Jan & Dean	#77
#78	1965	Bye, Bye, Baby (Baby, Goodbye)	The Four Seasons	#12
#79	1966	We Can Work it Out	The Beatles	#1
#80	1968	Lady Willpower	Gary Puckett & The Union Gap	#2
#81	1969	Make Your Own Kind of Music	Mama Cass Elliot	#36
#82	1965	Girl Come Running	The Four Seasons	#30
#83	1961	Stand By Me	Ben E. King	#4
#84	1961	Hit the Road Jack	Ray Charles	#1
#85	1966	Paint It, Black	The Rolling Stones	#1
#86	1963	It's My Party	Lesley Gore	#1
#87	1963	Donna the Prima Donna	Dion	#6
#88	1964	Save It For Me	The Four Seasons	#10
#89	1962	She's Got You	Patsy Cline	#14
#90	1960	If You Need Me	Fats Domino	#98
#91	1968	Do It Again	The Beach Boys	#20
#92	1966	Paperback Writer	The Beatles	#1
#93	1966	Last Train to Clarksville	The Monkees	#1
#94	1960	Tonight's the Night	The Shirelles	#39
#95	1967	Pretty Ballerina	The Left Banke	#15
#96	1967	Hello Goodbye	The Beatles	#1
#97	1966	You Can't Hurry Love	The Supremes	#1
#98	1966	Monday, Monday	Mamas & Papas	#1
#99	1963	In My Room	The Beach Boys	#23
#100	1968	Jumpin' Jack Flash	The Rolling Stones	#3

THE BEST 241 SONGS OF THE 1960s (cont'd)

#101	1966	Uptight (Everything's Alright)	Stevie Wonder	#3
#102	1965	A Lover's Concerto	The Toys	#2
#103	1966	Opus 17 (Don't You Worry 'Bout Me)	The Four Seasons	#13
#104	1964	Baby Love	The Supremes	#1
#105	1965	The Boy from New York City	The Ad Libs	#8
#106	1963	If You Wanna Be Happy	Jimmy Soul	#1
#107	1963	Then He Kissed Me	The Crystals	#6
#108	1969	Pinball Wizard	The Who	#19
#109	1966	Snoopy Vs. the Red Baron	The Royal Guardsmen	#2
#110	1963	Candy Girl	Four Seasons	#3
#111	1964	Chapel of Love	The Dixie Cups	#1
#112	1963	Denise	Randy & The Rainbows	#10
#113	1963	Marlena	The Four Seasons	#36
#114	1962	Ahab the Arab	Ray Stevens	#5
#115	1963	Wipe Out	The Surfaris	#2
#116	1964	I Get Around	The Beach Boys	#1
#117	1967	All You Need is Love	The Beatles	#1
#118	1966	Stop Stop Stop	The Hollies	#7
#119	1966	Lightnin' Strikes	Lou Christie	#1
#120	1967	Light My Fire	The Doors	#1
#121	1968	Piece of My Heart	Big Brother & The Holding Company	#12
#122	1968	Magic Carpet Ride	Steppenwolf	#3
#123	1969	Down on the Corner/Fortunate Son	Creedence Clearwater Revival	#3
#124	1966	Hold On! I'm a Comin'	Sam & Dave	#21
#125	1964	The Little Old Lady (From Pasadena)	Jan & Dean	#3
#126	1964	Baby, I Love You	The Ronettes	#24
#127	1965	Hey Mr. Tambourine Man	The Byrds	#1
#128	1965	Help Me, Rhonda	The Beach Boys	#1
#129	1968	Mission-Impossible	Lalo Schifrin	#41
#130	1969	Bad Moon Rising	Creedence Clearwater Revival	#2
#131	1963	My Boyfriend's Back	The Angels	#1
#132	1964	You Really Got Me	The Kinks	#7
#133	1965	You've Lost That Lovin' Feelin'	The Righteous Brothers	#1
#134	1964	She Loves You	The Beatles	#1
#135	1962	If I Had a Hammer (The Hammer Song)	Peter, Paul & Mary	#10
#136	1964	I Only Want to Be with You	Dusty Springfield	#12
#137	1968	Dream a Little Dream of Me	Mama Cass/Mamas & Papas	#12
#138	1963	Little Deuce Coupe	The Beach Boys	#15
#139	1966	Yellow Submarine	The Beatles	#2
#140	1964	Such a Night	Elvis Presley	#16
#141	1966	Good Lovin'	The Young Rascals	#1
#142	1965	I Can't Help Myself	Four Tops	#1

THE BEST 241 SONGS OF THE 1960s (cont'd)

#143	1965	You Were on My Mind	We Five	#3
#144	1969	I'm Free	The Who	#37
#145	1963	So Much in Love	The Tymes	#1
#146	1964	Leader of the Pack	The Shangri-Las	#1
#147	1966	But it's Alright	J.J. Jackson	#22
#148	1966	Day Tripper	The Beatles	#5
#149	1967	Ruby Tuesday	The Rolling Stones	#1
#150	1967	C'mon Marianne	The Four Seasons	#9
#151	1964	All My Loving	The Beatles	#45
#152	1962	Little Black Book	Jimmy Dean	#29
#153	1969	Get Back	The Beatles	#1
#154	1964	Wendy	The Beach Boys	#44
#155	1965	All Day and All of the Night	The Kinks	#7
#156	1962	I've Been Everywhere	Hank Snow	#68
#157	1967	Penny Lane	The Beatles	#1
#158	1966	Cherry, Cherry	Neil Diamond	#6
#159	1964	The Way You Do the Things You Do	The Temptations	#11
#160	1960	Baby (You've Got What It Takes)	Dinah Washington & Brook Benton	#5
#161	1968	Folsom Prison Blues	Johnny Cash	#32
#162	1969	I Can Hear Music	The Beach Boys	#24
#163	1967	Words of Love	Mamas & Papas	#5
#164	1964	Hello, Dolly!	Louis Armstrong	#1
#165	1961	Will You Love Me Tomorrow	The Shirelles	#1
#166	1965	I Hear a Symphony	The Supremes	#1
#167	1960	Tell Me That You Love Me	Fats Domino	#51
#168	1960	The Twist	Chubby Checker	#1
#169	1965	I Can't Explain	The Who	#93
#170	1964	I Saw Her Standing There	The Beatles	#14
#171	1961	What a Surprise	Johnny Maestro	#33
#172	1962	Can't Help Falling in Love	Elvis Presley	#2
#173	1962	Duke of Earl	Gene Chandler	#1
#174	1963	I Will Follow Him	Little Peggy March	#1
#175	1961	Tonight I Fell in Love	The Tokens	#15
#176	1961	Runaround Sue	Dion	#1
#177	1960	Save the Last Dance for Me	The Drifters	#1
#178	1961	Pretty Little Angel Eyes	Curtis Lee	#7
#179	1964	No Particular Place to Go	Chuck Berry	#10
#180	1966	My World is Empty Without You	The Supremes	#5
#181	1963	Another Saturday Night	Sam Cooke	#10
#182	1967	Pata Pata	Miriam Makeba	#12
#183	1968	Born to Be Wild	Steppenwolf	#2
#184	1968	I Heart It Through the Grapevine	Marvin Gaye	#1

THE BEST 241 SONGS OF THE 1960s (cont'd)

#	Year	Title	Artist	Chart
#185	1962	Twist and Shout	The Isley Brothers	#17
#186	1960	I Gotta Know	Elvis Presley	#20
#187	1961	Cupid	Sam Cooke	#17
#188	1965	I'll Never Find Another You	The Seekers	#4
#189	1967	I Can See for Miles	The Who	#9
#190	1968	Walk Away Renee	Four Tops	#14
#191	1966	A Hazy Shade of Winter	Simon & Garfunkel	#13
#192	1966	Ain't Too Proud to Beg	The Temptations	#13
#193	1964	Baby I Need Your Loving	Four Tops	#11
#194	1966	Reach Out I'll Be There	Four Tops	#1
#195	1968	The Snake	Al Wilson	#27
#196	1968	All Along the Watchtower	Jimi Hendrix	#20
#197	1964	Please Please Me	The Beatles	#3
#198	1965	Let's Hang On	The Four Seasons	#3
#199	1964	It's All Over Now	The Rolling Stones	#26
#200	1963	Red Sails in the Sunset	Fats Domino	#35
#201	1967	Back on the Street Again	The Sunshine Company	#36
#202	1969	Something in the Air	Thunderclap Newman	#37
#203	1968	Paying the Cost to Be the Boss	B.B. King	#39
#204	1964	Under the Boardwalk	The Drifters	#4
#205	1961	I Love How You Love Me	The Paris Sisters	#5
#206	1965	Silhouettes	Herman's Hermits	#5
#207	1961	Who Put the Bomp (In the Bomp, Bomp, Bomp)	Barry Mann	#7
#208	1967	Gimme Some Lovin'	Spencer Davis Group	#7
#209	1966	I've Got You Under My Skin	The Four Seasons	#9
#210	1963	Bossa Nova Baby	Elvis Presley	#8
#211	1965	It Ain't Me Babe	The Turtles	#8
#212	1965	Nowhere to Run	Martha & The Vandellas	#8
#213	1968	Different Drum	Stone Poneys Feat. Linda Ronstadt	#13
#214	1966	These Boots Are Made for Walkin'	Nancy Sinatra	#1
#215	1968	Green Tambourine	The Lemon Pipers	#1
#216	1969	Give Peace a Chance	John Lennon	#14
#217	1960	A Fool in Love	Ike & Tina Turner	#27
#218	1967	Beggin'	The Four Seasons	#16
#219	1967	Silence is Golden	The Tremeloes	#11
#220	1966	This Old Heart of Mine (Is Weak For You)	Isley Brothers	#12
#221	1966	(I Washed My Hands In) Muddy Water	Johnny Rivers	#19
#222	1968	Lady Madonna	Fats Domino	#100
#223	1964	Memphis	Johnny Rivers	#2
#224	1966	Little Man	Sonny & Cher	#21
#225	1966	Love's Made a Fool of You	Bobby Fuller Four	#26
#226	1968	Some Velvet Morning	Nancy Sinatra & Lee Hazlewood	#26

THE BEST 241 SONGS OF THE 1960s (cont'd)

#227	1960	Chain Gang	Sam Cooke	#2
#228	1962	Swiss Maid	Del Shannon	#64
#229	1961	Let's Twist Again	Chubby Checker	#8
#230	1965	I Got You Babe	Sonny & Cher	#1
#231	1967	Can't Take My Eyes Off You	Frankie Valli	#2
#232	1967	Get Together	The Youngbloods	#62
#233	1961	Tragedy	The Fleetwoods	#10
#234	1960	First Name Initial	Annette	#20
#235	1967	Twelve Thirty (Young Girls Are Coming to the Canyon)	Mamas & Papas	#20
#236	1969	Gitarzan	Ray Stevens	#8
#237	1960	No	Dodie Stevens	#73
#238	1961	I'm Gonna Knock on Your Door	Eddie Hodges	#12
#239	1961	Foot Stomping - Part 1	The Flares	#25
#240	1968	Delilah	Tom Jones	#15
#241	1965	Don't Think Twice	The Wonder Who (The Four Seasons)	#12

THE WORST SONGS OF THE 1960s

SONG	ARTIST	HOT 100
1960		
Yogi	The Ivy Three	#8
Run Samson Run	Neil Sedaka	#28
The Puppet Song	Frankie Avalon	#56
Clementine	Jan & Dean	#65
That's How Much	Brian Hyland	#74
The Big Time Spender (Parts I & II)	Cornbread & Biscuits	#75
Last Chance	Collay & The Satellites	#82
Teenage Hayride	Tender Slim	#93
The Old Payola Roll Blues (Side 1)	Stan Freberg/Jesse White	#99
1961		
Little Egypt (Ying-Yang)	The Coasters	#23
African Waltz	Cannonball Adderley	#41
The Touchables in Brooklyn	Dickie Goodman	#42
The Peppermint Twist	Danny Peppermint	#54
Little Miss Stuck-Up	The Playmates	#70
The Lonely Crowd	Teddy Vann	#76
Greetings (This Is Uncle Sam)	Valadiers	#89
Santa and the Touchables	Dickie Goodman	#99
1962		
Conscience	James Darren	#11
She Can't Find Her Keys	Paul Petersen	#19
Lolita Ya-Ya	The Ventures	#61

THE WORST SONGS OF THE 1960s (cont'd)

Don't Go Near the Eskimos	Ben Colder (Sheb Wooley)	#62
Oliver Twist	Rod McKuen	#76
Pop Goes the Weasel	Anthony Newley	#85
Hail to the Conquering Hero	James Darren	#97
Motorcycle	Tico & The Triumphs	#99
Night Time	Pete Antell	#100
1963		
On Top of Spaghetti	Tom Glazer	#14
8 X 10	Bill Anderson	#53
Surfer Joe	The Surfaris	#62
Give Us Your Blessing	Ray Peterson	#70
The Popeye Waddle	Don Covay	#75
My Babe	The Righteous Brothers	#75
The Ten Commandments of Love	James MacArthur	#94
Hi Diddle Diddle	Inez Foxx	#98
1964		
Sweet William	Millie Small	#40
Dumb Head	Ginny Arnell	#50
The Cheer Leader	Paul Petersen	#78
The Dodo	Jumpin' Gene Simmons	#83
1965		
The Jolly Green Giant	The Kingsmen	#4
Let's Do the Freddie	Chubby Checker	#40
A Lifetime of Loneliness	Jackie DeShannon	#66
Danny Boy	Patti LaBelle & The Bluebells	#76
Somewhere	P.J. Proby	#91
I Want My Baby Back	Jimmy Cross	#92
1966		
They're Coming to Take Me Away, Ha-Haaa!	Napoleon XIV	#3
The Eggplant That Ate Chicago	Dr. West's Medicine Show and Junk Band	#52
Batman	Jan & Dean	#66
You're Nobody Till Somebody Loves You	The Wonder Who? (The Four Seasons)	#96
1967		
You Better Sit Down Kids	Cher	#9
Sing Along with Me	Tommy Roe	#91
Felicidad	Sally Field	#94
Red Roses for Mom	Bobby Vinton	#95
When the Good Sun Shines	Elmo & Almo	#98
Mellow Yellow	Senator Bobby & Senator McKinley	#99
1968		
MacArthur Park	Richard Harris	#2
Tip-Toe Thru' the Tulips with Me	Tiny Tim	#17
Here Comes the Judge	Pigmeat Markham	#19

THE WORST SONGS OF THE 1960s (cont'd)

Harper Valley P.T.A. (Later That Same Day)	Ben Colder (Sheb Wooley)	#67
Reach Out	Merrilee Rush	#79
Don't Make the Good Girls Go Bad	Della Humphrey	#79
Just a Little Bit	Blue Cheer	#92
Billy You're My Friend	Gene Pitney	#92
1969		
To Susan on the West Coast Waiting	Donovan	#35
Moonflight	Vik Venus	#38
On Campus	Dickie Goodman	#45
You Keep Me Hanging On	Wilson Pickett	#92

SINGERS WHO ALSO ACTED IN MOVIES/TV

ARTIST	# Hot 100 Hits	# TV Shows/ Movies	ARTIST	# Hot 100 Hits	# TV Shows/ Movies
Steve Alaimo	9	4	Engelbert Humperdinck	23	12
Rex Allen	1	45	Burl Ives	10	57
Steve Allen	5	49	Sonny James	19	2
Ed Ames	7	19	Waylon Jennings	11	17
Nancy Ames	2	2	Tom Jones	30	13
Bill Anderson	6	11	B.B. King	36	15
Julie Andrews	1	45	Claude King	4	135
Paul Anka	53	19	Ray Davies ("The Kinks")	23	5
Annette	10	34	Gladys Knight	42	31
Ann-Margret	3	83	Michele Lee	1	45
Ray Anthony	6	14	Peggy Lee	11	18
Louis Armstrong	9	30	Tommy Leonetti	3	7
Audrey Arno	1	5	Ketty Lester	4	62
Frankie Avalon	25	50	Tony Butala ("The Lettermen")	20	6
Chuck Woolery (of "The Avante-Garde")	1	10	Jerry Lee Lewis	18	5
Bobby Bare	8	1	Art Linkletter	1	16
Count Basie	6	14	Little Richard	21	23
The Beatles	73	5	Trini Lopez	13	7
Maurice Gibb (from "The Bee Gees")	49	3	Darlene Love	4	9
Tony Bennett	31	13	Lulu	10	22
Jane Birkin	1	88	Moms Mabley	1	5
Ray Bolger	1	37	James MacArthur	1	58
Johnny Bond	2	36	George Maharis	5	69
Sonny Bono ("Sonny & Cher")	20	30	Pigmeat Markham	1	10
Pat Boone	61	29	Guy Marks	1	22

SINGERS WHO ALSO ACTED IN MOVIES/TV (cont'd)

Name			Name		
Bob Braun	1	8	Dean Martin	30	67
Walter Brennan	4	244	Wink Martindale	2	9
Teresa Brewer	24	6	Al Martino	35	9
James Brown	99	10	Gene McDaniels	8	3
Ruth Brown	7	11	Buddy Miles (voice of California Raisins)	10	1
Richard Burton	1	77	Mitch Miller & His Orchestra and Chorus	14	2
Jerry Butler	39	3	Roger Miller	16	12
Hamilton Camp	1	204	Hayley Mills	2	46
Glen Campbell	38	11	Guy Mitchell	10	12
Jo Ann Campbell	4	1	Robert Mitchum	3	133
Thelma Carpenter	1	11	The Monkees	21	3
Vikki Carr	7	10	Jaye P. Morgan	20	20
Mel Carter	7	4	Johnny Nash	12	3
Johnny Cash	48	26	Anthony Newley	4	77
Richard Chamberlain	8	82	Wayne Newton	17	40
Ray Charles	77	10	Nitty Gritty Dirt Band	11	2
Chubby Checker	35	4	Tony Orlando	25	8
Cher ("Sonny & Cher")	20	23	Buck Owens	11	5
Thomas Chong (from "Cheech & Chong", played guitar for "Bobby Taylor and The Vancouvers")	3	52	Patti Page	43	10
Dave Clark Five	24	2	Paul Peterson	6	50
Petula Clark	22	34	Webb Pierce	6	3
Roy Clark	6	13	Perez Prado and His Orchestra	5	14
Jimmy Cliff	3	4	Elvis Presley	153	31
Mike Clifford	3	7	Billy Preston	16	12
Nat "King" Cole	60	24	Teddy Randazzo	3	2
Dorothy Collins	4	5	Lou Rawls	19	48
Perry Como	50	5	Red River Dave	1	9
Rita Coolidge	15	7	Jerry Reed	12	19
Bill Cosby	5	45	Della Reese	10	69
Johnny Crawford	8	61	Jim Reeves	23	1
Bing Crosby	24	103	Paul Revere ("Paul Revere & The Raiders")	24	2
Vic Damone	7	19	Debbie Reynolds	4	85
Bobby Darin	41	26	Cliff Richard	19	19
James Darren	10	53	Bill Medley ("The Righteous Brothers")	24	5
Sammy Davis Jr.	17	66	Tex Ritter	3	74
Doris Day	15	42	Marty Robbins	24	12
Jimmy Dean	13	9	Jimmie Rodgers	25	7
Joe Pesci (played briefly with Joey Dee & The Starliters)	9	41	Kenny Rogers	41	23
Jackie DeShannon	16	10	Linda Ronstadt	36	7

SINGERS WHO ALSO ACTED IN MOVIES/TV (cont'd)

Name			Name		
Neil Diamond	56	5	Bobby Rydell	30	14
Fats Domino	66	3	Soupy Sales	1	34
Ral Donner	5	1	Tommy Sands	11	25
Donovan	17	4	Linda Scott	11	1
Jim Morrison ("The Doors")	17	2	David Seville/The Chipmunks	22	20
Patty Duke	4	141	Allan Sherman	5	7
Jimmy Durante	1	46	Bobby Sherman	10	24
Bob Dylan	23	10	Paul Simon	21	12
Duane Eddy	28	6	Frank Sinatra	68	64
Vincent Edwards	2	84	Nancy Sinatra	21	11
Shelley Fabares	4	91	Red Skelton	1	48
Fabian	10	48	The Smothers Brothers	1	2
Adam Faith	2	17	Terry Stafford	2	1
Marianne Faithfull	5	34	The Standells	4	3
Jose Feliciano	12	10	Kay Starr	13	11
Sally Field	1	62	The Statler Brothers	3	2
Eddie Fisher	23	7	Candi Staton	10	2
Frankie Ford	5	1	Connie Stevens	6	70
Pete Fountain	2	1	Dodie Stevens	5	3
Levi Stubbs (of "The Four Tops")	45	3	Ray Stevens	28	4
Connie Francis	56	9	Sandy Stewart	1	1
Aretha Franklin	76	7	Barbra Streisand	44	22
Stan Freberg	7	102	Danny Thomas	1	37
Frank Gallop	2	6	The Three Degrees	9	2
Gale Garnett	2	41	Johnny Tillotson	26	2
Gerry and The Pacemakers	11	1	Tiny Tim	3	9
Bobby Goldsboro	27	5	Mel Torme	1	42
Lesley Gore	19	4	Conway Twitty	20	3
Eydie Gorme (On Steve Allen's "Tonight Show")	17	7	June Valli	4	1
Robert Goulet	4	64	Leroy Van Dyke	3	1
Don Grady (Drummer for "The Yellow Balloon")	1	31	Bobby Vee	38	1
Lorne Greene	2	81	Billy Vera	6	40
Merv Griffin	1	23	Bobby Vinton	47	8
Arlo Guthrie	2	9	Adam Wade	11	34
George Hamilton IV	11	4	Porter Wagoner	1	2
Richard Harris	4	76	Dionne Warwick	56	19
Rolf Harris	3	12	Lawrence Welk	21	1
Noel Harrison	2	38	Andy Williams	47	112
Isaac Hayes	15	70	Stevie Wonder	65	7
Bobby Helms	11	1	Sheb Wooley	9	62
Eddie Hodges	4	19	Betty Wright	10	2
John Lee Hooker	1	1	Faron Young	6	6

SINGERS WHO ALSO ACTED IN MOVIES/TV (cont'd)

Lena Horne	2	21

Most popular musicians who dabble in acting end up only acting in a few movies or TV shows. Likewise, many actors who try their hand at singing only have a few hits. There are several individuals, however, who became quite successful at both the music industry and acting. The chart below lists the 1960s stars who had at least 20 Hot 100 hits and had at least 20 TV and/or movie credits. Leading the list is, of course, Elvis Presley.

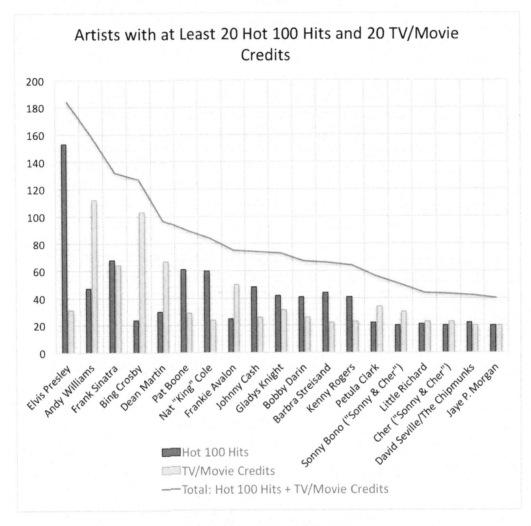

ONE-HIT WONDERS

This shouldn't need explaining, but every artist who appears in this list only had ONE hit. Just one.

YEAR	ARTIST	ARTIST'S ONLY HIT	HOT 100
1966	Abbey Tavern Singers	Off to Dublin in the Green	#94
1963	Billy Abbott and the Jewels	Groovy Baby	#55
1969	A.B. SKHY	Camel Back	#100
1963	Alice Wonder Land	He's Mine (I Love Him, I Love Him, I Love Him)	#62
1962	Rex Allen	Don't Go Near the Indians	#17
1960	Richie Allen	Stranger from Durango	#90
1963	Alley Cats	Puddin N' Tain (Ask Me Again, I'll Tell You the Same)	#43
1963	Allisons	Surfer Street	#93
1968	The Amboy Dukes	Journey to the Center of the Mind	#16

ONE-HIT WONDERS (cont'd)

Year	Artist	Song	Peak
1960	Elton Anderson	Secret of Love	#88
1961	Ernestine Anderson	A Lover's Question	#98
1961	Lale Anderson	(A Ship Will Come) Ein Schiff Wird Kommen	#88
1966	Chris Andrews	Yesterday Man	#94
1965	Julie Andrews	Super-cali-fragil-istic-expi-ali-docious	#66
1962	Anita & the So and Sos	Joey Baby	#91
1962	Pete Antell	Night Time	#100
1963	Appalachians	Bony Moronie	#62
1964	Ginny Arnell	Dumb Head	#50
1961	Audrey Arno	La Pachanga	#87
1968	Calvin Arnold	Funky Way	#72
1964	Clarence Ashe	Trouble I've Had	#99
1965	The Astors	Candy	#63
1963	The Astronauts	Baja	#94
1968	Avante-Garde	Naturally Stoned	#40
1963	Baby Jane & the Rockabyes	How Much Is That Doggie in the Window	#69
1966	Baby Ray	There's Something on Your Mind	#69
1968	The Ballads	God Bless Our Love	#65
1968	The Balloon Farm	A Question of Temperature	#37
1967	The Baltimore & Ohio Marching Band	Lapland	#94
1969	The Banana Splits	The Tra La La Song (One Banana, Two Banana)	#96
1964	Barbara and the Browns	Big Party	#97
1969	Keith Barbour	Echo Park	#40
1961	H.B. Barnum	Lost Love	#35
1963	Ray Barretto	El Watusi	#17
1963	Barry and the Tamerlanes	I Wonder What She's Doing Tonight	#21
1969	The Baskerville Hounds	Hold Me	#88
1969	Duke Baxter	Everybody Knows Matilda	#52
1960	The Beau-Marks	Clap Your Hands	#45
1963	Johnny Beecher	Sax Fifth Avenue	#65
1968	Madeline Bell	I'm Gonna Make You Love Me	#26
1964	The Bermudas	Donnie	#62
1964	Harold Betters	Do Anything You Wanna (Part 1)	#74
1967	Big Maybelle	96 Tears	#96
1962	Big Sambo and the House Wreckers	The Rains Came	#74
1962	Billy Joe and the Checkmates	Percolator (Twist)	#10
1963	Birdlegs and Pauline	Spring	#94
1961	Oscar Black	I'm a Fool to Care	#94
1969	Blackwell	Wonderful	#89
1967	Blades of Grass	Happy	#87
1964	The Blendells	La La La La La	#62
1963	The Blenders	Daughter	#61
1961	The Blossoms	Son-In-Law	#79

ONE-HIT WONDERS (cont'd)

1960	The Blue Diamonds	Ramona	#72
1961	The Blue Jays	Lover's Island	#31
1969	Eddie Bo	Hook and Sling-Part 1	#73
1965	Bonnie and the Treasures	Home of the Brave	#77
1960	James Booker	Gonzo	#43
1962	Bob Braun	Till Death Do Us Part	#26
1960	Larry Bright	Mojo Workout (Dance)	#90
1968	Arthur Brown	Fire	#2
1961	Louise Brown	Son-In-Law	#76
1969	The Bubble Puppy	Hot Smoke & Sasafrass	#14
1960	Bud and Travis	Ballad of the Alamo	#64
1968	Bull and the Matadors	The Funky Judge	#39
1965	Richard Burton	Married Man	#64
1963	The Busters	Bust Out	#25
1961	The Butanes	Don't Forget I Love You	#96
1965	Billy Butler and the Chanters	I Can't Work No Longer	#60
1963	Carl Butler	Don't Let Me Cross Over	#88
1961	Russell Byrd	You'd Better Come Home	#50
1961	Frankie Calen	Joanie	#78
1963	Bobby Callender	Little Star	#95
1961	The Cambridge Strings and Singers	Theme from Tunes of Glory	#60
1968	Hamilton Camp	Here's to You	#76
1965	Candy and the Kisses	The 81	#51
1967	The Candymen	Georgia Pines	#81
1960	Gary Cane and his Friends	The Yen Yet Song	#99
1965	Cannibal and the Headhunters	Land of 1000 Dances	#30
1964	The Carefrees	We Love You Beatles	#39
1968	Henson Cargill	Skip a Rope	#25
1961	Thelma Carpenter	Yes, I'm Lonesome Tonight	#55
1963	Andrea Carroll	It Hurts to Be Sixteen	#45
1964	Bernadette Carroll	Party Girl	#47
1962	Cathy Carroll	Poor Little Puppet	#91
1963	Ronnie Carroll	Say Wonderful Things	#91
1962	Carroll Bros.	Sweet Georgia Brown	#100
1966	Flip Cartridge	Dear Mrs. Applebee	#91
1961	The Caslons	Anniversary of Love	#89
1965	The Castaways	Liar, Liar	#12
1962	The Castle Sisters	Goodbye Dad	#100
1964	Cathy and Joe	I See You	#82
1963	Kenny Chandler	Heart	#64
1965	The Changin' Times	Pied Piper	#87
1963	Chantays	Pipeline	#4
1961	The Chanters	No, No, No	#41

ONE-HIT WONDERS (cont'd)

Year	Artist	Song	Peak
1960	Paul Chaplain and His Emeralds	Shortnin' Bread	#82
1963	The Charmettes	Please Don't Kiss Me Again	#100
1968	The Cherry People	And Suddenly	#45
1966	The Chicago Loop	(When She Needs Good Lovin') She Comes to Me	#37
1967	The Choir	It's Cold Outside	#68
1962	Dean Christie	Heart Breaker	#87
1966	Susan Christie	I Love Onions	#63
1962	Claudine Clark	Party Lights	#5
1968	Otis Clay	She's About a Mover	#97
1966	Clefs of Lavender Hill	Stop! - Get a Ticket	#80
1961	Buzz Clifford	Baby Sittin' Boogie	#6
1966	The C.O.D.s	Michael	#41
1962	Ann Cole	Don't Stop the Wedding	#99
1968	Bobby Cole	Mister Bo Jangles	#79
1960	Collay and the Satellites	Last Chance	#82
1963	Keith Colley	Enamorado	#66
1963	Chris Columbo Quintet	Summertime	#93
1963	Les Cooper and the Soul Rockers	Wiggle Wobble	#22
1960	Cowboy Copas	Alabam	#63
1960	Cornbread and Biscuits	The Big Time Spender (Parts I & II)	#75
1966	Count Five	Psychotic Reaction	#5
1964	The Crampton Sisters	I Didn't Know What Time It Was	#92
1969	Crazy Elephant	Gimme Gimme Good Lovin'	#12
1964	The Crescents	Pink Dominos	#69
1961	Cleveland Crochet and Band	Sugar Bee	#80
1965	G.L. Crockett	It's a Man Down There	#67
1964	Chris Crosby	Young and In Love	#53
1965	Jimmy Cross	I Want My Baby Back	#92
1963	The Cupids	Brenda	#57
1967	Clifford Curry	She Shot a Hole in My Soul	#95
1962	Florraine Darlin	Long as the Rose Is Red	#62
1968	Dave Dee, Dozy, Beaky, Mick and Tich	Zabadak	#52
1966	David and Jonathan	Michelle	#18
1961	Debbie Dean	Don't Let Him Shop Around	#92
1969	Nick DeCaro	If I Only Had Time	#95
1966	Dee Jay and the Runaways	Peter Rabbit	#45
1969	Desmond Dekker and the Aces	Israelites	#9
1961	The Delacardos	Hold Back the Tears	#78
1968	Jimmy Delphs	Don't Sign the Paper Baby (I Want You Back)	#96
1960	Nicky DeMatteo	Suddenly	#90
1964	The Devotions	Rip van Winkle	#36
1965	"Little" Jimmy Dickens	May the Bird of Paradise Fly Up Your Nose	#15
1961	Kenny Dino	Your Ma Said You Cried in Your Sleep Last Night	#24

ONE-HIT WONDERS (cont'd)

Year	Artist	Song	Peak
1961	Paul Dino	Ginnie Bell	#38
1967	Senator Everett McKinley Dirksen	Gallant Men	#29
1965	The Dixie Drifter	Soul Heaven	#99
1966	Dr. West's Medicine Show and Junk Band	The Eggplant That Ate Chicago	#52
1967	Micky Dolenz	Don't Do It	#75
1967	Lou Donaldson	Alligator Bogaloo	#93
1960	Harold Dorman	Mountain of Love	#21
1966	Mike Douglas	The Men in My Little Girl's Life	#6
1961	Ronny Douglas	Run, Run, Run	#75
1963	Debbie Dovale	Hey Lover	#81
1966	Drafi	Marble Breaks and Iron Bends	#80
1962	Charlie Drake	My Boomerang Won't Come Back	#21
1964	Pete Drake	Forever	#25
1961	Roy Drusky	Three Hearts in a Tangle	#35
1961	Duals	Stick Shift	#25
1960	The Dyna-Sores	Alley-Oop	#59
1966	The Dynatones	The Fife Piper	#53
1963	The Earls	Remember Then	#24
1969	Earth Opera	Home to You	#97
1961	The Edsels	Rama Lama Ding Dong	#21
1962	Jimmy Elledge	Funny How Time Slips Away	#22
1967	Elmo and Almo	When the Good Sun Shines	#98
1963	The Emotions	Echo	#76
1967	The Emperors	Karate	#55
1961	The Enchanters	I Lied to My Heart	#96
1968	The Epic Splendor	A Little Rain Must Fall	#87
1968	The Equals	Baby, Come Back	#32
1968	Eternity's Children	Mrs. Bluebird	#69
1961	Jack Eubanks	Searching	#83
1967	Every Father's Teenage Son	A Letter to Dad	#93
1969	Everything Is Everything	Witchi Tai To	#69
1963	The Excellents	Coney Island Baby	#51
1961	The Excels	Can't Help Lovin' That Girl of Mine	#100
1967	The Fascinations	Girls are Out to Get You	#92
1962	Victor Feldman Quartet	A Taste of Honey	#88
1960	The Fendermen	Mule Skinner Blues	#5
1967	Helena Ferguson	Where Is the Party	#90
1960	Johnny Ferguson	Angela Jones	#27
1968	Fever Tree	San Francisco Girls (Return of the Native)	#91
1967	Sally Field	Felicidad	#94
1967	The Fifth Estate	Ding Dong! The Witch Is Dead	#11
1962	Larry Finnegan	Dear One	#11
1961	Mary Ann Fisher	I Can't Take It	#92

ONE-HIT WONDERS (cont'd)

Year	Artist	Song	Peak
1968	Five by Five	Fire	#52
1963	The Five Du-Tones	Shake a Tail Feather	#51
1965	The Five Emprees	Little Miss Sad	#74
1961	The Flares	Foot Stomping - Part 1	#25
1968	Flavor	Sally Had a Party	#95
1966	Darrow Fletcher	The Pain Gets a Little Deeper	#89
1969	The Flirtations	Nothing but a Heartache	#34
1968	The Formations	At the Top of the Stairs	#83
1967	The Forum	The River Is Wide	#45
1963	Roosevelt Fountain	Red Pepper I	#78
1964	The Four-Evers	Be My Girl	#75
1968	The Four Sonics	You Don't Have to Say You Love Me	#89
1961	The Four Sportsmen	Pitter-Patter	#76
1967	Erma Franklin	Piece of My Heart	#62
1966	Dallas Frazier	Elvira	#72
1961	The Frogmen	Underwater	#44
1968	Max Frost and The Troopers	Shape of Things to Come	#22
1969	Thoomas and Richard Frost	She's Got Love	#83
1969	The Fun and Games	The Grooviest Girl in the World	#78
1963	The Furys	Zing! Went the Strings of My Heart	#92
1962	Gabriel and The Angels	That's Life (That's Tough)	#51
1960	Mel Gadson	Comin' Down with Love	#69
1963	The Galens	Baby I Do Love You	#70
1965	The Gants	Road Runner	#46
1964	John Gary	Soon I'll Wed My Love	#89
1966	Gary and The Hornets	Hi Hi Hazel	#96
1964	The Gestures	Run, Run, Run	#44
1962	Johnny Gibson	Midnight	#76
1963	James Gilreath	Little Band of Gold	#21
1964	The Girlfriends	My One and Only, Jimmy Boy	#49
1969	Tompall and The Glaser Brothers	California Girl (And the Tennessee Square)	#92
1963	Tom Glazer	On Top of Spaghetti	#14
1963	The Glencoves	Hootenany	#38
1967	The Glories	I Stand Accused (Of Loving You)	#74
1969	The Goodees	Condition Red	#46
1960	Rosco Gordon	Just a Little Bit	#64
1968	Grapefruit	Dear Delilah	#98
1961	Claude Gray	I'll Just Have a Cup of Coffee (Then I'll Go)	#84
1962	Maureen Gray	Dancin' the Strand	#91
1969	Charles Randolph Grean Sounde	Quentin's Theme	#13
1969	Garland Green	Jealous Kind of Fella	#20
1969	Steve Greenberg	Big Bruce	#97
1968	Barbara Greene	Young Boy	#86

ONE-HIT WONDERS (cont'd)

Year	Artist	Song	Peak
1967	Jack Greene	There Goes My Everything	#65
1963	Vince Guaraldi Trio	Cast Your Fate to the Wind	#22
1960	Larry Hall	Sandy	#15
1962	Jack Halloran Singers	The Little Drummer Boy	#96
1961	The Halos	"Nag"	#25
1961	Karl Hammel Jr.	Summer Souvenirs	#68
1966	The Harden Trio	Tippy Toeing	#44
1969	Tim Hardin	Simple Song of Freedom	#50
1967	The Hardtimes	Fortune Teller	#97
1961	The Harptones	What Will I Tell My Heart	#96
1962	Jennell Hawkins	Moments	#50
1963	The Hearts	Dear Abby	#94
1966	Hedgehoppers Anonymous	It's Good News Week	#48
1966	Neal Hefti	Batman Theme	#35
1963	The High Keyes	Que Sera, Sera (Whatever Will Be, Will Be)	#47
1962	Bunker Hill	Hide & Go Seek, Part I	#33
1963	The Hippies	Memory Lane	#63
1967	Don Ho and The Aliis	Tiny Bubbles	#57
1960	Ron Holden	Love You So	#7
1966	The Holidays	I'll Love You Forever	#63
1964	The Hollyridge Strings	All My Loving	#93
1960	Hollywood Argyles	Alley-Oop	#1
1967	The Hombres	Let It out (Let It All Hang Out)	#12
1962	John Lee Hooker	Boom Boom	#60
1960	Jamie Horton	My Little Marine	#84
1963	"Pookie" Hudson	I Know I Know	#96
1963	T.K. Hulin	I'm Not a Fool Anymore	#92
1968	Della Humphrey	Don't Make the Good Girls Go Bad	#79
1965	Danny Hutton	Roses and Rainbows	#73
1966	The In Crowd	Questions and Answers	#92
1968	Autry Inman	Ballad of Two Brothers	#48
1963	Big Dee Irwin	Swinging on a Star	#38
1965	The Ivy League	Tossing & Turning	#83
1960	The Ivy Three	Yogi	#8
1964	Hank Jacobs	So Far Away	#91
1967	Jesse James	Believe in Me Baby - Part 1	#92
1960	Jan and Kjeld	Banjo Boy	#58
1961	The Jarmels	A Little Bit of Soap	#12
1963	Morty Jay and The Surferin' Cats	Saltwater Taffy	#93
1967	Jerry Jaye	My Girl Josephine	#29
1963	The Jaynetts	Sally, Go 'Round the Roses	#2
1967	Jean and The Darlings	How Can You Mistreat the One You Love	#96
1969	Joe Jeffrey Group	My Pledge of Love	#14

ONE-HIT WONDERS (cont'd)

Year	Artist	Song	Peak
1963	Donald Jenkins and The Delighters	(Native Girl) Elephant Walk	#64
1962	Kris Jensen	Torture	#20
1964	The Jewels	Opportunity	#64
1968	Jim and Jean	People World	#94
1964	Jim and Monica	Slipin' and Slidin'	#96
1961	Jose Jimenez	The Astronaut (Parts 1 & 2)	#19
1966	Mable John	Your Good Thing (Is About to End)	#95
1966	Johnny and The Expressions	Something I Want to Tell You	#79
1960	Joiner Arkansas Junior High School Band	National City	#53
1965	Roddie Joy	Come Back Baby	#86
1966	Just Us	I Can't Grow Peaches on a Cherry Tree	#34
1967	Gunter Kallmann Chorus	Wish Me a Rainbow	#63
1968	Frankie Karl and The Dreams	Don't Be Afraid (Do as I Say)	#93
1968	Kasandra	Don't Pat Me On the Back and Call Me Brother	#91
1968	Kasenetz-Katz Singing Orchestral Circus	Quick Joey Small (Run Joey Run)	#25
1968	Manny Kellem, His Orchestra and Voices	Love Is Blue (L'Amour Est Bleu)	#96
1963	Murry Kellum	Long Tall Texan	#51
1960	Monty Kelly and His Orchestra	Summer Set	#30
1967	Al Kent	You've Got to Pay the Price	#49
1968	Troy Keyes	Love Explosion	#92
1965	The Kids Next Door	Inky Dinky Spider (The Spider Song)	#84
1961	Adrian Kimberly	The Graduation Song… Pomp and Circumstance	#34
1968	Rev. Martin Luther King	I Have a Dream	#88
1962	Sleepy King	Pushin' Your Luck	#92
1963	The King Pins	It Won't Be This Way (Always)	#89
1965	Kathy Kirby	The Way of Love	#88
1967	Pete Klint Quintet	Walkin' Proud	#98
1965	The Knight Bros.	Temptation 'Bout to Get Me	#70
1960	The Knockouts	Darling Lorraine	#46
1961	Kokomo	Asia Minor	#8
1962	The LaFayettes	Life's Too Short	#87
1965	Jack LaForge, His Piano and Orchestra	Goldfinger	#96
1961	Herb Lance and The Classics	Blue Moon	#50
1964	Mickey Lee Lane	Shaggy Dog	#38
1961	The Larks (Philadelphia group)	It's Unbelievable	#69
1965	The Larks (Los Angeles group)	The Jerk	#7
1967	The Last Word	Can't Stop Loving You	#78
1960	Rod Lauren	If I Had a Girl	#31
1968	Leapy Lee	Little Arrows	#16
1966	The Leaves	Hey Joe	#31
1961	Dick Lee	Oh Mein Papa	#94
1966	Jackie Lee (not to be confused with 50s one-hit wonder of the same name from Philadelphia)	The Duck	#14

ONE-HIT WONDERS (cont'd)

1968	Michele Lee	L. David Sloane	#52
1961	Hank Levine and Orchestra	Image - Part 1	#98
1961	The Limeliters	A Dollar Down	#60
1969	Art Linkletter	We Love You, Call Collect	#42
1965	Little Caesar and The Consuls	(My Girl) Sloopy	#50
1960	The Little Dippers	Forever	#9
1962	Little Jo Ann	My Daddy Is President	#67
1962	Little Joey and The Flips	Bongo Stomp	#33
1966	Liverpool Five	Any Way That You Want Me	#98
1961	Ronnie Love and His Orchestra	Chills and Fever	#72
1963	Matt Lucas	I'm Movin' On	#56
1960	Bob Luman	Let's Think About Living	#60
1967	Victor Lundberg	An Open Letter to My Teenage Son	#10
1961	The Ly-Dells	Wizard of Love	#54
1966	Lyme and Cybelle	Follow Me	#65
1964	Donna Lynn	My Boyfriend Got a Beatle Haircut	#83
1966	Johnny Lytle	The Loop	#80
1969	Moms Mabley	Abraham, Martin, and John	#35
1963	James MacArthur	James MacArthur	#94
1966	The Magic Mushrooms	It's-A-Happening	#93
1964	Siw-Umberto Marcato Malmkvist	Sole Sole Sole	#58
1967	Johnny Mann Singers	Up-Up and Away	#91
1961	The Marathons	Peanut Butter	#20
1960	Bobby Marchan	There's Something On Your Mind Part 2	#31
1961	Marcy Joe	Ronnie	#81
1962	Ernie Maresca	Shout! Shout! (Knock Yourself Out)	#6
1968	Pigmeat Markham	Here Comes the Judge	#19
1960	The Mark II	Night Theme	#75
1968	Guy Marks	Loving You Has Made Me Bananas	#51
1965	Derek Martin	You Better Go	#78
1962	Trade Martin	That Stranger Used to Be My Girl	#28
1965	The Marvelows	I Do	#37
1968	The Masqueraders	I Ain't Got to Love Nobody Else	#57
1960	Sammy Masters	Rockin' Red Wing	#64
1960	Tobin Matthews and Co.	Ruby Duby Du	#30
1963	The Matys Bros.	Who Stole the Keeshka?	#55
1968	The Mauds	Soul Drippin'	#85
1969	John Mayall	Don't Waste My Time	#81
1962	Nathaniel Mayer	Village of Love	#22
1963	Percy Mayfield	River's Invitation	#99
1969	MC5	Kick Out the Jams	#82
1961	Charlie McCoy	Cherry Berry Wine	#99
1967	Freddie McCoy	Peas 'N' Rice	#92

ONE-HIT WONDERS (cont'd)

Year	Artist	Song	Peak
1963	George McCurn	I'm Just a Country Boy	#55
1969	Brother Jack McDuff	Theme from Electric Surfboard	#95
1962	Rod McKuen	Oliver Twist	#76
1966	Tommy McLain	Sweet Dreams	#15
1962	Phil McLean	Small Sad Sam	#21
1961	Wyatt (Earp) McPherson	Here's My Confession	#97
1962	The Megatons	Shimmy, Shimmy Walk, Part 1	#88
1960	The Melodeers	Rudolph the Red Nosed Reindeer	#71
1967	The Metros	Sweetest One	#88
1960	Garry Miles	Look for a Star	#16
1961	Frankie Miller	Black Land Farmer	#82
1960	Garry Mills	Look for a Star - Part 1	#26
1961	Mina	This World We Love In (Il Cielo in Una Stanza)	#90
1962	The Miniature Men	Baby Elephant Walk	#87
1967	Moby Grape	Omaha	#88
1963	The Moments (Folk group, not to be confused with the R&B group with the same name from New Jersey, who had 14 hits)	Walk Right In	#82
1964	The Monarchs	Look Homeward Angel	#47
1966	Julie Monday	Come Share the Good Times with Me	#96
1966	The Monitors	Greetings (This Is Uncle Sam)	#100
1968	The Montanas	You've Got to Be Loved	#58
1961	Bob Moore and His Orchestra	Mexico	#7
1965	Lee Morgan	The Sidewinder, Part 1	#81
1962	Johnnie Morisette	Meet Me at the Twistin' Place	#63
1962	Marlow Morris Quintet	Play the Thing	#95
1969	Motherlode	When I Die	#18
1964	The Murmaids	Popsicles and Icicles	#3
1967	Mickey Murray	Shout Bamalama	#54
1964	The Mustangs	The Dartell Stomp	#92
1969	The New Establishment	(One of These Days) Sunday's Gonna' Come On Tuesday	#92
1961	The New Yorkers	Miss Fine	#69
1967	The Nightcrawlers (Not to be confused with the 90s one-hit wonder group of the same name from Scotland)	The Little Black Egg	#85
1961	Nino and The Ebb Tides	Juke Box Saturday Night	#57
1962	Jimmy Norman	I Don't Love You No More (I Don't Care About You)	#47
1968	Tom Northcott	1941	#88
1965	The Novas	The Crusher	#88
1964	Brooks O'Dell	Watch Your Step	#58
1968	Esther and Abi Ofarim	Cinderella Rockefella	#68
1964	Lenny O'Henry	Across the Street	#98
1969	Ola and The Janglers	Let's Dance	#92
1968	Ollie and The Nightingales	I Got a Sure Thing	#73

ONE-HIT WONDERS (cont'd)

1964	The Overlanders	Yesterday's Gone	#75
1965	The Packers	Hole in the Wall	#43
1967	The Parade	Sunshine Girl	#20
1960	The Paradons	Diamonds and Pearls	#18
1961	The Paragons	If	#82
1961	The Parkays	Late Date	#89
1961	Bobby Parker	Watch Your Step	#51
1966	Dean Parrish	Tell Her	#97
1963	The Pastel Six	The Cinnamon Cinder (It's a Very Nice Dance)	#25
1964	Patty and The Emblems	Mixed-Up, Shook-Up, Girl	#37
1964	Rita Pavone	Remember Me	#26
1967	The Peanut Butter Conspiracy	It's a Happening Thing	#93
1962	Pearlettes	Duchess of Earl	#96
1966	The Peels	Juanita Banana	#59
1968	People	I Love You	#14
1961	Danny Peppermint and The Jumping Jacks	The Peppermint Twist	#54
1963	The Percells	What are Boys Made Of	#53
1962	Emilio Pericoli	Al Di La'	#6
1963	Joe Perkins	Little Eeefin Annie	#76
1965	James Phelps	Love Is a 5-Letter Word	#66
1967	Pieces of Eight	Lonely Drifter	#59
1960	The Piltdown Men	Brontosaurus Stomp	#75
1966	The Poets	She Blew a Good Thing	#45
1966	The Poppies	Lullaby of Love	#56
1964	Joey Powers	Midnight Mary	#10
1967	The Precisions	If This Is Love (I'd Rather Be Lonely)	#60
1961	The Preludes Five	Starlight	#80
1964	The Premiers	Farmer John	#19
1966	Alan Price Set	I Put a Spell on You	#80
1967	Prince Buster	Ten Commandments	#81
1968	Professor Morrison's Lollipop	You Got the Love	#88
1966	Leroy Pullins	I'm a Nut	#57
1967	Pretty Purdie	Funky Donkey	#87
1963	Bill Pursell	Our Winter Love	#9
1964	The Pyramids	Penetration	#18
1964	Christine Quaite	Tell Me Mamma	#85
1967	The Rainy Daze	That Acapulco Gold	#70
1965	Eddie Rambeau	Concrete and Clay	#35
1960	The Ramblers (group from Connecticut)	Rambling	#73
1964	The Ramblers	Father Sebastian	#86
1961	Ramrods	(Ghost) Riders in the Sky	#30
1963	The Ran-Dells	Martian Hop	#16
1966	The Rationals	Respect	#92

ONE-HIT WONDERS (cont'd)

Year	Artist	Song	Peak
1963	Diane Ray	Please Don't Talk to the Lifeguard	#31
1968	Ricardo Ray	Nitty Gritty	#90
1962	Ray and Bob	Air Travel	#99
1966	The Razor's Edge	Let's Call It a Day Girl	#77
1960	Red River Dave	There's a Star Spangled Banner Waving #2 (Ballad of Francis Powers)	#64
1960	Denny Reed	A Teenager Feels It Too	#94
1965	Del Reeves	Girl on the Billboard	#96
1968	Rejoice!	Golden Gate Park	#96
1966	Googie Rene Combo	Smokey Joe's La La	#77
1962	Rene and Ray	Queen of My Heart	#79
1969	Lawrence Reynolds	Jesus Is a Soul Man	#28
1969	Rhinoceros	Apricot Brandy	#69
1963	The Ribbons	Ain't Gonna Kiss Ya	#81
1966	Richard and The Young Lions	Open Up Your Door	#99
1961	Rick and The Keens	Peanuts	#60
1967	John Roberts	Sockin' 1-2-3-4	#71
1961	Tina Robin	Dear Mr. D.J. Play It Again	#95
1964	Alvin Robinson	Something You Got	#52
1966	Rosco Robinson	That's Enough	#62
1961	Rochell and The Candles	Once Upon a Time	#26
1969	Rock and Roll Dubble Bubble	Bubble Gum Music	#74
1963	David Rockingham Trio	Dawn	#62
1961	The Rollers	The Continental Walk	#80
1966	Dana Rollin	Winchester Cathedral	#71
1962	Dick Roman	Theme from A Summer Place	#64
1969	Romeo and Juliet Soundtrack	Farewell Love Scene	#86
1967	The Romeos	Precious Memories	#67
1961	The Rondels	Back Beat No. 1	#66
1965	The Ron-Dels	If You Really Want Me to, I'll Go	#97
1962	Ronnie and The Hi-Lites	I Wish That We Were Married	#16
1967	The Rose Garden	Next Plane to London	#17
1967	Jimmy Roselli	There Must Be a Way	#93
1964	Round Robin	Kick That Little Foot Sally Ann	#61
1969	The Rugbys	You, I	#24
1963	The Rumblers	Boss	#87
1963	Lonnie Russ	My Wife Can't Cook	#57
1963	Charlie Russo	Preacherman	#92
1969	Barry Ryan	Eloise	#86
1969	John and Anne Ryder	I Still Believe in Tomorrow	#70
1969	John Wesley Ryles I	Kay	#83
1963	Kirby St. Romain	Summer's Comin'	#49
1965	Soupy Sales	The Mouse	#76

ONE-HIT WONDERS (cont'd)

Year	Artist	Song	Peak
1962	Saverio Saridis	Love Is the Sweetest Thing	#86
1969	Peter Sarstedt	Where Do You Go To (My Lovely)	#70
1961	Ronnie Savoy	And the Heavens Cried	#84
1968	The Scaffold	Thank U Very Much	#69
1967	Harvey Scales and The Seven Sounds	Get Down	#79
1968	Lalo Schifrin	Mission-Impossible	#41
1961	Neil Scott	Bobby	#58
1966	Johny Sea	Day for Decision	#35
1963	The Secrets	The Boy Next Door	#18
1964	Pete Seeger	Little Boxes	#70
1966	Jeannie Seely	Don't Touch Me	#85
1961	The Sevilles	Charlena	#84
1963	The Shacklefords	A Stranger in Your Town	#70
1964	Bobby Shafto	She's My Girl	#99
1969	Shango	Day After Day (It's Slippin' Away)	#57
1966	Bud Shank	Michelle	#65
1961	Helen Shapiro	Walkin' Back to Happiness	#100
1967	Mike Sharpe	Spooky	#57
1966	Sharpees	Tired of Being Lonely	#79
1967	Marlena Shaw	Mercy, Mercy, Mercy	#58
1964	Timmy Shaw	Gonna Send You Back to Georgia (A City Slick)	#41
1966	The Sheep	Hide & Seek	#58
1961	The Shells	Baby Oh Baby	#21
1963	Joe Sherman, His Orchestra and Chorus	Toys in the Attic	#85
1966	The Shindogs	Who Do You Think You Are	#91
1962	Mikey Shorr and the Cutups	Dr. Ben Basey	#60
1968	The Show Stoppers	Ain't Nothin' but a House Party	#87
1966	The Sidekicks	Suspicions	#55
1965	The Silkie	You've Got to Hide Your Love Away	#10
1961	Sims Twins	Soothe Me	#42
1960	The Singing Belles	Someone Loves You, Joe	#91
1963	The Singing Nun	Dominique	#1
1960	Sir Chauncey and His Exciting Strings	Beautiful Obsession	#89
1964	The Ska Kings	Jamaica Ska	#98
1969	Red Skelton	The Pledge of Allegiance	#44
1960	Felix Slatkin Orchestra	Theme from The Sundowners	#70
1962	Frank Slay and His Orchestra	Flying Circle	#45
1965	P.F. Sloan	The Sins of a Family	#87
1969	Jerry Smith and His Pianos	Truck Stop	#71
1967	Whistling Jack Smith	I Was Kaiser Bill's Batman	#20
1969	The Smoke Ring	No Not Much	#85
1963	The Smothers Brothers	Jenny Brown	#84
1961	Piero Soffici	That's the Way with Love	#59

ONE-HIT WONDERS (cont'd)

Year	Artist	Song	Peak
1967	Soul Brothers Six	Some Kind of Wonderful	#91
1968	The Soul Clan	Soul Meeting	#91
1968	The Soulful Strings	Burning Spear	#64
1968	Southwest F.O.B.	Smell of Incense	#56
1964	The Spats	Gator Tails and Monkey Ribs	#96
1962	Benny Spellman	Lipstick Traces (On a Cigarette)	#80
1965	The Spokesmen	The Dawn of Correction	#36
1966	Buddy Starcher	History Repeats Itself	#39
1964	Lucille Starr	The French Song (Quand Le Soleil Dit)	#54
1960	The Statues	Blue Velvet	#84
1969	The Steelers	Get It from the Bottom	#56
1961	The Stereos	I Really Love You	#29
1963	Sandy Stewart	My Coloring Book	#20
1962	The Stompers (Not to be confused with 80s one-hit wonder group of the same name from Boston)	Quarter to Four Stomp	#100
1961	The Strollers	Come on Over	#91
1960	Barrett Strong	Money (That's What I Want)	#23
1964	The Superbs	Baby Baby All the Time	#83
1964	The Swans	The Boy with the Beatle Hair	#85
1966	Norma Tanega	Walkin' My Cat Named Dog	#22
1967	Felice Taylor	It May Be Winter Outside (But in My Heart It's Spring)	#42
1969	Gloria Taylor	You Got to Pay the Price	#49
1966	Ko Ko Taylor	Wang Dang Doodle	#58
1962	Teddy and The Twilights	Woman Is a Man's Best Friend	#59
1965	Willie Tee	Teasin' You	#97
1960	The Temptations (Not to be confused with the 53-hit wonder group from Detroit)	Barbara	#29
1960	Tender Slim	Teenage Hayride	#93
1965	Thee Midniters	Land of a Thousand Dances Part 1	#67
1969	Thee Prophets	Playgirl	#49
1967	The Third Rail	Run, Run, Run	#53
1966	The Thirteenth Floor Elevators	You're Gonna Miss Me	#55
1966	Jamo Thomas	I Spy (For the FBI)	#98
1960	Jon Thomas and Orchestra	Heartbreak (It's Hurtin' Me)	#48
1962	Pat Thomas	Desafinado (Slightly Out of Tune)	#78
1960	Hank Thompson	She's Just a Whole Lot Like You	#99
1962	David Thorne	The Alley Cat Song	#76
1961	The 3 Friends	Dedicated (To the Songs I Love)	#89
1969	Thunderclap Newman	Something in the Air	#37
1962	Bertha Tillman	Oh My Angel	#61
1961	The Timetones	In My Heart	#51
1966	Tim Tam and The Turn-Ons	Wait a Minute	#76
1966	Cal Tjader	Soul Sauce (Guacha Guaro)	#88
1968	George Torrence and The Naturals	(Mama Come Quick, and Bring Your) Lickin' Stick	#91

ONE-HIT WONDERS (cont'd)

1963	The Toy Dolls	Little Tin Soldier	#84
1960	The Tree Swingers	Kookie Little Paradise	#73
1966	The Trolls	Every Day and Every Night	#96
1963	Doris Troy	Just One Look	#10
1969	The T.S.U. Toronadoes	Getting the Corners	#75
1967	2 of Clubs	Walk Tall	#92
1969	Piero Umiliani	Mah-Na-Mah-Na	#55
1969	Underground Sunshine	Birthday	#26
1966	The Unknowns	Melody for an Unknown Girl	#74
1961	Philip Upchurch Combo	You Can't Sit Down Part 2	#29
1965	The Vacels	You're My Baby (And Don't You Forget It)	#63
1961	Valadiers	Greetings (This Is Uncle Sam)	#89
1960	Danny Valentino	Biology	#95
1962	Mark Valentino	The Push and the Kick	#27
1966	The Van Dykes (Not to be confused with the other 60s group with the same name who had two hits)	No Man Is an Island	#94
1961	Teddy Vann	The Lonely Crowd	#76
1965	The Vejtables	I Still Love You	#84
1961	The Velaires	Roll Over Beethoven	#51
1969	Vik Venus	Moonflight	#38
1960	The Videls	Mister Lonely	#73
1963	Vito and The Salutations	Unchained Melody	#66
1962	The Volumes	I Love You	#22
1969	Porter Wagoner	The Carroll County Accident	#92
1960	Billy Walker	Forever	#83
1967	Boots Walker	They're Here	#77
1964	Wallace Brothers	Lover's Prayer	#97
1966	Walter Wanderley	Summer Samba (So Nice)	#26
1964	Dale Ward	Letter from Sherry	#25
1963	Robin Ward	Wonderful Summer	#14
1969	Ella Washington	He Called Me Baby	#77
1965	Billy Edd Wheeler	Ode to the Little Brown Shack Out Back	#50
1969	Marva Whitney	It's My Thing (You Can't Tell Me Who to Sock It To)	#82
1969	Harlow Wilcox and The Oakies	Groovy Grubworm	#30
1967	The Wildweeds	No Good to Cry	#88
1966	Mike Williams	Lonely Soldier	#69
1968	The Will-O-Bees	It's Not Easy	#95
1968	Wilmer and The Dukes	Give Me One More Chance	#80
1961	Phill Wilson	Wishin' on a Rainbow	#91
1963	Kai Winding and Orchestra	More	#8
1965	Jimmy Witherspoon	You're Next	#98
1961	Jimmy Witter	A Cross Stands Alone	#89
1964	The Womenfolk	Little Boxes	#83

ONE-HIT WONDERS (cont'd)

1964	Bobby Wood	If I'm a Fool for Loving You	#74
1967	The Woolies	Who Do You Love	#95
1963	Marion Worth	Shake Me I Rattle (Squeeze Me I Cry)	#42
1967	The Yellow Balloon	Yellow Balloon	#25
1962	Dave York and The Beachcombers	Beach Party	#95
1965	The "You Know Who" Group	Roses are Red My Love	#43
1966	Barry Young	One Has My Name (The Other Has My Heart)	#13
1968	Young Hearts	I've Got Love for My Baby	#94
1969	Zager and Evans	In the Year 2525 (Exordium & Terminus)	#1
1961	Si Zentner and His Orchestra	Up a Lazy River	#43
1961	Pat Zill	Pick Me Up on Your Way Down	#91

ARTISTS WHO USED A STAGE NAME

Stage Name	Actual Name	Stage Name	Actual Name
Billy Abbott and The Jewels	William Vaughn	Little Milton	James Milton Campbell
Johnny Adams	Lathan John Adams	Little Richard	Richard Wayne Penniman
"Cannonball" Adderley	Julian Edwin Adderley	Hank Locklin	Lawrence Hankins Locklin
Alice Wonder Land	Alice Faye Henderson	Lolita	Ditta Zuza Einzinger
Richie Allen	Richard Podolor	Shorty Long	Frederick Earl Long
Ed Ames	Ed Urick	Trini Lopez	Trinidad Lopez
Nancy Ames	Nancy Alfaro	Darlene Love	Darlene Wright
Bill Anderson	James William Anderson III	Lulu	Marie Lawrie
Julie Andrews	Julia Wells	Barbara Lynn	Barbara Lynn Ozen
Ruby Andrews	Ruby Stackhouse	Gloria Lynne	Gloria Alleyne
Annette	Annette Funicello	Moms Mabley	Loretta Mary Aiken
Ann-Margret	Ann-Margret Olsson	Lonnie Mack	Lonnie McIntosh
Pete Antell	Peter Blaise Antonio	Miriam Makeba	Zensi Miriam Makeba
Ray Anthony	Raymond Antonini	Mama Cass	Ellen Naomi Cohen
Louis Armstrong	Daniel Louis Armstrong	Manfred Mann	Michael Lubowitz
Eddy Arnold	Richard Edward Arnold	Barry Mann	Barry Iberman
Frankie Avalon	Francis Avallone	Herbie Mann	Herbert Jay Solomon
Baby Ray	Ray Eddlemon	Mantovani and His Orchestra	Annunzio Paolo Mantovani
LaVern Baker	Delores Williams	Little Peggy March	Margaret Battivio
Hank Ballard & The Midnighters	John Kendricks	Bobby Marchan	Oscar James Gibson
Darrell Banks	Darrell Eubanks	Marcy Jo	Marcy Rae Sockel
J.J. Barnes	James Jay Barnes	Pigmeat Markham	Dewey Markham
Joe Barry	Joe Barrios	Guy Marks	Mario Scarpa
Len Barry	Leonard Borisoff	Bobbi Martin	Barbara Martin
Count Basie	William Basie	Dean Martin	Dino Crocetti
Johnny Beecher	John Johnson	Wink Martindale	Winston Martindale
William Bell	William Yarborough	Al Martino	Alfred Cini

ARTISTS WHO USED A STAGE NAME (cont'd)

Tony Bennett	Anthony Dominick Benedetto	Sammy Masters	Samuel Lawmaster
Brook Benton	Benjamin Franklin Peay	Tobin Mathews & Co.	Willy Henson
Chuck Berry	Charles Edward Anderson Berry	Jimmy McCracklin	James David Walker
Big Maybelle	Mabel Louise Smith	Brother Jack McDuff	Eugene McDuffy
Mr. Acker Bilk	Bernard Stanley Bilk	Buddy Miles	George Miles
Billy Joe & The Checkmates	Louis Bideu	Garry Miles	James Carson
Cilla Black	Priscilla White	Jody Miller	Myrna Joy Brooks
Jeanne Black	Gloria Jeanne Black	Mrs. Miller	Elva Miller
Eddie Bo	Eddie Bocage	Ned Miller	Henry Ned Miller
Ray Bolger	Raymond Bulcao	Garnet Mimms & The Enchanters	Garrett Mimms
Johnny Bond	Cyrus Whitfield Bond	Mina	Anna Mazzini
Gary "U.S." Bonds	Gary Anderson	Guy Mitchell	Al Cernik
Pat Boone	Charles Eugene Boone	Matt Monro	Terrence Parsons
Jan Bradley	Addie Bradley	Chris Montez	Ezekiel Christopher Montanez
Bob Braun	Robert Brown	Wes Montgomery	John Leslie Montgomery
Teresa Brewer	Theresa Breuer	Jaye P. Morgan	Mary Margaret Morgan
Larry Bright	Julian Ferebee Bright	Napoleon XIV	Jerry Samuels
Donnie Brooks	John Abahosh	Ricky Nelson	Eric Hilliard Nelson
Arthur Brown	Arthur Wilton	Sandy Nelson	Sander Nelson
Ruth Brown	Ruth Weston	Nilsson	Harry Nelson
Dave Brubeck Quartet	David Warren	Jack Nitzsche	Bernard Nitzsche
Ray Bryant	Raphael Bryant	Kenny O'Dell	Kenneth Gist
Richard Burton	Richard Jenkins	Lenny O'Henry	Daniel Cannon
Russell Byrd	Bertrand Berns	Oliver	William Oliver Swofford
Cab Calloway	Cabell Calloway	Tony Orlando	Michael Anthony Orlando Cassavitis
Freddy Cannon	Frederick Picariello	Johnny Otis Show	John Veliotes
Vikki Carr	Florencia Martinez Cardona	Buck Owens	Alvis Edgar Owens
Andrea Carroll	Andrea DeCapite	Patti Page	Clara Ann Fowler
David Carroll and His Orchestra	Nook Schrier	Little Junior Parker	Herman Parker, Jr.
Ronnie Carroll	Ronald Cleghorn	Dean Parrish	Phil Anastasi
Flip Cartridge	William Meshel	Les Paul and Mary Ford	Paul was born Lester Polsfuss
Alvin Cash	Alvin Welch	Paul and Paula	Paul =Ray Hildebrand, Paula =Jill Jackson
Richard Chamberlain	George Richard Chamberlain	Esther Phillips	Esther Mae Jones
Gene Chandler	Eugene Dixon	Edith Piaf	Edith Giovanna Gassion
Kenny Chandler	Kenneth Bolognese	Perez Prado and His Orchestra	Damaso Perez Prado
Ray Charles	Ray Charles Robinson	Johnny Preston	John Preston Courville
Ray Charles Singers	Charles Raymond Offenberg	Prince Buster	Cecil Bustamente Campbell
Chubby Checker	Ernest Evans	P.J. Proby	James Marcus Smith
Cher	Cherilyn Sarkisian	Leroy Pullins	Carl Leroy Pullins
Dee Clark	Delecta Clark	Pretty Purdie	Bernard Purdie

ARTISTS WHO USED A STAGE NAME (cont'd)

Patsy Cline	Virginia Patterson Hensley	Eddie Rambeau	Edward Flurie
Joe Cocker	John Robert Cocker	Boots Randolph	Homer Randolph
Nat "King" Cole	Nathaniel Adams Cole	James Ray	James Ray Raymond
Perry Como	Pierino Como	Ricardo Ray	Ricardo Maldonado
Bill Cosby	William Henry Cosby, Jr.	Red River Dave	David McEnery
Bing Crosby	Harry Lillis Crosby	Jerry Reed	Jerry Reed Hubbard
Joe Cuba Sextet	Joe Cuba born Gilberto Calderon	Jimmy Reed	Mathis James Reed
Vic Damone	Vito Farinola	Della Reese	Delloreese Patricia Early
Bobby Darin	Walden Robert Cassotto	Del Reeves	Franklin Delano Reeves
James Darren	James Ercolani	Diane Renay	Renee Diane Kushner
Skeeter Davis	Mary Frances Penick	Googie Rene Combo	Raphael Rene
Debbie Dean	Reba Jeanette Smith	Chris Montez	Mary Reynolds
Joey Dee & The Starliters	Joseph DiNicola	Cliff Richard	Harry Rodger Webb
Desmond Dekker & The Aces	Desmond Dacris	Jeannie C. Riley	Jeanne Carolyn Stephenson
Sugar Pie DeSanto	Umpeylia Balinton	Tex Ritter	Maurice Ritter
Jackie DeShannon	Sharon Myers	Johnny Rivers	John Ramistella
Frank DeVol	Herman Frank DeVol	Marty Robbins	Martin David Robinson
Bo Diddley	Otha Ellas Bates McDaniel	Julie Rogers	Julie Rolls
Paul Dino	Paul Dino Bertuccini, Jr.	Dick Roman	Ricardo DeGiacomo
Fats Domino	Antoine Domino	Spencer Ross	Robert Mersey
Lee Dorsey	Irving Lee Dorsey	Lonnie Rush	Gerald Lionel Russ
Mike Douglas	Michael Dowd	Barry Ryan	Barry Sapherson
Ronny Douglas	Ralph Bruce Douglas	Bobby Rydell	Robert Ridarelli
Charlie Drake	Charles Springall	Mitch Ryder and The Detroit Wheels	William Levise
Pete Drake	Roddis Franklin Drake	Crispian St. Peters	Peter Smith
Rusty Draper	Farrell Draper	Soupy Sales	Milton Supman
Dave Dudley	David Pedruska	Mongo Santamaria	Ramon Santamaria
Patty Duke	Anna Marie Duke	Santana	Carlos Santana
Bob Dylan	Robert Zimmerman	Ronnie Savoy	Eugene Hamilton
Bobby Edwards	Robert Moncrief	Lalo Schifrin	Boris Schifrin
Vincent Edwards	Vincent Edward Zoine	Jack Scott	Jack Scafone, Jr.
Shirley Ellis	Shirley Elliston	Linda Scott	Linda Joy Sampson
The Everly Brothers	Don was born Isaac Donald	Neil Scott	Neil Bogart
Shelley Fabares	Michele Fabares	Peggy Scott & Jo Jo Benson	Peggy Stoutmeyer
Fabian	Fabiano Forte	Johnny Sea	John Seay
Bent Fabric and His Piano	Bent Fabricius-Bjerre	Jeannie Seely	Marilyn Jeanne Seely
Adam Faith	Terence Nelhams	Senator Bobby	Bill Minkin
Georgie Fame	Clive Powell	David Seville/The Chipmunks	Ross Bagdasarian
The Fantastic Johnny C	Johnny Corley	Bud Shank	Clifford Shank
Don Fardon	Donald Maughn	Del Shannon	Charles Westover
Narvel Felts	Albert Narvel Felts	Dee Dee Sharp	Dione LaRue

ARTISTS WHO USED A STAGE NAME (cont'd)

Larry Finnegan	John Lawrence Finnegan*	Mike Sharpe	Michael Shapiro
	*some sources have "Finneran" as last name	Marlena Shaw	Marlena Burgess
Frankie Ford	Frank Guzzo	Sandie Shaw	Sandra Goodrich
Connie Francis	Concetta Rosa Maria Franconero	Allan Sherman	Allan Copelon
Thomas & Richard Frost	Thomas and Richart Martin	Troy Shondell	Gary Schelton
John Gary	John Gary Strader	Mickey Shorr and The Cutups	Mickey Moses
Bobbie Gentry	Roberta Streeter	Bunny Sigler	Walter Sigler
Stan Getz	Stan Gayetzsky	Jerry Landis	Paul Simon
Dickie Goodman	Richard Goodman	Nina Simone	Eunice Waymon
Cary Grant	Archibald Leach	Frank Sinatra	Francis Albert Sinatra
Gogi Grant	Audrey Arinsberg	Sir Chauncey and His Exciting Strings	Ernie Freeman
Janie Grant	Rose Marie Casilli	Red Skelton	Richard Skelton
Dobie Gray	Lawrence Darrow Brown	P.F. Sloan	Phillip "Flip" Sloan
R.B. Greaves	Ronald Bertram Greaves	Millie Small	Millicent Small
Buddy Greco	Armando Greco	O.C. Smith	Ocie Lee Smith
Garland Green	Garfield Green	Hank Snow	Clarence Snow
Bobby Gregg and His Friends	Robert Grego	Joanie Sommers	Joan Drost
Bonnie Guitar	Bonnie Buckingham	Jimmy Soul	James McCleese
Slim Harpo	James Moore	Joe South	Joe Souter
Jennell Hawkins	Jennell Grimes	Red Sovine	Woodrow Wilson Sovine
Deane Hawley	William Dean Hawley	Billie Jo Spears	Billie Jean Spears
Al Hirt	Alois Maxwell Hirt	Dusty Springfield	Mary O'Brien
Buddy Holly	Charles Hardin Holley	Buddy Starcher	Oby Edgar Starcher
Jamie Horton	Gayla Peevey	Edwin Starr	Charles Hatcher
"Pookie" Hudson	James Hudson	Kay Starr	Katherine Starks
T.K. Hulin	Alton James Hulin	Lucille Starr	Lucille Savoie
Engelbert Humperdinck	Arnold Dorsey	Candi Staton	Canzata Staton
Tommy Hunt	Charles Hunt	Connie Stevens	Concetta Ingolia
Janis Ian	Janis Eddy Fink	Dodie Stevens	Geraldine Ann Pasquale
Jorgen Ingmann & His Guitar	Jorgen Ingmann-Pedersen	Ray Stevens	Harold Ray Ragsdale
Autry Inman	Robert Autry Inman	Sandy Stewart	Sandra Galitz
Big Dee Irwin	Difosco Erwin	Barbra Streisand	Barbara Streisand
Bull Moose Jackson	Benjamin Jackson	Bettye Swan	Betty Champion
J.J. Jackson	Jerome Louis Jackson	Ko Ko Taylor	Cora Walton
Etta James	Jamesetta Hawkins	Little Johnny Taylor	Johnny Merrett
Jesse James	James McClelland	Ted Taylor	Austin Taylor
Joni James	Giavanna Carmello Babbo	Willie Tee	Wilson Turbinton
Sonny James	James Loden	Nino Tempo & April Stevens	Antonio Lo Tempio and Carol Lo Tempio
Tommy James and The Shondells	Thomas Jackson	Tammi Terrell	Thomasina Montgomery
Jerry Jaye	Gerald Jaye Hatley	Joe Tex	Joseph Arrington Jr.

ARTISTS WHO USED A STAGE NAME (cont'd)

Jefferson	Geoff Turton	Joe Tex	changed name to Joseph Hazziez in 1972
Kris Jensen	Peter Jensen	B.J. Thomas	Billy Joe Thomas
Jose Jimenez	William Szathmary	Danny Thomas	Muzyad Zakhoob
Little Willie John	William Edgar John	Irma Thomas	Irma Lee
Robert John	Robert John Pedrick	Sue Thompson	Eva Sue KcKee
Buddy Johnson and His Orchestra	Woodrow Wilson Johnson	Johnny Thunder	Gil Hamilton
Syl Johnson	Syl Thompson	Tiny Tim	Herbert Khaury
Tamiko Jones	Barbara Tamiko Ferguson	Cal Tjader	Callen Tjader
Tom Jones	Thomas Jones Woodward	Mel Torme	Melvin Howard
KaSandra	John W. Anderson	Doris Troy	Doris Higginson
Johnny Kaye	John Kaminsky	Tommy Tucker	Robert Higginbotham
Ernie K-Doe	Ernest Kador	Sammy Turner	Samuel Black
Keith	James Barry Keefer	Spyder Turner	Dwight Turner
Al Kent	Al Hamilton	Conway Twitty	Harold Jenkins
Andy Kim	Androwis Jovakim	Jerry Vale	Genaro Vitaliano
Albert King	Albert Nelson	Mark Valentino	Anthony Busillo
Anna King	Anna Williams	Valjean	Valjean Johns
B.B. King	Riley King	Frankie Valli	Francis Castellucio
Ben E. King	Benjamin Earl Nelson	Billy Vaughn and His Orchestra	Richard Vaughn
Carole King	Carole Klein	Bobby Vee	Robert Velline
Freddy King (also performed as "Freddie King")	Freddy Christian	Jimmy Velvet	James Tennant
Jonathan King	Kenneth King	Vik Venus	Jack Spector
King Curtis	Curtis Ousley	Billy Vera	William McCord
Sonny Knight	Joseph Smith	Larry Verne	Larry Vern Erickson
Kokomo	Jimmy Wisner	Bobby Vinton	Stanley Robert Vinton
Billy J. Kramer with The Dakotas	William Ashton	Jerry Jeff Walker	Ronald Clyde Crosby
Patti LaBelle	Patricia Holt	Jr. Walker & The All Stars	Autry DeWalt Walker
Frankie Laine	Frank Paul LoVecchio	Robin Ward	Jacqueline Eloise McDonnell
Mickey Lee Lane	Mickey Lee Schreiber	Baby Washington	Justine Washington
Steve Lawrence	Sidney Leibowitz	Dinah Washington	Ruth Lee Jones
Leapy Lee	Lee Graham	Kim Weston	Agatha Natalie Weston
Otis Leavill	Otis Leavill Cobb	Marty Wilde	Reginald Smith
Brenda Lee	Brenda Mae Tarpley	Hank Williams Jr.	Randall Hank Williams
Dick Lee	Richard Lee Beurer	Roger Williams	Louis Weertz
Dickey Lee	Dickey Lipscomb	Stevie Wonder	Steveland Morris
Laura Lee	Laura Lee Rundless	Brenton Wood	Alfred Smith
Michele Lee	Michele Dusick	Sheb Wooley	Shelby Wooley
Peggy Lee	Norma Jean Egstrom	Marion Worth	Mary Ann Ward
Julian Lennon	John Charles Julian Lennon	O.V. Wright	Overton Vertis Wright
Ketty Lester	Revoyda Frierson	Tammy Wynette	Virginia Wynette Pugh

ARTISTS WHO USED A STAGE NAME (cont'd)

Gary Lewis and The Playboys	Gary Levitch	Dave York and The Beachcombers	David Kinzie
Art Linkletter	Arthur Kelly	Si Zentner and His Orchestra	Simon Zentner
Little Jo Ann	Jo Ann Morse		

1960s ARTISTS WHO ARE RELATED TO OTHER HOT 100 ARTISTS

1960s Artist	Relatives who also appeared on the Hot 100 Chart
"Cannonball" Adderley	Julian Edwin Adderley's brother, Nat Adderley was in group
Steve Alaimo	Cousin of Jimmy Alaimo of "The Mojo Men"
The Ames Brothers	Ed, Gene, Joe, Vic, all brothers
The Angels	Two of the trio were sisters: Phyllis and Barbara Allbut
The Arbors	Brothers Edward and Fred Farran, and Scott and Tom Herrick
The Bachelors	Brothers Declan and Conleth Cluskey
Barbara and The Browns	All Sisters: Barbara, Roberta, Betty, Maurice
The Beach Boys	Brothers Brian, Carl, Dennis Wilson, and cousin Mike Love
	Brian Wilson's daughters Carnie and Wendy Wilson were members of "Wilson Phillips"
Bee Gees	Three brothers: Barry, Robin, Maurice Gibb
The Bermudas	Rickie Page and her two daughters
Birdlegs and Pauline	Husband and wife team: Sidney Banks and Pauline Shivers Banks, and brothers Mack and Floyd Murphy
Jane Birkin and Serge Gainsbourg	Birkin was married to John Barry
The Blossoms	Included sisters Annette and Nanette Williams
The Bobbettes	Included sisters Emma and Jannie Pought
Pat Boone	Brother to Nick Todd
Bill Cunningham (of The Box Tops)	Brother to B.B. Cunningham of "The Hombres"
The Browns	Jim Ed Brown and sisters Maxine and Bonnie
Dorsey Burnette	Father of Billy Burnette and brother of Johnny Burnette
Johnny Burnette	Brother of Dorsey Burnette, and father of Rocky Burnette
Billy Butler (of Billy Butler and The Chanters)	Brother of Jerry Butler
Jo Ann Campbell	Married Troy Seals of "Jo Ann & Troy"
Candy and The Kisses	Included sisters Candy and Suzanne Nelson
Clarence Carter	Married Candi Staton
Johnny Cash	Married June Carter, daughter Rosanne Cash, stepdaughter Carlene Carter, brother to Tommy Cash
Bud Johnson (of "The Chanters")	Son of Buddy Johnson
Eugene Record (of "The Chi-Lites")	Husband of Barbara Acklin
Janet Ertel (of "The Chordettes")	Wife of Archie Bleyer
Ike Clanton	Brother of Jimmy Clanton
Jimmy Clanton	Brother of Ike Clanton
Clefs of Lavender Hill	Brothers Fred and Bill Moss, Brother and sister Joseph and Lorraine Ximenes
Nat "King" Cole	Father of Natalie Cole

1960s ARTISTS WHO ARE RELATED TO OTHER HOT 100 ARTISTS (cont'd)

The Contours	Billy Gordon married Georgeanna Tillman (of "The Marvelettes"), and Hubert Johnson was cousin of Jackie Wilson
Sam Cooke	Uncle of R.B. Greaves
The Cookies	Dorothy Jones and Beulah Robertson were cousins, Darlene McCrea and Earl-Jean McCrea were sisters
Rita Coolidge	Married Kris Kristofferson
The Cowsills	Family group: Brothers Paul, Bob, Bill, Barry, and John, with sister Susan and mother Barbara
The Crampton Sisters	Sisters Peggy and Pat
Creedence Clearwater Revival	Included brothers John and Tom Fogerty
The Crests	Patricia Van Dross sister of Luther Vandross
Bing Crosby	Uncle of Chris Crosby
Chris Crosby	Nephew of Bing Crosby
Damita Jo	Married Steve Gibson of "Steve Gibson & The Red Caps"
Skeeter Davis	Married to Joey Spampinato (bassist for NRBQ)
Tyrone Davis	Brother of Jean Davis (from group "Facts of Life")
Doris Day	Son Terry Melcher was member of "The Rip Chords" and "Bruce and Terry"
The Delfonics	Included brothers William and Wilbert Hart
Jackie DeShannon	Married to Randy Edelman
Detroit Emeralds	Brothers Abrim, Cleophus, Ivory, and Raymond Tilmon- all were cousins of "Sweet" James Epps of the "Fantastic Four"
Dino, Desi & Billy	Dino was Dean Martin's son
The Dixie Cups	Sisters Barbara Ann Hawkins and Rosa Lee Hawkins and their cousin Joan Johnson
The Dolphins	Carl Edmonson (lead vocals) was married to Linda Parrish of "2 of Clubs"
Bob Dylan	Son Jakob is lead singer of "The Wallflowers"
The Easybeats	George Young (guitar) is older brother of AC/DC's Angus and Malcolm Young
Duane Eddy	Married Jessi Colter
The Edsels	Included brothers Larry and Harry Green
The Emotions	Included sisters Wanda, Sheila, Pamela, and Jeanette Hutchinson, and cousin Theresa Davis
The Esquires	Included brothers Gilbert and Alvis Moorer
The Everly Brothers	Brothers Don and Phil
The Exciters	Included Herb Rooney and his wife Brenda Reid
The Falcons	Joe Stubbs was brother of Levi Stubbs of "The Four Tops"
Fantastic Four	James Epps was cousin of the Tilmon brothers in the "Detroit Emeralds"
The 5th Dimension	Marilyn McCoo and Billy Davis, Jr. married
Eddie Fisher	Married Debbie Reynolds, later married Connie Stevens
The Five Americans	Drummer James Wright married Robin of "Jon & Robin and The In Crowd"
The "5" Royales	Included cousins Lowman Pauling, Clarence Pauling, and Windsor King
The Five Stairsteps	Family group: Brothers Clarence Jr., James, Kenneth, Cubie, and Dennis Burke, and their sister Alohe
The Flamingos	Included cousins Zeke and Jake Carey
The Flirtations	Included sisters Shirley and Earnestine Pearce
The Four Preps	Bruce Belland is father of Tracey and Melissa Belland of "Voice of the Beehive"
Aretha Franklin	Sister of Erma Franklin
Erma Franklin	Sister of Aretha Franklin
Friend and Lover	Husband and wife: Jim and Cathy Post

1960s ARTISTS WHO ARE RELATED TO OTHER HOT 100 ARTISTS (cont'd)

Thomas & Richard Frost	Brothers Thomas and Richard Martin
Bobby Fuller Four	Included brothers Bobby and Randy Fuller
The Fun and Games	Included brothers Rock and Joe Romano
Gary and The Hornets	Brothers Gary, Gregg, and Steve Calvert
Marvin Gaye	Father of Nona Gaye
The G-Clefs	Included brothers Teddy, Timmy, Chris, and Arnold Scott
Bobbie Gentry	Married Jim Stafford
Tompall and The Glaser Brothers	Brothers Tompall, Chuck, and Jim Glaser
The Glass House	Scherrie Payne is sister of Freda Payne
Lesley Gore	Sister of Michael Gore
Eydie Gorme	Married Steve Lawrence
Charles Randolph Grean Sound	Randolph married Betty Johnson
R.B. Greaves	Nephew of Sam Cooke
The Greenwood County Singers	Included brothers Van Dyke and C. Carson Parks
The Harden Trio	Siblings Bobby, Robbie, and Arlene Harden
The Hearts	Zell Sanders is mother of Johnnylouise Richardson of Johnnie & Joe
The Hesitations	Included brothers George "King" and Charles Scott
Don Ho and The Aliis	Don Ho father of Hoku
The Hombres	Singer B.B. Cunningham brother to Bill Cunningham, who was a member of "The Box Tops"
The Honeycombs	Included brother and sister John Lantree and Ann "Honey" Lantree
Jimmy Hughes	Cousin of Percy Sledge
The Impressions	Included brothers Arthur and Richard Brooks
The Irish Rovers	Included brothers Will and George Millar, and their cousin Joe Millar
The Isley Brothers	Brothers O'Kelly, Ronald, Ernie, Marvin, and Rudolph Isley; Ronald married Angela Winbush
The Jamies	Included Tom Jameson and his sister Serena Jameson
Jan and Kjeld	Brothers Jan and Kjeld Wennick
Jean & The Darlings	Sisters Jeanne, Phefe, and Dee Dolphus
The Jelly Beans	Included sisters Elyse and Maxine Herbert
Waylon Jennings	Married Jessi Colter
The Jewels	Singer Grace Ruffin is cousin of Billy Stewart
Jim & Jean	Jim and Jean Glover were married
Little Willie John	Brother of Mable John
Mable John	Sister of Little Willie John
Syl Johnson	Father of Syleena Johnson
Jon & Robin and The In Crowd	Javonne "Robin" Braga married James Wright of "The Five Americans"
George Jones	Married Tammy Wynette
The Kimberlys	Brothers Harold and Carl Kimberly, with their wives, sisters Verna and Vera Kimberly
Carole King	Mother of Louise Goffin
The King Pins	Included brothers Andrew, Curtis, and Robert Kelly
The Kinks	Included brothers Ray and Dave Davies
The Knickerbockers	Included brothers Beau and Johnny Charles
Gladys Knight & The Pips	Family group: siblings Glays, Merald, and Brenda Knight, and cousins William and Eleanor Guest. Also managed by their cousin James "Pip" Woods.

1960s ARTISTS WHO ARE RELATED TO OTHER HOT 100 ARTISTS (cont'd)

Kool & The Gang	Included brothers Robert "Kool" Bell and Ronald Bell
Sidney Leibowitz	Married Eydie Gorme
John Lennon	Married Yoko Ono, and father of Julian Lennon
Julian Lennon	Son of John Lennon
The Lennon Sisters	Sister group: Dianne, Peggy, Kathy, and Janet Lennon
The Lettermen	Included brothers Jim and Gary Pike
Gary Lewis and The Playboys	Son of Jerry Lewis
Jerry Lee Lewis	Cousin of Mickey Gilley
Claudine Longet	Married Andy Williams
Los Indios Tabajaras	Brothers Natalicio and Antenor Lima
Darlene Love	Sister of Edna Wright (member of "The Honey Cone")
The Love Generation	Included brothers Tom and John Bahler
Lulu	Married Maurice Gibb (of "Bee Gees")
The Mad Lads	William Brown was brother of Bertrand Brown (member of "The Newcomers")
Miriam Makeba	Married to Hugh Masekela
Mama Cass	Sister of Leah Kunkel (member of "The Coyote Sisters")
The Mamas & The Papas	John and Michelle Phillips were married, their daughter is Chynna Phillips of "Wilson Phillips"
The Marcels	Included brothers Fred and Allen Johnson
Martha & The Vandellas	Included sisters Martha and Lois Reeves
Dean Martin	Son Dino was in "Dino, Desi & Billy"
The Marvelettes	Georgeanna Marie Tillman Gordon married Billy Gordon (of "The Contours"), and Wanda Young married Bobby Rogers of "The Miracles"
Hugh Masekela	Married Miriam Makeba
Tobin Mathews & Co.	Related to Jeremy Jordan
MC5	Guitarist Fred "Sonic" Smith married Patti Smith
The McCoys	Included brothers Rick and Randy Zehringer
The McGuire Sisters	Sisters Phyllis, Christine, and Dorothy
Mel and Tim	Cousins Mel Hardin and Tim McPherson
Sergio Mendes & Brasil '66	Lani Hall (of "Brasil '66") married Herb Alpert
The Meters	Keyboardist Arthur Neville is brother to Aaron Neville
Mickey and Sylvia	McHouston "Mickey" Baker and Sylvia Vanderpool's son is Joey (of "West Street Mob")
The Mills Brothers	Family group: father John Mills with sons Herbert, Harry, and Donald.
The Miracles	Bobby Rogers married Wanda Young (of "The Marvelettes")
The Mojo Men	Singer Jimmy Alaimo was cousin of Steve Alaimo
The Monarchs	Included cousins Bob and Lou Lange
The Murmaids	Included sisters Carol and Terry Fischer
Ricky Nelson	Father of twin sons Gunnar and Matthew Nelson (the group "Nelson")
Aaron Neville	Brother Art Neville was member of "The Meters", Ivan Neville is his son
The Newbeats	Included brothers Dean and Marc Mathis
Esther & Abi Ofarim	Husband and wife Esther and Abraham Ofarim
The O'Jays	Sammy Strain married Yvonne Fair, Eddie Levert father of Gerald and Sean (of group "Levert")
100 Proof Aged in Soul	Singer Joe Stubbs brother of Levi Stubbs (of the "Four Tops")
The Paris Sisters	Sisters Albeth, Priscilla, and Sherrell Paris

1960s ARTISTS WHO ARE RELATED TO OTHER HOT 100 ARTISTS (cont'd)

Parliament/Funkadelic	Included brothers Phelps and William Collins
Pearlettes	Included sisters Lynda and Sheila Galloway
The Pentagons	Included brothers Ken and Ted Goodloe
The Peppermint Rainbow	Included sisters Bonnie and Pat Lamdin
The Peppermint Trolley Company	Included Danny and Jimmy Faragher
Louis Prima and Keely Smith	Prima and Smith were married
James & Bobby Purify	Cousins James Purify and Robert Lee Dickey
Quicksilver Messenger Service	Guitarist John Cipollina was brother of Mario Cipollina of "Huey Lewis & The News"
The Raindrops	Husband and wife Jeff Barry and Ellie Greenwich
The Rainy Daze	Included brothers Tim and Kip Gilbert
Ramrods	Cousins Vincent Bell Lee and Eugene Moore, and brother and sister Richard and Claire Lane
The Ran-Dells	Brothers Steve and Robert Rappaport and cousin John Spirt
Randy & The Rainbows	Included two sets of brothers: Dominick "Randy" Safuto and Frank Safuto, and Mike and Sal Zero
Otis Redding	Father of Dexter and Otis III, uncle of Mark Locket of "The Reddings"
Rejoice!	Husband and wife team: Tom and Nancy Brown
Debbie Reynolds	Married Eddie Fisher
The Rip Chords	Terry Melcher is Doris Day's son
The Rocky Fellers	Family group: Pop Feller and four sons; Eddie, Albert, Tony, and Junior feller
The Rollers	Included brothers Eddie and Al Wilson
The Romeos	Included brothers Karl and Roland Chambers
The Rondels	Included cousins Leonard and James Petze
The Ronettes	Ronnie Spector, sister Estelle Bennett Vann, and their cousin Nedra Talley Ross
The Royalettes	Included sisters Anita and Sheila Ross
David Ruffin	Brother of Jimmy Ruffin
Jimmy Ruffin	Brother of David Ruffin
Bobby Russell	Married to Vicki Lawrence
John & Anne Ryder	Husband and wife
Tommy Sands	Married Nancy Sinatra
San Remo Golden Strings	Bob Hamilton is brother of Ronnie Savoy
Santo & Johnny	Brothers Santo and Johnny Farina
The Scaffold	Mike McGear is Paul McCartney's brother
The Shangri-Las	Two sets of sisters: Mary and Betty Weiss, and Mary Ann and Marge Ganser
Shepherd Sisters	Group of sisters: Martha, Mary Lou, Gayle, and Judy Shepherd
The Sherrys	Included sisters Dinell and Delphine Cook
The Show Stoppers	Two sets of brothers: Laddie and Alec Burke, and Earl and Timmy Smith
The Sidekicks	Included brothers Zack and Randy Bocelle
The Simon Sisters	Lucy and Carly Simon
Sims Twins	Brothers Bobby and Kenneth Sims
Frank Sinatra	Father of Nancy Sinatra
Nancy Sinatra	Daughter of Frank Sinatra
The Singing Belles	Sisters Anne and Angela Berry
Percy Sledge	Cousin of Jimmy Hughes

1960s ARTISTS WHO ARE RELATED TO OTHER HOT 100 ARTISTS (cont'd)

Sly & The Family Stone	Lead singer Sylvester "Sly Stone" Stewart's brother (Freddie Stone), sister (Rosie Stone), and cousin (Larry Graham) also in band
The Smoke Ring	Included brothers Joe, Nick, and Bob Hupp
The Smothers Brothers	Brothers Tom and Dick Smothers
Sonny & Cher	Husband and Wife duo
Soul Survivors	Included brothers Charles and Richard Ingui
The Spats	Included brothers Dick, Bud, and Ronnie Johnson
Spiral Starecase	Organist Harvey Kaplan is father of Brenda K. Starr
Dusty Springfield	Sister of Tom Springfield (of "The Springfields")
The Staple Singers	Family group: Father Roebuck "Pop" Staples with song Pervis and daughters Cleotha and Yvonne
The Starlets	Maxine Edwards- sister of Earl Edwards (of "The Dukays")
The Statler Brothers	Included brothers Harold and Don Reid
Candi Staton	Married Clarence Carter
Connie Stevens	Married Eddie Fisher, mother of Tricia Leigh Fisher
Billy Stewart	Cousin of Grace Ruffin (of "The Jewels")
Jon Stewart	Brother of Mike Stewart (of "We Five")
Sunny & The Sunglows	Included brothers Jesse, Oscar, and Ray Villanueva
The Sweet Inspirations	Included Cissy Houston- mother of Whitney Houston and aunt of Dione Warwick
The Tams	Included brothers Charles and Joseph Pope
Nino Tempo & April Stevens	Brother and sister
The Temptations	Included David Ruffin, cousin of Billy Stewart
Carla Thomas	Daughter of Rufus Thomas
Rufus Thomas	Father of Carla Thomas
The 3 Friends	Included brothers Clay and Walter Hammond
Tim Tam and The Turn-Ons	Included brothers Rick "Tim Tam" Wiesend and Dan Wiesend
The Tokens	Included brothers Phil and Mitch Margo
The Tremeloes	Alan Blakely brother of Mike Blakely of "Christie"; Len Hawkes father of Chesney Hawkes
Ike & Tina Turner	Husband and Wife
2 of Clubs	Linda Parrish married Carl Edmonson (of "The Dolphins")
Underground Sunshine	Included brothers Egbert and Frank Kohl
The Vacels	Included brothers Vinnie and Peter Gutowski
The Valentinos	Family group of brothers: Bobby, Cecil, Curtis, Friendly Jr., and Harris Womack; Cecil married Mary Wells
The Velvelettes	Included sisters Millie and Carol Gill, and cousins Bertha and Norma Barbee
The Viscounts	Included brothers Bobby and Joe Spievak
Wallace Brothers	Ernest and Johnny Wallace
Dee Dee Warwick	Sister of Dionne Warwick, cousin of Whitney Houston, niece of Cissy Houston
Dionne Warwick	Sister of Dee Dee Warwick, niece of Cissy Houston, cousin of Whitney Houston
We Five	Mike Stewart brother of John Stewart
Marty Wilde	Father of Kim Wilde
Jackie Wilson	Cousin of Hubert Johnson of "The Contours"
Stevie Wonder	Married Syreeta Wright ("Syreeta")
The Woolies	Included brothers Bob and Jeff Baldori
Tammy Wynette	Married George Jones

1960s ARTISTS WHO ARE RELATED TO OTHER HOT 100 ARTISTS (cont'd)	
Kathy Young with The Innocents	Kathy married John Walker from "The Walker Bros."

GROUPS WITH STRANGE NAMES

The Balloon Farm	Grapefruit
The Bubble Puppy	Hedgehoppers Anonymous
Cat Mother and The All Night News Boys	Hollywood Argyles
Cookie and His Cupcakes	Pigmeat Markham
Cornbread & Biscuits	The Peanut Butter Conspiracy
Crazy Elephant	The Peppermint Rainbow
Dave Dee, Dozy, Beaky, Mick and Tich	Professor Morrison's Lollipop
Dr. West's Medicine Show and Junk Band	Quicksilver Messenger Service
The Electric Prunes	Soupy Sales
Every Father's Teenage Son	The "You Know Who" Group!
Every Mother's Son	

ARTISTS WITH POSTHUMOUS HITS

Janis Joplin and Otis Redding both had their first posthumous single reach #1. None of their other hits would reach the top spot. John Lennon's "(Just Like) Starting Over" peaked at #1 after he died in 1980. It was his second #1 hit.

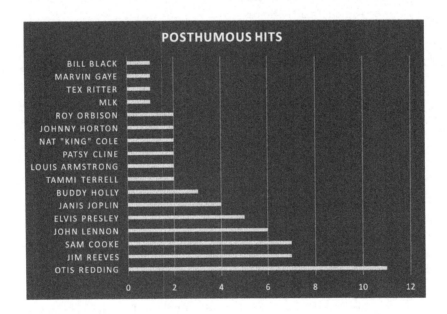

ARTISTS FROM FOREIGN COUNTRIES

The artists are organized according to where they were born, not where they lived, were raised, or, if they were a group, were formed. For example, Engelbert Humperdinck is not listed in the England section because, although he grew up there, he was born in India.

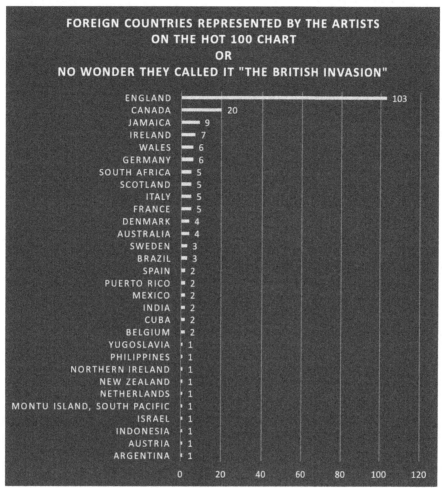

COUNTRY	ARTIST	COUNTRY	ARTIST
Argentina	Lalo Schifrin	England	The New Vaudeville Band
Australia	Duke Baxter	England	The Overlanders
Australia	The Easybeats	England	Peter and Gordon
Australia	Rolf Harris	England	Alan Price Set
Australia	The Seekers	England	Procol Harum
Austria	Lolita	England	Christine Quaite
Belgium	The Singing Nun	England	Julie Rogers
Belgium	The Waikikis	England	The Rolling Stones
Brazil	Los Indios Tabajaras	England	David Rose and His Orchestra
Brazil	Sergio Mendes & Brasil '66	England	Barry Ryan
Brazil	Walter Wanderley	England	John and Anne Ryder
Great Britain/Jamaica	The Equals	England	Crispian St. Peters
Canada	Paul Anka	England	Savoy Brown
Canada	The Beau-Marks	England	The Scaffold
Canada	Terry Black	England	The Searchers

ARTISTS FROM FOREIGN COUNTRIES (cont'd)

Canada	Dorothy Collins	England	Bobby Shafto
Canada	Bobby Curtola	England	Helen Shapiro
Canada	The Diamonds	England	Sandie Shaw
Canada	Percy Faith and His Orchestra	England	The Silkie
Canada	Lorne Greene	England	Small Faces
Canada	The Guess Who	England	Sounds Orchestral
Canada	Andy Kim	England	Dusty Springfield
Canada	Art Linkletter	England	The Status Quo
Canada	Little Caesar and The Consuls	England	The Swinging Blue Jeans
Canada	Motherlode	England	Thunderclap Newman
Canada	Tom Northcott	England	The Tornadoes
Canada	The Original Caste	England	Traffic
Canada	Jack Scott	England	The Tremeloes
Canada	Hank Snow	England	The Troggs
Canada	Lucille Snow	England	Unit Four Plus Two
Canada	Bobby Taylor and The Vancouvers	England	Vanity Fare
Canada	The Band	England	Ian Whitcomb
Cuba	Perez Prado and His Orchestra	England	The Who
Cuba	Mongo Santamaria	England	Marty Wilde
Denmark	Bent Fabric and His Piano	England	The Yardbirds
Denmark	Jorgen Ingmann & His Guitar	England	The Zombies
Denmark	Jan and Kjeld	France	Raymond LeFevre and His Orchestra
Denmark	Kai Winding and Orchestra	France	Les Compagnons de la Chanson
England	The Cambridge Strings and Singers	France	Claudine Longet
England	Chris Andrews	France	Paul Mauriat and His Orchestra
England	Julie Andrews	France	Jacky Noguez and His Orchestra
England	The Animals	Germany	Lale Anderson
England	Long John Baldry	Germany	Audrey Arno
England	Kenny Ball and His Jazzmen	Germany	Drafi
England	The Beatles	Germany	Horst Jankowski
England	Jeff Beck	Germany	Bert Kaempfert and His Orchestra
England	Bee Gees	Germany	Gunter Kallmann Chorus
England	Mr. Acker Bilk	India	Peter Sarstedt
England	Jane Birkin & Serge Gainsbourg	India	Engelbert Humperdinck (raised in England)
England	Cilla Black	Indonesia	The Blue Diamonds
England	Arthur Brown	Ireland	The Abbey Tavern Singers
England	Hamilton Camp	Ireland	The Bachelors
England	The Caravelles	Ireland	Ronnie Carroll
England	The Carefrees	Ireland	Richard Harris
England	Frank Chacksfield and His Orchestra	Ireland	Danny Hutton
England	Chad & Jeremy	Ireland	Van Morrison
England	Dave Clark Five	Ireland	The Irish Rovers (formed in Canada)

ARTISTS FROM FOREIGN COUNTRIES (cont'd)

England	Petula Clark	Israel	Esther Ofarim & Abi
England	Joe Cocker	Italy	Mantovani and His Orchestra
England	Cream	Italy	Rita Pavone
England	Dave Dee, Dozy, Beaky, Mick and Tich	Italy	Emilio Pericoli
England	David & Jonathan	Italy	Piero Soffici
England	Deep Purple	Italy	Piero Umiliani
England	Charlie Drake	Jamaica	Jimmy Cliff
England	Scott English	Jamaica	Desmond Dekker & The Aces
England	Adam Faith	Jamaica	Jimmy James & The Vagabonds
England	Marianne Faithfull	Jamaica	Eddie Lovette
England	Georgie Fame	Jamaica	Prince Buster
England	Don Fardon	Jamaica	Don Shirley
England	Victor Feldman Quartet	Jamaica	The Ska Kings
England	The Flying Machine	Jamaica	Millie Small
England	The Fortunes	Japan	Kyu Sakamoto
England	The Foundations	Mexico	Rudy Martinez
England	Freddie and The Dreamers	Mexico	Santana
England	Gerry and The Pacemakers	Montu Island, South Pacific	Johnnie Morisette
England	Cary Grant	Netherlands	The Shocking Blue
England	Grapefruit	New Zealand	Gale Garnett
England	The Harden Trio	Northern Ireland	Them
England	Noel Harrison	Philippines	The Rocky Fellers
England	Hedgehoppers Anonymous	Puerto Rico	Jose Feliciano
England	Herman's Hermits	Puerto Rico	Paul Venezuela
England	The Hollies	Scotland	Johnny Cymbal
England	The Honeycombs	Scotland	Lonnie Donegan and His Skiffle Group
England	The Hullaballoos	Scotland	Donovan
England	Frank Efield	Scotland	Lulu
England	Jefferson	Scotland	Andy Stewart
England	Davy Jones	South Africa	Four Jacks and a Jill
England	The Kinks	South Africa	Miriam Makeba
England	Kathy Kirby	South Africa	Manfred Mann
England	Billy J. Kramer with The Dakotas	South Africa	Hugh Masekela
England	Leapy Lee	South Africa	Danny Williams
England	Led Zeppelin	Spain	Los Bravos
England	John Lennon	Spain	Los Pop Tops
England	Liverpool Five	Sweden	Ann-Margret
England	The Magic Lanterns	Sweden	Siw-Umberto Marcato Malmkvist
England	John Mayall	Sweden	Ola & The Janglers
England	Gary Mills	Wales	Spencer Davis Group
England	Hayley Mills	Wales	Tom Jones
England	The Mindbenders	Wales	Badfinger

ARTISTS FROM FOREIGN COUNTRIES (cont'd)

England	Matt Monro	Wales	Shirley Bassey
England	The Montanas	Wales	Richard Burton
England	The Moody Blues	Wales	Mary Hopkin
England	The Nashville Teens	Yugoslavia	Ivo Robic
England	Anthony Newley		

ARTISTS WHOSE HITS EACH CHARTED LOWER THAN THEIR PREVIOUS HITS

This is a chart no artist wants to be a part of. Each of these artists' careers started off pretty well. Except for Harpers Bizarre, they all debuted with either a #1 hit or a #2 hit. Too bad it went straight downhill from there for all of them. To add insult to injury, not only did each hit chart lower than each previous hit, each hit for Johnny Preston and Strawberry Alarm Clock spent fewer weeks on the Hot 100 chart then each of their previous hits!

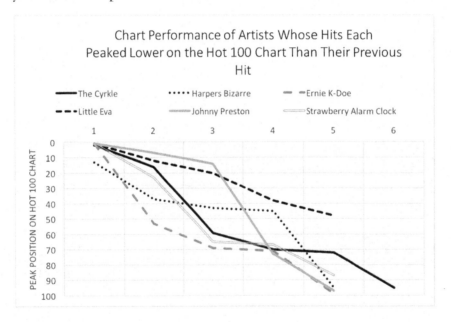

ARTISTS WITH THE MOST HITS, ONLY IN THE 60s

The artists in the chart below didn't have a single hit in any other decade.

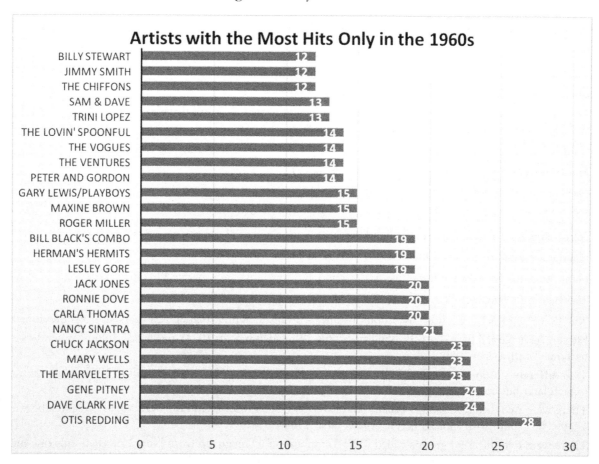

HONORABLE MENTION

These artists all had at least one hit in another decade.

	50s Hits	60s Hits	70s Hits	80s Hits
The Animals		18		1
Bobby Vee	1	36	1	
The Byrds		15	1	
Patsy Cline	1	12		
Floyd Cramer	1	10		
The Fireballs	1	10		
Etta James		27	1	
King Curtis		14	1	
Major Lance		11	1	
Mitch Ryder/Detroit Wheels		11		1
The Searchers		13	1	
Del Shannon		16		1
Percy Sledge		13	1	

OTHER TRIVIA/FACTS

- The Isley Brothers had hits in 6 decades (50s-2001).
- Little Richard had hits in the 50s, 60s, 70s, and 80s. Five years passed between last 50s hit and his first 60s hit.
- Five years between Richard's last 60s hit and his first 70s hit.
- Sixteen years passed between Richard's last 70s hit and his first 80s hit.
- Elvis Presley had hits in the 50s, 60s, 70s, 80s, and 2000s.
- Tex Ritter and Janis Ian both had only 3 hits, with each hit in a different decade. Ritter had one hit in the 50s, 60s, and 70s, while Ian had one hit in the 60s, 70s, and 80s.
- Chubby Checker had one hit in the 50s, 32 hits in the 60s, zero hits in the 70s, and two hits in the 80s.
- Janis Ian had only three hits, each at least 6 years apart.
- Darlene Love's fourth hit was 30 years after her third hit.
- Barry Mann had four hits. Three of them were separated by six years.
- Aaron Neville has nine hits. His 2nd and 3rd hits were released 22 years apart.
- Charlie Rich had three hits: One in 1960, 1965, and 1970.
- Hank Williams Jr. only had three hits. His second and third hits are separated by 36 years.
- The Belmonts had six hits in the 60s. Their 7th and final hit was 18 years later.
- Nat "King" Cole's last hit was a posthumous duet with his daughter, Natalie, 25 years after his previous hit.
- Fifteen years passed between B.B. King's 34th hit ("Philadelphia" in 1974) and his 35th hit ("When Love Comes to Town" with U2 in 1989).
- Two different groups were called "The Moments". The folk group had only one hit in 1963, while the R&B group (which later became "Ray, Goodman & Brown") had 14 hits between 1969-1980.
- There were two different groups called "The Rivieras". The group from New Jersey had three hits between 1958-1960. The group from Indiana had four hits, all in 1964.
- There were two different groups called "The Temptations". The group from New York had only one hit in 1960. The group from Michigan had 55 hits between 1964-1991.
- There were two different groups called the "The Van Dykes". The group from Texas had one hit in 1966. The other group had two hits in 1961.
- Two groups had very similar names: "The Rondels" and the "The Ron-Dels".
- The Miracles released 36 songs before their first #1. Also, their last hit was their 2nd #1.
- Brian Hyland had three top-five hits. His other 19 hits charted lower than #20.
- Bobby Bland had 37 hits, but his most popular song ("Ain't Nothing You Can Do") only got to #20 on the charts.
- Solomon Burke had 26 hits, but his most popular song ("Got to Get You off My Mind") only got to #22 on the charts.
- Chuck Jackson had 23 hits over a span of eight years, but none charted higher than #23.
- Herman's Hermits had 19 Hot 100 hits. Only their last hit ("Sleepy Joe") didn't make the top 40.
- Bobby Vinton had 44 hits. His first 15 hits all made the top 40.
- Laura Lee had eight hits, but only one made the top 40 ("Women's Love Rights", in 1971).
- After their first five hits failed to chart higher than #23, 14 of the Supremes next 15 hits made the top ten, including ten number one songs.
- The Royal Guardsmen had seven hits. Three of them were about Snoopy from the "Peanuts" comic strip.
- The Harry Simeone Chorale had the same song hit the Hot 100 five consecutive years. "The Little Drummer Boy" charted each year from 1958-1962. It was their only hit.
- All five of Bing Crosby's 60s hits were Christmas songs.
- The Five Satins had seven hits. Three of them were "In the Still of the Nite". It charted in 1956, 1960, and 1961. Their last hit was a medley in 1982 that featured "In the Still of the Nite".
- One of Bobby Helms' eleven Hot 100 hits charted six different years. "Jingle Bell Rock" was a hit in 1957, 1958, 1960, 1961, 1962, and 1997. Its highest mark on the Hot 100 was in 1957, when it peaked at #6.

OTHER TRIVIA/FACTS (cont'd)

- The Lovin' Spoonful charted 14 hits in the U.S. The average peak position on the Hot 100 chart for their first seven hits was #6. The average peak position on the Hot 100 chart for their last seven hits was #51.
- James Ray "Jimmy" Hart (Professional wrestling manager known as "Mouth of the South") was part of The Gentrys (6 hits).
- Moms Mabley was 75 years old when she had her one and only hit.
- Martin Luther King had a hit. It was a single that consisted of excerpts from his famous "I Have a Dream" speech. The single was also titled, "I Have a Dream".
- Thomas Chong (From the comedy duo "Cheech & Chong") had three hits as part of Bobby Taylor and The Vancouvers.
- Marvin Gaye had some impressive backup singers: Martha and The Vandellas (sang on three of his hits), the Supremes (two hits), and the Temptations (one hit).
- A U.S. Senator had a top 40 hit: Senator Everett Mckinley Dirksen (Illinois) had a hit with "Gallant Men" in 1967.
- The Four Seasons released songs under three different names. For their first hit, in 1956, they called themselves "The Four Lovers". For almost all of their other hits, they used the name "The Four Seasons", or some similar variation like "Frankie Valli & The Four Seasons", but they also had three hits using the name "The Wonder Who?".

The 60s Music Compendium
QUOTE SOURCES

1 July, 2017 Clapton, Eric. "Quotes." *www.brianwilson.com*. Web. 19 July 2017.
2 July, 2017 Runtagh, Jordan. "Beach Boys' 'Pet Sounds': 15 Things You Didn't Know." Rolling Stone 16 May 2016: Print.
3 July, 2017 Garfunkel, Art. "Quotes." *www.brianwilson.com*. Web. 19 July 2017.

4 July, 2017 Mastropolo, Frank. "Top 11 Musicians Influenced By the Beatles." *www.rockcellarmagazine.com*. 5 Feb. 2014. Web. 19 July 2017.
5 July, 2017 Barker, Emily. "The 50 Greatest Ever Beatles Songs - Picked by Johnny Marr, Royal Blood, Brian Wilson And More." *www.nme.com*. 23 Dec. 2015. Web. 19 July 2017.
6 July, 2017 "Beatles Splitting? Maybe, Says John." *Rolling Stone* 21 Jan. 1970: Print.
7 July, 2017 Battaglia, Andy. "Brian Wilson." *www.avclub.com*. 30 Aug. 2005. Web. 19 July 2017.
8 July, 2017 Hilburn, Robert. "Chuck Berry Sets The Record Straight." *Los Angeles Times* 4 Oct. 1987: *www.articles.latimes.com*. Web. 19 July 2017.
9 July, 2017 Almasy, Steve. "Musicians remember Chuck Berry's genius." *CNN*. N.p., 18 Mar. 2017. Web. 19 July 2017.
10 July, 2017 Trott, Bill. "Factbox: Famous musicians on Chuck Berry, rock 'n' roll master." *Reuters*. Ed. Diane Craft and Tom Brown. 18 Mar. 2017. Web. 19 July 2017.
11 July, 2017 Trott, Bill. "Factbox: Famous musicians on Chuck Berry, rock 'n' roll master." *Reuters*. Ed. Diane Craft and Tom Brown. 18 Mar. 2017. Web. 19 July 2017.
12 Brown, Yamma and Robin Gaby Fisher. Cold Sweat: My Father James Brown and Me. Chicago: Chicago Review Press, 2016.
13 July, 2017 Getlen, Larry. "Mick Jagger on James Brown: "I Copied All His Moves"." *Time* 24 July 2014: *Time*. Web. 19 July 2017.
14 Simmons, Sylvie. "Interview: Michael Jackson." *The Guardian*. The Guardian, 27 June 2009. Web. 19 July 2017.
15 "Ray Charles Dies." *www.rollingstone.com*. Rolling Stone, 10 June 2004. Web. 19 July 2017.
16 "A Tribute to Ray Charles". Rolling Stone, nos. 952–953, July 8–22, 2004.
17 Coleman, Mark. "Q&A: Ray Charles." *Rolling Stone* 16 Oct. 1977: Print.
18 *American Bandstand*. 4 Apr. 1964. Web. 19 July 2017.
19 Soul Deep: The Story of Black Popular Music (Ep. 3). 2005. Television.
20 *VH1 Legends: Sam Cooke*. 16 Dec. 2001. Television.
21 Robins, Wayne. "Frankie Valli Q&A: Looking Back at 50 Years of The Four Seasons." *www.billboard.com*. 3 Sept. 2013. Web. 20 July 2017.
22 "100 Greatest Singers of All Time." *www.rollinstone.com*. 2 Dec. 2010. Web. 20 July 2017.
23 Hammann, Lynn. "60s music book quote." Message to the author. 18 July 2017. E-mail.
24 "Connie Francis: America's Sweetheart of Song ." *Biography*. A&E. 25 Oct. 1998. Television.
25 "Connie Francis: America's Sweetheart of Song ." *Biography*. A&E. 25 Oct. 1998. Television.
26 "Connie Francis: America's Sweetheart of Song ." *Biography*. A&E. 25 Oct. 1998. Television.
27 "Connie Francis: America's Sweetheart of Song ." *Biography*. A&E. 25 Oct. 1998. Television.
28 Suer, Kinsley. "The Many Musical Influences of Janis Joplin." *www.pcs.org*. 17 May 2011. Web. 20 July 2017.
29 Soeder, John. "R-E-S-P-E-C-T: The inside story behind Aretha Franklin's chart-topping anthem." www.cleveland.com. 30 Oct. 2011. Web. 20 July 2017.
30 *Aretha Franklin: The Queen of Soul Documentary #1*. Web. 20 July 2017. <https://www.youtube.com/watch?v=RKfkvbOP1sc>.
31 "Aretha Franklin: Queen of Soul, Documentary # 2." Web. 20 July 2017. <https://www.youtube.com/watch?v=vpo0RG4zGNo>.
32 *Hour Magazine*. 1981. Web. 20 July 2017. <https://www.youtube.com/watch?v=5Xf_-2kx9xM>.
33 *One on One with Becky Magura*. WCTE. Cookeville, TN, 25 Nov. 2014. Web. 20 July 2017. <https://www.youtube.com/watch?v=R4azPN36qts>.
34 *Jewel Inducts Brenda Lee into the Rock and Roll Hall of Fame*. 27 Jan. 2011. Web. 20 July 2017. <https://www.youtube.com/watch?v=yPCSi5ZE1ow>.
35 Hutchinson, Lydia. "Stories From Elvis Presley's Band." *www.performingsongwriter.com*. 8 Jan. 2016. Web. 20 July 2017.
36 "Return of the Pelvis." *Newsweek* 11 Aug. 1969: Print.
37 "Quotes About Elvis." *www.graceland.com*. Web. 20 July 2017.
38 "Quotes About Elvis." *www.graceland.com*. Web. 20 July 2017.
39 West, Jessica Pallington. *What Would Keith Richards Do?: Daily Affirmations with a Rock and Roll Survivor*. Bloomsbury Publishing PLC, 2009. Print.
40 Green, Joey. *Dumb History: The Stupidest Mistakes Ever Made*. Penguin, 2012. Print.
41 *The Rolling Stones - Full Biography*. Biography. Web. 20 July 2017. <https://www.biography.com/video/the-rolling-stones-full-biography-15260739516>.
42 Pine, Joslyn, ed. *Book of African-American Quotations*. Dover Publications, 2011. Print.
43 *Girl Groups: The Story of a Sound*. Dir. Steve Alpert. Delilah Films, 1983.
44 *100 Greatest Women of Rock & Roll*. VH1. 26 July 1999. Television.

OTHER SOURCES

All 6,886 1960s hits were listened to via YouTube, iTunes streaming, CDs and records from libraries, and the author's personal music collection. All other information was gathered from the following sources:

"Record Reviews, Streaming Songs, Genres & Bands." *AllMusic*. N.p., n.d. Web. 08 Aug. 2017.

"Movies, TV and Celebrities." *IMDb*. IMDb.com, n.d. Web. 08 Aug. 2017.

Whitburn, Joel. *Joel Whitburn's Top Pop Singles 1955-2002*. Menomonee Falls, Wisc.: Record Research, 2003. Print.

Whitburn, Joel. *Joel Whitburn's Pop Annual, 1955-2011*. Menomonee Falls, WI: Record Research, 2012. Print.

Made in United States
North Haven, CT
15 March 2023

34071175R00246